OXFORD READINGS IN PHILOSOPHY

FREE WILL

Published in this series

The Problem of Evil, edited by Marilyn McCord Adams and
Robert Merrihew Adams
The Philosophy of Artificial Intelligence, edited by Margaret A. Boden
The Philosophy of Artificial Life, edited by Margaret A. Boden
Self-Knowledge, edited by Quassim Cassam
Locke, edited by Vere Chappell
Descartes, edited by John Cottingham
Virtue Ethics, edited by Roger Crisp and Michael Slote
The Philosophy of Law, edited by R. M. Dworkin
Environmental Ethics, edited by Robert Elliot
Plato I and II, edited by Gail Fine
Theories of Ethics, edited by Philippa Foot
Scientific Revolutions, edited by Ian Hacking
Bioethics, edited by John Harris
The Philosophy of Mathematics, edited by W. D. Hart
The Philosophy of Biology, edited by David L. Hull and Michael Ruse
The Philosophy of Time, edited by Robin Le Poidevin and Murray MacBeth
The Philosophy of Action, edited by Alfred R. Mele
Properties, edited by D. H. Mellor and Alex Oliver
The Philosophy of Religion, edited by Basil Mitchell
Meaning and Reference, edited by A. W. Moore
The Philosophy of Science, edited by David Papineau
Ethical Theory, edited by James Rachels
Nietzsche, edited by John Richardson and Brian Leiter
Consequentialism and its Critics, edited by Samuel Scheffler
Applied Ethics, edited by Peter Singer
Causation, edited by Ernest Sosa and Michael Tooley
Theories of Rights, edited by Jeremy Waldron
Free Will, edited by Gary Watson
Demonstratives, edited by Palle Yourgrau

Other volumes are in preparation

FREE WILL

Edited by
GARY WATSON

OXFORD
UNIVERSITY PRESS

OXFORD

UNIVERSITY PRESS

Great Clarendon Street, Oxford OX2 6DP

Oxford University Press is a department of the University of Oxford.
It furthers the University's objective of excellence in research, scholarship,
and education by publishing worldwide in

Oxford New York

Auckland Bangkok Buenos Aires Cape Town Chennai
Dar es Salaam Delhi Hong Kong Istanbul Karachi Kolkata
Kuala Lumpur Madrid Melbourne Mexico City Mumbai Nairobi
São Paulo Shanghai Taipei Tokyo Toronto

Oxford is a registered trade mark of Oxford University Press
in the UK and in certain other countries

Published in the United States
by Oxford University Press Inc., New York

British Library Cataloguing in Publication Data

Data available

Library of Congress Cataloging in Publication Data

Data available

ISBN 978-0-19-925494-1

10

Typeset in Times
by RefineCatch Limited, Bungay, Suffolk
Printed in Great Britain by
CPI Antony Rowe
Chippenham, Wilts.

CONTENTS

Introduction 1
Gary Watson

1. Human Freedom and the Self 26
Roderick M. Chisholm

2. An Argument for Incompatibilism 38
Peter van Inwagen

3. Free Will, Praise and Blame 58
J. J. C. Smart

4. Freedom and Resentment 72
Peter Strawson

5. Towards a Reasonable Libertarianism 94
David Wiggins

6. Are We Free to Break the Laws? 122
David Lewis

7. Freedom and Practical Reason 130
Hilary Bok

8. Alternate Possibilities and Moral Responsibility 167
Harry G. Frankfurt

9. Libertarianism and Frankfurt's Attack on the Principle of
Alternative Possibilities 177
David Widerker

10. Frankfurt-Style Compatibilism 190
John Martin Fischer

11. The Impossibility of Moral Responsibility 212
Galen Strawson

12. Freedom 229
Thomas Nagel

13. Agent Causation 257
Timothy O'Connor

14. Toward a Credible Agent-Causal Account of Free Will   285
    Randolph Clarke

15. Responsibility, Luck, and Chance: Reflections on Free Will
    and Indeterminism   299
    Robert Kane

16. Freedom of the Will and the Concept of a Person   322
    Harry G. Frankfurt

17. Free Agency   337
    Gary Watson

18. The Significance of Choice   352
    T. M. Scanlon

19. Sanity and the Metaphysics of Responsibility   372
    Susan Wolf

20. Freedom in Belief and Desire   388
    Philip Pettit and Michael Smith

21. Freedom of Will and Freedom of Action   408
    Rogers Albritton

22. Addiction as Defect of the Will: Some Philosophical Reflections   424
    R. Jay Wallace

    Notes on the Contributors   453
    Selected Bibliography   455
    Index of Names   458

INTRODUCTION

GARY WATSON

Samuel Johnson famously said, 'We *know* our will is free, and there's an end on't.'[1] Most of us share this opinion, perhaps, but we are deeply divided about what it is that we claim to know.[2] And that is where the philosophical conversation begins. This volume collects some of the most interesting and influential contributions to this conversation during the last fifty years or so. They have both refined the disagreements and developed the topic in new directions. This introduction is an attempt to characterize the basic issues and to describe some of these developments.[3]

Our sense of ourselves as free is perplexing not only because of hard questions about necessity and contingency, actions and events, reasons and causes. The perplexity is ethical as well as metaphysical. Our view of the nature of free will is bound up with our view of why free will matters. As Thomas Nagel points out in Essay 12 of this volume, free will matters in at least two interrelated ways. Both our autonomy (or capacity for self-determination) and our accountability seem to hinge on it. The sense of autonomy is the sense that one is not merely a witness to one's life but rather fashions it from the world as one finds it. This capacity for authorship is important to responsibility; it renders us accountable for what we finally

For advise about the contents of this volume, I am very grateful to Michael Bratman, John Fischer, Paul Hoffman, Jennifer Rosner, Tim Scanlon, Dan Speak, Jay Wallace, Nathan Westbrook, Susan Wolf, Gideon Yaffe, and anonymous advisers for Oxford University Press. For help, encouragement, and patience during the editorial process, I thank Ruth Anderson, Angela Griffin, and Peter Momtchiloff of Oxford University Press. Thanks too to the staff of the Department of Philosophy at University of California, Riverside, expecially Jan Martuscelli, for helping me put the materials together.

[1] James Boswell, *The Life of Samuel Johnson* (1791).

[2] We find ourselves in this kind of position in philosophy frequently, that although real scepticism is relatively rare, there is no shared confidence in the characterization of the phenomenon in question.

[3] I have benefited from helpful comments by Dan Speak on a draft of this Introduction. I make free use of passages from the following of my writings: 'Introduction', in Gary Watson (ed.), *Free Will* (New York: Oxford University Press, 1982), 'Free Action and Free Will', *Mind*, 96 (1987), and 'Free Will', in J. Kim and E. Sosa (eds.), *A Companion to Metaphysics* (Oxford: Basil Blackwell, 1995).

make of ourselves. But the value of self-determination is not confined to our relation to others. The denial of free will seems threatening to the meaning of human life. (This might explain Dr Johnson's anxiety to close the conversation altogether.) A satisfactory account of freedom will have to make sense of all this.

FREEDOM AND NECESSITY

Why, then, has the belief in free will seemed so problematic? For one thing, it looks to be inconsistent with a prevalent view about how the world is causally structured. The most familiar version of this outlook is *determinism*, according to which the state of the world at any given time is fixed in all of its details by prior states and by the laws of nature.[4] This appears to have alarming implications for our understanding of our own behaviour. There are two related ways of putting the threat. First, if a deterministic explanatory scheme is valid, it looks as though I do not originate my actions; I am merely a confluence of causal processes that were initiated long before my existence. So antecedent conditions, not I, determine my behaviour. Autonomy is then an illusion. Another way to put it is to say that determinism entails that I had to do what I did; there were no other possibilities. On the second formulation, I am not a free agent because I am not free to act otherwise; on the first, the problem is to see how we can be agents at all.

Peter van Inwagen puts the concern about alternative possibilities concisely: 'If determinism is true, then our acts are the consequences of the laws of nature and events in the remote past. But it is not up to us what went on before we were born, and neither is it up to us what the laws of nature are. Therefore, the consequences of these things (including our present acts) are not up to us.' (See Essay 2.) The so-called Consequence Argument (which van Inwagen carefully develops in Essay 2) aims to establish *incompatibilism* about human freedom and determinism. Incompatibilists fall into two camps, depending on whether they affirm determinism (and therefore deny freedom) or affirm freedom (and therefore deny determinism). The former are *sceptics*; the latter are known as *libertarians*.

Since the Consequence Argument is contested at several points, it will be useful to set out the argument stepwise.

1. If determinism is true, everything, including human actions, is causally

---

[4] In this essay, I often use the term 'determinism' loosely, applying it both to this *thesis* and to *universal causal determination*, the way the world is structured if this thesis is true.

necessitated by the prior state of the universe in accordance with the laws of nature.

2. If human actions are causally necessitated by the past together with the laws of nature, then we cannot ever do otherwise than what we do, unless we can falsify the laws of nature or falsify the description of the past.

3. We cannot falsify the laws of nature or the description of the past.

4. If we cannot act otherwise than we do, then we lack free will.

5. Hence, if determinism is true, we lack free will.

This reasoning is often extended to the question of responsibility as follows:

6. If we lack free will, we cannot appropriately hold one another responsible.

7. Hence, if determinism is true, we cannot appropriately hold one another responsible.

Unsurprisingly, the notions of 'causal necessity' and 'laws of nature' are one focus of controversy. Some writers try to dissolve the problem by appealing to an analysis of causation first suggested by David Hume. According to this view, we should avoid thinking of causes as events that 'compel' their effects. Causal relations are merely instances of unbroken regularities of the form, 'when an event of one type occurs, an event of another type occurs also, in a certain temporal or spatio-temporal relation to the first.'[5] If this is right, the appearance of conflict is illusory.

But this way out has not appealed to many philosophers. 'Nothing travels faster than the speed of light' is a law (if it is) only because nothing *can* travel at that speed, not just because nothing in fact ever has or will. Whatever else a regularity must be to count as a law of nature, it must be beyond the power of human beings to falsify. All that is required for the Consequence Argument is the notion of natural regularities that are not only unbroken but also unbreakable (by us, at least). (For a discussion of some complexities concerning the notion of natural laws, see David Wiggins, Essay 5.)

A related objection concerns the *scope* of determinism. Determinism is worth considering only when it is restricted to what Wiggins calls the 'science of matter'. The idea of a deterministic social science seems a fantasy. In that case, it might be thought, nothing follows about human action and choice, for these are not the subjects of the natural sciences. However, the implications of physical determinism cannot be so easily isolated. As Wiggins observes, even if action and choice are not reducible to material processes, determinism still rules out virtually every significant human

[5] See A. J. Ayer, 'Freedom and Necessity', in A. J. Ayer, *Philosophical Essays* (London: Macmillan, 1954), 271–84.

option. For determinism implies that your body cannot move in any different way from the way it in fact moves. It follows that you cannot choose to do anything—say, to dance or write or talk—that requires your body to move in another manner. Even if we supposed, absurdly, that our mental lives were entirely independent of the physical world, our autonomy, as Wiggins says, 'would be something utterly inert'. So the threat cannot be deflected in this way.

By far the most common compatibilist complaint concerns premiss 2. The sense in which actions are 'causally necessitated', compatibilists typically argue, is not inconsistent with the ordinary belief in our ability to act otherwise. For what we think when we think we could do otherwise is not that determinism is false but that what we do depends on our choice. To say we could have done otherwise implies only that *we would have done otherwise if we had decided or chosen to*. (See Essays 3 and 7 for this suggestion.) Determinism does not imply that nothing depends on one's choices in this way.

This line of defence has seemed so plainly defective to its critics that they often entertain unfriendly suspicions about the philosophical integrity of those who pursue it. (Kant dismissed it as a 'wretched subterfuge'.) For I am able to do otherwise only if I am able to choose to do otherwise, which, the critics insist, I am not able to do if determinism is true. Suppose someone suffers from severe addiction or claustrophobia; the fact that she would have avoided the drug, or would have entered the cave, *if* she had so chosen hardly settles the question of whether she could have done these things in her actual, pathological condition.

Recognizing the deficiencies of the original suggestion, most contemporary compatibilists have sought to refine it, and to provide it with a better rationale. For example, the foregoing objection shows that even when an individual's behaviour depends on her choice, she will lack freedom if her choice is impaired in the way we suppose a kleptomaniac's to be. This recognition has been developed in importantly different ways. We will describe some of these developments later, but suffice it to say that according to the refined analysis, an agent is free when her behaviour depends on her unimpaired capacity for rational choice. These refinements are thought to support compatibilism because nothing in the thesis of determinism implies that anyone's capacity for choice is defective in these kinds of ways.

This strategy—namely, to identify a reading of 'can do otherwise' that is both consistent with determinism and not open to clear counterexamples— will seem strained as long as the third premiss of the Consequence Argument seems to us (as van Inwagen thinks) 'evidently true'. The critic must give general reasons to doubt that this premiss identifies the sense of ability that is relevant to human freedom.

In their contributions to this collection, David Lewis and Hilary Bok do just this. Lewis's response to the Consequence Argument focuses on a seemingly absurd implication of the supposition that one can do otherwise in a deterministic world: that then one could either falsify the laws of nature or falsify some propositions about the past. Lewis distinguishes a strong from a weak reading of this implication, and argues that, in the case of the first disjunct, 'it is the strong version that is incredible and the weak version that is the consequence.' On the strong version, to say I could have falsified a proposition p, in a deterministic world, implies that I was able to do something such that either my act itself falsifies p or my act causes another event that falsifies p. Where 'p' expresses a law of nature, L, this strong reading yields the incredible consequence that I can perform an act that violates a law of nature or perform an act that causes another law-breaking event. Lewis agrees that if p is a law, no one can do that. But Lewis argues that this strong version does not follow from determinism. What follows is something weaker, and not absurd: I am able to do something such that if I did it, L would be false. This is not absurd because it does not imply that if I did that, I would be violating a law, or causing a law to be violated. For in a world in which I did otherwise, L would not be a law.[6] On the weak reading, Lewis contends, premiss 2 is true, but premiss 3 is false; on the strong reading, premiss 3 is obvious, but then premiss 2 is doubtful. There is no univocal reading of these two premisses on which they both come out true, or at least not self-evidently true.

While Lewis's critique of the Consequence Argument is hardly decisive, it does succeed in dispelling the argument's air of self-evidence. It shows that the compatibilist reading of 'could do otherwise' cannot be dismissed as merely *ad hoc*. In Essay 7, Bok provides positive grounds for such a reading by connecting it with the requirements of deliberation. Incompatibilists complain that the conditional interpretation preserves alternative possibilities only by arbitrarily abstracting from the agent's causal environment. The charge is that the notion of alternative possibility identified in this interpretation is utterly artificial, rather like stipulating that my radio can operate here and now, even without a fuse, because it *would* operate if it had one. The important notion for human freedom, they insist, is possibility *tout court* (in Bok's phrase), not possibility relative to some merely hypothetical conditions.

---

[6] See also Lewis's 'Counterfactual Dependence and Time's Arrow', *Journal of Philosophy*, 70 (1973). Some other writers, but not Lewis, present the same argument regarding the disjunct, 'I could have falsified a proposition about the past.' See, for example, John Fischer, 'Incompatibilism', *Philosophical Studies* (1983), and 'Van Inwagen on Free Will', *Philosophical Quarterly* (1986).

Bok answers this challenge by grounding the conditional interpretation in the distinction between practical and theoretical reason. These forms of reason have different aims, and answer to different norms, each of which supplies a distinctive sense of 'possibility'. From the standpoint of theoretical explanation and prediction, an individual's choices or intentions are indeed on a par with any other *sine qua non* concerning the operations of her limbs, muscles, and central nervous system. In contrast, Bok argues, it is crucial to our practical lives to distinguish between our decisions and other conditions of action in just the way that the conditional analysis suggests. The relevant notion of an 'alternative' is 'defined for use in practical reasoning', and the conditional notion of what we would do if we chose is precisely what we need for that purpose. From the standpoint of practical reason, the question of what is possible *tout court* is only indirectly relevant: 'we cannot narrow our conception of our alternatives beyond the set of alternatives that we would perform if we chose, since, when we deliberate, we either cannot know which action we will in fact choose to perform or cannot use that knowledge in making our choice.' Of course, as we have seen, this conditional notion of what is possible must be supplemented by an account of unimpaired practical reason, but Bok has supplied a principled ground for the claim that it, rather than the 'all-in' 'can', provides the relevant notion of alternatives. This is a significant dialectical advance. (In the rest of the book from which this essay is adapted, Bok tries to show how the distinction between practical and theoretical reason can be the basis for a satisfactory overall theory of freedom and responsibility.)

ACTING FREELY AND FREEDOM TO ACT OTHERWISE

The importance of the classical debate about the existence and meaning of alternative possibilities is called into question by Harry Frankfurt in Essay 8. Perhaps free will requires alternative possibilities in some sense, but Frankfurt argues that the availability of alternative possibilities is not necessary for responsibility. To show this, he imagines a circumstance in which an individual, *A*, is considering whether to shoot *B*. Suppose that a third agent, *C*, somehow is able to detect whether or not *A* is about to choose to shoot *B*, and has it within his power to see to it that *A* chooses to shoot *B*, in case *A* is about to choose otherwise. In short, *C*'s intention, together with his ability to implement it, stands as a kind of 'fail-safe' to guarantee the result he desires. As it turns out, *C* never has to exercise this power, because *A* chooses on her own to do the deed. In these circumstances, Frankfurt argues, the following both seem to be true. (1) *A* could not have chosen otherwise, because C would have seen to it that she chose to shoot B. (2) Since C did not actually have to intervene, and A chose to shoot B independently of the fail-safe plan, A is fully responsible for what she chose to do. Hence the principle that someone is morally responsible for what he does only if he could have done otherwise is false. Frankfurt calls this the Principle of Alternate Possibilities (PAP). If PAP is false, in Frankfurt's view, there is no basis for incompatibilism.

Frankfurt's essay has given rise to a vast and complex array of responses. Here we can only mention a few. Let us suppose, to begin with, that Frankfurt's examples succeed in refuting PAP. Still, as John Fischer points out in Essay 10, the denial of PAP does not establish compatibilism about responsibility. For determinism may undermine responsibility for different reasons. What Frankfurt-style examples establish is the weaker but still important conclusion that determinism does not conflict with responsibility simply by virtue of foreclosing alternatives. As Fischer says, this conclusion 'shifts the debate away from issues pertaining to alternative possibilities to issues related to the actual sequence of events leading to the behavior in question'. And some incompatibilists have indeed shifted ground in just this way, embracing Frankfurt's conclusion that free will is irrelevant to responsibility while attempting to locate the responsibility-undermining features of determinism directly in deterministic processes. Frankfurt's essay teaches us that what matters for responsibility is the actual explanation of our behaviour. For example, as some 'Frankfurt libertarians' have argued, determinism threatens responsibility, not because it precludes alternative possibilities, but because a deterministic history prevents us from being the sources or originators or authors of our lives. (See Fischer's essay for relevant references.)

But Fischer himself argues that determinism does not threaten responsibility in any of the other ways urged by these incompatibilists. Since he agrees that determinism rules out the 'genuine ability and freedom to choose and do otherwise' (or at least that there is a powerful case for this), and he is convinced by Frankfurt that responsibility does not require this ability, Fischer favours an intermediate position—'semi-compatibilism'. Determinism is incompatible with the freedom to will, choose, or do otherwise but not with responsibility. Ascriptions of responsibility require, in Fischer's view, that an individual's behaviour results from 'reasons-sensitive mechanisms' that have a certain historical development in the individual's life. What is required is not 'that he make a certain sort of difference to the world, but rather, that he expresses himself in a certain way. And this sort of self-expression does not require alternative possibilities.'

The moral of Frankfurt's story, we should emphasize, is not that responsibility comes apart from freedom. This would be an apt description only if free will is stipulated to be the capacity to will or do otherwise. The conclusion of the argument is rather that acting and willing freely does not require being free to act or will otherwise. The main basis for the judgement that A is responsible in a Frankfurt case is that, since C did not actually intervene, *A acted freely*, indeed *willed freely*. (This is a point that Frankfurt emphasizes in Essay 16.) Hence, a crucial connection of responsibility with freedom remains in place. A exercises free will, acts of her own free will, even though she would not have willed otherwise.

Not everyone is convinced by this claim, however. One kind of libertarian rebuttal is forcefully presented in David Widerker's essay. Widerker argues that PAP is not impugned by Frankfurt's examples because the cases either beg the question against the libertarian conception of responsibility or leave the individual's freedom to choose otherwise intact. We can see the worry about begging the question when we reflect on how the would-be intervener is supposed to ensure that A will choose to shoot. To use Frankfurt's own example, we might imagine that C could detect a distinctive physical sign, a twitch, say, whenever A decides to shoot someone. If we suppose that the twitch is causally sufficient, or correlated with a condition that is causally sufficient, for the decision, then arguably C's fail-safe capacity depends on the assumption of a deterministic relation between such conditions and A's decisions. But if that is so, Frankfurt's scenario is not one in which libertarians can concede that A is responsible. For even if the presence of the counterfactual intervener does not itself rob A of responsibility, C's power depends on a knowledge of conditions that do, namely the deterministic processes that C is monitoring. On the other hand, if the relation between the twitch and the decision is not deterministic, then there is no reason to concede that A could not have done otherwise. If A's deciding not to shoot is compatible with the signs on which C relies, then for all that the argument shows, it is open to A to decide not to shoot even when the twitch occurs. And many writers have underscored this point by arguing that the fail-safe mechanism still leaves it open to A to choose to shoot *on her own* or not. Widerker concludes that Frankfurt's argument against PAP (when formulated in terms of decisions or intentions) is unsuccessful; it either fails to provide a scenario in which A lacks the power to decide differently, or it illicitly assumes that determinism and responsibility are compatible. (For a response to this alleged dilemma, see Fischer's essay.)

SCEPTICISM AND THE LIBERTARIAN DILEMMA

For a long time, determinism seemed to bear the imprimatur of science. Libertarians were often on the defensive in this debate, for fear of appearing unscientific. That is no longer so. Determinism has always been conceptually questionable. For, as we have seen, there are difficulties with the concept of a *law*, and it is not clear what sense can be made of the idea of a complete description of the world. (See Wiggins's essay for an illuminating discussion of these issues.) So the doctrine is far from being a presupposition of rational thought. In the twentieth century, moreover, determinism ceased to be the dominant scientific conception of the physical world. Why, then, does the issue of compatibilism deserve our attention, unless we think that determinism stands a real chance of being true?

The answer is that there is a worry about indetermination as well,[7] and that if incompatibilism is true, we seem to be led to scepticism. The assumption that determinism is false is not enough to vouchsafe free agency. The 'space opened up by the falsity of determinism would be relevant', T. M. Scanlon points out in Essay 18, 'only if it were filled by something other than the cumulative effects of indeterministic physical processes.' Suppose that we are causal systems whose operations are highly probable, but not certain, given their antecedents. This supposition satisfies the incompatibilist requirement, but it hardly gives us what we are after.

This point suggests that what is ultimately threatening about determinism is that it is a version of a generic explanatory scheme according to which our behaviour is an output (deterministic or not) of a complex of internal states together with environmental inputs. The intuitive worry here is that this form of explanation—which Bok calls *mechanism*—treats people as *loci* at which the forces of nature (deterministic or not) play themselves out, rather than as authors or originators of their behaviour.[8] The fundamental problem raised by determinism, it seems, is a problem about self-determination; the question of alternative possibilities is at most ancillary.

Since the appeal to indeterministic mechanism gets us nowhere, the challenge for libertarians is to say what alternative form of explanation is available once determinism is denied. In Essay 3, J. J. C. Smart complains that libertarians somehow 'want our choices to be neither determined nor a

---

[7] For a forceful argument that the indeterministic interpretation of quantum mechanics does not further the libertarian cause, see Barry Loewer, 'Freedom from Physics: Quantum Mechanics and Free Will', *Philosophical Topics*, 24/2 (1996), 91–112.

[8] For more on this point about mechanism, see the essays of Bok, Nagel, and Albritton in this volume, and J. D. Velleman, *The Possibility of Practical Reason* (New York: Oxford University Press, 2000).

matter of chance'. These are logically exhaustive alternatives, Smart argues, so the libertarians are in trouble. If determinism is true, then we are not free and responsible agents, according to them. However, by the foregoing reasoning, if determinism is not true of our actions, we are not free and responsible agents of undetermined events, because those are a matter of 'chance'. Call this the libertarian dilemma, since it is a challenge to any incompatibilist who wants to avoid scepticism. (For critical discussion of this problem, see Wiggins's essay and Robert Kane's discussion in Essay 15.)

This argument is in an important way question begging, since it is precisely the libertarian thesis that there *is* a non-deterministic form of explanation distinctive of free agency. Nevertheless, the dilemma is worth pressing because it usefully frames the challenge facing any incompatibilist account of freedom. Different versions of libertarianism are different accounts of how to fill the space opened up by indeterminism.

Inspired by Thomas Reid, many modern libertarians have responded to this challenge by invoking a distinction between agent-causation and event-causation. In his seminal paper, 'Human Freedom and the Self', Roderick Chisholm argues that alternatives presented by the dilemma are not exhaustive. It rests on the false assumption that all causal explanation appeals to event-causation. In that case, Chisholm concedes, conduct could never be attributed to us as free and responsible individuals. But some events are explained simply by invoking the agents of those actions. That some events are not determined by other events does not entail that they were 'accidental, or random', for they might be determined by the agents themselves. For the same reason, the conduct of free agents is not 'contra-causal', as Smart supposes, but agent-causal. This conclusion has striking implications regarding the nature of human beings, Chisholm maintains. Free and responsible agents have, as he dramatically puts it, 'a prerogative which some would attribute only to God: each of us, when we act, is a prime mover unmoved.' (See Essay 1.)

Chisholm defends this notion against the charges of emptiness or incoherence, but most philosophers have remained very unsympathetic. At best, the term 'agent cause' seems to be just a label for what is needed. To say that we achieve self-determination in an indeterministic world by exercising agent-causation seems unhelpfully close to saying that we are self-determining in virtue of determining our actions. At worst, the theory commits us, in Wiggins's words, to a 'metaphysical, totally non-empirical and characterless self'. If free and responsible actions were not lawfully related to the states and processes of individuals, including their beliefs, values, and critical reasoning, then exercises of agent-causation would seem

to be divorced from psycho-physical reality, the rationally inexplicable out-
bursts of a structureless substance.

For these reasons, most have emphatically rejected Chisholm's interpretation of freedom and responsibility. Galen Strawson, however, argues that
Chisholm's interpretation is right, and that what should be rejected instead
is our common belief in freedom and responsibility. Here is one version of
Strawson's argument for scepticism: '(1) nothing can be *causa sui*—nothing
can be the cause of itself. (2) In order to be truly morally responsible for
one's actions one would have to be *causa sui*. . . . (3) Therefore nothing can
be truly morally responsible.' (See Essay 11.)

Thomas Nagel also thinks that scepticism about our ordinary view of
ourselves is in order. On his analysis, the problem arises from a clash of two
perspectives we can take on our own lives. We necessarily act from an
internal perspective, from which we appear to ourselves as sources of activity, determining which of a number of open alternatives is realized. But this
appearance is not validated by an objective or external point of view, according to which 'the agent and everything about him is swallowed up by the
circumstances of action; nothing of him is left to intervene in those circumstances. . . . We and our lives are seen as products and manifestations of the
world as a whole.' (See Rogers Albritton's discussion in Essay 21 for a similar diagnosis.) This clash places us in the untenable position of thinking of
ourselves as at once 'part of the order of nature' and intervening in nature.
We cannot coherently put these perspectives together, nor can we abandon
either altogether. (Compare Nagel's view with Bok's, who argues in her
book that there is no real disharmony between the first-personal stance and
the external perspective.)

The problem of freedom is part of the problem of finding room in the world
for ourselves, a problem that faces compatibilists as well. A credible defence of
incompatibilist free agency must fill the space opened up by the denial of
determinism with something besides an impossible power of self-creation.

LIBERTARIAN REFINEMENTS

In response to this challenge, the past few decades have seen a resurgence of
creative work in a libertarian vein. Unsurprisingly, the burden of this work is
to acquit libertarianism of the charge of metaphysical incredibility. These
attempts have been mainly of two kinds. Some have tried to demystify the notion
of agent causation. Others have tried to do without it. The papers by Timothy
O'Connor and Randolph Clarke are important efforts of the first kind.

Both of their essays offer an interpretation of agent-causation as a non-miraculous power that is tied essentially to our rational capacities. For O'Connor, both agent- and event-causation are instances of a primitive relation of causal production, or bringing about. Different objects have distinctive causal powers depending on their specific properties. In the case of event-causation, 'an object's possession of property P in circumstances C necessitates or makes probable a certain effect' (for example, the power of an acid to produce a corrosive effect on metal). Similarly, the properties of 'intelligent, purposive agents' enable them, in a law-like way, purposely (or at will) to bring about certain effects. The contrast with event-causation is that these properties *make possible*, rather than necessitate, our bringing about one effect rather than another. That's what makes us self-determining agents. O'Connor concludes his essay with an account of the connection between agent-causation and explanation by reasons.

Although O'Connor and Clarke both hold that agent-causation is an instance of something more general, they characterize the contrast in importantly different ways. Whereas O'Connor thinks 'there are two fundamental sorts of causation', Clarke argues that 'agent-causation, if there is such a thing, is (or involves) *exactly* the same relation as event-causation'. Moreover, Clarke insists on the consistency of the assertion of agent-causation and explaining the agent's choices and preferences in terms of the event-causal nexus; it is just that this nexus must be seen as probabilistic rather than necessitating. What the agent causes is her acting on a certain 'ordering of reasons', and event-causal explanations play an essential role in our understanding of this.

The papers by David Wiggins and Robert Kane represent, in very different ways, the attempt to defend libertarianism without agent-causation. Both think that the appeal to agent-causation is neither necessary nor helpful. They each try to defend versions of libertarianism with more modest resources. Wiggins argues that the non-deterministic form of explanation that is needed for free and responsible agency is just ordinary *practical intelligibility*: an account of 'a world in which agents are natural things among others, albeit natural things whose motions and capacities invite appraisal by subtle, exacting (and utterly familiar) standards of practical rationality'. What distinguishes a human being from other natural kinds is not his remarkable causal powers but

simply that his biography unfolds not only non-deterministically but also intelligibly; non-deterministically in that personality and character are never something complete, and need not be the deterministic origin of action; intelligibly in that each new action or episode constitutes a comprehensible phase in the unfolding of character, a further specification of what the man has by now *become*.

Recall that libertarian theories have both a negative and a positive component. The negative component is incompatibilism and the positive component is an account of what it takes to be a free and responsible agent in an indeterministic world. Chisholm, Clarke, and O'Connor posit an indeterministic form of causal relation between human beings and their decisions or behaviour. Wiggins's view provides a straightforward and metaphysically minimal alternative. Causally undetermined occurrences are not random if they are explained in the ordinary way by reference to the agent's ends and beliefs—if they are, in short, intelligible in terms of practical reason. In contrast to versions of libertarianism that try, in Nagel's words, 'to force autonomy into the natural order', Wiggins connects freedom with a distinctive kind of explanation, in which a reference to the individual as an agent is essential. (Wiggins's position is in this respect like Bok's. For both, freedom is connected with the validity of a certain standpoint on behaviour that is different from that of causal explanation.)

But this plausible claim[9] raises a question about the relation between this account of self-determination and the two parts of Wiggins's version of libertarianism. Why isn't practical intelligibility *sufficient* for viewing individuals as free and responsible? If so, and if this form of explanation can apply in a deterministic world, why can't the compatibilist give the same account? To be sure, the Consequence Argument (which Wiggins himself forcefully elaborates) offers an answer to this. But if practical intelligibility is enough to secure the relevant kind of self-determination in an indeterministic world, and if that kind of explanation is consistent with determinism,[10] then that seems to reinforce the suspicion that the Consequence Argument turns on an interpretation of possibility that is beside the point. Agent-causation theorists do not face a parallel question because, typically at least, the positive condition for self-determination, agent-causation, is taken to entail or presuppose the incompatibilist condition and therefore cannot be satisfied in a deterministic world.

Kane's essay is a careful, extended rebuttal of the idea, central to the libertarian dilemma, that the outcomes of indeterministic processes can only be a matter of luck. Like Wiggins, Kane wants to eschew any metaphysical commitments (beyond the denial of determinism) that non-libertarians do not also need. But Kane thinks the libertarian must appeal to more than practical intelligibility. It is not enough, as Wiggins has it, to see one's actions as 'a comprehensible phase of the unfolding of character, a further

---

[9] However, see Nagel's essay for doubts about its plausibility.

[10] Some philosophers would deny this, but, as far as I know, Wiggins does not declare himself on this question. For example, see Norman Malcolm, 'The Conceivability of Mechanism', *The Philosophical Review*, 77/1 (1968), and a reply by Daniel Dennett, 'Mechanism and Responsibility', reprinted in D. C. Dennett, *Brainstorms* (Montgomery, Vt.: Bradford Books, 1978), 233–55.

specification of what [one] has by now *become*'. According to Kane, we must be able to assign a causal role to 'self-forming actions' in the development of our characters. The conceptualization of this causal role does not require anything fancier than event-causation, Kane thinks. Nevertheless, the development of this idea leads him to some very speculative remarks about the importance of 'chaotic' brain processes in the formative stages of the self.

On the one hand, the positive half of Kane's version of libertarianism tries to put indeterminism to work in a way that cannot be appropriated by compatibilists. So the worry about Wiggins's account does not seem to apply here. But the complexities and uncertainties of Kane's conjectures raise a worry of a different kind. On this account, it is very unclear how, in general or in particular cases, we could ever be as confident as we seem to be in our ascriptions of responsibility. This worry applies to one degree or another to all of the libertarian theories we have considered, except for Wiggins's.

It may be, however, that libertarians' confidence (like our own in our unreflective lives) is in the end practical rather than theoretical. They may be content to sketch out a metaphysically coherent and scientifically consistent picture of human capacities that does justice to what they take to be our moral understanding of ourselves. Clarke is explicit about this. At the end of his essay, he suggests that the occurrence of agent-causation is not recommended (nor contradicted) by scientific inquiry but rather by a 'transcendental argument' from our moral commitments. What recommends this metaphysical position is its role in 'an explication of how we can be what we seem, from the moral point of view, to be.'

FREEDOM AND BLAME

So far we have been assuming that we want a theory that provides an adequate basis for moral responsibility and related values; the question has been whether or not only some sort of libertarian view can do that. In Essay 3, Smart not only challenges (on now familiar grounds) the coherence of such views; he thinks we should discard much of the 'moral understanding' that libertarianism is trying to preserve. Smart accuses libertarianism of underwriting 'righteous indignation', and a 'pharisaical attitude toward sinners' that fosters callousness towards the poor. (Compare the target of Galen Strawson's sceptical argument: 'As I understand it, true moral responsibility is responsibility of such a kind that, if we have it, then it *makes sense*, at least, to suppose that it could be just to punish some of us with (eternal) torment in hell and reward others with (eternal) bliss in heaven.') Smart thinks of himself as revising, rather than abandoning ordinary conceptions of freedom and responsibility. 'Though some of our ordinary talk about moral responsibility is frequently vitiated by a confused metaphysics of free will, much of it can be salvaged.' So part of the essay attempts to identify the sort of praise and blame that can be practised in a 'dispassionate and clear-headed way', while junking the rest. What is salvageable is the idea of praise and blame as ways of *grading people with a view to influencing their attitudes and conduct*, rather than *judging* them (where judging is understood as retributive in a punitive sense).

Although he shares Smart's distaste for what he regards as the 'panicky metaphysics' of libertarianism, Peter Strawson argues in Essay 4 that libertarians are right to 'recoil' from Smart's instrumentalist rationale for our common practices. He suggests that compatibilists like Smart go wrong in the same way as libertarians and sceptics do: they all suppose that our conception of one another as free and responsible requires a foundation. Sceptics see that the different candidates are deeply inadequate, so they conclude (with Galen Strawson) that these practices are indefensible. But this demand for some kind of external justification of the attitudes expressed by our practices 'overintellectualizes' them.

Strawson takes the ordinary concepts of freedom and responsibility to be rooted in a 'complicated web of attitudes and feelings which form an essential part of the moral life as we know it.' The prominent strands of this web are 'participant' or 'reactive' attitudes and responses, such as gratitude, resentment, love, and hurt feelings, as well as the practices of asking and granting forgiveness, moral indignation, and approbation. These responses and attitudes are expressions of the natural concern for 'the qualities of others' wills'—for 'whether the actions of other people . . . reflect . . . goodwill, affection, or esteem, . . . contempt, indifference or malevolence'. These attitudes and responses reflect 'the demand for the manifestation of a reasonable degree of good will or regard, on the part of others, not simply towards oneself, but towards all those on whose behalf moral indignation may be felt'. Our notion of freedom and responsibility is so bound up with our sense of the value and meaning of human life that it is just wrong-headed to suppose that an external critique of that form of life could have any real purchase.

The complex of reactive attitudes is affected by the ordinary excusing conditions ('She didn't realize you were there', 'He lost his balance'), and also by the extent to which others are capable of real involvement in the general range of adult interpersonal relationships. Towards the small child, the 'deranged', or 'sociopathic', we tend to take up an 'objective', 'detached' stance characterized by a concern for treatment or general consequences. Smart's instrumentalism distorts our practices because it sees them from this disengaged perspective. But the libertarian's and sceptic's emphasis on abstract questions about the character of the laws of nature or of the causal structure of the world is equally out of focus. No general thesis of the kind that determinism is supposed to be could possibly entail that everyone falls under one or another of the excusing or exempting conditions; otherwise it could be dismissed out of hand as contrary to ordinary experience. Hence, its truth or falsity is irrelevant to the propriety of the participant attitudes that constitute our conceptions of ourselves as free and responsible. Those attitudes do not rest on any theoretical or metaphysical commitments at all, beyond the familiar considerations that are relevant to the basic human concern for the quality of the attitudes manifested in interpersonal affairs. Holding responsible is as natural and basic to human life as friendship and hard feelings, as sympathy and antipathy. It rests on needs and concerns that are not so much to be justified as acknowledged.[11]

In Essay 18, T. M. Scanlon objects that both Smart and Peter Strawson (in different ways) tie the analysis of our judgements of blameworthiness and praiseworthiness too closely to the question of what we are doing when we make these judgements. Strawson's idea of participant attitudes highlights the important point that judging someone blameworthy is not just a matter of 'unwelcome description', coupled with the ambition to discourage certain kinds of behaviour. So his characterization fits our practices better than Smart's instrumentalism. But Strawson does not give a sufficiently illuminating account of the general capacities that are absent or compromised in such conditions as nonage or insanity, in virtue of which our reactive attitudes are affected. Furthermore, Scanlon denies that judgements of responsibility (even if they are expressed) must reflect sentiments of the kind Strawson emphasizes. Scanlon's thesis is that the connection of the requirement of freedom to judgements of praise and blame is to be explained by the appeal to the *content* of those judgements. He suggests that the freedom required for responsibility is best explained by a 'contractualist' theory of moral criticism. According to contractualism, the judgement that someone has wronged me, for example, implies that she has violated demands that none of us could reasonably reject as 'a basis for deliberation and . . . criticism'.[12] So 'moral judgments apply to people considered as possible participants in a system of co-deliberation.'

---

[11] Nagel disputes the contention that scepticism involves taking an illegitimate external or objective view. He argues that the assessment from such a standpoint is authorized by our practices. Wiggins agrees with Strawson that our fundamental concerns and attitudes require no general justification and that in particular we need not refute the thesis of determinism to carry on in our practices with good conscience. But it does not follow, Wiggins argues, that our practices do not conflict with that thesis.

[12] Scanlon has further developed contractualism and his account of responsibility in *What We Owe to Each Other* (Cambridge, Mass.: Harvard University Press, 1998).

The requirements of freedom identify some of the capacities necessary for this form of criticism to make sense. To criticize others' intentions in this way is not merely to grade them in negative terms, or to express our reactive attitudes, but to imply that their decisions or intentions have failed to answer to certain important reasons. Such criticism therefore presupposes 'the capacity for critically reflective, rational self-governance', the capacity to reflect on the reasons that bear on one's behaviour and to be governed in thought and action by that reflection.

FREEDOM, REFLECTION, AND NORMATIVE COMPETENCE

Scanlon's essay exemplifies two themes that characterize much recent work in this area: the importance of the capacity for critical reflection, and the bearing of normative considerations on the theory of freedom. This work construes autonomy or self-determination in terms of the powers of critical reflection. Like Scanlon, these writers generally find that the possession of these powers is not put in jeopardy by determinism. The most influential recent contribution to this first theme is Harry Frankfurt's 'Freedom of the Will and the Concept of a Person' (Essay 16). Frankfurt complains that the literature on freedom too often fails to distinguish freedom of action from freedom of will. Like other animals, human beings can be chained and caged. But as reflective beings, we are capable of a kind of freedom, as well as a corresponding form of bondage, that is not available to the other creatures. Like us, they are moved by their specific impulses and appetites, but they neither have nor lack freedom of the will because they lack the capacity to form preferences about what their 'will' should be. In contrast, we have the capacity to critically evaluate the motivational forces to which we are subject. This capacity is manifested in 'higher-order volitions': desires that some first-order desire (say, to eat or to strike back) be (or not be) effective in action. Freedom of the will is the capacity to conform our first-order motivation (our 'wills', in Frankfurt's technical sense) to our highest-order volitions. It is this capacity that can be destroyed by addictions or phobias. To be dominated by these desires contrary to our higher-order volitions is tantamount to being subject to external forces. Because these motivational forces are in the most important sense not our own, we are not autonomous when we are led by them.[13]

---

[13] For further developments of Frankfurt's views on free will and responsibility, see his *The Importance of What We Care About* (Cambridge: Cambridge University Press, 1988).

In 'Free Agency', I agree with the importance of critical reflection in an account of freedom and responsibility but reject the attempt to construe evaluation in non-normative terms. Reflective evaluation involves practical reason or judgement, which depends on an irreducible distinction between valuing and desiring. What gives 'higher-order volitions' their significance is that they typically reflect the agent's conception of what she has reason to do (or be). An agent is free, and acts freely, when what she chooses depends on and expresses that conception. This view is thus closer to Scanlon's in its conception of freedom as the capacity to respond to reasons.[14]

The essays by Frankfurt, Scanlon, and myself are different interpretations of the idea of freedom as (the capacity for) (rational) self-governance. Although she is sympathetic to the general idea, Susan Wolf argues that the aforementioned views leave out something crucial: *normative competence*. Self-governance, as these views characterize it, is compatible with the total incapacity to see the force of moral reasons. It is compatible, as Wolf puts it, with *insanity* in something like the legal sense—an inability to know the difference between good and bad reasons as they relate to legal or moral requirements. Someone might be wholeheartedly behind his actions, and completely capable of governing his life by his reflective conception of what is most valuable, but altogether lack the competence to recognize the validity of the norms to which we would hold him responsible. Such an individual has the capacity to revise and adjust his motivation in accordance with his higher-order volitions or values or conception of reasons; but unless he is capable of *knowing* the right reasons, Wolf thinks, he is not truly responsible for not complying with moral demands.

According to Wolf, sceptics and libertarians are right to deny that the capacity for self-revision is sufficient. What is further required, she thinks, is not the impossible capacity to create ourselves to which Galen Strawson reacts, but the capacity for self-*correction*, the ability to get it right.[15] We need not only autonomy (governance by the self), but the competence to apprehend and appreciate 'the reasons there are.'[16]

---

[14] Recall Bok's appeal to practical vision in Essay 7, as well as John Fischer's appeal to the notion of reasons-responsive mechanisms in Essay 10. Fischer and Mark Ravizza spell out this analysis in *Responsibility and Control: A Theory of Moral Responsibility* (Cambridge: Cambridge University Press, 1998).

[15] Paul Benson emphasizes the importance of normative competence in 'Freedom and Value', *Journal of Philosophy*, 84 (Sept. 1987). Wolf further develops her views on these issues in *Freedom Within Reason* (New York: Oxford University Press, 1990). R. Jay Wallace develops a systematic account of moral responsibility as the capacity for moral competence in *Responsibility and the Moral Sentiments* (Cambridge, Mass.: Harvard University Press, 1994).

[16] As a condition for moral responsibility, I find Wolf's insistence on moral competence persuasive. However, I am not inclined to see such competence as a condition of free will. Responsibility requires competencies that go beyond freedom, and this is one of them.

In their essay, Philip Pettit and Michael Smith call this conception of freedom and responsibility *orthonomy*. In contrast to the idea of autonomy as internal harmony, they point out, orthonomy requires the possibility of 'coming into line with something outside the realm of desire', namely with interpersonal norms. Pettit and Smith's use of this idea goes beyond Wolf's in two important ways. They interpret the idea of orthonomy in terms of our conversational practices, and they apply it to freedom of thought as well as to freedom of will. In contrast to Strawson, Pettit and Smith's analysis of the social context in which we hold one another responsible centres on the notion of a *conversational stance*,[17] rather than reactive attitudes. It is the requirements of this stance that dictate the conditions of freedom and responsibility. To treat someone as responsible is to 'authorize' him 'as an interlocutor' on certain practical or theoretical questions. This presumes not only that there are objective norms bearing on the question of what to do or believe, matters about which one can go wrong, but also that the interlocutor has the capacity to recognize and respond appropriately to the demands of these norms—that their belief and intention forming capacities are not disabled. (The authors emphasize that this is a matter of degree.)

Pettit and Smith's discussion of freedom of thought is salutary, for until recently, the ideas of epistemic and assertoric freedom and responsibility have been relatively neglected.[18] But their unification project is important for another reason. It might reorient our views of freedom of will and moral responsibility. For seeing free will and moral responsibility as a species of a more generic notion removes the emphasis from punishment and blame, and brings other dimensions of answerability and accountability to the foreground. As we have seen, a good bit of scepticism about free will and responsibility stems from worries about punishment and retribution, about 'true responsibility of the heaven and hell variety', in Galen Strawson's words. The recognition of freedom and responsibility of belief brings out the multidimensional character of answerability. This makes it easier to see how one could reasonably deny retributive accountability without discrediting responsibility and the freedom it entails altogether.

---

[17] This notion has obvious connections with the work of discourse theorists such as Jürgen Habermas. See, for example, *The Theory of Communicative Action*, trans. Thomas McCarthy (Boston: Beacon Press, vol. i, 1984, vol. ii, 1987).

[18] Pettit pursues some of these themes further in *A Theory of Freedom* (Oxford: Oxford University Press, 2001). For an alternative view on belief, see David Owens, *Reason without Freedom* (London: Routledge, 2000).

FREE WILL AND FREE ACTION

Scepticism about free will is a familiar position. What is striking about Rogers Albritton's contribution to this volume is its denial of *unfree* will. In his witty and challenging essay, Albritton defends the surprising doctrine of René Descartes that the will is 'so free in its nature that it cannot be constrained'. 'Most philosophers seem to think it quite easy to rob the will of some freedom,' Albritton notes, but in his view they tend to mistake unfreedom of will for something else. His essay insists on a distinction among four concepts: freedom of action, efficacy of will, freedom of will, and strength of will. What Albritton means by the will is the capacity to form intentions or to decide in favour of one course of action or another. 'What we propose to do is up to us, if our wills are free. But what the world will make of what we do is of course up to the world.' He agrees with Frankfurt that 'my freedom of will wouldn't be reduced if you chained me up', but he also disagrees that free will is diminished by such familiar obstacles to implementing your reflective evaluations as addictions and phobias. 'None of these examples shows that our wills—our capacities to form alternative intentions—are not "in perfect working order"'. Some of these conditions might involve the vice of weakness of will (the tendency to decide against your better judgement). Alternatively, they could constitute internal obstacles to implementing your will. In the latter case, they would undermine your will's efficacy—your ability to implement your will—but not its freedom to adopt different intentions. Indeed, the idea of unfree will, Albritton concludes, is 'incomprehensible'.

This perfect freedom of the will does not mean that human beings are not vulnerable to a variety of subtle manipulations, in addition to brute physical constraint. You might control someone by inducing a kind of automatism, or by manipulating her beliefs. In the first case, you would not be controlling her will, but eliminating that capacity. In the second case, you would control the information in the light of which she made her decisions, but not her power to make up her mind on the basis of that information. Thus, Albritton's claim about freedom of the will is not that human beings are omnipotent, but that it is a mistake to conceptualize these limitations in terms of limitations on the will.

In the final essay in this volume, R. Jay Wallace tries to account for the sense in which the will of a severely addicted person can indeed (contrary to Albritton) fail to be in 'perfect working order'. Addiction, as we have seen, is commonly invoked as a kind of paradigm of unfree will. But very little detailed attention is paid in this literature to what addiction is or to how to understand its effects on freedom. Wallace's essay rectifies this neglect. It makes two notable contributions. First, it avoids some prevailing unrealistic conceptions of the phenomena—for example, that addictions threaten freedom because they overwhelm the will by generating literally irresistible impulses, or because they bypass the will altogether, resulting in non-voluntary behaviour. (Compare Frankfurt's image in Essay 16 of the 'unwilling addict, helplessly violated by his own desires'.) Addictions rarely if ever have these effects. Wallace would thus be sympathetic with much of Albritton's scepticism about the ways in which philosophers have discussed the affects of alcoholism on freedom. Nevertheless, Wallace wants to account for the way these conditions can render someone vulnerable to significant volitional impairment. The second notable contribution of the essay is that it takes seriously the concept of will, so that the diminishment of freedom is an impairment of the will in precisely the sense Albritton has in mind.

Wallace's explanation depends on a contrast between two accounts of the relation of desires to deliberative agency. The 'hydraulic model', which presumes a kind of psychological determinism, or at least mechanism, reduces agency to relations among such causal forces as impulses and perceptions. (Note that these might be first- or second-order in Frankfurt's sense; thus the hierarchical model readily—though not necessarily—fits the hydraulic interpretation. Higher-order volitions are simply features of more complex causal systems.) This model fails to give an adequate role to agency, Wallace insists, and thus cannot give a satisfactory treatment of the distinction between weakness of will, addiction, and compulsion. What we need instead, Wallace thinks, is a volitionalist account, according to which the will is not one impulse among others (of whatever order of complexity), but a capacity to form intentions independently of whatever motivational influences one may be subject to.

It is this basic capacity that is impaired by conditions such as addiction. Being subject to addictive urges, Wallace notes, makes it 'more difficult for me to act well by my own lights' by making me persistently and vividly aware both of the immediate discomfort entailed by acting as I think I should and of the promise of immediate pleasure and relief available if I take the drug. This property of addictive desires distorts the 'phenomenological field of agency' in such a way that my 'powers of reflective self-control' are vitiated but not destroyed. For the same reason, Wallace concludes, addictions should be understood as conditions that potentially diminish accountability without exempting the addict entirely.

While the impairment of the addict's will is an impairment of her capacity to respond to reasons, Wallace's account of the will distinguishes his theory from the other attempts to understand freedom in terms of responsiveness to reasons. For Wallace, free agency can be understood neither in terms of certain motivational structures (however complex), nor in terms of normative judgement (however perspicacious). It requires the capacity actively to form intentions in view of one's motivational tendencies and one's normative conclusions. Only by reference to such a capacity can we explain something that remains obscure on normative accounts such as Pettit and Smith's: how free agency can be exercised not only in response to 'the true and the good', but in defiance of them.[19] In this respect, his volitionist moral psychology brings Wallace closer to libertarianism than to classical compatibilism. (For his own sense of his relation to libertarianism, see note 14 of his essay.)

SCEPTICISM, SUBSTITUTION, AND REVISION

In the remainder of this Introduction, I want to reflect on some issues that are raised by the seemingly intractable character of the controversies regarding the nature of freedom.

Writing in particular of what he takes to be clearly inadequate compatibilist proposals, David Wiggins says: 'Substitution of another notion may be called for, but substitution is not the same as the philosophical elucidation of what we have. The practical and metaphysical imports of substitution and analysis are totally different.' (See Essay 5.) This caution is well taken. If substitution is called for, then we should face up to that, and not pretend that we are delivering the original thing. But when *is* substitution called for, and how is that to be distinguished from analysis and from scepticism? What would a clear case of substitution look like, and what would be its point?

The project of substitution is well illustrated by Thomas Nagel's proposal in the last sections of his essay. Having critiqued the belief in autonomy as unintelligible, Nagel himself is entirely forthright about what he is doing. His proposal, he says, 'is not autonomy, not a solution to the problem of free will, but a substitute—one which falls short of the impossible aspiration to act from outside ourselves, but which nevertheless has value in its own right.' Nagel's candidate for *quasi*-autonomy is the ideal of living 'in a way that wouldn't have to be revised in light of anything more that could be known about us'.[20] Of course, we can never attain this vantage-point, which would

---

[19] In 'Three Conceptions of Rational Agency' (*Ethical Theory and Moral Practice*, 3 (1999), 217–42), Wallace makes it clear that on his version of volitionism, this counter-normative capacity is integral to the will and to 'self-determination'.

[20] I think a large part of the appeal of hierarchical theories is that they seem to capture the ideal of being affirmable from a more comprehensive perspective.

be a kind of self-transcendence,[21] but we can approximate it by minimizing the constraints of subjectivity. According to Nagel, this approach to objectivity is manifested in one's values, which (in contrast to preferences) aspire to interpersonal validity. But it is manifested in morality especially, wherein one acknowledges oneself as merely one person among others, equally real.

Now there is a certain tension (not a contradiction) between the two conditions for substitution. How easy will it be for a candidate to be an approximation of autonomy and preserve much of its distinctive value while still clearly lacking central features of the concept? The success of the candidate as a 'substitution' tends to recommend it, after all, as a pretty good *analysans*. Consider Nagel's proposal with these doubts in mind. Why shouldn't we simply regard his description to be a better account of what we intuitively take to be real freedom? *Quasi*-autonomy is after all a version of *orthonomy*, which, as we have seen, many writers offer as the thing itself. It is a canon of interpretation that one account of a practice or concept is better than another, other things equal, if the practice or concept makes sense on the one account but not on the other. (The only respect in which *orthonomy* seems to fall short of the real thing is that it is intelligible, and we should not hold that against it.) If we can have such a close approximation, isn't it strained to insist that this is substitution *rather than* 'true analysis'? For no non-sceptical philosophical account of an important concept can do any more than regiment pretheoretical intuitions.[22] And even if it fails fully to satisfy our everyday sense of things, as any account inevitably will, if orthonomy is indeed a form of freedom, to wave the banner of scepticism will seem melodramatic.

Nevertheless, Nagel gives plausible reasons for thinking that *quasi*-autonomy lacks central features of the target concept after all. Most importantly, it cannot underwrite responsibility in the way autonomy is supposed to do. We ordinarily think that people are responsible for their bad conduct because they are self-determining. In contrast, orthonomy is realized and expressed only in good conduct, not in action that goes against reason. So here is a major function of autonomy that Nagel's substitute cannot serve. Attributions of autonomy presume not just the ability to be fully responsive to reasons, but also our capacity freely to disregard them. If Nagel is right about responsibility, then, there is significant room

---

[21] For another discussion of freedom as transcendence, see Gideon Yaffe, 'Free Will and Agency at its Best', in James E. Tomberlin (ed.), *Action and Freedom* (Philosophical Perspectives, 14; Boston: Blackwell Publishers, 2000).

[22] Compare Quine's notion of analysis as *explication* in *Word and Object* (Cambridge, Mass.: MIT Press, 1960), 258–62. Compare also John Rawls's idea in *A Theory of Justice* that philosophical analysis attempts to achieve not synonymy, but a state of 'reflective equilibrium' among disparate theoretical and practical *desiderata* (Cambridge, Mass.: Harvard University Press, 1971).

for scepticism here and hence for a meaningful contrast between analysis and substitution.

CONCLUSION

Regarding the long-standing problems of philosophy, including this one, Rogers Albritton once said: 'The reason these disputes never end is that both sides are right about important things. I am inclined to think there is truth and nonsense on both sides, but the truth is very hard to find.'[23] I think that Albritton's message should affect the way we theorize on this and other philosophical problems. That the truth is hard to find on this topic, most philosophers will readily accept. But the other part of Albritton's message is less often taken to heart. One reality that compatibilists seldom acknowledge is the disparity between what they offer and what we naturally believe in our daily lives about our agency (a disparity upon which incompatibilists insist). For this reason, they are often vulnerable to the charge of 'revisionism'. On the other hand, if compatibilists tend to proceed as though what they proposed were merely common sense, libertarians tend to regard the phenomenon identified in compatibilist conceptions as worthless—about as valuable, in Kant's contemptuous phrase, as 'the freedom of the turnspit'.[24] Both of these tendencies are, at this stage of the game, dialectically unhelpful. (See Bok's discussion of 'dialectical stalemates' in Essay 7.)

The history of this problem indicates that these controversies are reflections of irresolvable tensions in our thought about agency. Any constructive philosophical account of our practices will have to emphasize certain of its conflicting features at the expense of others. So any consistent, non-sceptical philosophical account will strike some as 'revisionist' to one degree or another. Although we can sometimes agree that some proposals are so off-centre that they in effect change the subject (that seems to be the general reaction to Smart's suggestion), the persistently attractive options in this area all seem to have too much going for them to be dismissed in this way.

For the same reasons, flat-out scepticism will always be extravagant at best. There is nonsense in our conception of freedom, to be sure, but it, too, must be 'right about important things'. Scepticism about this or that feature of our self-understanding makes sense, but to reject that understanding as

---

[23] Quoted by Elaine Woo, 'Obituary of Rogers Albritton', *Los Angeles Times*, Monday, 3 June 2002.

[24] Near the end of his essay, Randolph Clark complains that 'any freedom of the will that we enjoy [on a compatibilist] view, if not a complete fraud, is a pale imitation of the freedom that is characterized by an agent-causal account.' There is at least the slight concession here that a compatibilist reading of freedom might not be a total sham.

thoroughly corrupt (as though freedom must be the capacity for self-creation or nothing at all) is either obtuse or itself a kind of nonsense. The issue can only be what, short of self-creation, is available to us. Competing interpretations must make some kind of sense of our status as beings who are, in some respects and to various degrees, in charge of our lives and accountable to others. These interpretations will inevitably turn on judgements about 'the varieties of free will worth wanting' (in Daniel Dennett's phrase).[25] Here, as elsewhere, ethics is the mother of metaphysics. (For a discussion of the values that might be at stake in our attributions of free and responsible agency, see Fischer, Essay 10.)

[25] This is the sub-title of Dennett's important book, *Elbow Room* (Cambridge, Mass.: MIT Press, 1984).

1

HUMAN FREEDOM AND THE SELF

RODERICK M. CHISHOLM

A staff moves a stone, and is moved by a hand, which is moved by a man.

(Aristotle, *Physics*, 256a)

1. The metaphysical problem of human freedom might be summarized in the following way: Human beings are responsible agents; but this fact appears to conflict with a deterministic view of human action (the view that every event that is involved in an act is caused by some other event); and it *also* appears to conflict with an indeterministic view of human action (the view that the act, or some event that is essential to the act, is not caused at all.) To solve the problem, I believe, we must make somewhat far-reaching assumptions about the self or the agent—about the man who performs the act.

Perhaps it is needless to remark that, in all likelihood, it is impossible to say anything significant about this ancient problem that has not been said before.[1]

2. Let us consider some deed, or misdeed, that may be attributed to a responsible agent: one man, say, shot another. If the man *was* responsible for what he did, then, I would urge, what was to happen at the time of the shooting was something that was entirely up to the man himself. There was a moment at which it was true, both that he could have fired the shot and also that he could have refrained from firing it. And if this is so, then, even

The University of Kansas Lindley Lecture, 1964, pp. 3–15. Copyright © 1964 by the Department of Philosophy, University of Kansas. Reprinted by permission of the Department of Philosophy of the University of Kansas.

[1] The general position to be presented here is suggested in the following writings, among others: Aristotle, *Eudemian Ethics*, bk. ii, ch. 6: *Nicomachean Ethics*, bk. iii, chs. 1–5; Thomas Reid, *Essays on the Active Powers of Man*; C. A. Campbell, 'Is "Free Will" a Pseudo-Problem?' *Mind* (1951), 441–65; Roderick M. Chisholm. 'Responsibility and Avoidability', and Richard Taylor. 'Determination and the Theory of Agency', in *Determinism and Freedom in the Age of Modern Science*, ed. Sidney Hook (New York, 1958).

though he did fire it, he could have done something else instead. (He didn't find himself firing the shot 'against his will', as we say.) I think we can say, more generally, then, that if a man is responsible for a certain event or a certain state of affairs (in our example, the shooting of another man), then that event or state of affairs was brought about by some act of his, and the act was something that was in his power either to perform or not to perform.

But now if the act which he *did* perform was an act that was also in his power *not* to perform, then it could not have been caused or determined by any event that was not itself within his power either to bring about or not to bring about. For example, if what we say he did was really something that was brought about by a second man, one who forced his hand upon the trigger, say, or who, by means of hypnosis, compelled him to perform the act, then since the act was caused by the *second* man it was nothing that was within the power of the *first* man to prevent. And precisely the same thing is true, I think, if instead of referring to a second man who compelled the first one, we speak instead of the *desires* and *beliefs* which the first man happens to have had. For if what we say he did was really something that was brought about by his own beliefs and desires, if these beliefs and desires in the particular situation in which he happened to have found himself caused him to do just what it was that we say he did do, then, since *they* caused it, *he* was unable to do anything other than just what it was that he did do. It makes no difference whether the cause of the deed was internal or external; if the cause was some state or event for which the man himself was not responsible, then he was not responsible for what we have been mistakenly calling his act. If a flood caused the poorly constructed dam to break, then, given the flood and the constitution of the dam, the break, we may say, *had* to occur and nothing could have happened in its place. And if the flood of desire caused the weak-willed man to give in, then he, too, had to do just what it was that he did do and he was no more responsible than was the dam for the results that followed. (It is true, of course, that if the man is responsible for the beliefs and desires that he happens to have, then he may also be responsible for the things they lead him to do. But the question now becomes: *is* he responsible for the beliefs and desires he happens to have? If he is, then there was a time when they were within his power either to acquire or not to acquire, and we are left, therefore, with our general point.)

One may object: But surely if there were such a thing as a man who is really *good*, then he would be responsible for things that he would do; yet, he would be unable to do anything other than just what it is that he does do, since, being good, he will always choose to do what is best. The answer, I think, is suggested by a comment that Thomas Reid makes upon an ancient author. The author had said of Cato, 'He was good because he could not be otherwise', and Reid observes: 'This saying, if understood literally and strictly, is not the praise of Cato, but of his constitution, which was no more the work of Cato than his existence'.[2] If Cato was himself responsible for the good things that he did, then Cato, as Reid suggests, was such that, although he had the power to do what was not good, he exercised his power only for that which was good.

All of this, if it is true, may give a certain amount of comfort to those who are tender-minded. But we should remind them that it also conflicts with a familiar view about the nature of God—with the view that St. Thomas Aquinas expresses by saying that 'every movement both of the will and of nature proceeds from God as the Prime Mover'.[3] If the act of the sinner *did* proceed from God as the Prime Mover, then God was in the position of the second agent we just discussed—the man who forced the trigger finger, or the hypnotist—and the sinner, so-called, was *not* responsible for what he did. (This may be a bold assertion, in view of the history of western theology, but I must say that I have never encountered a single good reason for denying it.)

There is one standard objection to all of this and we should consider it briefly.

3. The objection takes the form of a stratagem—one designed to show that determinism (and divine providence) is consistent with human responsibility. The stratagem is one that was used by Jonathan Edwards and by many philosophers in the present century, most notably, G. E. Moore.[4]

One proceeds as follows: The expression

(a) He could have done otherwise,

it is argued, means no more nor less than

(b) If he had chosen to do otherwise, then he would have done otherwise.

(In place of 'chosen', one might say 'tried', 'set out', 'decided', 'undertaken', or 'willed'.) The truth of statement (b), it is then pointed out, is consistent with determinism (and with divine providence); for even if all of the man's actions were causally determined, the man could still be such that, *if* he had chosen otherwise, then he would have done otherwise. What the murderers saw, let us suppose, along with his beliefs and desires, *caused* him to fire the

[2] Thomas Reid, *Essays on the Active Powers of Man*, essay iv, ch. 4 (*Works*, 600).

[3] *Summa Theologica*. First Part of the Second Part. qu. vi ('On the Voluntary and Involuntary').

[4] Jonathan Edwards, *Freedom of the Will* (New Haven, 1957); G. E. Moore, *Ethics* (Home University Library, 1912), ch. 6.

shot; yet he was such that *if*, just then, he had chosen or decided *not* to fire the shot, then he would not have fired it. All of this is certainly possible. Similarly, we could say, of the dam, that the flood caused it to break and also that the dam was such that, *if* there had been no flood or any similar pressure, then the dam would have remained intact. And therefore, the argument proceeds, if (b) is consistent with determinism, and if (a) and (b) say the same thing, then (a) is also consistent with determinism; hence we can say that the agent *could* have done otherwise even though he was caused to do what he did do; and therefore determinism and moral responsibility are compatible.

Is the argument sound? The conclusion follows from the premises, but the catch, I think, lies in the first premise—the one saying that statement (a) tells us no more nor less than what statement (b) tells us. For (b), it would seem, could be true while (a) is false. That is to say, our man might be such that, if he had chosen to do otherwise, then he would have done otherwise, and yet *also* such that he could not have done otherwise. Suppose, after all, that our murderer could not have *chosen*, or could not have *decided*, to do otherwise. Then the fact that he happens also to be a man such that, if he had chosen not to shoot he would not have shot, would make no difference. For if he could *not* have chosen *not* to shoot, then he could not have done anything other than just what it was that he did do. In a word: from our statement (b) above ('If he had chosen to do otherwise, then he would have done otherwise'), we cannot make an inference to (a) above ('He could have done otherwise') unless we can *also* assert:

(c) He could have chosen to do otherwise.

And therefore, if we must reject this third statement (c), then, even though we may be justified in asserting (b), we are not justified in asserting (a). If the man could not have chosen to do otherwise, then he would not have done otherwise—*even if* he was such that, if he *had* chosen to do otherwise, then he would have done otherwise.

The stratagem in question, then, seems to me not to work, and I would say, therefore, that the ascription of responsibility conflicts with a deterministic view of action.

4. Perhaps there is less need to argue that the ascription of responsibility also conflicts with an indeterministic view of action—with the view that the act, or some event that is essential to the act, is not caused at all. If the act—the firing of the shot—was not caused at all, if it was fortuitous or capricious, happening so to speak out of the blue, then, presumably, no one—and nothing—was responsible for the act. Our conception of action, therefore,

should be neither deterministic nor indeterministic. Is there any other possibility?

5. We must not say that every event involved in the act is caused by some other event; and we must not say that the act is something that is not caused at all. The possibility that remains, therefore, is this: We should say that at least one of the events that are involved in the act is caused, not by any other events, but by something else instead. And this something else can only be the agent—the man. If there is an event that is caused, not by other events, but by the man, then there are some events involved in the act that are not caused by other events. But if the event in question is caused by the man then it *is* caused and we are not committed to saying that there is something involved in the act that is not caused at all.

But this, of course, is a large consequence, implying something of considerable importance about the nature of the agent or the man.

6. If we consider only inanimate natural objects, we may say that causation, if it occurs, is a relation between *events* or *states of affairs*. The dam's breaking was an event that was caused by a set of other events—the dam being weak, the flood being strong, and so on. But if a man is responsible for a particular deed, then, if what I have said is true, there is some event, or set of events, that is caused, *not* by other events or states of affairs, but by the agent, whatever he may be.

I shall borrow a pair of medieval terms, using them, perhaps, in a way that is slightly different from that for which they were originally intended. I shall say that when one event or state of affairs (or set of events or states of affairs) causes some other event or state of affairs, then we have an instance of *transeunt* causation. And I shall say that when an *agent*, as distinguished from an event, causes an event or state of affairs, then we have an instance of *immanent* causation.

The nature of what is intended by the expression 'immanent causation' may be illustrated by this sentence from Aristotle's *Physics*: 'Thus, a staff moves a stone, and is moved by a hand, which is moved by a man.' (VII, 5, 256a, 6–8) If the man was responsible, then we have in this illustration a number of instances of causation—most of them transeunt but at least one of them immanent. What the staff did to the stone was an instance of transeunt causation, and thus we may describe it as a relation between events: 'the motion of the staff caused the motion of the stone.' And similarly for what the hand did to the staff: 'the motion of the hand caused the motion of the staff'. And, as we know from physiology, there are still other events which caused the motion of the hand. Hence we need not introduce the agent at this particular point, as Aristotle does—we *need* not, though we *may*. We *may* say that the hand was moved by the man, but we may *also* say that the motion of the hand was caused by the motion of certain muscles; and we may say that the motion of the muscles was caused by certain events that took place within the brain. But some event, and presumably one of those that took place within the brain, was caused by the agent and not by any other events.

There are, of course, objections to this way of putting the matter; I shall consider the two that seem to me to be most important.

7. One may object, firstly: 'If the *man* does anything, then, as Aristotle's remark suggests, what he does is to move the *hand*. But he certainly does not *do* anything to his brain—he may not even know that he *has* a brain. And if he doesn't do anything to the brain, and if the motion of the hand was caused by something that happened within the brain, then there is no point in appealing to "immanent causation" as being something incompatible with "transeunt causation"—for the whole thing, after all, is a matter of causal relations among events or states of affairs.'

The answer to this objection, I think, is this: It is true that the agent does not *do* anything with his brain, or to his brain, in the sense in which he *does* something with his hand and does something to the staff. But from this it does not follow that the agent was not the immanent cause of something that happened within his brain.

We should note a useful distinction that has been proposed by Professor A. I. Melden—namely, the distinction between 'making something A happen' and 'doing A'.[5] If I reach for the staff and pick it up, then one of the things that I *do* is just that—reach for the staff and pick it up. And if it is something that I do, then there is a very clear sense in which it may be said to be something that I know that I do. If you ask me, 'Are you doing something, or trying to do something, with the staff?', I will have no difficulty in finding an answer. But in doing something with the staff, I also make various things happen which are not in this same sense things that I do: I will make various air-particles move; I will free a number of blades of grass from the pressure that had been upon them; and I may cause a shadow to move from one place to another. If these are merely things that I make happen, as distinguished from things that I do, then I may know nothing whatever about them; I may not have the slightest idea that, in moving the staff, I am

---

[5] A. I. Melden, *Free Action* (London, 1961), especially ch. 3. Mr. Melden's own views, however, are quite the contrary of those that are proposed here.

bringing about any such thing as the motion of air-particles, shadows, and blades of grass.

We may say, in answer to the first objection, therefore, that it is true that our agent does nothing to his brain or with his brain; but from this it does not follow that the agent is not the immanent cause of some event within his brain; for the brain event may be something which, like the motion of the air-particles, he made happen in picking up the staff. The only difference between the two cases is this: in each case, he made something happen when he picked up the staff; but in the one case—the motion of the air-particles or of the shadows—it was the motion of the staff that caused the event to happen; and in the other case—the event that took place in the brain—it was this event that caused the motion of the staff.

The point is, in a word, that whenever a man does something A, then (by 'immanent causation') he makes a certain cerebral event happen, and this cerebral event (by 'transeunt causation') makes A happen.

8. The second objection is more difficult and concerns the very concept of 'immanent causation', or causation by an agent, as this concept is to be interpreted here. The concept is subject to a difficulty which has long been associated with that of the prime mover unmoved. We have said that there must be some event A, presumably some cerebral event, which is caused not by any other event, but by the agent. Since A was not caused by any other event, then the agent himself cannot be said to have undergone any change or produced any other event (such as 'an act of will' or the like) which brought A about. But if, when the agent made A happen, there was no event involved other than A itself, no event which could be described as *making* A happen, what did the agent's causation consist of? What, for example, is the difference between A's just happening, and the agents' *causing* A to happen? We cannot attribute the difference to any event that took place within the agent. And so far as the event A itself is concerned, there would seem to be no discernible difference. Thus Aristotle said that the activity of the prime mover is nothing in addition to the motion that it produces, and Suarez said that 'the action is in reality nothing but the effect as it flows from the agent'.[6] Must we conclude, then, that there is no more to the man's action in causing event A than there is to the event A's happening by itself? Here we would seem to have a distinction without a difference—in which case we have failed to find a *via media* between a deterministic and an indeterministic view of action.

---

[6] Aristotle, *Physics*, bk. iii, ch. 3; Suarez, *Disputations Metaphysicae*, Disputation 18, s 10.

The only answer, I think, can be this: that the difference between the man's causing A, on the one hand, and the event A just happening, on the other, lies in the fact that, in the first case but not the second, the event A *was* caused and was caused by the man. There was a brain event A; the agent did, in fact, cause the brain event; but there was nothing that he did to cause it.

This answer may not entirely satisfy and it will be likely to provoke the following question: 'But what are you really *adding* to the assertion that A happened when you utter the words "The agent *caused* A to happen"?' As soon as we have put the question this way, we see, I think, that whatever difficulty we may have encountered is one that may be traced to the concept of causation generally—whether 'immanent' or 'transeunt'. The problem, in other words, is not a problem that is peculiar to our conception of human action. It is a problem that must be faced by anyone who makes use of the concept of causation at all; and therefore, I would say, it is a problem for everyone but the complete indeterminist.

For the problem, as we put it, referring just to 'immanent causation', or causation by an agent, was this: 'What is the difference between saying, of an event A, that A just happened and saying that someone caused A to happen?' The analogous problem, which holds for 'transeunt causation', or causation by an event, is this: 'What is the difference between saying, of two events A and B, that B happened and then A happened, and saying that B's happening was the *cause* of A's happening?' And the only answer that one can give is this—that in the one case the agent was the cause of A's happening and in the other case event B was the cause of A's happening. The nature of transeunt causation is no more clear than is that of immanent causation.

9. But we may plausibly say—and there is a respectable philosophical tradition to which we may appeal—that the notion of immanent causation, or causation by an agent, is in fact more clear than that of transeunt causation, or causation by an event, and that it is only by understanding our own causal efficacy, as agents, that we can grasp the concept of *cause* at all. Hume may be said to have shown that we do not derive the concept of *cause* from what we perceive of external things. How, then, do we derive it? The most plausible suggestion, it seems to me, is that of Reid, once again: namely that 'the conception of an efficient cause may very probably be derived from the experience we have had . . . of our own power to produce certain effects'.[7] If we did not understand the concept of immanent causation, we would not understand that of transeunt causation.

---

[7] Reid. *Works*, 524.

10. It may have been noted that I have avoided the term 'free will' in all of this. For even if there is such a faculty as 'the will', which somehow sets our acts agoing, the question of freedom, as John Locke said, is not the question '*whether the will be free*'; it is the question '*whether a man be free*'.[8] For if there is a 'will', as a moving faculty, the question is whether the man is free to will to do these things that he does will to do—and also whether he is free *not* to will any of those things that he does will to do, and, again, whether he is free to will any of those things that he does not will to do. Jonathan Edwards tried to restrict himself to the question—'Is the man free to do what it is that he wills?'—but the answer to this question will not tell us whether the man is responsible for what it is that he *does* will to do. Using still another pair of medieval terms, we may say that the metaphysical problem of freedom does not concern the *actus imperatus*; it does not concern the question whether we are free to accomplish whatever it is that we will or set out to do; it concerns the *actus elicitus*, the question whether we are free to will or to set out to do those things that we do will or set out to do.

11. If we are responsible, and if what I have been trying to say is true, then we have a prerogative which some would attribute only to God: each of us, when we act, is a prime mover unmoved. In doing what we do, we cause certain events to happen, and nothing—or no one—causes us to cause those events to happen.

12. If we are thus prime movers unmoved and if our actions, or those for which we are responsible, are not causally determined, then they are not causally determined by our *desires*. And this means that the relation between what we want or what we desire, on the one hand, and what it is that we do, on the other, is not as simple as most philosophers would have it.

We may distinguish between what we might call the 'Hobbist approach' and what we might call the 'Kantian approach' to this question. The Hobbist approach is the one that is generally accepted at the present time, but the Kantian approach, I believe, is the one that is true. According to Hobbism, if we *know*, of some man, what his beliefs and desires happen to be and how strong they are, if we know what he feels certain of, what he desires more than anything else, and if we know the state of his body and what stimuli he is being subjected to, then we may *deduce*, logically, just what it is that he will do—or, more accurately, just what it is that he will try, set out, or undertake to do. Thus Professor Melden has said that 'the connection between wanting

---

[8] *Essay concerning Human Understanding*, bk. ii, ch. 21.

and doing is logical'.[9] But according to the Kantian approach to our problem, and this is the one that I would take, there is no such logical connection between wanting and doing, nor need there even be a causal connection. No set of statements about a man's desires, beliefs, and stimulus situation at any time implies any statement telling us what the man will try, set out, or undertake to do at that time. As Reid put it, though we may 'reason from men's motives to their actions and, in many cases, with great probability', we can never do so 'with absolute certainty'.[10]

This means that, in one very strict sense of the terms, there can be no science of man. If we think of science as a matter of finding out what laws happen to hold, and if the statement of a law tells us what kinds of events are caused by what other kinds of events, then there will be human actions which we cannot explain by subsuming them under any laws. We cannot say, 'It is causally necessary that, given such and such desires and beliefs, and being subject to such and such stimuli, the agent will do so and so'. For at times the agent, if he chooses, may rise above his desires and do something else instead.

But all of this is consistent with saying that, perhaps more often than not, our desires do exist under conditions such that those conditions necessitate us to act. And we may also say, with Leibniz, that at other times our desires may 'incline without necessitating'.

13. Leibniz's phrase presents us with our final philosophical problem. What does it mean to say that a desire, or a motive, might 'incline without necessitating'? There is a temptation, certainly, to say that 'to incline' means to cause and that 'not to necessitate' means not to cause, but obviously we cannot have it both ways.

Nor will Leibniz's own solution do. In his letter to Coste, he puts the problem as follows: 'When a choice is proposed, for example to go out or not to go out, it is a question whether, with all the circumstances, internal and external, motives, perceptions, dispositions, impressions, passions, inclinations taken together, I am still in a contingent state, or whether I am necessitated to make the choice, for example, to go out; that is to say, whether this proposition true and determined in fact, *In all these circumstances taken together I shall choose to go out*, is contingent or necessary.'[11] Leibniz's answer might be put as follows: in one sense of the terms 'necessary' and 'contingent', the proposition 'In all these circumstances taken together I

---

[9] Melden, 166.

[10] Reid, *Works*, 608, 612.

[11] 'Lettre à Mr. Coste de la Nécessité et de la Contingence' (1707) in *Opera Philosophica*, ed. Erdmann, 447–9.

shall choose to go out', may be said to be contingent and not necessary, and in another sense of these terms, it may be said to be necessary and not contingent. But the sense in which the proposition may be said to be contingent, according to Leibniz, is only this: there is no logical contradiction involved in denying the proposition. And the sense in which it may be said to be necessary is this: since 'nothing ever occurs without cause or determining reason', the proposition is causally necessary. 'Whenever all the circumstances taken together are such that the balance of deliberation is heavier on one side than on the other, it is certain and infallible that that is the side that is going to win out'. But if what we have been saying is true, the proposition 'In all these circumstances taken together I shall choose to go out', may be causally as well as logically contingent. Hence we must find another interpretation for Leibniz's statement that our motives and desires may incline us, or influence us, to choose without thereby necessitating us to choose.

Let us consider a public official who has some moral scruples but who also, as one says, could be had. Because of the scruples that he does have, he would never take any positive steps to receive a bribe—he would not actively solicit one. But his morality has its limits and he is also such that, if we were to confront him with a *fait accompli* or to let him see what is about to happen ($10,000 in cash is being deposited behind the garage), then he would succumb and be unable to resist. The general situation is a familiar one and this is one reason that people pray to be delivered from temptation. (It also justifies Kant's remark: 'And how many there are who may have led a long blameless life, who are only *fortunate* in having escaped so many temptations'.)[12] Our relation to the misdeed that we contemplate may not be a matter simply of being able to bring it about or not to bring it about. As St. Anselm noted, there are at least four possibilities. We may illustrate them by reference to our public official and the event which is his receiving the bribe, in the following way: (i) he may be able to bring the event about himself (*facere esse*), in which case he would actively cause himself to receive the bribe; (ii) he may be able to refrain from bringing it about himself (*non facere esse*), in which case he would not himself do anything to insure that he receive the bribe; (iii) he may be able to do something to prevent the event from occurring (*facere non esse*), in which case he would make sure that the $10,000 was *not* left behind the garage; or (iv) he may be unable to do anything to prevent the event from occurring (*non facere non esse*), in which case, though he may not solicit the bribe, he would allow

[12] In the Preface to the *Metaphysical Elements of Ethics*, in *Kant's Critique of Practical Reason and Other Works on the Theory of Ethics*, ed. T. K. Abbott (London, 1959), 303.

himself to keep it.[13] We have envisaged our official as a man who can resist the temptation to (i) but cannot resist the temptation to (iv): he can refrain from bringing the event about himself, but he cannot bring himself to do anything to prevent it.

Let us think of 'inclination without necessitation', then, in such terms as these. First we may contrast the two propositions:

(1) He can resist the temptation to do something in order to make A happen;

(2) He can resist the temptation to allow A to happen (i.e. to do nothing to prevent A from happening).

We may suppose that the man has some desire to have A happen and thus has a motive for making A happen. His motive for making A happen, I suggest, is one that *necessitates* provided that, because of the motive, (1) is false; he cannot resist the temptation to do something in order to make A happen. His motive for making A happen is one that *inclines* provided that, because of the motive, (2) is false; like our public official, he cannot bring himself to do anything to prevent A from happening. And therefore we can say that this motive for making A happen is one that *inclines but does not necessitate* provided that, because of the motive, (1) is true and (2) is false; he can resist the temptation to make it happen but he cannot resist the temptation to allow it to happen.

---

[13] Cf. D. P. Henry, 'Saint Anselm's *De "Grammatico"*', *Philosophical Quarterly*, x (1960), 115–26. St. Anselm noted that (i) and (iii), respectively, may be thought of as forming the upper left and the upper right corners of a square of opposition, and (ii) and (iv) the lower left and the lower right.

2

AN ARGUMENT FOR INCOMPATIBILISM

PETER VAN INWAGEN

3.1 The main contested question in current discussions of free will is not, as one might expect, whether we *have* free will. It is whether free will is compatible with determinism. It seems to me that free will and determinism are incompatible, and in this chapter I shall try to demonstrate this incompatibility.

Discussions of this question are usually not on a very high level. In the great majority of cases, they are the work of compatibilists and consist to a large degree in the ascription of some childish fallacy or other to incompatibilists (conflation of "descriptive" and "prescriptive" laws; failure to distinguish between causal necessity and compulsion; equation of freedom and mere randomness). Donald Davidson places himself in this tradition when he writes:

I shall not be directly concerned with [arguments for the incompatibility of freedom and causal determination], since I know of none that is more than superficially plausible. Hobbes, Locke, Hume, Moore, Schlick, Ayer, Stevenson, and a host of others have done what can be done, or ought ever to have been needed, to remove the confusions that can make determinism seem to oppose freedom.[1]

It is not my purpose in this book to defend any previous writer against a charge of fallacious argument. My own arguments will be explicit, and any fallacies they commit should be correspondingly visible. (It is doubtful whether anyone has ever been seduced by the fallacies with which incompatibilists are customarily charged; if anyone indeed has achieved such a level of philosophical incompetence, I, at least, fall short of it.) Now the line between arguing for a certain view and ascribing fallacious reasoning to the opponents of that view, while clear enough in theory, is often blurred in practice. Entangled with the charges of fallacy and confusion made in the writings of the philosophers Davidson mentions, there are positive

---

[1] "Freedom to Act" in Ted Honderich, ed., *Essays on Freedom of Action* (London: 1973), 139.

arguments for the compatibility of free will and determinism. In so far as these arguments can be disentangled from diagnoses of ills *I* am not heir to—if, indeed, these ills exist at all—I shall examine them in Chapter IV [omitted here].[2]

3.2 In Chapter I, I mentioned the following simple argument for incompatibilism, the Consequence Argument:

> If determinism is true, then our acts are the consequences of the laws of nature and events in the remote past. But it is not up to us what went on before we were born, and neither is it up to us what the laws of nature are. Therefore, the consequences of these things (including our present acts) are not up to us.

This, I think, is a *good* argument. But I must admit it's rather sketchy. The present chapter is an attempt to fill in the details of this sketch . . .

3.3 In this section, and in the following section, I shall explain what I mean by certain terms that will be used in the first argument for incompatibilism.

I shall begin by attempting to say what I mean by *determinism*. In order to define determinism I shall need three subordinate notions: the notion of a *proposition* (and allied notions such as *truth*, *denial*, *conjunction*, and *entailment*) and the notion of *the state of the entire physical world at an instant*, and the notion of a *law of nature*.

Propositions (that is, non-linguistic bearers of truth-value) were introduced in Section 2.4. I have little to add to what I said there and in 2.7 about propositions, truth, and falsity. I shall assume only that propositions have the following four properties. (i) To every possible way the world could be, there corresponds at least one proposition, a proposition that is necessarily such that it is true if and only if the world *is* that way. Since there are doubtless ways things could be that are too complex to be described in any natural language, this means that there are propositions that cannot be

---

[2] I know of only one fallacy that incompatibilists have been accused of that is not childish. In *Will, Freedom and Power* (Oxford: 1976), 175–6, Anthony Kenny charges that incompatibilists make use of the following rule of inference, which he contends is invalid:

I cannot do so-and-so
To do such-and-such is, in this case, to do so-and-so
hence, I cannot do such-and-such.

(The incompatibilist, Kenny says, proceeds by substituting 'violate a law of nature' for 'do so-and-so' and expressions denoting unperformed acts for 'do such-and-such'.) Whether or not this inference form is valid, and I do not think Kenny presents a clear counter-example to it, I cannot see that any of the arguments of the present chapter depends on it, despite the fact that these arguments do depend on our inability to render false any proposition that is a law of nature.

expressed in any natural language. (ii) Every proposition is either true or false. (iii) The conjunction of a true and a false proposition is a false proposition. (iv) Propositions obey the Law of Contraposition with respect to entailment. That is, for every x and every y, if x and y are propositions, and if it is impossible for x to be true and y false, then it is impossible for the denial of y to be true and the denial of x false.

One "model" for propositions that gives them these features is this: propositions are identified with sets of possible worlds.[3] A proposition in this sense is *true* if it contains the actual world; the *denial* of a proposition is its complement on the set of all possible worlds; the *conjunction* of two propositions is their intersection; one proposition *entails* a second if the former is a subset of the latter. I am not wedded to this model. It has features that unfit the "propositions" it models for certain tasks traditionally assigned to things called 'propositions'. For example, in Section 2.4, "propositions" were introduced as things that could be accepted, asserted, proved, denied, and so on. But the objects of such activities can hardly be modelled on sets of possible worlds, for on that model, for example, the proposition that some Albanian barber shaves all those and only those Albanians who do not shave themselves is identical with the proposition that there are Greek geometers who know how to trisect the angle: each is the empty set. Yet if these propositions are objects of assertion or denial, surely they must be distinct propositions. Still, this model yields all the features of propositions that I need for my present purposes, and shows, assuming the consistency of the notions of *set* and *possible world*, that these features are consistent.

Let us now turn to *the state of the entire physical world* (hereinafter, *the state of the world*) *at an instant*. I shall leave this notion largely unexplained, since my argument is very nearly independent of its content. Provided the following two conditions are met, one may flesh out 'the state of the world' in any way one likes.

(i) Our concept of *state* must be such that, given that the world is in a certain state at a certain instant, nothing *follows* about its state at any other instant: if x and y are any "states", and some possible world is in x at t_1 and y at t_2, there is a world that is in x at t_1 and *not* in y at t_2. For example, we must not choose a concept of *state* that would allow as a part of a description of the momentary state of the world, the clause, '. . . and, at T, the world is such that someone's left hand will be raised 10 seconds later than T'.

The theory of relativity has the consequence that this notion—the state of the world at an instant—has no application to things as they are, and is perhaps even incoherent. But there is a relativistically acceptable concept—

---

[3] In sec. 3.6 [omitted here] I shall explain in detail what I mean by *possible world* and related notions like that of truth "in" a world.

the state of things on the surface of a light-cone—that could be used in its place. This refinement, however, could be implemented only by tedious and philosophically irrelevant (in the present context) elaboration of definitions and arguments that are already rather more elaborate than I like. I shall therefore ignore relativistic considerations in the sequel. The second and third arguments will be similarly unsophisticated.

(ii) If there is some observable change in the way things are—if a white cloth becomes blue, a warm liquid cold, or if a man raises his hand—this change must entail some change in the state of the world. That is, our concept of *state* must not be so theoretical, so divorced from what is observably true, that, for example, it be possible for the world to be in the *same* state at t_1 and t_2, despite the fact that someone's hand is raised at t_1 and not at t_2. It is arguable that this requirement is incompatible with our interpreting *state* as *quantum-mechanical state*, for it is arguable that there exists a moment t and possible worlds w_1 and w_2 such that w_1 and w_2 are in the same quantum-mechanical state at t, although a certain cat is, in w_1, alive at t and, in w_2, dead at t.[4] But I shall say nothing about the deep and difficult problems this contention raises.

Having defined—or, at any rate, discussed—the notions of *proposition* and *state of the world at an instant*, we shall now combine them. Let us say that a proposition *expresses the state of the world at t* provided it is a true proposition that asserts of some state that, at t, the world is in that state. (We may put the matter this way in terms of our "sets of possible worlds" model of propositions: a proposition *p purports to express the state of the world at t* if there is some state such that p contains all those and only those worlds that are in that state at t; *p expresses the state of the world at t* if it purports to express the state of the world at t and is, moreover, true.)

Finally, I need the notion of a *law of nature*. I have no idea how to explain this term, much less define it. But I can say what I do *not* mean by it: as I said in Section 1.3, it is not an *epistemological* term. Ontologically speaking, a law of nature is a proposition: some propositions have the feature *being a law of nature* and some don't, and which do and which don't is a matter utterly independent of the present state of scientific knowledge and the history of scientific knowledge. The laws of nature would be just as they are even if there had never been any human beings or other rational animals. *Law of nature*, at least in my usage, is no more an epistemological term than is *star*. (Ontologically speaking, a star is a material body: some material bodies have

---

[4] This point has nothing to do with the so-called "many-worlds" interpretation of quantum mechanics. What I call possible worlds are abstract objects: ways the universe might be. The "worlds" of the many-worlds interpretation of quantum mechanics, however, are concrete objects: universes.

the feature *being a star* and some don't, and which do and which don't is a matter utterly independent of the present state of astronomical knowledge and of the history of astronomy. The stars would be just as they are even if there had never been any human beings or other rational animals.)

Despite the parallels I want to draw between the stars and the laws of nature, I want also to insist on an important difference between our *powers* with respect to these two classes of objects. It is quite conceivable that human power will grow to the extent that we shall one day be able to alter the stars in their courses. But we shall never be able to do anything about the laws of nature. There are presumably many propositions that are in fact true, but which it is within our power to falsify. Probably the proposition that no one ever has read or ever will read all of the *Oxford English Dictionary* aloud is true. I should think, however, that someone *could* falsify this proposition if he were willing to devote a large part of his life to this pointless task. But suppose someone has set out to falsify the Principle of the Conservation of Angular Momentum. That is, suppose someone is attempting to construct a piece of laboratory apparatus the behaviour of which would violate this principle. If the principle is a law of nature, he cannot succeed. If he *can* succeed (even if he doesn't), that is, if he has it within his power to succeed, then it is not a law. We might even imagine that the principle is in fact *true* but is not a law simply because someone can falsify it. Suppose that a certain physicist designs a certain piece of apparatus and that all competent physicists agree that if this piece of apparatus were built and put into operation it would violate the Principle of the Conservation of Angular Momentum. Suppose a respected firm of engineering contractors, having examined the physicist's specifications, state that it would be possible, given "the state of the art", to build the device. Suppose the physicists and engineers are right. But suppose that actually to construct the device would require an *enormous* expenditure of resources, a fact that results in its never being constructed. We may consistently add to these suppositions the supposition that angular momentum is conserved, that is, that the Principle of the Conservation of Angular Momentum is *true*. But this principle would simply not be a law of nature if such a device *could* be constructed: if human beings *can* (have it within their power to) conduct an experiment or construct a device that would falsify a certain proposition, then that proposition is not a law of nature. A law of nature must be immune to such possible disconfirmation. This of course is consistent with our saying that for any given law we could *conceive* of an experiment that would disconfirm it.

The conclusion of the above argument may be restated this way: the laws of nature impose limits on our abilities: they are partly determinative of what it is possible for us to do. And indeed this conclusion is hardly more than a tautology. The oddness of denying it can be brought out if we think of someone ordering a subordinate to violate a law of nature. Suppose a bureaucrat of the future orders an engineer to build a spaceship capable of travelling faster than light. The engineer tells the bureaucrat that it's a law of nature that nothing travels faster than light. The bureaucrat concedes this difficulty, but counsels perseverance: "I'm sure", he says, "that if you work hard and are very clever, you'll find some way to go faster than light, even though it's a law of nature that nothing does." Clearly his demand is simply incoherent.

I should point out that the above conclusion does not rest on the premiss that the laws of nature are *true* propositions. I am not saying that it is impossible for us to alter the laws of nature owing simply to the fact that it is logically impossible to cause any proposition simultaneously to satisfy the conditions 'x is a law of nature' and 'x is false' (laws of nature being by definition true).[5] If this argument were valid, one could derive fatalism from the premiss that it is logically impossible to cause any proposition simultaneously to satisfy the conditions 'x is a true proposition' and 'x is false'. But, as I said in Chapter II, many true propositions are such that one can render them false: the schema 'If P is a true proposition, then no one can render P false' has many counter-instances, at least in my opinion. The instance got by replacing 'P' with 'the proposition that no one ever reads all of the *OED* aloud' is one. No law of nature, however, is such that anyone can render it false: the schema, 'If P is a law of nature, then no one can render P false' has *no* counter-instances. Or put the matter this way: it is true and trivial, and not what I am arguing for, to say, "It is impossible for there to be a person x and a proposition y such that x can bring it about that y is a law of nature and y is false". Call this 'the *de dicto* principle'. It is also true to say, "It is necessary that, for every person x and every proposition y, if y is a law of nature, then x cannot render y false". This is at least *less* trivial and it is what I have been arguing for. Call this 'the *de re* principle'. From the *de re* principle and 'the proposition that momentum is conserved is a law of nature', we may validly deduce, 'Feynman cannot render the proposition that momentum is conserved false'. But from this premiss and the *de dicto* principle, no such conclusion follows. Note that such applications of *modus ponens* to instances of the *de re* principle may yield contingent truths, since the proposition that a given proposition is a law of nature may very well be a contingent truth. Feynman, for example, may be unable to render the proposition that momentum is conserved false because this proposition is a law

[5] Not that I *believe* that laws of nature are by definition true. See sec. 1.5. But I shall from now on assume that lawhood entails truth. This assumption could be dispensed with at the cost of minor complications.

of nature. But, for all I know, there are possible worlds in which he exists and in which this proposition (though perhaps true) is not a law of nature and in which he is able to render it false.

If we interpret 'law of nature' very broadly, there seem to be exceptions to the *de re* principle, and these must be dealt with. Consider *psychological* laws, including laws, if such there be, about the voluntary behaviour of rational agents. If there are such laws, it is at least arguable that they should be included among the "laws of nature"; rational agents are, after all, in some sense part of "nature". But it is hard to see how to avoid the conclusion that, if we have free will, we have it within our power to act differently from the way such laws say we shall act. Let us look at a particular case.

Suppose psychologists discover that no one who has received moral training of type A in early childhood ever spreads lying rumours about his professional colleagues. Suppose you and I in fact received such training. Does it follow that we *can't* engage in this odious activity? I don't see why it should be supposed to follow. (Mark Twain: "I am morally superior to George Washington. He couldn't tell a lie. I can and I don't.") Suppose further that you and I are in fact *able* to spread lying rumours about our colleagues. Does it follow that a statement of the regularity we have imagined psychologists to have discovered is, though true, not a law? Well, suppose the existence of this regularity is a logical consequence of some well-confirmed theory of human moral development that has great explanatory and predictive power. In that case, it would certainly be very *tempting* to call this statement a 'law'; I should hardly want to counsel resistance to this temptation. "But why", someone may ask, "does this regular pattern of behaviour occur if people don't *have* to conform to it?" Note that the only people in a position to depart from it are those who have in fact had training of type A. Perhaps it is just these people who *see the point* in not spreading lying rumours. To come to see the point in not exercising an ability one has is not to *lose* that ability.

So it seems at least plausible to suppose that the *de re* principle might be false if 'law of nature' were interpreted broadly enough. I shall simply narrow the interpretation of 'law of nature' by fiat: "laws of nature" in the sequel shall be by definition propositions that apply non-vacuously to things that are *not* rational agents. (Things such as teacups, electrons, and galaxies.) For such laws, I maintain, the *de re* principle holds good. This stipulation has an important consequence. It may well be that, for all that is said in this book, human behaviour is wholly predictable on the basis of laws that are about the voluntary behaviour of rational agents. Moreover, I see no reason to think that such predictability would be incompatible with free will.

Let us make one further stipulation about the laws of nature: the logical consequences of any set of laws of nature are also laws. This stipulation produces what is in some ways a rather artificial notion of a law of nature. It has, for example, the consequence that the conjunction of Snell's Law with the Principle of the Conservation of Angular Momentum (assuming these propositions to be laws) is a law. If anyone is troubled by this stipulation, which I adopt only because it will simplify the statement of my argument, he may read 'the laws of nature' in the sequel as 'the logical consequences of the laws of nature'. Thus, on our "sets of possible worlds" model for propositions, a law of nature is any set of worlds that has as a subset the set of all worlds in which the laws of nature are the same as those of the actual world, or, as we might say, are *nomologically congruent with* the actual world.

We may now define 'determinism'. We shall apply this term to the conjunction of these two theses:

> For every instant of time, there is a proposition that expresses the state of the world at that instant;[6]
>
> If *p* and *q* are any propositions that express the state of the world at some instants, then the conjunction of *p* with the laws of nature entails *q*.

This definition seems to me to capture at least one thesis that could properly be called 'determinism'. Determinism is, intuitively, the thesis that, given the past and the laws of nature, there is only one possible future. And this definition certainly has that consequence. It *also* has the consequence that the future determines a unique past. This consequence, however, does not trouble me. The only *physical* theories that are known to be deterministic "from-past-to-future" (two-particle classical mechanics and certain mathematically similar theories) are also known to be deterministic "from-future-to-past". There are "theories" in a certain broad sense of the word that are only "one-way" deterministic—"theories" describing the behaviour of certain Turing machines, for example—but I should be at least mildly surprised to see any plausible *physical* theory that had that feature. But if anyone is really troubled about this, he may add a suitable "later than" clause to the definition. Such an addition will not affect the use I shall make of this definition in what follows.

The reader will note that the horrible little word 'cause' does not appear in this definition. Causation is a morass in which I for one refuse to set foot. Or

---

[6] This thesis would seem to entail that there are at least as many propositions as there are moments of time; and, presumably, there are as many moments of time as there are real numbers. To postulate an indenumerable infinity of propositions, most of which are not things that could possibly be thought of, owing to their unimaginable complexity, may seem to some people to be extravagant. But I do not see how to state the thesis of determinism without some "extravagant" assumption. Compare Richard Montague's criticism, in the opening paragraphs of "Deterministic Theories", of the characterization of determinism that he attributes to Laplace and Ernest Nagel. (*Formal Philosophy* (New Haven: 1974), 303 f.)

not unless I am pushed. Certain arguments for the compatibility of free will and determinism will force me to say something about the relation between determinism and "universal causation". (See Section 4.4 [omitted here].)

3.4 Determinism is a thesis about propositions, but the free-will thesis is a thesis about agents. If we are going to investigate the conceptual relations between these two theses, we shall do well to state the free-will thesis as a thesis about agents and propositions. I propose to do this by devising a way to describe our powers to act—and, by acting, to modify the world—as powers over the truth-values of propositions. This can be done as follows. Consider the propositions I should express if I were to utter any of the following sentences at the present moment:

(a) $27 \times 15 = 405$;
(b) Magnets attract iron;
(c) Mary Queen of Scots was put to death in 1587;
(d) I have never read *The Teachings of Don Juan*;
(e) No one has ever read all of Hume's *Enquiry* aloud;
(f) The cup on my desk has never been broken.

(All these propositions are, I think, true.) There is at least one important and interesting difference between the relations I bear to (a)–(c) and those I bear to (d)-(f). The difference I have in mind might be described in various ways: there is nothing I can do, or ever could have done, about the fact that (a)–(c) are true, and this is not the case with (d)–(f); the truth of (a)–(c) is something it is not and never has been within my power to change, though the truth of (d)–(f) is something that it is within my power, or once was within my power, to change; (a)–(c) are true and I do not have, and never have had, any choice about this, but, though (d)–(f) are true, this is something I have a choice about, or is something I once had a choice about. (In making these assertions about the difference between (a)–(c), on the one hand, and (d)–(f), on the other, I assume I have free will. If I don't, then this apparent difference between the two sets of statements is illusory.)

I shall mark this distinction by using an idiom I introduced in Section 2.5: I *can render*, or once *could have rendered*, all of (d)–(f) *false*; I *cannot render*, and never *could have rendered*, any of (a)-(c) *false*. I rather like the name *being able to render false* for this relation that I bear to (d)–(f) and do not bear to (a)–(c). But I admit that this name could be misleading. In fact it has been misleading. My use of this phrase has on occasion created the impression that I believe that human beings can somehow enter into *causal* relations with propositions.[7] But being able to render a proposition false is

---

[7] See Jan Narveson, "Compatibilism Defended", *Philosophical Studies* (1977).

nothing so metaphysically exotic as that; to be able to render a proposition false is to be able to arrange or modify the concrete objects that constitute one's environment—shoes, ships, bits of sealing wax—in a way sufficient for the falsity of that proposition.

But how shall we understand this sufficiency? We might understand 'sufficient' to mean 'logically sufficient'. That is, we might understand '*s* can render *p* false' to mean 'It is within *s*'s power to arrange or modify the concrete objects that constitute his environment in some way such that it is not possible "in the broadly logical sense" that he arrange or modify these objects in that way and *p* be true'.[8] For example, I can, according to this proposal, render false the proposition that this cup is never broken, since I can break this cup—at least if I have free will—and it is not possible that I break this cup and this cup never be broken. If I *could* move my hand faster than light, then I *could*, in the sense proposed, render false the proposition that nothing ever travels faster than light, since it is not possible that I should move my hand faster than light and nothing ever travel faster than light.

I do not believe that this proposal exactly captures the intuitive notion of being able to render a proposition false, that is, the notion of "having control over" the truth-value of a proposition. Let us suppose that in 1550 Nostradamus predicted that the Sphinx would endure till the end of the world. And let us suppose that this prediction was correct and, in fact, that *all* Nostradamus's predictions were correct. Let us also suppose that it was within Gamal Abdel Nasser's power to have the Sphinx destroyed. Then, I should think, it was within Nasser's power to render false the proposition that all Nostradamus's predictions were correct. But this would not be the case according to the definition proposed in the preceding paragraph, since it is possible in the broadly logical sense that Nasser have had the Sphinx destroyed and yet all Nostradamus's predictions have been correct. That is, there are possible worlds in which the proposition that all Nostradamus's predictions were correct is true and in which Nasser had the Sphinx destroyed: worlds in which Nostradamus did *not* predict that the Sphinx would endure till the end of the world and made no other predictions that would have been falsified by Nasser's destruction of the Sphinx.

The best way to rule out such counter-examples would seem to be to "build the past into" our definition. More precisely, we may define '*s* can render *p* false' as follows:

> It is within *s*'s power to arrange or modify the concrete objects that constitute his environment in some way such that it is not possible in the broadly

---

[8] The phrase 'possible in the broadly logical sense' is Alvin Plantinga's. See *The Nature of Necessity* (Oxford: 1974), 1 f.

logical sense that he arrange or modify those objects in that way and the past have been exactly as it in fact was and *p* be true.

I believe that this definition captures the notion that is suggested by the words 'being able to render a proposition false', except, perhaps, for the case of false propositions about the past.[9] For example, it has the consequence that I can render the proposition that Socrates died of old age false, since it is not possible that the past should have been exactly as it in fact was and Socrates have died of old age. There are three reasons why this feature of our definition need not trouble us, however. First, it would be easy enough to remove it by some *ad hoc* fiat. Moreover, the first argument for the incompatibility of free will and determinism will involve only *true* propositions. Finally, the 'can render false' idiom will not appear in the *conclusion* of the argument. Thus the odd consequences of the definition can affect the conclusion of the argument only if they result in some defect (such as falsity) in at least one of its premisses.

3.5 Now the first argument. I shall imagine a case in which a certain man, after due deliberation, refrained from performing a certain contemplated act. I shall then argue that, if determinism is true, that man *could not have* performed that act. Because this argument will not depend on any features peculiar to our imagined case, the incompatibility of free will and determinism in general will be established, since, as will be evident, a parallel argument could easily be devised for the case of any agent and any unperformed act.

Let us suppose that there was once a judge who had only to raise his right hand at a certain time, T, to prevent the execution of a sentence of death

---

[9] There is one other way in which this definition may diverge from our intuitive notion of one's having the truth-value of a proposition within one's power. Consider the proposition that the safe is locked. Even if we were normally in the habit of talking of rendering propositions false, we should not normally say that an agent had it within his power to render this proposition false if he did not know, and had no way of discovering, the combination. But it may well be that a certain agent, who has no way of finding out the combination, is in the following situation: (i) he has it within his power to turn the dial left to 26, right to 32, left to 5; (ii) it is not possible that he should do this and the past be as it was and the safe remain locked. Thus, by the strict terms of our definition, he can render false the proposition that the safe is locked. Therefore, it might be argued, what our definition really captures is something that is more like '*s* could, if he were lucky enough, render *p* false' than it is like '*s* can render *p* false'. But if this is so, it will not materially affect our argument. Our argument will, loosely speaking, proceed by deducing 'It is not the case that *s* can render *p* false', for arbitrary values of *p*, from determinism. If this thesis deduced from determinism is really best read '*s* could not, no matter how lucky he was, render *p* false', this fact would hardly undermine my claim to have demonstrated the incompatibility of free will and determinism. Moreover, the present definition has the useful consequence that '*s* can render *p* false' is a purely extensional context, a feature that might very well have to be sacrificed in order to produce a more intuitive result in cases like the case of 'He can render the proposition that the safe is locked false'.

upon a certain criminal, such a hand-raising being the sign, according to the conventions of the judge's country, of a granting of special clemency. Let us further suppose that the judge—call him 'J'—refrained from raising his hand at T, and that this inaction resulted in the criminal's being put to death. We may also suppose that J was unbound, uninjured, and free from any paralysis of the limbs; that he decided not to raise his hand at T only after a suitable period of calm, rational, and relevant deliberation; that he had not been subjected to any "pressure" to decide one way or the other about the criminal's death; that he was not under the influence of drugs, hypnosis, or anything of that sort; and, finally, that there was no element in his deliberations that would have been of any special interest to a student of abnormal psychology. I shall argue that, despite all these advantages, J could not have raised his hand at T if determinism is true.

My argument for this conclusion will take the form of comments on the premises of an "argument" in the logic-text sense: a numbered sequence of propositions, all but the last of which are the argument's *premises* and the last of which is its *conclusion*. One critic has supposed that my use of an argument in the logic-text sense constituted my attempting to provide a "formal proof" for a philosophical thesis, and has derided the very possibility of such an enterprise.[10] I applaud his values while deploring his exegesis. Formal proofs of philosophical theses are not to be had and I should be a fool to attempt any. My critic has mistaken what is really no more than a bookkeeping device for an argument, and, in fact, for a proof. The numbered sequence of propositions below is not my first argument for incompatibilism. My first argument for incompatibilism, rather, takes the form of a commentary on the premises of the "argument in the logic-text sense". My argument, in fact, is conterminous with Section 3.5 of this book. I shall distinguish my argument from the numbered sequence of propositions it discusses by calling the former the First Argument and the latter the First Formal Argument. These are mere convenient labels and should be understood in the light of the present paragraph.

In the First Formal Argument and in my subsequent commentary upon it, I shall use 'T_0' to denote some arbitrarily chosen instant of time earlier than J's birth, 'P_0' to denote a proposition that expresses the state of the world at T_0, 'P' to denote a proposition that expresses the state of the world at T, and 'L' to denote the conjunction into a single proposition of all the laws of nature. All these symbols are to be regarded as "rigid designators". Thus, if I discuss certain counter-factual situations or unrealized possibilities or such, and if I use, for example, 'P' in the course of this discussion, I mean 'P' to

[10] Narveson, *op. cit.*

designate a proposition that *in fact* expresses the state of the world at T, whether or not it would express the state of the world at T if those situations obtained or those possibilities were realized.

The First Formal Argument consists of seven propositions, the seventh of which follows from the first six:

(1) If determinism is true, then the conjunction of P_0 and L entails P

(2) It is not possible that J have raised his hand at T and P be true

(3) If (2) is true, then if J could have raised his hand at T, J could have rendered P false

(4) If J could have rendered P false, and if the conjunction of P_0 and L entails P, then J could have rendered the conjunction of P_0 and L false

(5) If J could have rendered the conjunction of P_0 and L false, then J could have rendered L false

(6) J could not have rendered L false

(7) If determinism is true, J could not have raised his hand at T.

That (7) follows from (1)–(6) can easily be established by truth-functional logic. Note that all the conditionals that occur in (1)–(7) are material conditionals: the 'could have' that occurs in them is merely the past indicative of 'can'. ("John hasn't read this letter, has he?" "I don't know, but I hope you've kept it under lock and key. You know what a dedicated snoop he is. If he could have read it, he did read it.")

One critic has supposed that the premises of this argument are supposed to be necessary truths.[11] But this is not the case. If the premises of the argument were necessary truths, then its conclusion would be a necessary truth. But its conclusion is false in any possible world in which determinism is true and J raised his hand at T. Of course, in such worlds at least one of the premises will be false. This is a simple consequence of the formal validity of the argument. Take, for example, a world in which L is the conjunction of all laws of nature, determinism is true, and J raised his hand at T. In such a world, (5) is false, since its consequent is false and its antecedent true. The antecedent of (5) is true in such a world because J could in that world have done something incompatible with the truth of the (false) conjunction of P_0 and L: raising his hand. He could have done this in that world simply in virtue of the fact that he did.

So I don't say that all the premises of the First Formal Argument are necessary truths. But I do say that they are true in all possible worlds in which the story we have told about J is true. That is, the premises of the

---

[11] André Gallois, "Van Inwagen on Free Will and Determinism", *Philosophical Studies* (1977).

First Formal Argument, and hence its conclusion, *follow from* our story about J. The story of J is, or we are pretending it is, true. But it's obviously only contingently true: there are possible worlds in which J raised his hand at T; there are possible worlds in which J never existed at all. And in many such worlds, (7) will be false and at least one among (1)–(6) will therefore be false. And this is just the way things should be, for the conclusion of the First Formal Argument *oughtn't* to be a logical consequence of incompatibilism alone.

Let us now examine the premises of the First Formal Argument. The preceding paragraph should make it clear that in this examination we are entitled to draw upon any facts about J and his situation that were presented in the story we told about J.

Premiss (1). This premiss follows from our definition of determinism and our specifications of the designations of 'P$_o$', 'L', and 'P'.

Premiss (2). The symbol 'P' is our name for the proposition that expresses the state the world was in fact in at T, a time at which J's hand was not raised. It is therefore impossible for P to be true if J's hand was raised at T, or, indeed, if things were in any way different at T from the way they actually were.

Premiss (3). The clause 'J could have raised his hand at T' is ambiguous. Using the system of disambiguating brackets introduced in Section 2.6, we may represent this ambiguity as follows: this clause could mean either 'J could have (raised his hand at T)' or 'J could have (raised his hand) at T'. I mean this clause to be understood in the former sense.[12]

As to the *truth* of (3): it is obvious that if (2) is true and if J could have raised his hand at T, then there is a certain "arrangement or modification of the concrete objects constituting J's environment"—J's hand rising at T—such that (i) it is not possible that J should arrange things this way and P be true, and (ii) J could have arranged things this way.

---

[12] Many philosophers think that a "double temporal reference" is required to make ascriptions of ability fully explicit. That is, they think that the "real form" of ascriptions of ability is something like this: s could at t_1 have done A at t_2. I am not convinced by their arguments. I find 'Tom could have raised his hand at noon' ambiguous but clear—that is, I think it's clear what the two individually clear things this sentence might be used to say are—and 'Tom could at eleven o'clock have raised his hand at noon' sounds rather strange to me. I think the best way to understand sentences of this latter sort is like this: 's could at t_1 have done A at t_2' = df 's could have (done A at t_2) and at t_1 it was not yet too late for s to do A at t_2'. That is, I prefer to take sentences of the form 's could have done A at t' as "basic" (whatever precisely that means) and to define sentences containing a "double temporal reference" in terms of these basic sentences, disambiguating brackets, and the notion of "not yet too late". I do not believe that my argument requires this rather special notion.

Premiss (4). This premiss is an instance, allowing for a shift of tense, of the following general principle:

If s can render r false, and if q entails r, then s can render q false.

(Substitute 'J' for 's', 'P' for 'r', and 'the conjunction of P_o and L' for 'q'.) This principle is a trivial truth. For if q entails r, the denial of r entails the denial of q. Thus anything sufficient in the broadly logical sense for the falsity of r is also sufficient for the falsity of q. Therefore, if there is some arrangement of objects that s can produce, which is such that s's producing it would be sufficient for the falsity of r, there is some arrangement of objects—the very same one—that s can produce, which is such that his producing it would be sufficient for the falsity of q.

Premiss (5). This premiss is an instance of the following general principle:

If q is a true proposition that concerns only states of affairs that obtained before s's birth, and if s can render the conjunction of q and r false, then s can render r false.

Consider, for example, the propositions

The Spanish Armada was defeated in 1588

and

Peter van Inwagen never visits Alaska.

For all I know, the conjunction of these two propositions is true. At any rate, let us assume it is true. Given that it is true, it seems quite clear that I can render it false if and only if I can visit Alaska. If, for some reason, it is not within my power ever to visit Alaska, then I *cannot* render it false. This is a quite trivial assertion, and the general principle of which it is an instance is hardly less trivial. And it seems incontestable that premiss (5) is also an instance of this principle.

The general principle of which (5) is an instance need not be defended only by an appeal to intuition. Let us assume that the antecedent of this principle is true. That is, let us assume the truth of both:

(a) q is a true proposition that concerns only states of affairs that obtained before s's birth,

and

(b) s can render the conjunction of q and r false.

We shall proceed to derive the consequent of the principle.

Let W (for 'was') be the conjunction into a single proposition of all true propositions about the past. Then we have, from (b) and from the definition of 's can render p false' that was given in Section 3.4:

(c) There is a possible arrangement of objects a such that s can bring it about that a is realized and such that the conjunction of W with the proposition that a is realized (call this conjunction 'W & a') entails the denial of the conjunction of q and r ("$d(q \& r)$").

It follows from (a) that W entails q and thus that W & a entails q. From this and (c) it follows that W & a entails the conjunction of q and $d(q \& r)$. And from this it follows that W & a entails the denial of r. And, therefore, since s can bring it about that a is realized, s can render r false.

Premiss (6). This premiss would seem to be an obvious consequence of what we said about our powers with respect to the laws of nature in Section 3.3. But a compatibilist might reject this contention. I can imagine a compatibilist arguing as follows:

> Suppose determinism is true and suppose I am not in fact going to raise my hand one minute from now. It follows that there is a certain possible arrangement of objects—any arrangement that includes my hand's being raised would do—such that it is not possible in the broadly logical sense that I should arrange objects in that way and the past have been exactly as it was and L be true. But since I *can* raise my hand one minute from now, I therefore *can* render L false, though, of course, I am not going to do so. If this result *sounds* queer, that's not my fault; the queerness derives entirely from your definition of 's can render p false'.

Well, there is obviously *some* sense in which I can't render the laws of nature false: I have no choice about what the laws of nature are; there's nothing I can *do* about them. There are many propositions whose truth-values are within my power, but surely the laws of nature are not among them. Let us therefore simply set aside the definition of 's can render p false' that was given in Section 3.4 and ask: aren't the premisses of the First Formal Argument evidently true, however 's can render p false' may be defined? Isn't our pre-analytic understanding of the notion of one's power over a proposition sufficiently clear that we can simply *see* that the premisses of the First Formal Argument are true? The unregenerate compatibilists is likely to respond to these questions this way:

> I'm not willing to grant that. The premisses of the First Formal Argument may be plausible at first glance, but that can be said of many false propositions. I can't say for sure which of your premisses is false since, now that you have set aside the definition given in Section 3.4, I'm not clear about what you mean by *can render false*. But I am confident that for any reasonably precise specification of this notion—one, that is, that is as clear as

that given in Section 3.4—I shall be able to show that at least one of your premises is false when it is interpreted according to that definition. If you should devise a definition that does justice to our pre-analytic conviction that no one can render false a law of nature, then, I predict, I shall be able to show, according to the strict terms of that definition, that one of the other premises of the argument—I expect it would be either (4) or (5)—is false if compatibilism is true.[13]

But now, I think the compatibilist is doing no more than calling our attention to the fact that, if compatibilism is true, then some premiss of our argument is false. That is, he is calling our attention to the fact that the argument is valid.

The reader who accepts the characterization of *can render false* that was presented in Section 3.4 will perceive a certain ironic consequence of the compatibilist's argument (which is perfectly correct) for the conclusion that compatibilism entails the falsity of premiss (6): it is the compatibilist, and not the incompatibilist, who believes in "contra-causal freedom".

This completes my presentation of the First Argument. While this argument contains a great deal of detail, the general idea behind it is a simple one. Consider any act that (logically) someone might have performed. If it should turn out that this act was incompatible with the state of the world before that person's birth taken together with the laws of nature, then it follows that that person could not have performed that act. Moreover, if determinism is true, then just *any* deviation from the actual course of events would be incompatible with any past state of the world taken together with the laws of nature. Therefore, if determinism is true, it never has been within my power to deviate from the actual course of events that has constituted my history.

Some philosophers seem to think the statement, 'if an act was incompatible with the state of the world before a person's birth taken together with the laws of nature, then it follows that that person could not have performed that act' *must* be based on some sort of muddle. But if one examines an actual case in which a certain act is "ruled out" by the state of the world before someone's birth and the laws of nature, then this conclusion does *seem* to follow, and it is very hard indeed to see what muddle one's conviction that this is so is based on. Let us ask, for example, whether I could have visited the star Arcturus half an hour ago. My having visited Arcturus at that moment seems to be ruled out by the state of the world before I was born and the laws of nature. Let us consider the state of the world one

---

[13] Cf. Narveson, *op. cit.* The possibility of this line of argument was first pointed out to me in conversation by Raymond Martin and Michael Gardner.

minute before I was born. At that moment, I was approximately 3.6×10^{17} metres from Arcturus. The temporal interval separating the moment one minute before I was born from the moment that occurred one half hour before now is about 1.16×10^9 seconds. It is a law of nature—or so we believe at present; let's suppose we're right—that no two objects have a relative velocity greater than 3×10^5 metres per second.[14] It follows, by simple arithmetic, that I did not visit Arcturus one half hour ago.

Here we have a case in which the proposition that I *did not* do a certain thing is deducible from the state of the world before I was born taken together with a law of nature. And it certainly *seems* to follow from the fact that this deduction is possible that I *could not* have done this thing. It is at any rate *true* that I could not have done this thing (could not have visited Arcturus one half hour ago). Is there some further fact, beyond the fact of the deducibility of my non-visit to Arcturus from the state of the world before I was born and the laws of nature, to which we should need to refer to justify our belief that I couldn't have visited Arcturus one half hour ago? I don't see what this further fact could be. Is there some feature of this "deduction of non-performance" that is not a universal feature of deductions of non-performance, which we have capitalized upon? What is it, then? In order to drive this point home, I shall construct an argument parallel to the First Formal Argument for the conclusion that I *could not* have visited Arcturus one half hour ago. Let us use 'T' to designate the moment of time that occurred one half hour ago. Let 'P' designate the proposition that I did not visit Arcturus at T. Let 'P_0' designate the proposition that expresses the state of the world one minute before my birth. (Note that P_0 entails the proposition that at that moment Arcturus and I were separated by a distance of about 3.6×10^{17} metres.) Let 'L' designate the proposition that nothing travels faster than 3×10^8 metres per second. We may now argue:

(1) The conjunction of P_0 and L entails P

(2) It is not possible that I have visited Arcturus at T and P be true

(3) If (2) is true, then if I could have visited Arcturus at T, I could have rendered P false

(4) If I could have rendered P false, and if the conjunction of P_0 and L entails P, then I could have rendered the conjunction of P_0 and L false

(5) If I could have rendered the conjunction of P_0 and L false, then I could have rendered L false

(6) I could not have rendered L false

(7) I could not have visited Arcturus at T.

[14] The speed of light is just under 3×10^8 metres per second. The difference is minuscule—about ninety times the muzzle velocity of a high-speed rifle bullet.

This seems to be a perfectly cogent and unexceptionable argument for the conclusion that I could not have visited Arcturus at T. Anyone who thinks he can demonstrate that one of the premisses of the First Formal Argument is false, must either show that his argument does not also "demonstrate" the falsity of the corresponding premiss of the "Arcturus" argument, or else he must accept this conclusion and explain why the apparent truth of the premisses of the "Arcturus" argument is only apparent. Perhaps someone will be able to do one of these things, but this project does not look very promising to me.

On page 74, I said that "the unregenerate compatibilist" was likely to maintain that if premiss (6) of the First Formal Argument is true, then either premiss (4) or premiss (5) is false, or, at least, is inconsistent with compatibilism. (*Which* of (4) and (5) is false, according to this compatibilist, would depend on exactly how one defines 'can render false'.) This thesis about (4) and (5) is quite implausible when it is applied, *mutatis mutandis*, to the corresponding premisses of the "Arcturus" argument. Perhaps the reader will find it instructive to reflect on this implausibility and to ask himself whether some of it doesn't rub off on the compatibilist's thesis concerning the First Formal Argument.

Let us look at premiss (4). Suppose I could have rendered P false, that is, could so have arranged things that I have visited Arcturus at T. If P_o and L entail that I did *not* visit Arcturus at T, then I could so have arranged things that the conjunction of these two propositions is false: my so arranging things as to visit Arcturus at T is logically sufficient for the falsity of this conjunction.

Let us look at premiss (5). P_o is a proposition about the arrangement of the furniture of the world before I was born—and therefore before I was capable of arranging things. L is a proposition whose truth imposes an upper limit on the relative velocities of physical objects at any time. Surely if I could ever have done something sufficient for the falsity of the conjunction of these two propositions, it would be just this: getting two objects to exhibit a relative velocity incompatible with the truth of L.

These arguments for the truth of (4) and (5) may be combined in the following intuitive way. I believe that one minute before my birth the star Arcturus and I were separated by a distance of about 3.6×10^{17} metres. I believe that between the moment one minute before my birth and the moment that occurred one half hour ago, there elapsed approximately 1.16×10^9 seconds. I believe that no two physical objects ever move toward each other with a velocity greater than 3×10^8 metres per second. Now suppose someone trustworthy—God, say—tells me that, while these beliefs of mine are *true*, I should be wrong to infer from them that it was not within my power to have visited Arcturus one half hour ago. For, God says, this *was* within my power. What could I conclude from this revelation? Only one conclusion seems possible: it was within my power to do something that has in fact never been done, namely to travel (relative to a certain object) at a speed greater than 3×10^8 metres per second. If God should also tell me that it is a *law of nature* that nothing exceeds this velocity, then I could only conclude that it was within my power to violate a law of nature, that is, to work a miracle. This might be an unpalatable conclusion, but not so unpalatable as the conclusion that it was within my power to have been born over a year earlier than I in fact was.

3

FREE WILL, PRAISE AND BLAME

J. J. C. SMART

In this article I try to refute the so-called "libertarian" theory of free will, and to examine how our conclusions ought to modify our common attitudes of praise and blame. In attacking the libertarian view, I shall try to show that it cannot be consistently stated. That is, my discussion will be an "analytic-philosophical" one. I shall neglect what I think is in practice an equally powerful method of attack on the libertarian: a challenge to state his theory in such a way that it will fit in with modern biology and psychology, which are becoming increasingly physicalistic.

It is difficult to state clearly just what is the metaphysical view about free will to which I object. This is because it seems to me to be a self-contradictory one, and in formal logic any proposition whatever can be shown to follow from a contradiction. However in practice a confused and contradictory view does lead to a certain fairly characteristic set of propositions and attitudes. (In the case we are considering, one of these is that righteous indignation is an appropriate emotion in certain circumstances.[1]) The reason why a contradictory position can in practice lead to a circumscribed set of propositions is that the contradiction is not recognised by those who hold the views in question. Hence the logical proof schema which enables you to deduce any proposition whatever from a contradiction cannot be applied. It follows that a confused metaphysical view can have important practical consequences and may, for example, mean the difference between life and death to a criminal or a heretic.

When, in nineteenth-century England, the rich man brushed aside all consideration for his unsuccessful rivals in the battle for wealth and position, and looking at them as they starved in the gutter said to himself, "Well, they had the same opportunities as I had. If I took more advantage of them than

J. J. C. Smart, 'Free Will, Praise and Blame' from *Mind*, 70 (1961), 291–306. Reprinted by permission of Oxford University Press.

[1] See Paul Edwards, "Hard and soft determinism," and John Hospers, "What means this freedom?" in Sydney Hook, ed., *Determinism and Freedom in the Age of Modern Science* (New York: New York University Press, 1958), pp. 104–13 and 113–30.

they did, that is not my fault but theirs," he was most probably not only callous but (as I shall try to show) metaphysically confused. A man who said "Heredity and environment made me what I am and made them what they are" would be less likely to fall a prey to this sort of callousness and indifference. Metaphysical views about free will are therefore practically important, and their importance is often in inverse proportion to their clarity.

What is this metaphysical view about free will that I wish to attack? Its supporters usually characterise it negatively, by contrasting it with what it is not, namely determinism on the one hand and pure chance or caprice on the other. This is a dangerous procedure, because a negative characterisation may rule out absolutely every possibility; as if we defined a new sort of natural number, a "free" number, as one which is neither prime nor divisible by a number which is greater than one and smaller than itself. Our negative characterisation, that is, may be so comprehensive as to leave room for no possibility whatever. However let us play the metaphysician's game as long as we can, and let us try to see what the metaphysical doctrine of free will is, at least by investigating what it is not. And what it is not is, first of all, determinism.

"What would become of your laws, your morality, your religion, your gallows, your Paradise, your Gods, your Hell, if it were shown that such and such fluids, such fibres, or a certain acridity in the blood, or in the animal spirits, alone suffice to make a man the object of your punishments or your rewards?" So wrote the notorious Marquis de Sade.[2] According to Nigel Balchin, "The modern endocrinologist sometimes goes far to support de Sade, and draws a rather humiliating picture of a man as a sort of chemico-electric experiment, in which a drop too much of this, or a grain too little of that, is the origin of personality. The psychologist insists that an apparently minor incident or accident in the early stages of our development may affect the whole course of our lives. In the face of this comparison of views most of us are inclined to compromise. We believe that heredity, accident, and incident have a bearing on man's character and actions, and may even sometimes have a determinative one. But we do not accept the complete suspension of moral judgment implicit in de Sade's view."[3]

These quotations come from literary, rather than professionally philosophical sources, but there is nothing in them, I think, which would not be endorsed by the ablest philosophical defenders of the metaphysical notion of freedom, for example, C. A. Campbell. Two comments are important at this stage. The first is that not only de Sade, but his biographer Nigel Balchin

[2] Quoted by Nigel Balchin, *The Anatomy of Villainy*, p. 174.
[3] Ibid., p. 251.

and the philosopher Campbell, and very many men in the street, hold that to accept the deterministic position is to give up the notion of moral responsibility. The second is that the view outlined by Balchin does not entail the absurdity that we can never predict what people will do. According to Balchin, heredity and environment are important, though they do not exhaust the matter. And, as Campbell holds, free will need only be supposed to operate in cases of moral conflict, when our nature as determined by heredity and environment pulls us away from the path of duty. Since cases of moral conflict are rare, we can usually predict people's behaviour just as confidently as if we believed wholeheartedly in the determinist position. So the common argument against metaphysical freedom, that it makes nonsense of our confidence in predicting human behaviour, falls to the ground. (Hume, for example,[4] pointed out that the condemned prisoner prefers to attack the stone walls of his cell rather than the inflexible nature of his gaolers.) So I shall not press this particular objection.

Those who hold that determinism and moral responsibility are incompatible with one another do not, of course, hold that we are responsible for those of our actions which are due to pure chance. Somehow they want our moral choices to be neither determined nor a matter of chance. Campbell has a word for it: he says that our moral choices are instances of "contra-causal freedom."[5] There is not "unbroken causal continuity" in the universe, but we are sometimes able to choose between "genuinely open possibilities." None of these concepts is at all precisely defined by Campbell, but I propose to give definitions of "unbroken causal continuity" and of "pure chance" that may be acceptable to him, and to like-minded thinkers, and I shall then enquire whether in the light of these definitions there is any room for "contra-causal freedom" and "genuinely open possibilities."

(D1.) I shall state the view that there is "unbroken causal continuity" in the universe as follows. It is in principle possible to make a sufficiently precise determination of the state of a sufficiently wide region of the universe at time t_0, and sufficient laws of nature are in principle ascertainable to enable a superhuman calculator to be able to predict any event occurring within that region at an already given time t_1.[6]

(D2.) I shall define the view that "pure chance" reigns to some extent within the universe as follows. There are some events that even a superhuman calculator could not predict, however precise his knowledge of however wide a region of the universe at some previous time.

---

[4] *Treatise* (London: Oxford University Press, 1941), Bk. II, Pt. iii, Sec. 1.

[5] "Is 'Freewill' a Pseudo-Problem?" *Mind*, LX (1951).

[6] Cf. Laplace: *Théorie Analytique des Probabilités*, second edition (Paris, 1814), p. ii of the Introduction.

These definitions are themselves far from being precise. What does it mean to say that "sufficient laws of nature are in principle ascertainable"? The difficulty here comes from talking of the universe as deterministic or indeterministic. A perfectly precise meaning can be given to saying that certain *theories* are deterministic or indeterministic (for example that Newtonian mechanics is deterministic, quantum mechanics indeterministic), but our talk about actual events in the world as being determined or otherwise may be little more than a reflection of our faith in prevailing types of physical theory. It may therefore be that when we apply the adjectives "deterministic" and "indeterministic" to the *universe* as opposed to *theories*, we are using these words in such a way that they have no sense. This consideration does not affect our present inquiry, however. For the believer in free will holds that *no* theory of a deterministic sort or of a pure chance sort will apply to everything in the universe: he must therefore envisage a theory of a type which is neither deterministic nor indeterministic in the senses of these words which I have specified by the two definitions *D1* and *D2*; and I shall argue that no such theory is possible.

In giving a definition of determinism in terms of predictability, moreover, I neglect K. R. Popper's interesting demonstration ("Indeterminism in Quantum Physics and in Classical Physics," *British Journal for the Philosophy of Science*, I, 117–33 and 173–95) that there is a sense in which even within classical physics some events must be unpredictable. If there are two predictors P and Q, they cannot predict one another's behaviour. For by the definition of a predictor, small changes in P must lead to large changes in Q and *vice versa*. So in order for P to predict Q it must predict itself, but it cannot do this, for reasons similar to those in Ryle's *Concept of Mind*, pages 195 and following. In particular, if the Laplacian demon is to predict the universe it cannot itself be part of the universe, nor can it interact with the universe. The notion of a Laplacian demon is thus a physically unrealisable one. However the notion of a Laplacian demon which was nonphysical and which gained information about the world without energy interchanges does seem to be a *logically* possible, though a physically impossible one, and that is enough for present purposes. In any case I do not think that the libertarian would be satisfied by the assertion that human beings have merely that sort of unpredictability in principle that mechanical predictors made of springs, weights, levers and so on might have.

In the sense of *D2* the change of state, at a certain time, of a particular atom of radium would, according to modern quantum theory, be an event of "pure chance." It is important to distinguish "pure chance" from "chance" or "accident." Things may happen by chance or accident in a purely deterministic universe. (More precisely, we can have a use for the words "chance" and "accident" even within a purely deterministic theory.) A man walks along the street and is hit on the head by a falling tile. This is "chance"[7] or "accident" in the sense that it is the result of two separate causal chains, the first involving the causes of his walking along just that route at just that time, the second involving the causes of just that tile falling at just that time. There is no law which explains the event in question, as there would have been if the man had just walked under a ladder and if it had been a law of nature that men who walk under ladders get hit on the head by a falling body within the next thirty seconds. Nevertheless, though the man's being hit on the head is a case of "chance," Laplace's superhuman calculator could have predicted the occurrence. It is not this sense of "chance" that I am meaning when I refer to "pure chance."

Campbell (like Balchin and de Sade) holds that if the whole universe is deterministic in the sense of $D1$, then no one is morally responsible, for on this hypothesis if a person does a certain action "he could not have done otherwise," and that he could have done otherwise is a condition of moral responsibility. Now there is perhaps a sense of "could not have done otherwise" in which whether or not a person could or could not have done otherwise depends on whether or not the universe is deterministic in the sense of $D1$. But it does not follow that if a person could not have done otherwise in this special sense then he could not have done otherwise in any *ordinary* sense. Taken in any ordinary sense, within some concrete context of daily life, "he could have done otherwise" has no metaphysical implications. Does a child have to learn about Laplacian determinism before he can say that his little sister could have eaten her apple instead of his candy? Now it is the ordinary sense which we use when we talk about moral responsibility. How then can it follow that if a person "could not have done otherwise," in the *special* sense, that he was not morally responsible?

Campbell also holds, we may feel sure, that if an action comes about by "pure chance" in the sense of $D2$, then the agent is not morally responsible. He says, for example, that "a man cannot be morally responsible for an act which does not express his own choice but is, on the contrary, attributable to chance."[8] It is true that a little lower down Campbell uses the word "accident," and by "an accident" we mean "chance" in the weak sense, not "pure chance," but this is obviously a slip of the pen. I am sure that Campbell would agree that if one of our actions happened by "pure chance" in the sense in which, according to modern physics, the change of state of a particular radium atom happens by pure chance, then this action would not be

[7] Cf. Aristotle, *Physics*, 196b–97b.
[8] "Is 'Freewill' a Pseudo-Problem?" p. 460.

one for which we could be held *responsible*. We may therefore interpret Campbell as holding that if there is such a thing as moral responsibility then people's actions must not always be determined in the sense of *D1*, nor must they happen by pure chance in the sense of *D2*: they must occur as the result of something else, namely "contra-causal freedom."

The difficulty I find in the above conception is as follows. If we accept the definitions *D1* and *D2*, the following propositions are contradictories:

p: This event happened as a result of unbroken causal continuity.

q: This event happened by pure chance.

That is, *q* if and only if not *p*.

But *p* or not *p*.

So *p* or *q*, and not both not *p* and not *q*.

Therefore there is no *third* possibility outside *p* and *q*. What room, then, does logic leave for the concept of "contra-causal freedom?"

Are *D1* and *D2* good definitions of "unbroken causal continuity" and "pure chance"? Campbell might deny that they are, and up to a point I should agree with him. The notions of "causal necessity" and "chance" as used by philosophers are pretty vague, and it is to some extent uncertain just what are the rules of the game when we use these words. I want to show that there are imaginable cases which, if we adhered strictly to *D2*, we should have to call cases of pure chance, but which it would be natural to assimilate to "necessity." But I want also to suggest that any such imaginable cases would only lead us to revise *D1* and *D2* in *this* sense, that what was before "pure chance" would now become "unbroken causal continuity" or *vice versa:* the precise description of an intermediate possibility (a possibility which it would be natural for Campbell to call "contra-causal freedom") must forever elude us. That is, it might be natural to redefine "unbroken causal continuity" and "pure chance" so as to redistribute possible cases between them, but logic leaves me no room for a modification of *D1* and *D2* which would allow me to slap my knee and say "Ah! *That* must be the sort of thing Campbell means by 'contra-causal freedom.'" I shall illustrate my point by means of two examples.

(i) The universe might be such that it would be impossible for Laplace's superhuman calculator to predict a given event E from a knowledge of however many laws of nature and a determination, however precise, of however wide a region of the universe, at time t_0. Nevertheless we can conceive that he could calculate the occurrence of E from a knowledge of the initial conditions at two different times t_1 and t_2, plus certain laws of nature which would clearly be of a novel type. That is, the laws of nature together with the initial conditions at t_1 would determine not a single possibility but a linear *range* of possibilities, but with a fresh cross-bearing based on conditions at t_2 we should be able to make a unique prediction. In such a universe (or perhaps better, in the case of our having such a picture of the universe) it would be natural to say that E was "determined." Nevertheless according to $D1$ and $D2$ taken as they stand it would be a matter of "pure chance." We might make an appropriate modification of $D1$ and $D2$ so that this was no longer so.

(ii) The universe might consist of two regions A and B such that from a complete knowledge of the state of A at time t_1 together with a complete knowledge of the state of B at time t_2 you could predict the occurrence of any event E occurring in A at t_2, though from the state of the whole universe at t_1 no such prediction could be made. According to $D1$ and $D2$, taken strictly, E would have to be said to occur by "pure chance," but it might be natural, if such a universe (or such a type of law of nature) were more than a theoretical possibility, to remodel $D1$ and $D2$ so that E would now be said to occur "by necessity." For I do not think that a philosopher like Campbell would be inclined to call a moral choice "free" if it could be predicted from a knowledge of a previous state of a part of the universe in which the event took place together with a knowledge of the present state of a different part of the universe.

The above two examples show how there might be formulated a novel type of natural law which would be quasi-deterministic—that is, which would not be deterministic in the strict sense of $D1$ but which nevertheless would be such that we should feel like modifying $D1$ to accommodate it. (Of course if we did find it useful to formulate laws of such types we should find ourselves involved in a radical revolution in physical theory: the new physics would probably be at least as far removed from present-day physics as quantum theory is from classical physics.) But could any such case of quasi-determinism be accepted as a case of "contra-causal freedom?" Thinking of these cases may induce us to modify $D1$ and $D2$ so that the frontier between "necessity" and "pure chance" is moved a little one way or another, but this will not provide us with a buffer zone between the two territories.

Campbell holds that if determinism in the sense of $D1$ is true then a man could never correctly be said to have been able to do otherwise than he did. That this is not so can be seen if we consider the following example. Suppose that when washing the dishes you drop a plate, but that fortunately it does not break. You say, however, that it *could* have broken. That is, within the range of possible initial conditions covered by possible cases of "dropping," the known dispositional characteristics of the plate do not allow us to rule out the proposition "it will break." If, however, it had been an aluminium plate, then it would not have broken. That is, whatever the initial conditions had been (within a wide range) it would not have broken. Whether dropped flat or on its edge, with a spinning motion or with no spinning motion, from three feet or four feet or five feet, it still would not have broken. Thus such cases in which we use the words "could have" or "could not have" are cases in which we either cannot or can use a law or a law-like proposition to rule out a certain possibility despite our uncertainty as to the precise initial conditions. Briefly: E could not have happened if there are laws or law-like propositions which rule out E. Campbell wants to use "could not have happened" in a different way: he will say that E could not have happened if E is ruled out by certain laws or law-like propositions *together with the initial conditions*.[9]

However it is pretty certain that Campbell would resist the suggestion that "John Smith could have done otherwise" is analogous to "the plate could have broken." He would say[10] that it is an actual particular person in a particular set of circumstances with whom we are concerned when we ask "Could he have done otherwise? Was he morally responsible?" and that we are in no way concerned with hypothetical possibilities. It is difficult to see the force of this sort of criticism. It is but a tautology to say that if we ask whether John Smith could have done otherwise then we are asking a question about John Smith. Clearly we are interested in John Smith as an individual who has to deal with a particular situation, but what follows? That nothing follows can be made evident if we develop our example of the dropped plate. Suppose that I have a very valuable plate, made in China and once the property of some ancient emperor and the only one of its kind. While showing it to a friend I drop it but fortunately it does not break. Gasping with relief I say, "It could have broken but thank goodness it did not." Here we are using the words "could have" and yet our interest is very much in this particular plate in this set of circumstances. There is no suggestion here, however, that a very precise determination of the initial conditions together with an exact knowledge of the physical properties of the plate would not have enabled us to predict that in these (rather fortunate) circumstances it would not break.

On this analysis "could have" implies "would have if certain conditions had been fulfilled." In moral contexts the conditions that are of most importance are "if he had chosen," "if he had tried," and "if he had wanted to." This is not to say that in some cases we may not mean more than this.

---

[9] For a discussion of this sort of point see F. V. Raab, "Free Will and the Ambiguity of 'Could.'" *Philosophical Review*, LXIV (1955), 60–77.

[10] "Is 'Freewill' a Pseudo-Problem?" p. 453.

J. L. Austin, in a British Academy lecture,[11] has recently argued that whether or no determinism be the case, it is certainly contrary to what is suggested by ordinary language and ordinary thought. For example in part of an interesting footnote he says:[12]

"Consider the case where I miss a very short putt and kick myself because I could have holed it. It is not that I should have holed it if I had tried: I did try and missed. It is not that I should have holed it if conditions had been different: that might of course be so, but I am talking about conditions as they precisely were, and asserting that I could have holed it. There's the rub."

To elucidate this passage compare the sentence "I could have holed it if I had tried" with the sentence "this plate could have broken if it had been colder weather." This does not mean that it *would* have broken if had been colder weather. For a metal plate that becomes brittle due to intense cold may nevertheless be lucky in the way it falls, like the china plate in my example. When I say that I could have holed the putt (though I tried to and failed) I mean that I could have even if the *external* conditions had been precisely the same. It is surely compatible with this ordinary way of talking that I believe, like any determinist, that if the external conditions *and* the internal conditions (the state of my brain and nervous system) were precisely reproduced then my failure to hole the putt would be precisely reproduced. I cannot see, therefore, that Austin has shown that ordinary language favours indeterminism. Not that this matter is very important philosophically. Ordinary language may well enshrine a falsehood. Austin himself clearly distinguishes between the question of whether determinism is the case and the question of whether it is implied in ordinary language. Certainly Austin's careful discussion of "can" does not help me to guess what Campbell might mean by the word, for I can deal with all of Austin's cases on the lines of my china plate example. This is not to deny the intrinsic interest in many of Austin's suggestions, such as that the "if" in "I can if I choose" is not the conditional "if" familiar to logicians but is the "if" of doubt or hesitation. (Compare: "I can, but do I choose?" "I can but whether I choose to do so or not is another question."[13])

We can now consider Campbell's phrase "genuinely open possibility." If I drop a china plate it is an open possibility that it will break. It is not an open possibility that an aluminium plate will break. The possibility of an aluminium plate breaking can be ruled out for any likely range of initial conditions from a knowledge of the physical properties of aluminium. Whether the aluminium plate is dropped on its side or on its edge, with a rotary

---

[11] "Ifs and Cans," *Proceedings of the British Academy* (1956), pp. 109–32.

[12] Ibid., p. 119.

[13] These and other examples of this sort of "if" are given by Austin, "Ifs and Cans," pp. 114–15.

motion or without a rotary motion, in hot weather or cold weather, from a height of two feet or six feet, it still will not break. With the china plate, in some of these cases it will break and in some not. The phrases "an open possibility" and "not an open possibility" are therefore easily understood. What about "genuinely open possibility?" We might suggest that a possibility is "genuinely open" if from the relevant laws and law-like propositions together with a determination, however precise, of the initial conditions, not even Laplace's superhuman calculator could predict what will happen. This is, by *D2*, just a case of pure chance. Once more our endeavour to describe something intermediate between determinism and pure chance has failed.

Campbell tries by introspection to distinguish "contra-causal freedom" from both "causal necessitation" and "pure chance." That is, he hopes by appealing to introspection to give a sense to "could have done otherwise" which is different from both that in (*a*) "the plate could have broken" and that in (*b*) "even if the initial conditions had been precisely the same that atom could have shot out a photon." His appeal to introspection is an appeal to our feeling that in certain situations we can do either of two alternative things. Well, in certain situations I certainly do feel that I can do either of two things. That is, I say to myself, "I can do this and I can do that." *Either* I say this to myself using "can" in an ordinary way (as in "the plate could break, and it could fall without breaking") *or* I say these words to myself using "can" in some new way. In the former case introspection has yielded no new sense of "can," and in the latter case some new use of "can" must already have been established. For unless this new use of "can" can be explained antecedently to such introspection, introspection will only yield the fact of my saying to myself a meaningless sentence. But, as I have already argued, logic leaves no room for such a new sense of "can."

A similar situation arises if any alternative description of the predicament of moral choice is attempted. Thus Campbell says[14] that "I further find, if I ask myself just what it is I am believing when I believe that I 'can' rise to duty, that I cannot help believing that it lies with me here and now quite absolutely, which of two genuinely open possibilities I adopt." Our reply must be that we cannot say whether this is so or not. Perhaps we believe this, perhaps we do not, but we cannot tell until Campbell can explain to us what he means by "lies with me here and now quite absolutely" (as opposed to "lies with me here and now"), and until he can explain what is meant by "genuinely open possibilities" (as opposed to "open possibilities"). The same difficulty crops up[15] when he appeals to "creative activity." "Granted

[14] "Is 'Freewill' a Pseudo-Problem?" p. 463.
[15] Ibid., p. 462.

that creative activity is possible . . .," he says. But in any ordinary sense of these words creative activity is not only possible but actual. There are poets, novelists, mathematicians, architects and inventors. In what sense of "creative activity" is it an open question whether creative activity is possible or not? Some writers again bring in the concept of "spontaneity." But you do not have to reject metaphysical determinism before you can believe that your rubbish heap burst into flames as a result of spontaneous combustion.

Most of our ordinary senses of "could have" and "could not have" are not, in my view, incompatible with determinism. Though some of our ordinary talk about moral responsibility is frequently vitiated by a confused metaphysics of free will, much of it can be salvaged.

When in a moral context we say that a man could have or could not have done something we are concerned with the ascription of responsibility. What is it to ascribe responsibility? Suppose Tommy at school does not do his homework. If the schoolmaster thinks that this is because Tommy is really very stupid, then it is silly of him to abuse Tommy, to cane him or to threaten him. This would be sensible only if it were the case that this sort of treatment made stupid boys intelligent. With the possible exception of certain nineteenth-century schoolmasters, no one has believed this. The schoolmaster says, then, that Tommy is not to blame, he just *could not* have done his homework. Now suppose that the reason why Tommy did not do his homework is that he was lazy: perhaps he had just settled down to do it when some other boy tempted him to come out and climb a tree. In such a case the schoolmaster will hold Tommy responsible, and he will say that Tommy could have done his homework. By this he will not necessarily mean to deny that Tommy's behaviour was the outcome of heredity and environment. The case is similar to that of the plate which could have broken. The lazy boy is analogous to the china plate which could break and also could fall without breaking. The stupid boy is like the aluminium plate: whatever the initial conditions the same thing happens. If Tommy is sufficiently stupid, then it does not matter whether he is exposed to temptation or not exposed to temptation, threatened or not threatened, cajoled or not cajoled. When his negligence is found out, he is not made less likely to repeat it by threats, promises, or punishments. On the other hand, the lazy boy can be influenced in such ways. Whether he does his homework or not is perhaps solely the outcome of environment, but one part of the environment is the threatening schoolmaster.

Threats and promises, punishments and rewards, the ascription of responsibility and the nonascription of responsibility, have therefore a clear pragmatic justification which is quite consistent with a wholehearted belief in metaphysical determinism. Indeed it implies a belief that our actions are very largely determined: if everything anyone did depended only on pure chance (i.e. if it depended on nothing) then threats and punishments would be quite ineffective. But even a libertarian of course may admit that *most* of our actions are pretty well determined. (Campbell excepts only those acts which are done from a sense of duty against our inclination.)

It begins to appear that the metaphysical question of determinism is quite irrelevant to the rationality of our ascription of responsibility.

What about praise and blame? These concepts are more difficult. We must at the outset distinguish two ways in which we commonly use the word "praise." In one sense praise is the opposite of blame. We praise Tommy for his industry, blame him for his laziness. But when we praise a girl for her good looks this does not mean that we should have blamed her if her looks had been bad. When we praise one footballer for his brilliant run, we do not blame his unfortunate teammate who fumbled a pass. (Unless, of course, the fumble was due to carelessness.) When we praise Smith for his mathematical talent we do not imply that we blame Jones because, try as hard as he may, he cannot handle x's and y's. Of course we may well say that a girl is ugly, a footballer incompetent, or a man unmathematical, and this is the opposite of praise. But it is not blame. Praise and dispraise, in this sense, is simply grading a person as good or bad in some way. A young philosopher may feel pleasure at being praised by one of his eminent colleagues because he thereby knows that his work is assessed highly by one who is competent to judge, and he may be pained to hear himself dispraised because he thereby knows that his work is being assessed as of poor quality. Praise and dispraise of this sort has an obvious function just as has the grading of apples.[16] A highly graded apple is bought and a highly graded philosopher is appointed to a lectureship, while a low graded apple is not bought and the low graded philosopher is not appointed.

In general to praise or dispraise a man, a woman's nose, or a footballer's style is to grade it, and if the grader is competent we feel sure that there are good reasons for the grading. In practice, of course, reasons are frequently given, and this giving of reasons in itself can constitute what is called praise or dispraise. For example, if a philosopher writes about some candidate for a lecturership that he has some illuminating new ideas about the logic of certain psychological concepts, this is the sort of thing that is meant by "praise," and if he says that the candidate is muddleheaded and incapable of writing clear prose, this is the sort of thing which is meant by "dispraise." It is not the sort of thing we mean when we contrast praise with blame. To say

---

[16] On the notion of grading, see J. O. Urmson's article "On Grading," in A. G. N. Flew, ed., *Logic and Language* (Oxford: Blackwell, 1955), Second Series, pp. 159–88.

that a man cannot write clear prose is not necessarily to blame him. He may have been brought up among muddle-headed people and always given muddle-headed books to read. The fact that we do not feel like blaming him, however, does not alter the fact that we warn prospective employers about him.

Just as we may praise or dispraise a woman for her figure, a footballer for his fleetness or slowness of foot, a lecturer in philosophy for his intelligence or lack of intelligence, and a writer for clarity or obscurity, so naturally enough, we may praise or dispraise a man for his honesty or dishonesty, truthfulness or untruthfulness, kindness or unkindness and so on. In *this* sense of "praise" we may praise moral qualities and moral actions in exactly the same way as we may praise beauty, intelligence, agility, or strength. Either we may do so quite generally, using a grading word like "good," "excellent," or "first-class," or we may simply give a description. (For example: her cheeks are like roses, her eyes are like stars.) Praise has a primary function and a secondary function. In its primary function it is just to tell people what people are like. To say that one candidate for a lectureship writes clear prose whereas another cannot put a decent sentence together is to help the committee to decide who should be given the lectureship. Naturally enough, therefore, we like to be praised, hate to be dispraised. And even if no actual advantage is to come from praise, we like to be praised by a competent judge for work we have done because we take this as evidence that we have been on the right track and done something valuable. Because we come to like being praised and to hate being dispraised, praise and dispraise come to have an important secondary function. To praise a class of actions is to encourage people to do actions of that class. And utility of an action normally, but not always, corresponds to utility of praise of it.

So far I have talked of praise and dispraise, not of praise and blame. This is because I wanted a contrary for "praise" in the sense in which we can praise not only a moral action but a woman's nose. What about the contrast of praise with blame? Here I suggest that a clear-headed man will use the word "praise" just as before, and the word "blame" just like the previous "dispraise," with one proviso. This is that to praise (in this sense) or to blame a person for an action is not only to grade it (morally) but to imply that it is something for which the person is responsible, in the perfectly ordinary and nonmetaphysical sense of "responsible" which we have analysed earlier in this article. So we blame Tommy for his bad homework if this is due to laziness, not if it is due to stupidity. Blame in this sense can be just as dispassionate as dispraise of a woman's nose: it is just a grading plus an ascription of responsibility. It is perfectly compatible with a recognition that the lazy Tommy is what he is simply as a result of heredity plus environment (and perhaps pure chance).

Now most men do not, in my opinion, praise and blame people in this dispassionate and clear-headed way. This is brought out, in fact, by the quotations from de Sade and Balchin: most men do *not* feel that blame, in the way they use the word "blame," would be appropriate if a man's action was the result of heredity plus environment. The appropriateness of praise and blame is bound up, in the eyes of the ordinary man, with a notion of freewill which is quite metaphysical. Admittedly this metaphysics is incoherent and unformulated (as indeed it has to be, for when formulated it becomes self-contradictory). Nevertheless we can see that a rather pharisaical attitude to sinners and an almost equally unhealthy attitude to saints is bound up with this metaphysics in the thinking of the ordinary man if we look at the way in which very often his whole outlook and tendency to *judge* (not just to grade) other men changes when he is introduced to, and becomes convinced by, a philosophical analysis of freewill like the one in the present paper. How, again, can we explain the idea, held by so many religious people, that an omnipotent and benevolent God can *justly* condemn people to an eternity of torture? Must we not suppose that they have some confused idea that even with the same heredity and environmental influences, and quite apart from pure chance, the sinner *could* have done otherwise? (Of course, even granting this, the utility of Hell in the eyes of a benevolent God still remains obscure.) Or consider the man who excuses himself for his indifference to his less fortunate neighbour by saying, "Hadn't he the same opportunities as I had? He could have got on if he had acted with my drive, initiative, and so forth." There is sense in such a remark only in so far as the contempt for laziness and lack of drive to which it gives expression is socially useful in spurring others on to display more drive than they otherwise would.

But a man's drive is determined by his genes and his environment, and such a remark as the one above is after all a rather unimportant part of the environment. So I do not think that the remark can be regarded as just a way of influencing people to display drive and resourcefulness. It does depend on a metaphysics of free will. After all, if everyone had the genes that make for drive and energy they could not *all* get to the top. Dog would still eat dog.

The upshot of the discussion is that we should be quite as ready to *grade* a person for his moral qualities as for his nonmoral qualities, but we should stop *judging* him. (Unless "judge" just means "grade," as in "judging apples.") Moreover, if blame in general is irrational, so must be self-blame or self-reproach, unless this comes simply to resolving to do better next time.

4

FREEDOM AND RESENTMENT

PETER STRAWSON

I

Some philosophers say they do not know what the thesis of determinism is. Others say, or imply, that they do know what it is. Of these, some—the pessimists perhaps—hold that if the thesis is true, then the concepts of moral obligation and responsibility really have no application, and the practices of punishing and blaming, of expressing moral condemnation and approval, are really unjustified. Others—the optimists perhaps—hold that these concepts and practices in no way lose their *raison d'être* if the thesis of determinism is true. Some hold even that the justification of these concepts and practices requires the truth of the thesis. There is another opinion which is less frequently voiced: the opinion, it might be said, of the genuine moral sceptic. This is that the notions of moral guilt, of blame, of moral responsibility are inherently confused and that we can see this to be so if we consider the consequences either of the truth of determinism or of its falsity. The holders of this opinion agree with the pessimists that these notions lack application if determinism is true, and add simply that they also lack it if determinism is false. If I am asked which of these parties I belong to, I must say it is the first of all, the party of those who do not know what the thesis of determinism is. But this does not stop me from having some sympathy with the others, and a wish to reconcile them. Should not ignorance, rationally, inhibit such sympathies? Well, of course, though darkling, one has some inkling—some notion of what sort of thing is being talked about. This lecture is intended as a move towards reconciliation; so is likely to seem wrongheaded to everyone.

But can there be any possibility of reconciliation between such clearly opposed positions as those of pessimists and optimists about determinism? Well, there might be a formal withdrawal on one side in return for a

© The British Academy 1963. Reproduced by permission from *Proceedings of the British Academy*, 48 (1962), 1–25.

substantial concession on the other. Thus, suppose the optimist's position were put like this: (1) the facts as we know them do not show determinism to be false; (2) the facts as we know them supply an adequate basis for the concepts and practices which the pessimist feels to be imperilled by the possibility of determinism's truth. Now it might be that the optimist is right in this, but is apt to give an inadequate account of the facts as we know them, and of how they constitute an adequate basis for the problematic concepts and practices; that the reasons he gives for the adequacy of the basis are themselves inadequate and leave out something vital. It might be that the pessimist is rightly anxious to get this vital thing back and, in the grip of his anxiety, feels he has to go beyond the facts as we know them; feels that the vital thing can be secure only if, beyond the facts as we know them, there is the further fact that determinism is false. Might *he* not be brought to make a formal withdrawal in return for a vital concession?

II

Let me enlarge very briefly on this, by way of preliminary only. Some optimists about determinism point to the efficacy of the practices of punishment, and of moral condemnation and approval, in regulating behaviour in socially desirable ways.[1] In the fact of their efficacy, they suggest, is an adequate basis for these practices; and this fact certainly does not show determinism to be false. To this the pessimists reply, all in a rush, that *just* punishment and *moral* condemnation imply moral guilt and guilt implies moral responsibility and moral responsibility implies freedom and freedom implies the falsity of determinism. And to this the optimists are wont to reply in turn that it is true that these practices require freedom in a sense, and the existence of freedom in this sense is one of the facts as we know them. But what 'freedom' means here is nothing but the absence of certain conditions the presence of which would make moral condemnation or punishment inappropriate. They have in mind conditions like compulsion by another, or innate incapacity, or insanity, or other less extreme forms of psychological disorder, or the existence of circumstances in which the making of any other choice would be morally inadmissible or would be too much to expect of any man. To this list they are constrained to add other factors which, without exactly being limitations of freedom, may also make moral condemnation or punishment inappropriate or mitigate their force: as some forms of ignorance, mistake, or accident. And the general reason why moral

---

[1] Cf. P. H. Nowell-Smith, 'Freewill and Moral Responsibility', *Mind* (1948).

condemnation or punishment are inappropriate when these factors or conditions are present is held to be that the practices in question will be generally efficacious means of regulating behaviour in desirable ways only in cases where these factors are *not* present. Now the pessimist admits that the facts as we know them include the existence of freedom, the occurrence of cases of free action, in the negative sense which the optimist concedes; and admits, or rather insists, that the existence of freedom in this sense is compatible with the truth of determinism. Then what does the pessimist find missing? When he tries to answer this question, his language is apt to alternate between the very familiar and the very unfamiliar.[2] Thus he may say, familiarly enough, that the man who is the subject of justified punishment, blame or moral condemnation must really *deserve* it; and then add, perhaps, that, in the case at least where he is blamed for a positive act rather than an omission, the condition of his really deserving blame is something that goes beyond the negative freedoms that the optimist concedes. It is, say, a genuinely free identification of the will with the act. And this is the condition that is incompatible with the truth of determinism.

The conventional, but conciliatory, optimist need not give up yet. He may say: Well, people often decide to do things, really intend to do what they do, know just what they're doing in doing it: the reasons they think they have for doing what they do, often really are their reasons and not their rationalizations. These facts, too, are included in the facts as we know them. If this is what you mean by freedom—by the identification of the will with the act— then freedom may again be conceded. But again the concession is compatible with the truth of the determinist thesis. For it would not follow from that thesis that nobody decides to do anything; that nobody ever does anything intentionally; that it is false that people sometimes know perfectly well what they are doing. I tried to define freedom negatively. You want to give it a more positive look. But it comes to the same thing. Nobody denies freedom in this sense, or these senses, and nobody claims that the existence of freedom in these senses shows determinism to be false.

But it is here that the lacuna in the optimistic story can be made to show. For the pessimist may be supposed to ask: But *why* does freedom in this sense justify blame, etc.? You turn towards me first the negative, and then the positive, faces of a freedom which nobody challenges. But the only reason you have given for the practices of moral condemnation and punishment in cases where this freedom is present is the efficacy of these practices in regulating behaviour in socially desirable ways. But this is not a sufficient basis, it is not even the right *sort* of basis, for these practices as we understand them.

---

[2] As Nowell-Smith pointed out in a later article: 'Determinists and Libertarians', *Mind* (1954).

Now my optimist, being the sort of man he is, is not likely to invoke an intuition of fittingness at this point. So he really has no more to say. And my pessimist, being the sort of man he is, has only one more thing to say; and that is that the admissibility of these practices, as we understand them, demands another kind of freedom, the kind that in turn demands the falsity of the thesis of determinism. But might we not induce the pessimist to give up saying this by giving the optimist something more to say?

III

I have mentioned punishing and moral condemnation and approval; and it is in connection with these practices or attitudes that the issue between optimists and pessimists—or, if one is a pessimist, the issue between determinists and libertarians—is felt to be particularly important. But it is not of these practices and attitudes that I propose, at first, to speak. These practices or attitudes permit, where they do not imply, a certain detachment from the actions or agents which are their objects. I want to speak, at least at first, of something else: of the non-detached attitudes and reactions of people directly involved in transactions with each other; of the attitudes and reactions of offended parties and beneficiaries; of such things as gratitude, resentment, forgiveness, love, and hurt feelings. Perhaps something like the issue between optimists and pessimists arises in this neighbouring field too; and since this field is less crowded with disputants, the issue might here be easier to settle; and if it is settled here, then it might become easier to settle it in the disputant-crowded field.

What I have to say consists largely of commonplaces. So my language, like that of commonplace generally, will be quite unscientific and imprecise. The central commonplace that I want to insist on is the very great importance that we attach to the attitudes and intentions towards us of other human beings, and the great extent to which our personal feelings and reactions depend upon, or involve, our beliefs about these attitudes and intentions. I can give no simple description of the field of phenomena at the centre of which stands this commonplace truth: for the field is too complex. Much imaginative literature is devoted to exploring its complexities; and we have a large vocabulary for the purpose. There are simplifying styles of handling it in a general way. Thus we may, like La Rochefoucauld, put self-love or self-esteem or vanity at the centre of the picture and point out how it may be caressed by the esteem, or wounded by the indifference or contempt, of others. We might speak, in another jargon, of the need for love, and the loss of security which results from its withdrawal; or, in another, of human self-respect and its connection with the recognition of the individual's dignity. These simplifications are of use to me only if they help to emphasize how much we actually mind, how much it matters to us, whether the actions of other people—and particularly of *some* other people—reflect attitudes towards us of goodwill, affection, or esteem on the one hand or contempt, indifference, or malevolence on the other. If someone treads on my hand accidentally, while trying to help me, the pain may be no less acute than if he treads on it in contemptuous disregard of my existence or with a malevolent wish to injure me. But I shall generally feel in the second case a kind and degree of resentment that I shall not feel in the first. If someone's actions help me to some benefit I desire, then I am benefited in any case; but if he intended them so to benefit me because of his general goodwill towards me, I shall reasonably feel a gratitude which I should not feel at all if the benefit was an incidental consequence, unintended or even regretted by him, of some plan of action with a different aim.

These examples are of actions which confer benefits or inflict injuries over and above any conferred or inflicted by the mere manifestation of attitude and intention themselves. We should consider also in how much of our behaviour the benefit or injury resides mainly or entirely in the manifestation of attitude itself. So it is with good manners, and much of what we call kindness, on the one hand; with deliberate rudeness, studied indifference, or insult on the other.

Besides resentment and gratitude, I mentioned just now forgiveness. This is a rather unfashionable subject in moral philosophy at present; but to be forgiven is something we sometimes ask, and forgiving is something we sometimes say we do. To ask to be forgiven is in part to acknowledge that the attitude displayed in our actions was such as might properly be resented and in part to repudiate that attitude for the future (or at least for the immediate future); and to forgive is to accept the repudiation and to forswear the resentment.

We should think of the many different kinds of relationship which we can have with other people—as sharers of a common interest; as members of the same family; as colleagues; as friends; as lovers; as chance parties to an enormous range of transactions and encounters. Then we should think, in each of these connections in turn, and in others, of the kind of importance we attach to the attitudes and intentions towards us of those who stand in these relationships to us, and of the kinds of *reactive* attitudes and feelings to which we ourselves are prone. In general, we demand some degree of goodwill or regard on the part of those who stand in these relationships to us, though the forms we require it to take vary widely in different connections. The range and intensity of our *reactive* attitudes towards goodwill, its absence or its opposite vary no less widely. I have mentioned, specifically, resentment and gratitude; and they are a usefully opposed pair. But, of course, there is a whole continuum of reactive attitude and feeling stretching on both sides of these and—the most comfortable area—in between them.

The object of these commonplaces is to try to keep before our minds something it is easy to forget when we are engaged in philosophy, especially in our cool, contemporary style, viz. what it is actually like to be involved in ordinary inter-personal relationships, ranging from the most intimate to the most casual.

IV

It is one thing to ask about the general causes of these reactive attitudes I have alluded to: it is another to ask about the variations to which they are subject, the particular conditions in which they do or do not seem natural or reasonable or appropriate; and it is a third thing to ask what it would be like, what it *is* like, not to suffer them. I am not much concerned with the first question: but I am with the second; and perhaps even more with the third.

Let us consider, then, occasions for resentment: situations in which one person is offended or injured by the action of another and in which—in the absence of special considerations—the offended person might naturally or normally be expected to feel resentment. Then let us consider what sorts of special considerations might be expected to modify or mollify this feeling or remove it altogether. It needs no saying now how multifarious these considerations are. But, for my purpose, I think they can be roughly divided into two kinds. To the first group belong all those which might give occasion for the employment of such expressions as 'He didn't mean to', 'He hadn't realized', 'He didn't know'; and also all those which might give occasion for the use of the phrase 'He couldn't help it', when this is supported by such phrases as 'He was pushed', 'He had to do it', 'It was the only way', 'They left him no alternative', etc. Obviously these various pleas, and the kinds of situations in which they would be appropriate, differ from each other in striking and important ways. But for my present purpose they have something still more important in common. None of them invites us to suspend towards the agent, either at the time of his action or in general, our ordinary reactive attitudes. They do not invite us to view the *agent* as one in respect of whom these attitudes are in any way inappropriate. They invite us to view the *injury* as one in respect of which a particular one of these attitudes is inappropriate. They do not invite us to see the *agent* as other than a fully responsible agent. They invite us to see the *injury* as one for which he was not fully, or at all, responsible. They do not suggest that the agent is in any way an inappropriate object of that kind of demand for goodwill or regard which is reflected in our ordinary reactive attitudes. They suggest instead that the fact of injury was not in this case incompatible with that demand's being fulfilled, that the fact of injury was quite consistent with the agent's attitude and intentions being just what we demand they should be.[3] The agent was just ignorant of the injury he was causing, or had lost his balance through being pushed or had reluctantly to cause the injury for reasons which acceptably override his reluctance. The offering of such pleas by the agent and their acceptance by the sufferer is something in no way opposed to, or outside the context of, ordinary inter-personal relationships and the manifestation of ordinary reactive attitudes. Since things go wrong and situations are complicated, it is an essential and integral element in the transactions which are the life of these relationships.

The second group of considerations is very different. I shall take them in two sub-groups of which the first is far less important than the second. In connection with the first sub-group we may think of such statements as 'He wasn't himself', 'He has been under very great strain recently', 'He was acting under post-hypnotic suggestion'; in connection with the second, we may think of 'He's only a child', 'He's a hopeless schizophrenic', 'His mind has been systematically perverted', 'That's purely compulsive behaviour on his part'. Such pleas as these do, as pleas of my first general group do not, invite us to suspend our ordinary reactive attitudes towards the agent, either at the time of his action or all the time. They do not invite us to see the agent's action in a way consistent with the full retention of ordinary inter-personal attitudes and merely inconsistent with one particular attitude. They invite us to view the agent himself in a different light from the light in which we should normally view one who has acted as he has acted. I shall not linger over the first subgroup of cases. Though they perhaps raise, in the short term, questions akin to those raised, in the long term, by the second subgroup, we may dismiss them without considering those questions by taking that admirably suggestive phrase, 'He wasn't himself', with the seriousness that—for all its being logically comic—it deserves. We shall not feel resentment against the man he is for the action done by the man he is not; or at least we shall feel less. We normally have to deal with him under normal stresses; so we shall not feel towards him, when he acts as he does under abnormal stresses, as we should have felt towards him had he acted as he did under normal stresses.

---

[3] Perhaps not in every case *just* what we demand they should be, but in any case *not* just what we demand they should not be. For my present purpose these differences do not matter.

The second and more important subgroup of cases allows that the circumstances were normal, but presents the agent as psychologically abnormal—or as morally undeveloped. The agent was himself; but he is warped or deranged, neurotic or just a child. When we see someone in such a light as this, all our reactive attitudes tend to be profoundly modified. I must deal here in crude dichotomies and ignore the ever-interesting and ever-illuminating varieties of case. What I want to contrast is the attitude (or range of attitudes) of involvement or participation in a human relationship, on the one hand, and what might be called the objective attitude (or range of attitudes) to another human being, on the other. Even in the same situation, I must add, they are not altogether *exclusive* of each other; but they are, profoundly, *opposed* to each other. To adopt the objective attitude to another human being to see him, perhaps, as an object of social policy; as a subject for what, in a wide range of sense, might be called treatment; as something certainly to be taken account, perhaps precautionary account, of; to be managed or handled or cured or trained; perhaps simply to be avoided, though *this* gerundive is not peculiar to cases of objectivity of attitude. The objective attitude may be emotionally toned in many ways, but not in all ways: it may include repulsion or fear, it may include pity or even love, though not all kinds of love. But it cannot include the range of reactive feelings and attitudes which belong to involvement or participation with others in inter-personal human relationships; it cannot include resentment, gratitude, forgiveness, anger, or the sort of love which two adults can sometimes be said to feel reciprocally, for each other. If your attitude towards someone is wholly objective, then though you may fight him, you cannot quarrel with him, and though you may talk to him, even negotiate with him, you cannot reason with him. You can at most pretend to quarrel, or to reason, with him.

Seeing someone, then, as warped or deranged or compulsive in behaviour or peculiarly unfortunate in his formative circumstances—seeing someone so tends, at least to some extent, to set him apart from normal participant reactive attitudes on the part of one who sees him, tends to promote, at least in the civilized, objective attitudes. But there is something curious to add to this. The objective attitude is not only something we naturally tend to fall into in cases like these, where participant attitudes are partially or wholly inhibited by abnormalities or by immaturity. It is also something which is available as a resource in other cases too. We look with an objective eye on the compulsive behaviour of the neurotic or the tiresome behaviour of a very young child, thinking in terms of treatment or training. But we *can* sometimes look with something like the same eye on the behaviour of the normal and the mature. We *have* this resource and can sometimes use it: as a refuge,

say, from the strains of involvement; or as an aid to policy; or simply out of
intellectual curiosity. Being human, we cannot, in the normal case, do this
for long, or altogether. If the strains of involvement, say, continue to be too
great, then we have to do something else—like severing a relationship. But
what is above all interesting is the tension there is, in us, between the participant attitude and the objective attitude. One is tempted to say: between our
humanity and our intelligence. But to say this would be to distort both
notions.

What I have called the participant reactive attitudes are essentially natural
human reactions to the good or ill will or indifference of others towards us,
as displayed in *their* attitudes and actions. The question we have to ask is:
What effect would, or should, the acceptance of the truth of a general thesis
of determinism have upon these reactive attitudes? More specifically, would,
or should, the acceptance of the truth of the thesis lead to the decay or the
repudiation of all such attitudes? Would, or should, it mean the end of
gratitude, resentment, and forgiveness; of all reciprocated adult loves; of all
the essentially *personal* antagonisms?

But how can I answer, or even pose, this question without knowing *exactly*
what the thesis of determinism is? Well, there is one thing we do know: that
if there is a coherent thesis of determinism, then there must be a sense of
'determined' such that, if that thesis is true, then all behaviour whatever is
determined in that sense. Remembering this, we can consider at least what
possibilities lie formally open; and then perhaps we shall see that the question can be answered *without* knowing exactly what the thesis of determinism is. We can consider what possibilities lie open because we have already
before us an account of the ways in which particular reactive attitudes, or
reactive attitudes in general, may be, and, sometimes, we judge, should be,
inhibited. Thus I considered earlier a group of considerations which tend to
inhibit, and, we judge, should inhibit, resentment, in particular cases of an
agent causing an injury, without inhibiting reactive attitudes in general
towards that agent. Obviously this group of considerations cannot strictly
bear upon our question; for that question concerns reactive attitudes in
general. But resentment has a particular interest; so it is worth adding that it
has never been claimed as a consequence of the truth of determinism that
one or another of *these* considerations was operative in every case of an
injury being caused by an agent; that it would follow from the truth of
determinism that anyone who caused an injury *either* was quite simply
ignorant of causing it *or* had acceptably overriding reasons for acquiescing
reluctantly in causing it *or* . . ., etc. The prevalence of this happy state of
affairs would not be a consequence of the reign of universal determinism,
but of the reign of universal goodwill. We cannot, then, find here the

possibility of an affirmative answer to our question, even for the particular case of resentment.

Next, I remarked that the participant attitude, and the personal reactive attitudes in general, tend to give place, and, it is judged by the civilized, should give place, to objective attitudes, just in so far as the agent is seen as excluded from ordinary adult human relationships by deep-rooted psychological abnormality—or simply by being a child. But it cannot be a consequence of any thesis which is not itself self-contradictory that abnormality is the universal condition.

Now this dismissal might seem altogether too facile; and so, in a sense, it is. But whatever is too quickly dismissed in this dismissal is allowed for in the only possible form of affirmative answer that remains. We can sometimes, and in part, I have remarked, look on the normal (those we rate as 'normal') in the objective way in which we have learned to look on certain classified cases of abnormality. And our question reduces to this: could, or should, the acceptance of the determinist thesis lead us always to look on everyone exclusively in this way? For this is the only condition worth considering under which the acceptance of determinism could lead to the decay or repudiation of participant reactive attitudes.

It does not seem to be self-contradictory to suppose that this might happen. So I suppose we must say that it is not absolutely inconceivable that it should happen. But I am strongly inclined to think that it is, for us as we are, practically inconceivable. The human commitment to participation in ordinary inter-personal relationships is, I think, too thoroughgoing and deeply rooted for us to take seriously the thought that a general theoretical conviction might so change our world that, in it, there were no longer any such things as inter-personal relationships as we normally understand them; and being involved in inter-personal relationships as we normally understand them precisely is being exposed to the range of reactive attitudes and feelings that is in question.

This, then, is a part of the reply to our question. A sustained objectivity of inter-personal attitude, and the human isolation which that would entail, does not seem to be something of which human beings would be capable, even if some general truth were a theoretical ground for it. But this is not all. There is a further point, implicit in the foregoing, which must be made explicit. Exceptionally, I have said, we can have direct dealings with human beings without any degree of personal involvement, treating them simply as creatures to be handled in our own interests, or our side's, or society's—or even theirs. In the extreme case of the mentally deranged, it is easy to see the connection between the possibility of a wholly objective attitude and the impossibility of what we understand by ordinary inter-personal relationships. Given this latter impossibility, no other civilized attitude is available than that of viewing the deranged person simply as something to be understood and controlled in the most desirable fashion. To view him as outside the reach of personal relationships is already, for the civilized, to view him in this way. For reasons of policy or self-protection we may have occasion, perhaps temporary, to adopt a fundamentally similar attitude to a 'normal' human being; to concentrate, that is, on understanding 'how he works', with a view to determining our policy accordingly or to finding in that very understanding a relief from the strains of involvement. Now it is certainly true that in the case of the abnormal, though not in the case of the normal, our adoption of the objective attitude is a consequence of our viewing the agent as *incapacitated* in some or all respects for ordinary inter-personal relationships. He is thus incapacitated, perhaps, by the fact that his picture of reality is pure fantasy, that he does not, in a sense, live in the real world at all; or by the fact that his behaviour is, in part, an unrealistic acting out of unconscious purposes; or by the fact that he is an idiot, or a moral idiot. But there is something else which, *because* this is true, is equally certainly *not* true. And that is that there is a sense of 'determined' such that (1) if determinism is true, all behaviour is determined in this sense, and (2) determinism might be true, i.e. it is not inconsistent with the facts as we know them to suppose that all behaviour might be determined in this sense, and (3) our adoption of the objective attitude towards the abnormal is the result of prior embracing of the belief that the behaviour, or the relevant stretch of behaviour, of the human being in question *is* determined in this sense. Neither in the case of the normal, then, nor in the case of the abnormal is it true that, when we adopt an objective attitude, we do so *because* we hold such a belief. So my answer has two parts. The first is that we cannot, as we are, seriously envisage ourselves adopting a thoroughgoing objectivity of attitude to others as a result of theoretical conviction of the truth of determinism; and the second is that when we do in fact adopt such an attitude in a particular case, our doing so is not the consequence of a theoretical conviction which might be expressed as 'Determinism in this case', but is a consequence of our abandoning, for different reasons in different cases, the ordinary inter-personal attitudes.

It might be said that all this leaves the real question unanswered, and that we cannot hope to answer it without knowing exactly what the thesis of determinism is. For the real question is not a question about what we actually do, or why we do it. It is not even a question about what we would *in fact* do if a certain theoretical conviction gained general acceptance. It is a question about what it would be *rational* to do if determinism were true, a question about the rational justification of ordinary inter-personal attitudes in general. To this I shall reply, first, that such a question could seem real only to one who had utterly failed to grasp the purport of the preceding answer, the fact of our natural human commitment to ordinary inter-personal attitudes. This commitment is part of the general framework of human life, not something that can come up for review as particular cases can come up for review within this general framework. And I shall reply, second, that if we could imagine what we cannot have, viz. a choice in this matter, then we could choose rationally only in the light of an assessment of the gains and losses to human life, its enrichment or impoverishment; and the truth or falsity of a general thesis of determinism would not bear on the rationality of *this* choice.[4]

V

The point of this discussion of the reactive attitudes in their relation—or lack of it—to the thesis of determinism was to bring us, if possible, nearer to a position of compromise in a more usual area of debate. We are not now to discuss reactive attitudes which are essentially those of offended parties or beneficiaries. We are to discuss reactive attitudes which are essentially not those, or only incidentally are those, of offended parties or beneficiaries, but are nevertheless, I shall claim, kindred attitudes to those I have discussed. I put resentment in the centre of the previous discussion. I shall put moral indignation—or, more weakly, moral disapprobation—in the centre of this one.

The reactive attitudes I have so far discussed are essentially reactions to the quality of others' wills towards us, as manifested in their behaviour: to their good or ill will or indifference or lack of concern. Thus resentment, or what I have called resentment, is a reaction to injury or indifference. The reactive attitudes I have now to discuss might be described as the sympa-thetic or vicarious or impersonal or disinterested or generalized analogues of the reactive attitudes I have already discussed. They are reactions to the qualities of others' wills, not towards ourselves, but towards others. Because of this impersonal or vicarious character, we give them different names.

---

[4] The question, then, of the connection between rationality and the adoption of the objective attitude to others is misposed when it is made to seem dependent on the issue of determinism. But there is another question which should be raised, if only to distinguish it from the misposed question. Quite apart from the issue of determinism might it not be said that we should be nearer to being purely rational creatures in proportion as our relation to others was in fact dominated by the objective attitude? I think this might be said; only it would have to be added, once more, that if such a choice were possible, it would not necessarily be rational to choose to be more purely rational than we are.

Thus one who experiences the vicarious analogue of resentment is said to be indignant or disapproving, or morally indignant or disapproving. What we have here is, as it were, resentment on behalf of another, where one's own interest and dignity are not involved; and it is this impersonal or vicarious character of the attitude, added to its others, which entitle it to the qualification 'moral'. Both my description of, and my name for, these attitudes are, in one important respect, a little misleading. It is not that these attitudes are essentially vicarious—one can feel indignation on one's own account—but that they are essentially capable of being vicarious. But I shall retain the name for the sake of its suggestiveness; and I hope that what is misleading about it will be corrected in what follows.

The personal reactive attitudes rest on, and reflect, an expectation of, and demand for, the manifestation of a certain degree of goodwill or regard on the part of other human beings towards ourselves; or at least on the expectation of, and demand for, an absence of the manifestation of active ill will or indifferent disregard. (What will, in particular cases, *count* as manifestations of good or ill will or disregard will vary in accordance with the particular relationship in which we stand to another human being.) The generalized or vicarious analogues of the personal reactive attitudes rest on, and reflect, exactly the same expectation or demand in a generalized form; they rest on, or reflect, that is, the demand for the manifestation of a reasonable degree of goodwill or regard, on the part of others, not simply towards oneself, but towards all those on whose behalf moral indignation may be felt, i.e. as we now think, towards all men. The generalized and non-generalized forms of demand, and the vicarious and personal reactive attitudes which rest upon, and reflect, them are connected not merely logically. They are connected humanly; and not merely with each other. They are connected also with yet another set of attitudes which I must mention now in order to complete the picture. I have considered from two points of view the demands we make on others and our reactions to their possibly injurious actions. These were the points of view of one whose interest was directly involved (who suffers, say, the injury) and of others whose interest was not directly involved (who do not themselves suffer the injury). Thus I have spoken of personal reactive attitudes in the first connection and of their vicarious analogues in the second. But the picture is not complete unless we consider also the correlates of these attitudes on the part of those on whom the demands are made, on the part of the agents. Just as there are personal and vicarious reactive attitudes associated with demands on others for oneself and demands on others for others, so there are self-reactive attitudes associated with demands on oneself for others. And here we have to mention such phenomena as feeling bound or obliged (the 'sense of obligation'); feeling compunction;

feeling guilty or remorseful or at least responsible; and the more complicated phenomenon of shame.

All these three types of attitude are humanly connected. One who manifested the personal reactive attitudes in a high degree but showed no inclination at all to their vicarious analogues would appear as an abnormal case of moral egocentricity, as a kind of moral solipsist. Let him be supposed fully to acknowledge the claims to regard that others had on him, to be susceptible of the whole range of self-reactive attitudes. He would then see himself as unique both as one (*the* one) who had a general claim on human regard and as one (*the* one) on whom human beings in general had such a claim. This would be a kind of moral solipsism. But it is barely more than a conceptual possibility: if it is that. In general, though within varying limits, we demand of others for others, as well as of ourselves for others, something of the regard which we demand of others for ourselves. Can we imagine, besides that of the moral solipsist, any other case of one or two of these three types of attitude being fully developed, but quite unaccompanied by any trace, however slight, of the remaining two or one? If we can, then we imagine something far below or far above the level of our common humanity—a moral idiot or a saint. For all these types of attitude alike have common roots in our human nature and our membership of human communities.

Now, as of the personal reactive attitudes, so of their vicarious analogues, we must ask in what ways, and by what considerations, they tend to be inhibited. Both types of attitude involve, or express, a certain sort of demand for inter-personal regard. The fact of injury constitutes a prima-facie appearance of this demand's being flouted or unfulfilled. We saw, in the case of resentment, how one class of considerations may show this appearance to be mere appearance, and hence inhibit resentment, *without* inhibiting, or displacing, the sort of demand of which resentment can be an expression, without in any way tending to make us suspend our ordinary inter-personal attitudes to the agent. Considerations of this class operate in just the same way, for just the same reasons, in connection with moral disapprobation or indignation; they inhibit indignation without in any way inhibiting the sort of demand on the agent of which indignation can be an expression, the range of attitudes towards him to which it belongs. But in this connection we may express the facts with a new emphasis. We may say, stressing the moral, the generalized aspect of the demand, considerations of this group have no tendency to make us see the agent as other than a morally responsible agent; they simply make us see the injury as one for which he was not morally responsible. The offering and acceptance of such exculpatory pleas as are here in question in no way detracts in our eyes from the agent's status as a term of moral relationships. On the contrary, since things go wrong and situations are complicated, it is an essential part of the life of such relationships.

But suppose we see the agent in a different light: as one whose picture of the world is an insane delusion; or as one whose behaviour, or a part of whose behaviour, is unintelligible to us, perhaps even to him, in terms of conscious purposes, and intelligible only in terms of unconscious purposes: or even, perhaps, as one wholly impervious to the self-reactive attitudes I spoke of, wholly lacking, as we say, in moral sense. Seeing an agent in such a light as this tends, I said, to inhibit resentment in a wholly different way. It tends to inhibit resentment because it tends to inhibit ordinary inter-personal attitudes in general, and the kind of demand and expectation which those attitudes involve: and tends to promote instead the purely objective view of the agent as one posing problems simply of intellectual understanding, management, treatment, and control. Again the parallel holds for those generalized or moral attitudes towards the agent which we are now concerned with. The same abnormal light which shows the agent to us as one in respect of whom the personal attitudes, the personal demand, are to be suspended, shows him to us also as one in respect of whom the impersonal attitudes, the generalized demand, are to be suspended. Only, abstracting now from direct personal interest, we may express the facts with a new emphasis. We may say: to the extent to which the agent is seen in this light, he is not seen as one on whom demands and expectations lie in that particular way in which we think of them as lying when we speak of moral obligation; he is not, to that extent, seen as a morally responsible agent, as a term of moral relationships, as a member of the moral community.

I remarked also that the suspension of ordinary inter-personal attitudes and the cultivation of a purely objective view is sometimes possible even when we have no such reasons for it as I have just mentioned. Is this possible also in the case of the moral reactive attitudes? I think so; and perhaps it is easier. But the motives for a total suspension of moral reactive attitudes are fewer, and perhaps weaker: fewer, because only where there is antecedent personal involvement can there be the motive of seeking refuge from the strains of such involvement; perhaps weaker, because the tension between objectivity of view and the moral reactive attitudes is perhaps less than the tension between objectivity of view and the personal reactive attitudes, so that we can in the case of the moral reactive attitudes more easily secure the speculative or political gains of objectivity of view by a kind of setting on one side, rather than a total suspension, of those attitudes.

These last remarks are uncertain; but also, for the present purpose, unimportant. What concerns us now is to inquire, as previously in

connection with the personal reactive attitudes, what relevance any general
thesis of determinism might have to their vicarious analogues. The answers
once more are parallel; though I shall take them in a slightly different order.
First, we must note, as before, that when the suspension of such an attitude
or such attitudes occurs in a particular case, it is *never* the consequence of
the belief that the piece of behaviour in question was determined in a sense
such that all behaviour *might be*, and, if determinism is true, all behaviour *is*,
determined in that sense. For it is not a consequence of any general thesis of
determinism which might be true that nobody knows what he's doing or that
everybody's behaviour is unintelligible in terms of conscious purposes or
that everybody lives in a world of delusion or that nobody has a moral sense,
i.e. is susceptible of self-reactive attitudes, etc. In fact no such sense of
'determined' as would be required for a general thesis of determinism is ever
relevant to our actual suspensions of moral reactive attitudes. Second, suppose it granted, as I have already argued, that we cannot take seriously the
thought that theoretical conviction of such a general thesis would lead to
the total decay of the personal reactive attitudes. Can we then take seriously
the thought that such a conviction—a conviction, after all, that many have
held or said they held—would nevertheless lead to the total decay or
repudiation of the vicarious analogues of these attitudes? I think that the
change in our social world which would leave us exposed to the personal
reactive attitudes but not at all to their vicarious analogues, the generalization of abnormal egocentricity which this would entail, is perhaps even
harder for us to envisage as a real possibility than the decay of both kinds of
attitude together. Though there are some necessary and some contingent
differences between the ways and cases in which these two kinds of attitudes
operate or are inhibited in their operation, yet, as general human capacities
or pronenesses, they stand or lapse together. Finally, to the further question
whether it would not be *rational*, given a general theoretical conviction of
the truth of determinism, so to change our world that in it all these attitudes
were wholly suspended, I must answer, as before, that one who presses this
question has wholly failed to grasp the import of the preceding answer, the
nature of the human commitment that is here involved: it is *useless* to ask
whether it would not be rational for us to do what it is not in our nature to
(be able to) do. To this I must add, as before, that if there were, say, for a
moment open to us the possibility of such a godlike choice, the rationality of
making or refusing it would be determined by quite other considerations
than the truth or falsity of the general theoretical doctrine in question. The
latter would be simply irrelevant; and this becomes ironically clear when we
remember that for those convinced that the truth of determinism nevertheless really would make the one choice rational, there has always been the

insuperable difficulty of explaining in intelligible terms how its falsity would make the opposite choice rational.

I am aware that in presenting the argument as I have done, neglecting the ever-interesting varieties of case, I have presented nothing more than a schema, using sometimes a crude opposition of phrase where we have a great intricacy of phenomena. In particular the simple opposition of objective attitudes on the one hand and the various contrasted attitudes which I have opposed to them must seem as grossly crude as it is central. Let me pause to mitigate this crudity a little, and also to strengthen one of my central contentions, by mentioning some things which straddle these contrasted kinds of attitude. Thus parents and others concerned with the care and upbringing of young children cannot have to their charges either kind of attitude in a pure or unqualified form. They are dealing with creatures who are potentially and increasingly capable both of holding, and being objects of, the full range of human and moral attitudes, but are not yet truly capable of either. The treatment of such creatures must therefore represent a kind of compromise, constantly shifting in one direction, between objectivity of attitude and developed human attitudes. Rehearsals insensibly modulate towards true performances. The punishment of a child is both like and unlike the punishment of an adult. Suppose we try to relate this progressive emergence of the child as a responsible being, as an object of non-objective attitudes, to that sense of 'determined' in which, if determinism is a possibly true thesis, all behaviour *may* be determined, and in which, if it is a true thesis, all behaviour *is* determined. What bearing *could* such a sense of 'determined' have upon the progressive modification of attitudes towards the child? Would it not be grotesque to think of the development of the child as a progressive or patchy emergence from an area in which its behaviour is in this sense determined into an area in which it isn't? Whatever sense of 'determined' is required for stating the thesis of determinism, it can scarcely be such as to allow of compromise, borderline-style answers to the question, 'Is this bit of behaviour determined or isn't it?' But in this matter of young children, it is essentially a borderline, penumbral area that we move in. Again, consider—a very different matter—the strain in the attitude of a psychoanalyst to his patient. *His* objectivity of attitude, *his* suspension of ordinary moral reactive attitudes, is profoundly modified by the fact that the aim of the enterprise is to make such suspension unnecessary or less necessary. Here we may and do naturally speak of restoring the agent's freedom. But here the restoring of freedom means bringing it about that the agent's behaviour shall be intelligible in terms of conscious purposes rather than in terms only of unconscious purposes. *This* is the object of the enterprise; and it is in so far as *this* object is attained that the suspension, or half-suspension, of ordinary moral attitudes is deemed no longer necessary or appropriate. And in this we see once again the *irrelevance* of that concept of 'being determined' which must be the central concept of determinism. For we cannot both agree that this object is attainable and that its attainment has this consequence and yet hold (1) that neurotic behaviour is determined in a sense in which, it may be, all behaviour is determined, and (2) that it is because neurotic behaviour is determined in this sense that objective attitudes are deemed appropriate to neurotic behaviour. Not, at least, without accusing ourselves of incoherence in our attitude to psychoanalytic treatment.

VI

And now we can try to fill in the lacuna which the pessimist finds in the optimist's account of the concept of moral responsibility, and of the bases of moral condemnation and punishment; and to fill it in from the facts as we know them. For, as I have already remarked, when the pessimist himself seeks to fill it in, he rushes beyond the facts as we know them and proclaims that it cannot be filled in at all unless determinism is false.

Yet a partial sense of the facts as we know them is certainly present to the pessimist's mind. When his opponent, the optimist, undertakes to show that the truth of determinism would not shake the foundations of the concept of moral responsibility and of the practices of moral condemnation and punishment, he typically refers, in a more or less elaborated way, to the efficacy of these practices in regulating behaviour in socially desirable ways. These practices are represented solely as instruments of policy, as methods of individual treatment and social control. The pessimist recoils from this picture; and in his recoil there is, typically, an element of emotional shock. He is apt to say, among much else, that the humanity of the offender himself is offended by *this* picture of his condemnation and punishment.

The reasons for this recoil—the explanation of the sense of an emotional, as well as a conceptual, shock—we have already before us. The picture painted by the optimists is painted in a style appropriate to a situation envisaged as wholly dominated by objectivity of attitude. The only operative notions invoked in this picture are such as those of policy, treatment, control. But a thoroughgoing objectivity of attitude, excluding as it does the moral reactive attitudes, excludes at the same time essential elements in the concepts of *moral* condemnation and *moral* responsibility. This is the reason for the conceptual shock. The deeper emotional shock is a reaction, not simply to an inadequate conceptual analysis, but to the suggestion of a change in our world. I have remarked that it is possible to cultivate an exclusive objectivity of attitude in some cases, and for some reasons, where the object of the attitude is not set aside from developed inter-personal and moral attitudes by immaturity or abnormality. And the suggestion which seems to be contained in the optimist's account is that such an attitude should be universally adopted to all offenders. This is shocking enough in the pessimist's eyes. But, sharpened by shock, his eyes see further. It would be hard to make *this* division in our natures. If to all offenders, then to all mankind. Moreover, to whom could this recommendation be, in any real sense, addressed? Only to the powerful, the authorities. So abysses seem to open.[5]

But we will confine our attention to the case of the offenders. The concepts we are concerned with are those of responsibility and guilt, qualified as 'moral', on the one hand—together with that of membership of a moral community; of demand, indignation, disapprobation and condemnation, qualified as 'moral', on the other hand—together with that of punishment. Indignation, disapprobation, like resentment, tend to inhibit or at least to limit our goodwill towards the object of these attitudes, tend to promote an at least partial and temporary withdrawal of goodwill: they do so in proportion as they are strong; and their strength is in general proportioned to what is felt to be the magnitude of the injury and to the degree to which the agent's will is identified with, or indifferent to, it. (These, of course, are not contingent connections.) But these attitudes of disapprobation and indignation are precisely the correlates of the moral demand in the case where the demand is felt to be disregarded. The making of the demand *is* the proneness to such attitudes. The holding of them does not, as the holding of objective attitudes does, involve as a part of itself viewing their object other than as a member of the moral community. The partial withdrawal of goodwill which *these* attitudes entail, the modification *they* entail of the general demand that another should, if possible, be spared suffering, is, rather, the consequence of *continuing* to view him as a member of the moral community; only as one who has offended against its demands. So the preparedness to acquiesce in that infliction of suffering on the offender which is an essential part of punishment is all of a piece with this whole range of attitudes of which I have been speaking. It is not only moral reactive attitudes towards the offender which are in question here. We must mention also the self-reactive attitudes of offenders themselves. Just as the other-reactive attitudes are associated with a readiness to acquiesce in the infliction of suffering on an

---

[5] See J. D. Mabbott's 'Freewill and Punishment', in *Contemporary British Philosophy*, 3rd ser. (London: Allen & Unwin, 1956).

offender, within the 'institution' of punishment, so the self-reactive attitudes are associated with a readiness on the part of the offender to acquiesce in such infliction *without* developing the reactions (e.g. of resentment) which he would normally develop to the infliction of injury upon him: i.e. with a readiness, as we say, to accept punishment[6] as 'his due' or as 'just'.

I am not in the least suggesting that these readinesses to acquiesce, either on the part of the offender himself or on the part of others, are always or commonly accompanied or preceded by indignant boilings or remorseful pangs; only that we have here a continuum of attitudes and feelings to which these readinesses to acquiesce themselves belong. Nor am I in the least suggesting that it belongs to this continuum of attitudes that we should be ready to acquiesce in the infliction of injury on offenders in a fashion which we saw to be quite indiscriminate or in accordance with procedures which we knew to be wholly useless. On the contrary, savage or civilized, we have some belief in the utility of practices of condemnation and punishment. But the social utility of these practices, on which the optimist lays such exclusive stress, is not what is now in question. What is in question is the pessimist's justified sense that to speak in terms of social utility alone is to leave out something vital in our conception of these practices. The vital thing can be restored by attending to that complicated web of attitudes and feelings which form an essential part of the moral life as we know it, and which are quite opposed to objectivity of attitude. Only by attending to this range of attitudes can we recover from the facts as we know them a sense of what we mean, i.e. of *all* we mean, when, speaking the language of morals, we speak of desert, responsibility, guilt, condemnation, and justice. But we *do* recover it from the facts as we know them. We do not have to go beyond them. Because the optimist neglects or misconstrues these attitudes, the pessimist rightly claims to find a lacuna in his account. We can fill the lacuna for him. But in return we must demand of the pessimist a surrender of his metaphysics.

Optimist and pessimist misconstrue the facts in very different styles. But in a profound sense there is something in common to their misunderstandings. Both seek, in different ways, to overintellectualize the facts. Inside the general structure or web of human attitudes and feelings of which I have been speaking, there is endless room for modification, redirection, criticism, and justification. But questions of justification are internal to the structure or relate to modifications internal to it. The existence of the general framework of attitudes itself is something we are given with the fact of human society. As a whole, it neither calls for, nor permits, an external 'rational' justification. Pessimist and optimist alike show themselves, in different ways,

---

[6] Of course not *any* punishment for *anything* deemed an offence.

unable to accept this.[7] The optimist's style of over-intellectualizing the facts is that of a characteristically incomplete empiricism, a one-eyed utilitarianism. He seeks to find an adequate basis for certain social practices in calculated consequences, and loses sight (perhaps wishes to lose sight) of the human attitudes of which these practices are, in part, the expression. The pessimist does not lose sight of these attitudes, but is unable to accept the fact that it is just these attitudes themselves which fill the gap in the optimist's account. Because of this, he thinks the gap can be filled only if some general metaphysical proposition is repeatedly verified, verified in all cases where it is appropriate to attribute moral responsibility. This proposition he finds it as difficult to state coherently and with intelligible relevance as its determinist contradictory. Even when a formula has been found ('contra-causal freedom' or something of the kind) there still seems to remain a gap between its applicability in particular cases and its supposed moral consequences. Sometimes he plugs this gap with an intuition of fittingness—a pitiful intellectualist trinket for a philosopher to wear as a charm against the recognition of his own humanity.

Even the moral sceptic is not immune from his own form of the wish to over-intellectualize such notions as those of moral responsibility, guilt, and blame. He sees that the optimist's account is inadequate and the pessimist's libertarian alternative inane; and finds no resource except to declare that the notions in question are inherently confused, that 'blame is metaphysical'. But the metaphysics was in the eye of the metaphysician. It is a pity that talk of the moral sentiments has fallen out of favour. The phrase would be quite a good name for that network of human attitudes in acknowledging the character and place of which we find, I suggest, the only possibility of reconciling these disputants to each other and the facts.

There are, at present, factors which add, in a slightly paradoxical way, to the difficulty of making this acknowledgement. These human attitudes themselves, in their development and in the variety of their manifestations, have to an increasing extent become objects of study in the social and psychological sciences; and this growth of human self-consciousness, which we might expect to reduce the difficulty of acceptance, in fact increases it in several ways. One factor of comparatively minor importance is an increased historical and anthropological awareness of the great variety of forms which these human attitudes may take at different times and in different cultures.

---

[7] Compare the question of the justification of induction. The human commitment to inductive belief-formation is original, natural, non-rational (not *ir*rational), in no way something we choose or could give up. Yet rational criticism and reflection can refine standards and their application, supply 'rules for judging of cause and effect'. Ever since the facts were made clear by Hume, people have been resisting acceptance of them.

This makes one rightly chary of claiming as essential features of the concept of morality in general, forms of these attitudes which may have a local and temporary prominence. No doubt to some extent my own descriptions of human attitudes have reflected local and temporary features of our own culture. But an awareness of variety of forms should not prevent us from acknowledging also that in the absence of *any* forms of these attitudes it is doubtful whether we should have anything that *we* could find intelligible as a system of human relationships, as human society. A quite different factor of greater importance is that psychological studies have made us rightly mistrustful of many particular manifestations of the attitudes I have spoken of. They are a prime realm of self-deception, of the ambiguous and the shady, of guilt-transference, unconscious sadism and the rest. But it is an exaggerated horror, itself suspect, which would make us unable to acknowledge the facts because of the seamy side of the facts. Finally, perhaps the most important factor of all is the prestige of these theoretical studies themselves. That prestige is great, and is apt to make us forget that in philosophy, though it also is a theoretical study, we have to take account of the facts in *all* their bearings; we are not to suppose that we are required, or permitted, as philosophers, to regard ourselves, as human beings, as detached from the attitudes which, as scientists, we study with detachment. This is in no way to deny the possibility and desirability of redirection and modification of our human attitudes in the light of these studies. But we may reasonably think it unlikely that our progressively greater understanding of certain aspects of ourselves will lead to the total disappearance of those aspects. Perhaps it is not inconceivable that it should; and perhaps, then, the dreams of some philosophers will be realized.

If we sufficiently, that is *radically*, modify the view of the optimist, his view is the right one. It is far from wrong to emphasize the efficacy of all those practices which express or manifest our moral attitudes, in regulating behaviour in ways considered desirable; or to add that when certain of our beliefs about the efficacy of some of these practices turns out to be false, then we may have good reason for dropping or modifying those practices. What *is* wrong is to forget that these practices, and their reception, the reactions to them, really *are* expressions of our moral attitudes and not merely devices we calculatingly employ for regulative purposes. Our practices do not merely exploit our natures, they express them. Indeed the very understanding of the kind of efficacy these expressions of our attitudes have turns on our remembering this. When we do remember this, and modify the optimist's position accordingly, we simultaneously correct its conceptual deficiencies and ward off the dangers it seems to entail, without recourse to the obscure and panicky metaphysics of libertarianism.

5

TOWARDS A REASONABLE LIBERTARIANISM

DAVID WIGGINS

His own character is a man's destiny.

(Heraclitus)

Very well, my obliging opponent, we have now reached an issue. You think all the arbitrary specifications of the universe were introduced in one dose, in the beginning, if there was a beginning, and that the variety and complication of nature has always been just as it is now. But I, for my part, think that the diversification, the specification, has been continually taking place.

(C. S. Peirce)

1. INTRODUCTION

One of the many reasons, I believe, why philosophy falls short of a satisfying solution to the problem of the freedom of the will is that we still cannot refer to an unflawed statement of libertarianism. Perhaps libertarianism is in the last analysis untenable. But if we are to salvage its insights, we need to know what is the least unreasonable statement the position could be given. Compatibilist resolutions to the problem of freedom will always wear an

This text is based on chapter VIII of *Needs, Values, Truth*, 3rd edn. (Oxford University Press, 1998). That chapter was abbreviated from my contribution to *Essays on Freedom of Action*, edited by Ted Honderich (London: Routledge & Kegan Paul, 1973). I thank Routledge & Kegan Paul for permitting me to reprint it here. This was one part of a paper to the Oxford Philosophical Society in the summer of 1965. A version of another excerpt from that paper appeared as Part II of 'Freedom, Knowledge, Belief, and Causality', p. 13, in *Knowledge and Necessity*, ed. G. Vesey (London: Macmillan, 1970), and is cited at notes 4 and 5 below.

§4–§8 represent a rearrangement, revision, and extension of the three concluding sections of the original article. §9 is from a Postscript (p. 381) from 1998.

Every student of Richard Taylor's and Roderick Chisholm's path-breaking efforts to refurbish the credentials of libertarianism will perceive my indebtedness to them, as well as my various reservations about the positions they have taken. See especially Richard Taylor's *Action and Purpose* (New York: Prentice Hall, 1966) and Roderick Chisholm's 'He could have done otherwise', *Journal of Philosophy* (July 1967).

I thank Oxford University Press for their permission to make the quotation in note 16 and the British Academy for their permission to make that in note 28.

appearance of superficiality, however serious the reflections from which they arise,[1] until what they offer by way of freedom can be compared with something else, whether actual or possible or only seemingly imaginable, that is known to be the best that any indeterminist or libertarian could describe.[2] What follows is offered as a small step in the direction of a more reasonable or less fantastical exposition.

2. WHAT THE LIBERTARIAN MEANS BY 'HE COULD HAVE DONE OTHERWISE'

The libertarian says that someone is only responsible or free if sometimes he could do otherwise than he does do. It must at least sometimes be genuinely up to him what he chooses or decides to do. But what does this mean? Let us begin with three clarifications.

(i) It is characteristic of the libertarian to insist that, for at least some of the things that an agent with freedom does, or plans or decides to do, he must have a genuine alternative open to him. That is, for some act A and some act B, where A≠B, he must be able to do A and he must be able to do B. (In my usage 'act' denotes a thing done, *i.e.*, a *type* that particular actions exemplify. The auxiliary 'do' marks schematically the connexion of act and agent.) But does the same apply to what the agent with freedom thinks, believes or infers?[3] In another place,[4] I have given an argument, whatever it may be worth, whose purpose was to show that the notions *open choice, decision, alternative, up to me, freedom* have a different point in the realm of belief, the state whose distinctive aspiration it is to match or represent the

---

[1] By *compatibilism* (or dissolutionism) I mean the position which says that freedom (the freedom of being able to do otherwise) and physical determinism can coexist. By *incompatibilism* the position that they cannot coexist. *Libertarianism* is a species of incompatibilism, one which saves freedom by denying physical determinism. In refurbishing libertarianism I do not myself mean to subscribe to *a priori* or introspective or extra-scientific arguments against physical determinism but to subscribe to an interest in what the libertarian *wanted* by way of freedom, whether or not the world will allow of this freedom. Whether libertarianism is true or false, it is the only good source for the position which it entails (without being entailed by it), viz. incompatibilism. It is true that some classical determinists were incompatibilists of a sort, but for the most part libertarian writings are a better guide for the understanding of incompatibilism.

[2] It is only fair to say that more work has been done on this since the time of the complaint. See, for instance, the collection *Free Will* (Oxford University Press, 1982) edited by Gary Watson, and especially his Editorial Introduction.

[3] See, for instance, John Lucas in *Aristotelian Society Supplementary Volume*, 1967; Ted Honderich in *Punishment* (London, 1969) (recanted, *Aristotelian Society Supplementary Volume*, 1970).

[4] Cf. my 'Freedom', pp. 145–8 (*op. cit.*).

world as it is, from their point in the realm of action and volition. The proper province of action and volition is not to match anything in the physical world but to affect or act upon the world. Of course the world and its causal properties, whether or not these constitute it a deterministic world, are the unquestioned framework within which action takes place. But for the libertarian it is typical and proper to insist that nothing in that world should completely determine the ends, objectives and ideals with which the free agent, if he is truly free, deliberates about the changes he would seek to make to it. There is no question of requiring for ends and ideals the vindication by things in the world that a belief about the world requires from things in the world: on the other hand, the libertarian ought to be content to allow the world, if it will only do so, to convey to the free man who has questions that he wants to put and is suitably placed to answer them, how the world is.[5] Freedom does not consist in the exercise of the (colourable but irrelevant) right to go mad without interference or distraction by fact.[6] Alternatives of the kind that the libertarian defines and demands are alternatives in the realm not of theory but of practice.

(ii) To say that an agent is doing or will do B, and that there is something else, A, that he can do, is to say something ambiguous, even though (ignoring permissive and epistemic contexts) 'can' itself is most likely univocal (see (iii) below). A may be something the agent can generally do, for instance, or something he can for such and such a stretch of time do, given the opportunity. It is true and important that a claim about a persisting ability to do A is confirmed if the agent's wanting or trying to do A at an appropriate moment during the relevant period is a sufficient condition of his producing a non-fluke performance of act A. But, read in this way, the finding that the agent can do otherwise is irrelevant to the point that troubles the libertarian. What organises the whole dispute, that which holds the libertarian's position apart from his present day opponents' position, is rather his treatment of another question: if physical determinism is true, is there ever something different from what the agent will in fact do at some time t_i such that the agent can at t_i

---

[5] Historically speaking and common-sensically speaking, the point of the demand for freedom of thought was not to conceive one's beliefs in a manner untrammelled or underdetermined by external reality, but to remove civil and clerical obstacles to the spirit of enquiry that allows only the way things are to determine belief. The contrast I am drawing here between theoretical and practical does *not* depend on a conception of knowledge or discovery that excludes or ignores intellectual fertility or active invention. It simply imposes conditions upon its workings and possible outcomes. See, 'Freedom', p. 146.

[6] It is worth adding that the causal determination by the world of a rational man's particular true belief p cannot in itself entail that the world would have lodged this belief with him *even if it had not been true*—the conditional is both subjunctive and contrary to fact—or that nobody could have told that p was not true if it had not been true.

do this other thing at t_i instead? If physical determinism is true, the libertarian maintains, then such an alternative is never really or truly available to the agent (see below §4). Sometimes earlier doings, in their context, completely determine successions of later events and doings. According to the libertarian, however, there can only be real alternatives if there are at least some doings and decidings which, whether or not they completely determine their immediate successors, are not themselves entirely determined by earlier events. Of course, this is only a necessary condition of alternatives of freedom of action. The libertarian does not deny that, even if this freedom did not exist, we could, if we wished, having discovered that it didn't exist, continue mechanically to draw our conventional distinctions between different kinds of situations—between acting *voluntarily* and acting *reluctantly*, between *control* and *non-control*, between *freedom* and *constraint*. But determinism largely undermines their point, he says. It prunes off too much that was important. True freedom cannot be vindicated by holding onto distinctions whose rationale would be subverted by the discovery of the truth of determinism. (But of course, he will add, that is not what we have discovered. If anything, the reverse. See §7.)

(iii) Though the sentence schemata *he could have done otherwise* and *he could have done A instead of B* may import varying truth conditions, it is the libertarian's hope to explain all these variations by differences of complementation with respect to (a) the time or period for which the ability subsists, (b) the particular replacements of 'A' and 'B', and (c) the time specification for the doing A or B. *Can* itself is, in the libertarian's tentative opinion, a unitary semantical element.[7] But those who have distinguished, *e.g.*, a

---

[7] That is to say that the diversity of possible complementations is the *prima facie* best explanation of phenomena that writers have attributed to an ambiguity in the word *can* itself. If the schema 'he can X' has to be unpacked ('he (when?) can [(what?) (when?)]'); and if 'he can X if. . . .' (contrast Austin's discussion of this *if*, to which he gives a very peculiar treatment) has to be unpacked both in these ways and with respect to scope ('(he (when?) can [(what?) (when?)] if (. . .))' and 'he (when?) can [(what?) (when?) if . . .]'); and if there is also the phenomenon of ellipse (which seems to play an important role in sentences about what can and cannot be done *without undue cost* or *harm* to persons or property, etc.) to help explain the apparent diversity of truth-conditions; then I hope the way is open for an attempt to obtain a unified lexical account of *can* (ignoring permissive and epistemic uses). Such an attempt might attain the standard for lexical univocity suggested (for instance) in my 'Sentence Sense, Word Sense, and Difference of Word Sense' in *Semantics: An Interdisciplinary Reader in Philosophy, Linguistics, and Psycholinguistics*, ed. Steinberg and Jakobivits (Cambridge University Press, 1971).

There has been a temptation, among those of the compatibilist persuasion, to suppose that the commonness in pleas of justification and excuse of the 'cannot' that is to be interpreted as meaning 'cannot without undue cost or harm' counts somehow against the libertarian thesis. But libertarians and incompatibilists will reply that in doing A at t, x was only free if there was an act B other than A that x humanly could at t do at t despite the cost or prospective cost of doing B.

'general' *can* from 'particular' *can* have performed an important service in forcing us to be clear about what exactly it is that it is claimed an agent could or could not have done. The replacements for 'A' and 'B' must determine this fully. (The provision of two slots (a) and (c), for the times of the ability and the performance respectively, may seem questionable. But consider the fact that I may now, in Baker Street at 9.55 a.m., be able to catch the train from Paddington to Oxford at 10.15 a.m. Eight minutes later, however, at 10.03 a.m., if I have not progressed from Baker Street, then, given the state of the Inner Circle line and Marylebone Road, I shall certainly be unable to catch the train. What we have in this example is not a special case but a specially clear case. Both slots are always there—we cannot create them specially for cases like the train case—but when they both take the same temporal specification, as they must in 'he could have done otherwise' in at least some important occurrences, then the ellipse of one of them is surely natural and intelligible enough.)

So much for the sentence *he could have done otherwise* as it figures in the dispute, and as the libertarian construes its occurrence in the ordinary interchange of accusation, exoneration, exculpation, and the rest.[8] The other urgent need is for a clarification of the determinism that the libertarian takes to be incompatible with his understanding of the sentence.

3. WHAT DETERMINISM SIGNIFIES

J. L. Austin once maintained that determinism was 'the name of nothing clear'.[9] But as a second-level non-scientific theory that the world admits of explanation by a certain kind of ground level scientific theory, the thesis can be made as plain as terms like 'cause' and 'explain' can. Whatever his other difficulties, the incompatibilist need not find it impossible to indicate what it is that he is afraid of, or the libertarian what it is that he rejects.

---

[8] And not only there, but even within the expression of the moral sentiments that it is P. F. Strawson's conspicuous contribution to have insisted on bringing into the area of the controversy about free will. (See his 'Freedom and Resentment', *Proceedings of the British Academy*, vol. 48 (1962), pp. 1–25 [reprinted as Essay 4, this volume].) Consider Jonathan Bennett's claim:

If a benefactor was manifesting an insane compulsion to give things away, the beneficiary may welcome the gift but should not be grateful for it. In such cases the agent is not praiseworthy. ('Accountability' p. 15, in *Philosophical Subjects: Essays Presented to P. F. Strawson*, edited by Zak van Straaten (Oxford University Press, 1980).)

Consider why the claim might be accepted. We might ask: What was his intention towards me? Answer: that I have the object. Why then did he want me to have it? Answer: because he felt warmly towards me—as no doubt he felt towards others at that time. What then would be the matter with my feeling grateful for his making me a present of the thing? Sole possible answer(?): He couldn't help having that intention and those feelings.

[9] 'Ifs and Cans', *Collected Papers* (Oxford, 1961), p. 179.

Let us say that a scientific theory for a subject-matter s is deterministic if and only if (1) the theory possesses a store of predicates and relation-words for the characterisation of s-items (events, situations, etc.) and (2) the theory affirms lawlike general statements such that for every s-item s_j it can find a true description D_j, and find an s-item s_i with true description D_i such that s_i occurred some t seconds earlier than s_j, and some lawlike generalization in the form *if a D_i event occurs, then a D_j event occurs t seconds later* follows from the theory.

A deterministic theory is adequate if the law-like statements it affirms are true and will combine with the theory's descriptive categories $D_1, D_2, \ldots D_n$ to form explanations that are correct wherever $D_1, D_2, \ldots D_n$ apply.

As a first attempt, one might then say that determinism is the theory that *for every event (situation, state of the world or whatever) there is a true description and an adequate deterministic theory T that explains the event under that description.*

I suppose the reason for thinking that this might hold is science's spectacular success in extending again and again the number and variety of events for which it can find theories with the title to be in my sense adequate and deterministic. Someone may comment that it is hardly surprising that we have discovered the regularities which were there to be discovered; that our success shows nothing about the residue; nor does the possibility of such success really guarantee the operational or empirical intelligibility of the thesis of determinism. Perhaps it is not intelligible, it may be said, and J. L. Austin's doubts are borne out. Those, however, who want to persist in subscribing to determinism (in spite of, *e.g.* quantum phenomena) might reply to the objection with this question: 'How big *is* the residue? Can there really be, what the objection purports to achieve, an *a priori* estimation of it?'

At this point we stumble upon the widespread idea, very likely shared by Austinians, that every situation must be infinitely describable. All we can do in a causal investigation is to pick out and test causal *strands* from a total physical background that is provisionally regarded as the 'normal' background;[10] there is no logical question of this procedure (the only operational procedure, the objector says) either terminating or issuing in finished lawlike generalizations that are closed and not subject to a never ending process of qualification.

Let us first work out the determinist's answer to the difficulty about generalizations and then return to infinite describability. Adequacy in our first formulation required the strict and universal truth of the laws employed in

---

[10] I use here an idea of H. L. A. Hart and A. M. Honoré in *Causation in the Law* (Oxford, 1959), but there is no intention at all to ascribe to these authors any view at all about the import, sense, status or significance of the thesis of determinism.

deterministic explanation. If one says all Fs are Gs then one means *all* Fs; and if some restriction is needed of the conditions under which all D_i events at t_i are followed by D_j events at t_j, then the restriction must, for purposes of this determinism, be made explicit. A body falling near the surface of the earth for t seconds will cover a distance of $16t^2$ feet, for example, provided that it is in a vacuum and provided it is falling freely. The hypothesis of determinism that we are considering precisely entails that in due course such qualifications can be everywhere spelled out and completed.

It is true, of course, that Austinians are making an important point about the discovery of physical laws, and about the way in which everyday conceptions of causality lead into scientific ones. In deference to it, and in deference to Hart and Honoré's analysis, the determinist could meet the point in another way, by saying that an explanation holds universally if *either* (1) there are no apparent exceptions to the predictions made by the use of the law or laws L which cover it; *or* (2) every such apparent exception can be explained in terms of an interference (a) describable by the vocabulary of the body of theory to which L belongs, and (b) for which there is *in its own turn* an explanation in terms of an adequate theory, this theory itself being compatible with L. Whatever one thinks of this strategy, it enables one to suppose that every causal generalization starts life with a *ceteris paribus* clause, understood in line with (2) and in such a way that the escape clause does not trivialize L. Then in the revised set of definitions, deterministic in terms of *adequate, adequate* in terms of *universal*, and then *universal* in terms of *adequate* again, there would of course be a circle. It may perhaps be seen as matching a similar circle in the beginnings of a science. It is not necessarily a vicious circle, however, because by conjoining a larger and larger set of good and consistent theories it will become possible, *if determinism is true*, to diminish the apparent exceptions to nil. The determinist can then use the 'no exceptions' condition of clause (1) as a criterion of 'universality' and 'adequacy'.

If either of these replies is to carry the determinist the whole way against the objection, which has the virtue of bringing out just how exigent a thesis determinism is, then the next thing he must do is to combat directly the idea that every situation is without redundancy infinitely describable. This will be best achieved however by our first attending on his behalf to an important shortcoming in the first formulation of determinism. That formulation only undertook to find a theory to explain every item under *some description or other*. The flaw was this. What if the chosen descriptions were thin or uninformative (even as uninteresting as *something which happened at t*)? Such a determinism might leave almost every significant feature of reality perfectly free of determination by physical law.

It is no good for the determinist to try to stiffen the doctrine by requiring that for *every* description of every event there be an adequate deterministic theory T which explains the event under that description. How could *every* conceivable description, however arrived at, of anything, find its way into a law of nature or pull its weight in a serious theory?[11]

Both to amend the determinist thesis and to meet objections inspired by the question of indefinite describability, what the determinist needs, I think, is the notion of a *saturated* description. A description D of item x is saturated, let us say, if and only if (a) D is true of x, (b) there is no property P of x which can vary without variation in the property D stands for, and (c) D incorporates every projectible property of x.

(On pain of our new formulations collapsing into the amendment of determinism just dismissed, I emphasise that this idea has absolutely nothing to do with the *reduction* of all properties to saturated properties. If a picture is beautiful and serene and sad it cannot be modified in these respects without a modification in the chemical, structural, or physical properties which would enter into its saturated description. It does not of course follow from this tie between the aesthetic and scientific properties that we can find any complex description couched in the terms of physics or chemistry and satisfied by all and only pictures beautiful and serene and sad—or even by pictures which are these things to the very degree that x is.)

We can now state a sufficient but not necessary description of the holding of determinism. *For every event (situation . . .) there is a saturated description and a corresponding adequate and deterministic theory that explains that event under that description.* Saturated descriptions, if they exist, encode everything that is of any causal or scientific significance. Further refinements of this formulation might classify theories by the degree of computability of the functions they employ, by the degrees of solvability of the equations they invoke, or by other refinements into which there is no need to enter. The general character of the doctrine and the colour of its claims to be a factual doctrine[12] should now be apparent, as should the direction in which one

---

[11] Here, and in the ensuing paragraph, I am indebted to ideas of Davidson. See 'Mental Events', in Foster and Swanson (eds.), *Experience and Theory* (MIT Press, 1970).

[12] On this point see the problem stated by B. A. W. Russell, 'On the Notion of Cause' in *Mysticism and Logic* (London, 1921) and C. G. Hempel in Sidney Hook (ed.), *Determinism and Freedom* (New York, 1958).

An objection parallel to the plea of infinite describability has found some circulation (see J. Passmore, *Philosophical Review*, Vol. 68 (1959), pp. 93–102, and B. A. O. William's tentative exposition in D. F. Pears (ed.), *Freedom and the Will* (London, 1963)): that determinism is obliged to treat the universe as a sort of closed system or box, and to take seriously the idea of a total-state description of the world. It is certainly true that the classical Laplacean approach would characteristically have proceeded from outside to inside, from a total world state and total prediction to the prediction of constituent particular phenomena. (See La Place, Introduction to *Théorie Analytique des*

would have to look for its verification or falsification—*viz.*, the progress of the sciences of matter. The libertarian thinks modern science shows determinism is false. The incompatibilist hopes that it does. The compatibilist or dissolutionist usually assumes that it is true or as good as true.

Determinism is not always formulated as a thesis about the sciences of matter. So it may be helpful, and it will disarm objections to certain claims to be entered in §4 and §7, to pause here to express an attitude towards the psychological, sociological, or economic determinisms that attract some thinkers and still have a powerful effect on the institutions, practice and methodology of the social sciences.

It is not unusual to find social scientists who believe that some day, somehow, their sciences will grow up and produce results comparable in their way with the splendid things which in its maturity physics has achieved. In its adolescence, we are to suppose, social science practises and rehearses the methods of dispassionate enquiry and conscientious and accurate measurement that are the *sine qua non* of the spirit of science; but when the time comes, society will receive the instruments of stability and the dividend for which it has so presciently invested—namely applications of sociology, economics, psychology which will bear the same certain relation to the disciplines they apply as the products of modern technology do to chemistry, physics and the rest.

Unless the real message here is that in due course we shall see some of the predictions of social scientists positively brought about by the trend-planning that is 'based' upon them, or that certain sorts of social science can already be employed, without the benefit of any notable insight or understanding but to sinister effect, to protect our managers against the dangers of our facing the more open future that it might be more desirable for us to face, there is no very awesome reason to believe it. The only general argument I know for the likelihood of what social scientists hope (and libertarians disbelieve and incompatibilists fear) goes something like this: The physical sciences give good reason to believe that, at least on the macroscopic level, the world is a deterministic system. But every event that is economically described or sociologically described is also a physical event, so how could sociological events or economic events fail to make up a deterministic system themselves? They are physical events. So there must be

---

Probabilités, Oeuvres Complètes VII, Paris, 1847.) But if the world satisfies the thesis of determinism as I have expounded it by means of the notions of saturated description, adequacy, and universality—*if* this logical possibility is exemplified—then it is as unnecessary to describe the whole world in order to explain a particular event as it is unnecessary to reckon with indefinite describability. The only difficulty is one of establishing, however tentatively, that determinism is true. But in testing this we proceed from inside to out, from smaller to larger tracts of the universe.

universal laws and functional correlations out there awaiting the researcher who can make accurate enough measurements and can master (or hire enough computational brute force somehow to overwhelm) the multitude of variables required to hit upon and solve the relevant equations.

This argument, which rests on a greater confidence than many people can muster in physical determinism itself, comprises an instructive and fundamental mistake. Economic events, say, or commercial events, could be part of a larger deterministic system without themselves (or as such) comprising a self-contained deterministic system. And it would not follow from the fact that any system they helped to make up was deterministic that the laws in virtue of which it was deterministic would be *laws of economics* or *laws of sociology*.[13]

What determinism of the sort earlier envisaged says (where e_i, e_j, ... range over events, S represents all properties including sociological, economic, *etc.*, ones and P is the property of being physical, *i.e.* satisfying a description of a science of matter) is this:

$(e_i)S(e_i) \rightarrow (\exists e_j)(P(e_j) \& (e_i{=}e_j))$
For every economically or sociologically described event, there is a physical event identical with it.

Now when K ranges over natural or scientifically significant kinds,[14] K_S ranges over economically or socially categorized kinds, and K_P ranges over kinds of physical events, this no doubt entails

$(e_i)((e_i{\in}\ K_S) \rightarrow (\exists e_j)(\exists K_P)\ [(e_j \in K_P)\ \&\ (e_i{=}e_j)])$
For every event of a sociological or economic kind there is an event of a natural kind recognized by a science of matter which is identical with it.

But it does not entail the statement the argument crucially needs:

$(K_S)(\exists K_P)(e_i)[(e_i \in K_S) \rightarrow (\exists e_j)(e_j{=}e_i\ \&\ e_j{\in}\ K_P)]$
For every sociologically or economically characterized kind of event there is a natural kind of event recognized by a science of matter such that every event of the former kind belongs also to the latter kind.

---

[13] Cf. the situation in genetics. My parents' genotypes limit my genotype and hence my phenotype, but their phenotypes do not have anything like the same control over my phenotype. This is not the only kind of comparison possible, nor of course is it well calculated to gladden those who long for a stronger more independent status for social science or who ignore the other aspirations that linguistics or philosophy of language can suggest to social science. But the comparison might explain why it is that William Dray's 'How possibly?' pattern fits the explanations to be encountered in the actual practice of sociology, economics, anthropology, history, *etc.*, better than the covering law pattern fits them.

[14] See, e.g., W. V. Quine, 'Natural Kinds', in *Ontological Relativity and Other Essays* (New York, 1970).

4. THE LOGICAL CHARACTER OF THE
INCOMPATIBILITY OF DETERMINISM AND THE
ABILITY TO DO OTHERWISE

So much for serious determinism. It is a shaky hypothesis, and in its strict
and literal form wide open to disbelief. (See below §6.) It is not a thesis to be
disarmed by *a priori* arguments against its truth or significance. It is manifestly far stronger than the weak, almost undisputable thesis that every event
has some cause.[15] Unsurprisingly, therefore, the *denial* of the thesis does not
commit one to find any uncaused events, or to see agents, with Chisholm, as
'prime movers unmoved', or to anything else that is strange.

If determinism is true, and if every action of every agent in its particular
circumstances really is fixed in respect of its occurrence, in respect of its
mode of occurrence, and in respect of the characteristics upon which its
character as an action supervenes, and fixed in this way by some antecedent
physical condition; then obviously actions cannot be torn free from the
nexus of physical effects and fully determining causes.[16] It is this that creates
the incompatibility that the libertarian alleges between physical determinism
and statements of the form 'he could at *t'* have done otherwise at *t''*. But this
incompatibility needs to be stated carefully.

Richard Taylor writes on page 54 of *Action and Purpose*, 'If however,
existing conditions are causally sufficient for my moving my finger, then it
follows that it is causally impossible for me not to move [it] . . . Since, however, it is true that . . . I can hold it still, it follows that [this] is not causally
impossible.' What is the underlying argument of the first sentence of this
passage? For a moment one might suppose that the argument is this. (I) It is
a law of nature or a consequence of a law of nature that under conditions C
Taylor moves his finger. If this is a law of nature, it is true for all time. *A
fortiori* it is true for this time *t'* when Taylor does move his finger. Hence it is

---

[15] Maybe all events have causes but there is nothing in a cause or its circumstances to fix
everything about the character of its effect. On this and the problem of event reference and
individuation of events see Milton Fisk, 'A Defence of the Principle of Event Causality', *British
Journal of Philosophy of Science* (1967) and Donald Davidson, 'Causal Relations', *Journal of
Philosophy*, vol. 64 (1967).

[16] If that is the character of the causal nexus we live within, then it makes no particular
difference to this point whether or not actions are *identical* with movements of matter. Even if this
were the wrong thing to say, actions still could not be constitutively independent of the arrangement of matter or of physical events. On the constriction of freedom which would result from the
determinism of physics, whatever one thought of the identity view, see G. J. Warnock, *ab init.*, in
Freedom of the Will, ed. Pears (London, 1963). It should be added that even if we adopted the
mysterious view that mental events do not occur in the physical world, still, if physical determinism were true, bodily movements would fall within its ambit and the autonomy of the mental
would be limited to mental events with no proximate physical cause and no practical (acted)
outcome. Autonomy would be something utterly inert.

causally impossible at t' that C should obtain and Taylor not move his finger at t'. But (II) from t onwards C did obtain. Therefore (III) it was causally impossible at t' that Taylor should not move his finger at t'. Therefore (IV) Taylor could not at t' keep his finger still at t'—it was inevitable at t' that he move it. But we know (V) that he could at t' have kept his finger still at t'. Therefore (VI) some premiss must be false. So if we concede (II), the deterministic claim (I) is false.

This can scarcely be the argument Taylor had in mind, however. For its pattern at (I) (II) (III) reminds one of that patently invalid argument:

(I) $\Box$ (p is known $\supset$ p is true)
(II) I know q
(III) $\Box$ (q)

Nevertheless, I feel convinced, with Taylor,[17] that there is some valid inference from (I) to (III). The problem is to discover another form for it and to formulate its additional premisses. If this much can be accomplished, then, it will become worthwhile to try to characterise and define the notion of historical inevitability that makes the argument work. First then let us look for a better candidate form for the inference.

Suppose that a law of nature assures us that in the conditions obtaining at a particular juncture t'

(1) Inevitable at t' (if C at t then the agent does R at t'),

and suppose that we know that if the consequent is true this causally or logically excludes some particular agent's doing A, so that

(2) Inevitable at t' (if the agent does R at t' then the agent does not do A at t').

Then, if 'Inevitable at t' (if . . . then—)' is transitive, it follows that

(3) Inevitable at t' (if C at t then the agent does not do A at t').

Suppose for instance that 'R' is replaced by 'extend a finger' and 'A' is replaced by 'keep still'. And suppose the man failed to keep still. The question will be: Could he have kept still, even though, from the earlier moment t, C obtained? Proposition (1) is the particular contribution of determinism to the argument. What that thesis implies is that there exists this sort of

---

[17] And among many other Hobbes. His suggestive but equally incomplete formulation in the *De Corpore* runs as follows: 'Every act which is not impossible is possible. Every act therefore which is possible shall at some time be produced; for if it shall never be produced then those things shall never concur which are requisite for the production of it; wherefore that act is impossible by the definition; which is contrary to what was supposed.'

empirical truth. If the argument depends on (1) and (2), it will not be a fatalistic, but a deterministic argument.

The extra premiss which I believe the argument needs is the uncontroversial modal principle:

(4) $\Box p \supset (\Box(p \supset q) \supset \Box q)$.

Supposing that 'Inevitable at t'' is a modality (see below) and abbreviating this as '$\Box_{t'}$', we have as an instance of this:

(4') $\Box_{t'}$ (C at t) $\supset$ ($\Box_{t'}$ (C at $t \supset$ the agent does not do A at t') $\supset \Box_{t'}$ (the agent does not do A at t')).

Now suppose that the condition C did obtain at t. Surely then, by the time t' which is later than t, there was nothing to be done about the obtaining of this condition. So we have,

(5) $\Box_{t'}$ (C at t).

But, given (3), we have

(6) $\Box_{t'}$ (C at $t \supset$ the agent does not do A at t').

So by (4),

(7) $\Box_{t'}$ (the agent does not do A at t').

But if (7) is true, then (8) is false:

(8) He could at t' have kept still at t'.

We recognize this incompatibility when we allow the question of what was physically-cum-historically possible to organize our evaluation of excuses and pleas of non-responsibility. Therefore, given (3), and given that the condition C did obtain at t, we have

(9) He could not have kept still at t',

and this is the consequence, not of pure logic and the uncontroversial modal principle by themselves, but of empirical determinism and the nature of time.[18] At any given time a man has no real alternative but to do what he

[18] Some may doubt the incompatibility I claim between (7) and (8). It may disarm some of the misgivings that have been expressed if I point out that there is no question here of *analysing* the 'can' of agent ability in terms of historical-cum-physical possibility, or of any grammatical assimilation. All I claim is the incompatibility. Pending the production of another convincing principle to explain away what looks like a reliance on the incompatibility of (7) and (8) in our actual evaluation of excuses, I think that the denial of this incompatibility will continue to astonish those not already immersed in the philosophical controversy.

In his interesting article 'Alternate Possibilities and Moral Responsibility', *Journal of Philosophy*, vol. 20 (1969) [reprinted as Essay 8, this volume], Harry G. Frankfurt has suggested that

does at that time: in which case there is no way for him to exploit the fact that he could, if he were to do A now, do B in the future, and could, if he were to do not-A now, do D in the future. For it is already fixed which of A and not-A he will do. And the same argument will hamper the attempt to find his freedom at some earlier time.

Nobody will feel happy about this demonstration until more is said about the idea of historical inevitability at a time. But first, we must attend to the premisses (1)–(3). They rest, amongst other things, on the lawlike generalisation that entails (1) and the analytic truth or lawlike generalisation (as the case may be) that entails (2). But laws of nature themselves will usually be much more general than (1) or (2) and will rarely or never bear much resemblance to (3). Being very specific, (3) will depend heavily upon the particular situation at t'. It does what no proper law by itself would normally do. It links very different kinds of description. That it is possible to conjoin laws of nature, which could not by themselves perform this task, with facts about particular situations and *thereby* obtain particular statements like (3) is what makes it so difficult to find human freedom in the undoubted fact that there are most likely *no* exceptionless empirical principles at all about the causal antecedents (or consequences) of actions classed by action-kinds. But to make a bridge from propositions like (1) to propositions like (3), we simply do not need any exceptionless principle about the connexion between the condition recorded in 'C' and the sort of movement recorded in 'R at t''.

By 'it is historically inevitable at time t' that p' is intended something like this: whatever anybody or anything can do at t' or after t', it will make no difference to whether p, p being either a law of logic or a law of nature or at t' already history, or being the logical or physical consequence of what is

---

(i) He couldn't have done otherwise

is not a necessary condition or a sufficient condition of non-responsibility. What suffices for non-responsibility and will support our practice in the evaluation of excuses is

(ii) He did what he did *only* because (i).

What does (ii) mean? If it means that the only good explanation of the occurrence of his action is something like (i), then (ii) is rarely or never true. Its holding is much rarer than non-responsibility. On the other hand, if we omit the 'only' from (ii) and pretend that determinism is true, then we have something which will almost always be true (in so far as 'he couldn't do otherwise' is ever a straightforward causal explanation, which is dubious). So it will follow that there is little or no responsibility.

Suppose that (ii) concerned not causal explanation in general but explanations that go via the agent's own reasons—so that (ii) came down to 'his only reason for φ-ing was that he thought there was no alternative'. Then in this interpretation (ii) is not sufficient for non-responsibility. (Perhaps he *ought* to have realized that there was this other thing that he could do.) In the second place, (ii) then looks off the point in many cases. Many non-responsible acts are non-responsible for reasons quite other than the agent's having thought that he couldn't do otherwise.

already history. This definition includes the notion of possibility, but this is no objection. The purpose is only to fix from within the circle of modal notions a sense of necessity which satisfies principle (4′) and yields a strict implication which is transitive (for the passage from (1) and (2) to (3)). It is not necessary to break into the circle of modal notions from outside.

Briefly, one might say it is historically necessary at t that p just if it will hold that p whatever can happen at t or later (consistently with laws of nature).[19] Or in the sort of language that many people have come to prefer, and that David Lewis uses in his book *Counterfactuals* to characterise modal and counterfactual principles, one might stipulate that $\ulcorner \Box, p \urcorner$ is true if and only if it holds that p in every world whose history is indistinguishable from the history of the actual world up to (but not necessarily including) t. Here we should have to understand its natural laws as comprising a part of the history of a world.[20]

It remains to verify whether (4) and (4′) hold when the modality has its sense fixed in this way. Suppose then that it is historically necessary by time $t′$ that p. Then it holds that p in every world indistinguishable from the actual world with respect to times earlier than $t′$. Now suppose also that in every world indistinguishable from the actual world with respect to times earlier than $t′$ it holds that if p holds then q holds. But then in every world indistinguishable from the actual world with respect to times earlier than t it holds that q. So under the conditions that it is historically inevitable at $t′$ that p and that if p then q, it is historically inevitable at $t′$ that q.

---

[19] We are not defining a purely technical notion here. If we were it would be all too easy for someone to go back to premiss (6) and question that. We are characterising an existing everyday notion whose dual, historical possibility figures in such contexts as this one. 'It's too late. *H.M.S. Hermes* can't now intercept the *Bismarck* before *Bismarck* rounds the cape. It's no longer possible for her to get there in time.' And this, I have claimed, is the notion that figures not only in pleas of exoneration and exculpation, but also within the underlying dialectic of the moral sentiments. See note 8 above.

[20] It should be noted that none of these definitions makes 'Theaetetus sits at t' historically necessary at t just because Theaetetus sits at t. The sentence isn't true *whatever* Theaetetus does at t. And, unless determinism happens to be true, there is a possible world historically indistinguishable from ours up to t in which Theaetetus stands and does not sit at t. The proof of (9) does not therefore depend on the fatalistic type of puzzle revived at *Analysis*, vol. 25 (no. 4, 1965), or on a special view of truth, but on the absurdity of its being *now* possible for something *in the past* to have been different. I should not deny that the definition might be slightly improved by amending it to read 'indistinguishable from the history of the actual world *appreciably* before $t′$'. This abandons the precision of the Dedekind section in favour of a serviceable and perhaps indispensable vagueness. Two equally intelligible worlds can scarcely resemble one another up to t and differ in that in one Theaetetus sits promptly at t, and in the other he promptly stands at t. One or other world would involve a discontinuity.

It is important too that t is not a variable ranging only over instants, and that many truths of the form (6) involve imperfective (continuous) verbs. It is only in virtue of an abstraction that such verbs can be qualified by the use of the language of moments or instants. The variable t ranges over times in the ordinary sense.

This verifies (4) and with it (4') for the temporally indexed interpretation of □.

The reaction of some to this whole exercise will be to say that it fortifies a dislike they had always had for natural necessity—even before it was relativised to a time. I reply that such scepticism must in consistency apply equally aptly to physical possibility, relativised or unrelativised, wherever it outruns actuality. And here we notice a curious thing. This scepticism, by reducing possibility to actuality, seems to undermine 'can do otherwise' *directly*— unless it treats animate possibility, the *can* of human ability, with some special indulgence. But that would be a strange concession to make, especially in the presence of libertarians. Its effect would be to mark off animate agents from the rest of nature in just the sort of way in which many libertarians have wished to distinguish them.

5. VIEWS OPEN TO THE LIBERTARIAN OF THE SELF AND ITS ABILITIES

It may be said that the whole preceding demonstration turns on a confusion between what lies in the agent and what lies outside him.[21] It is perfectly absurd, it will be said, to lump together under the conditions C items as diverse as the character of the agent, the present state of mind of the agent, the external causes of that state of mind, and the concrete particularities of the conditions under which he acts. It makes as little sense as saying that one of the circumstances under which an agent did some specific thing was the circumstance that he was a man of a mean and murderous disposition. Nothing but confusion can come from such a way of speaking, it will be said; and the only possible philosophical outcome of speaking like this is a far-fetched theory of the metaphysical, totally non-empirical and character-less self whose difficulties match exactly the incoherences of the Lockean doctrine of substance—the thing with the property of having no properties, the substrate that explains the possibility of change by being both unchanged and identical with that which persists through change. Either the libertarian requires (cf. §2) that *nothing in the world outside the free agent himself* should determine for that agent how he will change or deliberate to change the world, or the libertarian simply requires that *nothing in the world* determine for the agent how he will change or deliberate to change the world. It will then be said that, if the requirement is stated in the former way,

---

[21] Cf. Aristotle's distinction between what is and is not *en to prattonti* in Book 3 of *Nicomachean Ethics*.

we can and must distinguish what lies within the agent from what lies without. If the requirement is stated in the latter way, however, then even the agent himself is excluded from determining anything—even *for himself*—unless the self is outside the world altogether. This is an unintelligible conception. Finally it may be said that the libertarian's expression 'determining for the agent' is pure rhetoric—the *agent* deliberates and thus determines for himself what change he will import.

I hope this states the objection as dissolutionists or compatibilists want to see it stated. But without the discovery of a specific mistake in the argument above, the absurdities of the metaphysical self cannot themselves suffice to disprove the inference from determinism to *nobody can do otherwise than they do*. How exactly the metaphysical self could be supposed to compensate for physical determinism is not at all clear. But, if determinism did really imply that if we were responsible, then the doctrine of the metaphysical self would be true, and if the doctrine of the metaphysical self is absurd (as I for one am sure that it is), then either we are not responsible or the doctrine of determinism is not true. But then if determinism is true, the conclusion follows that, in the full sense in which we commonly take ourselves to be responsible—*i.e.*, in the sense of 'responsible' fixed by the question whether a man can do otherwise—we are not responsible. But that after all is exactly what the libertarian said. The conditional 'if determinism is true then we are not responsible' is not *all* that he says. *If* he were also convinced of the antecedent (the truth of determinism), the libertarian would climb down to the weaker position (which is incompatibilism) and go on to say a great deal more. But first things first. His first point is that, if our actual notion of responsibility, unreformed, fails of application, then it can only darken counsel to pretend that our notion is another notion—some notion touted by utilitarians and dissolutionists, for instance—or to pretend that we never really had our notion. All sorts of things in our social, judicial, and penal institutions, and all sorts of things in our relations with human beings, depend, he says, upon the supposition that one *can* do other than one will do. Substitution of another notion of responsibility may be called for, but substitution is not the same as the philosophical elucidation of what we have. The practical and metaphysical imports of substitution and analysis are totally different. If a dilemma exists here, it should first be acknowledged and felt as such. Only barbarism and reaction can benefit by concealment, or so he will contend.

There is another way for his compatibilist opponent to move, however. If the conclusion of §4 is simply incredible—incredible regardless of the facts about scientific determinism—then perhaps this shows that *he could have done otherwise* never means what, in stating the doctrine of libertarianism in §§2–3, we took such trouble to make it mean where it occurs in §4. The step from (5) to (7) and the principle (6) are particularly relevant here. In the search for a compatibilist meaning for *can do otherwise*, some philosophers have tried to gain favour for some equivalence between *x can at t' (B at t')* and *if (. . . at t) then x does B at t'*; where . . . picks out some conditions distinguished from the rest of the circumstances of action by pertaining specially to what is *in* the agent. How should one react to this?

Perhaps the most promising-looking hypothetical analysis may be approached by way of a consideration of the non-animate dispositions. Carnap showed long ago the difficulties of trying to define such dispositions as brittleness or solubility in terms of conditionals like *if x is dropped then x breaks* or *if x is put into water x dissolves*. Instead of these conditionals he proposed 'reduction-sentences', which have the advantage of not verifying brittleness by the falsity of the antecedent. A typical reduction sentence would be *if x is dropped, then if x is brittle x breaks*. But even if a finite number of them could really fix the sense of 'brittle'—which is unclear and dubious—reduction-sentences are open to another difficulty. Brittle things may for various and divers reasons significantly frequently fail to break when dropped: and many things break when dropped even though they are not brittle. No satisfactory correction is obtained by converting the mood of the first or second sort of conditional into the subjunctive. But there is another remedy that suggests itself and has obvious relevance to the problem of animate abilities. Take 'is disposed' or 'tends' as *pro tempore* primitive, and analyse *x is fragile (during period t)* on something like these lines: *x is so disposed (during t) that (if x is hit or dropped then x breaks)*, where the hypothetical is now embedded within the characterisation of a categorically described disposition. The corresponding analysis of *x can at t A at t* might perhaps be *x is so disposed at t (that (if . . . then x does A at t))*, where . . . indicates some condition about something 'in' the agent. It could be the condition that he tries, or that he wants or whatever. In a further refinement one could transpose the conditional to the subjunctive mood.

No doubt this account represents some kind of advance on previous attempts. The specification of the categorical state of ability requires an *if*, but not in the manner of the more usual hypothetical analyses. What is noteworthy, however, is that the improvement in the analysis does nothing at all to block the question of the possibility of . . ., which is the condition mentioned in the antecedent. The analysis seems powerless to trump the circumstantial demonstration of the physical impossibility, taking everything into account, of . . . coming to pass. Till this problem is faced no subtleties about *in the agent* or the agent's *will* or his *will to will* can gain any purchase.

6. HUME'S FORK AND THE LIBERTARIAN VIEW OF THE SELF

Perhaps it is pointless to debate whether the sentence 'he could at *t'* have done otherwise at *t''* does have the sense I have ascribed to it in the incompatibilist demonstration of §4 above, pointless, that is, until it has been shown that an argument invoking that sense could ever, even if it were successful, do for the libertarian what he wanted. This problem is often taken to be equivalent to the following question: can the libertarian even specify a possible world in which there are things that people can (in the libertarian's sense) do, but do not do? Hume has been followed by a large number of philosophers in holding that not even a possible world of the right sort can be specified. If it were false that every event and every doing was causally determined, it is said, then causally underdetermined events and doings would surely, to that extent, be simply random. That someone could have φ-d would then mean no more than that it might at random have turned out that way. It is then asked whether it makes any better sense to hold someone responsible for actions that happen at random than for ones that arise from his character. Surely, the argument ends, if it doesn't, we ought to prefer that our actions be caused. Real freedom *requires* causal determinism.

This objection is question-begging. One cannot prove that determinism is a precondition of free will by an argument with a premiss tantamount to 'everything is either causally determined or random'. This is simply too close to the conclusion, that whatever is undetermined is random. That is what had to be shown. But in the form of a challenge, it may appear that at least something in the objection can stand. If an event is underdetermined, if nothing excluded an event of different specifications from taking the event's place, then what does it mean to deny that the event is random? What is it to be justified in ascribing the action identical with the event (or comprised by the event) to an agent whom one holds *responsible* for that action? In the unclaimed ground between the deterministically caused and the random, what is there in fact to be found?

In response to this challenge, some philosophers have ventured the idea that, within the field of physically underdetermined events, the thing that would make the difference between the random and the non-random is the presence or absence of a prior mental event such as a *volition*. It was in this tradition (which goes back at least as far as the *clinamen* or swerve of Epicurus and Lucretius) that Russell and Eddington tried to deploy the phenomena of quantum-indeterminacy as having a bearing upon the free-will issue.[22]

If—as seems likely—there is an uninterrupted chain of purely physical causation throughout the process from sense-organ to muscle, it follows that human actions are determined in the degree to which physics is deterministic. Now physics is only deterministic as regards macroscopic occurrences, and even in regard to them it asserts only very high probability, not certainty. It might be that, without infringing the laws of physics, intelligence could make improbable things happen, as Maxwell's demon would have defeated the second law of thermo-dynamics by opening the trap-door to fast-moving particles and closing it to slow-moving ones.

On these grounds it must be admitted that there is a bare possibility—not more—that, although occurrences in the brain do not infringe the laws of physics, neverthe-less their outcome is not what it would be if no psychological factors were involved . . . So for those who are anxious to assert the power of mind over matter it is possible to find a loophole. It may be maintained that one characteristic of living matter is a condition of unstable equilibrium, and that this condition is most highly developed in the brains of human beings. A rock weighing many tons might be so delicately poised on the summit of a conical mountain that a child could, by a gentle push, send it thundering down into any of the valleys below; here a tiny difference in the initial impulse makes an enormous difference to the result. Perhaps in the brain the unstable equilibrium is so delicate that the difference between two possible occurrences in one atom suffices to produce macroscopic differences in the movements of muscles. And since, according to quantum physics, there are no physical laws to determine which of several possible transitions a given atom will undergo, we may imagine that, in a brain, the choice between possible transitions is determined by a psychological cause called 'volition'. All this is possible, but no more than possible.

Russell is not enthusiastic, and it may be that the idea is even less free of difficulty than he allows. (Could not the incidence of human acts of 'vol-ition' upon quantum phenomena upset the probability distributions postu-lated by the quantum theory?) It is perplexing that he would base actions on occurrent mental events that he does not relate to personality or character, or even to purpose. If Russell tried to find room for such components as these in the genesis of action, then would that import the mysterious idea of an as it were 'immaterial realisation' of the agent to be the source of the volitions? What is an immaterial realization? Finally, is it likely that Russell's suggestion can give any clear account of what justifies him in comparing the role of volition to that of the child who gives the stone a *gentle push* in one or other of several possible directions?

If anything is to be salvaged from Russell's and Eddington's thought that the probable falsity of physical determination is relevant to the question of

[22] B. A. W. Russell, *Human Knowledge: Its Scope and Limits*, Chapter V: 'The Physiology of Sensation and Volition', p. 54.

free will, it will be far better for libertarians and incompatibilists to make it clear that their conception does not need to be so Cartesian. If their project is to describe a world that is a clear candidate to be the natural world, this had better be a world in which agents are natural things among others, albeit natural things whose motions and capacities invite appraisal by subtle, exacting (and utterly familiar) standards of practical rationality. Why should there not be actions that are not even in principle uniquely or deterministically derivable from laws and antecedent conditions but can, all the same, be fitted into practically meaningful sequences? We need not trace free actions back to volitions construed as little pushes aimed from outside the physical world. What we must find instead are patterns that are coherent and intelligible in the low level terms of practical deliberation, even if they are not amenable to the kind of generalisation or necessity that is the stuff of rigorous theory. On this conception the agent is conceived as an essentially and straightforwardly enmattered or embodied thing. His possible peculiarity as a natural thing among things in nature is simply that his biography unfolds not only non-deterministically but also intelligibly; non-deterministically in that personality and character are never something complete and need not be the deterministic origin of action; intelligibly in that each new action or episode constitutes a comprehensible phase in the unfolding of character, a further specification of what the man has by now *become*.

For help with such ideas, we might look first in the direction of J.-P. Sartre, and we should do best to look not to the crazily optimistic positions of the early plays *Les Mouches* or *Huis Clos* or *L'Etre et le Néant*, but to what he tried later, and more soberly, to make of his position.[23] Here is Sartre's 1969 account of it.[24]

For the idea which I have never ceased to develop is that in the end one is always responsible for what is made of one. Even if one can do nothing else besides assume this responsibility. For I believe that a man can always make something out of what is made of him. This is the limit I would today accord to freedom: the small movement which makes of a totally conditioned social being someone who does not render back completely what his conditioning has given him. What makes of Genet a poet when he had been rigorously conditioned to be a thief.

Perhaps the book where I have best explained what I mean by freedom is in fact, *Saint Genet*. For Genet was made a thief, he said 'I am a thief', and this tiny change was the start of a process whereby he became a poet, and then eventually a being no longer even on the margin of society, someone who no longer knows where he is, who

---

[23] Later, he was prepared to be 'scandalised' by his previous assertion (of Resistance times) that 'whatever the circumstances and whatever the site, a man is always free to choose to be a traitor or not . . .'. 'When I read this', he goes on, 'I said to myself: it's incredible, I actually believed that!' See *New Left Review*, no. 58, reproduced in *New York Review of Books*, 26 March 1970, p. 22.

[24] In *New Left Review*, *op. cit.*

falls silent. It cannot be a happy freedom, in a case like this. Freedom is not a triumph. For Genet, it simply marked out certain routes which were not initially given.

This is not the place to take up everything that is strange or interesting in the passage. It is surely not innocent of confusion where it employs the words *rigorously conditioned*, which belong with a view of the world that Sartre really ought to have seen the life of Genet as refuting. But the capital point that is got across to us is that it may not matter if the world *approximates* to a world that satisfies the principles of neurophysiological determinism, provided that this fails in the last resort to characterise the world completely, and provided that there are actions which, for all that they are causally under-determined, are answerable to practical reason, or are at least *intelligible* in that dimension. Surely *these* are not random. They are the mark left on the world by conscious agents who have freedom.

7. HUME'S CHALLENGE RE-EXAMINED

The developing or accumulating biography of people and their characters goes some way towards convincing at least some philosophers that the libertarian has more than nothing to offer in reply to the Humean challenge.[25] But perhaps the libertarian view is still presenting itself as needlessly peculiar—as insufficiently liberated from fixations that are proprietary to compatibilism and 'soft determinism'. What I think merits even more careful scrutiny is the challenge itself and the understanding of the free-will dispute that insists that it is not enough to expose (as above in §6 *ad init.*) the grossly question-begging nature of the Humean argument from which the challenge seeks to inherit its force. When the dialectical position is clarified, however, I hope it will be apparent that the libertarian does not have to have his own special or peculiar way of describing the perfectly ordinary case where an agent is free to do A and free to do B, A is not the same as B, and the agent chooses to do B. The libertarian need not speak of uncaused acts or efforts of the will, for instance, or see agents as unmoved movers or say anything that ordinary people do not say. *Any* account of acting freely that generally commends itself by its other descriptive, philosophical, and phenomenological merits, and commends itself to everyone else (as the Sartrean account might if it were filled out a little in the direction of perfect ordinariness), can commend itself to him too. His real concern is not with providing his own account of acting freely, but with how things have to be if the ordinary belief is to be vindicated that a person can sometimes, in the sense of the phrase

[25] See for instance Gary Watson's friendly account in *op. cit.* note 2 above.

relevant to responsibility, do otherwise than he does do. His concern is to block derivations such as (9) of §4. Where (9) lapses, faith returns.

The libertarian's account of the dialectical position might, if he wished, be this. Once upon a time, people used the language of deciding, choosing, and acting, the language of practical rationality, the language of moral character, and the language of incrimination and exculpation, quite unself-consciously. At that time, as even now, being fully responsible at t for doing A at t clearly implied being able at t to do something other than A at t, or entailed that at some earlier time than t there was something different from what you actually did then that you could then have done then; and it was sufficient for exculpation either to show that this condition was not satisfied or to show that, even if there was something else you could then have done then, it was then out of the question to do that then. (Or perhaps you could not then have been expected to know then that there was this other thing.) In that distant age from which we inherit our present concepts of *decision, action, ability*, and the rest, these were the thoughts that sustained the grasping of the senses of the words that stood for these concepts.

But then two things happened. First physiological and psychological discoveries suggested new possibilities of exculpation. New doubts arose whether a more profound knowledge might produce some conclusive exculpation for such and such acts done by such and such kinds of agent under such and such conditions. Secondly, with the arrival of the scientific conception of the world, the idea made its appearance that the human conception of the world and the scientific conception might be superimposed upon one another. At many points there might be nothing at all that was marked out by the intersection of the two conceptions (hence not even any question of inconsistency between the two world views). But sometimes there might be. It might be that, looking at the way in which events were articulated by the human conception, one would find that every event that registered there as a human action was an event that also registered in the scientific conception,[26] and registered there as an event that the scientific conception could envisage itself coming to see as historically necessary (in the §4 sense). And it might be that every interesting attribute that the human conception made it possible to ascribe to the action in question supervened upon, or was fixed by, the properties that the scientific conception attributed to the corresponding physical event.

That was how things seemed for a very long time after the end of the unreflecting first phase. But things need not seem like that any longer, the

---

[26] For doubts on this score, see Jennifer Hornsby 'Which Physical Events are Mental Events?', *Proceedings of the Aristotelian Society* (1980).

libertarian may say. What has now happened is that, quite apart from all sorts of doubts about the whole idea of a superposition of the human and scientific conceptions, those who work within the scientific conception have perceived significant limitations upon what could ever be shown therein to be physically-cum-historically necessary. *The sorts of premiss employed in the abstract or general demonstration in §4 are simply not available.* But in that case the intractable general problem that the incompatibilist and libertarian used to say that there was about physical determinism simply goes away. What is left is only the less general (albeit practically much more real and troublesome) form of exculpatory possibility—the worry about responsibility that arises from special physiological and psychological discoveries.[27]

Not only that. It is good that the intractable general problem goes away, the libertarian will claim. It is good because resentment, anger and indignation, gratitude and admiration, guilt, remorse, and the urge to make amends, plus all the other attitudes that make constant reference to what was possible or could in the circumstances have been expected of oneself or of others, are not things painted onto the surface of a going system of moral ideas already fully operational. They are integral to its workings. Of course, it was wrong for the libertarian to declare dogmatically that a reformed notion of responsibility would have to have recourse to the crude causal efficacy of punishment. For it is common ground between compatibilists and incompatibilists that this is not the same thing as the efficacy of moral norms or ideals working through consciousness. But that does not prevent it from being a real question *how* a reformed notion of responsibility, once dissociated from the question 'can he do otherwise?' (taken in the sense attributed to it by the libertarian), could reconstruct a rationale for the remorse or resentment (or whatever) that human beings direct at actual human doings of this or that or the other kind. When the reformed notion tries to make sense of the looking backwards that seems essential to these attitudes as we know them, how can it do otherwise than mimic the unreformed—except on pain of subverting the moral consciousness that arises from the generalization of these attitudes?

8. FREEDOM AND RESENTMENT

In his well-known British Academy lecture on this theme, P. F. Strawson claimed that, whatever we knew in favour of the hypothesis of total

---

[27] Even though the two ways of raising doubt proceed by radically different routes, they issue in a common interest in 'he could have done otherwise' and 'he could have helped it'. Nothing prevents the *sense* of such phrases from being the same in each context.

determinism, it could never be rational for us to opt out from all resentment or anger or gratitude or admiration, or from the conceptual framework of responsibility in which these and like responses or attitudes have their meaning; no one who supposed that it would be rational had thought into what it would really signify for human life to attempt to abandon them.

I hope that it will have struck the reader how much the libertarian whose position I am engaged in reconstructing would find to agree with in this. Even if the libertarian thinks there is more to be said about rationality,[28] what he will chiefly insist on pointing out is how singularly effective Strawson's lecture was in articulating, in fresh and novel detail, the full range and variety of things the libertarian always said were put in jeopardy by the classical utilitarian and crude substitutive resolutions of the problem of freedom. Strawson offers no such substitution. That would be wholly alien to his approach. What Strawson maintains is that, from the nature of the case, our ordinary ways of talking about responsibility, agency, human ability, human character and all the rest are best left unreplaced and unreduced. They require no justification at all beyond their manifest viability, and their proven capacity to animate the practices of everyday life. But here again the libertarian would agree, once more saluting the contribution that Strawson has made to the proper understanding of everything that would have been at stake if reform or substitution had been proposed.

Where then is the disagreement? Well, at least here: throughout his article Strawson proceeds as if it were simply obvious—he never argues for this— that, *if* the use of the ordinary language of responsibility, agency, human

---

[28] The transition by which Strawson reaches his conclusion is worth quoting.

Inside the general structure or web of human attitudes and feelings of which I have been speaking, there is endless room for modification, redirection, criticism, and justification. But questions of justification are internal to the structure or relate to modifications internal to it. The existence of the general framework of attitudes itself is something we are given with the fact of human society. As a whole, it neither calls for, nor permits, an external 'rational' justification. Pessimist and optimist alike show themselves, in different ways, unable to accept this. The optimist . . . seeks to find an adequate basis for certain social practices in calculated consequences, and loses sight (perhaps wishes to lose sight) of the human attitudes of which these practices are, in part, the expression. The pessimist does not lose sight of these attitudes, but is unable to accept the fact that it is just these attitudes themselves which fill the gap in the optimist's account. Because of this, *he thinks the gap can be filled only if some general metaphysical proposition is repeatedly verified, verified in all cases where it is appropriate to attribute moral responsibility.* This proposition *he finds it as difficult to state coherently and with intelligible relevance as its determinist contradictory. Even when a formula has been found ('contra-causal freedom' or something of the kind) there still seems to remain a gap between its applicability in particular cases and its supposed moral consequences (op. cit.* my italics).

Of course I object to the label 'pessimist' for the occupant of the libertarian/incompatibilist position. And the reason why I quote the passage is to point out that a libertarian with a healthy scepticism about the scientific basis of determinism can *agree* that the attitudes themselves fill the gap. Even better, he can declare that there is no gap. He can also insist that the falsehood of determinism need not be verified—even if there *would be a gap* if determinism were true. Finally— as we have several times insisted—he has no need to speak of such things as contra-causal freedom. Actions are events, and events have causes. What the libertarian dispenses with is only the metaphysical sort of cause that must *qua* cause exclude all outcomes except just one.

ability, character, etc. requires no justification, then the *untruth* of sentences in the form 'he could have helped it' ('he could then have done otherwise then') will never represent any threat at all to the sorts of things we express in that sort of language. It is the readiness to detach the consequent of this conditional that principally distinguishes Strawson from an incompatibilist. Indeed, without the conditional claim, Strawson's reconciliation is no reconciliation at all. But taking his position *with* the claim that the untruth of the sentence does not matter—taking it as intended to have the force of a reconciliation, *and* as a refutation of incompatibilism—Strawson's eirenic conclusion is a *non-sequitur*. The language of action and responsibility is not something one needs reason to opt into. Certainly. We just use it. But it does not follow that nothing could count as a reason to opt *out* from it.

The points I have been urging rest on delicate questions of onus and justification. Let me set them out as explicitly as possible.

(1) From the fact that I engage in a manner of thinking, feeling, and talking that is conditioned by a certain non-deterministic assumption, it never followed that I had to justify that assumption if I was to continue in that way of thinking, feeling, and talking. I didn't have to, and the libertarian never needed to suggest that I did. After all, there was nothing peculiar or odd about the assumption. (Rather, if the assumption has any peculiarity, the peculiarity is that it is almost certainly true. The thesis that has emerged as special, too special perhaps to be true, is the thesis of determinism.)

(2) From my not needing to justify the true non-deterministic assumption it does not follow that the *falsehood* of the assumption would have been irrelevant to the practice that was conditioned by the assumption. Maybe, even if the falsehood of the assumption were authoritatively revealed (*i.e.*, if it were authoritatively revealed that strict determinism in the sense of §3 obtained), it would *still* be rational for us to maintain the practices that are conditioned by the assumption. But, in so far as that could ever be shown, and in so far as it would really be rational for us to maintain the practices despite everything, well, perhaps what that really amounts to is this. By hook or by crook, Strawson would have managed to show that there were overwhelmingly good rational reasons—reasons that outweigh even the concern with truth—for us to distract our own attention from the falsehood of the non-deterministic assumption that conditions our practices.

(3) Under the given headings of the free-will dispute, this last contention can only be classified as a libertarian or incompatibilist doctrine. Reconciliationist or compatibilist it is not.

(4) The philosophical significance of determinism is that it threatens to subvert or upstage the meaning that an ordinary narration of an agent's acts and reasons shows as inhering in those acts. If determinism is not even true, then there is no such threat.

9. AN EVERYDAY CONCEPTION

Our picture of the capacity to choose or decide is part of the larger picture that we have of ourselves—a picture that is in part descriptive and in part normative—in which our individual autonomy is seen as residing positively in our pursuit of aims and ideals that are of our own reasonable and citizenly choosing, and residing negatively in the exclusion of the possibility that these particular aims or ideals *had* to be ours. This is to say that it is excluded from our picture that the generality of our individual deliberations or decisions or actions should be historically necessary. When we act at some point in the *now*, we do not normally think there was anything in the world *last year* or even *last week* (say) from which our act had, by virtue of natural laws and given circumstances, to ensue. Indeed it is a condition of human engagement that one should think that this is not so. Compare Kant, *Foundations of the Metaphysics of Morals* [448]. We are happy enough, of course, with the possibility that last week there was something *in us* from which our present act would ensue. But it is doubtful in the extreme that there exist the sort of laws about us either individually or collectively, laws seriously comparable with the laws of nature (and their applications and specializations) that would be required for the holding of historical necessity.

In this general picture, actions and decisions do not lie outside the causal nexus. But the causal nexus underdetermines them—if only because it underdetermines all sorts of things. And the way in which actions and decisions become explicable is by being seen as *intelligible*—and intelligible only by virtue of standing in the right relation to aims and ideals proposed to us by practical reason (cp. Plato, *Phaedo*, 98^d following). The fullest intelligibility of this latter sort is achieved in the whole story that not only recounts how the agent acted at this or that juncture but says what it was in the world—representing what sort of good or evil and engaging with what idea of the agent's—to which the agent was responding in acting so. In such a story, each succeeding episode in the sequence of the agent's doings will be an intelligible phase in the unfolding of an agent's mentality, a phase at once expressive of what the agent is and constitutive of what he is en route to become. Looking at the agent in this way, letting one part of the sequence impart significance to another, we have no difficulty in seeing the agent as one who exercises choice between alternatives (not necessarily making the choice that others would make). Nor do we have any difficulty in seeing the alternatives as real alternatives. Finally, availing ourselves of the said picture, we can see in the deliberations of agents a part of the culmination of the process by which striving has evolved into thought, and thought not only explores the world but colonizes it. At this point striving emerges finally in consciousness, a consciousness that holds itself answerable in action and reflection to the objects and properties thought discovers, subsumes objects under standards (in some sense) of its own making, yet refrains from hubristically supposing that, just because properties correspond to senses and practices that owe their existence to us, the properties thought finds in the world are its own creation.

In a philosophy that was happy to count itself as a recapitulation, extension and critique of ordinary experience, the details of such a phenomenological cum anecdotal cum philosophical account as this could be corrected or made more complete. But, improved and extended, why should it not stand as the best possible account of action and choice—or as the best possible account of action and choice as they are when practical reason has full sway over us?

6

ARE WE FREE TO BREAK THE LAWS?

DAVID LEWIS

Soft determinism seems to have an incredible consequence. It seems to imply, given certain acceptable further premises, that sometimes we are able to act in such a way that the laws of nature are broken. But if we distinguish a strong and a weak version of this incredible consequence, I think we shall find that it is the strong version that is incredible and the weak version that is the consequence.

Soft determinism is the doctrine that sometimes one freely does what one is predetermined to do; and that in such a case one is able to act otherwise though past history and the laws of nature determine that one will not act otherwise.

Compatibilism is the doctrine that soft determinism may be true. A compatibilist might well doubt soft determinism because he doubts on physical grounds that we are ever predetermined to act as we do, or perhaps because he doubts on psychoanalytic grounds that we ever act freely. I myself am a compatibilist but no determinist, hence I am obliged to rebut some objections against soft determinism but not others. But for the sake of the argument, let me feign to uphold soft determinism, and indeed a particular instance thereof.

I have just put my hand down on my desk. That, let me claim, was a free but predetermined act. I was able to act otherwise, for instance to raise my hand. But there is a true historical proposition H about the intrinsic state of the world long ago, and there is a true proposition L specifying the laws of nature that govern our world, such that H and L jointly determine what I did. They jointly imply the proposition that I put my hand down. They jointly contradict the proposition that I raised my hand. Yet I was free; I was able to raise my hand. The way in which I was determined not to was not the sort of way that counts as inability.

What if I had raised my hand? Then at least one of three things would

From *Theoria*, 47 (1981), 112–21. Copyright © Berghahn Books. Reprinted by permission of the publisher.

have been true. Contradictions would have been true together; or the historical proposition H would not have been true; or the law proposition L would not have been true. Which? Here we need auxiliary premises; but since I accept the premises my opponent requires to make his case, we may proceed. Of our three alternatives, we may dismiss the first; for if I had raised my hand, there would still have been no true contradictions. Likewise we may dismiss the second; for if I had raised my hand, the intrinsic state of the world long ago would have been no different.[1] That leaves the third alternative. If I had raised my hand, the law proposition L would not have been true. That follows by a principle of the logic of counterfactuals which is almost uncontroversial:[2] $A \mathrel{\Box\!\!\rightarrow} B \vee C \vee D$, $A \mathrel{\Box\!\!\rightarrow} - B$, $A \mathrel{\Box\!\!\rightarrow} - C$, $\therefore A \mathrel{\Box\!\!\rightarrow} D$.

If L had not been true, that implies that some law of nature would have been broken, for L is a specification of the laws. That is not to say that anything would have been both a law and broken—that is a contradiction in terms if, as I suppose, any genuine law is at least an absolutely unbroken regularity. Rather, if L had not been true, something that is in fact a law, and unbroken, would have been broken, and no law. It would at best have been an almost-law.

In short, as a (feigned) soft determinist, who accepts the requisite auxiliary premises and principle of counterfactual logic, I am committed to the consequence that if I had done what I was able to do—raise my hand—then some law would have been broken.

"That is to say," my opponent paraphrases, "you claim to be able to break the very laws of nature. And with so little effort! A marvelous power indeed! Can you also bend spoons?"

Distinguo. My opponent's paraphrase is not quite right. He has replaced the weak thesis that I accept with a stronger thesis that I join him in rejecting. The strong thesis is utterly incredible, but it is no part of soft determinism. The weak thesis is controversial, to be sure, but a soft determinist should not mind being committed to it. The two theses are as follows.

(Weak Thesis)   I am able to do something such that, if I did it, a law would be broken.
(Strong Thesis)   I am able to break a law.

To see the difference, consider not a marvelous ability to break a law but a commonplace ability to break a window. Perhaps I am able to throw a stone

---

[1] I argue for this in [4].

[2] The inference is valid in any system that treats the conditional as a propositionally (or even sententially) indexed family of normal necessities, in the sense of Brian F. Chellas ([1]).

in a certain direction; and perhaps if I did, the stone would hit a certain window and the window would break. Then I am able to break a window. For starters: I am able to do something such that, if I did it, a window would be broken. But there is more to be said. I am able to do something such that, if I did it, my act would cause a window-breaking event.

Or consider a commonplace ability to break a promise. Perhaps I am able to throw a stone; and perhaps if I did, I would break my promise never to throw a stone. Then I am able to break a promise. For starters: I am able to do something such that, if I did it, a promise would be broken. But there is more to be said. I am able to do something such that, if I did it, my act would itself be a promise-breaking event.

Next, consider what really would be a marvelous ability to break a law—an ability I could not credibly claim. Suppose that I were able to throw a stone very, very hard. And suppose that if I did, the stone would fly faster than light, an event contrary to law. Then I really would be able to break a law. For starters: I would be able to do something such that, if I did it, a law would be broken. But there is more to be said. I would be able to do something such that, if I did it, my act would cause a law-breaking event.

Or suppose that I were able to throw a stone so hard that in the course of the throw my own hand would move faster than light. Then again I would be able to break a law, regardless of what my act might cause. For starters: I would be able to do something such that, if I did it, a law would be broken. But there is more to be said. I would be able to do something such that, if I did it, my act would itself be a law-breaking event.

If no act of mine either caused or was a window-, promise-, or law-breaking event, then I think it could not be true that I broke a window, a promise, or a law. Therefore I am able to break a window, a promise, or a law only if I am able to do something such that, if I did it, my act either would cause or would be a window-, promise-, or law-breaking event.

Maybe my opponent will contend that according to soft determinism, there is another way of being able to break a law. But I see no reason to grant this contention.

Now consider the disputed case. I am able to raise my hand, although it is predetermined that I will not. If I raised my hand, some law would be broken. I even grant that a law-breaking event would take place. (Here I use the present tense neutrally. I mean to imply nothing about *when* a law-breaking event would take place.) But is it so that my act of raising my hand would cause any law-breaking event? Is it so that my act of raising my hand would itself be a law-breaking event? Is it so that any other act of mine would cause or would be a law-breaking event? If not, then my ability to raise my hand confers no marvelous ability to break a law, even though a law would be broken if I did it.[3]

Had I raised my hand, a law would have been broken beforehand. The course of events would have diverged from the actual course of events a little while before I raised my hand, and at the point of divergence there would have been a law-breaking event—a divergence miracle, as I have called it ([4]). But this divergence miracle would not have been caused by my raising my hand. If anything, the causation would have been the other way around. Nor would the divergence miracle have been my act of raising my hand. That act was altogether absent from the actual course of events, so it cannot get under way until there is already some divergence. Nor would it have been caused by any other act of mine, earlier or later. Nor would it have been any other act of mine. Nor is there any reason to say that if I had raised my hand there would have been some other law-breaking event besides the divergence miracle; still less, that some other law-breaking event would have been caused by, or would have been, my act of raising my hand. To accommodate my hypothetical raising of my hand while holding fixed all that can and should be held fixed, it is necessary to suppose one divergence miracle, gratuitous to suppose any further law-breaking.

Thus I insist that I was able to raise my hand, and I acknowledge that a law would have been broken had I done so, but I deny that I am therefore able to break a law. To uphold my instance of soft determinism, I need not claim any incredible powers. To uphold the compatibilism that I actually believe, I need not claim that such powers are even possible.

I said that if I had raised my hand, the divergence miracle beforehand would not have been caused by my raising my hand. That seems right. But my opponent might argue *ad hominem* that according to my own analysis of causation ([3]), my raising my hand does turn out to cause the divergence miracle. The effect would precede the cause, but I do not object to that. We seem to have the right pattern of counterfactual dependence between

---

[3] Up to a point, my strategy here resembles that of Keith Lehrer ([2], p. 199). Lehrer grants a weak thesis: the agent could have done somthing such that, if he had done it, there would have been a difference in either laws or history. He rejects, as I would, the step from that to a stronger thesis: the agent could have brought about a difference in laws or history. So far, so good. But Lehrer's reason for rejecting the stronger thesis is one I cannot accept. His reason is this: it is false that if the agent had preferred that there be a difference in laws or history, there would have been a difference in laws or history. I say, first, that this conditional may not be false. Suppose the agent is predetermined to prefer that there be no difference; had he preferred otherwise, there would have been a difference. (Had anything been otherwise than it was predetermined to be, there would have been a difference in either laws or history.) And second, if this conditional is not false, that is not enough to make the stronger thesis true. There must be some other reason, different from the one Lehrer gives, why the stronger thesis is false.

distinct events: (1) if I had raised my hand, the divergence miracle would have occurred, but (2) if I had not raised my hand, it would not have occurred.

I reply that we do not have this required pattern, nor would we have had it if I had raised my hand. Therefore I am safe in denying that the miracle would have been caused by my act.

We do not have the pattern because (1) is false. What is true is only that if I had raised my hand, then some or other divergence miracle would have occurred. There is no particular divergence miracle that definitely would have occurred, since the divergence might have happened in various ways.[4]

If I had raised my hand, (1) would have been true. But we still would not have had the right pattern, because in that case (2) would have been false. Consider a counterfactual situation in which a divergence miracle beforehand has allowed me to raise my hand. Is it so, from the standpoint of that situation, that if I had not raised my hand, the miracle would not have taken place? No; the miracle might have taken place, only to have its work undone straightway by a second miracle. (Even in this doubly counterfactual context, when I speak of a miracle I mean a violation of the actual laws.) What is true, at most, is that if I had not raised my hand, then the first miracle might not have taken place.

My incompatibilist opponent is a creature of fiction, but he has his prototypes in real life. He is modelled partly on Peter van Inwagen ([5], [6], [7]) and partly on myself when I first worried about van Inwagen's argument against compatibilism. He definitely is not van Inwagen; he does not choose his words so carefully. Still I think that for all his care, van Inwagen is in the same boat with my fictitious opponent.

Van Inwagen's argument runs as follows, near enough. (I recast it as a *reductio* against the instance of soft determinism that I feign to uphold.) I did not raise my hand; suppose for *reductio* that I could have raised my hand, although determinism is true. Then it follows, given four premises that I cannot question, that I could have rendered false the conjunction HL of a certain historical proposition H about the state of the world before my birth and a certain law proposition L. If so, then I could have rendered L false. (Premise 5.) But I could not have rendered L false. (Premise 6.) This refutes our supposition.

---

[4] Cf. [4], p. 463. At this point I am relying on contingent features of the world as we suppose it to be; as Allen Hazen has pointed out to me, we can imagine a world of discrete processes at which one divergent history in which I raise my hand clearly takes less of a miracle than any of its rivals. I think this matters little, since the task of compatibilism is to show how freedom and determinism might coexist at a world that might, for all we know, be ours.

To this I reply that Premise 5 and Premise 6 are not both true. Which one is true depends on whan van Inwagen means by "could have rendered false".

It does not matter what "could have rendered false" means in ordinary language; van Inwagen introduced the phrase as a term of art. It does not even matter what meaning van Inwagen gave it. What matters is whether we can give it any meaning that would meet his needs—any meaning that would make all his premises defensible without circularity. I shall consider two meanings. I think there is nothing in van Inwagen's text to suggest any third meaning that might work better than these two.[5]

First, a preliminary definition. Let us say that an event would falsify a proposition iff, necessarily, if that event occurs then that proposition is false. For instance, an event consisting of a stone's flying faster than light would falsify a law. So would an act of throwing in which my hand moves faster than light. So would a divergence miracle. But my act of throwing a stone would not itself falsify the proposition that the window in the line of fire remains intact; all that is true is that my act would cause another event that would falsify that proposition. My act of raising my hand would falsify any sufficiently inclusive conjunction of history and law. But it would not itself falsify any law—not if all the requisite law-breaking were over and done with beforehand. All that is true is that my act would be preceded by another event—the divergence miracle—that would falsify a law.

Let us say that I could have rendered a proposition false in the weak sense iff I was able to do something such that, if I did it, the proposition would have been falsified (though not necessarily by my act, or by any event caused by my act). And let us say that I could have rendered a proposition false in the strong sense iff I was able to do something such that, if I did it, the proposition would have been falsified either by my act itself or by some event caused by my act.

The Weak Thesis, which as a soft determinist I accept, is the thesis that I could have rendered a law false in the weak sense. The Strong Thesis, which I reject, is the thesis that I could have rendered a law false in the strong sense.

The first part of van Inwagen's argument succeeds whichever sense we take. If I could have raised my hand despite the fact that determinism is true

---

[5] Van Inwagen has indicated (personal communication, 1981) that he would adopt a third meaning for "could have rendered false", different from both of the meanings that I discuss here. His definition is roughly as follows: an agent could have rendered a proposition false iff he could have arranged things in a certain way, such that his doing so, plus the whole truth about the past, together strictly imply the falsehood of the proposition. On this definition, Premise 6 simply says that I could not have arranged things in any way such that I was predetermined not to arrange things in that way. It is uninstructive to learn that the soft determinist is committed to denying Premise 6 thus understood.

and I did not raise it, then indeed it is true both in the weak sense and in the strong sense that I could have rendered false the conjunction *HL* of history and law. But I could have rendered false the law proposition *L* in the weak sense, though I could not have rendered *L* false in the strong sense. So if we take the weak sense throughout the argument, then I deny Premise 6. If instead we take the strong sense, then I deny Premise 5.

Van Inwagen supports both premises by considering analogous cases. I think the supporting arguments fail because the cases produced are not analogous: they are cases in which the weak and strong senses do not diverge. In support of Premise 6, he invites us to reject the supposition that a physicist could render a law false by building and operating a machine that would accelerate protons to twice the speed of light. Reject that supposition by all means; but that does nothing to support Premise 6 taken in the weak sense, for the rejected supposition is that the physicist could render a law false in the strong sense. In support of Premise 5, he invites us to reject the supposition that a traveler could render false a conjunction of a historical proposition and a proposition about his future travels otherwise than by rendering false the nonhistorical conjunct. Reject that supposition by all means, but that does nothing to support Premise 5 taken in the strong sense. Given that one could render false, in the strong sense, a conjunction of historical and nonhistorical propositions (and given that, as in the cases under consideration, there is no question of rendering the historical conjunct false by means of time travel or the like), what follows? Does it follow that one could render the nonhistorical conjunct false in the strong sense? That is what would support Premise 5 in the strong sense. Or does it only follow, as I think, that one could render the nonhistorical conjunct false in at least the weak sense? The case of the traveler is useless in answering that question, since if the traveler could render the proposition about his future travels false in the weak sense, he could also render it false in the strong sense.

REFERENCES

[1] CHELLAS, B. F. "Basic conditional logic". *Journal of philosophical logic*, vol. 4 (1975), pp. 133–153.
[2] LEHRER, K. "Preferences, conditionals and freedom". In Peter van Inwagen, ed., *Time and cause*. Dordrecht: Reidel, 1980.
[3] LEWIS, D. "Causation". *Journal of Philosophy*, vol. 70 (1973), pp. 556–567.
[4] LEWIS, D. "Counterfactual dependence and time's arrow". *Noûs*, vol. 13 (1979), pp. 455–476.
[5] VAN INWAGEN, P. "A formal approach to the problem of free will and determinism". *Theoria*, vol. 40 (1974), pp. 9–22.

[6] VAN INWAGEN, P. "The incompatability of free will and determinism". *Philosophical studies*, vol. 27 (1975), pp. 185–199.
[7] VAN INWAGEN, P. "Reply to Narveson". *Philosophical studies*, vol. 32 (1977), pp. 89–98.

FREEDOM AND PRACTICAL REASON

HILARY BOK

My approach to the problem of freedom of the will relies on the distinction between theoretical and practical reasoning, and between the standpoints from which we engage in them. As I will use these terms, theoretical and practical reasoning are not distinguished by their subject-matter, by the modes of inference appropriate to each (in the sense suggested by investigations into the 'special logic of prescriptive utterances'), or by the idioms in which they allow us to describe the world. Instead, theoretical and practical reasoning are undertaken for different purposes, and the distinction between the theoretical and practical standpoints on which my arguments will rely is defined by this difference in purpose. The purpose of theoretical reasoning is to describe the world insofar as this can be done without engaging in practical reasoning; and to discover what causal connections exist between the objects and events which figure in that description. Theoretical claims are those claims which the best current theory takes to be descriptive or explanatory, excluding only those claims whose justification essentially depends on practical reasoning. The purpose of practical reasoning is to determine the will; to answer the question 'what should I do?'. Its aim is to ascertain what we have reason to do or not to do, to determine the relative importance of these various reasons for action, and thereby to arrive at a decision which we can regard as justifiable. Practical claims are those claims whose justification essentially involves practical reasoning.[1]

We can see, in general terms, how we might use the distinction between theoretical and practical reasoning to respond to libertarian objections to compatibilist accounts of freedom of the will and moral responsibility. Libertarians do not argue that either determinism or mechanism[2] implies

Hilary Bok, *Freedom and Responsibility*. Copyright © 1998 by PUP. Reprinted by permission of Princeton University Press.

[1] I develop this account further in chapter 2 of *Freedom and Responsibility*.
[2] By mechanism I mean the view that our deliberation and choices are as fully determined as other natural events, and that they can be explained in the same terms. Mechanistic views include both determinism and other views that hold that indeterministic natural events can figure in the explanation of our choices.

that there is no difference at all between those acts we ordinarily call free and other acts; or between behavior for which we ordinarily hold agents responsible and behavior for which we do not. But they claim that, if mechanism is true, those distinctions cannot possibly have the kind of significance which they would need to have were they to serve as the bases of a justification of our ascriptions of freedom and moral responsibility to persons.

This claim should raise our suspicions. After all, distinctions are not important or unimportant *per se*, but with respect to the purposes for which we invoke them. Because theoretical and practical reasoning serve different purposes, we might be able to argue that, for theoretical purposes, the distinctions invoked by a compatibilist justification of responsibility have no particular importance; but that for practical purposes, they are crucial, while the truth or falsity of the metaphysical hypotheses which libertarians take to be central to the problem of freedom of the will is irrelevant. If so, then we could explain both the strength of libertarians' objections to compatibilist accounts of freedom of the will and moral responsibility, and why, despite their strength, those objections are wrong.

I will argue that, from a practical point of view, we must regard ourselves as acting freely in (more or less) the situations in which we ordinarily take ourselves to do so; and that the truth or falsity of mechanism or determinism does not bear on the question whether or not we can ever be said to act freely in this sense. While I will address some libertarian objections to this account of freedom, I will not try to show here that my account of freedom is one that libertarians should find satisfactory.[3] My purpose here is simply to discover whether the requirements of practical reasoning give us reason to regard ourselves as free in any sense at all; and, if so, to determine what that sense is.

POSSIBILITY

We are free, we think, only when we can choose among courses of action that are truly open to us. And some course of action is truly open to us only if it is in fact possible for us to perform it. On this libertarians and compatibilists agree. They disagree, however, on the correct interpretation of these claims: on what it means to say that a course of action is 'truly open to us', and what kind of possibility its being truly open to us requires.

We can use the word 'possibility' in various senses. It is possible, in a

---

[3] To do so would require showing that this account of freedom allows us to justify the claim that we are morally responsible for our conduct in some satisfactory sense. I try to show this in *Freedom and Responsibility*, chapters 4–6.

general sense, for water to freeze or to evaporate, but not to tap-dance or to recite *Paradise Lost*. The claim that it is, in general, possible for water to freeze does not mean that it is possible for any given amount of water to freeze at any time, regardless of its circumstances and, in particular, of its temperature; that *every* bit of water *always* has freezing as an option. When we say that it is possible for some object to behave in a certain way, our claim is always made relative to some set of circumstances in which that object might find itself. Those circumstances can be specified more or less completely, and the possibilities we attribute to the object in question will vary accordingly. When, for instance, we claim that water can freeze, we consider water simply as such, in abstraction from the conditions in which any given amount of water finds itself. The claim that it is not possible for water to freeze at temperatures above 32 degrees Fahrenheit does not contradict that more general claim, but specifies the conditions over which it ranges in a way that affects our conception of the possibilities in question.

When we use the word 'possibility' in what I have called a general sense, we define the possibilities available to some object relative to an incomplete description of its circumstances: one which abstracts from certain types of information. Compatibilists use such a general conception of possibility in interpreting the claim that we act freely when we can choose among actions which it is possible for us to perform: we act freely, they claim, when we would perform any of several different actions if we chose to do so. This 'conditional analysis' defines our possibilities relative to a description of our circumstances which treats the course of our deliberation and the outcome of our choice as variables, whether or not antecedent events cause us to follow a particular line of reasoning or to make a particular choice. If we define our possibilities thus, then we can say that all of those actions which we would have performed had we chosen to perform them are possibilities for us, just as we can say that it is possible for a given amount of water to vaporize if we disregard the fact that it is sitting in my freezer.

Whereas compatibilists define our possibilities relative to a description of our circumstances which abstracts from certain kinds of information, libertarians allow no such omissions. They argue that our freedom requires that we be able to choose among alternatives which are possible given all relevant information about our state, our circumstances, and antecedent events, including those events (if any) which cause us to make a particular choice. I will refer to this 'all-in' sense of possibility as 'possibility *tout court*'.

In the arguments that follow, I will assume that determinism is true;[4] and

---

[4] I make this assumption for reasons of exposition, and not because I believe it to be true. I must make some assumption about the causal structure of the universe: to modify each step of my arguments to accommodate each such theory would make those arguments impossibly long. Since

therefore that, while a given agent at a given time might have any number of possibilities in the broader compatibilist sense, no agent can ever have more than one possibility *tout court*. If a free agent must have alternatives which are possible only in the compatibilists' general sense, then determinism is compatible with her freedom. But if she must have alternatives which are possible *tout court*, then determinism implies that she is not free.

The most common way of trying to show that freedom requires one or the other conception of possibility is to argue either that there is some sense of 'can' or 'possibility' that we do in fact use when we talk about freedom, or that to construe freedom using the other sense entails conclusions that we must find unacceptable. Arguments of this kind generally appeal to ordinary language, to various examples, or to our intuitions in support of their claims about the kind of possibility relevant to freedom of the will. Those to whom they are addressed generally respond by constructing alternative accounts which appeal to their preferred conception of possibility, and arguing that these accounts capture our intuitions about those examples at least as well as those of their opponents. For this reason, this type of argument is generally inconclusive. To see why, consider two prominent libertarian arguments, and the responses compatibilists might make to them.

First, libertarians claim that the fact that it is possible, in the compatibilists' general sense, for some agent at a given time to perform several actions does not show that that agent acts freely. In support of this claim, they argue that when we can perform some action only if we do something else, we do not claim that it is possible for us to perform that action unless we can do whatever performing it requires. So, for instance, while it might be true that I could pay off the Argentine national debt if I could transmute the dustballs under my bed into gold, this does not show that it is possible for me to pay off the Argentine national debt unless it is also true that I can transmute those dustballs into gold.

Similarly, if determinism is true, then while it may be possible for me to perform various actions if I choose to do so, what I will in fact choose to do is itself fully determined by antecedent events. I might now have various 'alternatives' in the compatibilists' sense: if I chose, I could continue to work on my book, call out for pizza, or chuck it all and head for Tibet. However, were a Laplacean demon to survey the universe shortly after the Big Bang, it

---

I believe that the truth or falsity of any such view is irrelevant to the question whether or not we are free, my main concern in selecting an assumption is not to choose the correct one, but to avoid the appearance of stacking the deck in my favor. I have therefore assumed the truth of determinism in particular because it is generally thought to be the hardest plausible view of the causal structure of the universe to reconcile with human freedom.

would be able to discern in that cosmic soup conditions which ensure that I will now type a paragraph, stare blankly into space for a few minutes, and then erase that paragraph in disgust; and which entirely preclude my picking up the telephone, buying a ticket to Lhasa, and arranging for sherpas. Given that those conditions existed, it is no more possible for me now to opt for the supposed 'alternative' of going to Tibet than it is possible for me to usher in an era of peace and good will by snapping my fingers. But if it is impossible for me now to choose to go to Tibet, then why should I take the fact that I would go to Tibet if (per impossibile) I were to make such a choice to show that I am now free to go to Tibet; or that going to Tibet is now a possibility for me in any sense in which paying off the Argentine national debt is not?[5]

Compatibilists might reply that this argument begs the question against them. For by allowing the conditions which determine what I will choose to do to constrain our conception of what I am free to do, libertarians must assume that the sense of 'possibility' relevant to freedom of the will is not the broader compatibilist conception of possibility (which, by definition, abstracts from information about what I will choose to do), but possibility *tout court*. Were we to assume instead that the conception of possibility relevant to freedom is the compatibilists' broader conception, we could easily explain why going to Tibet is an option for me, while paying off the Argentine national debt is not. For according to the compatibilists' general conception, it is possible for me to perform any action which I would perform if I chose. Since I would go to Tibet if I chose, but could not transmute dustballs into gold under any circumstances, only the first course of action is in this sense a possibility for me.

Second, Peter van Inwagen has argued[6] that if determinism is true, then we can never do anything other that what we actually do. He also claims that his argument presupposes no particular analysis of 'can'. Van Inwagen's argument is this: If determinism is true, we can infer all true statements about the world now from a complete description of the world at any previous time, together with the laws of nature. If it is true that A now (at T) raises her arm, then we can infer the truth of the statement 'A raises her arm at T' from a complete description of the world at some time preceding her birth, together with the laws of nature. If A could have refrained from raising her arm, then A could have rendered the statement 'A raises her arm

---

[5] This is a restatement of an argument made by Roderick Chisholm in "Human Freedom and the Self" [reprinted as Essay 1, this volume].

[6] In *An Essay on Free Will* (Oxford: Clarendon Press, 1983) [see Essay 2, this volume], and "The Incompatibility of Free Will and Determinism", in Gary Watson (ed.), *Free Will*, 1st edn. (New York: Oxford University Press, 1982). The summary of van Inwagen's argument that follows is drawn from "The Incompatibility of Free Will and Determinism".

at T' false. But since that statement follows from a complete description of the state of the world at some time before her birth, together with the laws of nature, then A could render that statement false only if she could falsify either the complete description of the world at a time before her birth or the laws of nature. But since no one can either alter the past or change the laws of nature, A cannot do so; and therefore determinism implies that she cannot perform any action other than the one she actually performs.

However, compatibilists need not accept van Inwagen's argument. They believe that we should interpret the claim that an agent can perform some action to mean that it is possible for her to perform that action if we abstract from any information about what she will choose to do. In this sense it is not possible for that agent to alter either the past or the laws of nature, since whatever she chooses to do, these will remain the same. Moreover, if determinism is true, we can derive claims about the particular action she will perform at T from the conjunction of a complete description of the world at some previous time and the laws of nature. However, it does not follow from this that she cannot perform any other action at T in the compatibilists' general sense unless we can infer the claim that she will not perform any other action from that conjunction without referring to any claims about what she will choose to do, or about the events which constitute her choice. Since we will not be able to infer claims about what she will choose to do without referring to claims about her choice whenever her actions depend on what she chooses to do, it will be true in all such cases that she can perform any of the actions which she would perform if she chose, if we use 'can' in its broader compatibilist sense. For this reason compatibilists can deny van Inwagen's argument on the grounds that it begs the question against them.

At this point we seem to have reached what John Fischer has called a "dia-lectical stalemate"[7]: a situation in which proponents of opposing views can explain our intuitions about various examples using different principles, and in which any example which seems to support one principle over the other can legitimately be rejected on the grounds that it presupposes the view it is meant to support. In dealing with dialectical stalemates, it is in general unhelpful to try to establish one view over the other by arguing that either our ordinary use of the terms in question, our intuitions, or consideration of some set of examples forces us to accept it. For our opponents will reject any examples which their view cannot explain; they will not share the intuitions to which we appeal; and they will reject the claim that they cannot use the

[7] John Martin Fischer, *The Metaphysics of Free Will* (Oxford: Blackwell, 1994), 83–5.

terms whose proper application is at issue in ways that accommodate their view.

This impasse exists because our ordinary use of the concept of freedom relies on the assumption that if I perform an action because I choose to do so, then I perform it freely, but if I perform it because something else causes me to do so, then I do not; that either we or the external world, but not both, cause us to act as we do. Mechanism implies that this assumption is false: that the actions we normally call 'free' are caused by choices which are themselves caused, ultimately, either by indeterministic events or by external causes. It therefore implies that our ordinary concept of freedom gives us reason both to affirm and to deny that we perform those actions freely. It is for this reason that appeals to intuition and ordinary language are not decisive: both libertarians and compatibilists draw on important features of our ordinary concept of freedom, both are trying to apply that concept to cases in which the conditions of its straightforward application are absent, both project that concept in ways that are not obviously unreasonable or illegitimate, and both can muster real intuitive support for their views. If this account is correct, then no appeal to our ordinary concept of freedom, or to the ways in which we ordinarily apply it, will settle the issue between libertarians and compatibilists, since that concept supports both views, and does not give us decisive grounds to reject either.

If this issue presents us with a dialectical stalemate, then it might seem that we must despair of finding a solution that would satisfy libertarians and compatibilists alike. In fact, however, I believe that it shows us the kind of argument we would need to make in order to find such a solution. We reach a dialectical stalemate when no arguments based on appeals to ordinary language, to the consideration of examples, or to our intuitions succeed in convincing our opponents, and when this is due not to our opponents' limitations, but to the fact that both sides can appeal to intuitions, accounts of apparent counterexamples, and claims about our ordinary use of the terms in question which are not unreasonable. In such situations we should abandon the attempt to convince our opponents that intuitions, examples, or ordinary language decisively favor our view, not only because such arguments are unlikely to convince them, but because the fact that we have reached a dialectical stalemate shows that such arguments are unsound. Instead, we should admit that there are several apparently legitimate ways of using the contested terms, that each way of using them will be supported by some apparently convincing intuitions, and that we will probably not find any example which will decisively show that one way of using these terms is right. Having made this concession, we should then proceed to ask what reasons we have to use the contested terms in either of these legitimate ways in the cases under discussion.

If this argument is correct, libertarians and compatibilists should agree that both the broader compatibilist conception of 'possibility' and the libertarian possibility *tout court* have something to be said for them, that both can usefully be employed in various circumstances, and that the claim that one of them is the conception of possibility relevant to discussions of freedom and responsibility is unlikely to be established by arguments either about what terms like 'possibility' or 'can' mean, by appeal to our ordinary concept of freedom, or by our intuitions. Were they to agree on this point, both sides would have to recast some of the arguments by which they had hoped to establish the illegitimacy of their opponents' position as demonstrations of the costs incurred by those who hold it.[8] Having done so, they could proceed to address the question: granted that we can legitimately use both the compatibilist conception of 'possibility' and the libertarian possibility *tout court*, what reasons do we have to construe our freedom and responsibility in terms of one rather than the other?

The claim that we should ask not which conception of freedom and responsibility are the real ones but which we have most reason to use might seem like a way of substituting questions about our motives for believing that we are free and responsible for questions about the justification of those beliefs, thereby deflecting libertarians' attention from the question whether we are in fact free or responsible in some satisfactory sense to timeworn compatibilist arguments about the social benefits of thinking that we are. This objection rests on two mistakes.

First, there is a difference between saying that we should be guided by what we care about in deciding which concepts to concern ourselves with, and saying that such considerations should guide our decisions about what beliefs to hold. I make only the former claim. I assume that given a particular conception of freedom or moral responsibility, we should decide whether we are free or responsible in that sense, and what would follow if we were, without respect to what we would like to be true. For this reason I will not try to argue, for instance, that we should regard ourselves as morally responsible because we would be less likely to behave badly if we did, since I am not aware of any reason for thinking that the truth of the latter claim is a reason for believing the former. I claim only that when we ask ourselves which conceptions of freedom and responsibility we should concern ourselves with, there is no conception that we must use, and that we are therefore at liberty to consider our reasons for using one or the other.

---

[8] See Fischer, *The Metaphysics of Free Will*, 199.

Second, one might object to this claim if one took an unduly narrow view of what we care about. Thus, for instance, Dennett claims that "unless we can tie (responsibility) to some recognizable social desideratum, it will have no rational claim on our esteem".[9] The idea that our concerns are so narrow seems wrong on two counts: first, not all desiderata are social, and second, not everything we might find desirable in a concept is an effect that concerning ourselves with that concept will produce. If we reject this restricted view of what we care about, we can regard as relevant to our assessment of concepts of freedom not only the consequences of accepting a particular conception of freedom, but features of that conception itself: for instance, its rational defensibility, its role in a justification of our ascriptions of moral responsibility, or its ability to help us to justify a satisfying account of our status as moral persons. Only if we construe what we care about broadly will we be able to accommodate libertarians' legitimate concerns; and only if we provide an account of freedom and responsibility which fully satisfies our concerns, broadly construed, will we be able to say that those who reject our account are not worried about anything worth wanting.

When we ask not which conception of freedom is the real one but which we have most reason to use, the force of libertarians' objections to compatibilist accounts of freedom is clear. For while libertarians cannot plausibly claim that the meanings of words like 'can' or 'possibility' ensure that their account of freedom is correct, or that our intuitions unequivocally favor their position, they can raise serious questions about what reason we have to construe our freedom in terms of the compatibilist conception of possibility. First, libertarians might ask why the conception of possibility relevant to freedom of the will should define our alternatives relative to a description of our situation which abstracts from any information at all. If determinism is true, then if we define our possibilities relative to all relevant information about our situation, we will conclude that no agent ever has more than one possibility available to her at a given time. We can decide to ignore some feature of her situation in formulating the description of that situation relative to which we will define her possibilities, and it will then seem to us that she has a variety of alternatives available to her. But from the fact that we have decided to ignore some feature of her situation, it does not follow that that feature has ceased to exist; nor does the fact that we have chosen to disregard the ways in which it limits her options imply that those limitations no longer constrain her. It might therefore seem that the compatibilists' general sense of possibility describes the possibilities which we would have if

    [9] Daniel Dennett, *Elbow Room* (Cambridge, Mass.: MIT Press, 1984), 163.

the course of our deliberation and the outcome of our choices were in fact undetermined, and not the possibilities which are actually available to us, things being as they are.[10] Unless compatibilists can explain why we should regard those actions which are possible in their sense as genuine alternatives, libertarians will take this argument to show that only those actions which are possible *tout court* are truly open to us.

Even if compatibilists could explain why we should regard those actions which are possible in their general sense as genuine possibilities, libertarians might ask why similar arguments would not show that all objects have alternatives which are truly open to them. The claim that persons are free and non-persons are not requires that persons have genuine alternatives in some sense in which non-persons do not. Compatibilists claim that we can choose among genuine alternatives whenever our actions depend on our choices. But given any object at any time, we can define some general sense of possibility according to which that object at that time had several possibilities open to it. If we abstract from information about the topography of the mountain down which it slides, we can claim that an avalanche could have buried any of a number of different sets of houses; if we abstract from information about the angle at which it was hit, we can claim that a pool ball could have knocked any of a range of other pool balls into the corner pocket; if we abstract from information about the causes of our choices, we can claim that we could have chosen to perform any of a number of actions. In all three cases, were we to consider all information relevant to an explanation of the behavior of the object under consideration, we would find that its actual behavior was its only possibility *tout court*; the compatibilist conception of our possibilities differs from the other two only in the particular type of information from which it abstracts. When compatibilists claim that the fact that we would have performed any of several actions had we chosen to do so shows that we have genuine alternatives, while the fact that a pool ball would have taken any of several paths had it been hit in the right way does not, they must therefore assume that when we incorporate information about the angle at which the pool ball was hit into an account of the alternatives available to it, we thereby show that some of those alternatives were not

---

[10] Note that, although I have discussed different conceptions of possibility, the sense of possibility involved in all of these conceptions is itself univocal. Each such conception uses the term 'possibility' to mean what I will call physical possibility: possibility given, first, some initial description of the object whose possibilities are in question, and of its situation; and, second, natural laws. They differ in that each defines our possibilities relative to descriptions which abstract from different types of information. This makes it natural to think that our "real" possibilities are those which are defined relative to a description of our circumstances which does not abstract from any information at all. I have discussed possibility in this way in part because it makes explicit the strength of the libertarian position on this point.

genuine; but when we incorporate information about the causes of our choices into an account of our alternatives, we do not. And this assumption seems to reflect an arbitrary attitude towards a particular type of natural cause, an attitude which libertarians will rightly require compatibilists to explain.

Finally, it is unclear why the compatibilist's general conception of our possibilities should be relevant to our moral evaluation of persons. It might be relevant if, in our ascriptions of moral responsibility, we were concerned with people in general and their possibilities. Just as water can freeze or vaporize, people can choose to act rightly or wrongly. But our evaluation of persons is typically not concerned with people in general, but with individuals. It is a desideratum of moral evaluation that it be subtle and fine-grained; that it be as sensitive as possible to differences in the capacities of agents and in their situations. We say that water can vaporize, but not that water in a functioning freezer can vaporize, and still less that *these ice cubes* could have vaporized *while they were locked in the deep-freeze*. Analogously, if determinism is true, we can say that people can refrain from acting selfishly, but not that a person who actually acted selfishly could have refrained from doing so, given the circumstances as they were. But the claim that an agent is morally responsible for her conduct seems to turn on the latter sort of claim, and therefore to require that we define the possibilities available to an individual relative to her actual situation, and not in abstraction from factors, like the causes of her choice, which seem obviously relevant to an understanding of how she came to act as she did.

Compatibilists must therefore explain why the conception of possibility which is relevant to freedom of the will should define our possibilities in abstraction from any information at all; why it should abstract, in particular, from information about the course of our deliberation and the outcome of our choices, but not from information about any other kind of event; and why we should regard a conception of possibility which does abstract from such information as relevant to our moral evaluation of persons. If compatibilists cannot answer these questions, libertarians will rightly reject their views. In what follows I will argue that the distinction between theoretical and practical reason allows us to answer these questions.

THEORETICAL POSSIBILITIES

Possibility *tout court* is central to theoretical reasoning. The aim of theoretical reasoning is to describe the world, and to explain the events which occur in it. Ideally, in explaining events it aims to provide a unified and systematic general explanation which would show all events to be either necessary or not susceptible to further explanation. To use that account to explain some particular event would be to show that event to be either the only event which could possibly have occurred, given all relevant natural laws and causes; or one of several such events which a complete specification of those laws and causes leaves open. To explain the behavior of any object, therefore, is to narrow our conception of the possibilities open to it as far as we can—that is, until we reach its possibilities *tout court*.

By contrast, the claim that an agent would have performed some action had she chosen to do so has no particular importance from a theoretical point of view. What would have happened had some condition obtained does not figure in an explanation of what happened when that condition did not obtain—though it might be indirectly relevant if, for instance, the agent's awareness of the fact that she would have performed certain actions had she chosen to do so was among the considerations which led her to act as she did. It is true that any number of actions might have been possible for her in the compatibilists' general sense, but this fact has, from a theoretical point of view, no particular significance.

Nor, from a theoretical point of view, can we explain the importance of the compatibilist conception of possibility by appealing to the idea that choices have some special significance. If mechanism is true, then our actions can be explained in the same terms as other natural events; and, qua cause, nothing sets our choices apart from the other natural events which might figure in such an explanation. For this reason, the claim that the distinction between those acts which depend on our choices and those which do not is more important or fundamental than the distinction between those events which depend on any other type of natural event and those which do not is, from a theoretical point of view, unfounded.

From a theoretical point of view, human actions are events to be described and explained. The whole point of the attempt to describe and explain events is to move from a general conception of the possibilities available to some object to an understanding of the causes which led that object to behave as it did; to specify the causes of its behavior more and more fully until that behavior can be seen to be either necessary or not susceptible to further explanation. From this point of view, compatibilists' insistence that we should define the possibilities available to us as those actions which we would perform if we chose will seem to reflect at best an unmotivated decision to disregard information which is clearly relevant to an explanation of her actions, and at worst a kind of willful blindness. For, from a theoretical point of view, there is no reason not to specify the causes of an agent's behavior fully, or to conclude our inquiries before we understand what caused her to act as she did.

PRACTICAL ALTERNATIVES

When we engage in practical reasoning, our purpose is not to explain what caused some event to occur, but to determine which of the actions available to us we have most reason to perform. Like theoretical reasoning, practical reasoning seeks in a sense to demonstrate the necessity of certain actions. But whereas theoretical reasoning seeks to show that some action which actually occurred was physically necessary in view of antecedent events and natural laws, practical reasoning seeks to determine which of the actions available to us is rationally required in view of our grounds for choice and the principles by which we govern our conduct.

Because the aims of theoretical and practical reasoning differ in this way, they require conceptions of possibility to serve different functions. Both the compatibilists' general conception of possibility and the libertarian possibility *tout court* are conceptions of physical possibility. They specify which events are possible for some object given some (more or less completely described) set of antecedent events and natural laws. As I have argued, one aim of theoretical reasoning is to narrow our conception of the physical possibilities available to some object until we can see that its behavior was either required by physical laws or not susceptible of further explanation. For this reason, the aim of theoretical reasoning itself requires that we employ a conception of physical possibility; and that this conception be the narrowest available to us, namely possibility *tout court*.[11] But because practical reasoning does not itself attempt to answer the question which of the alternatives available to us is physically possible or necessary, the aim of practical reasoning is not to determine whether or not any action is possible in either of the senses discussed above; and neither of those two conceptions of possibility can play in our practical reasoning a role analogous to that which possibility *tout court* plays in our theoretical reasoning. Instead, practical reasoning requires that we employ a conception of physical possibility in order to determine whether or not some action counts as one of our

---

[11] I do not mean to suggest that possibility *tout court* is the only conception of possibility which plays any role in theoretical reasoning, or that our attempts to describe and explain the world will never give us any reason to attend to the question what some object could, in any general sense, have done. My point is rather that the attempt to discover what it was possible *tout court* for some object to have done is itself one of the goals of theoretical reasoning, and that no conception of physical possibility plays an analogous role in practical reasoning.

alternatives at all: to define the set of alternatives among which we can choose.

In order to arrive at a decision about what to do, I must choose among some set of courses of action which I regard as my alternatives. This set will presumably not include all the courses of action which, in the least restrictive sense, I could conceivably perform. For instance, I might reject some courses of action out of hand as obviously undesirable or beneath consideration. To reject a course of action as clearly undesirable is to reject it on practical grounds. Since I must determine which actions I can rule out on these grounds by engaging in practical reasoning, I do not require such an account in order to engage in practical reasoning at all.

While practical reasoning does not itself require an account of which courses of action an agent regards as obviously undesirable, however, it does require some account of those other criteria, if any, which a proposed course of action must meet if she can legitimately consider it to be among her alternatives. We might conclude that there are no such criteria: that any action we can imagine can be counted among our alternatives. This would constitute an account of what must be true of some proposed course of action if it can be counted among our alternatives: namely, nothing. But we cannot dismiss the demand for such an account altogether. For without some conception of which proposed courses of action we can legitimately regard as alternatives and which we cannot, we would be unable to determine which courses of action we can legitimately regard as possible objects of choice.[12]

One criterion, clearly, is this: I can consider an action to be among my alternatives only if I do not know that it is impossible for me to perform that action. For if I know that I cannot possibly perform that action, then I need not ask myself whether or not I should perform it.[13] However, it is not sufficient to rule out those actions which I know that I cannot perform. For I can be wrong about which alternatives I have. I believe that I could go to a movie right now; but perhaps if I did decide to do so I would discover that my house has been encased in lucite. In this case, I would be wrong to think that going out to see a movie is a genuine alternative for me; had I known

---

[12] To say that an action is an alternative in this sense does not imply that it is an alternative that one should seriously consider, or even that it is an alternative to which one should give a moment's thought. While, as Susan Wolf suggests ("Asymmetrical Freedom", *Journal of Philosophy*, 67 (1980), 152–3), an agent might have to be crazy or immoral to regard abhorrent actions as alternatives worth considering, she would not have to be crazy or immoral to regard such actions as alternatives in the sense I discuss here, any more than she would have to be mathematically inept to claim that '1000' is a possible answer to the question 'What is 2 + 2?', while 'Blue' is not.

[13] I might consider trying to perform some action even though I know I will not succeed; but in this case the alternative which I consider is making a futile effort, not performing an impossible action.

that my house was encased in lucite, I would not have regarded it as one. If the criteria which an action must meet if it is to be counted among my alternatives are to accommodate the fact that I can be wrong about which alternatives I have, they cannot exclude only those actions which I know that I cannot perform. They must hold that it must really be possible, in some sense, for me to perform an action if I am to count it among my alternatives.

But while we cannot define our alternatives in terms of what we actually know or believe to be possible, the criteria that we use to define our alternatives must allow us, in principle, to know what it is possible, in the relevant sense, for us to do, and to know this while we deliberate. For the account of our alternatives which is currently under consideration is supposed to allow us to determine, while we deliberate, whether or not we can consider some course of action as one of the alternatives among which we can choose. Therefore, while our account of the criteria by which we decide whether or not some act should count as an alternative must allow for the possibility that we might apply them wrongly, they should not be such that the question whether or not some action counts as an alternative is in principle unanswerable from a practical point of view.

For this reason, the conception of possibility which we use to define our alternatives for the purposes of deliberation must define our possibilities relative to only those facts which we could conceivably know to be true while we deliberate. In the cases of error described above, I was wrong about which alternatives I had because I was ignorant of some fact that I might have known. In order for some course of action to count as one of my alternatives, it must be a course of action that I would regard as possible even if all such mistakes had been corrected, and all the relevant lacunae in my knowledge filled. But if there is some type of information that is in principle inaccessible to an agent engaged in deliberation, then we cannot define the alternatives available to a given agent as those which are possible relative to a description of her situation which includes information of that kind. For to define our alternatives in terms of such a conception of possibility would make it impossible in principle for any agent engaged in deliberation to know which proposed courses of action she could legitimately count among her alternatives. If a proposed course of action is to count among our alternatives, therefore, it must be possible for all we could conceivably know while we deliberate.

This raises the question: can we know what we will choose to do while we deliberate? Normally, when we predict what we will do, our predictions do not threaten either our need to deliberate or our reasons for regarding our alternatives as those actions we would perform if we chose. For instance, I am virtually certain that I will get out of bed tomorrow morning. But I predict that I will get out of bed tomorrow only because I am confident that I will in fact want to get out of bed tomorrow, and that this will be within my power. If, later this evening, I discover a revolutionary moral theory based on the idea that sloth is the ultimate human virtue, I will not think that my earlier prediction implies that I will be unable to live up to my new principles; if I am struck by a crippling attack of polio during the night, I will hardly be comforted by the thought that, according to that prediction, I will almost certainly get out of bed in the morning. I made that prediction because I assumed both that I would want to get out of bed tomorrow morning and that I would be able to; if, between the time when I made that prediction and the next morning, either of those assumptions turns out to be false, I no longer have reason to accept it. Among the ways in which I can falsify the assumptions on which it is based is to change my mind as the result of practical reasoning. For this reason, if I do decide to deliberate about whether or not to get out of bed tomorrow morning, I call my earlier prediction that I will get out of bed into question, and therefore it cannot give me reason not to count other courses of action among my alternatives.

The kinds of predictions which determinism seems to imply that we could make pose a threat of a different order. Those predictions are based on knowledge of the state of the world at a given time, and of the physical laws which govern it. If that time is, say, the time at which I make the prediction, the description of the state of the world at that time will include a description of my present views on the desirability of getting out of bed tomorrow morning. But the force of that prediction will depend not on my continuing to hold those views, but on my having held them at the time I made the prediction. There is therefore no way for me to deprive this prediction of its force by exercising my practical reason. If it were possible for me to predict what I will decide to do in this way, therefore, I might have reason to conclude that my only real alternatives are those actions that it is possible *tout court* for me to perform.

I will not dispute the claim that determinism implies that other people could in principle predict my actions with complete certainty on the basis of their knowledge of the state of the world at a given time, and of physical laws. But I will argue that I cannot predict my own actions in this way; and that others can do so only if their predictions do not themselves influence the process whereby I come to act as I do.[14]

[14] The argument that follows is similar to one made by Gilbert Ryle in *The Concept of Mind* (New York: Barnes and Noble Books, 1949), 195–8; by Karl Popper in "Indeterminism in Quantum Physics and in Classical Physics", *British Journal of the Philosophy of Science*, 1 (1951), 179–88; and by D. M. MacKay in "On the Logical Indeterminacy of a Free Choice", *Mind*, 69 (1960), 31–40.

Imagine that I have acquired the Pocket Oracle, a tiny yet unimaginably powerful computer which has been perfectly programmed to predict my behavior. If it does not show me its predictions, it will always know what I am about to do (or think, or choose). If it follows (so to speak) a step behind me, telling me at each instant what I have just thought or done, or if it keeps pace with me exactly, what it tells me will always be right—in either case, it might be considered a mechanical analog of my consciousness of myself. In none of these cases, obviously, will it threaten my practical reasoning.

If, however, the Pocket Oracle tries to tell me in advance what I am going to do or think or choose, it will run into problems. For in order to figure out what I am going to do, it must factor into its calculations all of the stimuli I receive, since these may be among the causes which lead me to act or choose as I do. And if it plans to tell me what I am about to do or choose, the information it gives me will be among the things it has to take into account. The Pocket Oracle, that is, must factor the result of its calculations into its calculations in order to arrive at a result; and it would have to know what that result was before arriving at it in order to do so.

Clearly, the best strategy for our Pocket Oracle would be to calculate the results of its telling me every prediction it could possibly make. For if there is some action which I will perform regardless of what the Pocket Oracle tells me I will do, then it can avoid an infinite regress, since it does not need to factor the result of its calculations into those calculations in order to arrive at a result.[15] Only if the Pocket Oracle concludes that all of its possible predictions converge on a single action will it be able to tell me what I am going to do; and only if it tells me what I am going to do can it make it unnecessary for me to engage in practical reasoning.

I might respond to any prediction the Pocket Oracle made by deciding to do something entirely different—perhaps I hate the idea of being so predictable, or perhaps I am simply perverse. Alternately, I might just do whatever it told me to do, perhaps on the grounds that, since an infallible oracle has told me that I will do this, I should resign myself to the inevitable. In either case, the Pocket Oracle would know what I would do if it predicted that I would choose heads and what I would do if it predicted that I would choose tails. But because, in both cases, what I do depends on what prediction it makes, these different predictions would not converge on a single action, and the Pocket Oracle would be unable to make any prediction at all.

---

[15] I leave aside the question how the Pocket Oracle could do this—while I can consider only a finite number of possible actions, the Pocket Oracle will have to consider everything which (in an everyday sense) I could possibly do, since the set of actions I will consider will presumably include the action which it predicts that I will perform. I will assume that only two actions—"heads" and "tails"—are available to me.

If what I do does not depend on what the Pocket Oracle predicts, however, its possible predictions will converge on a single action, and it will therefore be in a position to tell me what I am about to do. My future course of action might be independent of its predictions for several reasons. First, my future course of action might not be up to me at all. As Dennett observes, "there are genuine instances of what we might call *local fatalism* . . . Consider the man who has thrown himself off the Golden Gate Bridge and who thinks to himself, as he plummets, 'I wonder if this is really such a good idea.' Deliberation has indeed become impotent for this man. We can plot his future destination without bothering to factor in his intervening efforts at problem-solving; whatever they are, they will not yield a causal chain that will deflect him from the trajectory we have already plotted for him."[16] In such cases the predictions of the Pocket Oracle do not threaten my practical reasoning: it can predict my future behavior only because my practical reasoning is already completely irrelevant to it.

Second, I might simply not care what the Pocket Oracle tells me I am about to do. I am going to make up my own mind, thank you very much, and it can tell me whatever it pleases without affecting my decision in any way.[17] It would, of course, be very difficult for me to go on deliberating as usual if a Pocket Oracle which I knew to be infallible had just told me what I was about to decide to do.[18] But only when I succeed in ignoring its predictions can the Pocket Oracle predict my actions. In such cases those predictions cannot displace my practical reasoning—the moment I begin to do what the Pocket Oracle tells me I will do instead of deciding for myself is the moment it falls silent.

Third, I might be about to be subjected to some temptation which will cause me to perform one particular course of action regardless of what the Pocket Oracle tells me I will do. If, for instance, I were an alcoholic trying to

---

[16] Dennett, *Elbow Room*, 104.

[17] Obviously, it is not enough that I tell myself that the Pocket Oracle's predictions will have no effect on my decision; they must actually have no effect in order for the Pocket Oracle to be able to inform me of its prediction.

[18] One might think that it would be not just difficult, but impossible, for me to deliberate in these circumstances; that "(d)eliberating in the conviction that one will reach a certain decision is as impossible as trying to remember where one left his car keys in the conviction that one will conclude that they are in his overcoat." (David Perry, "Prediction, Explanation, and Freedom", *Monist*, 49/2 (1965), 239). It is certainly more plausible to think that, in the case at hand, I am simply refusing to listen to the Pocket Oracle than to imagine me attending to it, fully accepting the knowledge that the result of my deliberations will be x, and nonetheless deliberating as I would have done had the Pocket Oracle told me nothing. But I do not need to decide this issue for the purposes of my argument. If genuine deliberation is impossible when I know what I am about to do, then the Pocket Oracle cannot tell me what I am about to do in these cases; if it is possible, then it can tell me what I am about to do only when my knowledge of its predictions does not affect the course of my deliberations. In neither case can the prediction displace my practical reasoning.

give up drinking, the Pocket Oracle might be able to predict that, whatever it tells me, I will eventually find my way back to my neighborhood bar. This might happen for either of two reasons. It might be that the temptation to drink is simply too much for me: I do not now have the strength of will I would need to resist it, whatever virtuous resolutions I might make. It seems natural to describe such cases as cases of internal coercion: as in cases of local fatalism, my practical reasoning is not effective, and it is only because it is not effective that the Pocket Oracle can tell me what I am going to do. The Pocket Oracle's predictions should, therefore, be seen not as displacing my practical reasoning, but as informing me of the fact that my deliberation will, in this case, be useless.[19]

Alternately, it might be because the Pocket Oracle tells me *something* that I will end up starting to drink again. Were the Pocket Oracle to inform me that I would eventually start drinking again, I would decide to spare myself the (as I now realize) futile effort to remain sober; were it to tell me that I would stay sober, I would become complacent, fail to guard myself against temptations which I "knew" would not sway me, and eventually succumb. In this case, the Pocket Oracle can predict the results of my deliberation—not, however, because it simply *knows* what I will do, but because, given any intervention in my decision-making process, I will succumb to a temptation I might otherwise have resisted.

The Pocket Oracle's predictions have this effect because I make two assumptions. The first is that the Pocket Oracle's predictions are accurate— that I will in fact do what it says I will do. The second is that once the Pocket Oracle has predicted that I will do something, I no longer need to try to do what it has told me I will do. By definition, anything the Pocket Oracle tells me about my future is accurate; and therefore my first assumption is legitimate. It might also be rational, on these grounds, for me to stop trying to do something once the Pocket Oracle has told me that I will do something else. But it is not rational for me to stop trying to do something on the grounds that the Pocket Oracle has told me that I will do it, since it might be precisely because of my efforts that I will make that prediction come true. To think

---

[19] One might reject the idea that such cases should be characterized as 'internal coercion'. Being swept along by a flood of desire is different from being swept along by a flood of *water*: in the latter case the agent is literally helpless, while in the former (one might argue) the problem is not that she cannot choose to go against her desire, but that she does not choose to do so. (See, for instance, Kadri Vihvelin, "Stop Me Before I Kill Again", *Philosophical Studies*, 75 (1994), 115–48.) But I do not need to resolve this issue for the purposes of this argument. If an agent's actions are not up to her, then her situation is an instance of 'local fatalism'. If they are up to her, then she can learn what she is going to do because her decision will not be affected by her knowledge of this prediction. On either account, her situation can be assimilated to one of the two types of cases in which I have argued that our knowledge of some prediction concerning our future behavior cannot displace our practical reasoning.

that once the Pocket Oracle has told me that I will stay sober I need no longer try to do so is as irrational as deciding, when it tells me that my dinner will be cooked in an hour, that I can save money by not turning the stove on.

It is this second assumption which allows the Pocket Oracle to predict my actions in this group of cases. For if I did not react to the prediction that I would stay sober by abandoning my efforts to do so, then my efforts might well have made that prediction come true. If my efforts would have been unsuccessful then, as I argued above, we should view the case in question as one involving internal coercion. But if they would have succeeded, then the Pocket Oracle would not have been able to arrive at a prediction had it not known that I would respond to its prediction by abandoning them.

In this last group of cases, my actions are predictable because I have mistakenly identified determinism, which implies that my behavior is in principle predictable, with fatalism, which holds that there is some fate which will befall me whether I try to bring it about or to avoid it. It should not surprise us that the actions of a fatalist can be publicly predicted in situations where the actions of others cannot. To the extent that we abdicate either our power to decide for ourselves what we will do or our efforts to translate these decisions into action, we allow our behavior to be determined either by habit, by convenience, or by some external cause which determines our actions directly, rather than through our decisions. In so doing we allow the Pocket Oracle to avoid the problems posed by the effects of its predictions on our practical reasoning. But in such cases it is not the predictability of our behavior which threatens our need to determine our own actions through practical reasoning, but the fact that we have already chosen not to exercise this power which allows us to learn in advance what we will do.

If an agent does not confuse determinism with fatalism, or in some other way abdicate her power to choose her own conduct, then she can predict her own future behavior, or learn of such predictions from others, only when her knowledge of the outcome of her choice would not affect the course of her deliberation, or when her behavior does not depend on her choice. In the first case, since the agent can know which action is her only possibility *tout court* only if she would deliberate and choose exactly as she would have done had she not known what she would choose to do, the possibilities among which she must choose will be those among which she would have chosen had she not known which course of action she would choose. Whichever conception of possibility is relevant to the practical reasoning of an agent who does not know which course of action she will in fact choose to perform is the conception relevant to the practical reasoning of an agent who does know which action she will choose to perform, but on whose deliberation this knowledge has no effect. An agent whose behavior is entirely determined by factors other than her choice will have no reason to engage in practical reasoning at all; in any case, once she has correctly identified the set of actions which she would perform if she chose to, and has determined that that set has only one member, her conception of the possibilities available to her can hardly be criticized on the grounds that it is insufficiently narrow, nor will the statement that she has only one possibility *tout court* tell her anything she does not already know.

In all other cases, an agent cannot predict what she will choose to do, or learn of such predictions from others. But if it is in principle impossible for an agent to know, before making a choice, what she will choose to do, then no conceivable correction of her beliefs could allow her to narrow the set of actions which she regards as alternatives beyond those which she would perform if she chose to perform them. Because, while she deliberates, it is impossible in principle for her to predict the outcome of her choice, those actions are possible for all she could conceivably know. For this reason, the conception of our possibilities which we use to define the alternatives among which we can choose must be the compatibilists' general conception of possibility, rather than the narrower possibility *tout court*.

Libertarians argue that because, while I deliberate, conditions exist which will cause me to make some particular choice, the compatibilists' general conception of my possibilities is insufficiently narrow. They claim that, if determinism is true, only that action which I will in fact perform is a possibility *tout court* for me; and that that action is therefore my only genuine alternative. But to use the word 'alternative' in this sense renders it useless for the purposes of deliberation. While I deliberate I can, of course, believe that determinism is true; and therefore that I have only one possibility *tout court*. If I believe that the truth or falsity of determinism itself gives me reason to choose one or another of the alternatives available to me, then the claim that determinism is true or false will figure among my grounds for choice, and will be in that sense relevant to my practical reasoning. But my beliefs about the truth or falsity of determinism will not affect my conception of which alternatives I have. For in order to narrow my conception of the alternatives available to me to that one action which it is possible *tout court* for me to perform, I would have to know, while deliberating, which action that was; and to know this, I would have to be able to predict which action I would choose to perform. Because I cannot predict the outcome of my choices, I cannot know, while I deliberate, which of the actions which I would perform if I chose is possible *tout court*. Therefore, the belief that there is at any given time only one course of action which it is possible *tout court* for me to perform cannot lead me to conclude that any particular course of action is or is not among my alternatives. Whether or not I believe that determinism is true, I must choose among those actions which are possible for all I could conceivably know while I deliberate. Unless the belief that determinism is true figures among my grounds for choice it is, for practical purposes, empty.

Consider as an illustration Sartre's example of a young man torn between joining the Free French and caring for his aging mother.[20] Imagine that an incompatibilist, to whom he had described his dilemma, were to say to him: Although you may not realize it, you have only one genuine alternative. The young man begs for clarification: have the Allies invaded Berlin, ensuring the Nazis' defeat? Has his mother found someone else to care for her? Is this perhaps a particularly insensitive way of telling him that his mother has died? No, the incompatibilist replies: I mean that, because determinism is true, conditions now exist which ensure that you will choose one of those alternatives, and which entirely preclude your choosing the other.

Well, the young man might ask, which alternative *is* it inevitable that I choose? At this point, the incompatibilist would have to confess that, alas, she did not know which choice the young man would make; which of his alternatives was the genuine one, and which the spurious. If she were willing to try the young man's patience further, she might go on to explain why she would not be able to tell him which choice he would make even if she had an infallible Pocket Oracle. At the end of this recitation Sartre's young man might shrug his shoulders and say: If I were trying to decide what line to take in my work on causality, or to make some other decision in which the truth or falsity of determinism might figure among my grounds for choice, then this discussion would have helped me to see what decision I have most reason to make. And if the truth of determinism allowed me to eliminate all but one of my apparent alternatives from consideration, then it would have relieved me of the need to deliberate at all. But the truth of determinism gives me no reason to abandon either my mother or my country; and as for my 'alternatives', it implies only that whichever choice I make will have been the only choice that I could possibly have made. I don't know which choice that is; and your arguments imply that I cannot possibly know which of my alternatives you would call my only real possibility until I have already chosen one of them. So I am left with exactly the same decision, to be made among exactly the same alternatives, whether or not determinism is true. And now, if you will excuse me, I'll try to make it.

[20] Jean-Paul Sartre, "The Humanism of Existentialism", in Wade Baskin (ed.), *Sartre: Essays in Existentialism* (Secaucus, NJ: Citadel Press, 1965), 42–3.

ARE OUR ALTERNATIVES GENUINE?

I have argued that we cannot narrow our conception of our alternatives beyond the set of actions which we would perform if we chose since, when we deliberate, we either cannot know which action we will in fact choose to perform or cannot use that knowledge in making our choice. However, one might think that this claim does not imply that we have reason to regard all the actions which we could perform if we chose to do so as genuine alternatives. For it might be that to deliberate among various courses of action also requires that we believe those actions to be possible *tout court*. In this case, our conception of an alternative would have to meet two conditions. First, it would have to allow us to identify our alternatives while we deliberate; and thus, for the reasons given above, it could not restrict our alternatives beyond those actions which we would perform if we chose. Second, no action could count as one of our alternatives unless it were possible *tout court* for us to perform it. These conditions could not be jointly satisfied unless it were possible *tout court* for us to perform all those actions which we would perform if we chose; and thus they could not be jointly satisfied unless determinism were false. If deliberation requires that we regard our actions as possible *tout court*, then my arguments in the last section imply not that we have reason to regard those actions which we would perform if we chose as genuine alternatives, but that we cannot formulate a coherent conception of an alternative which meets the requirements of practical reasoning unless determinism is false.

Peter van Inwagen has argued on these grounds that a belief in determinism, if taken seriously, would make it impossible for us to deliberate.[21] Van Inwagen argues that deliberation "manifests" a belief that it is possible *tout court* for the agent to perform her various alternatives, since one cannot deliberate about whether or not to perform some course of action unless one believes it to be possible *tout court*. Determinism implies that only one such action is possible *tout court*, and therefore a determinist cannot believe that all of her supposed alternatives are in fact possible *tout court*. Since deliberation manifests the belief that one's alternatives are possible *tout court*, a determinist who deliberates thereby shows that she has inconsistent beliefs. On van Inwagen's view, determinists who recognize these facts must therefore either give up their belief in determinism, learn to live with the fact that they have beliefs that they know to be inconsistent, or give up on deliberation altogether (in which case van Inwagen claims that they will

---

[21] Van Inwagen, *An Essay on Free Will*, 153–61.

either "move about in random jerks and scuttles, or . . . withdraw into catatonia".[22])

The crucial step in van Inwagen's argument is the move from the uncontroversial claim that we cannot deliberate about whether or not to perform some action which we know that we cannot possibly perform, to the claim that we cannot deliberate about whether or not to perform some action unless we believe it to be possible *tout court*. Van Inwagen supports this move as follows: "Anyone who doubts that this is indeed the case may find it instructive to imagine that he is in a room with two doors and that he believes one of the doors to be unlocked and the other to be locked and impassable, though he has no idea which is which; let him then attempt to imagine himself deliberating about which door to leave by."[23]

Deliberation is the attempt to determine what one should do. If, in the situation van Inwagen describes, I were in any doubt about what to do, I might reasonably deliberate about whether or not I should try to leave the room at all, whether (if so) I should opt for a graceful exit through the unlocked door or try to scratch through the walls with my fingernails, and (if the former) how I should ascertain which door is unlocked. Deliberation is a perfectly good way of answering any of these questions. But, assuming that I do want to leave through a door, deliberation is not a good way to figure out which door to leave by. If I knew only that one of the two doors was locked, there might still be room for deliberation about which door to leave by: I might conceivably decide to try to smash through the locked door with my head, or to pick its lock with a hairpin. But if I know that one door is not only locked but impassable, I know that I cannot leave through it by any means; and therefore I cannot regard leaving through the locked door even as an undesirable alternative.

If I do want to leave the room through a door, then I must leave it through the door that is unlocked. And while there are some things about which I might reasonably deliberate in this situation, which door is unlocked is not one of them. When we deliberate, we try to answer the question 'What should I do?'. Under normal circumstances, the answer to this question is not, and does not imply, an answer to the question 'Which door is unlocked?', or to questions about any other matter of fact which is independent of my will. For this reason, deliberation is not a means of answering that question, any more than it is a means of discovering the precise value of the gravitational constant or the date of Dante's exile from Florence. Moreover, in the situation van Inwagen describes I have a perfectly

---

[22] Van Inwagen, *An Essay on Free Will*, 157.

[23] Ibid., 154.

good way of figuring out which door is unlocked: namely, to try the door-knobs and see. Because this is such an obvious way of discovering which door is unlocked, and because deliberation is not a way of doing so at all, deliberating about which door to leave by in the situation van Inwagen describes would, as he suggests, be absurd.

However, our ordinary choices are disanalogous to the situation van Inwagen describes in both respects. First of all, as I have argued, while we deliberate we cannot discover which of our alternatives is possible *tout court*; we cannot simply try the doorknobs and see. Second, in the situation van Inwagen describes, the question which door is unlocked is independent of my decision which door to leave through; and it is for this reason that delib-eration cannot help us to answer it. One door is locked; the other is not; and which door I choose to exit by has nothing to do with which is which. But when I face a choice among several courses of action which I would perform if I chose to, then which course of action is possible *tout court* depends on which I choose to perform; and any of those actions would be possible *tout court* if I chose to perform it.

Instead of imagining that I am in the situation van Inwagen describes, we should instead imagine that I am in a room with two doors, one of which is locked and one of which is unlocked; that I do not know which is which; but that I do know that the locks are set up in such a way that as soon as I choose to try to open one door, that door will unlock, and the door which I have not chosen will lock. We should also imagine that these doors do not open onto the same hallway. Perhaps one opens onto a Tahitian beach and the other into downtown Manhattan; in any case, imagine that I know which door opens onto which prospect. Would it be irrational to deliberate in *this* situ-ation? I cannot just try the doors and see which is unlocked, since I would have to try one before the other, thereby causing one to open and the other to lock. While it is true that one door is (now) locked and one unlocked, it is impossible for me to discover which is which without altering the conditions about which I seek to learn. Moreover, I have no reason to try to answer the question which door is now locked and which is unlocked. Since I can cause whichever door I wish to open, the question which is now unlocked has nothing to do with which door I actually leave by; and it can only be of academic interest to me.

In this situation, if I do not wish to remain in the room needlessly, I must somehow select one door to try to leave through. If I decide not to resolve this question through deliberation, I will have to select one door at random, or flip a coin, or find some other way of determining which door I will cause to become unlocked. Since I can leave through whichever door I want, and since the question which door I choose to try first will determine whether I find myself in Manhattan or Tahiti, it is unclear why I should not simply decide which door to leave by and act on my choice; why I should allow my future to be decided by the toss of a coin and not by my preferences or my practical principles. And if I could reasonably deliberate in this situation, despite my knowledge that at any given time only one door is unlocked, it is unclear why we should think that my deliberation must manifest the belief that both doors are unlocked.

Van Inwagen might object that the situation I have just described is not strictly analogous to our ordinary situations as determinists understand them. The most natural way to understand that situation is to suppose that the doorknobs are sensitive to my touch; and thus that my touching either doorknob causes that doorknob to unlock, and the other to lock. But in this case the fact that only one door is unlocked does not imply that it could not be possible *tout court* for me to leave through either door. For if my decision about which door to try to leave by were itself undetermined, and if that decision caused the door I chose to leave by to become unlocked, then it would be possible *tout court* for me to leave through either door. For this reason the fact that I can coherently deliberate in the situation I described above might not constitute a counterexample to his claim that we can coherently deliberate only when we believe our alternatives to be possible *tout court*.

Whether or not this objection succeeds depends on whether or not my reasons for supposing that it makes sense for me to deliberate in the situation I have described have anything to do with the question whether or not my choice is determined. They do not. It makes sense for me to deliberate in the situation just described for the following reasons: first, there are several actions which I would perform if I chose; second, which of those actions I end up performing is not a matter of complete indifference to me; third, if I ask myself which action to perform, I can try to figure out which action I think I have most reason to perform, choose to perform it, and act on my decision; fourth, no other means of selecting among those alternatives will reliably lead me to perform that action which I think I have most reason to perform. Whether or not these conditions obtain in any given case has nothing to do with the truth or falsity of determinism.[24]

---

[24] One might object that to take the question whether or not we can coherently deliberate if determinism is true to turn on the question whether or not we have reason to do so begs the question, since in so doing we must assume that it makes sense to ask whether we have reason to deliberate. If we cannot coherently engage in practical reasoning if determinism is true, then determinism implies that we cannot coherently ask ourselves whether or not we have reason to do anything, and thus a fortiori we cannot coherently ask ourselves what reason we have to deliberate. I have construed the question whether or not deliberation 'manifests' the belief that determinism

For this reason I conclude that deliberation does not, as van Inwagen suggests, manifest a belief that it is possible *tout court* for us to perform our various alternatives. Rather, it manifests a belief that we would perform any of those alternatives if we chose to do so. If this conclusion is correct, then determinism does not imply the impossibility of constructing a coherent conception of an alternative which meets the requirements of practical reasoning. Rather, practical reasoning requires that we regard all those actions which we would perform if we chose to perform them as our alternatives, and does not require that we believe those alternatives to be possible *tout court*. We can therefore regard ourselves as choosing among alternatives whether or not determinism is true.

DOES OUR BELIEF THAT WE CHOOSE AMONG ALTERNATIVES REFLECT ONLY OUR EPISTEMIC LIMITATIONS?

I have argued that because, while we deliberate, we either cannot know what we will choose to do or cannot use that knowledge, we cannot narrow our conception of our alternatives beyond those actions which we would perform if we chose; and therefore that no narrower conception of our alternatives can be relevant to practical reasoning. Because this argument shows only that no narrower conception of our alternatives is available to us while

is false in this way because I cannot see how else to construe it. Van Inwagen seems to think that it is unintelligible to deliberate if one believes in the truth of determinism. I have assumed that the clearest way of showing someone's conduct to be intelligible is to show it to be reasonable, given her beliefs; and have tried to argue that it is in this sense intelligible for a determinist to deliberate. It is unclear to me whether, in his discussion of this point, van Inwagen means to admit that we can ask whether a determinist's conduct is reasonable, and to deny that it is; or to deny that it makes sense to apply terms like 'reasonable' to a determinist's conduct at all. But on either construction, van Inwagen has not established his point.

If van Inwagen means to admit the possibility that we can describe the determinist's deliberation as reasonable or unreasonable, and to argue that it is unreasonable, then the arguments given above show that he is wrong. On the other hand, if van Inwagen were to object that I have begged the question in supposing that a determinist's conduct could ever be reasonable, given her beliefs, he must assume that a determinist's conduct must always be unintelligible, since her beliefs prevent us from assessing her conduct in the terms we use to determine the intelligibility of human action; and, in particular, from regarding her conduct either as reasonable or as unreasonable given her beliefs. This is a more substantial claim than van Inwagen seems to be making; and establishing its truth would require far more in the way of argument than his appeal to the example discussed above provides. In particular, it would require some explanation of why a determinist who had some conception of the kinds of actions she preferred to perform, and the kind of life she wished to lead, could not coherently ask which of the actions which she would perform if she chose to perform them her standards gave her most reason to perform; and of why, if she did try to decide among those actions, she could not coherently be described as deliberating, and as doing so for good reasons.

we deliberate, it might seem to show only that we must use this conception *faute de mieux*: that while ideally we might hope to narrow our conception of our alternatives to our possibilities *tout court*, our epistemic limitations prevent us from doing so, and thereby force us to settle for the broader compatibilist conception.

In fact, I believe that when we engage in practical reasoning it is not only unavoidable but rational to regard our alternatives as those actions which we would perform if we chose to do so since, for the purposes of deliberation, we have no reason to regard the various actions which we would perform if we chose as differing with respect to their possibility. When I deliberate, I evaluate the various alternatives available to me. I ask myself what would happen if I made one choice rather than another, and what reason I have to bring about the various states of affairs which would result from my choosing one alternative rather than another. In weighing my alternatives I take into account the effects of those choices; and while I must believe that each of the states of affairs I envision is consistent with my general beliefs about the way the world works, and that it would in fact occur were I to make the choice whose effect I take it to be, I need not believe that all of these states of the world could be simultaneously realized. If I choose to perform any action which I would perform if I chose it, then I will perform that action, and it will therefore be possible *tout court*. When I consider the respective merits of the states of affairs which would result from the various choices I might make, then if the actions among which I choose are actions which I would perform if I chose, I consider states of the world in which those actions are possible *tout court*. For the purposes of deliberation, therefore, I can regard all those alternatives as possible *tout court*, since each would be possible *tout court* were I to choose it; without thereby contradicting my belief that only one of them is in fact possible *tout court*.

When we deliberate, we take the question what we will in fact choose to do to be open—not because we believe the outcome of our choice to be physically undetermined, but because we regard the question what we will in fact choose to do as one whose answer depends on us, and which we have yet to answer. And we are right to regard it thus: since, when we engage in practical reasoning, we try to decide what to do, when we engage in practical reasoning we must regard the question what we will choose to do as one we have yet to resolve. Because we take the question what we will choose to do to be open, for the purposes of deliberation we regard all those actions which we would perform if we chose as genuine alternatives for us. And we are right to regard them thus: to say that we would perform some action if we chose is (trivially) to say that, if we chose, then we would perform it; and therefore if we regard the question what we will choose as open, we should regard all these actions as possible.

In the case discussed above, for instance, the fact that at any given time only one door is unlocked is irrelevant for the purposes of my deliberation. Because either door will become unlocked as soon as I choose it, I can regard my alternatives as 'leaving through the door on the left' and 'leaving through the door on the right', despite the fact that there is, at any given time, only one unlocked door through which I can leave. I can, that is, regard myself as having to choose between leaving through either of the two doors, without thereby contradicting my belief that only one door is in fact unlocked at any given time.

Similarly, when I try to decide what to do, I may believe that only one of my alternatives is possible *tout court*. But because which of the courses of action that I would perform if I chose is possible *tout court* depends on which course of action I choose to perform, any of those courses of action will be possible *tout court* if I choose to perform it. Since, while I deliberate, I must regard the question which of my alternatives I will choose to perform as open, for the purposes of deliberation I should not regard those alternatives as differing with respect to their possibility. Any of them will be possible *tout court* if I choose to perform it, and impossible *tout court* if I do not. Nothing prevents me from performing any of those actions which I would perform if I chose except my choosing to do something else.[25]

Still, a libertarian might say, in most cases that obstacle is insuperable, since there is in fact only one choice which we could possibly make. Again, I do not wish to deny that this is true,[26] but to insist on its irrelevance to practical reasoning. As I have said, when we deliberate we take the question what we will choose to do to be open, a question to be answered. In answering it, we ask not which action we will in fact perform, but which action we have reason to perform. We search not for the causes of an event whose nature is already specified, but for the grounds which determine which of our alternatives we have reason to choose. While we may conclude that some course of action is not among our alternatives on the grounds that we know that we could not possibly perform it, we reject courses of action which are among our alternatives not on the grounds that they are physically impossible, but because we do not have reason to perform them. And when at last we choose to perform one action, we do so not because we have discovered

---

[25] For a very different formulation of this point, see J. David Velleman, *Practical Reflection* (Princeton, NJ: Princeton University Press, 1989), especially chapter 5.

[26] One might deny this by denying determinism; but, as before, I assume the truth of determinism for the purposes of this argument.

that it is our only possibility *tout court*, but because we have determined that it is the choice we have most reason to make.

If the fact that there is, in any situation, some particular action which is our only possibility *tout court* implied that practical reasoning was pointless or futile, then it would imply that we have no reason to ask ourselves which of the alternatives available to us we have most reason to perform; no reason to search for grounds rather than causes. But no plausible theoretical claim could imply this; a fortiori, the claim under consideration does not. If that claim allowed us to narrow the set of actions which we could legitimately regard as alternatives beyond those which we would perform if we chose, then it would constrain our practical reasoning by limiting the set of possible objects of choice over which it ranges. But I have argued that it cannot allow us to do this. Finally, if the fact that some particular action was our only possibility *tout court* could serve as a reason to perform some action, then it would affect our practical reasoning by providing us with grounds for choice. But it cannot—not only because we can never know which action is possible *tout court* until we have already chosen, but because, when our actions depend on our choices, which action is our only possibility *tout court* depends on which action we choose to perform, and therefore the fact that some action is our only possibility *tout court* could not possibly serve as a reason to choose to perform one action rather than another. While the truth of determinism might figure among our grounds for choice, the fact that some particular action is our only possibility *tout court* cannot possibly play any role in the deliberation which leads us to perform it. That fact is, for practical purposes, empty.

Thus far I have argued that, from a practical point of view, we cannot narrow the set of actions which we regard as alternatives beyond those which we would perform if we chose; and that for the purposes of deliberation we can regard all of these actions as genuine alternatives. These arguments allow us to answer two of the libertarian objections discussed earlier.[27] To the question why we should define our alternatives relative to a description of our situation which does not incorporate information about the outcome of our choices, we can reply that our use of the compatibilists' general conception of possibility does not reflect an arbitrary decision to ignore information relevant to our understanding of the possibilities available to us, but the fact that that information is in principle inaccessible to us while we deliberate; and therefore that conceptions of

---

[27] The third ("why is the compatibilists' general conception of possibility relevant to our evaluation of individuals?") is addressed in chapters 4–6 of *Freedom and Responsibility*.

possibility which incorporate that information can play no role in practical reasoning.

To the question why we should regard ourselves as having alternatives on the grounds that we can choose among actions which we would perform if we chose to, while we do not regard pool balls as having alternatives on the grounds that they would take various trajectories if they were hit at various angles, we can reply that the concept of an alternative is defined for use in practical reasoning; and therefore that only beings who are capable of engaging in practical reasoning have reason to regard themselves as having alternatives. If a pool ball were capable of engaging in practical reasoning, then it might have reason to wonder what its alternatives were. Things being as they are, however, it does not.

Moreover, if a pool ball were capable of engaging in practical reasoning, it would not have reason to regard itself as having various alternative trajectories except in those situations in which its trajectory depended on its choice. If hitting such a pool ball at a particular angle caused it to roll along a particular path by causing it to make a particular choice, then it would have reason to regard the various trajectories which it would take if it chose to take them as its alternatives.[28] But if hitting it caused it to take a particular trajectory by any other means, then it could in principle predict its actual trajectory. It would therefore have no more reason to define its possible trajectories in abstraction from the angle at which it would be hit than someone about to be thrown off the Empire State building would have to define her possible trajectories in abstraction from information about the way in which she would be thrown.

It is only because we can think at all that we can so much as frame the question which alternatives we have. It is only because we can engage in practical reasoning that we have reason to raise that question, since the concept of an alternative is a practical one. And it is only because we can act on our decisions that we have reason to conclude that we do have alternatives. Only a being which met all three conditions would have reason to regard itself as choosing among genuine alternatives. Any being which met all three conditions would be a person; and that person would have reason to regard her alternatives as those actions which she would perform if she chose.

From a theoretical point of view, as I have said, human actions are events to be described and explained. Theoretical reasoning therefore gives us no reason to disregard the causes which lead us to choose as we do, or to ascribe

---

[28] I leave aside the question whether or not we could regard a being whose choices were determined in this way as having anything like a continuing self.

any particular importance to the conception of possibility on which the conditional analysis of freedom of the will relies. From the practical point of view, however, our use of this general conception of possibility, as opposed to the narrower possibility *tout court*, is both unavoidable and rational. It is unavoidable because while we deliberate we cannot possibly employ a conception of the alternatives which are available to us which is narrower than the set of actions which we would perform were we to choose to do so. It is rational because, for the purposes of deliberation, we must regard the question what we will choose to do as open, and because, if we regard that question as open, we should not regard the various actions which we would perform if we chose as differing with respect to their possibility, since any of them would be possible *tout court* if we chose to perform it. Moreover, to determine whether or not a particular action is one which we would perform if we chose is to determine whether or not we can regard it as a possible object of choice: an action about which the question whether or not we have reason to perform it can legitimately be raised. The question whether or not I would perform some action if I chose is as fundamental to practical reasoning as the question whether or not some object is a possible object of knowledge is to theoretical reasoning: in each case, the answer to the question determines whether the type of reasoning under consideration is appropriate to a given object at all. By contrast, the question whether or not some action is possible *tout court* is, for practical purposes, irrelevant. For all three reasons, practical reasoning requires that we regard those actions which we would perform if we chose as genuine alternatives.

FREEDOM

Freedom of the will has traditionally been held to involve two distinct conditions.[29] The first condition holds that our wills are free only if we can choose among genuine alternatives. I have argued that when we engage in practical reasoning, we should regard all those actions which we would perform if we chose as genuine alternatives. An agent can, as noted above, be wrong about which alternatives she actually has; because I have defined the concept of an alternative in terms of the actions which the agent would have performed had she chosen to perform them, and not in terms of those she believed that she could have performed when she made her choice, my account allows for the possibility that she might wrongly identify some course of action as one of her alternatives because she believes, falsely, that she would perform it if

---

[29] See G. Watson, "Free Action and Free Will", *Mind*, 96 (1987), 145.

she chose to. But because it incorporates those constraints on knowledge which are unavoidable when one occupies the practical point of view, and in particular the fact that while deliberating an agent either cannot know what the results of her deliberation will be or cannot use that knowledge, my account does not imply that she is wrong to think that those actions which she would perform if she chose to are, in the relevant sense, possibilities for her; or that when she decides to perform one of them and acts on her decision, she does not act freely.

The second condition which an agent must meet if his will is to be free has been described in different ways: as requiring that he be able to secure "the conformity of his will to his second-order volitions",[30] or that he have "the capacity to translate his values into action".[31] But it always involves the ability to step back and ask ourselves whether or not we should act on our various motivations and desires; to attain some critical distance from them and choose which to endorse, rather than acting on them unreflectively or accepting them uncritically. When we are capable of determining our conduct through practical reasoning, we must have this capacity, since evaluating our motivations and deciding which we have most reason to act on is one of the things that practical reasoning consists in.[32]

When we engage in practical reasoning, we ask ourselves what we have most reason to do: which facts about our situation and motivations we should regard as constituting reasons for action, which of those reasons are most compelling, and what, as a result, we should do. There are no theoretical claims about which we might not in principle raise the question whether they constitute reasons for action; no theoretical claims which, so to speak, carry their credentials as reasons for action in themselves, or whose natures guarantee them a place among our reasons for action whether or not we choose to regard them as such.

In particular, the fact that I have some desire, or feel impelled by some motivation, cannot lead me to conclude that I should satisfy that desire or act on that motivation unless I take the fact that I have that desire or motivation to constitute a reason for acting on it;[33] nor is there any desire or

---

[30] Harry Frankfurt, "Freedom of the Will and the Concept of a Person", in Frankfurt, *The Importance of What We Care About* (New York: Cambridge University Press, 1988), 20 [reprinted as Essay 16, this volume].

[31] Gary Watson, "Free Agency", this volume, Essay 17.

[32] This means that my account, like Frankfurt's and Watson's, is a hierarchical one. I differ from them in taking freedom to consist in our ability to determine our conduct through practical reasoning, not in our ability to act on our values or our second-order volitions.

[33] Cf. Immanuel Kant, *Religion within the Limits of Reason Alone*, trans. T. M. Greene and H. H. Hudson (New York: Harper & Row, 1960), 19–20; Henry Allison, *Kant's Theory of Freedom* (Cambridge: Cambridge University Press, 1990), chapter 2, especially pp. 39–41; Barbara Herman, "On the Value of Acting from the Motive of Duty", in Herman, *The Practice of Moral*

motivation about which I could not in principle raise the question whether or not the fact that I have that desire or motivation constitutes a reason for acting on it. I might conclude that that desire or motivation does constitute such a reason, and act accordingly. But in this case the fact that I had that desire or motivation would not suffice to explain my action, since, had I concluded that I did not have reason to act on it, either I would have performed some other action, or I would have performed that action for some other reason. If my desire or motivation does suffice to explain why I performed some action, without requiring the additional assumption that I regarded it as a reason for acting as I did, then it must be true that even had I concluded that it was not such a reason, I would nonetheless have performed that action. But if this is true, then I was not then capable of deciding which of the actions available to me I had most reason to perform, and of acting on my decision. I could not, that is, have been capable of determining my conduct through practical reasoning.

If we are capable of determining our conduct through practical reasoning, then we need not accept our various desires and motivations uncritically, or act on them blindly. We can ask ourselves which of our desires and motivations constitute reasons for action and which do not, and we can conclude that we have no reason whatsoever to satisfy some of our desires or to act on some of our motivations. If we can act on our decisions, then we will not satisfy those desires or act on those motivations. We might allow our various desires and motivations to dictate our actions, either by failing to exercise our capacity to evaluate them or by deciding that we have reason to allow our conduct to be governed by "the economy of (our) first-order desires".[34] But if we are capable of determining our conduct through practical reasoning, then we cannot explain such failures as the result of our inability to decide for ourselves which of our various desires and motivations provide us with reasons for action.[35]

Judgment (Cambridge, Mass.: Harvard University Press, 1993), 11–12; and Christine Korsgaard, "Morality as Freedom", in Yirmiyahu Yovel (ed.), *Kant's Practical Philosophy Reconsidered* (Dordrecht: Kluwer Academic Publisher, 1989), 26–9.

[34] Frankfurt, "Freedom of the Will and the Concept of a Person", 18.

[35] This is true regardless of the source of the desires in question. Even in the absence of mad scientists, drug addictions, and other sources of alien desires, we are subject to odd bouts of desire that spring up in us from unknown sources. When someone cuts us off on the freeway, a desire to run her off the road might sweep over us; when a particularly irritating person buttonholes us at a party, we might feel tempted to substitute withering disdain for our customary tact. We normally regard ourselves as capable of resisting these temptations, and hold ourselves responsible if we do not. If a resistible alien desire were to spring up in us, we could respond to it in the same way: by stepping back from it, asking ourselves whether or not we think we should act on it, and acting accordingly; in short, by engaging in practical reasoning and acting on our decision. If we endorse that desire and act on it, then in so doing we exercise our autonomy, rather than revealing its

When we are capable of determining our conduct through practical reasoning, we meet both of the conditions which freedom of the will requires. I will therefore define freedom as follows: a person is free if she is capable of determining her actions through practical reasoning; such an agent is free to choose among all those acts which she would perform if she chose to perform them, and she is free to perform a given action if she would perform it if she chose to do so. When we see these actions as possible or our wills as free in this sense, we need not believe that determinism is false, since we need not believe that all of these actions and choices are possible *tout court*, or that we are free in a libertarian sense. We simply recognize that, given the unavoidable constraints on our knowledge, we must choose among the actions which are possible for all we could possibly know. Because these constraints are unavoidable, such a belief in our freedom is not an unjustifiable concession to our desire to think ourselves metaphysically unique, or a belief which we might be persuaded to give up by some scientific theory, but a necessary feature of deliberation and choice.

For this reason, my arguments should not be confused with those which purport to show that we must believe that we are free, in a libertarian sense, when we decide what to do. I can see no reason to suppose that deliberation forces us to think of ourselves as free in a libertarian sense; and while I have argued that determinism and mechanism are, for practical purposes, empty, I have not tried to argue that deliberation requires us to believe that they are false. I have argued that the requirements of practical reasoning give us reason to regard ourselves as free in the sense defined above; but the claim that we are free in this sense does not require the falsity of determinism or mechanism, and therefore cannot be identified with a libertarian conception of freedom.

Nor should my arguments be confused with those which base the claim that we are free, in a libertarian sense, on an experience of freedom which is supposed to attend our choices. Such arguments have been widely and justifiably criticized by others;[36] I will not rehearse those criticisms here. My arguments differ from them in three important respects. First of all, as I have

---

absence. For this reason, so long as our ability to determine our conduct through practical reasoning were left intact, neither the strength of a resistible alien desire nor its external cause could properly be said to undermine our autonomy. See David Blumenfeld, "Freedom and Mind Control", *American Philosophical Quarterly*, 25/3 (1988), 215–27 and Daniel Dennett, "Mechanism and Responsibility", in Dennett, *Brainstorms* (Cambridge, Mass.: MIT Press, 1981), for development of this point, and for persuasive arguments against objections to compatibilism which turn on the possibility of implanting beliefs and desires in people's minds.

[36] See, for instance, John Stuart Mill, *An Examination of Sir William Hamilton's Philosophy and of the Principal Philosophical Questions Discussed in his Writings*, ed. J. M. Robson, vol. ix, *Mill: Collected Works* (Toronto: University of Toronto Press, 1979), chapter 26.

said, I have not tried to argue that we are free in a libertarian sense: that our choices are not determined by natural causes. Secondly, my arguments are not based on any claims about what we experience when we make choices. Indeed, this strategy would be directly opposed to my own: for to base the claim that we are free on some experience which we can supposedly explain only by assuming it to be veridical is to construe freedom as a theoretical, and not as a practical, concept. Finally, the claim that an experience of freedom inevitably attends our choices leaves open the possibility that the inevitability in question is merely psychological; that our choices might just as well produce in us the impression that our skin was purple. It does not, and (arguably) could not, warrant the claim that the belief that we are free is rationally required. By contrast, I have tried to argue not that people engaged in deliberation just do, for some unspecified reason, see their alternatives as the actions which they could perform if they chose, but that practical reasoning necessarily involves such a conception of our alternatives, and that this necessity derives not from our nature, but from the nature of practical reasoning itself.

Finally, I have not tried to argue that our freedom depends on our belief that we are free.[37] My arguments depend essentially on the following claims: that when we adopt the practical point of view, we have reason to employ certain concepts, like the concepts of an alternative and of a free agent; that the requirements of practical reasoning give us reason to define these concepts in certain ways; and that when we do so, we have reason to regard ourselves as free when we can determine our conduct through practical reasoning, whether or not determinism or mechanism is true. These are all claims about the concepts we have reason to use, and the beliefs we have reason to accept; and not about the concepts we actually use, or the beliefs we actually hold. For this reason my arguments do not make the truth of the claim that we are free agents dependent in objectionable ways on our belief that that claim is true.

One might think that I would see myself as free in the sense defined above only until I made my choice, since as soon as I choose and act I learn which act was possible *tout court*, and therefore the constraints on the knowledge available to practical reasoning, which led me to employ the more general conception of my possibilities, no longer restrict me. This would imply that though I must believe that I am free when I choose, that belief is mistaken, since the passage of time will inevitably dispel it. This conclusion might follow had I argued that when I choose I must see myself as free in the libertarian's sense; that I must act under the illusion of contracausal freedom. But I argued above that when I see myself as free I do not believe, mistakenly, that it is possible *tout court* for me to choose to perform any action which I could perform if I chose to. I simply recognize that my actions depend on my choices, that when I make those choices I do not know, or cannot use my knowledge of, which action I will choose to perform, that I can legitimately regard any action which I could perform if I chose as a genuine alternative, and therefore that I must, from a practical point of view, regard myself as free to perform any of the actions which I could perform if I chose to. If I subsequently discover that my actions were not up to me, for example because, unbeknownst to me, I was drugged, hypnotized, or coerced, then I will conclude that I was wrong to think that I was free in this sense. But I will not conclude that I was not really free in this sense simply because I discover which action it was inevitable that I choose.

8

ALTERNATE POSSIBILITIES AND MORAL RESPONSIBILITY

HARRY G. FRANKFURT

A dominant role in nearly all recent inquiries into the free-will problem has been played by a principle which I shall call "the principle of alternate possibilities." This principle states that a person is morally responsible for what he has done only if he could have done otherwise. Its exact meaning is a subject of controversy, particularly concerning whether someone who accepts it is thereby committed to believing that moral responsibility and determinism are incompatible. Practically no one, however, seems inclined to deny or even to question that the principle of alternate possibilities (construed in some way or other) is true. It has generally seemed so overwhelmingly plausible that some philosophers have even characterized it as an *a priori* truth. People whose accounts of free will or of moral responsibility are radically at odds evidently find in it a firm and convenient common ground upon which they can profitably take their opposing stands.

But the principle of alternate possibilities is false. A person may well be morally responsible for what he has done even though he could not have done otherwise. The principle's plausibility is an illusion, which can be made to vanish by bringing the relevant moral phenomena into sharper focus.

I

In seeking illustrations of the principle of alternate possibilities, it is most natural to think of situations in which the same circumstances both bring it about that a person does something and make it impossible for him to avoid doing it. These include, for example, situations in which a person is coerced into doing something, or in which he is impelled to act by a hypnotic suggestion, or in which some inner compulsion drives him to do what he does. In situations of these kinds there are circumstances that make it impossible for

From the *Journal of Philosophy*, 66/23 (1969), 829–39. Reprinted by permission of the publisher and the author.

the person to do otherwise, and these very circumstances also serve to bring it about that he does whatever it is that he does.

However, there may be circumstances that constitute sufficient conditions for a certain action to be performed by someone and that therefore make it impossible for the person to do otherwise, but that do not actually impel the person to act or in any way produce his action. A person may do something in circumstances that leave him no alternative to doing it, without these circumstances actually moving him or leading him to do it—without them playing any role, indeed, in bringing it about that he does what he does.

An examination of situations characterized by circumstances of this sort casts doubt, I believe, on the relevance to questions of moral responsibility of the fact that a person who has done something could not have done otherwise. I propose to develop some examples of this kind in the context of a discussion of coercion and to suggest that our moral intuitions concerning these examples tend to disconfirm the principle of alternate possibilities. Then I will discuss the principle in more general terms, explain what I think is wrong with it, and describe briefly and without argument how it might appropriately be revised.

II

It is generally agreed that a person who has been coerced to do something did not do it freely and is not morally responsible for having done it. Now the doctrine that coercion and moral responsibility are mutually exclusive may appear to be no more than a somewhat particularized version of the principle of alternate possibilities. It is natural enough to say of a person who has been coerced to do something that he could not have done otherwise. And it may easily seem that being coerced deprives a person of freedom and of moral responsibility simply because it is a special case of being unable to do otherwise. The principle of alternate possibilities may in this way derive some credibility from its association with the very plausible proposition that moral responsibility is excluded by coercion.

It is not right, however, that it should do so. The fact that a person was coerced to act as he did may entail both that he could not have done otherwise and that he bears no moral responsibility for his action. But his lack of moral responsibility is not entailed by his having been unable to do otherwise. The doctrine that coercion excludes moral responsibility is not correctly understood, in other words, as a particularized version of the principle of alternate possibilities.

Let us suppose that someone is threatened convincingly with a penalty he finds unacceptable and that he then does what is required of him by the issuer of the threat. We can imagine details that would make it reasonable for us to think that the person was coerced to perform the action in question, that he could not have done otherwise, and that he bears no moral responsibility for having done what he did. But just what is it about situations of this kind that warrants the judgment that the threatened person is not morally responsible for his act?

This question may be approached by considering situations of the following kind. Jones decides for reasons of his own to do something, then someone threatens him with a very harsh penalty (so harsh that any reasonable person would submit to the threat) unless he does precisely that, and Jones does it. Will we hold Jones morally responsible for what he has done? I think this will depend on the roles we think were played, in leading him to act, by his original decision and by the threat.

One possibility is that Jones$_1$ is not a reasonable man: he is, rather, a man who does what he has once decided to do no matter what happens next and no matter what the cost. In that case, the threat actually exerted no effective force upon him. He acted without any regard to it, very much as if he were not aware that it had been made. If this is indeed the way it was, the situation did not involve coercion at all. The threat did not lead Jones$_1$ to do what he did. Nor was it in fact sufficient to have prevented him from doing otherwise: if his earlier decision had been to do something else, the threat would not have deterred him in the slightest. It seems evident that in these circumstances the fact that Jones$_1$ was threatened in no way reduces the moral responsibility he would otherwise bear for his act. This example, however, is not a counterexample either to the doctrine that coercion excuses or to the principle of alternate possibilities. For we have supposed that Jones$_1$ is a man upon whom the threat had no coercive effect and, hence, that it did not actually deprive him of alternatives to doing what he did.

Another possibility is that Jones$_2$ was stampeded by the threat. Given that threat, he would have performed that action regardless of what decision he had already made. The threat upset him so profoundly, moreover, that he completely forgot his own earlier decision and did what was demanded of him entirely because he was terrified of the penalty with which he was threatened. In this case, it is not relevant to his having performed the action that he had already decided on his own to perform it. When the chips were down he thought of nothing but the threat, and fear alone led him to act. The fact that at an earlier time Jones$_2$ had decided for his own reasons to act in just that way may be relevant to an evaluation of his character; he may bear full moral responsibility for having made *that* decision. But he can hardly be said to be morally responsible for his action. For he performed the action simply as a result of the coercion to which he was subjected. His earlier decision played no role in bringing it about that he did what he did, and it would therefore be gratuitous to assign it a role in the moral evaluation of his action.

Now consider a third possibility. Jones$_3$ was neither stampeded by the threat nor indifferent to it. The threat impressed him, as it would impress any reasonable man, and he would have submitted to it wholeheartedly if he had not already made a decision that coincided with the one demanded of him. In fact, however, he performed the action in question on the basis of the decision he had made before the threat was issued. When he acted, he was not actually motivated by the threat but solely by the considerations that had originally commended the action to him. It was not the threat that led him to act, though it would have done so if he had not already provided himself with a sufficient motive for performing the action in question.

No doubt it will be very difficult for anyone to know, in a case like this one, exactly what happened. Did Jones$_3$ perform the action because of the threat, or were his reasons for acting simply those which had already persuaded him to do so? Or did he act on the basis of two motives, each of which was sufficient for his action? It is not impossible, however, that the situation should be clearer than situations of this kind usually are. And suppose it is apparent to us that Jones$_3$ acted on the basis of his own decision and not because of the threat. Then I think we would be justified in regarding his moral responsibility for what he did as unaffected by the threat even though, since he would in any case have submitted to the threat, he could not have avoided doing what he did. It would be entirely reasonable for us to make the same judgment concerning his moral responsibility that we would have made if we had not known of the threat. For the threat did not in fact influence his performance of the action. He did what he did just as if the threat had not been made at all.

III

The case of Jones$_3$ may appear at first glance to combine coercion and moral responsibility, and thus to provide a counterexample to the doctrine that coercion excuses. It is not really so certain that it does so, however, because it is unclear whether the example constitutes a genuine instance of coercion. Can we say of Jones$_3$ that he was coerced to do something, when he had already decided on his own to do it and when he did it entirely on the basis of that decision? Or would it be more correct to say that Jones$_3$ was not coerced to do what he did, even though he himself recognized that there was an irresistible force at work in virtue of which he had to do it? My own linguistic intuitions lead me toward the second alternative, but they are somewhat equivocal. Perhaps we can say either of these things, or perhaps we must add a qualifying explanation to whichever of them we say.

This murkiness, however, does not interfere with our drawing an important moral from an examination of the example. Suppose we decide to say that Jones$_3$ was *not* coerced. Our basis for saying this will clearly be that it is incorrect to regard a man as being coerced to do something unless he does it *because of* the coercive force exerted against him. The fact that an irresistible threat is made will not, then, entail that the person who receives it is coerced to do what he does. It will also be necessary that the threat is what actually accounts for his doing it. On the other hand, suppose we decide to say that Jones$_3$ *was* coerced. Then we will be bound to admit that being coerced does not exclude being morally responsible. And we will also surely be led to the view that coercion affects the judgment of a person's moral responsibility only when the person acts as he does because he is coerced to do so—i.e., when the fact that he is coerced is what accounts for his action.

Whichever we decide to say, then, we will recognize that the doctrine that coercion excludes moral responsibility is not a particularized version of the principle of alternate possibilities. Situations in which a person who does something cannot do otherwise because he is subject to coercive power are either not instances of coercion at all, or they are situations in which the person may still be morally responsible for what he does if it is not because of the coercion that he does it. When we excuse a person who has been coerced, we do not excuse him because he was unable to do otherwise. Even though a person is subject to a coercive force that precludes his performing any action but one, he may nonetheless bear full moral responsibility for performing that action.

IV

To the extent that the principle of alternate possibilities derives its plausibility from association with the doctrine that coercion excludes moral responsibility, a clear understanding of the latter diminishes the appeal of the former. Indeed the case of Jones$_3$ may appear to do more than illuminate the relationship between the two doctrines. It may well seem to provide a decisive counterexample to the principle of alternate possibilities and thus to show that this principle is false. For the irresistibility of the threat to which Jones$_3$ is subjected might well be taken to mean that he cannot but perform the action he performs. And yet the threat, since Jones$_3$ performs the action without regard to it, does not reduce his moral responsibility for what he does.

The following objection will doubtless be raised against the suggestion that the case of Jones$_3$ is a counterexample to the principle of alternate possibilities. There is perhaps a sense in which Jones$_3$ cannot do otherwise than perform the action he performs, since he is a reasonable man and the threat he encounters is sufficient to move any reasonable man. But it is not this sense that is germane to the principle of alternate possibilities. His knowledge that he stands to suffer an intolerably harsh penalty does not mean that Jones$_3$, strictly speaking, *cannot* perform any action but the one he does perform. After all it is still open to him, and this is crucial, to defy the threat if he wishes to do so and to accept the penalty his action would bring down upon him. In the sense in which the principle of alternate possibilities employs the concept of "could have done otherwise," Jones$_3$'s inability to resist the threat does not mean that he cannot do otherwise than perform the action he performs. Hence the case of Jones$_3$ does not constitute an instance contrary to the principle.

I do not propose to consider in what sense the concept of "could have done otherwise" figures in the principle of alternate possibilities, nor will I attempt to measure the force of the objection I have just described.[1] For I believe that whatever force this objection may be thought to have can be deflected by altering the example in the following way.[2] Suppose someone— Black, let us say—wants Jones$_4$ to perform a certain action. Black is prepared to go to considerable lengths to get his way, but he prefers to avoid showing his hand unnecessarily. So he waits until Jones$_4$ is about to make up his mind what to do, and he does nothing unless it is clear to him (Black is an excellent judge of such things) that Jones$_4$ is going to decide to do something *other* than what he wants him to do. If it does become clear that Jones$_4$ is going to decide to do something else, Black takes effective steps to ensure that Jones$_4$ decides to do, and that he does do, what he wants him to do.[3]

---

[1] The two main concepts employed in the principle of alternate possibilities are "morally responsible" and "could have done otherwise." To discuss the principle without analyzing either of these concepts may well seem like an attempt at piracy. The reader should take notice that my Jolly Roger is now unfurled.

[2] After thinking up the example that I am about to develop I learned that Robert Nozick, in lectures given several years ago, had formulated an example of the same general type and had proposed it as a counterexample to the principle of alternate possibilities.

[3] The assumption that Black can predict what Jones$_4$ will decide to do does not beg the question of determinism. We can imagine that Jones$_4$ has often confronted the alternatives—A and B—that he now confronts, and that his face has invariably twitched when he was about to decide to do A and never when he was about to decide to do B. Knowing this, and observing the twitch, Black would have a basis for prediction. This does, to be sure, suppose that there is some sort of causal relation between Jones$_4$'s state at the time of the twitch and his subsequent states. But any

Whatever Jones$_4$'s initial preferences and inclinations, then, Black will have his way.

What steps will Black take, if he believes he must take steps, in order to ensure that Jones$_4$ decides and acts as he wishes? Anyone with a theory concerning what "could have done otherwise" means may answer this question for himself by describing whatever measures he would regard as sufficient to guarantee that, in the relevant sense, Jones$_4$ cannot do otherwise. Let Black pronounce a terrible threat, and in this way both force Jones$_4$ to perform the desired action and prevent him from performing a forbidden one. Let Black give Jones$_4$ a potion, or put him under hypnosis, and in some such way as these generate in Jones$_4$ an irresistible inner compulsion to perform the act Black wants performed and to avoid others. Or let Black manipulate the minute processes of Jones$_4$'s brain and nervous system in some more direct way, so that causal forces running in and out of his synapses and along the poor man's nerves determine that he chooses to act and that he does act in the one way and not in any other. Given any conditions under which it will be maintained that Jones$_4$ cannot do otherwise, in other words, let Black bring it about that those conditions prevail. The structure of the example is flexible enough, I think, to find a way around any charge of irrelevance by accommodating the doctrine on which the charge is based.[4]

Now suppose that Black never has to show his hand because Jones$_4$, for reasons of his own, decides to perform and does perform the very action Black wants him to perform. In that case, it seems clear, Jones$_4$ will bear precisely the same moral responsibility for what he does as he would have borne if Black had not been ready to take steps to ensure that he do it. It would be quite unreasonable to excuse Jones$_4$ for his action, or to withhold the praise to which it would normally entitle him, on the basis of the fact that he could not have done otherwise. This fact played no role at all in leading him to act as he did. He would have acted the same even if it had not been a fact. Indeed, everything happened just as it would have happened without Black's presence in the situation and without his readiness to intrude into it.

In this example there are sufficient conditions for Jones$_4$'s performing the

plausible view of decision or of action will allow that reaching a decision and performing an action both involve earlier and later phases, with causal relations between them, and such that the earlier phases are not themselves part of the decision or of the action. The example does not require that these earlier phases be deterministically related to still earlier events.

[4] The example is also flexible enough to allow for the elimination of Black altogether. Anyone who thinks that the effectiveness of the example is undermined by its reliance on a human manipulator, who imposes his will on Jones$_4$, can substitute for Black a machine programmed to do what Black does. If this is still not good enough, forget both Black and the machine and suppose that their role is played by natural forces involving no will or design at all.

action in question. What action he performs is not up to him. Of course it is in a way up to him whether he acts on his own or as a result of Black's intervention. That depends upon what action he himself is inclined to perform. But whether he finally acts on his own or as a result of Black's intervention, he performs the same action. He has no alternative but to do what Black wants him to do. If he does it on his own, however, his moral responsibility for doing it is not affected by the fact that Black was lurking in the background with sinister intent, since this intent never comes into play.

V

The fact that a person could not have avoided doing something is a sufficient condition of his having done it. But, as some of my examples show, this fact may play no role whatever in the explanation of why he did it. It may not figure at all among the circumstances that actually brought it about that he did what he did, so that his action is to be accounted for on another basis entirely. Even though the person was unable to do otherwise, that is to say, it may not be the case that he acted as he did *because* he could not have done otherwise. Now if someone had no alternative to performing a certain action but did not perform it because he was unable to do otherwise, then he would have performed exactly the same action even if he *could* have done otherwise. The circumstances that made it impossible for him to do otherwise could have been subtracted from the situation without affecting what happened or why it happened in any way. Whatever it was that actually led the person to do what he did, or that made him do it, would have led him to do it or made him do it even if it had been possible for him to do something else instead.

Thus it would have made no difference, so far as concerns his action or how he came to perform it, if the circumstances that made it impossible for him to avoid performing it had not prevailed. The fact that he could not have done otherwise clearly provides no basis for supposing that he *might* have done otherwise if he had been able to do so. When a fact is in this way irrelevant to the problem of accounting for a person's action it seems quite gratuitous to assign it any weight in the assessment of his moral responsibility. Why should the fact be considered in reaching a moral judgment concerning the person when it does not help in any way to understand either what made him act as he did or what, in other circumstances, he might have done?

This, then, is why the principle of alternate possibilities is mistaken. It asserts that a person bears no moral responsibility—that is, he is to be excused—for having performed an action if there were circumstances that made it impossible for him to avoid performing it. But there may be circumstances that make it impossible for a person to avoid performing some action without those circumstances in any way bringing it about that he performs that action. It would surely be no good for the person to refer to circumstances of this sort in an effort to absolve himself of moral responsibility for performing the action in question. For those circumstances, by hypothesis, actually had nothing to do with his having done what he did. He would have done precisely the same thing, and he would have been led or made in precisely the same way to do it, even if they had not prevailed.

We often do, to be sure, excuse people for what they have done when they tell us (and we believe them) that they could not have done otherwise. But this is because we assume that what they tell us serves to explain why they did what they did. We take it for granted that they are not being disingenuous, as a person would be who cited as an excuse the fact that he could not have avoided doing what he did but who knew full well that it was not at all because of this that he did it.

What I have said may suggest that the principle of alternate possibilities should be revised so as to assert that a person is not morally responsible for what he has done if he did it because he could not have done otherwise. It may be noted that this revision of the principle does not seriously affect the arguments of those who have relied on the original principle in their efforts to maintain that moral responsibility and determinism are incompatible. For if it was causally determined that a person perform a certain action, then it will be true that the person performed it because of those causal determinants. And if the fact that it was causally determined that a person perform a certain action means that the person could not have done otherwise, as philosophers who argue for the incompatibility thesis characteristically suppose, then the fact that it was causally determined that a person perform a certain action will mean that the person performed it because he could not have done otherwise. The revised principle of alternate possibilities will entail, on this assumption concerning the meaning of 'could have done otherwise', that a person is not morally responsible for what he has done if it was causally determined that he do it. I do not believe, however, that this revision of the principle is acceptable.

Suppose a person tells us that he did what he did because he was unable to do otherwise; or suppose he makes the similar statement that he did what he did because he had to do it. We do often accept statements like these (if we believe them) as valid excuses, and such statements may well seem at first glance to invoke the revised principle of alternate possibilities. But I think that when we accept such statements as valid excuses it is because we assume that we are being told more than the statements strictly and literally convey.

We understand the person who offers the excuse to mean that he did what he did *only because* he was unable to do otherwise, or *only because* he had to do it. And we understand him to mean, more particularly, that when he did what he did it was not because that was what he really wanted to do. The principle of alternate possibilities should thus be replaced, in my opinion, by the following principle: a person is not morally responsible for what he has done if he did it only because he could not have done otherwise. This principle does not appear to conflict with the view that moral responsibility is compatible with determinism.

The following may all be true: there were circumstances that made it impossible for a person to avoid doing something; these circumstances actually played a role in bringing it about that he did it, so that it is correct to say that he did it because he could not have done otherwise; the person really wanted to do what he did; he did it because it was what he really wanted to do, so that it is not correct to say that he did what he did only because he could not have done otherwise. Under these conditions, the person may well be morally responsible for what he has done. On the other hand, he will not be morally responsible for what he has done if he did it only because he could not have done otherwise, even if what he did was something he really wanted to do.

9

LIBERTARIANISM AND FRANKFURT'S ATTACK ON THE PRINCIPLE OF ALTERNATIVE POSSIBILITIES

DAVID WIDERKER

Harry Frankfurt's well-known attack (Frankfurt 1969 [Essay 8, this volume]) on the principle of alternative possibilities,

(PAP) A person is morally responsible for performing a given act A only if he could have acted otherwise,

has received considerable attention in recent philosophical literature. Except for a few dissenters, it has on the whole gone unchallenged.[1] In this paper, I wish to take a fresh look at Frankfurt's attack on PAP from a libertarian viewpoint. I shall try to show that it does not succeed when applied to mental acts such as deciding, choosing, undertaking, forming an intention, that is, mental acts that for the libertarian constitute the basic *loci* of moral responsibility. If correct, this result will enable us to formulate a necessary condition for moral responsibility that is more adequate than PAP and not vulnerable to Frankfurt's criticism.

At the outset, let me state a number of assumptions that I shall employ in the discussion to follow. First, the version of libertarianism I intend to defend is the view that an agent's decision (choice) is free in the sense of freedom required for moral responsibility only if (i) it is not casually determined, and (ii) in the circumstances in which the agent made that decision (choice), he could have avoided making it.[2] Second, I take 'a given act A' in

---

From *Philosophical Review*, 104 (1995), 247–61. Copyright © 1995 Cornell University. Reprinted by permission of the publisher and the author.

[1] The dissenters include Davidson (1973, 149–50); Naylor (1984); Heinaman (1986, 275–76); and Lamb (1993, 522–23). Among those who agree with Frankfurt in his rejection of PAP, we may find, for example, Blumenfeld (1971, 340–41); Fischer (1982, 33–34); Fischer and Ravizza (1991, 258–59); Dennett (1984, chap. 6); Berofsky (1987, 31–33); Zimmerman (1988, 119–27); and Stump (1990, 255–56). For an extensive bibliography on Frankfurt's attack on PAP, see Fischer 1987.

[2] Condition (i) is intended to rule out compatibilist construals of avoidability. A decision is not causally determined, as I use the expression, if prior to its occurrence there does not obtain a causally sufficient condition for it.

Some may want to strengthen the definition of libertarianism given in the text by also requiring

PAP to refer to an action such that the agent was aware, at the time, that he was performing it (or was trying to perform it) and with regard to which he believed that he could have done otherwise.[3] Third, I shall adopt a fine-grained account of action individuation,[4] and shall thus treat 'A' in PAP as a variable for actions themselves, rather than actions under A-descriptions. I believe, however, that the conclusions I reach will also be acceptable, *mutatis mutandi*, to someone who individuates actions coarsely, such as, for example, Davidson.

1

Frankfurt develops his attack on PAP in two steps. He first argues for the following thesis:

> (IRR) There may be circumstances in which a person performs some action which although they make it impossible for him to avoid performing that action, they in no way bring it about that he performs it. (Frankfurt 1969, 830, 837)

Then he claims that an agent who was in a situation of the sort described in IRR (henceforth "IRR-situation") cannot in order to absolve himself of moral responsibility claim that he acted in circumstances that left him no alternative to doing what he did. For, by hypothesis, these circumstances had nothing to do with what he did. He would have acted the same even if those circumstances had not obtained. Hence, PAP is false (ibid., 836–37).

As we can see, the success of Frankfurt's case against PAP depends crucially upon his ability to convince us of the plausibility of IRR. It is, therefore, important to see whether he succeeds in this endeavor. To establish IRR, Frankfurt asks us to consider the following situation, which, he claims, is an example of an IRR-situation.

Suppose someone—Black, let us say—wants Jones to perform a certain action. Black is prepared to go to considerable lengths to get his way, but he prefers to avoid

---

that a free decision not be *logically* necessitated by a state of affairs (hard facts) obtaining prior to it. See, for example, Alston 1989, 164–65. For definitions of libertarianism that are equivalent or closely related to the one employed here, see Plantinga 1974, 165–66; Ginet 1990, 124; van Inwagen 1983, 8, 13–14.

    Note that this version of libertarianism differs from Thomas Reid's version of libertarianism in that it does not employ the notion of agent-causation. For a libertarian response to Frankfurt of a Reidean type, see Rowe 1991, 82–85.

[3] Frankfurt's case against PAP would be considerably weaker without this assumption.

[4] Thus, I shall treat an action as a dated particular consisting at least in part in an agent's exemplifying an act-property at a time. I use 'act-property' in Goldman's sense, according to which an agent's having exemplified such a property does not entail that he performed an action, or that he acted intentionally (see Goldman 1970, 15–17). Although I adopt Goldman's use of 'act-property', I do not endorse his account of action.

showing his hand unnecessarily. So he waits until Jones is about to make up his mind what to do, and he does nothing unless it is clear to him (Black is an excellent judge of such things) that Jones is going to decide something other than what he wants him to do. If it does become clear that Jones is going to decide something else, Black takes effective steps to ensure that Jones decides to do, and that he does do, what he wants him to do. Whatever Jones's initial preferences and inclinations, then, Black will have his way. . . .

. . . Now, suppose that Black never has to show his hand because Jones, for reasons of his own, decides to perform and does perform the very action Black wants him to perform. (ibid., 835)

To better grasp the scenario Frankfurt wishes us to consider, let us describe it in more concrete terms. Let us suppose that Jones is deliberating about whether to kill a certain person Smith at time t3. Suppose further that, unbeknownst to Jones, there is another person Black who for some reason wants it to be the case that Jones decides at t2 to kill Smith and then carries out this decision. Although Black can force Jones to act in the way he wants him to act, he prefers not to show his hand unnecessarily. Black can be sure that he will have his way in view of his knowing the following facts about Jones and himself:

(1) If Jones is blushing at t1, then, provided no one intervenes, Jones will decide at t2 to kill Smith.
(2) If Jones is not blushing at t1, then, provided no one intervenes, he will not decide at t2 to kill Smith.
(3) If Black sees that Jones shows signs that he will not decide at t2 to kill Smith, that is, sees that Jones is *not* blushing at t1, then Black forces Jones to decide at t2 to kill Smith; but if he sees that he is blushing at t1, then he does nothing.

Finally, suppose that Black does not have to show his hand, because

(4) Jones is blushing at t1, and decides at t2 to kill Smith for reasons of his own.

Given that the action in question is Jones's decision to kill Smith, has Frankfurt given us an example of an IRR-situation? Or to put it more precisely, has he succeeded in describing a situation in which a decision for which an agent is morally responsible is such that, though there is no causally sufficient condition for its occurrence, it nevertheless is unavoidable? If he has, then he has refuted libertarianism. For he will have shown that, contrary to what is implied by that position, a decision can be free in the sense of freedom pertinent to moral responsibility without being avoidable. Consequently, he will also have refuted PAP as applied to decisions. I wish to claim, however, that he has not established this result. To see this, let us

examine (1) more closely. Note that the truth of (1) cannot be grounded in
the fact that Jones's blushing at t1 is, in the circumstances, causally sufficient
for his decision to kill Smith, or in the fact that it is indicative of a state that
is causally sufficient for that decision, since such an assumption would be
neither in accordance with IRR nor accepted by the libertarian. On the
other hand, if (1) is not thus grounded, then the following two options are
available to the libertarian to resist the contention that Jones's decision to
kill Smith is unavoidable. He may either reject (1), claiming that the most
that he would be prepared to allow is

   (1a) If Jones is blushing at t1, then Jones will *probably* decide at t2 to kill
         Smith. (Adams 1977, 111)

But (1a) is compatible with Jones's having the power to decide not to kill
Smith, since there is the possibility of Jones's acting out of character. Or the
libertarian may construe (1) as a conditional of freedom in Plantinga's sense
(Plantinga 1974, chap. 9), that is, as

   (1b) If Jones is blushing at t1, then Jones will *freely* decide at t2 to kill
         Smith,[5]

in which case the libertarian may again claim that in the actual situation
when Jones is blushing at t1, it is within his power to refrain from deciding to
kill Smith at t2. To be sure, as things turned out Jones did not exercise that
power, but this fact is irrelevant, claims the libertarian. Thus, in either case,
Jones's power *not* to decide to kill Smith is preserved, and hence again we
have not been given an example of an IRR-situation.

   That Frankurt has failed to give us an example of an IRR-situation for
decisions can be argued for in another way. We know that if Jones were *not*
to blush at t1, then he would be forced to decide at t2 to kill Smith. But this
fact by itself does not imply that in the actual scenario, where he was blushing at t1, Jones did not have it within his power at t1 to refrain from deciding
to kill Smith. After all, he could have exercised this power immediately after
blushing at t1. *Nothing* in the assumptions cited above rules out this possibility.[6] To put it in terms of possible worlds, nothing in the assumptions cited
above rules out the possibility that the causally possible worlds, relative to t1,
in which Jones can be said to exercise his power of not deciding at t2 to kill
Smith are such that in some of them he is blushing at t1. To rule out this
possibility, we must assume that Jones's *not* blushing at t1 is a causally
necessary condition for his *not* deciding at t2 to kill Smith. But this means

---

[5] The term 'freely' is used by Plantinga in the libertarian's sense.
[6] Cf. Lamb 1993, 522.

that his blushing at t1 is causally sufficient for his decision to kill Smith. For if p is a causally necessary condition for q, then the absence of p is a causally sufficient condition for the absence of q. But if so, then, as argued above, what we have is not an IRR-situation.[7]

My strategy, then, of resisting Frankfurt's argument for IRR is to put before Frankfurt the following dilemma: Either the truth of (1) is grounded in some fact that is causally sufficient (in the circumstances) for Jones's decision at t2 to kill Smith, or it is not. If it is, then the situation described by Frankfurt is not an IRR-situation, since the factor that makes it impossible for Jones to avoid his decision to kill Smith *does* bring about that decision. On the other hand, if the truth of (1) is not thus grounded, it is hard to see how Jones's decision is unavoidable.[8] In either case the truth of IRR has not been established. In view of these considerations, I conclude that Frankfurt's attack on PAP as applied to decisions fails.

At this point a defender of Frankfurt might make the following move. First, he might ask us to consider a situation in which the sign that Black uses as an indication of whether Jones is going to decide to kill Smith is Jones's inclination to act so.[9] (If immediately after the deliberation process, Jones shows an inclination to decide to kill Smith, Black does nothing. On the other hand, if Jones shows an inclination to the contrary, Black intervenes and forces Jones to decide to kill Smith.) He might then claim that my rebuttal of Frankfurt rests on a mistaken assumption as to the relation between an agent's decision to perform some act and his inclination to decide to perform it. The latter, he might claim, does not precede the decision, but is rather a part of it. That is, a decision to do A, on this view, is a temporal process that begins with an inclination to decide to do A, and is then followed by some appropriate set of mental events that taken together make up the decision. This being the case, Frankfurt's point remains intact, since the sort of dilemma that I developed earlier does not arise. Frankfurt might agree that Jones's showing an inclination to decide to kill Smith is not a causally sufficient condition of his actual decision to kill Smith, but still insist that Jones lacks the power to decide otherwise. For to be able to exercise that power, Jones would first have to show an inclination for

[7] Fischer (1982, 33) also tries to describe an IRR-situation with regard to decisions. I criticize his attempt in "Libertarianism and the Avoidability of Decisions" (forthcoming in *Faith and Philosophy*), employing considerations similar to those that I have used above against Frankfurt. For Fischer's response, see his "Libertarianism and Avoidability" (also forthcoming in *Faith and Philosophy*).

[8] Frankfurt seems to concede that to ensure that Jones's decision to kill Smith is unavoidable, the decision has to be caused by an earlier state of Jones's (Frankfurt 1969, n. 3). This is puzzling given that he undertakes to establish a thesis such as IRR.

[9] The possibility that the inclination to make a certain decision can be used as a sign of that decision is suggested by Fischer (see Fischer 1982, 26).

deciding not to kill Smith. But then Black would intervene, and would force him to decide to kill Smith nevertheless.[10]

However, this attempt to rescue Frankfurt's argument is unconvincing for two reasons. First, it only pushes the debate between Frankfurt and the libertarian back one step. Instead of claiming that a free agent has it within his power to decide otherwise, the libertarian might now insist that such an agent has it within his power to form an inclination to decide otherwise. Second, and more importantly, the libertarian might reject the objector's conception of a decision. He might claim that a decision, being the forming of an intention, is a *simple* mental action[11] that does not exhibit the sort of complex structure assumed by the objector. This point, he might stress, is also borne out by our everyday talk about decisions. Thus, it would be conceptually wrong for one to describe what Jones is doing at a given moment by saying that he is in the *process* of deciding to kill Smith, or that he has not yet finished deciding to kill Smith. Jones, to be sure, can be said to be in the process of *trying to reach a decision* about whether to kill Smith. But that process and the event of deciding to kill Smith are two different things. To reject this libertarian reply, Frankfurt's defender would have to refute the conception of decision underlying it. And as long he has not done so, the libertarian position is immune to Frankfurt's attack on PAP.

2

So far I have argued that Frankfurt's attack on the principle of alternative possibilities does not work for decisions. But how about actions other than deciding, for example, killing, stealing, voting, insulting, intentional omission such as an agent's intentionally not obeying an order, etc.? Frankfurt seems to be right in rejecting PAP when applied to this latter type of act. For example, assuming that Jones kills Smith for reasons of his own, the passive presence of a counterfactual intervener who, if he were to detect in Jones a pro-attitude or inclination not to kill Smith, would prevent Jones from acting so, would be sufficient to rob Jones of his freedom to act otherwise, without in any way forcing him to act as he actually did. What we want to understand is what accounts for this difference between the two sorts of cases. Our previous remarks on the nature of decisions suggest an answer to this question. Note that, unlike a decision, an act such as Jones's act of intentionally not killing Smith (which in this case may count as Jones's acting otherwise) is a *complex* act. It is a complex act in the sense that it

---

[10] This possible line of defense, along with the refutation that follows it, is also mentioned in my "Libertarianism and the Avoidability of Decisions."

[11] I am borrowing 'simple mental action' from Ginet 1990, chap. 1.

requires both an intention on Jones's part not to kill Smith, as well as his being later, at t3, in the state of not killing Smith. The performance of such an act, could, therefore, be prevented by a powerful enough counterfactual intervener, who being able to detect the said intention in Jones, is in a position to prevent him from being in that state (the state of not killing Smith). The same, however, cannot be said in the case of Jones's decision to kill Smith. To act otherwise in this case, it is sufficient for Jones to decide not to kill Smith, which is a decision that Jones can make without (necessarily) having to form a *prior* intention not to decide to kill Smith, and which does not depend for its occurrence on the occurrence of any later events. Hence, the sort of way in which a counterfactual intervener can prevent an agent from acting otherwise in the case of an act like killing is not available to the intervener in the case of a decision.

This asymmetry between a complex action such as killing and the act of deciding can be also brought out by the following consideration. Suppose again that Jones kills Smith at t3, and consider what is known as the conditional analysis of 'could have done otherwise' as applied to this act, namely,

(5C) Had Jones chosen at t2 not to kill Smith at t3, he would have succeeded in doing so.

It seems intuitive to view (5C) as a necessary condition of

(5) Jones could have acted otherwise; that is, Jones could have performed the act of not killing Smith.

This fact also explains why the presence of a Frankfurt-type counterfactual intervener like Black would deprive Jones of his ability to act otherwise. His presence would render (5C) false, and consequently would also falsify (5). Note, however, that this sort of consideration would not count against Jones's ability to decide otherwise. And the reason here is not that a conditional analysis of

(6) Jones could have decided otherwise; that is, Jones could have decided at t2 *not* to kill Smith at t3

as

(6C) Had Jones chosen at t1 to decide at t2 *not* to kill Smith, he would have succeeded in doing so

would not make sense, in view of the obscurity of 'Jones chooses at t1 to decide not to perform a certain action'. (We certainly can conceive of circumstances in which such a locution would make sense. For example, a person S who is strongly inclined to kill another person X may, in order not to succumb to this temptation, choose to visit a hypnotist who is able to cause him to decide to act otherwise, and in such circumstances it would be true to say that S chose at t1 not to decide at t2 to kill X.) Rather, it is that the truth of (6C) is simply not a necessary condition of the truth of (6). One easy way to see this is to conceive of a Frankfurt-type scenario in which the counterfactual intervener is intent on preventing Jones from deciding not to kill Smith if and only if Jones chooses at t1 to so decide. In such circumstances, (6C) would be false, whereas (6) might still be true, since, as explained above, Jones need not, in order to exercise his power to decide *not* to kill Smith, *first* choose to decide not to do so. He can decide directly not to kill Smith, without having to go through any prior process of choosing.

The salient point that emerges is that insofar as the performance of a given action by an agent involves the realization of a certain want (volition) or intention of the agent by events that are distinct from that want or intention and that occur after the latter is formed, a Frankfurt-type counterfactual intervener can in principle prevent the occurrence of those events, and can consequently prevent the performance of the action. But we have not been given a good reason to think that the intervener can prevent the agent from forming that want (volition) or intention, provided of course that the agent believes that what he wants (wills) or intends to do is in his power. Putting this point in terms of freedom, we may say that a Frankfurt-type counterfactual intervener can deprive an agent of his *freedom to carry out* a given want or intention, but he cannot deprive him of his *freedom to form* it.

3

If my argument so far is correct, there arises an important distinction between the following two principles:

(PAP′) Where A is a complex act, a person is morally responsible for performing A only if he could have performed some other complex act instead of A;[12]

(PAV) A person is morally responsible for performing a given act A only if he could have avoided performing it,

where the latter does not fall prey to Frankfurt's criticism. I have already defended PAV in the case where A is a decision, or the forming of an intention, etc. I wish now to defend it for the case where A is a complex action

[12] Alternatively, this principle might be formulated as follows:

(PAP′) Where A is a complex act, a person S is morally responsible for performing A only if it was within S's power to perform some complex act other than A, and not to perform A.

such as Jones's action of killing Smith, or Jack's action of stealing a book, etc. To see this, let us consider once more a situation in which at t2 Jones forms on his own an intention to kill Smith at t3, and carries it out. Assume also that lurking in the background there is Black, who, if he were to notice that Jones decided at t2 *not* to kill Smith, would intervene and force Jones to kill him. I wish to claim that though in the situation under consideration Jones cannot (at t1) prevent Smith's death, and cannot avoid exemplifying the property of killing Smith at t3, he nevertheless can avoid the performance of his *actual* act of killing Smith, or can bring about the nonoccurrence of that act. My defense of this claim rests on the following two considerations: (a) I assume a version of action theory according to which Jones's act of killing Smith, a complex action, consists at least in part of an intention or volition by Jones to bring about Smith's death, where that intention or volition stands in some appropriate causal relation to the *event* of Jones's killing Smith.[13] Moreover, I assume that the said action (qua acttoken), *essentially* contains that volition or intention.[14] (b) I then claim that by having the power to form at t1 the intention *not* to kill Smith, which Frankfurt's counterfactual intervener cannot prevent him from doing, Jones can prevent the occurrence of his intention to kill Smith (qua intentiontoken), and hence, given (a), can also be said to have the power to bring about the non-occurrence of his act of killing Smith (qua act-token).[15]

Note that the above defense of PAV differs importantly from Peter Van Inwagen's recent defense of the principle:

(PPP2) A person is morally responsible for a certain state of affairs only if that state of affairs obtains, and he could have prevented it from obtaining. (1983, 171–75)

[13] For "component" conceptions of action of this type, see, for example, Searle 1983, 84–93; McCann 1974; and Costa 1987. The intention in question might be an "intention in action" in Searle's sense or a "proximal intention" in Mele's sense. See Mele 1992a, 208–9 and Mele 1992b, chaps. 9–10.

[14] Strictly speaking, there is a further essentialist assumption that I need to make, which is that the exact time at which an event occurs is essential to it. For an interesting defense of this assumption, see Lombard 1982.

[15] Note also that a further consideration in favor of PAV is that the part of it that deals with moral blame.

(PAV1) A person S is morally blameworthy for performing a given act A only if S could have avoided performing A

is entailed by the following two principles, which seem intuitively correct:

(MB) A person S is morally blameworthy for performing a given act A only if S has a moral obligation *not* to perform A.

(K) A person S has a moral obligation *not* to perform a given act A only if it was within S's power *not* to perform A.

In this connection, see Widerker 1991, 222–24, and Widerker and Katzoff 1993, 102–4.

For one thing, his defense applies only to states of affairs that can be deemed consequences or results of acts, such as the state of affairs of Smith's being dead (ibid., 165). It does *not* apply to what van Inwagen calls "act-universals" (which correspond to my act-tokens), such as Jones's act of killing Smith at t, or Jones's decision to kill Smith at t, with which PAV is concerned.[16] Second, van Inwagen defends PPP2 assuming that in a Frankfurt-type setting an act-consequence, such as Smith's being dead, is unavoidable, whereas in my defense of PAV, I insist on the avoidability of Jones's act of killing Smith in such a setting.[17]

PAV brings out nicely the difference between acting otherwise and avoiding the performance of an act, stressing that the latter does not imply the former. It also enables the libertarian to give a simple explanation of why, in the case of Jones's unjustifiably killing Smith, we may hold Jones blameworthy for performing that act, even though he could not have done otherwise. He is blameworthy because he had a moral obligation not to perform

---

[16] In his 1978 (220–21), van Inwagen expresses serious doubts whether his defense of PPP2 could be applied to defend what he calls "the Principle of Alternate Possibilities for act-universals," namely

(PAP2)   A person S is morally responsible for a certain act-universal only if that act-universal obtains, and S could have prevented it from obtaining.

[17] Note also that my defense of PAV is also not vulnerable to John Fischer's recent criticism (1982, 29–30) of

(PPP1)   A person is morally responsible for a certain event-particular only if he could have prevented it.

Fischer takes the defender of PPP1 to be (i) assuming

(E)   If an event x is the product of some causes, then it is essentially the product of those causes,

and then (ii) arguing that PPP1 is not falsified by a Frankfurt-type counterexample to PAP. The alleged reason for this is that in the alternate scenario in which Jones is forced by Black or by some other factor to kill Smith, Jones's *actual* act of killing Smith does not occur, since *it* has a different causal history than Jones's act of killing Smith in that scenario. Hence, Jones's power to prevent his actual act of killing Smith (qua act-token) is not threatened. Aside from finding (E) problematic, Fischer charges the proponent of this defense of PPP1 with confusing the idea of Jones's having the power to prevent his act of killing Smith with the logical possibility of that act's not occurring. Note, however, that his criticism of the above defense of PPP1 is based on the assumption that in the alternative scenario in which Jones is forced by Black or by some other factor to kill Smith (Fischer talks about a mechanism installed in Jones's brain which does this task) Jones *never* succeeds in making the decision *not* to kill Smith. As Fischer sees it, in that scenario Jones is merely inclined towards making that decision, and is then forced by Black to decide to kill Smith nevertheless and to kill him. This assumption is not true in the case of my defense of PAV. For, as I explicitly argue, in the alternate scenario that I am envisaging, Jones *does* succeed in making that decision, and hence does succeed in forming an intention *not* to kill Smith, in which case he can properly be said to have the power to prevent his actual act of killing Smith. Now it is true that in that scenario, immediately after having formed the intention *not* to kill Smith, Jones may be forced by Black to form the contrary intention, and then to act on it. But this would be a different intention from the one he actually formed, and a different act from the one he actually performed. On this point see also note 14.

this act and could have avoided performing it, but failed to do so. The fact that, in the circumstances, Jones could not have done otherwise, in the sense of not having the power to perform some other complex act instead of the killing, is irrelevant. His obligation was to avoid killing Smith, and not to do something else instead. To be sure, Jones's power to avoid the killing, as well as his responsibility for it, are grounded, for the libertarian, in the avoidability of and his responsibility for his *decision* to kill Smith. But this is as it should be, since, on his view, it is decisions and the like to which responsibility attaches in the first instance.

To sharpen the results of our investigation, it may be useful at this point to state exactly how the libertarian's position differs from Frankfurt's. The libertarian maintains that Frankfurt has not given a good reason to reject the following principles:

(PAPD)   A person is morally responsible for his *decision* (choice, undertaking) to do A only if he could have decided otherwise.

(PAV)   A person is morally responsible for performing a given act A only if he could have avoided performing it.

(PAV′)   Where V is a complex act-property (killing, voting, insulting, etc.), and t* is the exact time at which a person S Vs intentionally, S is morally responsible for his Ving *intentionally* at t* only if it was within his power not to V intentionally at t*.

However, the libertarian agrees with Frankfurt that

(PAP′)   Where A is a complex act, a person is morally responsible for performing A only if he could have performed some other complex act instead of A

is false.[18]

Frankfurt's argument against PAP presents a formidable challenge to the libertarian conception of freedom and moral responsibility. In this paper, we have examined his argument and found that one central assumption of it,

---

[18] As for Jones's responsibility for the event of Smith's dying, the libertarian I am representing has a choice. He may adopt van Inwagen's view that Jones is not morally responsible for this event ("event-universal" in van Inwagen's terms), since

(a)   no person x is responsible for the obtaining of a state of affairs that would have obtained no matter what choices or decisions x had made (van Inwagen 1983, 171–80).

Or he may regard Jones as being indirectly or derivatively responsible for the said event by virtue of being responsible for the decision that led to it. For accounts of indirect or derivative responsibility, see Berofsky 1987, 35, and Zimmerman 1988, 55–57. Similar remarks would apply to Jones's responsibility for his exemplifying the act-property of killing Smith at t3. Ginet (unpublished manuscript) has recently argued that van Inwagen's thesis (a) needs to be modified as follows: If a certain state of affairs would have obtained no matter what choices or decisions x had made *that x could have made*, then x is not responsible for it.

IRR, is unwarranted, because it does not hold for decisions, formings of intentions, etc.—mental acts that for the libertarian constitute the primary *loci* of moral responsibility. This being the case, I conclude that, contrary to much opinion, libertarians have nothing to fear from Frankfurt's attack on PAP.[19]

REFERENCES

Adams, R. 1977. "Middle Knowledge and the Problem of Evil." *American Philosophical Quarterly*, 14: 109–17.

Alston, William P. 1989. *Divine and Human Language*. Ithaca: Cornell University Press.

Berofsky, B. 1987. *Freedom from Necessity*. London: Routledge and Kegan Paul.

Blumenfeld, D. 1971. "The Principle of Alternate Possibilities." *Journal of Philosophy*, 67: 339–45.

Costa, M. 1987. "Causal Theories of Action." *Canadian Journal of Philosophy*, 17: 831–54.

Davidson, D. 1973. "Freedom to Act." In *Essays on Freedom of Action*, ed. Ted Hondrich. London: Routledge and Kegan Paul.

Dennett, D. 1984. *Elbow Room: Varieties of Free Will Worth Wanting*. Cambridge: MIT Press.

Fischer, J. M. 1982. "Responsibility and Control." *Journal of Philosophy*, 89: 24–40. Reprinted in Fischer 1987.

——. Forthcoming. "Libertarianism and Avoidability."

——, ed. 1987. *Moral Responsibility*. Ithaca: Cornell University Press.

Fischer, J. M., and M. Ravizza. 1991. "Responsibility and Inevitability." *Ethics*, 101: 258–78.

Frankfurt, H. 1969. "Alternate Possibilities and Moral Responsibility." *Journal of Philosophy*, 66: 829–39. [Reprinted as Essay 8, this volume.]

Ginet, C. 1990. *On Action*. Cambridge: Cambridge University Press.

——. Comments on Van Inwagen, "Ability and Responsibility." Unpublished manuscript.

Goldman, A. 1970. *A Theory of Human Action*. Englewood Cliffs, N.J.: Prentice Hall.

Heinaman, R. 1986. "Incompatibilism without the Principle of Alternative Possibilities." *Australasian Journal of Philosophy*, 64: 266–76.

Lamb, James W. 1993. "Evaluative Compatibilism and the Principle of Alternate Possibilities." *Journal of Philosophy*, 90: 497–516.

Lombard, L. 1982. "Events and the Essentiality of Time." *Canadian Journal of Philosophy*, 12: 1–17.

McCann, H. 1974. "Volition and Basic Action." *Philosophical Review*, 83: 451–73.

Mele, A. 1992a. *Springs of Action*. Oxford: Oxford University Press.

——. 1992b. "Recent Work on Intentional Action." *American Philosophical Quarterly*, 29: 200–17.

[19] I would like to thank Eddy Zemach, William Alston, Charlotte Katzoff, Brian Shanley, and, most especially, Dale Gottlieb, Carl Ginet, William Rowe, and Elmar Kremer for excellent discussions and comments on earlier versions of this paper. I have also benefited from the comments of the referees for the *Philosophical Review*.

Naylor, M. 1984. "Frankfurt on the Principle of Alternate Possibilities." *Philosophical Studies*, 46: 249–58.

Plantinga, A. 1974. *The Nature of Necessity*. Oxford: Oxford University Press.

Rowe, W. L. 1991. *Thomas Reid on Freedom and Morality*. Ithaca: Cornell University Press.

Searle J. 1983. *Intentionality*. Cambridge: Cambridge University Press.

Stump, E. 1990. "Intellect, Will and the Principle of Alternate Possibilities." In *Christian Theism and the Problems of Philosophy*, ed. Michael D. Beaty. Notre Dame: University of Notre Dame Press.

Van Inwagen, P. 1978. "Ability and Responsibility." *Philosophical Review*, 87: 201–24. Reprinted in Fischer 1987.

——. 1983. *An Essay on Free Will*. Oxford: Oxford University Press.

Widerker, D. 1991. "Frankfurt on 'Ought Implies Can' and Alternate Possibilities." *Analysis*, 51: 222–24.

——. Forthcoming. "Libertarianism and the Avoidability of Decisions."

Widerker, D., and Katzoff C. 1993. Review of B. Berofsky, *Freedom from Necessity. Journal of Philosophy*, 90: 98–104.

Zimmerman, M. 1988. *An Essay on Moral Responsibility*. Totowa, N.J.: Rowman and Littlefield.

10

FRANKFURT-STYLE COMPATIBILISM

JOHN MARTIN FISCHER

I INTRODUCTION

Many philosophers have worried that God's existence (understood in a certain way) or causal determinism (the doctrine that nonrelational features of the past, together with the laws of nature, are causally sufficient for all truths about the present and future) would rule out moral responsibility. One influential reason for this discomfort, although certainly not the only reason, is that it is plausible to suppose that God's existence (construed in a certain way) or causal determinism would rule out "genuine" alternative possibilities. If moral responsibility requires this sort of alternative possibility (at least at some relevant point along the path to behavior), then it would seem that God's existence or causal determinism would be incompatible with moral responsibility.

The thought that moral responsibility requires genuine alternative possibilities—the freedom to will, choose, or do otherwise—has been and continues to be an important motivation for incompatibilism about such doctrines as God's existence or causal determinism and moral responsibility. It is quite natural to suppose that if we have only one option that is genuinely available to us, then we *have* to do what we actually do, and that if we have to do what we actually do, we are *compelled* so to behave. But if we are compelled to behave as we actually do, then surely we cannot legitimately be held morally responsible for what we do.

Joel Feinberg employs the analogy between an individual making decisions about his life and a train going down the railroad tracks. Having genuine freedom—the sort that grounds our moral responsibility—corresponds, on Feinberg's model, to a train's having more than one track available to it. If our lives correspond to a train chugging down a track

'Frankfurt-Style Compatibilism' from *The Contours of Agency: Essays on Themes from Harry Frankfurt*, edited by Sarah Buss and Lee Overton, 1–26. Reprinted by permission of The MIT Press.

which is the only track it can take, then it follows, according to Feinberg, that we "could take no credit or blame for any of [our] achievements, and [we] could no more be responsible for [our] lives than are robots, or the trains in our . . . metaphor that must run on 'predestined grooves.' "[1] Feinberg here articulates the powerful and influential idea that in order to be morally responsible, we must have more than one option. The future must be a branching, treelike structure; following Borges, the future must be a "garden of forking paths."

Because of the presupposed link between moral responsibility (and even personhood) and alternative possibilities, an extraordinary amount of attention has been given to arguments purporting to establish that God's existence or causal determinism do indeed rule out the relevant sorts of alternative possibilities. Much ingenuity has been displayed on both sides. But today, after literally thousands of years of debates about these issues, there is still heated disagreement about whether God's existence (understood in certain ways) or causal determinism rules out alternative possibilities.

Given this disagreement, and the fact (I believe it to be a fact) that rational people can disagree about whether the doctrines in question are indeed incompatible with the relevant sort of alternative possibilities (that is, the fact that there is no *knockdown* argument for incompatibilism), we seem to have arrived at a certain kind of stalemate. In my view, Harry Frankfurt has helped us to make considerable progress in this dialectic context. Frankfurt has presented a set of examples that appear to show that moral responsibility does not after all require alternative possibilities. If he is correct about this, then we can admit that it is plausible that God's existence or causal determinism would rule out alternative possibilities but still maintain that we can reasonably be thought to be morally responsible (even in a causally determined world or a world in which an essentially omniscient, temporal God exists). Slightly more carefully, Frankfurt has helped us to shift the debate away from issues pertaining to alternative possibilities to issues related to the actual sequence of events leading to the behavior in question. In my view, this is an important contribution, even if it does not in itself decisively establish compatibilism about (say) causal determinism and moral responsibility.

In this essay I shall begin by sketching a "Frankfurt-type example." I shall then lay out a disturbing challenge to the claim I have made above that these examples help us to make significant progress in the debates about the relationship between moral responsibility and causal determinism. (In the

---

[1] Joel Feinberg, "The Interest of Liberty on the Scales," in his *Rights, Justice, and the Bounds of Liberty: Essays in Social Philosophy* (Princeton: Princeton University Press, 1980), 36–40.

discussion that follows, I focus mainly on causal determinism, although I believe the points will in most instances apply equally to God's existence.)[2] I then will provide a reply to this challenge, and the reply will point toward a more refined formulation of the important contribution I believe Frankfurt has made to defending a certain sort of compatibilism.

II FRANKFURT-TYPE EXAMPLES

Here is a particular version of a "Frankfurt-type example."[3] In this sort of case, a crucial role is played by some kind of involuntary sign or indication of the agent's future choices and behavior.[4] So suppose Jones is in a voting booth deliberating about whether to vote for Gore or Bush. (He has left this decision until the end, much as some restaurant patrons wait until the waiter asks before making a final decision about their meal.) After some reflection, he chooses to vote for Gore, and does vote for Gore by marking his ballot in the normal way. Unbeknownst to him, Black, a liberal neurosurgeon working with the Democratic party, has implanted a device in Jones's brain that monitors Jones's brain activities. If he is about to choose to vote Democratic, the device simply continues monitoring and does not intervene in the process in any way. If, however, Jones is about to choose to vote (say) Republican, the device triggers an intervention that involves electronic stimulation of the brain sufficient to produce a choice to vote for the Democrat (and a subsequent Democratic vote).

How can the device tell whether Jones is about to choose to vote Republican or Democrat? This is where the "prior sign" comes in. If Jones is about to choose at t_2 to vote for Gore at t_3, he shows some involuntary sign—say a neurological pattern in his brain—at t_1. Detecting this, Black's device does not intervene. But if Jones is about to choose at t_2 to vote for Bush at t_3, he shows an involuntary sign—a different neurological pattern in his brain—at t_1. This brain pattern would trigger Black's device to intervene and cause Jones to choose at t_2 to vote for Gore, and to vote for Gore at t_3.

Given that the device plays no role in Jones's deliberations and act of voting, it seems to me that Jones acts freely and is morally responsible for voting for Gore. And given the presence of Black's device, it is plausible to

---

[2] Whether this is the case will depend on how one understands God's attributes, and, in particular, whether God's providential activities involve causation of the human will.

[3] The classic presentation is in Harry Frankfurt, "Alternate Possibilities and Moral Responsibility," in *The Importance of What We Care About* (Cambridge: Cambridge University Press, 1988) [reprinted as Essay 8, this volume].

[4] For this kind of Frankfurt-type case, see David Blumenfeld, "The Principle of Alternate Possibilities," *Journal of Philosophy*, 67 (1971): 339–344.

think that Jones does not have alternative possibilities with regard to his choice and action. Thus Frankfurt-type cases seem to sever the putative connection between moral responsibility and alternative possibilities; they appear to show the falsity of the Principle of Alternate Possibilities (PAP): A person is morally responsible for what he has done only if he could have done otherwise. And if moral responsibility does not require alternative possibilities, then if causal determinism threatens moral responsibility, it would not do so in virtue of ruling out alternative possibilities.

III THE CHALLENGE

The idea that Frankfurt-type examples help to pave the way for compatibilism has been challenged by various philosophers.[5] The challenge can usefully be put in terms of a dilemma: the Frankfurt-type stories presuppose either that causal determinism is true, or that it is false. If the former, then the claim that the relevant agent is morally responsible is question-begging, and if the latter, then the claim that the agent lacks alternative possibilities is false.

Let us start with the presupposition that causal determinism obtains. It does appear as if the relevant agent—Jones, in the example above—cannot choose or do otherwise (cannot choose at t_2 to vote for Bush or vote for Bush at t_3). This is because the "counterfactual intervener"—the liberal neurosurgeon, Black—can know, given the prior sign exhibited by Jones at t_1, that Jones will indeed choose to vote for Gore at t_2. If Jones were to choose at t_2 to vote for Bush, the prior sign would have had to have been different; thus Jones cannot at t_2 choose to vote for Bush. But the problem is that the contention that Jones is morally responsible for choosing to vote for Gore, and actually voting for Gore, is put in doubt, given the assumption of causal determinism.

That is, if causal determinism is assumed, it does not seem that someone could say that Jones is obviously morally responsible for his actual choice

---

[5] For such skepticism, see (among others) David Widerker, "Libertarian Freedom and the Avoidability of Decisions," *Faith and Philosophy*, 12 (1995): 113–118; and "Libertarianism and Frankfurt's Attack on the Principle of Alternative Possibilities," *Philosophical Review*, 104 (1995): 247–261 [reprinted as Essay 9, this volume]; Robert Kane, *Free Will and Values* (Albany: State University of New York Press, 1985), 51; and *The Significance of Free Will* (New York and Oxford: Oxford University Press, 1996), esp. 142–145; Carl Ginet, "In Defense of the Principle of Alternative Possibilities: Why I Don't Find Frankfurt's Argument Convincing," *Philosophical Perspectives*, 10 (1996): 403–417; Keith D. Wyma, "Moral Responsibility and Leeway for Action," *American Philosophical Quarterly*, 34 (1997): 57–70; and Laura Ekstrom, "Protecting Incompatibilist Freedom," *American Philosophical Quarterly*, 35 (1998): 281–291.

and action in a context in which the relationship between causal determinism and moral responsibility is at issue. To do so would appear to beg the question against the incompatibilist.

Laura Ekstrom is a good example of a philosopher who insists that if causal determinism is assumed to be true, then one cannot infer that the agent in question is morally responsible for his behavior.[6] Ekstrom says:

[Let us] focus our attention on the fact that causal determinism might be true. If it is true, then past events together with the laws of nature are together sufficient for Jones's making the particular decision he makes. . . . So Jones's subjective perception of available options is irrelevant; in fact, the past pushes him into one particular decision state, the only state physically possible at the time, given the past and the laws of nature. . . . In fact, according to the incompatibilist, if determinism is true, Jones should not be judged as morally responsible for his decision and his act, given the pushing feature of determinism . . . so P.A.P. is not defeated.[7]

In further support of her view, Ekstrom says:

Whether or not determinism is true *ought* to be relevant [to our intuitions concerning Jones's moral responsibility]—this is precisely what incompatibilist arguments are designed to show. According to the incompatibilists, our everyday notions concerning our own and others' freedom and moral responsibility in acting can be shown to be, upon reflection, in need of revision if the thesis of causal determinism is true.[8]

Now consider the other horn of the dilemma: that is, suppose that indeterminism (of a certain relevant sort) obtains. Under this supposition it would not be dialectically inappropriate to claim that Jones is morally responsible for his actual choice at t_2 to vote for Gore and his vote for Gore at t_3. But now the contention that Jones cannot choose at t_2 to vote for Bush at t_3 is called into question. This is because there is no deterministic relationship between the prior sign exhibited by Jones at t_1 and Jones's subsequent choice at t_2. So, if we consider the time just prior to t_2, everything about the past can be just as it is consistently with Jones's choosing at t_2 to vote for Bush. Someone might think that if it takes some time for Jones to make the choice, Black can intervene to prevent the completion of the choice; but then Jones will still have the possibility of "beginning to make the choice."

The proponents of the Frankfurt-type examples contend that they are non-question-begging cases in which an agent is morally responsible for his choice and action and yet has no sufficiently robust alternative possibilities. But the challenge appears to show that the examples in question are either not uncontroversial cases in which the agent is morally responsible for his

---

[6] Ekstrom, "Protecting Incompatibilist Freedom."
[7] Ibid., 284–285.
[8] Ibid., 284.

choice and subsequent behavior, or not cases in which the agent lacks alternative possibilities.

IV REPLY

The Assumption of Indeterminism

In giving my strategy for replying to the challenge, I want to start with the assumption of causal indeterminism. The idea behind the worry here is that although the agent can legitimately be deemed morally responsible, there are ineliminable alternative possibilities (given the assumption of indeterminism). I will only sketch the sort of reply I would be inclined to pursue, because I want to focus here on the assumption of causal determinism.

The first thing to say is that various philosophers, including Eleonore Stump, Alfred Mele and David Robb, and David Hunt, have argued that one can indeed construct versions of the Frankfurt-type examples in which it is both the case that indeterminism obtains and there are *no* alternative possibilities.[9] As I have discussed these versions of the Frankfurt-type examples in some detail elsewhere, I shall here simply say that I find these examples, and similar indeterministic Frankfurt-type examples, intriguing and highly suggestive.[10] They may indeed show that one can construct Frankfurt-type

---

[9] Hunt employs what might be called a "blockage" case, rather than a "prior-sign" case. This sort of case takes its cue from John Locke's example of a man who is, unbeknownst to him, locked in a room and decides voluntarily to remain in the room. In Hunt's case, although the brain actually works by an indeterministic process, all other neural pathways (all neural pathways not actually taken) are blocked (as in the locked door of John Locke's example). David P. Hunt, "Moral Responsibility and Unavoidable Action," *Philosophical Studies*, 97 (2000): 195–227. Mele and Robb present a case in which there are two actually operating sequences—one indeterministic and the other deterministic—which simultaneously result in the agent's decision (in which case the indeterministic sequence preempts the deterministic sequence). Alfred R. Mele and David Robb, "Rescuing Frankfurt-Style Cases," *Philosophical Review*, 107 (1998): 97–112. And Stump employs the plausible idea that one could correlate a certain stream of neural events with mental events such as choices or decisions; in her cases, the "counterfactual interveners" (the analogues to Black) can anticipate an impending mental event (of the relevant sort) by "reading" or detecting the *beginnings* of the neural sequence. Stump argues that they can thereby cut off the *mental event* (as opposed to the correlated neural sequence) before it even begins. Eleonore Stump, "Non-Cartesian Dualism and Materialism with Reductionism," *Faith and Philosophy*, 12 (1995): 505–531; "Libertarian Freedom and the Principle of Alternate Possibilities," in *Faith, Freedom and Rationality: Philosophy of Religion Today*, ed. Daniel Howard-Snyder and Jeff Jordan (Lanham, Maryland: Rowman and Littlefield, 1996), 73–88; and "Alternative Possibilities and Responsibility: The Flicker of Freedom," unpublished manuscript delivered at the American Philosophical Association Pacific Division Meetings, March 1998, Los Angeles, California.

[10] For a more careful description and evaluation of these sorts of indeterministic Frankfurt-type cases, see John Martin Fischer, "Recent Work on Moral Responsibility," *Ethics*, 110 (1999): 93–139, esp. 113–123.

examples that explicitly presuppose indeterminism in which there are *no* alternative possibilities.

It may, however, turn out that even in these examples there emerge alternative possibilities of certain sorts; here I would, however, pursue the argument (which I have developed elsewhere) that the alternative possibilities in question are not sufficiently *robust* to ground attributions of moral responsibility.[11] That is, I would argue that it is not enough for the critic of the Frankfurt-type examples to argue that there exist *some* alternative possibilities in the cases, no matter how flimsy or exiguous; if one grounds moral responsibility in alternative possibilities, I believe they must be *of a certain sort*. Someone who believes in the "garden of forking paths" picture (according to which alternative possibilities are necessary for moral responsibility) should also believe that those alternative possibilities are sufficiently robust. The mere possibility of unintentional or involuntary behavior—behavior for which the agent is not morally responsible—does not seem to me to offer sufficient substance on which to base one's attributions of moral responsibility. As in the debates about the relationship between libertarianism and control, there is a crucial difference between the *ability* to do otherwise and the *mere possibility* of something different happening. The same point applies to the debates about the Frankfurt-type cases.

So my view is that either one can entirely expunge alternative possibilities—even in the context of indeterminism in the actual sequence—or the remaining alternative possibilities will not be sufficiently robust. This is not surprising, because I would suggest that what we *value* in action for which an agent can legitimately be held morally responsible is *not* that he makes a certain sort of difference to the world, but rather, that he expresses himself in a certain way. And this sort of self-expression does not require alternative possibilities. I have argued elsewhere that adopting this view about the intuitive picture behind our ascriptions of moral responsibility—that what we value, in behavior for which the agent can fairly be held morally responsible, is a distinctive kind of self-expression—can make it considerably more plausible that moral responsibility does not in fact require alternative possibilities.[12]

---

[11] John Martin Fischer, *The Metaphysics of Free Will: An Essay on Control* (Oxford: Blackwell Publishers, 1994), 131–159; and "Responsibility and Self-Expression," *Journal of Ethics*, 3 (1999): 277–297.

[12] Fischer, "Responsibility and Self-Expression."

The Assumption of Causal Determinism

Let's now suppose that causal determinism is true. Under this assumption, it is unfair and question-begging simply to assert that the relevant agent—say, Jones—is morally responsible for his behavior. But the proponent of Frankfurt-style compatibilism should not—and need not—make such an assertion at this point.[13] Rather, the argument is in two parts. The first step is to argue—based on the Frankfurt-type examples—that intuitively it is plausible that alternative possibilities are irrelevant to ascriptions of moral responsibility. If one agrees with this point, the preliminary conclusion could be stated as follows: if the agent (say, Jones) is not morally responsible for his behavior, this is *not* in virtue of his lacking alternative possibilities. That is, the proponent of Frankfurt-style compatibilism does *not* assert, simply on the basis of Frankfurt-type examples, that the relevant agent is morally responsible for his behavior. Such a compatibilist should not take any stand about the responsibility of the agent simply on the basis of reflection on the Frankfurt-type examples. He should just say, "I don't know at this point whether the agent is morally responsible for his behavior, but *if* he is not, it is *not* because he lacks alternative possibilities."

Thus Frankfurt-type examples have the important function of *shifting the debate* away from considerations pertinent to the relationship between causal determinism and alternative possibilities. What now becomes important is to consider whether causal determinism in the actual sequence can plausibly be thought *directly* to rule out moral responsibility, independently of considerations relating to alternative possibilities. It is important to see that the issues here are different. That is, causal determinism is alleged to rule out alternative possibilities in virtue of deeply plausible principles encapsulating the "fixity of the past" and the "fixity of the natural laws." If causal determinism is true, then the past, together with the natural laws, entails all truths about the present and future. So, if the past is fixed and the natural laws are fixed, it would seem that this leaves room for only one present and one future.[14] But such principles (encapsulating the fixity of the past and natural laws) can be embraced by a "semicompatibilist"—a compatibilist about causal determinism and moral responsibility who separates this claim from the claim of the compatibility of causal determinism and alternative possibilities. The factors that would allegedly show that causal determinism directly rules out moral responsibility are *different* from

[13] I sketch this sort of reply in Fischer, "Recent Work on Moral Responsibility."

[14] For a development and discussion of such arguments, and the parallel argument with respect to God's foreknowledge, see Fischer, *The Metaphysics of Free Will*.

those that appear to show that causal determinism rules out alternative possibilities.

Some philosophers have evidently thought that Frankfurt-type compatibilism must fail insofar as the Frankfurt-type examples in themselves do not decisively establish the compatibility of causal determinism and moral responsibility. Michael Della Rocca argues that the relevance of alternative possibilities—even if they are mere flickers of freedom—is that they are a *sign* of the existence of actual-sequence indeterminism. If causal determination obtains in the actual sequence, then Della Rocca claims that one cannot conclude that the relevant agent is morally responsible.[15] Similarly, recall that Ekstrom has claimed that if causal determinism is assumed to be true, one cannot assert that the relevant agent is morally responsible, and thus "PAP is not defeated."

But the success of the Frankfurt-type strategy should not be judged on the basis of whether the Frankfurt-type cases in themselves decisively establish that moral responsibility is compatible with causal determinism. That they do not do *all* the work does not show that they do not do *some* important work. For example, I believe that the Frankfurt-type cases *do* show the following principle false: (PAP*): Lacking alternative possibilities is a condition which in itself—and apart from anything that accompanies it (either contingently or necessarily)—makes it the case that an agent is not morally responsible for his behavior. That (PAP*) is shown to be false is real progress: now we should turn to the issue of whether something that (perhaps) accompanies the lack of alternative possibilities—actual-sequence causal determination—rules out moral responsibility *directly*. Of course, if the reasons to think that causal determination in the actual sequence rules out moral responsibility directly are just as strong as the reasons to think that causal determinism rules out alternative possibilities, then the progress would be illusory; but I shall be arguing in the rest of this paper that the reasons are *not* as strong.

V CAUSAL DETERMINATION IN THE ACTUAL SEQUENCE

The question now is this: does causal determination in the actual sequence *directly* rule out moral responsibility (i.e., does causal determinism rule out moral responsibility apart from ruling out alternative possibilities)? In my

---

[15] Michael Della Rocca, "Frankfurt, Fischer and Flickers," *Noûs*, 32 (1998): 99–105. Indeed, he begins the article with the statement, "In this paper, I argue that John Martin Fischer's most recent argument for the compatibility of causal determinism and moral responsibility does not succeed" (99).

book, *The Metaphysics of Free Will: An Essay on Control*, I considered a number of reasons someone might think that causal determination directly rules out moral responsibility.[16] For example, an incompatibilist might insist that the presence of causal determination in the actual sequence is inconsistent with notions of "initiation," "origination," "being active rather than passive," or "creativity," where some (or all) of these notions are requirements of moral responsibility. On this approach, the incompatibilist does not rest his case on principles encapsulating the fixity of the past and the fixity of the laws (or modal "transfer principles" of any sort); rather, he rests his case on factors whose presence in the actual sequence allegedly directly rules out moral responsibility.

None of these notions, however, provides a compelling reason to opt for incompatibilism about causal determinism and moral responsibility. My argument (in *The Metaphysics of Free Will: An Essay on Control*) was that with respect to each of the notions in question—origination, initiation, activity, creativity, and so forth—there are compatibilist and incompatibilist interpretations, and, further, that there is no strong reason to opt for the incompatibilist interpretation, *apart from considerations pertaining to alternative possibilities.*[17] Thus there is no reason that a fair, reflective, and reasonable person not already committed to incompatibilism should conclude that causal determinism, in itself, and apart from considerations about alternative possibilities, is incompatible with moral responsibility. In the rest of this paper, I want to consider some other reasons it might be thought that causal determinism directly rules out moral responsibility; basically I will be defending and developing my view that there is no good reason a fair-minded person (not already committed to incompatibilism) should be convinced that causal determination in the actual sequence directly precludes moral responsibility.

Robert Kane's book, *The Significance of Free Will*, together with related articles, is perhaps the most comprehensive and thoughtful presentation of the motivation of incompatibilism (and also a positive account of libertarian freedom) of which I am aware.[18] Kane distinguishes two separate motivations for incompatibilism: a worry about alternative possibilities, and a worry about "ultimacy." To have "ultimate responsibility," according to Kane, agents must

have the power to be the *ultimate* producers of their own ends. . . . They have the *power to make choices which can only and finally be explained in terms of their own wills*

---

[16] Fischer, *The Metaphysics of Free Will*, esp. 149–154.
[17] For an elaboration of this argument, see Fischer, *The Metaphysics of Free Will*, 147–154.
[18] Kane, *The Significance of Free Will*.

(i.e., character, motives, and efforts of will). No one can have this power in a determined world.[19]

Thus Kane contends that quite apart from issues about alternative possibilities, the presence of causal determination in the actual sequence would be inconsistent with an agent's being "ultimately responsible" and so would rule out the agent's being morally responsible.

But why exactly must an agent have this sort of ultimate responsibility in order to be morally responsible? Someone could say that on reflection we have a deep preference not to be intermediate links in a deterministic causal chain that begins in events prior to our births. Perhaps *this* is the reason causal determinism rules out moral responsibility (quite apart from threatening alternative possibilities).

I find this answer puzzling and difficult to assess. One reason is that it seems to me to be dangerously close to, if not identical with, simply asserting that on reflection we have a deep preference that causal determinism (as applied to us) not be true. The question at issue is why exactly causal determinism in the actual sequence rules out moral responsibility *directly*. The answer that is proposed is that we can just see that we do not want it to be the case that our deliberations are simply intermediate links in a causally deterministic chain that begins before our births. But this answer does seem to me to be the assertion that we do not want it to be the case that causal determinism is true and thus that our behavior be causally determined. Perhaps this answer could be deemed "question-begging," or perhaps it is simply dialectically unhelpful. In any case, if the question at issue is why there is some reason to suppose that causal determination in the actual sequence directly rules out moral responsibility, and the dialectical context is one in which it is supposed that it is not *immediately obvious* that mere causal determination in the actual sequence directly rules out moral responsibility, then one must say more than that we object to being intermediate links in a deterministic causal chain.

When it is not the case that a person's choice and action are produced by a deterministic causal chain that starts with factors "external" to the person, Kane points out that it can be said of the person, "The buck stops here." Quite apart from wanting alternative possibilities, Kane suggests that we want it to be the case that the buck stops here. But, obviously, in this context, "The buck stops here" is a metaphor. If it simply stands for not being an intermediate link in a deterministic causal chain, then we are back to the problem that this does not make any dialectic progress.

---

[19] Robert Kane, "Two Kinds of Incompatibilism," *Philosophy and Phenomenological Research*, 50 (1989), 254.

A similar problem afflicts the view of Derk Pereboom, who claims that "if all of our behavior was 'in the cards' before we were born, in the sense that things happened before we came to exist that, by way of a deterministic causal process, inevitably result in our behavior, then we cannot legitimately be blamed for our wrongdoing."[20] Our behavior's "being in the cards" is obviously a metaphor. Pereboom means by this that conditions prior to our births "inevitably result in our behavior by a deterministic causal process." If the problematic notion of inevitability simply implies the notion of entailment, then Pereboom's claim just comes down to the unargued-for assumption that causal determination in the actual sequence rules out responsibility. Again, this is dialectically unhelpful. If "inevitability" also implies some sort of actual-sequence compulsion, this is question-begging within the dialectic context. *Why* exactly is it the case that one's behavior's being "in the cards," in the relevant sense, involves problematic compulsion and thus directly rules out moral responsibility?

I think it is interesting that, once the debate is shifted away from the relationship between causal determinism and alternative possibilities, it is difficult to present a non-question-begging reason why causal determinism rules out moral responsibility. I can however identify various additional resources in Kane's work which could be employed to explain why it is that we would object to the presence of causal determination in the actual sequence (apart from worries about alternative possibilities). The first idea seems to be that if we allow for moral responsibility when there is actual-sequence causal determination, then we will need to say that agents who are covertly manipulated in objectionable ways are also morally responsible.

Kane distinguishes between "constraining" and "nonconstraining" manipulation or "control."[21] Constraining control thwarts preexisting desires, values, ends, and purposes. But nonconstraining manipulation (or, in Kane's term, "control") actually implants the desires, values, ends, and purposes. When the nonconstraining control is covert (CNC), the agent is unaware of it. Kane says:

We are well aware of these two ways to get others to do our bidding in everyday life. We may force them to do what we want by coercing or constraining them against their wills, which is constraining or CC control. Or we may manipulate them into doing what we want while making them feel that they have made up their own minds and are acting "of their own free wills"—which is covert non-constraining or CNC control. Cases of CNC control in larger settings are provided by examples of behavioral engineering such as we find in utopian works like Aldous Huxley's *Brave New World*

[20] Derk Pereboom, "Alternative Possibilities and Causal Histories," chapter 1 of *Living without Free Will* (Cambridge: Cambridge University Press, 2001).

[21] Kane, *The Significance of Free Will*, 64–71.

or B. F. Skinner's *Walden Two*. Frazier, the fictional founder of Skinner's Walden Two, gives a clear description of CNC control when he says that in his community persons can do whatever they want or choose, but they have been conditioned since childhood to want and choose only what they can have or do.[22]

As Kane points out, the citizens of Walden Two are "satisfied" with themselves; they do not have inner motivational conflicts and they are marvelously "wholehearted" in their attitudes and engagements.[23] Indeed, Frazier, the founder of Walden Two, describes it as the "freest place on earth."[24]

Kane's point is that someone who allows for moral responsibility in the presence of actual-sequence causal determination will also have to allow for it in contexts like Walden Two. His suggestion is that once one concerns oneself with the *sources* of one's purposes and ends, this will necessarily lead to incompatibilism.[25] But I disagree. A compatibilist will certainly insist that not all causal chains are relevantly similar. The kind of manipulation that takes place in Walden Two does indeed rule out moral responsibility; for a compatibilist, this can be in virtue of the *specific nature* of the causal sequences that issue in behavior, rather than the *mere fact* of causal determination.

For example, on the approach to compatibilism I favor, one looks carefully at the *history* of the behavior in question. If there is unconsented-to covert manipulation of certain sorts, this can be the sort of historical factor that rules out moral responsibility. On my approach, one demands that the behavior issue from the agent's own suitably reasons-sensitive mechanism. That is, the agent must—in a specified sense—have "ownership" of the process that leads to the behavior, and this process must be appropriately sensitive to reasons. These conditions are not met in the objectionable cases

---

[22] Ibid., 65.

[23] Ibid., 65.

[24] B. F. Skinner, *Walden Two* (New York: MacMillan, 1962), 297; as cited in Kane, *The Significance of Free Will*, 65.

[25] A similar point is made by Ekstrom:

But the model of a person as chugging along on a certain line of straight train tracks, without any forks in the path, is the antithesis of a deep-seated and pervasive image of ourselves as free agents. The idea that we can direct our behavior by our thoughts (desires, beliefs, intentions) is welcome, but it is only superficially comforting. It comforts until we think about the possibility that even our thoughts are driven to be what they are by previous neurophysiological events which themselves stand in a chain of events (between which there are deterministic causal links), a chain going backward through events in our childhood brains and to events prior to our birth. (Ekstrom, "Protecting Incompatibilist Freedom," 285.)

Also, Kane says:

But, as Martha Klein has pointed out, an interest in ultimacy adds a different set of concerns [from those pertaining to alternative possibilities] about the "sources," "grounds," "reasons," and "explanations" of actions and events—that is, concerns about where they came from, what produced them, and who was responsible for them. It is by focusing on such concerns about origins and responsibility, I would argue, and not merely on alternative possibilities, that one arrives at incompatibilism. (Kane, *The Significance of Free Will*, 74.)

of CNC, and yet I would argue that they can be met in a context of mere causal determination.[26]

One might press all sorts of worries about the particular account I have simply gestured at here. But the key point is that a compatibilist can offer a robustly historical theory of moral responsibility. A compatibilist may well offer plausible ways of distinguishing between objectionable sorts of manipulation and mere causal determination. In reply to this sort of point, Kane says that in the cases of CNC and mere causal determination, the agents are *equally* unable to choose or do otherwise; that is, alternative possibilities are expunged as effectively by mere determination as by problematic manipulation.[27] I am willing to grant this, but this point is irrelevant to the issue of whether causal determination in the actual sequence *directly* rules out moral responsibility. It is in no way obvious that a compatibilist cannot usefully distinguish between the *actual sequences* involved in problematic manipulation and those involved in mere causal determination.

It is helpful to see how the sort of compatibilism envisaged here— semicompatibilism—differs from old-style compatibilism. Both sorts of compatibilism insist on the point that not all causal sequences are relevantly similar. But old-style compatibilism sought to defend the idea that when the causally deterministic sequence is not "problematic," then the agent has a genuine ability or freedom to choose and do otherwise. In contrast, semicompatibilism concedes that the mere fact of causal determination rules out alternative possibilities; nevertheless, it seeks to sort through the actual pathways to the behavior in question, distinguishing between those pathways that confer responsibility and those that do not. In doing so, the view can look carefully at the *sources* of an agent's values, preferences, purposes, and ends; it can attend to how the agent got to be the way he is.[28]

Kane gives great emphasis to a second point, which is related to his view that a compatibilist cannot adequately account for contexts of covert non-

---

[26] For developments of this sort of view, see Fischer, *The Metaphysics of Free Will*; and John Martin Fischer and Mark Ravizza, *Responsibility and Control: A Theory of Moral Responsibility* (Cambridge: Cambridge University Press, 1998). The conditions on ownership of the mechanism that issues in behavior are set out in *Responsibility and Control*, 207–239; the sort of reasons-sensitivity required for moral responsibility is developed on pp. 62–150. Throughout the book we argue that the conditions on reasons-sensitivity and mechanism ownership can indeed be met in a causally deterministic world; for a discussion of the relevant sorts of "manipulation," and how they would run afoul especially of the ownership condition, see pp. 230–236.

[27] Kane, *The Significance of Free Will*, 67–69.

[28] In her review of my book, *The Metaphysics of Free Will: An Essay on Control*, Sarah Buss says:

... I do not see how [Fischer's] semicompatibilism differs in any very important way from good old-fashioned compatibilism. Compatibilists have always readily conceded that if causal determinism is true, then no one has the ability to do-otherwise-even-when-the-past-and-the-laws-are-held-fixed. They have simply insisted that agents do not need *this* ability to be morally responsible for their behavior. According to the familiar compatibilist view, the

constraining control. He claims that the causal determination of all of an agent's behavior is inconsistent with the agent's having "objective worth."[29] To develop the notion of objective worth, Kane tells the story of Alan the artist:

Alan has been so despondent that a rich friend concocts a scheme to lift his spirits. The friend arranges to have Alan's paintings bought by confederates at the local art gallery under assumed names for $10,000 apiece. Alan mistakenly assumes his paintings are being recognized for their artistic merit by knowledgeable critics and collectors, and his spirits are lifted. Now let us imagine two possible worlds involving Alan. The first is the one just described, in which Alan thinks he is a great artist, and thinks he is being duly recognized as such, but really is not. The other imagined world is a similar one in which Alan has many of the same experiences, including the belief that he is a great artist. But in this second world he really is a great artist and really is being recognized as such; his rich friend is not merely deceiving him to lift his spirits. Finally, let us imagine that in both these worlds Alan dies happily, believing he is a great artist, though only in the second world was his belief correct.[30]

Kane points out that although Alan would feel equally happy in both worlds, most of us would say that there is an important difference in value in the two worlds for Alan. To say this, for Kane, is to accept some notion of "objective worth," according to which value is not simply a function of subjective states or experiences. So far so good. But Kane goes on to say:

I want to suggest that the notion of ultimate responsibility is of a piece with this

---

ability to do otherwise relevant to moral responsibility is the ability to do otherwise *if* certain counterfactual conditions obtain—if, for example one chooses to do otherwise. . . . (Sarah Buss, "Review of *The Metaphysics of Free Will*, by John Martin Fischer," *Philosophical Books* [1997]: 117–121, esp. 120.)

I admit that there has been some confusion about the "target" of various compatibilist analyses of "could" or "ability." Some compatibilists have indeed taken the relevant notion to be a *conditional ability*, corresponding to "can, if the agent were to choose differently," or something like this. But this seems to me to open the compatibilist to an obvious and devastating objection; it is simply irrelevant that the agent would have been able to do the thing in question *under different circumstances*. What one is interested in is whether the agent can do the thing in question in the particular circumstances he is in. Most compatibilists have understood their project to be to give an analysis of precisely this notion of "can, in the agent's particular circumstances." They take it that they are giving an account of the intuitive notion of "can"—what Austin called the "all-in sense of 'can' "—that corresponds to the notion of "can" that plays a role in our deliberations as agents (where we take it that we have more than one path into the future genuinely available to us—here and now). Given this project, however, their analyses do not necessarily embrace the fixity of the past or the fixity of the natural laws. It is important to distinguish between taking some sort of conditional ability to be the target of one's compatibilist analysis of an unconditional ability, on the one hand, and denying the fixity of the past or the fixity of the natural laws as part of one's compatibilist analysis, on the other. For good examples of such compatibilist approaches, see Keith Lehrer, " 'Can' in Theory and Practice: A Possible Worlds. Analysis," in *Action Theory: Proceedings of the Winnipeg Conference on Human Action*, ed. M. Brand and D. Walton (Dordrecht: D. Reidel, 1976), 241–270; and Terence Horgan, " 'Could,' Possible Worlds, and Moral Responsibility," *Southern Journal of Philosophy*, 17 (1979): 345–358.

[29] Kane, *The Significance of Free Will*, 97–98.
[30] Ibid., 97.

notion of objective worth. If, like Alan, we think that the objective worth of our acts or accomplishments is something valuable over and above the felt satisfaction the acts have or bring, then I suggest we will be inclined to think that a freedom requiring ultimate responsibility is valuable over and above compatibilist freedoms from coercion, compulsion, and oppression.... [I]f objective worth means little to us, or makes no sense—if we believe that the final perspective Alan or anyone should take is *inside* the worlds, in which subjective happiness is all that counts (even if it is based on deception)—we are likely to see no point or significance as well in ultimate responsibility and incompatibilist freedom.[31]

But, again, I disagree with Kane's contention that the compatibilist is saddled with the unattractive view. It is admittedly the case that some compatibilist views focus solely on structural arrangements of mental states.[32] But this is not essential to compatibilism. As I pointed out above, the view I favor is *historical*. I have argued elsewhere that there are two problems with purely structural accounts of moral responsibility (such as the hierarchical model): they are ahistorical, and they do not attend to the *connections* between the agent and the world.[33] My compatibilist account of moral responsibility is sensitive to history and it demands certain connections between the agent and the reasons provided by the world.[34] Just as a compatibilist account of moral responsibility can have these features (in virtue of which it is not purely structural), so a compatibilist can certainly agree with the view that there is "objective" worth in the sense that value is not purely a function of experiences—one must be connected to the world in the right way. (I also do not see why even a purely structural or "internalistic" compatibilist could not have an objective view about value, which is, after all, a *different* notion from moral responsibility.) There is absolutely *nothing* about compatibilism that requires a purely subjective account of value.

The attempts discussed above to argue that causal determination of behavior rules out moral responsibility apart from considerations pertinent to alternative possibilities are unconvincing. I now want to explore what Kane takes to be a related theme—the idea of independence. Kane says:

... when one traces the desires we have for incompatibilist free will to their roots, by way of [the idea of ultimate responsibility], one eventually arrives at two elemental (and I think interrelated) desires—(i) the desire to be independent sources of activity

---

[31] Kane, *The Significance of Free Will*, 98.

[32] Harry Frankfurt's "hierarchical" view of moral responsibility is a salient and important example of such a view. The classic presentation is in Harry Frankfurt, "Freedom of the Will and the Concept of the Person," in *The Importance of What We Care About* [reprinted as Essay 16, this volume].

[33] See, for example, Fischer and Ravizza, *Responsibility and Control*, esp. 252–253.

[34] I believe that a mechanism becomes the "agent's own" in virtue of the process whereby he "takes responsibility" for it; this renders may approach to moral responsibility a historical theory: *Responsibility and Control*, 170–239. Further, the reasons-responsiveness requirement ensures the appropriate sort of connection between the agent and the world.

in the world, which is connected, I maintain, from the earliest stages of childhood to the sense we have of our uniqueness and importance as individuals; and (ii) the desire that some of our deeds and accomplishments (such as Alan's paintings in my example) have objective worth. . . .[35]

But what exactly is it to be an "independent" source of activity? At this point in the dialectical context, one cannot say that the relevant notion of independence requires that, given the agent's past and environmental niche, he has alternative possibilities; and as we have seen, one cannot simply argue that the relevant notion of independence is captured by the claim that we prefer not to be an intermediate link in a deterministic causal chain.

Alfred Mele has offered a useful suggestion here.[36] This is the idea: an agent is independent, in the relevant sense, according to the incompatibilist, insofar as he makes an explanatory contribution to his behavior, the making of which cannot be fully explained by the laws of nature and the state of the world at some time prior to his having any sense of the apparent options.[37] If an agent's making a contribution to his behavior is fully explained by reference to prior conditions and the laws of nature, then he is not independent in the relevant sense; and of course if there is causal determination in the actual sequence leading to behavior, then the agent's contributions can in fact be entirely explained by prior conditions and the laws of nature. The desire for this sort of independence can then be offered as a reason why causal determination in the actual sequence would rule out moral responsibility quite apart from issues pertaining to alternative possibilities.

Kane attributes great importance to the requirement of incompatibilistic independence. As we saw above, Kane connects this sort of independence to one's "uniqueness and importance as an individual." Kane says, "What determinism takes away is a certain sense of the importance of oneself as an individual."[38] In a further elaboration of this view, Kane quotes William James, from his essay, "The Dilemma of Determinism": "The great point [about the incompatibilist view] is that the possibilities are really *here*. At those soul-trying moments when fate's scales seem to quiver [we acknowledge] that the issue is decided nowhere else than *here* and *now*. *That* is what gives the palpitating reality to our moral life and makes it tingle . . . with so strange and elaborate an excitement."[39] About this passage

[35] Kane, *The Significance of Free Will*, 98.

[36] Alfred R. Mele, "Soft Libertarianism and Frankfurt-Style Scenarios," *Philosophical Topics*, 24 (1996): 123–142; "Flickers of Freedom," *Journal of Social Philosophy*, 29 (1998): 144–156; "Kane, Luck, and the Significance of Free Will," *Philosophical Explorations*, 2 (1999): 96–104: and "Ultimate Responsibility and Dumb Luck," *Social Philosophy and Policy*, 16 (1999): 274–293.

[37] Mele, "Ultimate Responsibility and Dumb Luck," 285–287.

[38] Kane, *Free Will and Values*, 178.

[39] William James, "The Dilemma of Determinism," in *The Will to Believe and Other Essays* (New York: Dover, 1956), 183; as cited in Kane, *The Significance of Free Will*, 88.

from James, Kane says, "It may be easy to ridicule James's assertion that a certain passion and excitement would be taken out of present and future choice situations if we believed their outcomes were determined. But many ordinary persons and philosophers, myself included, would say that it is true."[40]

If causal determinism were true, would our importance as individuals be diminished? Would the passion, the thrill of life be gone? I don't have any inclination to think so. Imagine that a consortium of scientists from Cal Tech, Stanford, and MIT announced that despite the previous scientific views, it turns out that the equations that describe the universe are deterministic. That is, the previous indeterministic views—which posited tiny residual indeterminacies at the macro-level based on quantum indeterminacies at the micro-level—were based on inadequacies in our understanding of nature, and the new view is that the equations are universal generalizations. Would you conclude that your life lacks importance, that its importance is significantly diminished, or that your deliberations are empty and meaningless? I certainly would not.

I grant that those who are strongly predisposed to incompatibilism will cling to the requirement of independence (interpreted as above). They think of us as having what might be called the "importance of independence." But there is another sort of importance, which is, in my view, at least as compelling; let us call this the "importance of indispensability." Note that even if causal determinism obtains, invocation of prior states of the world plus the natural laws cannot explain our behavior and its upshots without *also* explaining that *we make a certain sort of contribution to them*. That is, the prior conditions and laws of nature explain what happens only by also explaining that we make a certain sort of contribution—that our deliberations have a certain character, for example. The very factors that explain what happens cannot explain the way the world actually unfolds without *also* explaining that we make a certain sort of contribution through (for example) our unhindered deliberations.[41]

Thus, in a causally deterministic world, although we would lack the importance of independence (interpreted as above), we could have the

[41] Michael Zimmerman has pointed out that in a case of actual (as opposed to preemptive) overdetermination, reference to one's (unhindered) deliberations may not be necessary in order to explain the fact that some state of affairs obtains, given that the same state of affairs is caused to obtain by some other route, as well as by one's deliberations. But it is nevertheless true that reference to one's unhindered deliberations is essential to an explanation of *how the actual sequence unfolds*, and thus, *of how it comes about* that the state of affairs obtains. The intended notion of explanation is not simply an explanation *that* a state of affairs obtains; it is an explanation of how it comes about that the state of affairs obtains.

importance of indispensability. By "unhindered" deliberations I mean deliberations not impaired by factors *uncontroversially* thought to rule out moral responsibility, such as certain sorts of hypnosis, manipulation, subliminal advertising, coercion, and so forth.[42] I believe that when one engages in unhindered deliberation in a causally deterministic world, one can exercise a certain sort of control; this is a kind of "actual-sequence" control, which does not require the presence of alternative possibilities. If this view is correct, then in a causally deterministic world, invocation of prior conditions together with the laws of nature cannot explain what happens without also explaining that the agent exercises a certain sort of control in contributing to it. Such an agent can surely be important, and—leaving aside the tingling sensation referred to by James—his deliberations can certainly have all the passion and engagement that it is reasonable to want.

Recall Robert Kane's metaphor, "The buck stops here." With apologies to Harry Truman, the compatibilist can suggest an alternative metaphor. To quote—or perhaps I should concede, paraphrase—the former Green Bay Packer, Ray Nitschke (not to be confused with the philosopher, Friedrich Nietzsche!), "To get there from here, you have to go through me, baby."

Now the dialectical situation is as follows. We have discussed two different notions of importance related to the explanatory role of prior conditions, the laws of nature, and the self—the importance of independence and the importance of indispensability. I suppose that certain people who are strongly predisposed to incompatibilism will insist on the requirement of independence (as interpreted above) for moral responsibility. But it seems to me that the importance of indispensability is at least an equally attractive notion. It is not obvious that one should prefer the requirement of independence (as interpreted above) to the requirement of indispensability. Given the compatibilistic notion of the importance of indispensability, I do not think that a fair-minded, reasonable person not already committed to incompatibilism will conclude that incompatibilistic independence is a requirement of moral responsibility. The compatibilist, then, can offer an attractive account of the sort of importance related to the explanatory role of prior conditions. Further, it is clear that the compatibilist can offer his own account of "independence," which would posit a freedom from certain

---

[42] Of course, an incompatibilist will contend that causally determined deliberations are not *unhindered*. I cannot here argue against the incompatibilist's contention; I am not here seeking to "prove" that my notion of "unhindered" is somehow the "correct" notion. Rather, I am employing what I admit to be a compatibilist notion. My claim is that this notion can be employed to present something—the importance of indispensability—that is at least as attractive (to the target audience—reasonable and fair-minded people not already committed to incompatibilism) as the incompatibilistically construed importance of independence.

objectionable kinds of influences (but not necessarily all prior states of the universe and the laws of nature).

Return now to Laura Ekstrom's contention that, if there is causal determination in the actual sequence, "the past pushes [the agent] into one particular decision state, the only state physically possible at the time, given the past and the laws of nature. . . ." It seems to me that Ekstrom's idea faces the same problems as the various suggestions discussed above. There is a commonsense notion of "pushing," according to which there is a difference between (say) being pushed by a strong gust of wind and simply walking normally down a trail. On this notion of "pushing," one would not necessarily be pushed by the past and laws of nature, given causal determinism. Of course, one could adopt a special incompatibilist notion of pushing, but this will only be attractive to those already strongly inclined toward incompatibilism, and not to reasonable and fair-minded persons not already strongly committed to a particular view about the compatibility issue.

I suppose Ekstrom could seek to argue that on the commonsense notion of "pushing," the laws of nature push. But there are various different accounts of what makes a generalization a law of nature. On many of these accounts, which have considerable plausibility, there would be no inclination whatsoever to say that laws of nature must "push." On some views, laws of nature do not "necessitate";[43] on other views, laws of nature necessitate, but this necessitation may be cashed out in ways which should not incline one to say that the laws push. So, for example, some would argue that one feature that makes a generalization a law of nature is that it "supports its counterfactuals" in a certain way; surely, however, this feature in itself does not entail problematic "pushing."

To elaborate. On the Stalnaker/Lewis account of the semantics for counterfactuals, the truth of a counterfactual is determined by the similarity-relations among possible worlds.[44] (Very roughly, "If *P* were the case, then *Q* would be the case" is true, on this approach, just in case *Q* is true in the possible world or worlds most similar to the actual world in which *P* is true.) Employing this approach to the truth conditions for counterfactuals, one could say that what helps to distinguish between mere generalizations and the laws of nature is the similarity-relations among various possible worlds. But this in itself does not seem to imply that the laws of nature "push" in any objectionable way, and it is hard to see how this, in combination with other

[43] For such a view, and its role in rendering compatibilism more appealing, see Bernard Berofsky, *The Metaphysical Basis of Responsibility* (New York: Routledge and Kegan Paul, 1987).
[44] Robert Stalnaker, "A Theory of Conditionals," in *Studies in Logical Theory, American Philosophical Quarterly* Series, ed. N. Rescher (Oxford: Blackwell Publishers, 1968): 98–112; and David Lewis, *Counterfactuals* (Cambridge: Harvard University Press, 1973).

factors, would have this sort of implication. Thus, as far as I can see, there is *no* reason that would compel a person not already committed to incompatibilism to think that causal determination in the actual sequence rules out moral responsibility *directly* (i.e., apart from ruling out alternative possibilities).

VI CONCLUSION

I said above that the Frankfurt-type examples have helped to shift the debates about free will and moral responsibility from considerations about alternative possibilities to factors present in the "actual-sequence." I now want to return explicitly to the issue of whether this is genuine—or merely illusory—progress. The progress would be merely illusory if the reasons to think that causal determination in the actual sequence rules out moral responsibility are just as strong as the reasons to think that causal determinism rules out alternative possibilities.

But I do *not* think that this is so. I believe that a reasonable person, having fairly considered the arguments, should conclude that causal determinism rules out alternative possibilities. The argument to this conclusion from the principles encapsulating the fixity of the past and the fixity of the natural laws seems to me to be strong. I do not think that the argument here is knockdown, or that any rational person needs to accept it simply in virtue of his rationality. But I believe that the argument that causal determinism rules out alternative possibilities is a valid argument based on premises that any fair-minded and reasonable person really *should* accept: the relevant notions of the fixity of the past and laws are deeply embedded in common sense.

In contrast, I do not think that any reasonable and fair-minded person, not already strongly predisposed to or antecedently committed to incompatibilism, should conclude that causal determination in the actual sequence *directly* rules out moral responsibility. There are various factors one might consider here: initiation, creativity, activity, freedom from objectionable manipulation, objective value, importance, and so forth. But for each notion there is a compatibilist account as well as an incompatibilist account. And it seems to me that there is no good reason to think that a reasonable and fair-minded person, not already committed to incompatibilism, should embrace the incompatibilist notion. Of course, the arguments sketched above will not convince a person who comes to the discussion with strong incompatibilist inclinations or is already firmly committed to incompatibilism; but I don't think any argument could do that, and this is certainly not a fair test of success.

So we should not accept the conclusion of the party-poopers who claim that Frankfurt-style compatibilism is not successful. Frankfurt-style compatibilism does represent a genuine advance; Frankfurt has helped to shift the debates from a context in which incompatibilism has an advantage to one in which incompatibilism has no such advantage.[45] If one believes—as I do—that there is a good "positive" reason to adopt compatibilism insofar as our basic views about ourselves—our views of ourselves as persons and as morally responsible—should not be held hostage to the discoveries of a consortium of scientists about the precise nature of the equations that describe the universe, then the progress made by Frankfurt can at least help to clear the way to embracing compatibilism.[46]

ACKNOWLEDGMENTS

I am indebted to thoughtful questions and comments by Michael Zimmerman, Win-Chiat Lee, and Harry Frankfurt at the conference, "Contours of Agency: The Philosophy of Harry Frankfurt," Wake Forest University, November 1999. I am especially grateful to the probing and detailed written comments by the editors, Sarah Buss and Lee Overton. I am privileged to be included among such distinguished philosophers in this volume in honor of a man whose work sets the standard for originality and elegance: Harry Frankfurt.

[45] In Della Rocca, "Frankfurt, Fischer, and Flickers," he says:

... I should like to call attention to a connection between my criticism of Fischer and what is, perhaps, Fischer's guiding insight in his approach to moral responsibility. For Fischer, in accounting for moral responsibility, we should focus not directly on any alternative sequence of events there may be, but on properties of the actual sequence, including especially facts about the actual causes of the relevant action. In criticizing Fischer, I have, in effect, used this insight or at least an implication of it against Fischer himself. The problem I have raised stems from his focusing on what the flicker of freedom shows about the alternative scenario (viz. that Jones does not do A freely in the alternative scenario), but not on what the flicker shows about the actual situation (viz. that Jones' action is not externally determined in the actual situation). If my objection to Fischer succeeds, it does so in virtue of drawing our attention to a connection between the presence of the flicker and a feature of the actual causal sequence. My procedure here thus reinforces, in a way that is perhaps not entirely welcome to Fischer, his exhortation to focus on the actual sequence. (103–104)

But Della Rocca's "procedure" is not at all unwelcome to me. If his point is that once one focuses on the actual sequence, there will be no *knockdown* argument (acceptable even to those already strongly inclined toward incompatibilism), I do not disagree. Rather, my point is that the debate will have been shifted to terrain considerably more hospitable to compatibilism. This is why I think it is useful to see that the presence of alternative possibilities does not *in itself* ground ascriptions of moral responsibility, and why I welcome the focus on the actual sequence.

[46] I do not believe that our personhood and moral responsibility should be insulated from *every* empirical discovery about the world. Rather, I believe that these central notions should be resilient with respect to this particular issue—whether the equations that describe the macroscopic universe are universal generalizations or probabilistic generalizations with extremely high probabilities attached to them. For discussions, see Fischer and Ravizza, *Responsibility and Control*, 253–254, and Fischer, "Recent Work on Moral Responsibility."

11

THE IMPOSSIBILITY OF MORAL RESPONSIBILITY

GALEN STRAWSON

I

There is an argument, which I will call the Basic Argument, which appears to prove that we cannot be truly or ultimately morally responsible for our actions. According to the Basic Argument, it makes no difference whether determinism is true or false. We cannot be truly or ultimately morally responsible for our actions in either case.

The Basic Argument has various expressions in the literature of free will, and its central idea can be quickly conveyed. (1) Nothing can be *causa sui*— nothing can be the cause of itself. (2) In order to be truly morally responsible for one's actions one would have to be *causa sui*, at least in certain crucial mental respects. (3) Therefore nothing can be truly morally responsible.

In this paper I want to reconsider the Basic Argument, in the hope that anyone who thinks that we can be truly or ultimately morally responsible for our actions will be prepared to say exactly what is wrong with it. I think that the point that it has to make is obvious, and that it has been underrated in recent discussion of free will—perhaps because it admits of no answer. I suspect that it is obvious in such a way that insisting on it too much is likely to make it seem less obvious than it is, given the innate contrasuggestibility of human beings in general and philosophers in particular. But I am not worried about making it seem less obvious than it is so long as it gets adequate attention. As far as its validity is concerned, it can look after itself.

A more cumbersome statement of the Basic Argument goes as follows.[1]

(1) Interested in free action, we are particularly interested in actions that are performed for a reason (as opposed to 'reflex' actions or mindlessly habitual actions).

Galen Strawson, 'The Impossibility of Moral Responsibility' from *Philosophical Studies*, 75/1–2 (1994), 5–24. Copyright © 1994 Kluwer Academic Publishers. Reprinted with kind permission of Kluwer Academic Publishers.

[1] Adapted from G. Strawson (1986), pp. 28–30.

(2)   When one acts for a reason, what one does is a function of how one is, mentally speaking. (It is also a function of one's height, one's strength, one's place and time, and so on. But the mental factors are crucial when moral responsibility is in question.)

(3)   So if one is to be truly responsible for how one acts, one must be truly responsible for how one is, mentally speaking—at least in certain respects.

(4)   But to be truly responsible for how one is, mentally speaking, in certain respects, one must have brought it about that one is the way one is, mentally speaking, in certain respects. And it is not merely that one must have caused oneself to be the way one is, mentally speaking. One must have consciously and explicitly chosen to be the way one is, mentally speaking, in certain respects, and one must have succeeded in bringing it about that one is that way.

(5)   But one cannot really be said to choose, in a conscious, reasoned, fashion, to be the way one is mentally speaking, in any respect at all, unless one already exists, mentally speaking, already equipped with some principles of choice, 'P1'—preferences, values, pro-attitudes, ideals—in the light of which one chooses how to be.

(6)   But then to be truly responsible, on account of having chosen to be the way one is, mentally speaking, in certain respects, one must be truly responsible for one's having the principles of choice P1 in the light of which one chose how to be.

(7)   But for this to be so one must have chosen P1, in a reasoned, conscious, intentional fashion.

(8)   But for this, i.e. (7), to be so one must already have had some principles of choice P2, in the light of which one chose P1.

(9)   And so on. Here we are setting out on a regress that we cannot stop. True self-determination is impossible because it requires the actual completion of an infinite series of choices of principles of choice.[2]

(10) So true moral responsibility is impossible, because it requires true self-determination, as noted in (3).

This may seem contrived, but essentially the same argument can be given in a more natural form. (1) It is undeniable that one is the way one is, initially, as a result of heredity and early experience, and it is undeniable that these are things for which one cannot be held to be in any way responsible (morally or otherwise). (2) One cannot at any later stage of life hope to accede to true moral responsibility for the way one is by trying to change the

---

[2] That is, the infinite series must have a beginning and an end, which is impossible.

way one already is as a result of heredity and previous experience. For (3) both the particular way in which one is moved to try to change oneself, and the degree of one's success in one's attempt at change, will be determined by how one already is as a result of heredity and previous experience. And (4) any further changes that one can bring about only after one has brought about certain initial changes will in turn be determined, via the initial changes, by heredity and previous experience. (5) This may not be the whole story, for it may be that some changes in the way one is are traceable not to heredity and experience but to the influence of indeterministic or random factors. But it is absurd to suppose that indeterministic or random factors, for which one is ex hypothesi in no way responsible, can in themselves contribute in any way to one's being truly morally responsible for how one is.

The claim, then, is not that people cannot change the way they are. They can, in certain respects (which tend to be exaggerated by North Americans and underestimated, perhaps, by Europeans). The claim is only that people cannot be supposed to change themselves in such a way as to be or become truly or ultimately morally responsible for the way they are, and hence for their actions.

II

I have encountered two main reactions to the Basic Argument. On the one hand it convinces almost all the students with whom I have discussed the topic of free will and moral responsibility.[3] On the other hand it often tends to be dismissed, in contemporary discussion of free will and moral responsibility, as wrong, or irrelevant, or fatuous, or too rapid, or an expression of metaphysical megalomania.

I think that the Basic Argument is certainly valid in showing that we cannot be morally responsible in the way that many suppose. And I think that it is the natural light, not fear, that has convinced the students I have taught that this is so. That is why it seems worthwhile to restate the argument in a slightly different—simpler and looser—version, and to ask again what is wrong with it.

Some may say that there is nothing wrong with it, but that it is not very interesting, and not very central to the free will debate. I doubt whether any

---

[3] Two have rejected it in fifteen years. Both had religious commitments, and argued, on general and radical sceptical grounds, that we can know almost nothing, and cannot therefore know that true moral responsibility is not possible in some way that we do not understand.

non-philosopher or beginner in philosophy would agree with this view. If one wants to think about free will and moral responsibility, consideration of some version of the Basic Argument is an overwhelmingly natural place to start. It certainly has to be considered at some point in a full discussion of free will and moral responsibility, even if the point it has to make is obvious. Belief in the kind of absolute moral responsibility that it shows to be impossible has for a long time been central to the Western religious, moral, and cultural tradition, even if it is now slightly on the wane (a disputable view). It is a matter of historical fact that concern about moral responsibility has been the main motor—indeed the *ratio essendi*—of discussion of the issue of free will. The only way in which one might hope to show (1) that the Basic Argument was not central to the free will debate would be to show (2) that the issue of moral responsibility was not central to the free will debate. There are, obviously, ways of taking the word 'free' in which (2) can be maintained. But (2) is clearly false none the less.[4]

In saying that the notion of moral responsibility criticized by the Basic Argument is central to the Western tradition, I am not suggesting that it is some artificial and local Judaeo-Christian-Kantian construct that is found nowhere else in the history of the peoples of the world, although even if it were that would hardly diminish its interest and importance for us. It is natural to suppose that Aristotle also subscribed to it,[5] and it is significant that anthropologists have suggested that most human societies can be classified either as 'guilt cultures' or as 'shame cultures'. It is true that neither of these two fundamental moral emotions necessarily presupposes a conception of oneself as truly morally responsible for what one has done. But the fact that both are widespread does at least suggest that a conception of moral responsibility similar to our own is a natural part of the human moral-conceptual repertoire.

In fact the notion of moral responsibility connects more tightly with the notion of guilt than with the notion of shame. In many cultures shame can attach to one because of what some member of one's family—or government—has done, and not because of anything one has done oneself; and in such cases the feeling of shame need not (although it may) involve some obscure, irrational feeling that one is somehow responsible for the behaviour of one's family or government. The case of guilt is less clear. There is no doubt that people can feel guilty (or can believe that they feel guilty) about things for which they are not responsible, let alone morally

---

[4] It is notable that both Robert Kane (1989) and Alfred Mele (forthcoming), in two of the best recent incompatibilist discussions of free will and autonomy, have relatively little to say about moral responsibility.

[5] Cf. *Nicomachean Ethics* III. 5.

responsible. But it is much less obvious that they can do this without any sense or belief that they are in fact responsible.

III

Such complications are typical of moral psychology, and they show that it is important to try to be precise about what sort of responsibility is under discussion. What sort of 'true' moral responsibility is being said to be both impossible and widely believed in?

An old story is very helpful in clarifying this question. This is the story of heaven and hell. As I understand it, true moral responsibility is responsibility of such a kind that, if we have it, then it *makes sense*, at least, to suppose that it could be just to punish some of us with (eternal) torment in hell and reward others with (eternal) bliss in heaven. The stress on the words 'makes sense' is important, for one certainly does not have to believe in any version of the story of heaven and hell in order to understand the notion of true moral responsibility that it is being used to illustrate. Nor does one have to believe in any version of the story of heaven and hell in order to believe in the existence of true moral responsibility. On the contrary: many atheists have believed in the existence of true moral responsibility. The story of heaven and hell is useful simply because it illustrates, in a peculiarly vivid way, the *kind* of absolute or ultimate accountability or responsibility that many have supposed themselves to have, and that many do still suppose themselves to have. It very clearly expresses its scope and force.

But one does not have to refer to religious faith in order to describe the sorts of everyday situation that are perhaps primarily influential in giving rise to our belief in true responsibility. Suppose you set off for a shop on the evening of a national holiday, intending to buy a cake with your last ten pound note. On the steps of the shop someone is shaking an Oxfam tin. You stop, and it seems completely clear to you that it is entirely up to you what you do next. That is, it seems to you that you are truly, radically free to choose, in such a way that you will be ultimately morally responsible for whatever you do choose. Even if you believe that determinism is true, and that you will in five minutes time be able to look back and say that what you did was determined, this does not seem to undermine your sense of the absoluteness and inescapability of your freedom, and of your moral responsibility for your choice. The same seems to be true even if you accept the validity of the Basic Argument stated in section I, which concludes that one cannot be in any way ultimately responsible for the way one is and decides. In both cases, it remains true that as one stands there, one's freedom and true moral responsibility seem obvious and absolute to one.

Large and small, morally significant or morally neutral, such situations of choice occur regularly in human life. I think they lie at the heart of the experience of freedom and moral responsibility. They are the fundamental source of our inability to give up belief in true or ultimate moral responsibility. There are further questions to be asked about why human beings experience these situations of choice as they do. It is an interesting question whether any cognitively sophisticated, rational, self-conscious agent must experience situations of choice in this way.[6] But they are the experiential rock on which the belief in true moral responsibility is founded.

IV

I will restate the Basic Argument. First, though, I will give some examples of people who have accepted that some sort of true or ultimate responsibility for the way one is is a necessary condition of true or ultimate moral responsibility for the way one acts, and who, certain that they are truly morally responsible for the way they act, have believed the condition to be fulfilled.[7]

E. H. Carr held that "normal adult human beings are morally responsible for their own personality". Jean-Paul Sartre talked of "the choice that each man makes of his personality", and held that "man is responsible for what he is". In a later interview he judged that his earlier assertions about freedom were incautious; but he still held that "in the end one is always responsible for what is made of one" in some absolute sense. Kant described the position very clearly when he claimed that "man *himself* must make or have made himself into whatever, in a moral sense, whether good or evil, he is to become. Either condition must be an effect of his free choice; for otherwise he could not be held responsible for it and could therefore be *morally* neither good nor evil." Since he was committed to belief in radical moral responsibility, Kant held that such self-creation does indeed take place, and wrote accordingly of "man's character, which he himself creates". and of "knowledge of oneself as a person who . . . is his own originator". John Patten, the

---

[6] Cf. MacKay (1960), and the discussion of the 'Genuine Incompatibilist Determinist' in G. Strawson (1986, pp. 281–6).

[7] I suspect that they have started out from their subjective certainty that they have true moral responsibility. They have then been led by reflection to the realization that they cannot really have such moral responsibility if they are not in some crucial way responsible for being the way they are. They have accordingly concluded that they are indeed responsible for being the way they are.

current British Minister for Education, a Catholic apparently preoccupied by the idea of sin, has claimed that "it is . . . self-evident that as we grow up each individual chooses whether to be good or bad." It seems clear enough that he sees such choice as sufficient to give us true moral responsibility of the heaven-and-hell variety.[8]

The rest of us are not usually so reflective, but it seems that we do tend, in some vague and unexamined fashion, to think of ourselves as responsible for—answerable for—how we are. The point is quite a delicate one, for we do not ordinarily suppose that we have gone through some sort of active process of self-determination at some particular past time. Nevertheless it seems accurate to say that we do unreflectively experience ourselves, in many respects, rather as we might experience ourselves if we did believe that we had engaged in some such activity of self-determination.

Sometimes a part of one's character—a desire or tendency—may strike one as foreign or alien. But it can do this only against a background of character traits that are not experienced as foreign, but are rather 'identified' with (it is a necessary truth that it is only relative to such a background that a character trait can stand out as alien). Some feel tormented by impulses that they experience as alien, but in many a sense of general identification with their character predominates, and this identification seems to carry within itself an implicit sense that one is, generally, somehow in control of and answerable for how one is (even, perhaps, for aspects of one's character that one does not like). Here, then, I suggest that we find, semi-dormant in common thought, an implicit recognition of the idea that true moral responsibility for what one does somehow involves responsibility for how one is. Ordinary thought is ready to move this way under pressure.

There is, however, another powerful tendency in ordinary thought to think that one can be truly morally responsible even if one's character is ultimately wholly non-self-determined—simply because one is fully self-consciously aware of oneself as an agent facing choices. I will return to this point later on.

---

[8] Carr in *What Is History?*, p. 89; Sartre in *Being and Nothingness, Existentialism and Humanism*, p. 29, and in the *New Left Review* 1969 (quoted in Wiggins, 1975) [reprinted as Essay 5, this volume]; Kant in *Religion within the Limits of Reason Alone*, p. 40, *The Critique of Practical Reason*, p. 101 (Ak. V. 98), and in *Opus Postumum*, p. 213; Patten in *The Spectator*, January 1992.

These quotations raise many questions which I will not consider. It is often hard, for example, to be sure what Sartre is saying. But the occurrence of the quoted phrases is significant on any plausible interpretation of his views. As for Kant, it may be thought to be odd that he says what he does, in so far as he grounds the possibility of our freedom in our possession of an unknowable, non-temporal noumenal nature. It is, however, plausible to suppose that he thinks that radical or ultimate self-determination must take place even in the noumenal realm, in some unintelligibly non-temporal manner, if there is to be true moral responsibility.

V

Let me now restate the Basic Argument in very loose—as it were conversational—terms. New forms of words allow for new forms of objection, but they may be helpful nonetheless.

(1) You do what you do, in any situation in which you find yourself, because of the way you are.

So

(2) To be truly morally responsible for what you do you must be truly responsible for the way you are—at least in certain crucial mental respects.

Or:

(1) What you intentionally do, given the circumstances in which you (believe you) find yourself, flows necessarily from how you are.

Hence

(2) you have to get to have some responsibility for how you are in order to get to have some responsibility for what you intentionally do, given the circumstances in which you (believe you) find yourself.

Comment. Once again the qualification about 'certain mental respects' is one I will take for granted. Obviously one is not responsible for one's sex, one's basic body pattern, one's height, and so on. But if one were not responsible for anything about oneself, how one could be responsible for what one did, given the truth of (1)? This is the fundamental question, and it seems clear that if one is going to be responsible for any aspect of oneself, it had better be some aspect of one's mental nature.

I take it that (1) is incontrovertible, and that it is (2) that must be resisted. For if (1) and (2)) are conceded the case seems lost, because the full argument runs as follows.

(1) You do what you do because of the way you are.

So

(2) To be truly morally responsible for what you do you must be truly responsible for the way you are—at least in certain crucial mental respects.

But

(3) You cannot be truly responsible for the way you are, so you cannot be truly responsible for what you do.

Why can't you be truly responsible for the way you are? Because

(4) To be truly responsible for the way you are, you must have intentionally brought it about that you are the way you are, and this is impossible.

Why is it impossible? Well, suppose it is not. Suppose that

(5) You have somehow intentionally brought it about that you are the way you now are, and that you have brought this about in such a way that you can now be said to be truly responsible for being the way you are now.

For this to be true

(6) You must already have had a certain nature N in the light of which you intentionally brought it about that you are as you now are.

But then

(7) For it to be true you and you alone are truly responsible for how you now are, you must be truly responsible for having had the nature N in the light of which you intentionally brought it about that you are the way you now are.

So

(8) You must have intentionally brought it about that you had that nature N, in which case you must have existed already with a prior nature in the light of which you intentionally brought it about that you had the nature N in the light of which you intentionally brought it about that you are the way you now are . . .

Here one is setting off on the regress. Nothing can be *causa sui* in the required way. Even if such causal 'aseity' is allowed to belong unintelligibly to God, it cannot be plausibly be supposed to be possessed by ordinary finite human beings. "The *causa sui* is the best self-contradiction that has been conceived so far", as Nietzsche remarked in 1886:

it is a sort of rape and perversion of logic. But the extravagant pride of man has managed to entangle itself profoundly and frightfully with just this nonsense. The desire for "freedom of the will" in the superlative metaphysical sense, which still holds sway, unfortunately, in the minds of the half-educated; the desire to bear the entire and ultimate responsibility for one's actions oneself, and to absolve God, the world, ancestors, chance, and society involves nothing less than to be precisely this *causa sui* and, with more than Baron Münchhausen's audacity, to pull oneself up into existence by the hair, out of the swamps of nothingness . . . (*Beyond Good and Evil*, §21).

The rephrased argument is essentially exactly the same as before, although the first two steps are now more simply stated. It may seem pointless to repeat it, but the questions remain. Can the Basic Argument simply be dismissed? It is really of no importance in the discussion of free will and moral responsibility? (No and No) Shouldn't any serious defense of free will and moral responsibility thoroughly acknowledge the respect in which the Basic Argument is valid before going on to try to give its own positive account of the nature of free will and moral responsibility? Doesn't the argument go to the heart of things if the heart of the free will debate is a concern about whether we can be truly morally responsible in the absolute way that we ordinarily suppose? (Yes and Yes)

We are what we are, and we cannot be thought to have made ourselves *in such a way* that we can be held to be free in our actions *in such a way* that we can be held to be morally responsible for our actions *in such a way* that any punishment or reward for our actions is ultimately just or fair. Punishments and rewards may seem deeply appropriate or intrinsically 'fitting' to us in spite of this argument, and many of the various institutions of punishment and reward in human society appear to be practically indispensable in both their legal and non-legal forms. But if one takes the notion of justice that is central to our intellectual and cultural tradition seriously, then the evident consequence of the Basic Argument is that there is a fundamental sense in which no punishment or reward is ever ultimately just. It is exactly as just to punish or reward people for their actions as it is to punish or reward them for the (natural) colour of their hair or the (natural) shape of their faces. The point seems obvious, and yet it contradicts a fundamental part of our natural self-conception, and there are elements in human thought that move very deeply against it. When it comes to questions or responsibility, we tend to feel that we are somehow responsible for the way we are. Even more importantly, perhaps, we tend to feel that our explicit self-conscious awareness of ourselves as agents who are able to deliberate about what to do, in situations of choice, suffices to constitute us as morally responsible free agents in the strongest sense, whatever the conclusion of the Basic Argument.

VI

I have suggested that it is step (2) of the restated Basic Argument that must be rejected, and of course it can be rejected, because the phrases 'truly responsible' and 'truly morally responsible' can be defined in many ways. I will briefly consider three sorts of response to the Basic Argument, and I will concentrate on their more simple expressions, in the belief that truth in philosophy, especially in areas of philosophy like the present one, is almost never very complicated.

(I) The first is *compatibilist*. Compatibilists believe that one can be a free and morally responsible agent even if determinism is true. Roughly, they claim, with many variations of detail, that one may correctly be said to be truly responsible for what one does, when one acts, just so long as one is not caused to act by any of a certain set of constraints (kleptomaniac impulses, obsessional neuroses, desires that are experienced as alien, post-hypnotic commands, threats, instances of *force majeure*, and so on). Clearly, this sort of compatibilist responsibility does not require that one should be truly responsible for how one is in any way at all, and so step (2) of the Basic Argument comes out as false. One can have compatibilist responsibility even if the way one is is totally determined by factors entirely outside one's control.

It is for this reason, however, that compatibilist responsibility famously fails to amount to any sort of true *moral* responsibility, given the natural, strong understanding of the notion of true moral responsibility (characterized above by reference to the story of heaven and hell). One does what one does entirely because of the way one is, and one is in no way ultimately responsible for the way one is. So how can one be justly punished for anything one does? Compatibilists have given increasingly refined accounts of the circumstances in which punishment may be said to be appropriate or intrinsically fitting. But they can do nothing against this basic objection.

Many compatibilists have never supposed otherwise. They are happy to admit the point. They observe that the notions of true moral responsibility and justice that are employed in the objection cannot possibly have application to anything real, and suggest that the objection is therefore not worth considering. In response, proponents of the Basic Argument agree that the notions of true moral responsibility and justice in question cannot have application to anything real; but they make no apologies for considering them. They consider them because they are central to ordinary thought about moral responsibility and justice. So far as most people are concerned, they are the subject, if the subject is moral responsibility and justice.

(II) The second response is *libertarian*. Incompatibilists believe that freedom and moral responsibility are incompatible with determinism, and some of them are libertarians, who believe that that we are free and morally responsible agents, and that determinism is therefore false. In an ingenious statement of the incompatibilist-libertarian case, Robert Kane argues that agents in an undetermined world can have free will, for they can "have the power to make choices for which they have ultimate responsibility". That is, they can "have the power to make choices which can only and finally be explained in terms of their own wills (i.e. character, motives, and efforts of will)".[9] Roughly, Kane sees this power as grounded in the possible occurrence, in agents, of efforts of will that have two main features: first, they are partly indeterministic in their nature, and hence indeterminate in their outcome; second, they occur in cases in which agents are trying to make a difficult choice between the options that their characters dispose them to consider. (The paradigm cases will be cases in which they face a conflict between moral duty and non-moral desire.)

But the old objection to libertarianism recurs. How can this indeterminism help with *moral* responsibility? Granted that the truth of determinism rules out true moral responsibility, how can the falsity of determinism help? How can the occurrence of partly random or indeterministic events contribute in any way to one's being truly morally responsible either for one's actions or for one's character? If my efforts of will shape my character in an admirable way, and in so doing are partly indeterministic in nature, while also being shaped (as Kane grants) by my already existing character, why am I not merely lucky?

The general objection applies equally whether determinism is true or false, and can be restated as follows. We are born with a great many genetically determined predispositions for which we are not responsible. We are subject to many early influences for which we are not responsible. These decisively shape our characters, our motives, the general bent and strength of our capacity to make efforts of will. We may later engage in conscious and intentional shaping procedures—call them S-procedures—designed to affect and change our characters, motivational structure, and wills. Suppose we do. The question is then why we engage in the particular S-procedures that we do engage in, and why we engage in them in the particular way that we do. The general answer is that we engage in the particular S-procedures that we do engage in, given the circumstances in which we find ourselves, because of certain features of the way we already are. (Indeterministic factors may also play a part in what happens, but these will not help to make us responsible for what we do.) And these features of the way we already are—call them character features, or C-features—are either wholly the products of genetic or environmental influences, deterministic or random, for which we are not responsible, or are at least partly the result of earlier S-procedures, which are in turn either wholly the product of C-features for which we are not responsible, or are at least partly the product of still earlier S-procedures, which are turn either the products of C-features for which we are not responsible, or the product of such C-features together with still earlier S-procedures—and so on. In the end, we reach the first S-procedure, and this will have been

<hr>

[9] Kane (1989) p. 254. I have omitted some italics.

engaged in, and engaged in the particular way in which it was engaged in, as a result of genetic or environmental factors, deterministic or random, for which we were not responsible.

Moving away from the possible role of indeterministic factors in character or personality formation, we can consider their possible role in particular instances of deliberation and decision. Here too it seems clear that indeterministic factors cannot, in influencing what happens, contribute to true moral responsibility in any way. In the end, whatever we do, we do it either as a result of random influences for which we are not responsible, or as a result of non-random influences for which we are not responsible, or as a result of influences for which we are proximally responsible but not ultimately responsible. The point seems obvious. Nothing can be ultimately *causa sui* in any respect at all. Even if God can be, we can't be.

Kane says little about moral responsibility in his paper, but his position seems to be that true moral responsibility is possible if indeterminism is true. It is possible because in cases of "moral, prudential and practical struggle we ... are truly 'making ourselves' in such a way that we are ultimately responsible for the outcome". This 'making of ourselves' means that "we can be ultimately responsible for our present motives and character by virtue of past choices which helped to form them and for which we were ultimately responsible" (op. cit., p. 252). It is for this reason that we can be ultimately responsible and morally responsible not only in cases of struggle in which we are 'making ourselves', but also for choices and actions which do not involve struggle, flowing unopposed from our character and motives.

In claiming that we can be ultimately responsible for our present motives and character, Kane appears to *accept* step (2) of the Basic Argument. He appears to accept that we have to 'make ourselves', and so be ultimately responsible for ourselves, in order to be morally responsible for what we do.[10] The problem with this suggestion is the old one. In Kane's view, a person's 'ultimate responsibility' for the outcome of an effort of will depends essentially on the partly indeterministic nature of the outcome. This is because it is only the element of indeterminism that prevents prior character and motives from fully explaining the outcome of the effort of will (op. cit, p. 236). But how can this indeterminism help with moral responsibility? How can the fact that my effort of will is indeterministic in such a way that its outcome is indeterminate make me truly responsible for it, or even help to make me truly responsible for it? How can it help in any way at all with moral responsibility? How can it make punishment—or reward—ultimately just?

---

[10] He cites van Inwagen (1989) in support of this view.

There is a further, familiar problem with the view that moral responsibility depends on indeterminism. If one accepts the view, one will have to grant that it is impossible to know whether any human being is ever morally responsible. For moral responsibility now depends on the falsity of determinism, and determinism is unfalsifiable. There is no more reason to think that determinism is false than that it is true, in spite of the impression sometimes given by scientists and popularizers of science.

(III) The third option begins by accepting that one cannot be held to be ultimately responsible for one's character or personality or motivational structure. It accepts that this is so whether determinism is true or false. It then directly challenges step (2) of the Basic Argument. It appeals to a certain picture of the self in order to argue that one can be truly free and morally responsible in spite of the fact that one cannot be held to be ultimately responsible for one's character or personality or motivational structure. This picture has some support in the 'phenomenology' of human choice—we sometimes experience our choices and decisions as if the picture were an accurate one. But it is easy to show that it cannot be accurate in such a way that we can be said to be truly or ultimately morally responsible for our choices or actions.

It can be set out as follows. One is free and truly morally responsible because one's self is, in a crucial sense, independent of one's character or personality or motivational structure—one's CPM, for short. Suppose one is in a situation which one experiences as a difficult choice between A, doing one's duty, and B, following one's non-moral desires. Given one's CPM, one responds in a certain way. One's desires and beliefs develop and interact and constitute reasons for both A and B. One's CPM makes one tend towards A or B. So far the problem is the same as ever: whatever one does, one will do what one does because of the way one's CPM is, and since one neither is nor can be ultimately responsible for the way one's CPM is, one cannot be ultimately responsible for what one does.

Enter one's self, S. S is imagined to be in some way independent of one's CPM. S (i.e. one) considers the deliverances of one's CPM and decides in the light of them, but it—S—incorporates a power of decision that is independent of one's CPM in such a way that one can after all count as truly and ultimately morally responsible in one's decisions and actions, even though one is not ultimately responsible for one's CPM. Step (2) of the Basic Argument is false because of the existence of S.[11]

The trouble with the picture is obvious. S (i.e. one) decides on the basis of the deliverances of one's CPM. But whatever S decides, it decides as it does

[11] Cf. C.A. Campbell (1957).

because of the way it is (or else because partly or wholly because of the occurrence in the decision process of indeterministic factors for which it— i.e. one—cannot be responsible, and which cannot plausibly be thought to contribute to one's true moral responsibility). And this returns us to where we started. To be a source of true or ultimate responsibility, S must be responsible for being the way it is. But this is impossible, for the reasons given in the Basic Argument.

The story of S and CPM adds another layer to the description of the human decision process, but it cannot change the fact that human beings cannot be ultimately self-determining in such a way as to be ultimately morally responsible for how they are, and thus for how they decide and act. The story is crudely presented, but it should suffice to make clear that no move of this sort can solve the problem.

'Character is destiny', as Novalis is often reported as saying.[12] The remark is inaccurate, because external circumstances are part of destiny, but the point is well taken when it comes to the question of moral responsibility. Nothing can be *causa sui*, and in order to be truly morally responsible for one's actions one would have to be *causa sui*, at least in certain crucial mental respects. One cannot institute oneself in such a way that one can take over true or assume moral responsibility for how one is in such a way that one can indeed be truly morally responsible for what one does. This fact is not changed by the fact that we may be unable not to think of ourselves as truly morally responsible in ordinary circumstances. Nor is it changed by the fact that it may be a very good thing that we have this inability—so that we might wish to take steps to preserve it, if it looked to be in danger of fading. As already remarked, many human beings are unable to resist the idea that it is their capacity for fully explicit self-conscious deliberation, in a situation of choice, that suffices to constitute them as truly morally responsible agents in the strongest possible sense. The Basic Argument shows that this is a mistake. However self-consciously aware we are, as we deliberate and reason, every act and operation of our mind happens as it does as a result of features for which we are ultimately in no way responsible. But the conviction that self-conscious awareness of one's situation can be a sufficient foundation of strong free will is very powerful. It runs deeper than rational argument, and it survives untouched, in the everyday conduct of life, even after the validity of the Basic Argument has been admitted.

---

[12] e.g. by George Eliot in *The Mill on the Floss*, book 6, chapter 6. Novalis wrote "Oft fühl ich jetzt . . . [und] je tiefer einsehe, dass Schicksal und Gemüt Namen eines Begriffes sind"—"I often feel, and ever more deeply realize, that fate and character are the same concept". He was echoing Heracleitus, Fragment 119 DK.

VII

There is nothing new in the somewhat incantatory argument of this paper. It restates certain points that may be in need of restatement. "Everything has been said before", said André Gide, echoing La Bruyère, "but since nobody listens we have to keep going back and beginning all over again." This is an exaggeration, but it may not be a gross exaggeration, so far as general observations about the human condition are concerned.

The present claim, in any case, is simply this: time would be saved, and a great deal of readily available clarity would be introduced into the discussion of the nature of moral responsibility, if the simple point that is established by the Basic Argument were more generally acknowledged and clearly stated. Nietzsche thought that thoroughgoing acknowledgement of the point was long overdue, and his belief that there might be moral advantages in such an acknowledgement may deserve further consideration.[13]

REFERENCES

Aristotle, 1953. *Nicomachean Ethics*, trans. J. A. K. Thomson, Allen and Unwin, London.

Campbell, C. A., 1957. 'Has the Self "Free Will"?', in C. A. Campbell, *On Selfhood and Godhood*, Allen and Unwin, London.

Carr, E. H., 1961. *What Is History?*, Macmillan, London.

Kane, R., 1989. 'Two Kinds of Incompatibilism', *Philosophy and Phenomenological Research*, 50, pp. 219–254.

Kant, I., 1956. *Critique of Practical Reason*, trans. L. W. Beck, Bobbs-Merrill, Indianapolis.

—— 1960. *Religion within the Limits of Reason Alone*, trans. T. M. Greene and H. H. Hudson, Harper and Row, New York.

—— 1993. *Opus postumum*, trans. E. Förster and M. Rosen, Cambridge University Press, Cambridge.

MacKay, D. M., 1960. 'On the Logical Indeterminacy of Free Choice', *Mind*, 69, pp. 31–40.

Mele, A., 1995. *Autonomous Agents: From Self-Control to Autonomy*, Oxford University Press, New York.

Nietzsche, F., 1966. *Beyond Good and Evil*, trans. Walter Kaufmann, Random House, New York.

Novalis, 1802. *Heinrich von Ofterdingen*.

Sartre, J.-P., 1969. *Being and Nothingness*, trans. Hazel E. Barnes, Methuen, London.

—— 1989. *Existentialism and Humanism*, trans. Philip Mairet, Methuen, London.

Schacht, R., 1983. *Nietzsche*, Routledge and Kegan Paul, London.

---

[13] Cf. R. Schacht (1983) pp. 304–9. The idea that there might be moral advantages in the clear headed admission that true or ultimate moral responsibility is impossible has recently been developed in another way by Saul Smilansky (1994).

Smilansky, S., 1994. 'The Ethical Advantages of Hard Determinism', *Philosophy and Phenomenological Research*.

Strawson, G., 1986. *Freedom and Belief*, Clarendon Press, Oxford.

Van Inwagen, P., 1989. 'When Is the Will Free?', *Philosophical Perspectives*, 3, pp. 399–422.

Wiggins, D., 1975. 'Towards a Reasonable Libertarianism', in T. Honderich, ed., *Essays on Freedom of Action*, Routledge, London.

12

FREEDOM

THOMAS NAGEL

1. TWO PROBLEMS

Something peculiar happens when we view action from an objective or external standpoint. Some of its most important features seem to vanish under the objective gaze. Actions seem no longer assignable to individual agents as sources, but become instead components of the flux of events in the world of which the agent is a part. The easiest way to produce this effect is to think of the possibility that all actions are causally determined, but it is not the only way. The essential source of the problem is a view of persons and their actions as part of the order of nature, causally determined or not. That conception, if pressed, leads to the feeling that we are not agents at all, that we are helpless and not responsible for what we do. Against this judgment the inner view of the agent rebels. The question is whether it can stand up to the debilitating effects of a naturalistic view.

Actually the objective standpoint generates three problems about action, only two of which I shall take up. Those two both have to do with freedom. The first problem, which I shall simply describe and put aside, is the general metaphysical problem of the nature of agency. It belongs to the philosophy of mind.

The question "What is action?" is much broader than the problem of free will, for it applies even to the activity of spiders and to the peripheral, unconscious or subintentional movements of human beings in the course of more deliberate activity (see Frankfurt [Essay 16, this volume]). It applies to any movement that is not involuntary. The question is connected with our theme because *my doing* of an act—or the doing of an act by someone else—seems to disappear when we think of the world objectively. There seems no room for agency in a world of neural impulses, chemical reactions, and bone and muscle movements. Even if we add sensations, perceptions, and feelings we don't get action, or doing—there is only what happens.

In line with what was said earlier about the philosophy of mind, I think the only solution is to regard action as a basic mental or more accurately psychophysical category—reducible neither to physical nor to other mental terms. I cannot improve on Brian O'Shaughnessy's exhaustive defense of this position. Action has its own irreducibly internal aspect as do other psychological phenomena—there is a characteristic mental asymmetry between awareness of one's own actions and awareness of the actions of others—but action isn't anything else, alone or in combination with a physical movement: not a sensation, not a feeling, not a belief, not an intention or desire. If we restrict our palette to such things plus physical events, agency will be omitted from our picture of the world.

But even if we add it as an irreducible feature, making subjects of experience also (and as O'Shaughnessy argues, inevitably) subjects of action, the problem of free action remains. We may act without being free, and we may doubt the freedom of others without doubting that they act. What undermines the sense of freedom doesn't automatically undermine agency.[1] I shall leave the general problem of agency aside in what follows, and simply assume that there is such a thing.

What I shall discuss are two aspects of the problem of free will, corresponding to the two ways in which objectivity threatens ordinary assumptions about human freedom. I call one the problem of autonomy and the other the problem of responsibility; the first presents itself initially as a problem about our own freedom and the second as a problem about the freedom of others.[2] An objective view of actions as events in the natural order (determined or not) produces a sense of impotence and futility with respect to what we do ourselves. It also undermines certain basic attitudes toward all agents—those reactive attitudes (see Strawson (2)) that are conditional on the attribution of responsibility. It is the second of these effects that is usually referred to as the problem of free will. But the threat to our conception of our own actions—the sense that we are being carried along by the universe like small pieces of flotsam—is equally important and equally deserving of the title. The two are connected. The same external view that poses a threat to my own autonomy also threatens my sense of the autonomy of others, and this in turn makes them come to seem inappropriate

---

[1] Here I agree with R. Taylor, *Action and Purpose* (Englewood Cliffs, NJ: Prentice-Hall, 1966), p. 140.

[2] Jonathan Bennett makes this distinction, calling them the problems of agency and accountability, respectively (Bennett, *Kant's Dialectic* (Cambridge: Cambridge University Press, 1974), ch. 10).

objects of admiration and contempt, resentment and gratitude, blame and praise.

Like other basic philosophical problems, the problem of free will is not in the first instance verbal. It is not a problem about what we are to *say* about action, responsibility, what someone could or could not have done, and so forth. It is rather a bafflement of our feelings and attitudes—a loss of confidence, conviction or equilibrium. Just as the basic problem of epistemology is not whether we can be *said to know* things, but lies rather in the loss of belief and the invasion of doubt, so the problem of free will lies in the erosion of interpersonal attitudes and of the sense of autonomy. Questions about what we are to say about action and responsibility merely attempt after the fact to express those feelings—feelings of impotence, of imbalance, and of affective detachment from other people.

These forms of unease are familiar once we have encountered the problem of free will through the hypothesis of determinism. We are undermined but at the same time ambivalent, because the unstrung attitudes don't disappear: they keep forcing themselves into consciousness despite their loss of support. A philosophical treatment of the problem must deal with such disturbances of the spirit, and not just with their verbal expression.

I change my mind about the problem of free will every time I think about it, and therefore cannot offer any view with even moderate confidence; but my present opinion is that nothing that might be a solution has yet been described. This is not a case where there are several possible candidate solutions and we don't know which is correct. It is a case where nothing believable has (to my knowledge) been proposed by anyone in the extensive public discussion of the subject.

The difficulty, as I shall try to explain, is that while we can easily evoke disturbing effects by taking up an external view of our own actions and the actions of others, it is impossible to give a coherent account of the internal view of action which is under threat. When we try to explain what we believe which seems to be undermined by a conception of actions as events in the world—determined or not—we end up with something that is either incomprehensible or clearly inadequate.

This naturally suggests that the threat is unreal, and that an account of freedom can be given which is compatible with the objective view, and perhaps even with determinism. But I believe this is not the case. All such accounts fail to allay the feeling that, looked at from far enough outside, agents are helpless and not responsible. Compatibilist accounts of freedom tend to be even less plausible than libertarian ones. Nor is it possible simply to dissolve our unanalyzed sense of autonomy and responsibility. It is something we can't get rid of, either in relation to ourselves or in relation to others. We are apparently condemned to want something impossible.

2. AUTONOMY

The first problem is that of autonomy. How does it arise?

In acting we occupy the internal perspective, and we can occupy it sympathetically with regard to the actions of others. But when we move away from our individual point of view, and consider our own actions and those of others simply as part of the course of events in a world that contains us among other creatures and things, it begins to look as though we never really contribute anything.

From the inside, when we act, alternative possibilities seem to lie open before us: to turn right or left, to order this dish or that, to vote for one candidate or the other—and one of the possibilities is made actual by what we do. The same applies to our internal consideration of the actions of others. But from an external perspective, things look different. That perspective takes in not only the circumstances of action as they present themselves to the agent, but also the conditions and influences lying behind the action, including the complete nature of the agent himself. While we cannot fully occupy this perspective toward ourselves while acting, it seems possible that many of the alternatives that appear to lie open when viewed from an internal perspective would seem closed from this outer point of view, if we could take it up. And even if some of them are left open, given a complete specification of the condition of the agent and the circumstances of action, it is not clear how this would leave anything further for the agent to contribute to the outcome—anything that he could contribute as source, rather than merely as the scene of the outcome—the person whose act it is. If they are left open given everything about him, what does he have to do with the result?

From an external perspective, then, the agent and everything about him seems to be swallowed up by the circumstances of action; nothing of him is left to intervene in those circumstances. This happens whether or not the relation between action and its antecedent conditions is conceived as deterministic. In either case we cease to face the world and instead become parts of it; we and our lives are seen as products and manifestations of the world as a whole. Everything I do or that anyone else does is part of a larger course of events that no one "does," but that happens, with or without explanation. Everything I do is part of something I don't do, because I am a part of the world. We may elaborate this external picture by reference to biological, psychological, and social factors in the formation of ourselves and other agents. But the picture doesn't have to be complete in order to be threatening. It is enough to form the idea of the possibility of a picture of this kind. Even if we can't attain it, an observer literally outside us might.

Why is this threatening, and what does it threaten? Why are we not content to regard the internal perspective of agency as a form of clouded subjective appearance, based as it inevitably must be on an incomplete view of the circumstances? The alternatives are alternatives only relative to what we know, and our choices result from influences of which we are only partly aware. The external perspective would then provide a more complete view, superior to the internal. We accept a parallel subordination of subjective appearance to objective reality in other areas.

The reason we cannot accept it here, at least not as a general solution, is that action is too ambitious. We aspire in some of our actions to a kind of autonomy that is not a mere subjective appearance—not merely ignorance of their sources—and we have the same view of others like us. The sense that we are the authors of our own actions is not just a feeling but a belief, and we can't come to regard it as a pure appearance without giving it up altogether. But what belief is it?

I have already said that I suspect it is no intelligible belief at all; but that has to be shown. What I am about to say is highly controversial, but let me just describe what I take to be our ordinary conception of autonomy. It presents itself initially as the belief that antecedent circumstances, including the condition of the agent, leave some of the things we will do undetermined: they are determined only by our choices, which are motivationally explicable but not themselves causally determined. Although many of the external and internal conditions of choice are inevitably fixed by the world and not under my control, some range of open possibilities is generally presented to me on an occasion of action—and when by acting I make one of those possibilities actual, the final explanation of this (once the background which defines the possibilities has been taken into account) is given by the intentional explanation of my action, which is comprehensible only through my point of view. My reason for doing it is the *whole* reason why it happened, and no further explanation is either necessary or possible. (My doing it for no particular reason is a limiting case of this kind of explanation.)

The objective view seems to wipe out such autonomy because it admits only one kind of explanation of why something happened—causal explanation—and equates its absence with the absence of any explanation at all. It may be able to admit causal explanations that are probabilistic, but the basic idea which it finds congenial is that the explanation of an occurrence must show how that occurrence, or a range of possibilities within which it falls, was necessitated by prior conditions and events. (I shall not say anything about the large question of how this notion of necessity is to be interpreted.) To the extent that no such necessity exists, the occurrence is unexplained. There is no room in an objective picture of the world for a type of explanation of action that is not causal. The defense of freedom requires the acknowledgment of a different kind of explanation essentially connected to the agent's point of view.

Though it would be contested, I believe we have such an idea of autonomy. Many philosophers have defended some version of this position as the truth about freedom: for example Farrer, Anscombe, and Wiggins. (The metaphysical theories of agent-causation espoused by Chisholm and Taylor are different, because they try to force autonomy into the objective causal order—giving a name to a mystery.) But whatever version one picks, the trouble is that while it may give a correct surface description of our prereflective sense of our own autonomy, when we look at the idea closely, it collapses. The alternative form of explanation doesn't really explain the action at all.

The intuitive idea of autonomy includes conflicting elements, which imply that it both is and is not a way of explaining why an action was done. A free action should not be determined by antecedent conditions, and should be fully explained only intentionally, in terms of justifying reasons and purposes. When someone makes an autonomous choice such as whether to accept a job, and there are reasons on both sides of the issue, we are supposed to be able to explain what he did by pointing to his reasons for accepting it. But we could equally have explained his refusing the job, if he had refused, by referring to the reasons on the other side—and he could have refused for those other reasons: that is the essential claim of autonomy. It applies even if one choice is significantly more reasonable than the other. Bad reasons are reasons too.[3]

---

[3] Some would hold that we have all the autonomy we should want if our choice is determined by compelling reasons. Hampshire, for example, attributes to Spinoza the position that "a man is most free, ... and also feels himself to be most free, when he cannot help drawing a certain conclusion, and cannot help embarking on a certain course of action in view of the evidently compelling reasons in favor of it . . . The issue is decided for him when the arguments in support of a theoretical conclusion are conclusive arguments" (S. Hampshire, "Spinoza and the Idea of Freedom", *Proceedings of the British Academy* (1960), p. 198). And Wolf proposes as the condition of freedom that the agent "could have done otherwise if there had been good and sufficient reason" (S. Wolf, "Asymmetrical Freedom", *Journal of Philosophy* (1980), p. 159)—which means that if there wasn't a good reason to act differently, the free agent needn't have been able to as differently.

Something like this has more plausibility with respect to thought, I believe, than it has with respect to action. In forming beliefs we may hope for nothing more than to be determined by the

Intentional explanation, if there is such a thing, can explain either choice in terms of the appropriate reasons, since either choice would be intelligible if it occurred. But for this very reason it cannot explain why the person accepted the job for the reasons in favor instead of refusing it for the reasons against. It cannot explain on grounds of intelligibility why one of two intelligible courses of action, both of which were possible, occurred. And even where it can account for this in terms of further reasons, there will be a point at which the explanation gives out. We say that someone's character and values are revealed by the choices he makes in such circumstances, but if these arc indeed independent conditions, they too must either have or lack an explanation.

If autonomy requires that the central element of choice be explained in a way that does not take us outside the point of view of the agent (leaving aside the explanation of what faces him with the choice), then intentional explanations must simply come to an end when all available reasons have been given, and nothing else can take over where they leave off. But this seems to mean that an autonomous intentional explanation cannot explain precisely what it is supposed to explain, namely *why I did what I did rather than the alternative that was causally open to me*. It says I did it for certain reasons, but does not explain why I didn't decide not to do it for other reasons. It may render the action subjectively intelligible, but it does not explain why this rather than another equally possible and comparably intelligible action was done. That seems to be something for which there is no explanation, either intentional or causal.

Of course there is a trivial intentional explanation: my reasons for doing it are also my reasons against not doing it for other reasons. But since the same could be said if I had done the opposite, this amounts to explaining what happened by saying it happened. It does not stave off the question why these reasons rather than the others were the ones that motivated me. At some point this question will either have no answer or it will have an answer that takes us outside of the domain of subjective normative reasons and into the domain of formative causes of my character or personality.[4]

---

truth (see D. Wiggins, "Freedom, Knowledge, Belief and Causality", in *Knowledge and Necessity*, Royal Institute of Society Lectures, vol. iii (London: MacMillan, 1970), pp. 145–8; see also Wefald, ch. 15), but in action our initial assumption is different. Even when we feel rationally compelled to act, this does not mean we are causally determined. When Luther says he *can* do nothing else, he is referring to the normative irresistibility of his reasons, not to their causal power, and I believe that even in such a case causal determination is not compatible with autonomy.

[4] Lucas notices this but is not, I think, sufficiently discouraged by it: "There remains a tension between the programme of complete explicability and the requirements of freedom. If men have free will, then no complete explanation of their actions can be given, except by reference to themselves. We can give their reasons. But we cannot explain why their reasons were reasons for

So I am at a loss to account for what we believe in believing that we are autonomous—what intelligible belief is undermined by the external view. That is, I cannot say what would, if it were true, support our sense that our free actions originate with us. Yet the sense of an internal explanation persists—an explanation insulated from the external view which is complete in itself and renders illegitimate all further requests for explanation of my action as an event in the world.

As a last resort the libertarian might claim chat anyone who does not accept an account of what I was up to as a basic explanation of action is the victim of a very limited conception of what an explanation is—a conception locked into the objective standpoint which therefore begs the question against the concept of autonomy. But he needs a better reply than this. Why aren't these autonomous subjective explanations really just descriptions of how it seemed to the agent—before, during, and after—to do what he did; why are they something more than impressions? Of course they are at least impressions, but we take them to be impressions *of* something, something whose reality is not guaranteed by the impression. Not being able to say what that something is, and at the same time finding the possibility of its absence very disturbing, I am at a dead end.

I have to conclude that what we want is something impossible, and that the desire for it is evoked precisely by the objective view of ourselves that reveals it to be impossible. At the moment when we see ourselves from outside as bits of the world, two things happen: we are no longer satisfied in action with anything less than intervention in the world from outside; and we see clearly that this makes no sense. The very capacity that is the source of the trouble—our capacity to view ourselves from outside—encourages our aspirations of autonomy by giving us the sense that we ought to be able to encompass ourselves completely, and thus become the absolute source of what we do. At any rate we become dissatisfied with anything less.

When we act we are not cut off from the knowledge of ourselves that is revealed from the external standpoint, so far as we can occupy it. It is, after all, *our* standpoint as much as the internal one is, and if we take it up, we can't help trying to include anything it reveals to us in a new, expanded basis of action. We act, if possible, on the basis of the most complete view of the circumstances of action that we can attain, and this includes as complete a view as we can attain of ourselves. Not that we want to be paralyzed by self-consciousness. But we can't regard ourselves, in action, as subordinate to an external view of ourselves, because we automatically subordinate the

them. . . . Asked why I acted, I give my reasons: asked why I chose to accept them as reasons, I can only say 'I just did'" (J. R. Lucas, *The Freedom of the Will* (Oxford: Oxford University Press, 1970), pp. 171–2).

external view to the purposes of our actions. We feel that in acting we ought to be able to determine not only our choices but the inner conditions of those choices, provided we step far enough outside ourselves.

So the external standpoint at once holds out the hope of genuine autonomy, and snatches it away. By increasing our objectivity and self-awareness, we seem to acquire increased control over what will influence our actions, and thus to take our lives into our own hands. Yet the logical goal of these ambitions is incoherent, for to be really free we would have to act from a standpoint completely outside ourselves, choosing everything about ourselves, including all our principles of choice—creating ourselves from nothing, so to speak.

This is self-contradictory: in order to do anything we must already be something. However much material we incorporate from the external view into the grounds of action and choice, this same external view assures us that we remain parts of the world and products, determined or not, of its history. Here as elsewhere the objective standpoint creates an appetite which it shows to be insatiable.

The problem of freedom and the problem of epistemological skepticism are alike in this respect. In belief, as in action, rational beings aspire to autonomy. They wish to form their beliefs on the basis of principles and methods of reasoning and confirmation that they themselves can judge to be correct, rather than on the basis of influences that they do not understand, of which they are unaware, or which they cannot assess. That is the aim of knowledge. But taken to its logical limit, the aim is incoherent. We cannot assess and revise or confirm our entire system of thought and judgment from outside, for we would have nothing to do it with. We remain, as pursuers of knowledge, creatures inside the world who have not created ourselves, and some of whose processes of thought have simply been given to us.

In the formation of belief, as in action, we belong to a world we have not created and of which we are the products; it is the external view which both reveals this and makes us wish for more. However objective a standpoint we succeed in making part of the basis of our actions and beliefs, we continue to be threatened by the idea of a still more external and comprehensive view of ourselves that we cannot incorporate, but that would reveal the unchosen sources of our most autonomous efforts. The objectivity that seems to offer greater control also reveals the ultimate givenness of the self.

Can we proceed part way along the inviting path of objectivity without ending up in the abyss, where the pursuit of objectivity undermines itself and everything else? In practice, outside of philosophy we find certain natural stopping places along the route, and do not worry about how things would look if we went further. In this respect too the situation resembles that in epistemology, where justification and criticism come fairly peacefully to an end in everyday life. The trouble is that our complacency seems unwarranted as soon as we reflect on what would be revealed to a still more external view, and it is not clear how we can reestablish these natural stopping places on a new footing once they are put in doubt.

It would require some alternative to the literally unintelligible ambition of intervening in the world from outside (an ambition expressed by Kant in the unintelligible idea of the noumenal self which is outside time and causality). This ambition arises by a natural extension or continuation of the pursuit of freedom in everyday life. I wish to act not only in light of the external circumstances facing me and the possibilities that they leave open, but in light of the internal circumstances as well: my desires, beliefs, feelings, and impulses. I wish to be able to subject my motives, principles, and habits to critical examination, so that nothing moves me to action without my agreeing to it. In this way, the setting against which I act is gradually enlarged and extended inward, till it includes more and more of myself, considered as one of the contents of the world.

In its earlier stages the process does genuinely seem to increase freedom, by making self-knowledge and objectivity part of the basis of action. But the danger is obvious. The more completely the self is swallowed up in the circumstances of action, the less I have to act with. I cannot get completely outside myself. The process that starts as a means to the enlargement of freedom seems to lead to its destruction. When I contemplate the world as a whole I see my actions, even at their empirically most "free," as part of the course of nature, and this is not my doing or anyone else's. The objective self is not in a position to pull the strings of my life from outside any more than TN is.

At the end of the path that seems to lead to freedom and knowledge lie skepticism and helplessness. We can act only from inside the world, but when we see ourselves from outside, the autonomy we experience from inside appears as an illusion, and we who are looking from outside cannot act at all.

3. RESPONSIBILITY

It seems to me that the problem of responsibility is insoluble, or at least unsolved, for similar reasons. We hold ourselves and others morally responsible for at least some actions when we view them from the inside; but we cannot give an account of what would have to be true to justify such judgments. Once people are seen as parts of the world, determined or not, there seems no way to assign responsibility to them for what they do. Everything about them, including finally their actions themselves, seems to blend in with the surroundings over which they have no control. And when we then go back to consider actions from the internal point of view, we cannot on close scrutiny make sense of the idea that what people do depends ultimately on them. Yet we continue to compare what they do with the alternatives they reject, and to praise or condemn them for it. (My examples will generally involve negative judgments, but everything I say is meant to apply to praise as well as to condemnation.)

What is going on here? Let me begin with a prephilosophical account of what a judgment of responsibility is. It always involves two parties, whom I shall call the *judge* and the *defendant*. These may be the same person, as when someone holds himself responsible for doing or having done something. But it will be easier to examine the complexities of the phenomenon if we concentrate first on the interpersonal case, and how it ultimately breaks down.

The defendant is an agent, and in a judgment of responsibility the judge doesn't just decide that what has been done is a good or a bad thing, but tries to enter into the defendant's point of view as an agent. He is not, however, concerned merely with how it felt: rather, he tries to assess the action in light of the alternatives presenting themselves to the defendant—among which he chose or failed to choose, and in light of the considerations and temptations bearing on the choice—which he considered or failed to consider. To praise or blame is not to judge merely that what has happened is a good or a bad thing, but to judge the person for having done it, in view of the circumstances under which it was done. The difficulty is to explain how this is possible—how we can do more than welcome or regret the event, or perhaps the psychology of the agent.

The main thing we do is to compare the act or motivation with alternatives, better or worse, which were deliberately or implicitly rejected though their acceptance in the circumstances would have been motivationally comprehensible. That is the setting into which one projects both an internal understanding of the action and a judgment of what should have been done. It is the sense of the act in contrast with alternatives not taken, together with a normative assessment of those alternatives—also projected into the point of view of the defendant—that yields an internal judgment of responsibility. What was done is seen as a selection by the defendant from the array of possibilities with which he was faced, and is defined by contrast with those possibilities.

When we hold the defendant responsible, the result is not merely a description of his character, but a vicarious occupation of his point of view and evaluation of his action from within it. While this process need not be accompanied by strong feelings, it often is, and their character will depend on the makeup of the judge. Condemnatory judgments, for example, may be accompanied by impulses of retribution and punishment. These are most likely to appear in their full ferocity when the psychic configuration of the judge subjects him to strong conflicts with respect to the defendant's situation of choice. A judgment of responsibility involves a double projection: into the actual choice and into the possible alternatives, better or worse. If the judge identifies strongly with the bad act done or avoided, his contempt or admiration will be correspondingly strong. It is a familiar fact that we hate most the sins that tempt us most, and admire most the virtues we find most difficult.

The kinds of things we judge others for vary. We condemn a rattle-snake for nothing, and a cat for nothing or practically nothing. Our understanding of their actions and even of their point of view puts us too far outside them to permit any judgments about what they should have done. All we can do is to understand why they have done what they did, and to be happy or unhappy about it. With regard to small children the possibilities of moral judgment are somewhat greater, but we still cannot project ourselves fully into their point of view in order to think about what they should do, as opposed to what would be required of an adult in corresponding circumstances. Similar limits apply to judgments of other people's intelligence or stupidity. Someone has not made a stupid mistake if he completely lacks the capacity of thought needed to draw the correct conclusion from the evidence available to him. The larger his intellectual capacities, the greater his opportunities for stupidity, as well as for intelligence, It is the same with good and evil. A five-year-old can be blamed for throwing the cat out the window, but not for a gross failure of tact.

Two kinds of thing may undermine a judgment of responsibility, and familiar excusing conditions fall into one or other of these classes. First, it may emerge that the character of the choice or the circumstances of action facing the defendant are different from what they at first appeared to be. He may not have full knowledge of the consequences of what he is doing; he may be acting under severe coercion or duress; certain alternatives which seemed available may not be, or he may be unaware of them. Such discoveries alter the character of the action to be assessed, but do not block a judgmenueof responsibility altogether.

Second, something may prevent the judge from projecting his standards into the point of view of the defendant—the initial move needed for any judgment of responsibility. Certain discoveries render the judge's projection into the defendant's perspective irrelevant to the assessment of what the defendant has done, because he is quite different from the defendant in crucial ways. For example, the defendant may have been acting under hypnotic suggestion, or under the influence of a powerful drug, or even, in the vein of science fiction, under the direct control of a mad scientist manipulating his brain. Or he may turn out not to be a rational being at all. In these cases the judge will not regard the vantage point of the defendant as the correct one to take up for purposes of assessment. He will not project himself into the defendant's point of view, but will stay outside him—so that the contemplation of alternative possibilities will not support praise or blame but only relief or regret.

The philosophical disappearance of all responsibility is an extension of this second type of disengagement. The essence of a judgment of responsibility is an *internal* comparison with alternatives—choices the agent did not make which we contrast with what he did, for better or for worse. In ordinary judgments of responsibility an objective view of the agent may lead us to alter our assumption about which alternatives are eligible for such comparison. Even alternatives that seemed to the agent to be available at the time may seem to us out of the running, once our external view of him becomes more complete.

The radically external standpoint that produces the philosophical problem of responsibility seems to make every alternative ineligible. We see the agent as a phenomenon generated by the world of which he is a part. One aspect of the phenomenon is his sense of choosing among alternatives, for good or bad reasons. But this makes no difference. Whether we think of his practical reasoning and his choices as causally determined or not, we cannot project ourselves into his point of view for the purpose of comparing alternatives once we have ascended to that extreme objective standpoint which sees him merely as a bit of the world. The alternatives that he may think of as available to him are from this point of view just alternative courses that the world might have taken. The fact that what didn't happen would have been better or worse than what did doesn't support an internal judgment of responsibility about a human being any more than it does about a rattlesnake.

Furthermore, as is true with respect to autonomy, there is nothing we can imagine being true of the agent, even taking into account his own point of view, which would support such a judgment. Once we are in this external position, nothing about the intentional explanation of action will help. Either something other than the agent's reasons explains why he acted for the reasons he did, or nothing does. In either case the external standpoint sees the alternatives not as alternatives for the agent, but as alternatives for the *world*, which *involve* the agent. And the world, of course, is not an agent and cannot be held responsible.

The real problem is the external vantage point. In ordinary judgments of responsibility we do not go that far outside, but stay inside our natural human point of view and project it into that of other, similar beings, stopping only where it will not fit. But judgments so based are vulnerable to the more external view, which can take in both the defendant and the judge. Then the whole complex—the defendant's choice and the judge's projection into it and resulting judgment—is seen as a phenomenon also. The judge's sense of the defendant's alternatives is revealed as an illusion which derives from the judge's projection of his own illusory—indeed unintelligible—sense of autonomy into the defendant.

I can no more help holding myself and others responsible in ordinary life than I can help feeling that my actions originate with me. But this is just another way in which, from some distance outside, I seem to myself to be trapped.

As usual, a radically external view presents me with an unfulfillable demand. It gives me the idea that to be truly autonomous I would have to be able to act in light of everything about myself—from outside myself and indeed from outside the world. And it makes any projection into the point of view of an ordinary agent seem unreal. What he sees as alternatives among which he can decide are really, from this point of view, alternative courses the world might take, within which his actions fall. While I can compare the course of events which includes his actual conduct with an alternative which includes his doing something else, my evaluation of these alternatives will not yield a judgment of his action from within. Alternatives for the world are not alternatives *for* him just because they include him. In a sense, the radically external standpoint is not a standpoint of choice at all. It is only when I forget about it and return to my status as fellow creature that I can project myself into the point of view of another agent in the way required for a judgment of responsibility. Only then can I evaluate the alternatives facing *him*, and thereby judge him for what he did.

The bafflement of moral judgments by objective detachment is unstable. We may be able temporarily to view William Calley, for example, as a phenomenon—a repulsive and dangerous bit of the zoosphere—without condemning him on the basis of a projection into his standpoint of our own sense of genuine alternatives in action. But it is next to impossible to remain in the attitude of inability to condemn Lieutenant Calley for the murders at My Lai: our feelings return before the ink of the argument is dry. That is because we don't stay in the rarefied objective atmosphere but drop back into our point of view as agents, which then allows us to see Calley's point of view, as he entered the village to encounter only peasants eating breakfast, and no resistance, as the point of view within which evaluation must proceed.[5] We cannot stay outside Lieutenant Calley because we cannot stay outside ourselves. Nevertheless, the external standpoint is always there as a possibility, and once having occupied it we can no longer regard our internal judgments of responsibility in the same way. From a point of view that is available to us, they can suddenly seem to depend on an illusion—a forgetting of the fact that we are just parts of the world and our lives just parts of its history.

4. STRAWSON ON FREEDOM

Let me contrast my view of the problem, specifically of its genuineness, with Strawson's. In his classic essay "Freedom and Resentment" he argues that though we can on occasion adopt the objective attitude toward other persons, it is not possible for the reactive attitudes to be philosophically undermined *in general* by any belief about the universe or human action, including the belief in determinism. The essence of his view, expressed toward the end of the essay, is this:

Inside the general structure or web of human attitudes and feelings of which I have been speaking, there is endless room for modification, redirection, criticism, and justification. But questions of justification are internal to it. The existence of the general framework of attitudes itself is something we are given with the fact of human society. As a whole, it neither calls for, nor permits, an external 'rational' justification.[6]

His view here is the same as his view about knowledge (and in a footnote to the passage, he draws an explicit parallel with the problem of induction). Justification and criticism make sense only within the system: justification of the system from outside is unnecessary, and therefore criticism from outside is impossible.

I believe this position is incorrect because there is no way of preventing the slide from *internal* to *external* criticism once we are capable of an external view. It needs nothing more than the ordinary idea of responsibility. The problem of free will, like the problem of skepticism, does not arise because of a philosophically imposed demand for external justification of the entire system of ordinary judgments and attitudes. It arises because there is a continuity between familiar "internal" criticism of the reactive attitudes on the basis of specific facts, and philosophical criticisms on the basis of supposed general facts. When we first consider the possibility that all human

---

[5] See S. M. Hirsch, *My Lai 4* (New York: Random House, 1970) for the details.

[6] Peter Strawson, "Freedom and Resentment," *Proceedings of the British Academy* (1962), p. 23 [reprinted as Essay 4, this volume].

actions may be determined by heredity and environment, it threatens to defuse our reactive attitudes as effectively as does the information that a particular action was caused by the effects of a drug—despite all the differences between the two suppositions. It blocks the projection into the point of view of the agent on which the reactive attitudes depend. The same is true when we expand the point to cover every way in which our lives can be seen as part of the course of nature, whether determined or not. No new standards come into it; in fact no demand for justification comes into it, since the challenge depends only on generalizing familiar standards of criticism. We cease to resent what someone has done if we cease to see the alternatives as alternatives for him.

The parallel with skepticism in epistemology is again clear. The extremely general possibilities of error that the skeptic imagines undermine confidence in all our beliefs in just the way that a more mundane particular possibility of error undermines confidence in a particular belief. The possibility of complete erosion by skeptical possibilities is built into our ordinary beliefs from the start: it is not created by the philosophical imposition of new standards of justification or certainty. On the contrary, new justifications seem to be required only in response to the threat of erosion from ordinary criticisms, sufficiently generalized.

Similarly with action. Some of the externally imposed limitations and constraints on our actions are evident to us. When we discover others, internal and less evident, our reactive attitudes toward the affected action tend to be defused, for it seems no longer attributable in the required way to the person who must be the target of those attitudes. The philosophical challenges to free will are nothing but radical extensions of this encroachment. As the unchosen conditions of action are extended into the agent's makeup and psychological state by an expanded objectivity, they seem to engulf everything, and the area of freedom left to him shrinks to zero. Since this seems to happen whether determinism is true or not, we are threatened with the conclusion that the idea of free agency with which we began is really unintelligible. It only seemed to mean something when we located it in the space left open by those familiar limits on action imposed by the external world—and only because we did not think enough about what would have to occupy that blank space. Nothing, it seems, could.

This is a genuine challenge to our freedom and the attitudes that presuppose it, and it cannot be met by the claim that only internal criticisms are legitimate, unless that claim is established on independent grounds. The push to objectivity is after all a part of the framework of human life. It could only be stopped from leading to these skeptical results if the radically external view of human life could be shown to be illegitimate—so that our questions had to stop before we got there.[7]

5. THE BLIND SPOT

I am now going to change the subject. I have said this problem has no available solution and will not contradict myself by proposing one. But I want to do something else, and that is to describe a kind of reconciliation between the objective standpoint and the inner perspective of agency which reduces the radical detachment produced by initial contemplation of ourselves as creatures in the world. This does not meet the central problem of free will. But it does reduce the degree to which the objective self must think of itself as an impotent spectator, and to that extent it confers a kind of freedom. It is a bit like the relation between the ordinary pursuit of objective knowledge and philosophical skepticism—to explain the obscure by the equally obscure: a limited harmony between external and internal, in the shadow of an even more external view.

We cannot act from outside ourselves, nor create ourselves *ex nihilo*. But the impulse to this logically impossible goal also pushes us toward something else, which is not logically impossible and which may assuage the original impulse somewhat to the extent that we can attain it. We want to bring the external view of ourselves back into connection with our actions, as far as we can. We must learn to act from an objective standpoint as well as to view ourselves from an objective standpoint.

The problem here is continuous with the prephilosophical problem of seeking freedom from inner bondage in ordinary life. We all want external freedom, of course: the absence of obstacles to doing what we want. We don't want to be locked or tied up, or closed off from opportunities, or too poor or weak to do what we would like. But reflective human beings want something more. They want to be able to stand back from the motives and reasons and values that influence their choices, and submit to them only if they are acceptable. Since we can't act in light of *everything* about ourselves, the best we can do is to try to live in a way that wouldn't have to be revised in light of anything more that could be known about us. This is a practical analogue of the epistemological hope for harmony with the world.

[7] See B. Stroud, *The Significance of Philosophical Skepticism* (Oxford: Oxford University Press, 1984) for the analogous point that skepticism is unavoidable unless we can somehow show the demand for an 'external' account of knowledge to be illegitimate. Once the question has been raised, it can't be answered. This makes it tempting to look for a way of showing that it can't be raised—but I am skeptical about the prospects of such a strategy.

Let me repeat that this is not autonomy, not a solution to the problem of free will, but a substitute—one which falls short of the impossible aspiration to act from outside ourselves, but which nevertheless has value in its own right. I want to discuss some of the ways in which we can reduce the detachment from our own actions that initially results from taking up the objective standpoint, by coming to act from that standpoint.

We might try, first, to develop as complete an objective view of ourselves as we can, and include it in the basis of our actions, wherever it is relevant. This would mean consistently looking over our own shoulders at what we are doing and why (though often it will be a mere formality). But this objective self-surveillance will inevitably be incomplete, since some knower must remain behind the lens if anything is to be known. Moreover, each of us knows this—knows that some of the sources of his actions are not objects of his attention and choice. The objective view of ourselves includes both what we know and can use, and what we know that we do not know, and therefore know that we cannot use.

Let me call this the *essentially incomplete objective view*, or *incomplete view* for short. The incomplete view of ourselves in the world includes a large blind spot, behind our eyes, so to speak, that hides something we cannot take into account in acting, because it is what acts. Yet this blind spot is part of our objective picture of the world, and to act from as far out as possible we must to some extent include a recognition of it in the basis of our actions.

We may discover our freedom to be limited if the objective view turns up an irrational impulse or fear whose influence on our conduct we can't prevent, but which we know to be irrational and cannot accept as justified. But we can also reflect that our actions may be constrained by an influence we know nothing about. This might be either something we could successfully resist if we did know about it, or something we wouldn't be able to resist even then, but which we also couldn't accept as a legitimate ground for action.

The incomplete view faces us with the possibility that we are constrained in one of these ways without knowing it, by factors operating in the blind spot. It also faces us with the certainty that however much we expand our objective view of ourselves, something will remain beyond the possibility of explicit acceptance or rejection, because we cannot get entirely outside ourselves, even though we know that there is an outside.

We hope we aren't under influences that we would see grounds for resisting if we became aware of them—various forms of prejudice, irrationality, and narrow-mindedness. This is a fairly ordinary limitation on freedom, which we can take measures to avoid. Some of these measures involve widening the range of our self-awareness, and some require rather an attunement to the selective need for seeking it. The real difficulty, though, is to say what it is reasonable to hope for with respect to the core of the self that lies at the center of the blind spot.

It is clear that we can't decisively and irrevocably endorse our actions, any more than we can endorse our beliefs, from the most objective standpoint we can take toward ourselves, since what we see from that standpoint is the incomplete view. All we can do to avoid the disengagement of that standpoint from action is to try to satisfy a negative condition: the absence of positive reasons to detach. The best we can hope for is to act in a way that permits some confidence that it would not prove unacceptable no matter how much more completely we developed the objective view—no matter how many more steps we took outside ourselves, even beyond all real possibility.

This involves the idea of an unlimited hypothetical development on the path of self-knowledge and self-criticism, only a small part of which we will actually traverse. We assume that our own advances in objectivity are steps along a path that extends beyond them and beyond all our capacities. But even allowing unlimited time, or an unlimited number of generations, to take as many successive steps as we like, the process of enlarging objectivity can never be completed, short of omniscience. First, every objective view will contain a blind spot, and cannot comprehend everything about the viewer himself. But second, there will not even be a limiting point beyond which it is impossible to go. This is because each step to a new objective vantage point, while it brings more of the self under observation, also adds to the dimensions of the observer something further which is not itself immediately observed. And this becomes possible material for observation and assessment from a still later objective standpoint. The mind's work is never done.

So the creation of an objective will is not a completable task. What is wanted is some way of making the most objective standpoint the basis of action: subordinating it to my agency instead of allowing it, and therefore me, to stay outside of my actions as a helpless observer. Given that I cannot do this by acting from outside the world, on the basis of a complete objective view of myself and it, the next best thing is to act from within the world on the basis of the most objective view of which I am capable—the incomplete view—in such a way as to guard against rejection by its successors in the objective sequence, both those that I can achieve and those that I can't. The attempt to achieve immunity from later objective revision (independently of whether I will actually reach the later objective stages) is the only way to make the incomplete objective view a continuing part of the basis of my actions. That is the closest I can come to acting on the world from outside myself while being part of it.

This form of integration between the standpoints must be distinguished from the position of a creature that doesn't suffer from the sense of helplessness because it can't take up the external view toward itself. When a cat stalks a bird, no element of the cat's self can remain outside as a detached observer of the scene, so there is no sense in which the cat can feel that *he* is not doing it. But because there is more to me than there is to a cat, I am threatened by the feeling that I do not really act when I act only on the basis of that internal view which suffices for a cat.

The cat's immunity to the problem of autonomy does not mean that it is free. We can consider the cat from outside and it may be that we will see it as trapped, in certain respects, by ignorance, fear, or instinct. Its nature is given and cannot be subjected by the cat to endorsement, criticism, or revision. It cannot increase its own rationality.

We would not be in much better shape than the cat if, though we remained engaged in our actions however objective a standpoint we achieved, nevertheless there was a standpoint more objective than any open to us, from which we would appear to an outside observer as the cat appears to us. But in fact, unlike the cat, we can form the idea of views of ourselves more objective than any we can reach, and can make our own detachment or engagement parasitic on what we suppose those views would reveal. We wish to believe that the possibility of engagement is not limited to the maximum level that we can actually attain, and we would like to be able to regard this level as a link to unlimited objectivity—so that there is no view of us, no matter how external, that permits complete detachment. This is to extend the ambition of rationalism to practical reason.

Descartes tried to recapture knowledge by imagining his relation to the world from the point of view of God. Finding one's feet within the world in a way that will withstand criticism from more objective standpoints than one can take up is a Cartesian enterprise, and like Descartes' it can hope at best for only partial success. But with this qualification, there are several strategies for increasing objective engagement with one's actions—or at least decreasing objective disengagement from them.

6. OBJECTIVE ENGAGEMENT

The most ambitious strategy would be to seek positive grounds for choice that commanded the assent of the objective will no matter how far removed it was from my particular perspective. This, if it were possible, would amount to acting *sub specie aeternitatis*. It would be analogous to the epistemological strategy of grounding belief in a priori certainties: mathematical or logical truths or methods of reasoning of whose falsehood one cannot conceive—of which one can't even conceive that a far wiser being might see that they were false, though it was beyond one's own powers.

Since such absolute objective grounds are even harder to come by in practical than in theoretical reason, a less ambitious strategy seems called for. One such strategy—a strategy of objective tolerance as opposed to objective affirmation—is to find grounds for acting within my personal perspective that will not be *rejected* from a larger point of view: grounds which the objective self can tolerate because of their limited pretensions to objectivity. Such latitude would be acceptable within the constraints imposed by any more positive results of the objective view.

The epistemological analogue would be the identification of certain beliefs as limited in the objectivity of their claims. These would be about the world of appearance, and an objective view could admit them as such. The danger with this strategy is that it can be misused as a general escape from skepticism by reducing all apparently objective judgments to subjective claims about the appearances. But if we avoid this kind of escapist reductionism, there certainly remain some beliefs which are just about the appearances. Beliefs about the subjective character of my sensory experiences, for example, are not threatened by the prospect that they might be overthrown from a much more objective standpoint.

With respect to decision and action, the strategy of objective tolerance is appropriate in areas where I do not aspire to the highest degree of self-command. When I choose from a menu I am interested only in opening myself to the play of inclinations and appetites, in order to see what I most feel like having (providing it's a cheap restaurant and I'm not on a diet). I am content here to be guided by my strongest appetite, without fear that from a more detached perspective it might appear that one of the weaker ones should really be preferred.

In fact I don't know what it would mean to wonder whether, *sub specie aeternitatis*, wanting a chicken salad sandwich was perhaps really preferable as a ground for action to wanting a salami sandwich. Nothing happens when I put myself outside of these desires and contemplate the choice: it can be made only from an internal perspective, for the preferences are neither undermined nor endorsed from an external one. Perhaps there could be some objective endorsement of the satisfaction of the preferences without endorsement of the preferences themselves. But even this principle of prima facie hedonism seems superfluous until I am faced with the problem of weighing these preferences against other motives and values.

In these kinds of cases, then, I do not feel trapped or impotent when I consider my situation objectively, because I do not aspire to more control than I have if my choice is dictated by my immediate inclinations. I am content with the freedom of a cat choosing which armchair to curl up in. External assessment can add nothing to this, nor does it detract.

The strategy of finding areas for objective tolerance rather than objective endorsement may have application at higher levels than that of choosing from a menu. It may be that from a standpoint sufficiently external to that of ordinary human life, not only chicken salad and salami but much of what is important to human beings—their hopes, projects, ambitions, and very survival—cannot be seen positively to matter. Insofar as I can regard that standpoint as part of my own, I may be able to endorse objectively almost nothing that I do. Whether this makes me the helpless victim of most of the motives and values that govern my life depends on whether from this most objective standpoint such values would be rejected as erroneous, or whether, like a taste for pecan pie, they could be tolerated as limited in their objective pretensions, and therefore subjectively legitimate as grounds for action. If in the sequence of more and more external perspectives they would be endorsed up to a certain point and thereafter tolerated, then I need not fear radical objective separation from acts that depend on them—though there will be a certain detachment.

This form of "reentry" leaves us in a different position with respect to our impulses from the one we are in prereflectively. The belief that they do not make strongly objective claims, and therefore are not liable to being over-thrown or discredited from a more objective standpoint, is now in the back-ground of our motives. As with sensory impressions, they have a different status in our picture of the world once we have distinguished between appearance and reality. When we act on such impulses we need not feel objectively dissociated, because if we consider the possibility that they would be rejected from a higher standpoint, we can conclude that because of their limited pretensions they would not.

But while many choices have this uncomplicated character, more difficult questions arise in connection with the characteristically human capacity to move to a higher vantage point and a higher order of desires—particularly where there is conflict among different types of first-order desires. Then practical judgment originates with the objective standpoint, and we look for some assurance that it will not be overthrown by a still more objective or detached view.

An important method of objective integration is ordinary practical rationality, which is roughly analogous to the process of forming a coherent set of beliefs out of one's prereflective personal impressions. This involves not mere tolerance, but actual endorsement of some motives, suppression or revision of others, and adoption of still others, from a standpoint outside that within which primary impulses, appetites, and aversions arise. When these conflict we can step outside and choose among them. Although such rationality can be exercised purely with respect to present desires, it is naturally extended to prudential rationality, which is exercised from an objective standpoint detached from the present, and decides on the weight to be accorded to all one's interests, present and future.

Prudence may itself conflict with other motives, and then it becomes itself subject to assessment from outside. But if it is just one's own present and future desires that are in question, prudence consists in taking up a standpoint outside the present—and perhaps refusing to permit one's choices to be dictated by the strongest present desire. Most simply, preference may be given to the satisfaction of stronger or longer-term expected desires; but other interests may also count.

The conflict between prudence and impulse is not like the conflict between chicken salad and salami, for it is a conflict between levels; the immediate perspective of the present moment and the (partly) transcendent perspective of temporal neutrality among the foreseeable moments of one's life. It is an example of the pursuit of freedom because through prudence we try to stand back from the impulses that press on us immediately, and to act in a temporal sense from outside of ourselves. If we could not do this, we would as agents be trapped in the present moment, with temporal neutrality reduced to a vantage point of observation.[8] And we would be even more trapped if we couldn't exercise practical rationality by harmonizing our desires even in the present: we would just have to watch ourselves being pushed around by them.

Prudence itself does not hold comparable dangers unless it is viewed from a larger perspective in competition with motives of a quite different kind. One must be careful here: prudence itself can be a kind of slavery, if carried too far. The dominance of a timeless view of one's life may be objectively unwise. And compulsiveness or neurotic avoidance based on repressed desires can easily be disguised as rational self-control. But in its normal form, prudence increases one's freedom by increasing one's control over the operation of first-order motives, through a kind of objective will.

The objective stance here is not merely permissive, but active. The prudential motives do not exist prior to the adoption of an objective standpoint, but are produced by it. Even the direct motivation of present desires is replaced by the objective weight they are given in a timeless prudential assessment,

---

[8] I've said more about this in T. Nagel, *The Possibility of Altruism* (New York: Oxford University Press, 1970).

when they are thrown into a class with future ones. (I shall not try to discuss the difficult problems that arise about past desires in relation to the analysis of prudence—problems vividly exposed and thoroughly explored in Parfit.)[9]

Although prudence is only the first stage in the development of an objective will, it is selective in its endorsement of more immediate motives and preferences. From outside of the present moment, not all the impulses and goals of each present moment can be equally endorsed, especially if they conflict with one another. Certain basic and persistent desires and needs will be natural candidates for prudential endorsement, but passing whims won't be, as such—although the general capacities and liberties that enable one to indulge such whims may be objectively valued. (Parfit has suggested to me that this same division may also show up in ethics, for the desires that provide the material for prudence may be the ones we have to consider in according objective weight to the interests of other people.) This does not mean that motives which cannot be endorsed from a timeless standpoint must be crushed completely. Their immediate operation is objectively tolerable, but they do have to compete with prudential reasons in whose formation they do not have a significant voice, so to speak.

Even when I choose not to submit entirely to prudential considerations as against present impulse, this depends on squaring my acts with the objective view. For I must objectively tolerate those impulses and their success, even if I do not endorse them with their full weight. Otherwise it is not freedom that I display but weakness of will.

The timeless standpoint may to some extent take a hands-off attitude toward the motives of the present moment. This restrained manifestation of objectivity is an example of something more general and very important in the relation between subjective and objective: there are limits to the degree to which the objective standpoint can simply take over and replace the original perspectives which it transcends.

Nevertheless, we are led outside the standpoint of the present, to a position from which we can at least subject our immediate impulses to objective scrutiny. And this first step into objective time is taken with the hope that its results would not be overthrown by more advanced steps not yet taken, or perhaps not even takable by us. The essential activity of the objective will, in assessing, endorsing, rejecting, and tolerating immediate impulses, is to recognize or form values, as opposed to mere preferences.[10]

---

[9] D. Parfit, *Reasons and Persons* (Oxford: Oxford University Press, 1984), ch. 8.

[10] See G. Watson "Free Agency", *Journal of Philosophy* (April 1975 [Essay 17, this volume]), for a discussion of the relation between freedom and values. The present discussion of objective will is an attempt to say more about what values are and how they provide an alternative to the autonomy we cannot have.

7. MORALITY AS FREEDOM

More external than the standpoint of temporal neutrality is the standpoint from which one sees oneself as just an individual among others, viewing one's interests and concerns entirely from outside. In some respects, the appropriate attitude from this standpoint may be tolerance rather than endorsement. But we are not in general content to regard our lives in this way once we have taken up an external view, nor are we content to act without a more positive endorsement from the objective self.

Moreover, tolerance runs into difficulty when the interests of different individuals conflict. I can't continue to regard my impulses and desires as making no objective claims if I wish to pursue them in opposition to the desires of others—unless I am prepared to regard the outcome of all such conflicts with objective indifference, like the choice between chicken salad and salami. But if I'm going to take a dim view, from an external standpoint, of the situation in which I don't get any lunch at all because a greedy fellow picnicker has eaten all the sandwiches, then I must move beyond objective tolerance to objective endorsement.

This is a different connection between the objective standpoint and action: engagement not just from outside the present moment, but from outside one's life.[11] Thus in a sense I come to act on the world from outside my particular personal place in it—to control the behavior of TN from a standpoint that is not mine qua TN. The objective self for whom the problem of free will arises is co-opted into agency.

All this manifests itself in the formation of impersonal values, and the modification of conduct and motivation in accordance with them. It imposes serious constraints. Values are judgments from a standpoint external to ourselves about how to be and how to live. Because they are accepted from an impersonal standpoint, they apply not only to the point of view of the particular person I happen to be, but generally. They tell me how I should live because they tell me how anyone should live.

A proper discussion of this form of inner-outer integration belongs to ethics, and I shall undertake it later. In a sense, I am agreeing with Kant's view that there is an internal connection between ethics and freedom: subjection to morality expresses the hope of autonomy, even though it is a hope that cannot be realized in its original form. We cannot act on the world from outside, but we can in a sense act from both inside and outside our particular position in it. Ethics increases the range of what it is about ourselves that we

---

[11] See Parfit, *Reasons and Persons*, ch. 7, for an argument that if one accepts the first, one has to accept the second. Prudence, he argues, cannot be identified with practical rationality, because it is unreasonable to hold that reasons cannot be relative to time but must be relative to persons.

can will—extending it from our actions to the motives and character traits and dispositions from which they arise. We want to be able to will the sources of our actions down to the very bottom, reducing the gap between explanation and justification. To put it another way, we want to reduce the size of the range of determinants of our actions that are not willable but merely observable—that from outside we can only *watch*.

Naturally there are many determinants of action to which the will cannot extend. Ethics cannot make us omnipotent: if we wished to close the gap between explanation and justification completely, it would mean willing the entire history of the world that produced us and faced us with the circumstances in which we must live, act, and choose. Such *amor fati* is beyond the aspiration of most of us.

There is a way of extending the will beyond ourselves to the circumstances of action, but it is through the extension of ethics into politics. Objective engagement is increased not only if we can will the sources of our actions relative to the circumstances, but also if the circumstances of life are such that we can will from an objective standpoint that the conditions in which we must act should be as they are. Then in a sense the harmony between observation and will, or between explanation and justification, is extended into the world. (The epistemological analogue would be objective endorsement of the intellectual environment and process of education that led to the formation of one's capacity for reasoning, assessing evidence, and forming beliefs.)

What we hope for is not only to do what we want given the circumstances, but also to be as we want to be, to as deep a level as possible, and to find ourselves faced with the choices we want to be faced with, in a world that we can want to live in. If we were interested only in eliminating the external barriers to freedom, we would not be led into ethics, but only into the attempt to increase control over our environment. This would involve politics too, but only a politics based on our interests, like that of Hobbes, not an ethical politics. It is the attack on inner barriers that leads to the development of ethics, for it means that we hope to be able to will that our character and motives should be as they are, and not feel simply stuck with them when viewing ourselves objectively.

Values express the objective will. Ethical values in particular result from the combination of many lives and sets of interests in a single set of judgments. The demands of balancing, coordination, and integration that this imposes have consequences for what can be objectively willed for each individual, and therefore for oneself. Ethics is one route to objective engagement because it supplies an alternative to pure observation of ourselves from outside. It permits the will to expand at least some of the way along the path of transcendence possible for the understanding. How far we can travel on this path is partly a matter of luck. We may be so constituted that our objective judgments cannot keep pace with our capacity for doubt. And of course we can always raise the purely abstract doubt that even the strongest sense of harmony between internal and external views might be an illusion, identifiable as such only from a superior vantage point that we cannot reach.

None of this, as I have said, solves the traditional problem of free will. However much harmony with an objective view we may achieve in action, we can always undermine the sense of our own autonomy by reflecting that the chain of explanation or absence of explanation for this harmony can be pursued till it leads outside our lives.

When it comes to moral responsibility and the internal comparison of action with the alternatives, nothing is changed by the possibilities of object-ive engagement I have discussed. If there is such a thing as responsibility, it would have to be found in bad actions as well as good ones—that is, in actions which one could not endorse from an objective standpoint. This means that any attempt to locate freedom in the development of rational and moral self-command will run into the problem Sidgwick posed as an objection to Kant. The problem is that if freedom can be pursued and approached only through the achievement of objective and ultimately eth-ical values of some kind, then it is not clear how someone can be both free and bad, hence not clear how someone can be morally responsible for doing wrong, if freedom is a condition of responsibility.[12]

In practice we project ourselves for purposes of judgment into the stand-point of anyone whose actions we can interpret subjectively as a manifest-ation of his values.[13] This is perfectly natural, but it cannot defuse the problem of responsibility, which can always be raised again, both about us and about the people we feel able to understand and evaluate from inside.

I can see no way to bring judgments of responsibility back into line with the external view—no way to reengage it with such judgments as it can be partially reengaged with action. Judgments of responsibility depend on a kind of projection into the standpoint of the defendant which we cannot carry out unless we forget the external view to a certain extent. I can't simultaneously think of Lieutenant Calley as a natural phenomenon from outside and assess his actions from inside by contrasting them with the

---

[12] H. Sidgwick, *The Methods of Ethics* (7th Edition, 1907), bk. 1, ch. 5, sec. 1. Kant grapples with this problem in I. Kant, *Religion within the Limits of Reason Alone* (1794), bk. 1, which deals explicitly with responsibility for evil.
[13] This includes actions which go against the values he holds explicitly—as when someone out of fear fails to decide to do what he thinks he should, or fails to do what he has decided to do. The failure to act on one's values shows something about their strength, as well as about the strength of one's will.

alternatives that appeared subjectively available to him at the time. Nothing analogous to partial objective engagement is available here. Unless there is a way to block the ascent to the external view, we cannot find a place to stand inside the world which will permit us to make such judgments without the threat that they will seem senseless from farther out. But we seem locked into a practice of projection in which we take the sense of our own autonomy, intelligible or not, as our measure for the judgment of others.

As I have said, it seems to me that nothing approaching the truth has yet been said on this subject.

13

AGENT CAUSATION

TIMOTHY O'CONNOR

I. INTRODUCTION

A natural way of characterizing our typical experience of making decisions and acting upon them—one that would, I think, gain widespread assent—goes something like this: When I decide, say, to go for a walk on a cool autumn evening, I am conscious of various factors at work (some consciously articulated, some not) motivating me either to do so or to do something else instead. And there are some courses of action which, while it is *conceivable* that I might choose to follow them, are such that they do not represent 'genuine' possibilities for me at that time, given my current mood, particular desires and beliefs, and, in some cases, long-standing intentions of a general sort. But within the framework of possibilities (and perhaps even relative likelihoods) that these present conative and cognitive factors set, it seems for all the world to be *up to me* to decide which particular action I will undertake. The decision I make is no mere vector sum of internal and external forces acting upon me during the process of deliberation (if, indeed, I deliberate at all). Rather, *I* bring it about—directly, you might say—in response to the various considerations: I am the source of my own activity, not merely in a relative sense as the most proximate and salient locus of an unbroken chain of causal transactions leading up to this event, but fundamentally, in a way not prefigured by what has gone before. Or, again, so it seems.

But a thesis that enjoys unusual consensus among contemporary philosophers is that this pretheoretic conception is not at all like the way things

From *Agents, Causes, and Events: Essays on Indeterminism and Free Will*, edited by Timothy O'Connor. Copyright © 1995 by Oxford University Press, Inc. Used by permission of Oxford University Press, Inc.
    Many people have given me helpful suggestions and criticisms of material presented in this paper, some of which was presented in a pair of lectures at the Free University in Amsterdam. I wish to acknowledge in particular the help of Randolph Clarke, Mark Crimmins, Norman Kretzmann, Al Plantinga, Dave Robb, Sydney Shoemaker, René van Woudenberg, and, especially, Carl Ginet.

really are with respect to ordinary human activity. Indeed, most would claim that any attempt to theoretically articulate this commonsense picture of agency will inevitably be incoherent or, at best, irremediably mysterious. However, arguments on behalf of this thesis are not nearly as strong as the confidence with which it is generally held. This observation, together with an examination of the nature of such arguments, leads me to suspect that many philosophers are deeply in the grip of a certain broad picture of the physical world, one which has come to seem overwhelmingly obvious to them, despite the fact that it rests, so far as I can see, on certain empirical assumptions that are as yet unsubstantiated. I will address this intoxicating picture below, though I fear that my rhetorical skills are not up to the task of breaking the grip it has on some.

In what follows, I will contend that the commonsense view of ourselves as fundamental causal agents—for which some have used the term "unmoved movers" but which I think might more accurately be expressed as "not wholly moved movers"—is theoretically understandable, internally consistent, and consistent with what we have thus far come to know about the nature and workings of the natural world. In the section that follows, I try to show how the concept of 'agent' causation can be understood as a distinct species (from 'event' causation) of the primitive idea, which I'll term "causal production," underlying realist or non-Humean conceptions of event causation. In Section III, I respond to a number of contemporary objections to the theory of agent causation. Sections IV and V are devoted to showing that the theory is compatible with ordinary reasons explanations of action, which then places me in a position to respond, in the final section, to the contention that we could never know, in principle, whether the agency theory actually describes a significant portion of human activity.

Let me be clear from the outset about two tasks that I do not propose to undertake here. First, I will in no way attempt to argue or adduce evidence for the claim that the theory described actually applies to human action. (I will, however, briefly suggest what sort of considerations could count as evidence in favor of its applicability.) Nor will I attempt to address the epistemological question of whether it is reasonable to suppose, in the absence of strong, directly confirming evidence, that the agency theory gives a correct schematic account of (a significant portion of) human activity, though I am inclined to answer this in the affirmative. What follows is strictly an essay in "descriptive metaphysics," charting the internal relationship among concepts in what I believe to be part of the commonsense picture of the world.

II. EVENT CAUSATION AND AGENT CAUSATION

I begin with a strong, highly controversial assumption about the general concept of causality. This assumption is that the core element of the concept is a *primitive* notion of the 'production' or 'bringing about' of an effect. This entails the negative thesis that a satisfactory reductive analysis of causality along Humean lines (in any of its versions) cannot be given. It should be readily apparent that if, contrary to this anti-Humean assumption, a satisfactory reductive analysis of causality *can* be given, the agency theorists's project of defending a variant species of causality immediately collapses into incoherence. For such reductive analyses are either committed to a general connection between certain *types* of causes and effects or equate causation with a form of counterfactual dependence. Neither approach is consistent with the agency theorist's claim that a causal relation can obtain between an agent and some event internal to himself, since his understanding of this is such as not to imply that the sort of event effected on that occasion will or would always (or generally) be produced given relevantly similar internal and external circumstances.

Acceptance of this assumption naturally (though not inevitably) points one in the direction of some sort of 'necessitarian' account of event causation. It is debatable, of course, whether the necessity in question is to be identified with broadly logical (or metaphysical) necessity or is rather to be thought of as a special, contingent form. Though the accounts I rely on in sketching a broadly necessitarian view take the former route, all that I want to assume here is that there is some form or other of objective necessity attaching to event-causal relations, as it is quite compatible with my purposes that this be held to be a primitive, contingent variety.[1] (Let me forestall confusion by emphasizing at the outset that, in drawing upon the necessitarian view of *event* causation in order to explicate the notion of agent causation, I am not suggesting that there is anything analogous to a necessary connection between prior circumstances and agent-caused events. Indeed, I will argue below that this is impossible. Rather, as will become clear shortly, the sole aspect of the necessitarian view that I carry over to agent causation is the necessary connection between an object's instantiating a certain set of properties and its possession of a causal power or powers. The two sorts of causation differ sharply, however, in terms of the manner in which causal powers are exercised: of necessity, when the object is placed in the

---

[1] As has recently been suggested, for example, by David M. Armstrong (*What Is a Law of Nature?* [Cambridge: Cambridge University Press, 1984]) and Michael Tooley (*Causation: A Realist Approach* [Oxford: Clarendon Press, 1987]).

appropriate circumstances, for event causation; under the voluntary, unnecessitated control of the agent, for agent causation.)

A recent elucidation of a necessitarian approach to causality is found in Harré and Madden.[2] The central notion in their theory is that of the "powerful particular." When placed in the appropriate circumstances, an object manifests its inherent causal powers in observable effects. The particular powers had by a given object have their basis in its underlying nature—its chemical, physical, or genetic constitution and structure. Events figure in the causal relation in virtue of "stimulat[ing] a suitable generative mechanism to action, or [clearing away] impediments to the activity of a powerful particular already in a state of readiness to act" (p. 5). An example of the first sort of causal event is the detonation of a stick of dynamite. The other sort—the removal of an impediment to action—is exemplified by the removal of the air from an underwater cylinder, thereby enabling the body of water to exercise its power to crush the object. Certain effects are 'characteristic' of objects in the appropriate circumstances in a strong sense—"given the specification of the causal powers of the things and substances of the world, the denial of statements describing these effects of those powers, when the environment allows them to be exercised, would be inconsistent with the nature of those things" (p. 5). "While natures are preserved, the world must go on in its usual way," although "[n]ecessity might, and probably, does, hold in some cases only between the productive circumstances and a certain distribution of possible outcomes or productions" (p. 153).

Now it is natural to link the causal powers an object possesses at a given time directly to its properties. Shoemaker[3] provides a helpful explication of this idea. First we are told that the possession of a causal power by an object is to be thought of as its being the case that "its presence in circumstances of a particular sort will [of necessity] have certain effects" (p. 211). Properties figure into the picture in the following way:

Just as powers can be thought of as functions from circumstances to causal effects, so the properties on which powers depend can be thought of as functions from properties to powers (or, better, as functions from sets of properties to sets of powers). One might even say that properties are second-order powers; they are powers to produce first-order powers (powers to produce certain sorts of events) if combined with certain other properties. (p. 212)

This implies that the relationship between an object's properties and its causal powers is a logically necessary one: "what makes a property the

---

[2] *Causal Powers: A Theory of Natural Necessity* (Oxford: Basil Blackwell, 1975).
[3] "Causality and Properties," in *Identity, Cause and Mind* (Cambridge: Cambridge University Press, 1984).

property it is, what determines its identity, is its potential for contributing to the causal powers of the things that have it" (p. 212).

If one wishes to hold, by contrast, that causal necessity is logically contingent, then one may say that properties are contingently associated with such functions from properties to powers, rather than being identified with (or logically connected to) them. And another possible wrinkle on the broad position, as Shoemaker notes, is to allow that

the [causal] laws . . . may be statistical, the powers to which the properties contribute, may, accordingly, be statistical tendencies or propensities, and the causation may be nonnecessitating. (p. 232)

With this thumbnail sketch of a standard necessitarian account of event causation before us, I now turn to the central task of showing how the notion of agent causation may be seen as a distinct species or embodiment of the basic, primitive notion of causal production. The core idea is quite simple: First of all, according to my preferred understanding of the agency theory, wherever the agent-causal relation obtains, the agent bears a *property* or set of properties that is volition-enabling (i.e., in virtue of this property, the agent has a type of causal power which, in accordance with traditions, we may term "active power"). In this way, then, claims of the form "agent A caused event e" also satisfy a weak version of Davidson's Humean dictum that "causal statements are implicitly general": such assertions may be thought to imply that a similarly situated agent (i.e., such that the relevant internal and external properties are instantiated) will always *have it directly within his power to* cause an event of the e-type.

Thus, the agency theory (as I interpret it) affirms the completely general claim (i.e., one applicable to both of the basic sorts of causation) that objects have causal powers in virtue of their properties, so that objects sharing the same properties share the same causal capacities, but it denies that all such causal powers may be thought of as (or as being intimately associated with) simple "functions from circumstances to effects" (as Shoemaker puts it). For it maintains that some properties contribute to the causal powers of the objects that bear them in a very different way from the event-causal paradigm, in which *an object's possession of property P in circumstance C* necessitates or makes probable a certain effect. On this alternative picture, a property of the right sort can (in conjunction with appropriate circumstances) *make possible* the direct, purposive bringing about of an effect *by the agent* who bears it.

Such a property thus plays a different functional role in the associated causal process. It gives rise to a fundamentally different type of causal power—one that in suitable circumstances is exercised at will by the agent, rather than of necessity, as with objects that are not partly self-determining agents.

To repeat, then, the fundamental tenet of the agency theory may be taken to be the claim that there are two basic *sorts* of (causal) properties, one of which applies uniquely to intelligent, purposive agents.[4] The thesis that there are two fundamental sorts of causation is a consequence of the thesis concerning types of properties.

Now some may be willing to grant the basic internal coherence of this alternative paradigm, but will maintain that special assumptions would have to be made concerning the nature of the agent in whom such a property were instantiated, assumptions that are not plausible. The most common thought here is that it presuppose some form of substance dualism.

Let us consider, therefore, the compatibility of the agency theory with the view that the only substances to be found in the natural world are material substances. (I intend this to be noncommital on the question of whether certain material substances, such as living human brains, can have irreducibly mental [i.e., nonphysical] *properties.*) A human agent, in particular, is a wholly biological organism, whose macroproperties are either constituted by or dependent on the properties of certain elementary physical particles, organized into complex subsystems at a number of levels. Now some philosophers, it seems, are convinced that this basic picture inexorably leads to the following:

Since all of the surface features of the world are entirely caused by and realized in systems of microelements, the behavior of microelements is sufficient to determine everything that happens. Such a 'bottom up' picture of the world allows for top-down causation (our minds, for example, can affect our bodies). But top-down causation only works because the top level is already caused by and realized in the bottom levels.[5]

But why does the author (John Searle) consider it an assured result that this bottom up picture is applicable to everything that happens in nature? Certain passages in the text from which this quotation is taken seem to suggest that it simply *follows* from the view that nature consists of material

---

[4] As Reid clearly saw, the notion of a particular actively (or agent-causally) bringing about an effect is intelligible only on the supposition that the particular be an agent capable of representing possible courses of action to himself and having certain desires and beliefs concerning those alternatives. (The reader is invited to try to form the conception of an object constituting a counter example to this claim.) This simple observation is sufficient to dismiss the derisive query of Watson ("Free Action and Free Will," *Mind*, 94 [1987], pp. 145–72) as to whether it is conceivable that spiders should turn out to be "agent-causes in Chisholm's sense" (p. 168).

[5] Searle, in *Minds, Brains, and Science* (Cambridge, Mass.: Harvard University Press, 1984), p. 94.

substances built up out of elementary particles, while others may be read as claiming that there are strongly confirming *empirical* grounds.

Surely the former reason is without merit. How can we deduce a priori that the organization of matter into certain highly complex systems will never result in novel *emergent* properties—either properties that themselves exert (in certain circumstances) an irreducibly "downward" form of causal influence, or ones that enable the objects that bear them to do so "at will"? Thomas Reid saw this point clearly. Although he was a substance dualist who thought that no purely material substances are capable of thought, he considered the implications for material agency if he were mistaken in this assumption:

[But if matter] require only a certain configuration to make it think rationally, it will be impossible to show any good reason why the same configuration may not make it act rationally and freely. . . . Those . . . who reason justly from this system of materialism, will easily perceive, that the doctrine of necessity[6] is so far from being a direct inference, that it can receive no support from it.[7]

Unfortunately, I haven't the space here to explore at any length the concept of an emergent property on which I'm relying. Suffice it to say that an emergent property is a macroproperty that is generated by the properties of an object's microstructure, but whose role in the causal processes involving that object are not reducible to those of the microproperties.[8] I'm inclined to think that any tendency to suppose that the emergence of macrodeterminative properties in material substances is strictly inconceivable must be diagnosed as an instance of the withering effect on one's imagination that results from long-standing captivation by a certain picture of the world.

So whether there are any emergent properties of matter is an empirical question to be decided ultimately on the basis of our success in identifying macrolevel properties of complex systems with relational complexes of microlevel properties. Now the agency theorist, as we have seen,[9] is committed (on the assumption of a substance monism) to the emergence of a very different *sort* of property altogether. Instead of producing certain effects in

---

[6] Reid would not have recognized *in*deterministic natural processes as an alternative to causal necessity. Hence, his claim that there is no reason to suppose that intelligent material substances (if such there be) could not be capable of free action is a defense of the possibility of a material system's exercising agent-causality.

[7] Reid, *Essays on the Active Powers of the Human Mind* (Cambridge, Mass.: MIT Press, 1969), p. 367.

[8] For further details, see my "Emergent Properties" (*American Philosophical Quarterly*, 31 [April 1994], pp. 91–104, cf. Brian McLaughlin, "The Rise and Fall of British Emergentism," in A. Beckermann, H. Flohr, and J. Kim, eds., *Emergence or Reduction? Essays on the Prospects of Nonreductive Physicalism* (Berlin: Walter de Gruyter, 1992).

[9] Because agent-causality is a distinct species of causation, only an emergent type of property could enable its occurrence.

the appropriate circumstances itself, of necessity, such a property enables the *particular* that possesses it (within a certain range of circumstances) to freely and directly bring about (or not bring about) any of a range of effects. (The number of alternatives genuinely open to an agent will doubtless vary from case to case.) This further commitment leaves the theory's proponent open to a special sort of objection, not applicable to emergentist claims generally: given the unique nature of the *sort* of property the theory postulates, it is unclear whether it is really conceivable that such a property could *emerge* from other natural properties. It will be claimed that only a very different sort of *substance* from material substances, such as is posited by Cartesian dualism, could possess such a property. It is noteworthy that many philosophers who discuss the agency theory seem to simply *assume* that its adherents are dualists.[10] But given that there is nothing inconsistent about the emergence of an "ordinary" causal property, having the potential for exercising an irreducible causal influence on the environments in which it is instantiated, it is hard to see just why there could not be a sort of emergent property whose novelty consists in its capacity to enable its possessor directly to effect changes at will (within a narrowly limited range, and in appropriate circumstances). And if such a possibility claim is difficult to evaluate on a purely abstract level, it is perhaps more plausible when considered in relation to entities such as ourselves, conscious, intelligent agents, capable of representing diverse, sophisticated plans of action for possible implementation and having appetitive attitudes that are efficacious in bringing about a desired alternative.

The likely reply to this, of course, is that the incoherency of such a view cannot be demonstrated only because we have been given so very "thin" a model to go on. Here, too, I believe, it must be admitted that there is some truth to this charge. Taking the agency theory seriously within a basically materialist framework brings forth a whole host of theoretical problems and issues such as the following:[11] When does a physical system qualify as an "agent"? What structural transformations in the human nervous system would result in long-standing (or permanent) loss of the agent-causal capacity generally? Precisely to what extent is an ordinary human's behavior directly regulated by the agent himself, and to what extent is it controlled by microdeterministic processes? (Put more generally, how do event- and agent-causal processes interact?) These, however, are obviously empirical matters,

---

[10] Two examples among many are Honderich (*A Theory of Determinism*, Oxford: Oxford University Press, 1988) and Levison ("Chisholm and 'the Metaphysical Problem of Human Freedom'," *Philosophia*, 8 [1978], pp. 537–41).

[11] Actually, an adherent of a viable dualist version of the agency theory would have to answer much the same sort of questions as those suggested above.

requiring extensive advancements within neurobiological science (and advancements favorable, of course, to the agency theorist's commitment to a significant measure of indeterminacy in human behavior). The answers to such questions will not be shown by philosophical work in action theory.

III. SOME CONTEMPORARY OBJECTIONS TO THE AGENCY THEORY

However, we have yet to examine a few other challenges to the tenability of the agency theory that have been raised in the literature, challenges that clearly are within the province of the philosophical theorist.

Donald Davidson has famously contended that the agency theorist faces an inescapable dilemma, once the question is posed, how well does the idea of agent causality account for the relation between an agent and his action?[12] The dilemma that Davidson sees may be expressed thus: either the causing by an agent of a primitive action[13] is a further event, distinct from the primitive action, or it is not.

Suppose first that the agent-causing is a further event. If so, then it is either an action or it is not. If it is an action, then the action we began with was not, contrary to the assumption, primitive. If it is not an action, then we have the absurdity of a causing that is not a doing. Therefore, it seems that we should not say that an agent's causing a primitive action is an event distinct from the action.

Suppose, then, that we grasp the second horn of the original dilemma and maintain that the agent's causing his action does not consist of some further event distinct from his primitive action. Davidson replies:

[T]hen what more have we said when we say the agent caused the action than when we say he was the agent of the action? The concept of *cause* seems to play no role. . . . What distinguishes agent causation from ordinary causation is that no expansion into a tale of two events is possible, and no law lurks. By the same token, nothing is explained. There seems no good reason, therefore, for using such expressions as 'cause', 'bring about', 'make the case' to illuminate the relation between an agent and his act. (pp. 52–53)

Now there are several highly dubious assumptions being made in this passage, but the first response to be made to the putative dilemma is to deny

---

[12] "Agency," in *Essays on Actions and Events* (Oxford: Oxford University Press, 1980), p. 52.

[13] That is, an action that one performs without doing anything else in order to perform it. Theories of action differ on the question of the class of actions that fall within one's repertoire of primitive or basic actions, but plausible candidates include decisions and simple bodily movements.

Davidson's assumption that the agency theory maintains that there is an irreducible causal relation between the agent and his (free) *action*. For from this perspective, what is most intimately my activity is the causal *initiation* of my behavior, the causal production of determinate (immediately executive) intentions or volitions. Thus, Bishop writes that on the agency theory.

[T]he action *is* the existent relation, and may not be collapsed into one of its terms. The object of the agent-causal relation, then, is not the action itself but certain events or sequences of events which, in virtue of their standing in this relation, count as *intrinsic* to the agent's intentional action.[14]

In the case of an observable bodily movement such as waving my hand, my action consists of the causal relation I bear to the coming-to-be of the state of determinate intention to wave my hand, plus the sequence of events that flow from that decision.[15] How shall we think of the primitive mental action at the core of this larger action? Does it simply consist, as Bishop suggests, of an existent (agent-causal) relation alone? I think that this suggestion is ill conceived, for the reason that the *production* of the internal event is not to be identified with the instantiated relation alone, somehow isolable from its relata, but rather it is the complex event or state of affairs, *S's production of e*.

Now this, of course, is somewhat at odds with the conventional analysis of actions as consisting of the events or sequences of events *produced by* an appropriate causal factor. There is good reason to think the conventional analysis is mistaken, however. Consider first the orthodox account of the production of action, viz., the causal theory. On this account, actions are causally produced (at least in part) by desires and beliefs. Such theorists generally claim that there is a sense in which an action may be thought of as produced by its agent on the causal theory—*I* am the source of my decision to wave my hand in virtue of the fact that my desire to raise my hand (together with certain beliefs) is causally efficacious in bringing that decision about. Thinking of the matter in this way, the event that is my decision, then, is (at least partially) constitutive of an action of mine not solely in virtue of

---

[14] "Agent-causation," *Mind*, 92 (1983), p. 71.

[15] It would be a mistake, I think, to characterize a decision of the action-triggering type as simply the *occurrence* of an event that is, as I've been putting it, the coming-to-be of a state of intention to Φ. While this construal is natural, of course, on causal theories of action, the agency theory conceives of the activity of decision formation as centrally involving the agent causation of such an event. Consequently, the formation of decision is most properly defined as a complex state of affairs consisting of the agent's bearing a causal relation to a causally simple mental event (which, I have suggested, we may take to be the coming-to-be of a state of intention to Φ). Some agency theorists have spoken of "causing one's own decision"; I suggest that they are best interpreted as expressing the above idea in shorthand. In what follows, I will make use of this convenience also from time to time, and the reader should interpret such statements in the preceding manner.

its intrinsic features, but also in virtue of the fact that it is causally related to me in a certain way. But this is problematic. Is not the production of internal mental events and/or bodily movements an essential part of my activity? If so, then we cannot avoid the conclusion that my primitive action (on the causal account) is to be identified with *DB's causing e*, where 'DB' is the causally efficacious desire-belief complex.[16]

It will be objected by many that it is simply a mistake to think of the relevant beliefs and desires as components of the action. But whatever unnaturalness this claim appears to possess is to be attributed to the failure of the causal theory to reflect the commonsense view of the etiology of ordinary behavior. If we *are* inclined to adopt this picture of the springs of action, then since I am active only in virtue of the productivity of properties that constitute my mental state, my being in that state is inseparable from my core activity—that of producing, e.g., a bodily movement.

I will hazard the suggestion that the fact that most action theorists do not individuate actions in this way is in part a result (in some cases indirect) of the influence of Hume's views on causation. Hume and his followers conceive a sequence of events over time as composed of discrete and essentially unconnected elements, "time slices." We may, as a wholly contingent matter of fact, discern various patterns of regularity in the sequences we observe over time, but there are no existent causal relations in nature between events. But if we repudiate this reductionist picture of causality, and allow that causes truly *produce* their effects, then, as I've just argued, the causal theorist ought to allow that actions are partly constituted by the causal relations that (he maintains) exist between an agent's reasons and resulting behavior.

To return, though, to the task of responding to the dilemma that Davidson attempts to construct, we thus begin by noting that on the agency theory, rather than there being a causal relation between agent and action, the relational complex *constitutes* the action. Suppose, however, that Davidson were to reformulate his dilemma in terms of the relation between the agent and the event constituents of a primitive (or core) action.[17] The first horn of the dilemma (which assumes that the agent's causing some event is distinct from his action) will then clearly be idle. But what of the second horn? If we say that the agent's causal activity is identical to his action, is it true, as Davidson asserts, that the concept of cause plays no role in what we assert?

---

[16] Fred Dretske has argued for just this claim in *Explaining Behavior* (Cambridge, Mass.: MIT Press, 1988), ch. 2.

[17] Bishop, "Agent-causation," pp. 72–73, suggests this reformulation of Davidson's argument. However, I have differed with Bishop's interpretation of Davidson's remarks in posing the second horn of the dilemma, and consequently my response to it takes on a different form from his.

That nothing is explained, since we are not connecting the event-constituents of the action to a law?

As far as I can see, Davidson offers absolutely no reason to think we should say this. And, prima facie, such an assertion does seem at least partly explanatory: for if one points to that which causally produced an event, how could one have nonetheless failed to so much as contribute to an explanation of its occurrence? To he sure, such an explanation is far from *complete*. We have yet to indicate, for example, with what reasons the agent acted as he did. And we have said nothing in specific terms of the sort of nature possessed by the agent, in virtue of which he was capable of bringing about such effects. But one has surely been given *something* by way of explanation. It seems that Davidson's understanding of the matter here has been clouded by the deleterious effects of Hume, to the effect that explanation of events can only come about through subsumption under a law. But this dogma is essentially tied to the Humean framework, and I take it that there are good reasons for rejecting this.[18] We may safely conclude, therefore, that Davidson's supposed dilemma poses no serious threat to the agency theory.

Another well-known attack on the coherence of the agency theory is made by C. D. Broad.[19] Broad writes:

I see no *prima facie* objection to there being events that are not completely determined. But, in so far as an event *is* determined, an essential factor in its total cause must be other *events*. How can an event possibly be determined to happen at a certain date if its total cause contained no factor to which the notion of date has any application? And how can the notion of date have any application to anything that is not an event? (p. 215)

It is far from clear to me just what the difficulty is that Broad takes himself to be pointing out here. It is true that persisting objects such as human agents are not, in the ordinary sense, 'datable' entities, although we may specify the temporal interval through which they exist. But we may, of course, quite unproblematically speak of certain facts being true of an agent at one time that do not hold of him at another. And such is the claim of the

---

[18] Most fundamentally, I fail to see how merely indicating that an event falls under a pattern of regularity—no matter how "lawlike" the formal characteristics of that pattern may be—is, in and of itself, explanatory. It is only by indicating something concerning the causal mechanism(s) at work (as a broadly realist position understands this notion) that genuine explanation can be accomplished. Most Humeans, of course, do not see the matter this way.

[19] "Determinism, Indeterminism, and Libertarianism," in *Ethics and the History of Philosophy* (London: RKP, 1952). Broad's argument has been endorsed by Ginet (*On Action* [Cambridge: Cambridge University Press, 1990], pp. 13–14), although Prof. Ginet has told me in conversation that he no longer feels certain that the apparent difficulty Broad raises is decisive. And a similar (though, to my mind, less clear) sort of objection to Reid's agency theory is raised by Baruch Brody in his introduction to a 1969 edition of Reid's *Essays on the Active Powers* (Cambridge, Mass.: MIT Press).

agency theorist. Consider, for example, my deliberation a while ago concerning whether to continue working on this paper for another hour or to stop and do something else. After a brief moment of consideration, I formed the intention (at time t, say) to continue working. According to the agency theory, we may suppose that at t I possessed the power to choose to continue working or to choose to stop, where this is understood as the capacity to cause either of these mental occurrences. And, in fact, that capacity was exercised at t in a particular way (in choosing to continue working), allowing us to say truthfully that Tim at time t causally determined his own choice to continue working. But we needn't, in order to make sense of this, analyze it as the claim (of dubious intelligibility) that a 'datable entity', Tim-at-t, was the occurrent cause of the decision to continue working.

But, you might say, given the fact that your producing your decision occurs at a specific time (and how could it be otherwise?), doesn't it seem appropriate to identify the particular *mental state* you were in at that time as what was ultimately responsible for that decision (though perhaps in a causally indeterministic fashion, if you like)? What is it about the nature of the causal process as you envision it that prevents us from properly saying this?

My answer is that the alternative wrongly implies that it is whatever is *distinctive* about the state that the agent was in at the time of his action— distinguishing it from his state just prior to that moment, say—that triggers the action. But while there are various *necessary* conditions on an agent's producing a decision to X, these conditions may obtain over a protracted period of time, and so cannot be thought to be themselves causally efficacious (with respect to the decision).

Perhaps underlying Broad's remarks, though, is the thought (made explicit in Ginet, *On Action*) that the proposition that I caused the decision at t cannot explain why I decided *when* I did, nor can it explain *why* I decided as I did. Now this is certainly true, and, we may add, it is further true that analogous questions are answered when we give an event-causal explanation of an event (setting aside complications raised by indeterministic event-causal processes). For causal properties are (ordinarily) such as to immediately give rise to their characteristic effects in the right circumstances, and the effects to which they give rise are *characteristic*, i.e., it is impossible (either physically or metaphysically) that any *other* effect should come about in just those circumstances.

But, as I have been at pains to emphasize, agent-causes operate in a different fashion, and corresponding to this is a difference in the way they are involved in the *explanation* of the effects they produce.[20] An agent-cause

---

[20] As I noted above in responding to Davidson.

does not produce a certain effect by virtue of its very nature, as does an event-cause, but does so at will in the light of considerations accessible to the agent at that time. And so a full explanation of why an agent-caused event occurred will include, among other things, an account of the reasons upon which the agent acted. (The nature of such reasons-explanations, and their degree of explanatory power vis-à-vis fully event-causal explanations, will be considered in the following two sections.)

Yet another instance of an objection that attempts to insist that the agency theory meet standard requirements within an event-causal paradigm, which, upon reflection, are seen to be simply inappropriate in the context of agent-causality, is noted by the agency theorist Chisholm:

> Our account presupposes that there are certain events which men, or agents, cause to happen. Suppose, then, that on a certain occasion a man does cause a certain event e to happen. What, now, of that event—the event which is his thus causing e to happen? We have assumed that there is no sufficient condition for his causing e to happen. Shall we say it was not caused by anything? If we say this, then we cannot hold *him* responsible for his causing e to happen.[21]

I believe that the proper line of response here begins with the observation that the very idea of there being sufficient causal conditions for an agent-causal event is unintelligible. One agency theorist who has endorsed the opposing view is Richard Taylor:

> [T]here is nothing in the concept of agency [where this involves an irreducible causal relation between agent and act], as such, to entail that any events must be causally undetermined, and in that sense "free," in order for some of them to be the acts of agents. Indeed, it might well be that everything that ever happens, happens under conditions which are such that nothing else could happen, and hence that in the case of every act that any agent ever performs there are conditions that are causally sufficient for his doing just what he does. This is the claim of determinism, but it does not by itself require us to deny that there are agents who sometimes initiate their own acts. What is entailed by this concept of agency, according to which men are the initiators of their own acts, is that for anything to count as an act there must be an essential reference to an agent as the cause of that act, whether he is, in the usual sense, caused to perform it or not.[22]

We may say that I am free and responsible for some behavior of mine, then, just in case I originate or cause it and am not determined to do so. This would be allowed by Reid and other agency theorists who followed him. Taylor departs from the standard view of agency theorists only in suggesting that the first of these conditions may obtain in the absence of the second. He suggests as a simple, likely case of this sort my grasping my seat tightly while on a ski lift (where my timidity and fright are causally sufficient in the

---

[21] "Reflections on Human Agency," *Idealistic Studies*, 1 (1971), p. 40.
[22] *Action and Purpose* (Englewood Cliffs, NJ: Prentice-Hall, 1966), pp. 114–15.

circumstances for my doing so). He notes that it would be odd to say that this is not something I *did* (compare my concurrent perspiration), and concludes from such examples that it is perfectly intelligible that I should be determined to (agent) cause my own actions. (In Reid's terminology, one may be unfree in the exercise of one's active power.)

Now it is one thing to argue in this way: it is perfectly intelligible that one should be determined on occasion to act as one does; on this theory, one is always the agent cause of one's acts; hence, this theory is constrained to allow for the possibility that an agent is determined to cause his own action. But it is quite another directly to defend the idea of causally determined agent causation against the charge of incoherence. Just how are we to understand the notion of there being a sufficient causal condition for an exercise of active power?

Unfortunately, Taylor himself never tries to spell this out, and he is apparently unaware of the difficulty one faces in trying to do so coherently. Note that what we are to envisage is not that there are sufficient causal conditions for event e independently of my causing it, but rather conditions sufficient precisely for the event that is *my causing e* (and only *thereby* for *e*). (This event is constituted by the holding of a causal relation between myself and the subevent *e*). It is *this* sort of event for which, Taylor claims, there may be sufficient causal conditions.

For the purpose of evaluating this claim, it will be useful to consider first the case of event causation. The cause of *A's causation of B* is none other than the cause of A itself.[23] What, then, of *S's causation of e*? There appears to be no way of getting a grip on the notion of an event of *this* sort's having a sufficient, efficient cause. Because of its peculiar causal structure, there is no event at its front end, so to speak, but only an enduring agent. And there cannot be an immediate, efficient cause of a causal relation (i.e., independently of the causation of its front end relatum). In general, that which is causally produced in the first instance is always an event or state having a causally *simple* structure: an object O's exemplifying *intrinsic* properties p_1, p_2, ... at time t_0. Causally complex events can also be caused, of course, but only in a derivative way: where they have the form *event X's causing event Y*, whatever causes event X is a cause *thereby* of *X's causing Y*. In the special case of an *agent's* causing an event internal to his action, however, there is no causally simple component event forming its initial segment, such that one might cause the complex event (*S's causing e*) in virtue of causing *it*.

---

[23] Assuming, that is, that what we are after is the "triggering" cause of the event, rather than what Fred Dretske calls a "structuring" cause—roughly, that which establishes a causal pathway between two objects or systems so that when the first is operated upon (by the triggering cause) in the right manner, it brings about a result in the latter.

Therefore, it is problematic to suppose that there could *be* sufficient causal conditions for an agent-causal event.

If I am right in claiming that it is strictly impossible for there to be sufficient causal conditions for an agent-causal event, we may readily dispose of the objection introduced by Chisholm that if *my causing e* itself has no cause, then I cannot be responsible for it. For it would appear from the above that no answer *could* be given to the question of what was the cause of a given agent-causal event, and hence that the question is ill framed, resulting from a failure to understand the peculiar nature of such an event. In this type of complex event, there is no first subevent bearing a causal relation to a second. So it seems that the libertarian may acknowledge without embarrassment that events of *this* type are uncaused.[24]

To support the point I am trying to make here, I want to emphasize the contrast between the scenarios envisaged by the agency theorist and those envisaged by the simple indeterminist. The simple indeterminist claims that a (causally) simple mental event of the proper sort (e.g., a volition), if causally undetermined, is intrinsically such as to be under the control of the agent who is its subject.[25] I have tried elsewhere to give reasons for supposing that the claim is in fact false.[26] Agent-control—the type of immediate control we take ourselves to have over our own actions—is clearly causal in nature.

But now consider an instance of *S's causing e*. This event is intrinsically a doing, owing to its internal causal structure (i.e., an agent's bearing a direct causal relation to another event). Its very nature precludes the possibility of there being a sufficient causal condition for it (as I argued earlier), being an event that is the agent's causing the event internal to it (*e*). Now the event *e* is itself clearly under the control of the agent, since *he* caused it (directly). But would it not, then, be perfectly absurd to raise a doubt concerning whether the agent controlled *his causing e?* Indeed, it seems to me that the question of

---

[24] Of course, there will be a large number of *necessary* causal conditions for the occurrence of any instance of an agent's directly causing some internal mental event at a particular time *t*. (And, hence, where any of these are absent, a sufficient condition for the *non*occurrence of such events.) Many of these will have to do with the internal state of the agent prior to *t*. To note only the most obvious such conditions, for an agent to cause, say, his decision to immediately engage in Φ-ing, the option must be one that is accessible to his conscious awareness, he must believe it to be within his power, and, it would seem, he must have some positive inclination to Φ. There will of course also be numerous conditions in terms of the structural constitution of the agent's neurophysiological system. It is evident from our acquaintance with pathological cases that very subtle forms of malfunctioning can vitiate or even negate altogether the agent's capacity to act with a normal degree of autonomy.

[25] See, e.g., Carl Ginet, "Reasons Explanation of Action: An Incompatibilist Account," *Philosophical Perspectives*, 3 (1989), pp. 17–46.

[26] "Indeterminism and Free Agency: Three Recent Views," *Philosophy and Phenomenological Research*, 53 (no. 3, 1993), pp. 499–526.

whether the agent has control over this event is ill framed—*it* is simply an instance of an agent's *exercising* direct control over another event.

Chisholm, by contrast, would have the agency theorist maintain that the agent himself causes his agent-causing. It seems that the following line of thought underlies Chisholm's commitment to this perplexing suggestion:

(1) An agent S bears responsibility for an event x only if S has causally contributed to the occurrence of x.

(2) Any instance of an agent's causing an event is itself an event.

(3) Agents are responsible for their agent-causings.

∴ (4) Agents cause the events which are their agent-causings.

And, of course, if the agent is responsible for an instance of agent-causing by causing *it*, then we must say that he is responsible for this further event of his causing his agent-causing. And thus in this way we are led (with Chisholm) to fabricate an infinity of simultaneous events. But while statement (1) seems quite evident when we focus on events that either lack internal causal structure or are constituted by two or more such simple events causally connected to one another, if one allows for the possibility of events that simply are the direct causal activity of agents, then one ought not to suppose that (1) holds with unrestricted generality.

IV. TWO OBJECTIONS TO INDETERMINISTIC REASONS EXPLANATION

I have yet to address an issue that critically bears on the viability of the agency theorist's general project of providing an adequate theoretical framework for understanding how free agency operates. We explain the actions of ourselves and others around us by citing or ascribing reasons for which the action was performed. How do reasons figure into the performance of actions as the agency theorist conceives them? It is astonishing to me to see how often critics of the agency theory make the mistaken assumption that the agency theory is either incompatible with reasons-based accounts of action or is advanced as an independent alternative to such accounts. This leads naturally enough to the conclusion that it is simply confused[27] or explanatorily superfluous.[28] In this section and in the one that follows, I try to show how agent causality plays a necessary role in reasons explanations,

---

[27] See Honderich, *Determinism*, pp. 196–97.
[28] See Stewart Goetz, "A Noncausal Theory of Agency," *Philosophy and Phenomenological Research*, 49 (1988), pp. 303–16.

once we abandon the causal theory's model of reasons as influencing actions by causally producing them.

I begin by considering two recent objections of a highly general character against the possibility of a satisfactory account of noncausal reasons explanations. The first of these is Galen Strawson's claim that the indeterminist's conception of of an agent as acting in view of prior motives while not being determined by them ineluctably leads to a vicious regress. For, he claims, we can conceive of an agent sitting in detached judgment on the matter of whether to act in accordance with motive X or motive Y only if he has some *further* desires or principles of choice that decisively inclines him in one of these directions. But if this is the case, then the agent is self-determining in making his choice only if he is somehow responsible for the presence of those further factors, which requires his having chosen to be that way. . . . [29]

Strawson is not alone in holding that the libertarian is unwittingly committed to this (problematic) picture. The same suggestion was colorfully made by Leibniz:

One will have it that the will alone is active and supreme, and one is wont to imagine it to be like a queen seated on her throne, whose minister of state is the understanding, while the passions are her courtiers or favourite ladies, who by their influence often prevail over the counsel of her ministers. One will have it that the understanding speaks only at this queen's order; that she can vacillate between the arguments of the ministers and the suggestions of the favourites, even rejecting both, making them keep silence or speak, and giving them audience as it seems good to her. But it is a personification or mythology somewhat ill-conceived. [30]

But while we may wholeheartedly agree with Leibniz's assessment of this conception as "somewhat ill-conceived," we should also reject the suggestion that the libertarian *must* be assuming (if the account is to avoid positing fortuitous, irrational choices) that the agent has further, second-order reasons that explain why he chose to act in accordance with one set of motives rather than another. Consider a scenario in which an agent is deliberating between two courses of action X and Y, each of which has considerations in its favor. (I will refer to these sets of considerations as {X} and {Y}, respectively.) Suppose further that the agency theory is correct and the agent herself brings about the decision to take option X. The question, "Why did the agent perform that action?", is meaningfully answered by citing {X}, even though these reasons did not produce the agent's decision, and she could have chosen differently in those very same circumstances. In citing {X}, we are explaining the motivating factors that were in view when the

[29] *Freedom and Belief* (Oxford: Oxford University Press, 1986), pp. 53–54.
[30] *Theodicy* (LaSalle, Ill.: Open Court, 1985), p. 421.

agent made a self-determining choice. It is not necessary to try to ascend to a level of second-order reasons (for acting on first-order reasons) in a desperate bid to render this conception of action intelligible.

Perhaps underlying Strawson's charge is the belief that an action would be irrational or at least arbitrary (in a pejorative sense of that term) if, at the time of acting, the agent did not believe that her reasons decisively favored the course of action chosen, that she had reasons for performing X *rather than* Y. The first thing to notice here is that even if we were to accept this, it does not clearly imply that the agent-causationist model must be mistaken. For we should then say, in any given case, that while the agent has it in her power to choose any of a range of alternatives, only one choice would be rational from the standpoint of her own reasons. Why would it still be "rationally-speaking random," as Strawson puts it (in a portion of the text not quoted here), if the agent makes the *preferable* choice? And, further-more, don't we sometimes make irrational decisions? It is open to Strawson to accept my claim that choices of the most preferable option would be rational, but then suggest that the power the agency theory confers on free agents is worthless. For it is nothing but the power to make irrational decisions, and who wants *that?* I do not accept the suggestion that there is no value in an agent's *freely* choosing to be (for the most part) rational. But we can say something further. And that is that many situations of choice simply do not point to one course of action as "the thing to do" in the circum-stances, as being preferable to all the rest.[31] Moral choices are commonly of this sort, but it is not limited to these. And if this claim is right, then there will be situations in which the agency theory confers a power on agents beyond that of determining whether they shall act rationally or irrationally.

In responding to Strawson's contention that the indeterministic aspect of the agency theory leads to a regress of reasons, I have begun to stray into the territory of the second, related objection to indeterministic reasons explanation that I want to consider, and so it is appropriate now to make this objection explicit. Suggested by various remarks in Kane,[32] the objection I have in mind may be put thus: Any genuinely explanatory response to the question, "Why did S do X?", will ipso facto be an answer to the question, "Why did S do X rather than any of the available alternatives?", and a proper answer to the latter of these must incorporate *all* the relevant psycho-logical features of the agent at the moment of choice. This requires some

---

[31] Helpful discussions of such choice scenarios are found in Robert Kane's *Free Will and Values* (Buffalo: SUNY Press, 1985) and Peter van Inwagen's "When Is the Will Free?".

[32] "Two Kinds of Incompatibilism," *Philosophy and Phenomenological Research*, 50 (1989), pp. 219–54 (see, e.g., pp. 227–28). Kane's remarks in this connection are endorsed by Richard Double in *The Non-Reality of Free Will* (New York: Oxford University Press, 1991).

elaboration. The question, "Why did S do X rather than, say, Y or Z?", might be interpreted as simply a request for the reason that motivated S's making the choice S made (as opposed to reasons there may have been for any of the alternatives to X). When the question is construed in this way, however, we needn't cite all the considerations before S's mind at the time of the decision, but only those that provided a motive for doing X. But the sort of reading of this question that Kane has in mind is a much stronger one, which requests an account of why it was *necessary* that S do X in those circumstances rather than any of the alternatives. And citing whatever motive(s) there were for doing X at that time is clearly insufficient for this purpose. Rather, we need an account that implies that those motives were enough to tip the balance in favor of the actual outcome, as against its competitors.

Consider the following remarks in Kane ("Two Kinds of Incompatibilism"):

> How can we explain either outcome, should it occur, *in terms of exactly the same past?* If we say, for example, that the agent did [X] rather than [Y] here and now because the agent had such and such reasons or motives and engaged in such and such a deliberation before choosing to act, how would we have explained the doing of [Y] rather than [X] *given exactly the same reasons or motives and the same prior deliberation?* (p. 228, emphasis added)

In simply assuming that an explanation of the action will cite *all* the salient psychological features of the agent at the time of his decision, Kane is clearly presuming that there is only one type of adequate explanation of a choice, the type that explains why only that choice *could* have been made at that point in the agent's psychological history. But this is unsupported. The agency theorist may cheerfully concede that explanations of *that* sort are precluded by actions that are described by his theory—i.e., explanations that cite factors that could put an observer in a position to predict outcomes with certainty. And though we may grant that explanations of that sort are highly desirable for scientific purposes (among others), no reason has been given why we cannot allow explanations that account for an occurrence by characterizing it as the freely initiated behavior of an agent motivated by such and such a reason.[33]

The element of causal initiation is critical, I think, to the viability of this alternative explanatory framework. Some philosophers have failed to see

---

[33] In a recent discussion, Randolph Clarke helpfully calls attention to the fact that a strong case has been made (quite apart from the special case of reasons explanation) by contemporary philosophers of science that explanation of an event needn't involve showing why it rather than *any* other possible outcome obtained. See his "A Principle of Rational Explanation?" *Southern Journal of Philosophy*, 30 (no. 3, 1992), pp. 1–12, and the articles he cites there.

that the prior presence of consciously considered reasons and agent-causal initiation are each necessary components in the agency theorist's explanatory scheme, and so have drawn the conclusion that the role of reasons in explaining actions obviates appeal to agent causation. Thus, Goetz, for example,[34] writes:

[I]f the reasons for which an agent acts help explain her freedom and responsibility with respect to that action, and her causing of her action can only be explained by appeal to the reason for which she acts, it is clear that the agent's causing of her action cannot help explain how it is that the agent is free and responsible with respect to her action. *Any explanatory power which the causation by the agent of her action might have would have to be derived from or parasitic upon the explanatory power of the reason she has for performing that action.* Thus, not only is it the case that agent-causation cannot help explain an agent's performance of a free action, but also it is not needed for this explanatory role, once the agent's reason for performing that action has been invoked to explain it. (p. 310, emphasis added)

The sentence I have highlighted in the preceding passage involves a mistaken claim. It is doubtful that we can form a conception of an agent's causing an event internal to his action without his having any sort of pro-attitude toward that action, and so to that extent the agent's causing the component event is dependent on the reason he has (or, his having *a* reason) for acting in that way. Nonetheless, the relative dependency of reasons and agent-causal initiation with respect to explanatory power is precisely the reverse of what Goetz suggests. For the agent's free exercise of his causal capacity provides a necessary link between reason and action, without which the reason could not in any significant way explain the action. It allows us to claim that the reason had an influence on the *production* of the decision, while not causing it. Were we to remove the element of causal production of decision altogether, and simply claim that the decision was uncaused, then noting the fact that the agent had a reason that motivated acting in that way would not suffice to explain it (as Davidson has famously argued). For in that case, any number of actions may have been equally likely to occur, *and* the agent would not have exercised any sort of *control* over which of these was actually performed (either via the efficacy of his reasons or in the direct fashion suggested by the agency theory). And it seems sufficiently obvious that where there are no controlling agents or factors of even a relatively weak, indeterministic sort, there can be no explanation of the occurrence.

It will be observed that the crucial claim I am making here is that any genuine explanation of an occurrence must involve an account of how that occurrence was *produced*. It has often been thought that, given this

[34] A similar claim is made by Irving Thalberg in "How Does Agent Causation Work?" in M. Brand and D. Walton, eds., *Action Theory* (Dordrecht: D. Reidel, 1976), pp. 213–38, esp. p. 234 f.

requirement, the only way in which reasons can play a role in the explanation of an action is by functioning as the central features of a set of conditions that determine the action. One alternative to this is to suppose that reasons cause actions without determining them. I do not deny that this is a viable indeterministic account of reasons explanation rival to the one I am offering here. But while it provides for the possibility of reasons explanation, I think it must be rejected ultimately on the grounds that it fails to show how it can be up to an agent to determine which among a range of possible courses of action he will actually undertake.[35] If I am right in supposing this, then the only account of reasons explanation that is consonant, in the final analysis, with a picture of free and responsible agency is the one suggested by the agency theory.

V. AN ACCOUNT OF REASONS EXPLANATION

So far, however, I have only spoken impressionistically of the sort of reasons explanation appropriate to the agency theory. I now attempt to give a more careful account by laying out conditions sufficient for the truth of each of two general sorts of ordinary reasons explanation. (What I say about these cases is readily adaptable to other sorts, such as explanation by a prior intention.)

The first sort that I want to consider involves explaining action by reference to a prior desire that Φ, where this is construed broadly (and beyond everyday usage) as including any kind of "pro-attitude" or positive inclination towards the state of affairs Φ. The following general conditions seem to me to suffice for the truth of an explanation of an action in terms of an antecedent desire:

S V-ed, then, in order to satisfy her antecedent desire that Φ if:
   (i)   prior to this V-ing, S had a desire that Φ, and believed that by V-ing, she would satisfy (or contribute to satisfying) that desire, and
   (ii) S's V-ing was initiated (in part) by her own self-determining causal activity,[36] and
   (iii) concurrent with this V-ing, S continued to desire that Φ and intended of this V-ing that it satisfy (or contribute to satisfying) that desire.

---

[35] I argue this claim at length in O'Connor, "Three Recent Views." See also ch. 4 of P. van Inwagen's *An Essay on Free Will* (New York: Oxford University Press, 1983).

[36] As I suggested above, I am inclined to term the agent-causal event (*S's causation of e*) a "decision," the event component of which is the-coming-to-be-of-an-action-triggering-intention-to-V-here-and-now. It is plausible to take it that the intention one has concurrent with the full performance of the action (required in condition (iii) in the text) is a direct causal consequence of the action-triggering-intention that is directly brought about by the agent.

Condition (iii) is necessary[37] because were I to cease to have the original desire and act for a completely different reason, it clearly would not have a genuinely explanatory role to play. It also handles cases in which I continue to have the desire but it is not the reason for which I act (and hence I don't intend of my action that it satisfy that desire).

This third condition is an adaptation of the central component of Ginet's account[38] of reasons explanation, although there is an important difference in how it functions in our overall accounts. I am in agreement with Ginet that the part of the explanation that involves a connection between the prior desire and the present intention need not be causal in nature (apart from the causal connections involved in continuing to have the desire), but may, rather, be wholly *internal* (similarity of content) and *referential*. If it is my purpose or intention in V-ing that I carry out a prior desire that Φ, then the prior desire may figure in the explanation of this action even if it does not constitute part of a set of conditions that causally produce the action. *Contra* Ginet, however, this will be the case only if the noncausal connection between desire and intention is coupled with some other, appropriate sort of factor that produces or initiates the action, viz., the agent herself (hence, the necessity of condition (ii)).

In discussing Ginet's simple indeterminist, noncausal account of reasons explanations (which lacks anything analogous to my condition (ii)), Lawrence Davis writes:

> "[S]he opened the window in order to let in fresh air" only if she opened the window *because she believed* she would or might let in fresh air thereby. And this "because" must be causal—else I do not see a plausible distinction between [this sentence] and (1′) She opened the window knowing she would let fresh air in thereby. . . . If I am right that something causal is needed, . . . [then] Ginet has not shown that undetermined acts can be explained in terms of their antecedents.[39]

I think that Davis is right in supposing that "something causal is needed" to make possible an explanatory link between antecedent reason and action, but that causal element needn't be a *nomic* connection between reason and action. The agency theory provides a coherent framework in which reasons can influence the production of an action without themselves forming part of a causally sufficient condition for the action.

I might note that there may be further factors that enter into the explanation of my V-ing. Suppose my prior desire was relatively indeterminate with respect to *when* it should be realized. There will often be certain

---

[37] More precisely, *some* condition or other that is more or less like condition (iii) is needed to give a *sufficient* condition for acting in order to satisfy a prior desire.

[38] Ginet, "Reasons Explanation."

[39] Review of Ginet's *On Action* in *Mind*, 100 (no. 3, 1991), p. 393.

considerations or other factors at the time of acting that elicited my action (by suggesting that this was a particularly opportune time to satisfy the desire), and these will certainly figure in a full explanation of my action. But, by the same token, it's not obvious that there *needs* to be such environmental stimuli. Perhaps I am only concerned that I act within a certain time frame, and any particular moment is as good as any other. In such a case, there may not be an explanation of why I acted just *then* (rather than at some other time).

The set of sufficient conditions for an explanation of action by prior reasons just given are consistent with the agent not having a clear preference for the action performed over any available alternative. However, we often do act on such preferences; in such cases, we can explain (in terms of antecedent reasons) not only why the agent V-ed, but also why she V-ed *rather* than doing something else instead. Can we give nondeterministic sufficient conditions for the truth of such explanations, similar to those sketched above? I think that we clearly can. Consider the following:

S V-ed then rather than doing something else because she preferred V-ing to any alternative if:

(i)   prior to this V-ing, S had a desire that Φ, and believed that by V-ing, she would satisfy (or contribute to satisfying) that desire, and

(ii) S preferred V-ing as a means to satisfying the desire that Φ, and also preferred satisfying Φ over the satisfaction of any other desire, and

(iii) S's V-ing was initiated (in part) by her own self-determining causal activity, and

(iv) concurrent with this V-ing, (a) S continued to desire that Φ and intended of this V-ing that it satisfy (or contribute to satisfying) that desire, and (b) S continued to prefer V-ing to any alternative action she believed to be open to her.

It is quite consistent with the *antecedent* circumstances expressed in these conditions that S have *failed* to V at that time. She might, for example, have come to prefer on reflection some alternative (or have ceased to desire that Φ altogether), or she might have decided to continue seeking out further relevant considerations, or, finally, she might have simply succumbed to some temptations despite her continuing to believe that V-ing represented the best course of action open to her (thereby exhibiting the phenomenon of "weakness of will").[40]

It might be claimed, however, that the fact that our set of conditions does not rule out these possibilities goes to show that they are not truly *sufficient* for the truth of explanations of why an agent performed a particular action rather than any alternatives she had considered. Statements (i)–(iv) must be

---

[40] Compare Ginet, *On Action*, p. 149.

supplemented with conditions that rule out the possibility of these alternative scenarios. Only then, it will be claimed, will we have adequately explained why S performed the action she did, rather than some other action.

But while similar charges have often been made by critics of libertarianism, as best I can see, there are no good reasons to accept them. We may suppose that it is a wholly contingent matter of fact that none of the alternative scenarios I envisaged occurred, that the prior circumstances did not necessitate their nonoccurrence. How does this show our set of conditions to be inadequate? If what we are seeking to explain is why a particular action was *in fact* undertaken rather than some other, as opposed to why the action *had* to occur, why is it not enough that we refer to those antecedent reasons the agent had for preferring the chosen action over the alternatives, reasons the agent continued to have at the time of the action and that she intended to satisfy in performing it? Providing such an explanation clearly makes it teleologically intelligible that the agent chose to perform that action rather than any of the others, though it does not imply that no other action could have occurred in just those circumstances. Therefore, I cannot see why one should think that it fails genuinely to explain the action in any meaningful sense—unless, again, the critic is failing to note the difference between agent-causal and entirely noncausal reasons explanations, a difference that is embodied in my third condition above.

VI. IS AGENT CAUSATION DISTINGUISHABLE FROM MERE RANDOMNESS?

The final objection to the agency theory that I consider here is epistemological in nature: it seems that it is impossible, in principle, for us ever to know whether any events *are* produced in the manner that the agency theory postulates, because such an event would be indistinguishable from one which was essentially random, not connected by even probabilistic laws to events preceding it.[41] (Alternatively put, the objection claims that we could never know whether the unique sort of property or properties that give rise to active power is instantiated.)

However, if my earlier contention that simple indeterminism is incompatible with genuine reasons explanations of action is correct, then I believe that the present objection must be judged mistaken. The simple indeterminist supposes that (in many cases) an agent's decision is not the outcome of any determinative causal influence—neither the agent's prior reasons, as on

---

[41] An objection along these lines is presented by Alvin Goldman in *A Theory of Human Action* (Englewood Cliffs, NJ: Prentice Hall, 1970).

the causal theory, nor simply the agent qua agent (as on the agency theory). I claimed, though, that reasons explanations require a mechanism of control that 'hooks up', so to speak, the agent's reasons and consequent decision (and action). On the causal theory, this is supplied by an event-causal relation between the decision and matching reason(s). On the agency theory, an agent's capacity directly to produce a decision in the light of consciously held reasons fills the bill. We cannot *simply* appeal, as, for example, Ginet ("Reasons Explanation of Action") does, to *internal* (and referential) relations between concurrent intention and prior motives, on the one hand, and that same concurrent intention and the decision (or action), on the other. Without the mediation of a (necessarily causal) 'mechanism of control', prior motives cannot *explain* a decision, even though (as it happens) they may *coincide* with it.

Returning now to the objection under consideration, let us suppose that our knowledge of natural processes were to progress to such a point as to provide unmistakable evidence of significant indeterminism in the nature of ordinary human action. Would we have no reason, in such an eventuality, to prefer the agent-causal hypothesis to that of simple indeterminism? Surely not. Surely it would be preferable to adopt a theory of action in virtue of which our reasons-based explanations could remain largely intact. And it seems that, in such a scenario, only the agency theory would allow this. Furthermore, given a detailed knowledge of neurophysiological processes, we could go beyond the bare postulation of the appropriate property (i.e., one on which the power to cause directly any of a certain range of alternative events supervenes). We could explain in some detail, for instance, the systemic conditions under which such a property is instantiated, as well as the subtleties of its interplay with other causal processes involved in the production of behavior.

Thus, the employment of the concept of active power is not irremediably at odds with the attempt to give a scientific account of natural processes, including human behavior (as is sometimes alleged). The use of this concept in explaining human behavior is consonant with scientific methodology, broadly construed, and could in principle be mapped onto other explanatory theories concerning biological subsystems of the human organism. It does run counter to the general program of microreductive explanation, which has been highly successful in other contexts. But this, it surely must be recognized, is simply a research *strategy*. Given its explanatory potential, it obviously should be pushed as far as it can go in the understanding of human behavior. (And there is a further reason that agent-causal mechanisms should be appealed to in theoretical accounts only after the alternatives have been exhausted: we simply cannot know in advance the details of how event- and agent-causal processes interact, nor the precise sorts of circumstances in which agent-causal processes do not figure at all in the production of behavior.) But if limits of the right sort persist, I see no reason that explanatory theories invoking the concept of agent causality should not be adopted.[42] The alternative—to regard much of our behavior as without explanation (save for the fact that it falls within certain parameters)—is simply not credible.

This reply to the charge that we could never have reasons for preferring the agent-causal form of explanation to that of causal randomness may be bolstered by a simple appeal to how things seem to us when we act. It is not, after all, simply to provide a theoretical underpinning for our belief in moral responsibility that the agency theory is invoked. First and foremost (as I suggested at the outset), the agency theory is appealing because it captures the way we experience our own activity. It does not seem to me (at least ordinarily) that I am caused to act by the reasons which favor doing so; it seems to be the case, rather, that *I* produce my decision *in view of* those reasons, and could have, in an unconditional sense, decided differently. This depiction of the phenomenology of action finds endorsement not only, as might be expected, in agency theorists such as Reid, Campbell, and Taylor, but also in determinists such as Bradley,[43] Nagel,[44] and Searle,[45] and in Ginet's "actish phenomenal quality".[46] If these largely similar accounts of the experience of action are, as I believe, essentially on target, then it is natural for the agency theorist to maintain that they involve the *perception* of the agent-causal relation. Just as the non-Humean is apt to maintain that we not only perceive, e.g., the movement of the axe along with the separation of the wood, but the axe *splitting* the wood (Madden and Harré, *Causal Powers*, pp. 49–51), so I have the apparent perception of my actively and freely deciding to take Seneca Street to my destination and not Buffalo instead.[47] Such experiences could, of course, be wholly illusory, but do we not properly assume, in the absence of strong countervailing reasons, that

[42] For discussion of the possible use of the concept in the social sciences, see p. 84 of John Greenwood, "Agency, Causality, and Meaning," *Journal for the Theory of Social Behavior*, 18 (no. 1, 1988), pp. 95–115.

[43] "Free Will: Problem or Pseudo-Problem?" *Australasian Journal of Philosophy*, 36 (1958), pp. 33–45.

[44] *The View from Nowhere* (New York: Oxford University Press, 1986), ch. 7.

[45] See note 5.

[46] Ginet, *On Action*.

[47] Donagan, surprisingly, is an agency theorist who professes to find the notion of directly *perceiving* one's causal activity unintelligible (*Choice: The Essential Element in Human Action* [London: RKP, 1987], pp. 181–82). Judging by his remarks there, however, I suspect that he would reach a similar verdict with respect to the notion of perceiving certain instances of event-causal activity.

things are pretty much the way they appear to us? I will not delve into this further epistemological issue here, my concern being that of descriptive metaphysics, but I will note that skepticism about the veridicality of such experiences has numerous isomorphs that, if accepted, appear to lead to a greatly diminished assessment of our knowledge of the world, an assessment that most philosophers resist.

14

TOWARD A CREDIBLE AGENT-CAUSAL ACCOUNT OF FREE WILL

RANDOLPH CLARKE

Agent-causal accounts of free will, of the sort advanced in years past by Chisholm and Taylor,[1] are now widely regarded as discredited. Such accounts held that when an agent acts with free will, her action is not causally determined by any prior events. The agent herself was said to cause her action, and this causation by the agent was said not to consist in causation by an event or collection of events. An agent acting with this sort of freedom, it was claimed, acted with the ability to do otherwise. And what the agent did was not an accident or a matter of chance; the agent herself made it happen that she did what she did. She was an uncaused cause of her so acting.

Such accounts have been rejected chiefly for two reasons. First, they failed to provide an adequate account of the relations between an agent, her reasons for action, and her action, and hence they failed as accounts of rational free action.[2] Second, they did not provide an intelligible explication of what causation by an agent was supposed to be.[3]

From *Noûs*, 27 (1993), 191–203. Copyright © Blackwell Publishing. Reprinted by permission of the publisher.

I wish to thank audiences at Princeton University and North Carolina State University for comments on earlier versions of this paper. Many individuals provided helpful suggestions and criticisms; I am especially grateful to Gilbert Harman and David Lewis.

[1] Roderick M. Chisholm, "Freedom and Action," in Keith Lehrer, ed., *Freedom and Determinism* (New York: Random House, 1966); "The Agent as Cause," in Myles Brand and Douglas Walton, eds., *Action Theory* (Dordrecht: D. Reidel, 1976); and *Person and Object* (La Salle, Ill.: Open Court, 1976), pp. 53–88. Richard Taylor, *Action and Purpose* (Englewood Cliffs, NJ: Prentice-Hall, 1966), pp. 99–152; "Determinism and the Theory of Agency," in Sydney Hook, ed., *Determinism and Freedom in the Age of Modern Science* (New York: Collier Books, 1979); and *Metaphysics* (Englewood Cliffs, NJ: Prentice-Hall, 1983), pp. 33–50.

[2] The rationality objection is sometimes stated in terms of the intelligibility of the action or in terms of rational explicability. For versions of this objection, see C. D. Broad, *Ethics and the History of Philosophy* (London: Routledge & Kegan Paul, 1952), p. 215; Carl Ginet, *On Action* (Cambridge: Cambridge University Press, 1990), pp. 13–14; and Irving Thalberg, "Agent Causality and Reasons for Action," *Philosophia*, 7 (1978), pp. 555–66, esp. p. 564.

[3] For examples of the intelligibility objection, see R. Kane, *Free Will and Values* (Albany: State University of New York Press, 1985), p. 72; and Gary Watson, "Free Action and Free Will," *Mind*, 96 (1987), pp. 145–72, esp. p. 167.

It is, in my view, unfortunate that the notion of agent causation has been largely abandoned, and in this paper I hope to contribute to its rehabilitation. I will sketch an agent-causal account of free will that differs in important respects from those of Chisholm and Taylor; and I will argue that given this account, the first of the objections described above can be easily met, and that considerable progress can be made in meeting the second. If I am right, then the result is an important one for a viable agent-causal account would provide an attractive alternative to compatibilist accounts of free will.

I. RATIONAL FREE ACTION

On Chisholm's and Taylor's accounts, when an agent acts with free will, her action (or some event that is a part of her action) is not caused by any events.[4] Indeed, Chisholm seems to believe that *any* action must be caused by an agent and not by any event.[5] The rationality problem arises directly from these requirements, for if an agent's action is not caused by her having certain reasons for action, then it is unclear how she can be said to have acted on those reasons and how her action can be said to be rational (and rationally explicable).

There are, I believe, two errors in Chisholm's and Taylor's requirements regarding the causes of actions. First, agent causation should be seen as required for acting with free will, but not for acting. An agent-causal account of free will might then be made consistent with the familiar analyses of action. And second, an agent-causal account should not deny that free actions are caused by prior events. Both of these mistakes can be avoided without sacrificing what is of value in an agent-causal account.

According to one of our most familiar pictures of deliberation and action, it is frequently the case when an agent acts that there is a variety of things that she can do, and she brings it about that she does one of these things in particular. The chief virtue of an agent-causal view, I believe, is that it gives a non-Orwellian account of how these two conditions can obtain.

Like any libertarian view, an agent-causal account makes room for the first of these conditions by requiring that determinism be false. Given indeterminism, it may often be the case when an agent acts that there are several different actions each of which it is naturally possible that she perform, where "naturally possible" is explained as follows: at time t it is

---

[4] See, for example, Chisholm's "Freedom and Action," p. 17, and Taylor's *Action and Purpose*, p. 127.

[5] Chisholm writes that "we must say that at least one of the events that is involved in any act is caused, not by any other event, but by the agent, by the man" ("Freedom and Action," p. 29).

naturally possible that an event E occur (in our world) at time t' just in case there is at least one possible world with the same laws of nature as ours and with a history exactly like ours up through time t in which E occurs at t'.[6]

Unlike most other libertarian accounts, an agent-causal account secures the second condition by taking it seriously and quite literally. An agent's bringing it about that she performs one in particular of the naturally possible actions is taken as a condition of production, and producing is taken to be causally bringing about. An agent's causing her performing a certain action is taken to be really that, and not really something quite different, such as the causation of her action by an event involving the agent. Finally since agents or persons are held not to be themselves effects of prior causes, on agent-causal accounts agents constitute uncaused causes of their performing the particular actions they perform.

Agent-causal accounts thus secure an interesting condition of production, one that requires that, when an agent acts with free will, she is in a significant respect an originator of her action. This condition can be expressed as follows:

(CP)   When an agent acts with free will, her action is causally brought about by something that (a) is not itself causally brought about by anything over which she has no control, and that (b) is related to her in such a way that, in virtue of its causing her action, she determines which action she performs.

When CP is fulfilled, an agent is a real point of origin of her action. She determines that she perform that action, and that determination by her is not determined by anything beyond her control.

Any account of free will that allows that all events (except perhaps the world's first event) are caused, that all causes are events, and that all causal chains go back in time, if not forever, then to the beginning of the universe will fail to secure CP, regardless of whether causal relations are deterministic or merely probabilistic. CP appears unsecured, too, if an uncaused event is the immediate cause of the agent's action. For then it is unclear how the agent could be related to that uncaused event in such a way that she controlled its occurrence, and by controlling its occurrence determined which action she would perform. CP *is* secured if the relation in question is taken to be identity. For then when an agent acts with free will, she herself causes

---

[6] In this paper I focus on cases in which an agent acts with an ability to do otherwise. Certain features of the account I will sketch are more visibly displayed in light of such cases. However, I emphasize here that I do not believe that a libertarian need require, for free will, that an agent be able to do anything significantly different from what she actually does. If an agent has very good reason to perform an action of a certain type (A'ing), and if she has no reason not to, then, although it may be causally indeterminate *when* she A's, or exactly *how* she A's, it may not be naturally possible that she not A. So long as she is an undetermined determinant of her A'ing, it seems to me that it ought to be allowed that she acts with free will.

her performing a certain action, and qua agent or person she is not the effect of any causes (although events involving her are).

Now, it is consistent with this much of the agent-causal account that earlier events, including the agent's having or coming to have certain reasons to act, cause her performing a certain action. For suppose that all events in our world (except perhaps a first event) are caused by earlier events, but that event causation is "chancy" or probabilistic rather than deterministic.[7] Then, given the events up until now, there might be a certain chance, or single-case, objective probability (say, for example, .6) that a certain event E occur now, as well as a certain chance (.4) that E not occur now. Whatever happens now, past events cause it; but since they do not causally necessitate it, something else might have happened instead, in which case past events would have caused that something else. Suppose, further, that frequently when a human agent acts, it is naturally possible that she perform any one of several different actions each of which precludes her performing any of the others. Whichever of these actions she performs, earlier events probabilistically cause that action. It is consistent with these suppositions that often when a human agent acts, *she* causes her performing one rather than any of the other naturally possible actions. She brings it about that she performs that particular action. Yet, until her performance of that action, the chance that she would perform it remained somewhere between zero and one.

A libertarian view that affirms this account of human agency allows that an agent's behavior, besides being caused by her, is caused also by earlier events, among which are her having or coming to have certain beliefs, desires, preferences, aims, values, and so forth. This difference from the agent-causal views of Chisholm and Taylor stems from the recognition, here, that event causation may be probabilistic, and that probabilistic causation is not the threat to free will that causal necessitation is.[8] CP can thus be secured even if it is allowed that all events are caused by prior events.

[7] For a sample of discussions of nondeterministic causation, see G. E. M. Anscombe, "Causality and Determination," in *The Collected Philosophical Papers of G. E. M. Anscombe*, vol. 2 (Oxford: Basil Blackwell, 1981); Ellery Eells, *Probabilistic Causality* (Cambridge: Cambridge University Press, 1991); David Lewis, "Causation," in *Philosophical Papers*, vol. 2 (Oxford: Oxford University Press, 1986), esp. pp. 175–84; and Michael Tooley, *Causation: A Realist Approach* (Oxford: Clarendon Press, 1987), pp. 289–96.

[8] In fact, Chisholm, in one of his later discussions of free will, does draw a distinction that appears similar to this one. See Roderick M. Chisholm, "Comments and Replies," *Philosophia*, 7 (1978), pp. 597–636, esp. p. 629. However, he and Taylor generally take causation to be causal necessitation, and they deny that free will is compatible with universal causation.

John Bishop, too, has argued that an agent causal view need not rule out universal event causation. See his "Agent-Causation," *Mind*, 92 (1983), pp. 61–79, esp. pp. 76–79. However, there are two important differences between Bishop's approach and my own. First, his aim in "Agent-Causation" is to advance an agent-causal account of *action* and not just of acting with free will. (Hence, some of the problems with which he deals are not problems for me.) Second, Bishop

The agent-causal account that I have sketched, then, is itself a kind of reconciliationism. It reconciles a traditionally libertarian claim—that freedom consists in being an undetermined determinant of one's action—with the apparently undeniable fact that human beings are part of the causal order, that all events involving human beings are causally brought about by earlier events. Such a view reconciles free will not with determinism but with the highly plausible thesis of universal event causation. There is a clear advantage to be gained from this sort of reconciliation, for it allows for our ability to predict and explain human behavior.

The account suggested here thus provides a reply to the following version of the rational-explicability objection. The agent exists prior to, as well as during and after, the performance of any one of her actions. Yet the action occurs at a certain time. The fact that the action is caused by the agent, then, cannot explain why the action occurs when it does rather than earlier or later. Hence, it is objected, on an agent-causal account, the timing of human actions cannot be explained.[9]

The reply is that, on the view sketched here, the timing of an action is explained as well as it is on a wholly event-causal account of human agency, given the assumption that event causation is nondeterministic. On the view I suggest, the occurrence of certain prior events will be a necessary condition of an agent's causing a certain event. Absent those prior events, the later event will not be naturally possible, and an agent can cause only what is naturally possible. The agent-causal view thus has the same resources as does a wholly event-causal view of human agency to explain why an agent performs a certain action at a certain time, rather than earlier or later. If there is an event, such as her acquiring new reasons, that explains why she acted then and not at some other time, then both sorts of views have available an explanation. If there is no such event, then neither sort of view has available an explanation. As I explain in more detail in Section III, although agent causation adds nothing to our ability to explain human behavior, neither does it subtract anything.

suggests that agent causation is "conceptually primitive," and he does not attempt to explicate it. (In Section II, I take some steps toward such an explication.)

In his later work, Bishop defends an event-causal theory of action. See *Natural Agency: An Essay on the Causal Theory of Action* (Cambridge: Cambridge University Press, 1989).

[9] This version of the rational-explicability objection is expressed by Broad, *Ethics*, p. 215, and by Ginet, *On Action*, pp. 13–14. Ginet notes that the objection can be stated as well in terms of explaining why one particular action rather than another is performed. The reply to this variation is analogous to that given to the variation concerning the timing of the action. Given the assumption that event causation is nondeterministic, the agent-causal view has the same resources as does a wholly event-causal account to provide the contrastive explanation. This point is covered in more detail in the remainder of Section I.

On the agent-causal account sketched here, when an agent acts with free will, the agent's beliefs and desires are among the causes of her behavior. But if this is so, how are event and agent causation related, and can agent-caused actions still be rational?

The best reply here, I believe, is to maintain that what an agent directly causes, when she acts with free will, is her acting on (or for) certain of her reasons rather than on others, and her acting for reasons ordered in a particular way by weight, importance, or significance as the reasons for which she performs that action. Her acting for that ordering of reasons is itself a complex event, one that consists, in part, of her behavior's being caused by those reasons.[10] What is agent-caused, then, is her performing that action for that ordering of reasons rather than, say, that action for a different ordering of reasons or another action for different reasons.[11]

In the simplest case, an agent has her reasons and she acts on them. Pam attends a lecture on Mapplethorpe, say, primarily because she is interested in his work and secondarily because she knows the speaker. She might also have some desire to accompany a second friend to an interesting movie that is showing at the same time. But she causes her acting on the first set of reasons, and on a particular ordering of them, instead. What she directly causes is her attending the lecture primarily because of her interest in Mapplethorpe's work and secondarily because of her friendship with the lecturer.

Now, if an agent's action is rational, then her acting *for* a particular ordering of reasons will be rational in light of the reasons the agent *has* to act. It will be rational in light of her overall constellation of motivational states. And there are a couple of questions on this point that are waiting to be addressed.

One question concerning the rationality of agent-caused actions is whether, when an agent acts with this sort of freedom, there could be at least one ordering of the reasons *for* which she acts such that her acting for that

---

[10] I say "in part" because acting on or for certain reasons consists in more than the fact that one's action is caused by those reasons. The action must be nondeviantly caused by the reasons, and the reasons must constitute at least part of an explanation of the action. For a fuller account, see Robert Audi, "Acting for Reasons," *Philosophical Review*, 95 (1986), pp. 511–46.

[11] Even if agents can cause events, is it credible that an agent can affect whether her having certain reasons will have a certain effect, viz., her performing a certain action? I think so. After all, events can affect whether other events will have certain effects. Suppose that human agency is a wholly event-causal process. If it is cloudy, I acquire the belief that it is cloudy and might rain. If I believe that it is cloudy and might rain, then I might take my umbrella, but it is very likely that I will not. However, if I believe that it is cloudy and might rain, and then if my companion remarks that it is cloudy, then I will very likely take my umbrella. My companion's remark, or the absence of it, may causally affect whether the clouds and my belief will cause a certain action. The agent-causal case is disanalogous in that the agent, unlike my companion's remark, is not an event. But if agents, like events, can cause events, then it appears that agents can affect which effects certain events will have.

ordering would be rational in light of the reasons she *has* to act. The answer to this question is an easy "yes." If Pam has better reasons to attend the Mapplethorpe lecture than to go to the movie, then it is rational for her to act for those better reasons. It will be rationally explicable why she went to the lecture, and rationally explicable as well why she went to the lecture instead of going to the movies. Such explanations need refer to no more than the reasons for which she acted in going to the lecture.

It is important for a libertarian view that on a significant number of the occasions when an agent acts with free will, there is more than one action that she might rationally perform. Although our freedom of the will might consist partly in an ability to behave irrationally, free will is more desirable if it is the freedom to determine which of several genuine alternatives one will rationally pursue. A second rationality question, then, is whether the view sketched here allows for such alternative rationality.

It is often rationally indeterminate what we shall do and for what reasons we shall act. We are, for example, sometimes faced with choices among alternatives about which we are utterly indifferent. If I am given a choice of any one of several fine-looking apples, I may have no reason to pick any one of them rather than any other. In this kind of situation, my choice of any one of the apples will be as rational as would have been the choice of any other one. We also often face decisions where we have equally good reasons for making either of two or more choices. If I have until now taken as great an interest in surfing as in downhill skiing, I might as rationally choose to vacation at the beach as I might choose to go to the mountains.

There are other sorts of cases in which it is rationally indeterminate not only *for* which reasons an agent will act, but also how the reasons an agent *has* to act will be ordered. In making a decision, an agent will sometimes change the order in which she ranks considerations as reasons for action, and sometimes it may be as rational for her to change an ordering as it is for her to maintain it. Someone who smokes, for example, might have long judged that the health risks are less important to her than the pleasure she derives from smoking and the irritability and disruption that would result from quitting. If such a decision could be rational in the first place, then this agent might rationally continue to smoke: but it would surely not offend rationality if she one day reversed her ordering of reasons and decided to quit. Finally, an agent may face a decision that requires her to order considerations that she has not previously compared with each other; in some such cases there may be two or more new orderings each of which would be equally rational given her previous constellation of motivational states.

The important point to be made about all cases of rational indeterminacy is that the presence or absence of agent causation makes no difference to the rationality of the action. Whether such an action is agent-caused or not, there will be no contrastive rational explanation of it, one that would answer the question, "Why did you choose this apple rather than that one?" or "Why did you go to the beach rather than to the mountains?" This absence is due entirely to the structure of the situation and the agent's reasons. Such actions are nevertheless rationally explicable. I chose this apple because I wanted to eat an apple and it was as good as any other; I went to the beach because I like to surf. There is nothing rationally defective about an action of this sort; given the circumstances, it is as rational as can be.

II. CAUSATION BY AN AGENT

I turn now to the objection concerning the intelligibility of the notion of agent causation. Chisholm has offered a definition of agent causation in terms of 'undertaking' or 'endeavoring'.[12] However, both of these terms suggest that agent causation is a kind of intentional action; and if that is so, it is unclear that it deserves the name 'causation' at all, since event causation, about which there are at least intelligible accounts, is not any kind of intentional action. Van Inwagen has proposed a different kind of analysis, one on which the agent causation of an action is held to consist wholly in the performance of an action a component event of which is uncaused by any event.[13] However, this approach fails to tell us in positive terms in what the causation by the agent consists, and indeed why the component event could not be entirely uncaused.

Certain features drawn from the views of Chisholm and Taylor, as well as from the view I have sketched here, suggest the beginnings of an account of agent causation. Agent causation is a relation, the first relatum of which is an agent or person and the second relatum of which is an event. Agents enter into such relations only as first relata, never as second relata. And an agent that is a relatum of such a relation is not identical to any event, property, fact, or state of affairs, nor to any collection of such things.[14] What is directly caused by an agent is her acting for a particular ordering of reasons.

What remains is to say just what this relation is. The prevailing tendency

[12] Chisholm, "The Agent as Cause," and *Person and Object*, pp. 53–88.
[13] Peter van Inwagen, "A Definition of Chisholm's Notlon of Immanent Causation," *Philosophia*, 7 (1978), pp. 567–81.
[14] Only a very minimal commitment as to the nature of a person is implied here. All that is implied is a denial of the bundle view, the view that a person is simply a collection of qualities or events. It is certainly *not* implied here that a person is a Cartesian ego, or a monad, or any sort of nonphysical thing. Nor is it implied that a person is a bare particular; on the contrary, in the view sketched here, an agent's causal powers depend on her attributes.

among agent causalists and their critics alike on this point has been to stress how different agent causation is from event causation and indeed how "mysterious" the former is.[15] However, the proper line here, I believe, is to maintain that agent causation, if there is such a thing, is (or involves) *exactly* the same relation as event causation.[16] The only difference between the two kinds of causation concerns the types of entities related, not the relation. The question that needs to be addressed, then, is whether there is an intelligible account of the relation of causation that will serve in accounts of event causation as well as agent causation.

The most familiar accounts of event causation are reductionist, aiming to analyze causation in terms of such noncausal and nonnomological features as constant conjunction or counterfactual dependence, or in terms of the modalities of necessity and sufficiency. Certainly, if any of this type of account of event causation is correct, then agent causation cannot be the same relation as event causation. For agent causation plainly cannot be either the constant conjunction of an agent and an action type or the counterfactual dependence of an action on an agent, nor can it consist in an agent's being a necessary or sufficient condition for the performance of a particular action.[17] However, reductionist accounts are subject to grave difficulties,[18] and they are not the only sort of account around.

An attractive alternative is to take the causal relation to be among the basic constituents of the universe. Causation may be held to be a real relation between particulars, one that, although analyzable, is not reducible to noncausal and non-nomological properties and relations. There is a variety of such realist accounts of causation.[19] A common intuition underlying

[15] Taylor expresses this sort of view, as do Kane and Watson. See Taylor, *Metaphysics*, p. 49; Kane, *Free Will and Values*, p. 72; and Watson, "Free Action and Free Will," p. 167.

[16] Event causation may be probabilistic, and a single world might contain both kinds. The causal relation itself need not differ in the two cases; the difference between them might reside in the fact that the underlying laws involve different higher-order relations. For an account of this sort, see Tooley, *Causation*.

Perhaps it needs to be required that agent causation is deterministic. However, I am not sure that this is so. I see no problem in saying that, on the agent-causal account, the agent, together with her having certain reasons, jointly deterministically cause her acting on those reasons.

[17] Certainly, if the agent had not existed, her action would not have occurred. However, it is not the agent's existing, nor her coming to exist, but rather the agent that is said to cause her action. Furthermore, no agent causalist wants to claim that an agent causes every event that would not have occurred had she not existed.

[18] For criticism of reductionist accounts of causation, see Galen Strawson, "Realism and Causation," *The Philosophical Quarterly*, 37 (1987), pp. 252–77; Michael Tooley, "Causation: Reductionism Versus Realism," *Philosophy and Phenomenological Research*, 50 (1990), pp. 215–36; and the works cited in note 19.

[19] See, for example, John Bigelow and Robert Pargetter, "Metaphysics of Causation," *Erkenntnis*, 33 (1990), pp. 89–119; Adrian Heathcote and D. M. Armstrong, "Causes and Laws," *Noûs*, 25 (1991), pp. 63–73; and Tooley, *Causation*.

many is that reductionist accounts attempt to explain the more fundamental by the less fundamental. It is not, for example, because one event counterfactually depends on another that the second may be said to cause the first. Rather, according to a realist, such counterfactual dependence is to be explained in terms of causal relations and laws.[20]

One type of realist account of event causation can be sketched, in broad strokes, as follows. An event (particular) causes another just in case the relation of causation obtains between them. Two events can be so related only if they possess (or are constituted by) properties that are in turn related under a law of nature. Ultimately, then, causal relations are grounded in laws of nature, which consist of second-order relations among universals.

Such an account roughly resembles that favored by Tooley for event (or, as he would have it, state-of-affairs) causation.[21] Tooley maintains that the relations involved in this sort of account—causation, as well as the higher order relations among universals—can be adequately specified, without reduction, by a set of postulates indicating the roles of these relations within the domain of properties and states of affairs.[22] If he is correct about this, then we have an analysis of the causal relation that can be employed in an account of agent causation. An agent causalist can say that it is the relation thus analyzed that obtains between a person and her action when she acts with free will; it is the very relation that, within the domain of properties and events or states of affairs, occupies the specified role.[23]

Moreover, an account that runs parallel, at a certain level of description, to that suggested for event causation would seem to be available for agent causation. An agent may be held to cause a particular action (more

[20] Bigelow and Pargetter write:

We take causation to be part of the basic furniture of nature, and as such it functions as an input into the explanation of modalities. It is widely agreed that the best account of modalities make appeal to the framework of possible worlds. There is less agreement on how possible worlds are to be construed. Most of the details on the nature of worlds are unimportant here. What is important is only the direction of explanation between causation and the nature of worlds. We support theories which use causation as part of an account of what there is in any given possible world. Thus causation enters into the explanation of modalities, and in particular, into the explanation of 'necessary and sufficient conditions', and also of probabilities. Hence modal or probabilistic theories, even if they could be adjusted until they became extensionally correct, would nevertheless proceed in the wrong direction from an explanatory point of view. ("Metaphysics of Causation," p. 98)

[21] Tooley, *Causation*.

[22] The terms defined in this manner themselves appear in the postulates, but they can be replaced by variables to give us a theory that employs only antecedently understood observational, quasi-logical, and logical vocabulary. The theory succeeds in defining causation and the (two) relations involved in laws just in case there is a unique ordered triple of relations that satisfies the open formula of the theory.

The approach is one that is generally available for a realist treatment of theoretical terms. The technique employed is the Ramsey/Lewis method. For discussion of this method see David Lewis, "How to Define Theoretical Terms," in *Philosophical Papers*, vol. 1 (Oxford: Oxford University Press, 1983).

[23] I owe this suggestion to David Lewis.

precisely: an event of acting on a certain ordering of reasons) just in case the relation of causation obtains between these two particulars. And an agent can be said to be so related to one of her actions only if these two particulars exemplify certain properties. Perhaps the only agents who cause things are those who have the property of being capable of reflective practical reasoning,[24] and perhaps such an agent directly causes only those events that constitute her acting for reasons. There might, in that case, be a law of nature to the effect that any individual who acts with such a capacity acts with free will.

Here is one way in which such a law might be construed. Suppose that it is necessarily true that if an action is performed with free will, then the agent causes her acting on the reasons on which she acts. (That there is such a necessary truth seems to be what, at bottom, agent causalists have always argued.) Suppose, further, that a necessary, but not logically sufficient, condition of acting with free will is that an agent act with a capacity for reflective, rational self-governance. Now suppose that it is a law in our world that if an agent possessing that capacity acts on reasons, then she acts with free will.[25] Here we have a contingent statement of natural necessity. Together with the supposed necessary truth, it implies the obtaining of the causal relation between agent and action.

Natural law, then, may subsume all free action without undermining the freedom with which human beings act. On this sort of account, the agent causation on which free will is held to depend is seen as thoroughly natural.

On the suggested account, then, agent causation is the obtaining of a relation between two particulars; the relation involved is the very same one that is involved in event causation. An agent's exercise of her causal power is

---

[24] Several compatibilist accounts identify free will with a capacity to direct one's behavior by reflective practical reasoning. See, for example, T. M. Scanlon, "The Significance of Choice," in Sterling M. McMurrin, ed., *The Tanner Lectures on Human Values*, vol. 8 (Salt Lake City: University of Utah Press, 1988), esp. p. 174 [reprinted as Essay 18, this volume]; and Gary Watson, "Free Action and Free Will," esp. pp. 152–53. Acting with such a capacity is, I believe, a necessary condition of acting with free will, and an adequate libertarian account will need to affirm this. Whether having that capacity is lawfully associated with agent-causing one's actions is, of course, another matter.

[25] This way of expressing the law seems to imply that intentionality enters into the law of nature that governs agent causation, and it might be objected that such an implication is incredible. I am not sure that it is. Many of us believe, anyway, that intentional states (or our having them) can enter into causal relations, and that it can be *because* a certain state has a certain intentional content that that state causes what it does. If the intentionality of mental states really is relevant to their causal roles, then we have one good reason to believe that intentionality somehow enters into the laws of nature that govern the causal relations of those states.

On the other hand, what if the intentional is anomalous? In that case, anyone who claims that the intentionality of mental states is causally relevant owes us an account of how that relevance is captured in the laws of nature. When we have that account, an agent causalist can use it for her own purposes.

simply the obtaining of this relation between her and an event. An agent need not *do* anything—if by that is meant perform some action—in order to cause something. Thus, agent causation is not fundamentally the performance of some special kind of action that then causes one's bodily movements. Nevertheless, the causal power that such an account attributes to agents is no more "magical" than that which we attribute to events. For an event need not perform any action in order to cause another event, and event causation is not fundamentally the occurrence of some third event between cause and effect; it is fundamentally the obtaining of a relation between the two.

The upshot is that, on an agent-causal account, an agent's *control* over her behavior resides fundamentally in her *causing* what she does. Her control does not reside fundamentally in her performing some special sort of action. Since causing is bringing something about, producing it, or making it happen, causing seems to be the right sort of thing on which to base an agent's control over her behavior.

My suggestions concerning an account of agent causation are, of course, programmatic. It remains to be seen whether such an account can be fully worked out. Nevertheless, the alternative of a realist account of causation significantly weakens the charge that the notion of agent causation is mysterious or unintelligible. If a realist treatment of event causation is intelligible, then we fairly well understand, too, what is meant by the claim that agents cause their actions. And given a realist account of causation, what is expressed by the claim in question is, it seems to me, something that is true in some possible worlds. At this juncture, an objection that agent causation is metaphysically impossible would stand in need of some argument.[26]

III. WHY BELIEVE IT

Even if an agent-causal thesis is intelligible, however, and even if what it states is not something impossible, the question remains whether it is reasonable to believe that, in fact, human beings agent-cause at least some of

---

[26] It may be objected that, even if it is not impossible that a person should be a cause, nevertheless, on the view I have suggested, entities of two ontologically different sorts are said to be causes, and that (so the objection goes) is absurd. I do not think that it is. When it comes to accounts of "ordinary" causation, some say the relata are events, some say aspects of events, some say states of affairs, and some say properties. Consider the hypothesis that, in fact, at least two of these sorts of entities are causes. I do not think that it asserts something that is impossible.

For an argument that entities of several ontologically different kinds are indeed relata of causation, see David H. Sanford, "Causal Relata," in Ernest LePore and Brian P. McLaughlin, eds., *Actions and Events: Perspectives on the Philosophy of Donald Davidson* (Oxford: Basil Blackwell, 1985). I note that Sanford does *not* admit persons as causal relata.

their actions. I will first indicate what kind of argument is *not* available for such a view and then outline what seems to me the best argument that *can* be made.

First, if agent causation is as described here, then there is no observational evidence that could tell us whether our world is an indeterministic world with agent causation or an indeterministic world without it.[27] We do not introspectively observe agent causation, and even highly improbable behavior could occur in a world without agent causation.

A related point is that affirming agent causation would not improve our ability to predict and explain human behavior. Our beliefs about event causation play a crucial role in this kind of understanding of human agency. But those beliefs concern the conditions for the occurrence of some event, and beliefs about agent causation are about something quite different. Nevertheless, it should be evident that, since an agent-causal thesis does not require that there be any gaps in chains of event causes, agent causation does not undermine the predictive and explanatory significance of event causes. Indeed, agent causation is consistent with its being the case that probabilistic laws of nature apply as thoroughly to human beings and their behavior as such laws apply to anything else. Thus, contrary to what Chisholm claims, agent causation is not a reason why "there can be no complete science of man."[28]

If prediction and explanation are paradigmatic of scientific understanding, it appears that agent causation neither contributes to nor detracts from such understanding. Its contribution, rather, would be to our understanding of ourselves as moral agents. We believe, most of us, that we are morally responsible for much of what we do. Agent causation, it may be argued, is a condition of the possibility of morally responsible agency.[29] Affirming

---

[27] Perhaps we could have evidence that our world was a deterministic world; but I take it that we don't.

[28] Chisholm, "Freedom and Action," p. 24.

[29] There is a widespread conviction that it is just too much to believe that human beings have a causal power that is to be found nowhere else in nature. Here is one part of a reply to that conviction: If it is accepted that we are morally responsible for at least some of our actions, then it is already accepted that we are morally unique (at least among known natural agents). If it is, moreover, necessarily true that only an agent who agent-causes her actions is a morally responsible agent, then one cannot consistently believe that we are thus morally unique and at the same time reject the metaphysics of agent causation.

The second part of a reply is that, in fact, it is not necessary for an agent-causalist to maintain that only human agents are agent causes. It can be allowed that the laws governing agent causation are not as suggested above but also cover causation by agents who lack the reflective capacity that free agents have. In that case, agent causation is a necessary but not a sufficient condition for free will. A further necessary condition is that an agent act with a capacity rationally to reflect on the courses of action she might pursue and on the reasons for which she might pursue them, and to govern her behavior on the basis of such reflection.

something like the view sketched here, then, would give us an explication of how we can be what we seem, from the moral point of view, to be. Importantly, the explication provided would be one that is consistent with how we view ourselves from the scientific point of view.

The broader case for this view, as these last remarks suggest, constitutes a kind of transcendental argument, one that, in outline, runs as follows: (1) we are morally responsible agents; (2) if we are morally responsible agents, then we act with free will; (3) if we act with free will, then determinism is false; (4) if determinism is false and still we act with free will, then we agent-cause our actions; and (5) if our acting with free will requires that we agent-cause our actions, then that freedom is as presented in the account sketched above.

I have not, of course, established these five propositions here. My aim has been only to argue for serious consideration of the account referred to in the last of them. The crucial steps of the arguments are, of course, the rejection of compatibilism and of nonagent-causal libertarian views. What inclines many of us to follow those steps, I believe, is that we find unsatisfactory any view of free will that allows that everything that causally brings about an agent's action is itself causally brought about by something in the distant past. Certainly any freedom of the will that we enjoy on such a view, if not a complete fraud, is a pale imitation of the freedom that is characterized by an agent-causal account. If I am right that agent causation can be made intelligible and that agent-caused actions can be rational, then an agent-causal account certainly deserves close attention.

15

RESPONSIBILITY, LUCK, AND CHANCE: REFLECTIONS ON FREE WILL AND INDETERMINISM

ROBERT KANE

Ludwig Wittgenstein[1] once said that "to solve the problems of philosophers, you have to think even more crazily than they do" (ibid., p. 75). This task (which became even more difficult after Wittgenstein than it was before him) is certainly required for the venerable problem of free will and determinism.

I. THE LUCK PRINCIPLE

Consider the following principle:

(LP)   If an action is *undetermined* at a time *t*, then its happening rather than not happening at *t* would be a matter of *chance* or *luck*, and so it could not be a *free* and *responsible* action.

This principle (which we may call the *luck principle*, or simply LP) is false, as I shall explain shortly. Yet it seems true. LP and a related principle to be considered later in this paper are fueled by many of those "intuition pumps," in Daniel Dennett's[2] apt expression, which support common intuitions

From the *Journal of Philosophy*, 96/5 (1999), 217–40. Reprinted by permission of the publisher and the author.

   This paper was prompted by a recent objection made in various forms against my view and other incompatibilist views of freedom and responsibility by Galen Strawson, Alfred Mele, Bernard Berofsky, Bruce Waller, Richard Double, Mark Bernstein, and Ishtiyaque Haji. (See footnote 10 for references.) The paper has benefitted from interchanges with the above persons and with participants at a conference on my work on free will at the University of Arkansas in September, 1997: Gary Watson, Barry Loewer, Timothy O'Connor, Randolph Clarke, Christopher Hill, and Thomas Senor. It has also benefitted from interchanges in conferences or in correspondence with John Martin Fischer, William Rowe, Nicholas Nathan, David Hodgson, Saul Smilansky, Kevin Magill, Peter van Inwagen, Derk Pereboom, Laura Ekstrom, Hugh McCann, and Ilya Prigogine. I am especially grateful to Mele and Strawson for pursuing me assiduously on these issues since the publication of my latest work, and for perceptive comments on the penultimate draft by Mele, Berofsky, and George Graham.

[1] *Culture and Value* (New York: Blackwell, 1980).
[2] *Elbow Room* (Cambridge, Mass.: MIT, 1984), chapter 1 and pp. 32–34, 64–65, 119–20, 169–70.

about freedom and responsibility. LP and related principles lie behind the widespread belief that indeterminism, so far from being required for free will and responsibility, would actually undermine free will and responsibility. Dennett does not dwell on intuition pumps of this sort, as I shall do in this paper. As a compatibilist, he is more interested in criticizing intuition pumps that lead people to think (mistakenly, on his view) that freedom and responsibility are not compatible with determinism, whereas intuition pumps that support LP lead people to think freedom and responsibility are not compatible with *indeterminism*. Yet intuition pumps of the latter kind are every bit as pervasive and influential in free-will debates as those Dennett dwells upon; and they are as much in need of deconstruction, since they play a significant role in leading people to believe that freedom and responsibility must be compatible with determinism.

I think the modern route to compatibilism—which is the reigning view among contemporary philosophers—usually goes through principles like LP at some point or other. In my experience, most ordinary persons start out as natural incompatibilists. They believe there is some kind of conflict between freedom and determinism; and the idea that freedom and responsibility might be compatible with determinism looks to them at first like a "quagmire of evasion" (William James) or "a wretched subterfuge" (Immanuel Kant). Ordinary persons have to be talked out of this natural incompatibilism by the clever arguments of philosophers—who, in the manner of their mentor, Socrates, are only too happy to oblige. To weaken natural incompatibilist instincts, philosophers first argue that what we mean by freedom in everyday life is the power or ability to do whatever we choose or desire to do—in short, an absence of coercion, compulsion, oppression, and other impediments or constraints upon our behavior. They then point out that we can be free in these everyday senses to do what we choose or desire, even if our choices and desires are determined by causes that lie in our past.

But this line of argument does not usually dispose of incompatibilist intuitions by itself. Ordinary persons might grant that many everyday freedoms are compatible with determinism and still wonder if there is not also some deeper freedom—the freedom to have an *ultimate* say in what we choose or desire to do in the first place—that is incompatible with determinism. (I have argued elsewhere[3] that this deeper freedom is what was traditionally meant by "free *will*.") So the philosophers must add a second step to their case—an argument to the effect that any allegedly deeper freedom (of the will) that is not compatible with determinism is no intelligible

---

[3] *The Significance of Free Will* (New York: Oxford, 1996), pp. 10–14, 33–37.

freedom at all. And with this step, principles like LP come into the picture. For any freedom not compatible with determinism would require indeterminism; and what is undetermined, it seems, would happen by chance or luck and could not be a free and responsible action. This kind of argument is the one that usually puts the final nail in the coffin of incompatibilist instincts.

When philosophy professors go through this two-stage argument in the modern classroom, they are replicating the standard case against traditional (incompatibilist or libertarian) free will which is one of the defining characteristics of modernity. The goal is to consign incompatibilist freedom to the dustbin of history with other beliefs that a modern scientific age is encouraged to outgrow. Students and ordinary persons subjected to this argument may have an uneasy feeling they are being had by the clever arguments of philosophers. But, also seeing no obvious response, except an appeal to mystery, many of them become compatibilists.

II. INDETERMINISM, THE BOGEYMAN

The second stage of this two-stage argument in support of compatibilism will concern me here, the one that goes through LP and related principles in the attempt to show that indeterminism would not enhance, but in fact would undermine, freedom and responsibility. What is at stake here is not merely the clever arguments of philosophers; for it happens that the case for principles like LP is a powerful one. It *is* difficult to see how indeterminism and chance can be reconciled with freedom and responsibility. Philosophers have tried to bring this out in a number of ways which will be addressed here. We may think of these as the varied intuition pumps that support LP and principles like it.

(1) We are often asked to consider, for example, that whatever is undetermined or happens by chance is not under the *control* of anything, and so is not under the control of the agent. But an action that is not under the control of the agent could not be a free and responsible action. (Here it is evident that the notion of control is involved in the case for LP: indeterminism and chance imply lack of control to a degree that implies lack of freedom and responsibility.)

(2) Another line of argument often heard is this: suppose a choice occurred as the result of an undetermined event (say, a quantum jump) in one's brain. Would that be a free choice? Being undetermined, it would appear to be more of a fluke or accident than a free and responsible action. Some twentieth-century scientists and philosophers have suggested that free will might be rescued by supposing that undetermined quantum events in

the brain could be amplified to have large-scale effects on choice or action.[4] Unfortunately, this modern version of the ancient Epicurean "swerve" of the atoms seems to be subject to the same criticisms as its ancient counterpart. It seems that undetermined events in the brain or body, whether amplified or not, would occur spontaneously and would be more of a nuisance—or perhaps a curse, like epilepsy—than an enhancement of freedom and responsibility.

(3) Nor would it help to suppose that the indeterminism or chance came *between* our choices (or intentions) and our actions. Imagine that you are intending to make a delicate cut in a fine piece of cloth, but because of an undetermined twitching in your arm, you make the wrong cut. Here, indeterminism is no enhancement of your freedom, but a *hindrance* or *obstacle* to your carrying out your purposes as intended. Critics of libertarian freedom[5] have often contended that this is what indeterminism would always be—a hindrance or impediment to one's freedom. It would get in the way, *diminishing* control, and hence responsibility, instead of enhancing them.

(4) Even more absurd consequences follow if we suppose that indeterminism or chance is involved in the initiation of overt actions. Arthur Schopenhauer[6] imagined the case of a man who suddenly found his legs start to move *by chance*, carrying him across the room against his wishes. Such caricatures are popular among critics of indeterminist freedom for obvious reasons: undetermined or chance-initiated overt actions would represent the opposite of controlled and responsible actions.

(5) Going a little deeper, one may also note that, if a choice or action is undetermined, it might occur otherwise *given exactly the same past and laws of nature* up to the moment when it does occurs. This means that, if Jane is deliberating about whether to vacation in Hawaii or Colorado, and gradually comes to favor and choose Hawaii, she might have chosen otherwise (chosen Colorado), given *exactly the same deliberation* up to the moment of choice that in fact led her to favor and choose Hawaii (exactly the same thoughts, reasonings, beliefs, desires, dispositions, and other characteristics—not a sliver of difference). It is difficult to make sense of this. The choice of Colorado in such circumstances would seem irrational and inexplicable, capricious and arbitrary.[7] If it came about by virtue of

---

[4] For example, physicist A. H. Compton, *The Freedom of Man* (New Haven: Yale, 1935) and neurophysiologist John Eccles, *Facing Reality* (New York: Springer, 1970).

[5] See, for example, Galen Strawson, who argues that, even if free will should be incompatible with determinism, indeterminism would be "no help" in enhancing either freedom or responsibility—"The Unhelpfulness of Indeterminism," *Philosophy and Phenomenological Research* (forthcoming).

[6] *Essay on the Freedom of the Will* (Indianapolis: Bobbs-Merrill, 1960), p. 47.

[7] This dilemma for incompatibilist accounts of freedom is nicely described by Thomas Nagel, *The View from Nowhere* (New York: Oxford, 1986), chapter 7 [see Essay 12, this volume].

undetermined events in Jane's brain, this would not be an occasion for rejoicing in her freedom, but for consulting a neurologist about the waywardness of her neural processes.

(6) At this point, some defenders of incompatibilist freedom appeal to Gottfried Leibniz's[8] celebrated dictum that prior reasons or motives need not determine choice or action, they may merely "incline without necessitating"—that is, they may incline the agent toward one option without determining the choice of that option. This may indeed happen. But it will not solve the present problem; for it is precisely *because* Jane's prior reasons and motives (beliefs, desires, and the like) incline her toward the choice of Hawaii that choosing Colorado by chance at the end of exactly the same deliberation would be irrational and inexplicable. Similarly, if her reasons had inclined her toward Colorado, then choosing Hawaii by chance at the end of the same deliberation would have been irrational and inexplicable. And if prior reasons or motives had not inclined her either way (the celebrated medieval "liberty of indifference") and the choice was a matter of chance, then the choosing of one rather than the other would have been all the more a matter of luck and out of her control. (One can see why libertarian freedom has often been ridiculed as a mere "liberty of indifference.")

(7) Indeed, critics of indeterminist freedom have often argued that indeterminist free choices must always amount to *random* choices of this sort and hence the outcomes would be matters of mere luck or chance—like spinning a wheel to select among a set of alternatives. Perhaps there is a role for such random choices in our lives when we are genuinely indifferent to outcomes.[9] But to suppose that *all* of our free and responsible choices—including momentous ones, like whether to act heroically or treacherously—had to be by random selection in this way has been regarded by many philosophers as a *reductio ad absurdum* of the view that free will and responsibility require indeterminism.

(8) Consider one final argument which cuts more deeply than the others and to which I shall devote considerable attention. This paper was in fact prompted by new versions of this argument advanced in recent years against my incompatibilist account of free will by Galen Strawson, Alfred Mele, Bernard Berofsky, Bruce Waller, Richard Double, Mark Bernstein, and Ishtiyaque Haji[10]—though the argument is meant to apply generally to any view

---

[8] *Selections* (New York: Scribner's, 1951), p. 435.

[9] Stephen M. Cahn makes a persuasive case for there being such a role—"Random Choices," *Philosophy and Phenomenological Research*, XXXVII (1977): 549–51.

[10] Strawson, "The Impossibility of Moral Responsibility," *Philosophical Studies*, LXXV (1994): 5–24, [reprinted as Essay 11, this volume], and "The Unhelpfulness of Indeterminism," *op. cit.*; Mele, Review of my *The Significance of Free Will*, the *Journal of Philosophy*, XCV, 11 (November 1998): 581–84, and "Luck and the Significance of Free Will," *Philosophical Explorations*

requiring that free actions be undetermined up to the moment when they occur.

Suppose two agents had exactly the same pasts (as indeterminism requires) up to the point where they were faced with a choice between distorting the truth for selfish gain or telling the truth at great personal cost. One agent lies and the other tells the truth. As Waller puts it, if the pasts of these two agents "are really identical" in every way up to the moment of choice, "and the difference in their acts results from chance," would there "be any grounds for distinguishing between [them], for saying that one deserves censure for a selfish decision and the other deserves praise" (*op. cit.*, p. 151)? Mele poses the problem in terms of a single agent in different possible worlds. Suppose in the actual world, John fails to resist the temptation to do what he thinks he ought to do, arrive at a meeting on time. If he could have done otherwise given the same past, then his counterpart, John* in a nearby possible world, which is the same as the actual world up to the moment of choice, resists the temptation and arrives on time. Mele then argues that, "if there is nothing about the agents' powers, capacities, states of mind, moral character and the like that explains this difference in outcome, ... the difference is just a matter of luck" (*op. cit.*, pp. 582–83). It would seem that John* got lucky in his attempt to overcome temptation, whereas John did not. Would it be just to reward the one and punish the other for what appears to be ultimately the luck of the draw?

Considerations such as (1)–(8) lie behind familiar and varied charges that undetermined choices or actions would be "arbitrary," "capricious," "random," "uncontrolled," "irrational," "inexplicable," or "matters of luck or chance," and hence not free and responsible actions. These are the charges which principles like LP are meant to express. Responses to them in the history of philosophy have been many; but none to my mind has been entirely convincing. The charges have often led libertarians—those who believe in an incompatibilist free will—to posit "extra factors" in the form of unusual species of agency or causation (such as noumenal selves, immaterial egos, or nonoccurrent agent causes) to account for what would otherwise be arbitrary, uncontrolled, inexplicable, or mere luck or chance. I do not

(forthcoming); Berofsky, "Ultimate Responsibility in a Deterministic World," *Philosophy and Phenomenological Research* (forthcoming); Waller, "Free Will Gone Out of Control," *Behaviorism*, XVI (1988): 149–67; Double, *The Non-reality of Free Will* (New York: Oxford, 1991), p. 140; Bernstein, "Kanean Libertarianism," *Southwest Philosophy Review*, XI (1995): 151–57; Haji, "Indeterminism and Frankfurt-type Examples," *Philosophical Explorations* (forthcoming). Different, but related, concerns about indeterminism and agency are aired by Timothy O'Connor, "Indeterminism and Free Agency: Three Recent Views," *Philosophy and Phenomenological Research*, LIII (1993): 499–526; and Randolph Clarke, "Free Choice, Effort and Wanting More," *Philosophical Explorations* (forthcoming).

propose to appeal to any such extra factors in defense of libertarian freedom. Such appeals introduce additional problems of their own without, in my view, directly confronting the deep problems about indeterminism, chance, and luck to which considerations (1)–(8) are pointing. To confront these deep problems directly, I believe one has to rethink issues about indeterminism and responsibility from the ground up, without relying on appeals to extracausal factors—a task to which I now turn.

III. INDETERMINISM AND RESPONSIBILITY

First, one must question the intuitive connection in people's minds between "indeterminism's being involved in something's happening" and "its happening merely as a matter of chance or luck." 'Chance' and 'luck' are terms of ordinary language which carry the connotation of "its being out of my control" (as in (1) and (4) and above). So using them already begs certain questions, whereas 'indeterminism' is a technical term that merely precludes *deterministic* causation (though not causation altogether). Second, one must emphasize that indeterminism does not have to be involved in all free and responsible acts, even for incompatibilists or libertarians.[11] Frequently, we act from a will already formed; and it may well be that our actions are determined in such cases by our then existing characters and motives. On such occasions, to do otherwise by chance *would* be a fluke or accident, irrational and inexplicable, as critics of indeterminist freedom contend (in (3) and (4) above).

Incompatibilists about free will should not deny this. What they should rather say is that when we act from a will already formed (as we frequently do), it is "our own free will" by virtue of the fact that we formed it (at least in part) by earlier choices or actions which were not determined and for which we could have done otherwise voluntarily, not merely as a fluke or accident. I call these earlier undetermined actions *self-forming actions* or SFAs.[12]

---

[11] I defend this point at length in *Free Will and Values* (Albany: SUNY, 1985), chapters 4 and 5. It is also defended by Peter van Inwagen, "When Is the Will Free?" in J. Tomberlin, ed., *Philosophical Perspectives*, Volume 3 (Atascadero, Calif.: Ridgeview, 1989), pp. 399–422. John Martin Fischer has described the view that van Inwagen and I defend as "restricted libertarianism," and has criticized it in "When the Will Is Free," in Tomberlin, ed., *Philosophical Perspectives*, Volume 6 (Atascadero: Ridgeview, 1992), pp. 423–51. Another critic is Hugh McCann, "On When the Will Is Free," in G. Holmstrom-Hintikka and R. Tuomela, eds., *Contemporary Action Theory*, Volume 1 (Dordrecht: Kluwer, 1997), pp. 219–32. Van Inwagen responds to Fischer in "When Is the Will Not Free?" *Philosophical Studies*, LXXV (1994): 95–114; and I respond in *The Significance of Free Will*, pp. 32–43.

[12] See *The Significance of Free Will*, pp. 74–78. SFAs are also sometimes called "self-forming willings" or SFWs in that work (pp. 125 ff.).

Undetermined SFAs are a subset of all of the actions done of our own free wills (many of which may be determined by our earlier formed character and motives). But if there were no such undetermined SFAs in our lifetimes, there would have been nothing we could have ever voluntarily done to make ourselves different than we are—a condition that I think is inconsistent with our having the kind of responsibility for being what we are which genuine free will requires.

Now, let us look more closely at these undetermined SFAs. As I see it, they occur at times in life when we are torn between competing visions of what we should do or become. Perhaps we are torn between doing the moral thing or acting from self-interest, or between present desires and long-term goals, or we are faced with difficult tasks for which we have aversions. In all such cases, we are faced with competing motivations and have to make an effort to overcome temptation to do something else we also strongly want. In the light of this picture, I suggest the following incompatibilist account of SFAs.[13] There is a tension and uncertainty in our minds at such times of inner conflict which are reflected in appropriate regions of our brains by movement away from thermodynamic equilibrium—in short, a kind of stirring up of chaos in the brain that makes it sensitive to micro-indeterminacies at the neuronal level. As a result, the uncertainty and inner tension we feel at such soul-searching moments of self-formation is reflected in the indeterminacy of our neural processes themselves. What is experienced phenomenologically as uncertainty corresponds physically to the opening of a window of opportunity that temporarily screens off complete determination by the past. (By contrast, when we act from predominant motives or settled dispositions, the uncertainty or indeterminism is muted. If it were involved then, it *would* be a mere nuisance or fluke, capricious or arbitrary, as critics contend (in (2), (5) and (6) above).)

When we do decide under such conditions of uncertainty, the outcome is not determined because of the preceding indeterminacy—and yet it can be willed (and hence rational and voluntary) either way owing to the fact that in such self-formation, the agents' prior wills are divided by conflicting motives. If we overcome temptation, it will be the result of our effort; and if we fail, it will be because we did not *allow* our effort to succeed. And this is owing to the fact that, while we wanted to overcome temptation, we also wanted to fail, for quite different and incommensurable reasons. When we decide in such circumstances, and the indeterminate efforts we are making

---

[13] This, in broad outline, is the account developed in my *The Significance of Free Will*, chapters 8–10. In later sections below, I make important additions to it in response to criticisms.

become determinate choices, we *make* one set of competing reasons or motives prevail over the others then and there *by deciding*.

Return now to concerns about indeterminism and responsibility in the light of this picture. Consider a businesswoman who faces a conflict in her will of the kind typically involved in such SFAs. She is on the way to a meeting important to her career when she observes an assault in an alley. An inner struggle ensues between her moral conscience, to stop and call for help, and her career ambitions, which tell her she cannot miss this meeting—a struggle she eventually resolves by turning back to help the victim. Now suppose this woman visits some future neuroscientists the next day and they tell her a story about what was going on in her brain at the time she chose, not unlike the story just told. Prior to choice, there was some indeterminacy in her neural processes stirred up by the conflict in her will. The indeterminism made it uncertain (and undetermined) whether she would go back to help or press onward.

Suppose further that two recurrent and connected neural networks are involved in the neuroscientists' story. Such networks circulate impulses and information in feedback loops and generally play a role in complex cognitive processing in the brain of the kind that one would expect to be involved in human deliberation. Moreover, recurrent networks are nonlinear, thus allowing (as some recent research suggests) for the possibility of chaotic activity, which would contribute to the plasticity and flexibility human brains display in creative problem solving (of which practical deliberation is an example).[14] The input of one of these recurrent networks consists of the woman's moral motives, and its output the choice to go back; the input of the other, her career ambitions, and its output, the choice to go on to her meeting. The two networks are connected, so that the indeterminism that made it uncertain that she would do the moral thing was coming from her desire to do the opposite, and vice versa—the indeterminism thus arising, as we said, from a conflict in the will. When her effort to overcome self-interested desires succeeded, this corresponded to one of the neural pathways reaching an activation threshold, overcoming the indeterminism generated by the other.

To this picture, one might now pose the following objection: if it really was undetermined which choice the woman would make (in neural terms, which network would activate) right up to the moment when she chose, it

---

[14] See P. Huberman and G. Hogg, "Phase Transitions in Artificial Intelligence Systems," *Artificial Intelligence*, xxxiii (1987): 155–72; C. Skarda and W. Freeman, "How Brains Make Chaos in Order to Make Sense of the World," *Behavior and Brain Sciences*, x (1987): 161–95; A. Babloyantz and A. Destexhe, "Strange Attractors in the Human Cortex," in L. Rensing, ed., *Temporal Disorder in Human Oscillatory Systems* (New York: Springer, 1985), pp. 132–43.

seems that it would be a matter of luck or chance that one choice was made rather than the other, and so she could not be held responsible for the outcome. (Note that this is an expression of LP.) The first step in response is to recall a point made earlier: we must be wary of moving too hastily from 'indeterminism is involved in something's happening' to 'its happening merely as a matter of chance or luck'. 'Luck' and 'chance' have meanings in ordinary language that mere indeterminism may not have. The second step is to note that indeterminism of itself does not necessarily undermine control and responsibility.[15] Suppose you are trying to think through a difficult problem (say, a mathematical problem) and there is some indeterminacy in your neural processes complicating the task—a kind of chaotic background. It would be like trying to concentrate and solve a problem with background noise or distraction. Whether you are going to succeed in solving the mathematical problem is uncertain and undetermined because of the distracting neural noise. Yet if you concentrate and solve the problem nonetheless, I think we can say that you did it and are responsible for doing it even though it was undetermined whether you would succeed. The indeterministic noise would have been an obstacle to your solving the problem which you nevertheless overcame by your effort.

There are numerous other examples in the philosophical literature of this kind, where indeterminism functions as an obstacle to success without precluding responsibility. Consider an assassin who is trying to kill the prime minister but might miss because of some undetermined events in his nervous system which might lead to a jerking or wavering of this arm. If he does hit his target, can he be held responsible? The answer (as J. L. Austin and Philippa Foot[16] successfully argued decades ago) is "yes," because he intentionally and voluntarily succeeded in doing what he was *trying* to do—kill the prime minister. Yet his killing the prime minister was undetermined. We might even say in a sense that he got lucky in killing the prime minister, when he could have failed. But it does not follow, if he succeeds, that killing the prime minister was not his action, not something he did; nor does it follow, as LP would require, that he was not responsible for killing the prime minister. Indeed, if anything is clear, it is that he both killed the prime minister and was responsible for doing so.

Or consider a husband who, while arguing with his wife, swings his arm

---

[15] Important recent defenses of the claim that indeterminism does not necessarily undermine control and responsibility include Clarke, "Indeterminism and Control," *American Philosophical Quarterly*, xxxii (1995): 125–38; Carl Ginet, *On Action* (New York: Cambridge, 1990), chapter 6; O'Connor; and Laura Ekstrom, *Free Will* (Boulder: Westview, forthcoming).

[16] Austin, "Ifs and Cans," in his *Philosophical Papers* (New York: Oxford, 1961), pp. 153–80; Foot, "Free Will as Involving Determinism," in Berofsky, ed., *Free Will and Determinism* (New York: Harper and Row, 1966), pp. 95–108.

down in anger on her favorite glass table top, intending to break it. Again we suppose that some indeterminism in the husband's efferent neural pathways makes the momentum of his arm indeterminate, so it is undetermined if the table will break right up to the moment when it is struck. Whether the husband breaks the table or not is undetermined. Yet it does not follow, if he succeeds, that breaking the table was not something he did; nor again does it follow, as LP would require, that he was not responsible for breaking it.[17] The inference sanctioned by LP from 'it was undetermined' to 'he was not responsible', is not valid. The above cases are counterexamples to it; and there are many more.

IV. POSSIBLE WORLDS AND LP*

But one may grant this and still object that counterexamples to LP of these kinds do not amount to genuine exercises of free will involving SFAs, such as the businesswoman's, where there is conflict in the wills of the agents and they are supposed to choose freely and responsibly *whichever* way they choose. If the assassin and husband succeed in doing what they are trying to do (kill the prime minister, break the table) they will do it *voluntarily* (in accordance with their wills) and *intentionally* (knowingly and purposely). But if they *fail* because of the indeterminism, they will not fail voluntarily and intentionally, but "by mistake" or "accident," or merely "by chance." Thus, their "power" to do *otherwise* (if we should even call it a power) is not the usual power we associate with freedom of choice or action in self-formation, where the agents should be able to choose or act either way voluntarily or intentionally. The power to do otherwise of the assassin and the husband is more like Jane's "power" in (5) and (6) of section II, to choose to vacation in Colorado by a fluke or accident, after a long deliberation in which she had come to favor Hawaii.

As a consequence, while LP may fail for cases like those of the assassin, husband, and mathematical problem solver, another luck principle similar to LP might still be applicable to genuine exercises of free will involving SFAs, like the businesswoman's: if it is undetermined at t whether an agent *voluntarily* and *intentionally* does A at t or *voluntarily* and *intentionally* does otherwise, then the agent's doing one of these rather than the other at t

[17] We must, of course, assume in both these examples that other (compatibilist) conditions for responsibility are in place—for example, that, despite his anger, the husband was not acting compulsively and would have controlled himself, if he had wished; that he knew what he was doing and was doing it intentionally to anger his wife, and so on (and similarly for the assassin). But the point is that nothing in the facts of either case preclude these assumptions from also being satisfied.

would be a matter of *luck* or *chance*, and so could not be a free and responsible action. This principle—let us call it LP*—is fueled by the same intuitions that fuel LP. Indeed, it is a special case of LP, but one that is more
difficult to deal with because it is not subject to counterexamples like those
of the husband and the assassin; and it seems to be applicable to SFAs, like
the businesswoman's, where failure is not merely a matter of mistake or
accident.

To explore further the difficulties posed by LP*, let us look at the final
and, I think, most powerful of the intuition pumps in support of LP-type
principles mentioned in section II, namely, consideration (8). This was the
argument of Strawson, Mele, Berofsky, Waller, Double, Bernstein, and Haji
about two agents, or one agent in different possible worlds, with the same
pasts.

Consider the version of this argument by Mele, which appeared in this
JOURNAL and is a particularly revealing and challenging version of it. In the
actual world, an agent John succumbs to the temptation to arrive late to a
meeting, whereas his counterpart, John*, in a nearby possible world, whose
physical and psychological history is the same as John's up to the moment of
choice (as indeterminism requires), resists this temptation. Similarly, we can
imagine a counterpart to the businesswoman, businesswoman*, in a nearby
possible world who goes to her meeting instead of stopping to aid the assault
victim, given the same past. But then, Mele argues, "if there is nothing about
[these] agents' powers, capacities, states of mind, moral character and the
like that explains this difference in outcome," since they are the same up to
the moment of choice in the two possible worlds, "then the difference is just
a matter of luck" (*op. cit.*, p. 583).[18] It would seem that John* got lucky in his
attempt to overcome temptation, whereas John did not; and similarly, the
businesswoman got lucky in her attempt to overcome temptation, while
businesswoman* did not.

Let us first consider a general form of this argument that would support
LP.

    (a) In the actual world, person P (for example, John, the businesswoman)
        does A at t.

On the assumption that the act is undetermined at t, we may imagine that:

    (b) In a nearby-possible world which is the same as the actual world up to
        t, P^* (P's counterpart with the same past) does otherwise (does B) at t.

---

[18] I have elsewhere denied that the pasts of the agents can be exactly the same, since, with
indeterminist efforts, there is no exact sameness or difference (*The Significance of Free Will*,
pp. 171–74). Mele's argument is designed to work, however, whether this denial of exact sameness
is assumed or not. So I do not make an issue of it here.

(c) But then (since their pasts are the same), there is nothing about the agents' powers, capacities, states of mind, characters, dispositions, motives, and so on prior to t which explains the difference in choices in the two possible worlds.

(d) It is therefore a matter of luck or chance that P does A and P^* does B at t.

(e) P is therefore not responsible (praiseworthy or blameworthy, as the case may be) for A at t (and presumably P^* is also not responsible for B).

Call this the *luck argument*. The key assumption is the assumption of indeterminism, which leads to step (b). The remaining steps are meant to follow from (b), given (a).

Despite the fact that this argument looks like Mele's and has an initial plausibility, it is not his argument—and it is a good thing it is not. For the argument from (a)–(e) is invalid as it stands—for the same reasons that LP was invalid. Consider the husband and husband* (his counterpart in a nearby world who fails to break the wife's table). If the outcome is undetermined, husband and husband* also have "the same powers, capacities, states of mind, characters, dispositions, motives, and so on" up to the moment of breaking or not breaking the table, as the argument requires; and it is a matter of luck or chance that the table breaks in one world and not the other. But for all that, it does not follow, as (e) requires, that the husband is not responsible for breaking the table. The husband would have quite a task persuading his wife that he was not responsible for breaking the table on the grounds that it was a matter of luck or chance that it broke. ("Luck or chance did it, not me" is an implausible excuse.)

But, of course, as we noted, husband* is not also responsible for *failing* to break the table, since he does not fail to break it voluntarily or intentionally. He is responsible only for the attempt, when he fails. Similarly, assassin* would be responsible for the attempted murder of the prime minister, when he missed. What has to be explicitly added to the argument (a)–(e) to avoid counterexamples like these is the LP* requirement that *both* P and P^* *voluntarily* and *intentionally* do A and B respectively in their respective worlds. Specifically, we must add to premise (a) that P voluntarily and intentionally does A at t and to (b), that P^* voluntarily and intentionally does B at t, and then make the corresponding additions to (d) and (e). This will yield what we might call the LP* version of the luck argument rather than the LP version. And the stronger LP* version is clearly the one Mele intends, since John's choice in his example is supposed to be an SFA, like the businesswoman's choice in my example, where the agents can go either way voluntarily and intentionally. Moreover, this version of the argument—like LP* itself—is immune to counterexamples like those of the husband and the assassin.

V. PARALLEL PROCESSING

Nonetheless, despite immunity from these counterexamples, I think the LP* version of the luck argument, and LP* itself, also fail. But it is far less easy to show why. To do so, we have to take a closer look at SFAs and push the argument beyond where it has come thus far. Let it be granted that the businesswoman's case and other SFAs like John's are not like the examples of the husband and the assassin. The wills of the husband and assassin are already "set" on doing what they intend, whereas the wills of agents in SFAs, like the businesswoman and John, are not already settled or "formed" until they choose (hence the designation "self-forming actions").[19]

Thus, to get from examples like those of the husband and assassin to genuine SFAs, I think we must do two things. First, we must put the indeterminacy involved in the efferent neural pathways of the husband and assassin into the central neural processes of the businesswoman and other agents, like John, who are making efforts of will to overcome moral, prudential, and other temptations. This move has already been made in earlier sections. But to respond to LP* versions of the luck argument, like Mele's, I believe this move must also be combined with another—a kind of "doubling" of the example given earlier of solving the mathematical problem in the presence of background indeterministic noise.[20]

Imagine that the businesswoman is *trying* or making an effort to solve *two* cognitive problems at once, or to complete two competing (deliberative) tasks at once—to make a moral choice and to make a choice for her ambitions (corresponding to the two competing neural networks involved in the earlier description). With respect to each task, as with the mathematical problem, she is being thwarted in her attempt to do what she is trying to do by indeterminism. But in her case, the indeterminism does not have a mere external source; it is coming from her own will, from her desire to do the opposite. Recall that the two crossing neural networks involved are

---

[19] See *The Significance of Free Will*, pp. 112–14.

[20] This further "doubling" move is consistent with the theory put forward in *The Significance of Free Will*, and presupposes much of that theory, but is not made in that work. It is a further development especially provoked by Mele's argument discussed here as well as by criticisms of other persons since the book's publication, such as Strawson, Berofsky, Nicholas Nathan, Gary Watson, Clarke, O'Connor, Double, and Haji.

connected, so that the indeterminism which is making it uncertain that she will do the moral thing is coming from her desire to do the opposite, and vice versa. She may therefore fail to do what she is trying to do, just like the assassin, the husband, and the person trying to solve the mathematical problem. But I argue that, if she nevertheless *succeeds*, then she can be held responsible because, like them, she will have succeeded in doing *what she was trying to do*. And the interesting thing is that this will be true of her, *whichever choice is made*, because she was trying to make both choices and one is going to succeed.

Does it make sense to talk about agents trying to do two competing things at once in this way? Well, we know the brain is a parallel processor and that capacity, I believe, is essential for the exercise of free will. In cases of self-formation, agents are simultaneously trying to resolve plural and competing cognitive tasks. They are, as we say, of two minds. But they are not therefore two separate persons. They are not disassociated from either task.[21] The businesswoman who wants to go back and help the assault victim is the same ambitious woman who wants to go on to her meeting and close the sale. She is a complex creature, like most of us who are often torn inside; but hers is the kind of complexity needed for free will. And when she succeeds in doing one of the things she is trying to do, she will endorse that as *her* resolution of the conflict in her will, voluntarily and intentionally, as LP* requires. She will not disassociate from either outcome, as did Jane (in (5) of section II), who wondered what "happened to" her when she chose Colorado, or like the husband and assassin who did not also want to fail.[22]

But one may still object that the businesswoman makes one choice rather than the other *by chance*, since it was undetermined right up to the last moment which choice she would make. If this is so, we may have the picture of her first making an effort to overcome temptation (to go on to her meeting) and do the moral thing, and then at the last minute "chance takes over" and decides the issue for her. But this is the wrong picture. On the view just described, you cannot separate the indeterminism from the effort to overcome temptation in such a way that *first* the effort occurs *followed by* chance

---

[21] I account for this elsewhere in terms of the notion of a "self-network" (*The Significance of Free Will*, pp. 137–42), a more comprehensive network of neural connections representing the general motivational system in terms of which agents define themselves as agents and practical reasoners. For further discussion of such a notion, see Owen Flanagan, *Consciousness Reconsidered* (Cambridge: MIT, 1992), pp. 207 ff.

[22] In response to my claim (*The Significance of Free Will*, p. 215) that "free willers [who engage in SFAs] are always trying to be better than they are by their own lights," by trying to overcome temptations of various sorts, Strawson asks: but "can't they also try to be worse than they are?"— "The Unhelpfulness of Indeterminism." He is right, of course; they can. I should have added what I am saying here, that free willers can and do *also* try to be as bad or worse than they are by resisting efforts to be better. Strange creatures indeed.

or luck (or vice versa). One must think of the effort and the indeterminism as fused; the effort *is* indeterminate and the indeterminism is a property of the effort, not something separate that occurs after or before the effort. The fact that the woman's effort of will has this property of being indeterminate does not make it any less her *effort*. The complex recurrent neural network that realizes the effort in the brain is circulating impulses in feedback loops and there is some indeterminacy in these circulating impulses. But the whole process is her effort of will and it persists right up to the moment when the choice is made. There is no point at which the effort stops and chance "takes over." She chooses *as a result of* the effort, even though she might have failed because of the indeterminism.

And just as expressions like 'She chose *by* chance' can mislead us in these contexts, so can expressions like 'She got lucky'. Ask yourself this question: Why does the inference 'He got lucky, *so he was not responsible*' fail when it does fail, as in the cases of the husband and the assassin? The first part of an answer goes back to the claim that 'luck', like 'chance', has question-begging implications in ordinary language which are not necessarily implications of "indeterminism" (which implies only the absence of deterministic causation). The core meaning of 'He got lucky', which *is* implied by indeterminism, I suggest, is that 'He succeeded *despite the probability or chance of failure*'; and this core meaning does not imply lack of responsibility, if he succeeds.

If 'He got lucky' had further meanings in these contexts often associated with 'luck' and 'chance' in ordinary usage (for example, the outcome was not his doing, or occurred by *mere* chance, or he was not responsible for it), the inference would not fail for the husband and assassin, as it clearly does. But the point is that these further meanings of 'luck' and 'chance' do not follow *from the mere presence of indeterminism*. Second, the inference 'He got lucky, so he was not responsible' fails because *what* the assassin and husband succeeded in doing was what they were trying and wanting to do all along. Third, *when* they succeeded, their reaction was not "Oh dear, that was a mistake, an accident—something that *happened* to me, not something I *did*." Rather, they *endorsed* the outcomes as something they were trying and wanting to do all along, that is to say, knowingly and purposefully, not by mistake or accident.

But these conditions are satisfied in the businesswoman's case as well, *either way* she chooses. If she succeeds in choosing to return to help the victim (or in choosing to go on to her meeting) (i) she will have "succeeded despite the probability or chance of failure"; (ii) she will have succeeded in doing what she was trying and wanting to do all along (she wanted both outcomes very much, but for different reasons, and was trying to make those reasons prevail in both cases); and (iii) when she succeeded (in choosing to return to help) her reaction was not "Oh dear, that was a mistake, an accident—something that happened to me, not something I did." Rather, she endorsed the outcome as something she was trying and wanting to do all along; she recognized it as her resolution of the conflict in her will. And if she had chosen to go on to her meeting she would have endorsed that outcome, recognizing it as her resolution of the conflict in her will.

VI. THE LUCK ARGUMENT REVISITED

With this in mind, let us return to the LP* version of the argument from (a)-(e). I said that Mele clearly intends this stronger LP* version of the argument, since the force of his argument depends on the fact that John's choice in his example is a SFA, like the businesswoman's, instead of being like the actions of the husband and assassin. But if this is so, then John's situation will also be like the businesswoman's on the account just given of SFAs. Since both of them are simultaneously trying to do *both* of the things they may do (choose to help or go on, overcome the temptation to arrive late or not), they will do either with intent or on purpose, as a result of wanting and trying to do it—that is, intentionally and voluntarily. Thus, their "failing" to do one of the options will not be a mistake or accident, but a voluntary and intentional doing *of the other*.

Likewise, businesswoman* and John* are simultaneously trying to do both things in their respective worlds; and they will not "fail" to act on moral or weak-willed motives by mistake or accident, as the case may be, but by voluntarily and intentionally choosing to act on the opposing motives. The point is that in self-formation of these kinds (SFAs), failing is never *just* failing; it is always also a *succeeding* in doing something else we wanted and were trying to do. And we found that one can be responsible for succeeding in doing what one was trying to do, even in the presence of indeterminism. So even if we add the LP* requirement of more-than-one-way voluntariness and intentionality to the argument of (a)–(e), the argument remains invalid for cases like the businesswoman's and other SFAs, like John's.

But one might argue further, as Mele does, that John and John* (and businesswoman and businesswoman*) not only had the same capacities, motives, characters, and the like prior to choice, but they made exactly the same *efforts* as well. And this does seem to suggest that the success of one and failure of the other was a matter of mere luck or chance, so that John and the businesswoman were not responsible. But again the inference is too hasty. Note, first, that husband and husband* also made the same efforts (as well as having the same capacities, motives, and characters) up to the very moment of breaking of the table. Yet it does not follow that the husband is not responsible when he succeeds. And *both* the businesswoman and businesswoman*, and John and John*, are in the position of the husband in their respective worlds, since both will have succeeded in doing what they were trying to do.

But one may still want to object: if the businesswoman and businesswoman*, and John and John*, make exactly the same efforts, how can it *not* be a matter of chance that one succeeds and the other does not, in a way that makes them not responsible? To which I reply: But if they both succeeded in doing what they were trying to do (because they were simultaneously trying to do both things), and then having succeeded, they both *endorsed* the outcomes of their respective efforts (that is, their choices) as what they were trying to do, instead of disowning or disassociating from those choices, how then can we *not* hold them responsible? It just does not follow that, because they made exactly the same efforts, they chose *by* chance.

To say something was done "by chance" usually means (as in the assassin and husband cases when they fail), it was done "by mistake" or "accidentally," "inadvertently," "involuntarily," or "as an unintended fluke." But none of these things holds of the businesswoman and John either way they choose. Unlike husband*, businesswoman* and John do not fail to overcome temptation by mistake or accident, inadvertently or involuntarily. They consciously and willingly fail to overcome temptation *by* consciously and willingly choosing to act in selfish or weak-willed ways. So, just as it would have been a poor excuse for the husband to say to his wife when the table broke that "Luck or chance did it, not me," it would be a poor excuse for businesswoman* and John to say "Luck or chance did it, not me" when they failed to help the assault victim or failed to arrive on time.

Worth highlighting in this argument is the point that we cannot simply say the businesswoman and businesswoman* (or John and John*) made exactly the same *effort* (in the singular) in their respective possible worlds and one succeeded while the other failed. We must say they made exactly the same *efforts* (plural) in their respective worlds. Mentioning only one effort prejudices the case, for it suggests that the failure of that effort in one of the worlds was a *mere* mistake or accident, when the fact is that both of the agents (P and P^*) made *both* efforts in *both* worlds. In one world, one of the efforts issued in a choice and in the other world, a different effort issued in a different choice; but neither was merely accidental or inadvertent in either world. I would go even further and say that we may also doubt that the efforts they were both making really were exactly the same. Where events are indeterminate, as are the efforts they were making, there is no such thing as exact sameness or difference of events in different possible worlds. Their efforts were not exactly the same, nor were they exactly different, because they were not exact. They were simply unique.[23]

One might try another line: perhaps we are begging the question in assuming that the outcomes of the efforts of the businesswoman and her counterpart were *choices* at all. If they were not choices to begin with, they could not have been voluntary choices. One might argue this on the grounds that (A) "If an event is undetermined, it must be something that merely happens and cannot be somebody's choice"; and (B) "If an event is undetermined, it must be something that merely happens, it cannot be something an agent does (it cannot be an action)." But to see how question-begging these assumptions are, one has only to note that (A) and (B) imply respectively (A′) "If an event is a choice, it must be determined" ("All choices are determined") and (B′) "If an event is an action, it must be determined" ("All actions are determined"). Are these supposed to be a priori or analytic truths? If so, then long-standing issues about freedom and determinism would be settled by fiat. If an event were not determined, it could not be a choice or action necessarily or by definition.[24]

This explains the businesswoman's suspicions when she exited the neuroscientists' offices. They told her that when she "chose" to go back to help the assault victim the day before, there was some indeterminism in her neural processes prior to choice. She accepted this as a correct empirical finding. But she was suspicious when the neuroscientists tried to get her to make the further inference from those findings that she did not really *choose* to help the assault victim yesterday. She refused to accept that conclusion, and rightly so. For in drawing it, they were going beyond their empirical findings and trying to foist on her the a priori assumption that if an event was undetermined, it could not have been her choice or could not have been something she did. She rightly saw that there was nothing in the empirical evidence that required her to say that. To choose is consciously and deliberately to form an intention to do something; and she did that, despite the indeterminism in her neural processes (as did businesswoman* when she chose to go on to her meeting).

---

[23] See *The Significance of Free Will*, pp. 171–74.

[24] Ibid., pp. 183–86, for a fuller account of why indeterminism does not rule out action or choice.

VII. FINAL CONSIDERATIONS: CONTROL AND EXPLANATION

But it is one thing to say that she chose and another to say she chose *freely* and *responsibly*. This would require that she not only chose, but had voluntary *control* over her choice either way. We have not talked at length to this point about the matter of control (considerations (1) and (3) of section II) and must now do so. For this may be the reason why we may think the choices made by the businesswoman and businesswoman* (or John and John*) could not be responsible, if they were undetermined. We might deny that they had voluntary control over what they chose, where voluntary control means being able to bring about something in accordance with one's will or purposes (or, as we often say, the ability to bring something about "at will").

One thing does seem to be true about control which critics of indeterminist freedom have always maintained: indeterminism, wherever it appears, does seem to *diminish* rather than enhance agents' voluntary control (consideration (3) of section II). The assassin's voluntary control over whether or not the prime minister is killed (his ability to realize his purpose or what he is trying to do) is diminished by the undetermined impulses in his arm—and so also for the husband and his breaking the table. Moreover, this limitation is connected to another, which I think we must also grant—that indeterminism, wherever it occurs, functions as a *hindrance* or *obstacle* to our purposes that must be overcome by effort (consideration (3)).

But recall that in the businesswoman's case (and for SFAs generally, like John's), the indeterminism that is admittedly diminishing her ability to overcome selfish temptation, and *is* indeed a hindrance to her doing so, is coming from her own will—from her desire and effort to do the opposite—since she is simultaneously trying to realize two conflicting purposes at once. Similarly, her ability to overcome moral qualms is diminished by the fact that she also simultaneously wants and is trying to act on moral reasons. If we could look at each of the two competing neural networks involved separately, abstracting from the other, the situation would look analogous to the situations of the husband and the assassin. The agent would be trying to do something while being hindered by indeterminism coming from an external source. But, in fact, we cannot look at the two networks separately in this way because, in reality, they are connected and interacting. The indeterminism that is a hindrance to her fulfilling one is coming from its interactions with the other. The indeterminism, therefore, does not have an external source. It is internal to her will, and hence to her self, since she identifies with both networks and will identify with the choice reached by either of them as her choice.

The upshot is that, despite the businesswoman's diminished control over *each* option considered separately, due to a conflict in her will, she nonetheless has what I call *plural voluntary control* over the two options considered *as a set* (ibid., pp. 134–43). Having plural voluntary control over a set of options means being able to bring about *whichever* of the options you will or most want, *when* you will to do so, for the reasons you will to do so, without being coerced or compelled in doing so. And the businesswoman (or John) has this power, because whichever of the options she chooses (to help the victim or go on to her meeting) will be *endorsed* by her as what she wills or most wants to do at the moment when she chooses it (though not necessarily beforehand); she will choose it for the reasons she most wants to act on then and there (moral or selfish reasons, as the case may be); she need not have been coerced by anyone else into choosing one rather than the other; and she will not be choosing either compulsively, since neither choice is such that she could not have chosen it then and there, even if she most wanted to.[25]

One must add, of course, that such plural voluntary control is not the same as what may be called *antecedent determining control*—the ability to determine or guarantee which of a set of options will occur *before* it occurs (ibid., p. 144). With respect to undetermined self-forming choices (SFAs), agents cannot determine or guarantee which choice outcome will occur *beforehand*; for that could only be done by predetermining the outcome. But it does not follow that, because one cannot determine which of a set of outcomes will occur before it occurs, one does not determine which of them occurs *when* it occurs. When the conditions of plural voluntary control are satisfied, agents exercise control over their present and future lives then and there by deciding.

But can we not at least say that, if indeterminism is involved, then *which* option is chosen is "arbitrary"? I grant that there is a sense in which this is true. An ultimate arbitrariness remains in all undetermined SFAs because there cannot, in principle, be sufficient or overriding *prior* reasons for making one set of competing reasons prevail over the other. But I argue that such arbitrariness relative to prior reasons tells us something important about free will. It tells us, as I have elsewhere expressed it, that every undetermined self-forming choice (SFA) "is the initiation of a 'value experiment' whose justification lies in the *future* and is not fully explained by the *past*. [Making such a choice], we say in effect, 'Let's try this. It is not required by my past, but is consistent with my past and is one branching pathway my life could

---

[25] *The Significance of Free Will*, pp. 133–38, where a more detailed case is made for each of these claims.

now meaningfully take. I am willing to take responsibility for it one way or the other'" (ibid., pp. 145–46). To initiate and take responsibility for such value experiments whose justification lies in the future, is to "take chances" without prior guarantees of success. Genuine self-formation requires this sort of risk-taking and indeterminism is a part of it. If there are persons who need to be certain in advance just exactly what is the best or right thing to do in every circumstance (perhaps to be told so by some human or divine authority), then free will is not for them.

This point also throws light on why the luck argument fails, even in the stronger LP* version, despite its initial plausibility. Consider the move from step (c)—the agents P and P^* have the same powers, characters, motives, and the like, prior to t in the two possible worlds—to step (d), which says it was a matter of luck or chance that P did A and P^* did B at t. An important reason given for this move was that, if both agents have all the same prior powers, characters, motives, and the like, there can be no "explanation of the difference in choice" between the two agents in terms of their prior reasons or motives; and this is taken to imply that the difference in choices in the two worlds is a matter of luck or chance *in a way* that precludes responsibility.

But this move, like others discussed earlier, is too hasty. The absence of an explanation of the difference in choice in terms of prior reasons does not have the tight connection to issues of responsibility one might initially credit it with. For one thing, the absence of such an explanation does not imply (as I have been arguing throughout this paper) that businesswoman and businesswoman* (John and John*) (1) did not *choose* at all, nor does it imply that they did not both choose (2) *as a result of their efforts*, nor that they did not choose (3) *for reasons* (different reasons, of course) that (4) they most wanted to choose for *when* they chose, nor that they did not choose for those reasons (5) *knowingly* and (6) *on purpose* when they chose, and hence (7) *rationally*, (8) *voluntarily*, and (9) *intentionally*. None of these conditions is precluded by the absence of an explanation of the difference of choice in terms of prior reasons. Yet these are precisely the kinds of conditions we look for when deciding whether or not persons are responsible.

I suggest that the reason why these conditions are not excluded is that the explanation of the difference of choice in the two possible worlds which is missing is an explanation in terms of *sufficient* or *conclusive* reasons—one that would render an alternative choice, given the same prior reasons, irrational or inexplicable. And, of course, *that* sort of explanation is not possible for undetermined SFAs, when there is conflict in the will and the agent has good (but not decisive or conclusive) prior reasons for going either way. But neither is that sort of explanation required to say that an agent acts as the result of her effort for reasons she most wants to act on then and there.

In sum, *you can choose responsibly for prior reasons that were not conclusive or decisive prior to your choosing for them.*

I said a moment ago that such arbitrariness relative to prior reasons tells us something important about free will—that every self-forming choice is the initiation of a value experiment whose justification lies in the future and cannot be fully explained by the past. It is worth adding in this regard that the term 'arbitrary' comes from the Latin *arbitrium*, which means 'judgment'—as in *liberum arbitrium voluntatis* ("free judgment of the will")—the medieval designation for free will. Imagine a writer in the middle of a novel. The novel's heroine faces a crisis and the writer has not yet developed her character in sufficient detail to say exactly how she will react. The author must make a "judgment" (*arbitrium*) about how she will react that is not determined by the heroine's already formed past, which does not give unique direction. In this sense, the author's judgment of how she will act is "arbitrary," but not entirely so. It has input from the heroine's fictional past and, in turn, gives input to her projected future.

In a similar manner, agents who exercise free will are both authors of, and characters in, their own stories at once. By virtue of "self-forming" judgments of the will (*arbitria voluntatis*), they are "arbiters" of their own lives, taking responsibility for "making themselves" out of past that, if they are truly free, does not limit their future pathways to one. If someone should charge them with not having a sufficient or conclusive prior reason for choosing as they did, they may reply as follows: "Perhaps so. But that does not mean I did not *choose*, and it does not mean I did not choose for *good* reasons, which I stand by and for which I take responsibility. If I lacked sufficient or conclusive prior reasons, that is because, like the heroine of the novel, I was not a fully formed person before I chose—and still am not, for that matter.[26] Like the author of the novel, I am in the process of writing a story and forming a person (who, in my case, is myself). It is a heavy burden, but an eminently human one."

[26] Jan Branson (in "Alternatives of Oneself," *Philosophy and Phenomenological Research* (forthcoming)) has made an important distinction that is relevant here—between choosing "alternatives *for* oneself" and choosing "alternatives *of* oneself." Branson notes that some choices in life are for different courses of action that will make a difference in what sort of person the chooser will become in future. In such cases, agents are not merely choosing alternatives for themselves but are choosing alternatives of themselves. Many SFAs, as I understand them, would be of this kind.

16

FREEDOM OF THE WILL AND THE CONCEPT
OF A PERSON

HARRY G. FRANKFURT

What philosophers have lately come to accept as analysis of the concept of a person is not actually analysis of *that* concept at all. Strawson, whose usage represents the current standard, identifies the concept of a person as 'the concept of a type of entity such that *both* predicates ascribing states of consciousness *and* predicates ascribing corporeal characteristics ... are equally applicable to a single individual of that single type'.[1] But there are many entities besides persons that have both mental and physical properties. As it happens—though it seems extraordinary that this should be so—there is no common English word for the type of entity Strawson has in mind, a type that includes not only human beings but animals of various lesser species as well. Still, this hardly justifies the misappropriation of a valuable philosophical term.

Whether the members of some animal species are persons is surely not to be settled merely by determining whether it is correct to apply to them, in addition to predicates ascribing corporeal characteristics, predicates that ascribe states of consciousness. It does violence to our language to endorse the application of the term 'person' to those numerous creatures which do have both psychological and material properties but which are manifestly not persons in any normal sense of the word. This misuse of language is doubtless innocent of any theoretical error. But although the offence is 'merely verbal', it does significant harm. For it gratuitously diminishes our philosophical vocabulary, and it increases the likelihood that we will over-look the important area of inquiry with which the term 'person' is most naturally associated. It might have been expected that no problem would be

From the *Journal of Philosophy*, 68/1 (1971), 5–20. Reprinted by permission of the publisher and the author.

[1] P. F. Strawson, *Individuals* (London: Methuen, 1959), 101–2. Ayer's usage of 'person' is similar: 'it is characteristic of persons in this sense that besides having various physical proper-ties ... they are also credited with various forms of consciousness' (A. J. Ayer, *The Concept of a Person* (New York: St. Martin's, 1963), 82). What concerns Strawson and Ayer is the problem of understanding the relation between mind and body, rather than the quite different problem of understanding what it is to be a creature that not only has a mind and a body but is also a person.

of more central and persistent concern to philosophers than that of understanding what we ourselves essentially are. Yet this problem is so generally neglected that it has been possible to make off with its very name almost without being noticed and, evidently, without evoking any widespread feeling of loss.

There is a sense in which the word 'person' is merely the singular form of 'people' and in which both terms connote no more than membership in a certain biological species. In those senses of the word which are of greater philosophical interest, however, the criteria for being a person do not serve primarily to distinguish the members of our own species from the members of other species. Rather, they are designed to capture those attributes which are the subject of our most humane concern with ourselves and the source of what we regard as most important and most problematical in our lives. Now these attributes would be of equal significance to us even if they were not in fact peculiar and common to the members of our own species. What interests us most in the human condition would not interest us less if it were also a feature of the condition of other creatures as well.

Our concept of ourselves as persons is not to be understood, therefore, as a concept of attributes that are necessarily species-specific. It is conceptually possible that members of novel or even of familiar non-human species should be persons; and it is also conceptually possible that some members of the human species are not persons. We do in fact assume, on the other hand, that no member of another species is a person. Accordingly, there is a presumption that what is essential to persons is a set of characteristics that we generally suppose—whether rightly or wrongly—to be uniquely human.

It is my view that one essential difference between persons and other creatures is to be found in the structure of a person's will. Human beings are not alone in having desires and motives, or in making choices. They share these things with the members of certain other species, some of whom even appear to engage in deliberation and to make decisions based upon prior thought. It seems to be peculiarly characteristic of humans, however, that they are able to form what I shall call 'second-order desires' or 'desires of the second order'.

Besides wanting and choosing and being moved *to do* this or that, men may also want to have (or not to have) certain desires and motives. They are capable of wanting to be different, in their preferences and purposes, from what they are. Many animals appear to have the capacity for what I shall call 'first-order desires' or 'desires of the first order', which are simply desires to do or not to do one thing or another. No animal other than man, however, appears to have the capacity for reflective self-evaluation that is manifested in the formation of second-order desires.[2]

I

The concept designated by the verb 'to want' is extraordinarily elusive. A statement of the form '*A* wants to *X*'—taken by itself, apart from a context that serves to amplify or to specify its meaning—conveys remarkably little information. Such a statement may be consistent, for example, with each of the following statements: (a) the prospect of doing *X* elicits no sensation or introspectible emotional response in *A*; (b) *A* is unaware that he wants to *X*; (c) *A* believes that he does not want to *X*; (d) *A* wants to refrain from *X*-ing; (e) *A* wants to *Y* and believes that it is impossible for him both to *Y* and to *X*; (f) *A* does not 'really' want to *X*; (g) *A would rather die than X*; and so on. It is therefore hardly sufficient to formulate the distinction between first-order and second-order desires, as I have done, by suggesting merely that someone has a first-order desire when he wants to do or not to do such-and-such, and that he has a second-order desire when he wants to have or not to have a certain desire of the first order.

As I shall understand them, statements of the form '*A* wants to *X*' cover a rather broad range of possibilities.[3] They may be true even when statements like (a) through (g) are true: when *A* is unaware of any feelings concerning *X*-ing, when he is unaware that he wants to *X*, when he deceives himself about what he wants and believes falsely that he does not want to *X*, when he also has other desires that conflict with his desire to *X*, or when he is ambivalent. The desires in question may be conscious or unconscious, they need not be univocal, and *A* may be mistaken about them. There is a further source of uncertainty with regard to statements that identify someone's desires, however, and here it is important for my purposes to be less permissive.

Consider first those statements of the form '*A* wants to *X*' which identify first-order desires—that is, statements in which the term 'to *X*' refers to an

---

[2] For the sake of simplicity, I shall deal only with what someone wants or desires, neglecting related phenomena such as choices and decisions. I propose to use the verbs 'to want' and 'to desire' interchangeably, although they are by no means perfect synonyms. My motive in forsaking the established nuances of these words arises from the fact that the verb 'to want', which suits my purposes better so far as its meaning is concerned, does not lend itself so readily to the formation of nouns as does the verb 'to desire'. It is perhaps acceptable, albeit graceless, to speak in the plural of someone's 'wants'. But to speak in the singular of someone's 'want' would be an abomination.

[3] What I say in this paragraph applies not only to cases in which 'to *X*' refers to a possible action or inaction. It also applies to cases in which 'to *X*' refers to a first-order desire and in which the statement that '*A* wants to *X*' is therefore a shortened version of a statement—'*A* wants to want *X*'—that identifies a desire of the second order.

action. A statement of this kind does not, by itself, indicate the relative strength of A's desire to X. It does not make it clear whether this desire is at all likely to play a decisive role in what A actually does or tries to do. For it may correctly be said that A wants to X even when his desire to X is only one among his desires and when it is far from being paramount among them. Thus, it may be true that A wants to X when he strongly prefers to do something else instead; and it may be true that he wants to X despite the fact that, when he acts, it is not the desire to X that motivates him to do what he does. On the other hand, someone who states that A wants to X may mean to convey that it is this desire that is motivating or moving A to do what he is actually doing or that A will in fact be moved by this desire (unless he changes his mind) when he acts.

It is only when it is used in the second of these ways that, given the special usage of 'will' that I propose to adopt, the statement identifies A's will. To identify an agent's will is either to identify the desire (or desires) by which he is motivated in some action he performs or to identify the desire (or desires) by which he will or would be motivated when or if he acts. An agent's will, then, is identical with one or more of his first-order desires. But the notion of the will, as I am employing it, is not coextensive with the notion of first-order desires. It is not the notion of something that merely inclines an agent in some degree to act in a certain way. Rather, it is the notion of an *effective* desire—one that moves (or will or would move) a person all the way to action. Thus the notion of the will is not coextensive with the notion of what an agent intends to do. For even though someone may have a settled intention to do X, he may none the less do something else instead of doing X because, despite his intention, his desire to do X proves to be weaker or less effective than some conflicting desire.

Now consider those statements of the form 'A wants to x' which identify second-order desires—that is, statements in which the term 'to X' refers to a desire of the first order. There are also two kinds of situation in which it may be true that A wants to want to X. In the first place, it might be true of A that he wants to have a desire to X despite the fact that he has a univocal desire, altogether free of conflict and ambivalence, to refrain from x-ing. Someone might want to have a certain desire, in other words, but univocally want that desire to be unsatisfied.

Suppose that a physician engaged in psychotherapy with narcotics addicts believes that his ability to help his patients would be enhanced if he understood better what it is like for them to desire the drug to which they are addicted. Suppose that he is led in this way to want to have a desire for the drug. If it is a genuine desire that he wants, then what he wants is not merely to feel the sensations that addicts characteristically feel when they are gripped by their desires for the drug. What the physician wants, in so far as he wants to have a desire, is to be inclined or moved to some extent to take the drug.

It is entirely possible, however, that, although he wants to be moved by a desire to take the drug, he does not want this desire to be effective. He may not want it to move him all the way to action. He need not be interested in finding out what it is like to take the drug. And in so far as he now wants only to *want* to take it, and not to *take* it, there is nothing in what he now wants that would be satisfied by the drug itself. He may now have, in fact, an altogether univocal desire *not* to take the drug; and he may prudently arrange to make it impossible for him to satisfy the desire he would have if his desire to want the drug should in time be satisfied.

It would thus be incorrect to infer, from the fact that the physician now wants to desire to take the drug, that he already does desire to take it. His second-order desire to be moved to take the drug does not entail that he has a first-order desire to take it. If the drug were now to be administered to him, this might satisfy no desire that is implicit in his desire to want to take it. While he wants to want to take the drug, he may have *no* desire to take it; it may be that *all* he wants is to taste the desire for it. That is, his desire to have a certain desire that he does not have may not be a desire that his will should be at all different than it is.

Someone who wants only in this truncated way to want to X stands at the margin of preciosity, and the fact that he wants to want to X is not pertinent to the identification of his will. There is, however, a second kind of situation that may be described by 'A wants to X'; and when the statement is used to describe a situation of this second kind, then it does pertain to what A wants his will to be. In such cases the statement means that A wants the desire to X to be the desire that moves him effectively to act. It is not merely that he wants the desire to X to be among the desires by which, to one degree or another, he is moved or inclined to act. He wants this desire to be effective— that is, to provide the motive in what he actually does. Now when the statement that A wants to want to X is used in this way, it does entail that A already has a desire to X. It could not be true both that A wants the desire to X to move him into action and that he does not want to X. It is only if he does want to X that he can coherently want the desire to X not merely to be one of his desires but, more decisively, to be his will.[4]

---

[4] It is not so clear that the entailment relation described here holds in certain kinds of cases, which I think may fairly be regarded as non-standard, where the essential difference between the standard and the non-standard cases lies in the kind of description by which the first-order desire in question is identified. Thus, suppose that A admires B so fulsomely that, even though he does not know what B wants to do, he wants to be effectively moved by whatever desire effectively

Suppose a man wants to be motivated in what he does by the desire to concentrate on his work. It is necessarily true, if this supposition is correct, that he already wants to concentrate on his work. This desire is now among his desires. But the question of whether or not his second-order desire is fulfilled does not turn merely on whether the desire he wants is one of his desires. It turns on whether this desire is, as he wants it to be, his effective desire or will. If, when the chips are down, it is his desire to concentrate on his work that moves him to do what he does, then what he wants at that time is indeed (in the relevant sense) what he wants to want. If it is some other desire that actually moves him when he acts, on the other hand, then what he wants at that time is not (in the relevant sense) what he wants to want. This will be so despite the fact that the desire to concentrate on his work continues to be among his desires.

II

Someone has a desire of the second order either when he wants simply to have a certain desire or when he wants a certain desire to be his will. In situations of the latter kind, I shall call his second-order desires 'second-order volitions' or 'volitions of the second order'. Now it is having second-order volitions, and not having second-order desires generally, that I regard as essential to being a person. It is logically possible, however unlikely, that there should be an agent with second-order desires but with no volitions of the second order. Such a creature, in my view, would not be a person. I shall use the term 'wanton' to refer to agents who have first-order desires but who are not persons because, whether or not they have desires of the second order, they have no second-order volitions.[5]

The essential characteristic of a wanton is that he does not care about his will. His desires move him to do certain things, without its being true of him either that he wants to be moved by those desires or that he prefers to be

moves B; without knowing what B's will is, in other words, A wants his own will to be the same. It certainly does not follow that A already has, among his desires, a desire like the one that constitutes B's will. I shall not pursue here the questions of whether there are genuine counter-examples to the claim made in the text or of how, if there are, that claim should be altered.

[5] Creatures with second-order desires but no second-order volitions differ significantly from brute animals and, for some purposes, it would be desirable to regard them as persons. My usage, which withholds the designation 'person' from them, is thus somewhat arbitrary. I adopt it largely because it facilitates the formulation of some of the points I wish to make. Hereafter, whenever I consider statements of the form 'A wants to want to X'. I shall have in mind statements identifying second-order volitions and not statements identifying second-order desires that are not second-order volitions.

moved by other desires. The class of wantons includes all non-human animals that have desires and all very young children. Perhaps it also includes some adult human beings as well. In any case, adult humans may be more or less wanton; they may act wantonly, in response to first-order desires concerning which they have no volitions of the second order, more or less frequently.

The fact that a wanton has no second-order volitions does not mean that each of his first-order desires is translated heedlessly and at once into action. He may have no opportunity to act in accordance with some of his desires. Moreover, the translation of his desires into action may be delayed or precluded either by conflicting desires of the first order or by the intervention of deliberation. For a wanton may possess and employ rational faculties of a high order. Nothing in the concept of a wanton implies that he cannot reason or that he cannot deliberate concerning how to do what he wants to do. What distinguishes the rational wanton from other rational agents is that he is not concerned with the desirability of his desires themselves. He ignores the question of what his will is to be. Not only does he pursue whatever course of action he is most strongly inclined to pursue, but he does not care which of his inclinations is the strongest.

Thus a rational creature, who reflects upon the suitability to his desires of one course of action or another, may none the less be a wanton. In maintaining that the essence of being a person lies not in reason but in will, I am far from suggesting that a creature without reason may be a person. For it is only in virtue of his rational capacities that a person is capable of becoming critically aware of his own will and of forming volitions of the second order. The structure of a person's will presupposes, accordingly, that he is a rational being.

The distinction between a person and a wanton may be illustrated by the difference between two narcotics addicts. Let us suppose that the physiological condition accounting for the addiction is the same in both men, and that both succumb inevitably to their periodic desires for the drug to which they are addicted. One of the addicts hates his addiction and always struggles desperately, although to no avail, against its thrust. He tries everything that he thinks might enable him to overcome his desires for the drug. But these desires are too powerful for him to withstand, and invariably, in the end, they conquer him. He is an unwilling addict, helplessly violated by his own desires.

The unwilling addict has conflicting first-order desires: he wants to take the drug, and he also wants to refrain from taking it. In addition to these first-order desires, however, he has a volition of the second order. He is not a neutral with regard to the conflict between his desire to take the drug and his desire to refrain from taking it. It is the latter desire, and not the former, that he wants to constitute his will; it is the latter desire, rather than the former, that he wants to be effective and to provide the purpose that he will seek to realize in what he actually does.

The other addict is a wanton. His actions reflect the economy of his first-order desires, without his being concerned whether the desires that move him to act are desires by which he wants to be moved to act. If he encounters problems in obtaining the drug or in administering it to himself, his responses to his urges to take it may involve deliberation. But it never occurs to him to consider whether he wants the relation among his desires to result in his having the will he has. The wanton addict may be an animal, and thus incapable of being concerned about his will. In any event he is, in respect of his wanton lack of concern, no different from an animal.

The second of these addicts may suffer a first-order conflict similar to the first-order conflict suffered by the first. Whether he is human or not, the wanton may (perhaps due to conditioning) both want to take the drug and want to refrain from taking it. Unlike the unwilling addict, however, he does not prefer that one of his conflicting desires should be paramount over the other; he does not prefer that one first-order desire rather than the other should constitute his will. It would be misleading to say that he is neutral as to the conflict between his desires, since this would suggest that he regards them as equally acceptable. Since he has no identity apart from his first-order desires, it is true neither that he prefers one to the other nor that he prefers not to take sides.

It makes a difference to the unwilling addict, who is a person, which of his conflicting first-order desires wins out. Both desires are his, to be sure; and whether he finally takes the drug or finally succeeds in refraining from taking it, he acts to satisfy what is in a literal sense his own desire. In either case he does something he himself wants to do, and he does it not because of some external influence whose aim happens to coincide with his own but because of his desire to do it. The unwilling addict identifies himself, however, through the formation of a second-order volition, with one rather than with the other of his conflicting first-order desires. He makes one of them more truly his own and, in so doing, he withdraws himself from the other. It is in virtue of this identification and withdrawal, accomplished through the formation of a second-order volition, that the unwilling addict may meaningfully make the analytically puzzling statements that the force moving him to take the drug is a force other than his own, and that it is not of his own free will but rather against his will that this force moves him to take it.

The wanton addict cannot or does not care which of his conflicting first-order desires wins out. His lack of concern is not due to his inability to find a convincing basis for preference. It is due either to his lack of the capacity for reflection or to his mindless indifference to the enterprise of evaluating his own desires and motives.[6] There is only one issue in the struggle to which his first-order conflict may lead: whether the one or the other of his conflicting desires is the stronger. Since he is moved by both desires, he will not be altogether satisfied by what he does no matter which of them is effective. But it makes no difference *to him* whether his craving or his aversion gets the upper hand. He has no stake in the conflict between them and so, unlike the unwilling addict, he can neither win nor lose the struggle in which he is engaged. When a *person* acts, the desire by which he is moved is either the will he wants or a will he wants to be without. When a *wanton* acts, it is neither.

III

There is a very close relationship between the capacity for forming second-order volitions and another capacity that is essential to persons—one that has often been considered a distinguishing mark of the human condition. It is only because a person has volitions of the second order that he is capable both of enjoying and of lacking freedom of the will. The concept of a person is not only, then, the concept of a type of entity that has both first-order desires and volitions of the second order. It can also be construed as the concept of a type of entity for whom the freedom of its will may be a problem. This concept excludes all wantons, both infrahuman and human, since they fail to satisfy an essential condition for the enjoyment of freedom of the will. And it excludes those suprahuman beings, if any, whose wills are necessarily free.

Just what kind of freedom is the freedom of the will? This question calls for an identification of the special area of human experience to which the concept of freedom of the will, as distinct from the concepts of other sorts of freedom, is particularly germane. In dealing with it, my aim will be primarily to locate the problem with which a person is most immediately concerned when he is concerned with the freedom of his will.

According to one familiar philosophical tradition, being free is

---

[6] In speaking of the evaluation of his own desires and motives as being characteristic of a person, I do not mean to suggest that a person's second-order volitions necessarily manifest a *moral* stance on his part toward his first-order desires. It may not be from the point of view of morality that the person evaluates his first-order desires. Moreover, a person may be capricious and irresponsible in forming his second-order volitions and give no serious consideration to what is at stake. Second-order volitions express evaluations only in the sense that they are preferences. There is no essential restrictions on the kind of basis, if any, upon which they are formed.

fundamentally a matter of doing what one wants to do. Now the notion of an agent who does what he wants to do is by no means an altogether clear one: both the doing and the wanting, and the appropriate relation between them as well, require elucidation. But although its focus needs to be sharpened and its formulation refined, I believe that this notion does capture at least part of what is implicit in the idea of an agent who *acts* freely. It misses entirely, however, the peculiar content of the quite different idea of an agent whose *will* is free.

We do not suppose that animals enjoy freedom of the will, although we recognize that an animal may be free to run in whatever direction it wants. Thus, having the freedom to do what one wants to do is not a sufficient condition of having a free will. It is not a necessary condition either. For to deprive someone of his freedom of action is not necessarily to undermine the freedom of his will. When an agent is aware that there are certain things he is not free to do, this doubtless affects his desires and limits the range of choices he can make. But suppose that someone, without being aware of it, has in fact lost or been deprived of his freedom of action. Even though he is no longer free to do what he wants to do, his will may remain as free as it was before. Despite the fact that he is not free to translate his desires into actions or to act according to the determinations of his will, he may still form those desires and make those determinations as freely as if his freedom of action had not been impaired.

When we ask whether a person's will is free we are not asking whether he is in a position to translate his first-order desires into actions. That is the question of whether he is free to do as he pleases. The question of the freedom of his will does not concern the relation between what he does and what he wants to do. Rather, it concerns his desires themselves. But what question about them is it?

It seems to me both natural and useful to construe the question of whether a person's will is free in close analogy to the question of whether an agent enjoys freedom of action. Now freedom of action is (roughly, at least) the freedom to do what one wants to do. Analogously, then, the statement that a person enjoys freedom of the will means (also roughly) that he is free to want what he wants to want. More precisely, it means that he is free to will what he wants to will, or to have the will he wants. Just as the question about the freedom of an agent's action has to do with whether it is the action he wants to perform, so the question about the freedom of his will has to do with whether it is the will he wants to have.

It is in securing the conformity of his will to his second-order volitions, then, that a person exercises freedom of the will. And it is in the discrepancy between his will and his second-order volitions, or in his awareness that their coincidence is not his own doing but only a happy chance, that a person who does not have this freedom feels its lack. The unwilling addict's will is not free. This is shown by the fact that it is not the will he wants. It is also true, though in a different way, that the will of the wanton addict is not free. The wanton addict neither has the will he wants nor has a will that differs from the will he wants. Since he has no volitions of the second order, the freedom of his will cannot be a problem for him. He lacks it, so to speak, by default.

People are generally far more complicated than my sketchy account of the structure of a person's will may suggest. There is as much opportunity for ambivalence, conflict, and self-deception with regard to desires of the second order, for example, as there is with regard to first-order desires. If there is an unresolved conflict among someone's second-order desires, then he is in danger of having no second-order volition; for unless this conflict is resolved, he has no preference concerning which of his first-order desires is to be his will. This condition, if it is so severe that it prevents him from identifying himself in a sufficiently decisive way with *any* of his conflicting first-order desires, destroys him as a person. For it either tends to paralyse his will and to keep him from acting at all, or it tends to remove him from his will so that his will operates without his participation. In both cases he becomes, like the unwilling addict though in a different way, a helpless bystander to the forces that move him.

Another complexity is that a person may have, especially if his second-order desires are in conflict, desires and volitions of a higher order than the second. There is no theoretical limit to the length of the series of desires of higher and higher orders; nothing except common sense and, perhaps, a saving fatigue prevents an individual from obsessively refusing to identify himself with any of his desires until he forms a desire of the next higher order. The tendency to generate such a series of acts of forming desires, which would be a case of humanization run wild, also leads toward the destruction of a person.

It is possible, however, to terminate such a series of acts without cutting it off arbitrarily. When a person identifies himself *decisively* with one of his first-order desires, this commitment 'resounds' throughout the potentially endless array of higher orders. Consider a person who, without reservation or conflict, wants to be motivated by the desire to concentrate on his work. The fact that his second-order volition to be moved by this desire is a decisive one means that there is no room for questions concerning the pertinence of desires or volitions of higher orders. Suppose the person is asked whether he wants to want to concentrate on his work. He can properly insist that this question concerning a third-order desire does not arise. It would be a mistake to claim that, because he has not considered whether he wants the second-order volition he has formed, he is indifferent to the question of whether it is with this volition or with some other that he wants his will to accord. The decisiveness of the commitment he has made means that he has decided that no further question about his second-order volition, at any higher order, remains to be asked. It is relatively unimportant whether we explain this by saying that this commitment implicitly generates an endless series of confirming desires of higher orders, or by saying that the commitment is tantamount to a dissolution of the pointedness of all questions concerning higher orders of desire.

Examples such as the one concerning the unwilling addict may suggest that volitions of the second order, or of higher orders, must be formed deliberately and that a person characteristically struggles to ensure that they are satisfied. But the conformity of a person's will to his higher-order volitions may be far more thoughtless and spontaneous than this. Some people are naturally moved by kindness when they want to be kind, and by nastiness when they want to be nasty, without any explicit forethought and without any need for energetic self-control. Others are moved by nastiness when they want to be kind and by kindness when they intend to be nasty, equally without forethought and without active resistance to these violations of their higher-order desires. The enjoyment of freedom comes easily to some. Others must struggle to achieve it.

IV

My theory concerning the freedom of the will accounts easily for our disinclination to allow that this freedom is enjoyed by the members of any species inferior to our own. It also satisfies another condition that must be met by any such theory, by making it apparent why the freedom of the will should be regarded as desirable. The enjoyment of a free will means the satisfaction of certain desires—desires of the second or of higher orders—whereas its absence means their frustration. The satisfactions at stake are those which accrue to a person of whom it may be said that his will is his own. The corresponding frustrations are those suffered by a person of whom it may be said that he is estranged from himself, or that he finds himself a helpless or a passive bystander to the forces that move him.

A person who is free to do what he wants to do may yet not be in a position to have the will he wants. Suppose, however, that he enjoys both freedom of action and freedom of the will. Then he is not only free to do what he wants to do; he is also free to want what he wants to want. It seems to me that he has, in that case, all the freedom it is possible to desire or to conceive. There are other good things in life, and he may not possess some of them. But there is nothing in the way of freedom that he lacks.

It is far from clear that certain other theories of the freedom of the will meet these elementary but essential conditions: that it be understandable why we desire this freedom and why we refuse to ascribe it to animals. Consider, for example, Roderick Chisholm's quaint version of the doctrine that human freedom entails an absence of causal determination.[7] Whenever a person performs a free action, according to Chisholm, it's a miracle. The motion of a person's hand, when the person moves it, is the outcome of a series of physical causes; but some event in this series, 'and presumably one of those that took place within the brain, was caused by the agent and not by any other events' (18). A free agent has, therefore, 'a prerogative which some would attribute only to God: each of us, when we act, is a prime mover unmoved' (23).

This account fails to provide any basis for doubting that animals of sub-human species enjoy the freedom it defines. Chisholm says nothing that makes it seem less likely that a rabbit performs a miracle when it moves its leg than that a man does so when he moves his hand. But why, in any case, should anyone *care* whether he can interrupt the natural order of causes in the way Chisholm describes? Chisholm offers no reason for believing that there is a discernible difference between the experience of a man who miraculously initiates a series of causes when he moves his hand and a man who moves his hand without any such breach of the normal causal sequence. There appears to be no concrete basis for preferring to be involved in the one state of affairs rather than in the other.[8]

It is generally supposed that, in addition to satisfying the two conditions I have mentioned, a satisfactory theory of the freedom of the will necessarily provides an analysis of one of the conditions of moral responsibility. The most common recent approach to the problem of understanding the freedom of the will has been, indeed, to inquire what is entailed by the assumption that someone is morally responsible for what he has done. In my view, however, the relation between moral responsibility and the freedom of the will has been very widely misunderstood. It is not true that a person is morally responsible for what he has done only if his will was free when he did it. He may be morally responsible for having done it even though his will was not free at all.

---

[7] 'Freedom and Action', in *Freedom and Determinism*, ed. Keith Lehrer (New York: Random House, 1966), 11–44. [See Essay 1, this volume.]

[8] I am not suggesting that the alleged difference between these two states of affairs is unverifiable. On the contrary, physiologists might well be able to show that Chisholm's conditions for a free action are not satisfied, by establishing that there is no relevant brain event for which a sufficient physical cause cannot be found.

A person's will is free only if he is free to have the will he wants. This means that, with regard to any of his first-order desires, he is free either to make that desire his will or to make some other first-order desire his will instead. Whatever his will, then, the will of the person whose will is free could have been otherwise; he could have done otherwise than to constitute his will as he did. It is a vexed question just how 'he could have done otherwise' is to be understood in contexts such as this one. But although this question is important to the theory of freedom, it has no bearing on the theory of moral responsibility. For the assumption that a person is morally responsible for what he has done does not entail that the person was in a position to have whatever will he wanted.

This assumption *does* entail that the person did what he did freely, or that he did it of his own free will. It is a mistake, however, to believe that someone acts freely only when he is free to do whatever he wants or that he acts of his own free will only if his will is free. Suppose that a person has done what he wanted to do, that he did it because he wanted to do it, and that the will by which he was moved when he did it was his will because it was the will he wanted. Then he did it freely and of his own free will. Even supposing that he could have done otherwise, he would not have done otherwise; and even supposing that he could have had a different will, he would not have wanted his will to differ from what it was. Moreover, since the will that moved him when he acted was his will because he wanted it to be, he cannot claim that his will was forced upon him or that he was a passive bystander to its constitution. Under these conditions, it is quite irrelevant to the evaluation of his moral responsibility to inquire whether the alternatives that he opted against were actually available to him.[9]

In illustration, consider a third kind of addict. Suppose that his addiction has the same physiological basis and the same irresistible thrust as the addictions of the unwilling and wanton addicts, but that he is altogether delighted with his condition. He is a willing addict, who would not have things any other way. If the grip of his addiction should somehow weaken, he would do whatever he could to reinstate it; if his desire for the drug should begin to fade, he would take steps to renew its intensity.

The willing addict's will is not free, for his desire to take the drug will be effective regardless of whether or not he wants this desire to constitute his will. But when he takes the drug, he takes it freely and of his own free will. I am inclined to understand his situation as involving the overdetermination

---

[9] For another discussion of the considerations that cast doubt on the principle that a person is morally responsible for what he has done only if he could have done otherwise, see my 'Alternate Possibilities and Moral Responsibility', *Journal of Philosophy* (1969), 829–39 [reprinted as Essay 8, this volume].

of his first-order desire to take the drug. This desire is his effective desire because he is physiologically addicted. But it is his effective desire also because he wants it to be. His will is outside his control, but, by his second-order desire that his desire for the drug should be effective, he has made this will his own. Given that it is therefore not only because of his addiction that his desire for the drug is effective, he may be morally responsible for taking the drug.

My conception of the freedom of the will appears to be neutral with regard to the problem of determinism. It seems conceivable that it should be causally determined that a person is free to want what he wants to want. If this is conceivable, then it might be causally determined that a person enjoys a free will. There is no more than an innocuous appearance of paradox in the proposition that it is determined, ineluctably and by forces beyond their control, that certain people have free wills and that others do not. There is no incoherence in the proposition that some agency other than a person's own is responsible (even *morally* responsible) for the fact that he enjoys or fails to enjoy freedom of the will. It is possible that a person should be morally responsible for what he does of his own free will and that some other person should also be morally responsible for his having done it.[10]

On the other hand, it seems conceivable that it should come about by chance that a person is free to have the will he wants. If this is conceivable, then it might be a matter of chance that certain people enjoy freedom of the will and that certain others do not. Perhaps it is also conceivable, as a number of philosophers believe, for states of affairs to come about in a way other than by chance or as the outcome of a sequence of natural causes. If it is indeed conceivable for the relevant states of affairs to come about in some third way, then it is also possible that a person should in that third way come to enjoy the freedom of the will.

[10] There is a difference between being *fully* responsible and being *solely* responsible. Suppose that the willing addict has been made an addict by the deliberate and calculated work of another. Then it may be that both the addict and this other person are fully responsible for the addict's taking the drug, while neither of them is solely responsible for it. That there is a distinction between full moral responsibility and sole moral responsibility is apparent in the following example. A certain light can be turned on or off by flicking either of two switches, and each of these switches is simultaneously flicked to the 'on' position by a different person, neither of whom is aware of the other. Neither person is solely responsible for the light's going on, nor do they share the responsibility in the sense that each is partially responsible; rather, each of them is fully responsible.

17

FREE AGENCY

GARY WATSON

In this essay I discuss a distinction that is crucial to a correct account of free action and to an adequate conception of human motivation and responsibility.

I

According to one familiar conception of freedom, a person is free to the extent that he is able to do or get what he wants. To circumscribe a person's freedom is to contract the range of things he is able to do. I think that, suitably qualified, this account is correct, and that the chief and most interesting uses of the word 'free' can be explicated in its terms. But this general line has been resisted on a number of different grounds. One of the most important objections—and the one upon which I shall concentrate in this paper—is that this familiar view is too impoverished to handle talk of free actions and free will.

Frequently enough, we say, or are inclined to say, that a person is not in control of his own actions, that he is not a 'free agent' with respect to them, even though his behaviour is intentional. Possible examples of this sort of action include those which are explained by addictions, manias, and phobias of various sorts. But the concept of free action would seem to be pleonastic on the analysis of freedom in terms of the ability to get what one wants. For if a person does something intentionally, then surely he was able at that time to do it. Hence, on this analysis, he was free to do it. The familiar account would not seem to allow for any further questions, as far as freedom is concerned, about the action. Accordingly, this

From the *Journal of Philosophy*, 72/8 (1975), 205–20. Reprinted by permission of the publisher and the author.

I have profited from discussions with numerous friends, students, colleagues, and other audiences, on the material of this essay; I would like to thank them collectively. However, special thanks are due to Joel Feinberg, Harry Frankfurt, and Thomas Nagel.

account would seem to embody a conflation of free action and intentional action.

Philosophers who have defended some form of compatibilism have usually given this analysis of freedom, with the aim of showing that freedom and responsibility are not really incompatible with determinism. Some critics have rejected compatibilism precisely because of its association with this familiar account of freedom. For instance, Isaiah Berlin asks: if determinism is true,

... what reasons can you, in principle, adduce for attributing responsibility or applying moral rules to [people] which you would not think it reasonable to apply in the case of compulsive choosers—kleptomaniacs, dipomaniacs, and the like?[1]

The idea is that the sense in which actions would be free in a deterministic world allows the actions of 'compulsive choosers' to be free. To avoid this consequence, it is often suggested, we must adopt some sort of 'contra-causal' view of freedom.

Now, though compatibilists from Hobbes to J. J. C. Smart have given the relevant moral and psychological concepts an exceedingly crude treatment, this crudity is not inherent in compatibilism, nor does it result from the adoption of the conception of freedom in terms of the ability to get what one wants. For the difference between free and unfree actions—as we normally discern it—has nothing at all to do with the truth or falsity of determinism.

In the subsequent pages, I want to develop a distinction between wanting and valuing which will enable the familiar view of freedom to make sense of the notion of an unfree action. The contention will be that, in the case of actions that are unfree, the agent is unable to get what he most wants, *or values*, and this inability is due to his own 'motivational system'. In this case the obstruction to the action that he most wants to do is his own will. It is in this respect that the action is unfree: the agent is obstructed in and by the very performance of the action.

I do not conceive my remarks to be a defence of compatibilism. This point of view may be unacceptable for various reasons, some of which call into question the coherence of the concept of responsibility. But these reasons do not include the fact that compatibilism relies upon the conception of freedom in terms of the ability to get what one wants, nor must it conflate free action and intentional action. If compatibilism is to be shown to be wrong, its critics must go deeper.

---

[1] *Four Essays on Liberty* (Oxford University Press, 1969), xx–xxi.

II

What must be true of people if there is to be a significant notion of free action? Our talk of free action arises from the apparent fact that what a person most wants may not be what he is finally moved to get. It follows from this apparent fact that the extent to which one wants something is not determined solely by the *strength* of one's desires (or 'motives') as measured by their effectiveness in action. One (perhaps trivial) measure of the strength of the desire or want is that the agent acts upon that desire or want (trivial, since it will be non-explanatory to say that an agent acted upon that desire because it was the strongest). But, if what one most wants may not be what one most strongly wants, by this measure, then in what sense can it be true that one wants it?[2]

To answer this question, one might begin by contrasting, at least in a crude way, a Humean with a Platonic conception of practical reasoning. The ancients distinguished between the rational and the irrational parts of the soul, between Reason and Appetite. Hume employed a superficially similar distinction. It is important to understand, however, that (for Plato at least) the rational part of the soul is not to be identified with what Hume called 'Reason' and contradistinguished from the 'Passions'. On Hume's account, Reason is not a source of motivation, but a faculty of determining what is true and what is false, a faculty concerned solely with 'matters of fact' and 'relations among ideas'. It is completely dumb on the question of what to do. Perhaps Hume could allow Reason this much practical voice: given an initial set of wants and beliefs about what is or is likely to be the case, particular desires are generated in the process. In other words, a Humean might allow Reason a crucial role in deliberation. But its essential role would not be to supply motivation—Reason is not that kind of thing—but rather to calculate, within a context of desires and ends, how to fulfil those desires and serve those ends. For Plato, however, the rational part of the soul is not some kind of inference mechanism. It is itself a source of motivation. In general form, the desires of Reason are desires for 'the Good'.

Perhaps the contrast can be illustrated by some elementary notions from decision theory. On the Bayesian model of deliberation, a preference scale is imposed upon various states of affairs contingent upon courses of action open to the agent. Each state of affairs can be assigned a numerical value (initial value) according to its place on the scale; given this assignment, and

---

[2] I am going to use 'want' and 'desire' in the very inclusive sense now familiar in philosophy, whereby virtually any motivational factor that may figure in the explanation of intentional action is a want; 'desire' will be used mainly in connection with the appetites and passions.

the probabilities that those states of affairs will obtain if the actions are performed, a final numerical value (expected desirability) can be assigned to the actions themselves. The rational agent performs the action with the highest expected desirability.

In these terms, on the Humean picture, Reason is the faculty that computes probabilities and expected desirabilities. Reason is in this sense neutral with respect to actions, for it can operate equally on any given assignment of initial values and probabilities—it has nothing whatsoever to say about the assignment of initial values. On the Platonic picture, however, the rational part of the soul itself determines what has *value* and how much, and thus is responsible for the original ranking of alternative states of affairs.

It may appear that the difference between these conceptions is merely a difference as to what is to be called 'Reason' or 'rational', and hence is not a substantive difference. In speaking of Reason, Hume has in mind a sharp contrast between what is wanted and what is thought to be the case. What contrast is implicit in the Platonic view that the ranking of alternative states of affairs is the task of the rational part of the soul?

The contrast here is not trivial; the difference in classificatory schemes reflects different views of human psychology. For one thing, in saying this (or what is tantamount to this) Plato was calling attention to the fact that it is one thing to think a state of affairs good, worthwhile, or worthy of promotion, and another simply to desire or want that state of affairs to obtain. Since the notion of value is tied to (cannot be understood independently of) those of the good and worthy, it is one thing to value (think good) a state of affairs and another to desire that it obtain. However, to think a thing good is at the same time to desire it (or its promotion). Reason is thus an original spring of action. It is because valuing is essentially related to thinking or *judging* good that it is appropriate to speak of the wants that are (or perhaps arise from) evaluations as belonging to, or originating in, the rational (that is, *judging*) part of the soul; values provide *reasons* for action. The contrast is with desires, whose objects may not be thought good and which are thus, in a natural sense, blind or irrational. Desires are mute on the question of what is good.[3]

---

[3] To quote just one of many suggestive passages: 'We must . . . observe that within each one of us there are two sorts of ruling or guiding principle that we follow. One is an innate desire for pleasure, the other an acquired judgement that aims at what is best. Sometimes these internal guides are in accord, sometimes at variance; now one gains the mastery, now the other. And when judgement guides us rationally toward what is best, and has the mastery, that mastery is called temperance, but when desire drags us irrationally toward pleasure, and has come to rule within us, the name given to that rule is wantonness' (*Phaedrus*, 237e–238e; Hackforth trans.).

For a fascinating discussion of Plato's parts-of-the-soul doctrine, see Terry Penner's 'Thought and Desire in Plato', in Gregory Vlastos, ed., *Plato: A Collection of Critical Essays*, vol. ii (New

Now it seems to me that—given the view of freedom as the ability to get what one wants—there can be a problem of free action only if the Platonic conception of the soul is (roughly) correct. The doctrine I shall defend is Platonic in the sense that it involves a distinction between valuing and desiring which depends upon there being independent sources of motivation. No doubt Plato meant considerably more than this by his parts-of-the-soul doctrine; but he meant at least this. The Platonic conception provides an answer to the question I posed earlier: in what sense can what one most wants differ from that which is the object of the strongest desire? The answer is that the phrase 'what one most wants' may mean either 'the object of the strongest desire' or 'what one most *values*'. This phrase can be interpreted in terms of strength or in terms of ranking order or preference. The problem of free action arises because what one desires may not be what one values, and what one most values may not be what one is finally moved to get.[4]

The tacit identification of desiring or wanting with valuing is so common[5] that it is necessary to cite some examples of this distinction in order to illustrate how evaluation and desire may diverge. There seem to be two ways in which, in principle, a discrepancy may arise. First, it is possible that what one desires is not *to any degree* valued, held to be worthwhile, or thought good; one assigns *no* value whatever to the object of one's desire. Second, although one may indeed value what is desired, the strength of one's desire may not properly reflect the degree to which one values its object; that is, although the object of a desire is valuable, it may not be deemed the most valuable in the situation and yet one's desire for it may be stronger than the want for what is most valued.

York: Anchor, 1971). As I see it (and here I have been influenced by Penner's article), the distinction I have attributed to Plato was meant by him to be a solution to the socratic problem of *akrasia*.

   I would argue that this distinction, though necessary, is insufficient for the task, because it does not mark the difference between ('mere') incontinence or weakness of will and psychological compulsion. This difference requires a careful examination of the various things that might be meant in speaking of the strength of a desire.

[4] Here I shall not press the rational/non-rational contrast any further than this, though Plato would have wished to press it further. However, one important and anti-Humean implication of the minimal distinction is this: it is not the case that, if a person desires to do X, he therefore has (or even regards himself as having) a reason to do X.

[5] For example, I take my remarks to be incompatible with the characterization of value R. B. Perry gives in *General Theory of Value* (Harvard University Press, 1950). In ch. 5, Perry writes: 'This, then, we take to be the original source and constant feature of all value. That which is an object of interest is *eo ipso* invested with value.' And 'interest' is characterized in the following way: '. . . liking and disliking, desire and aversion, will and refusal, or seeking and avoiding. It is to this all-pervasive characteristic of the motor-affective life, this *state, act, attitude* or *disposition of favour* or disfavor, to which we propose to give the name of "interest".'

The cases in which one in no way values what one desires are perhaps rare, but surely they exist. Consider the case of a woman who has a sudden urge to drown her bawling child in the bath; or the case of a squash player who, while suffering an ignominious defeat, desires to smash his opponent in the face with the racquet. It is just false that the mother values her child's being drowned or that the player values the injury and suffering of his opponent. But they desire these things nonetheless. They desire them in spite of themselves. It is not that they assign to these actions an initial value which is then outweighed by other considerations. These activities are not even represented by a positive entry, however small, on the initial 'desirability matrix'.

It may seem from these examples that this first and radical sort of divergence between desiring and valuing occurs only in the case of momentary and inexplicable urges or impulses. Yet I see no conclusive reason why a person could not be similarly estranged from a rather persistent and pervasive desire, and one that is explicable enough. Imagine a man who thinks his sexual inclinations are the work of the devil, that the very fact that he has sexual inclinations bespeaks his corrupt nature. This example is to be contrasted with that of the celibate who decides that the most fulfilling life for him will be one of abstinence. In this latter case, *one* of the things that receive consideration in the process of reaching his all-things-considered judgement is the value of sexual activity. There is something, from his point of view, to be said for sex, but there is more to be said in favour of celibacy. In contrast, the man who is estranged from his sexual inclinations does not acknowledge even a prima-facie reason for sexual activity; that he is sexually inclined toward certain activities is not even *a* consideration. Another way of illustrating the difference is to say that, for the one man, foregoing sexual relationships constitutes a *loss*, even if negligible compared with the gains of celibacy; whereas from the standpoint of the other person, no loss is sustained at all.

Now, it must be admitted, any desire may provide the basis for a reason in so far as non-satisfaction of the desire causes suffering and hinders the pursuit of ends of the agent. But it is important to notice that the reason generated in this way by a desire is a reason for *getting rid* of the desire, and one may get rid of a desire either by satisfying it or by eliminating it in some other manner (by tranquillizers, or cold showers). Hence this kind of reason differs importantly from the reasons based upon the evaluation of the activities or states of affairs in question. For, in the former case, attaining the object of desire is simply a means of eliminating discomfort or agitation, whereas in the latter case that attainment is the end itself. Normally, in the pursuit of the objects of our wants we are not attempting chiefly to relieve ourselves. We aim to satisfy, not just eliminate, desire.

Nevertheless, aside from transitory impulses, it may be that cases wherein nothing at all can be said in favour of the object of one's desire are rare. For it would seem that even the person who conceives his sexual desires to be essentially evil would have to admit that indulgence would be pleasurable, and surely that is something. (Perhaps not even this should be admitted. For indulgence may not yield pleasure at all in a context of anxiety. Furthermore, it is not obvious that pleasure is intrinsically good, independently of the worth of the pleasurable object.) In any case, the second sort of divergence between evaluation and desire remains: it is possible that, in a particular context, what one wants most strongly is not what one most values.

The distinction between valuing and desiring is not, it is crucial to see, a distinction among desires or wants according to their content. That is to say, there is nothing in the specification of the objects of an agent's desires that singles out some wants as based upon that agent's values. The distinction in question has rather to do with the *source* of the want or with its role in the total 'system' of the agent's desires and ends. It has to do with why the agent wants what he does.

Obviously, to identify a desire or want simply in terms of its content is not to identify its source(s). It does not follow from my wanting to eat that I am hungry. I may want to eat because I want to be well-nourished; or because I am hungry; or because eating is a pleasant activity. This single desire may have three independent sources. (These sources may not be altogether independent. It may be that eating is pleasurable only because I have appetites for food.) Some specifications of wants or desires—for instance, as cravings—pick out (at least roughly) the source of the motivation.

It is an essential feature of the appetites and the passions that they engender (or consist in) desires whose existence and persistence are independent of the person's judgement of the good. The appetite of hunger involves a desire to eat which has a source in physical needs and physiological states of the hungry organism. And emotions such as anger and fear partly consist in spontaneous inclinations to do various things—to attack or to flee the object of one's emotion, for example. It is intrinsic to the appetites and passions that appetitive and passionate beings can be motivated in spite of themselves. It is because desires such as these arise independently of the person's judgement and values that the ancients located the emotions and passions in the irrational part of the soul;[6] and it is because of

---

[6] Notice that most emotions differ from passions like lust in that they involve beliefs and some sort of valuation (cf. resentment). This may be the basis for Plato's positing a third part of the soul which is in a way partly rational—namely, *Thumos*.

this sort of independence that a conflict between valuing and desiring is possible.[7]

These points may suggest an inordinately dualistic view according to which persons are split into inevitably alien, if not always antagonistic, halves. But this view does not follow from what has been said. As central as it is to human life, it is not often noted that some activities are valued only to the extent that they are objects of the appetites. This means that such activities would never be regarded as valuable constituents of one's life were it not for one's susceptibility to 'blind' motivation—motivation independent of one's values. Sexual activity and eating are again examples. We may value the activity of eating to the degree that it provides nourishment. But we may also value it because it is an enjoyable activity, even though its having this status depends upon our appetites for food, our hunger. In the case of sex, in fact, if we were not erotic creatures, certain activities would not only lose their value to us, they might not even be physiologically possible.

These examples indicate, not that there is no distinction between desiring and valuing, but that the value placed upon certain activities depends upon their being the fulfilment of desires that arise and persist independently of what we value. So it is not that, when we value the activity of eating, we think there are reasons to eat no matter what other desires we have; rather, we value eating when food appeals to us; and, likewise, we value sexual relationships when we are aroused. Here an essential part of the *content* of our evaluation is that the activity in question be motivated by certain appetites. These activities may have value for us only in so far as they are appetitively motivated, even though to have these appetites is not *ipso facto* to value their objects.

Part of what it means to value some activities in this way is this: we judge that to cease to have such appetites is to lose something of worth. The judgement here is not merely that, if someone has these appetites, it is worthwhile (*ceteris paribus*) for him to indulge them. The judgement is rather that it is of value to have and (having them) to indulge these appetites. The former judgement does not account for the eunuch's loss or sorrow, whereas the latter does. And the latter judgement lies at the bottom of the discomfort one may feel when one envisages a situation in which, say, hunger is consistently eliminated and nourishment provided by insipid capsules.

It would be impossible for a non-erotic being or a person who lacked the appetite for food and drink fully to understand the value most of us attach

---

[7] To be sure, one may attempt to cultivate or eliminate certain appetites and passions, so that the desires that result may be in this way dependent upon one's evaluations. Even so, the resulting desires will be such that they can persist independently of one's values. It is rather like jumping from an airplane.

to sex and to dining. Sexual activity must strike the non-erotic being as perfectly grotesque. Or consider an appetite that is in fact 'unnatural' (i.e. acquired): the craving for tobacco. To a person who has never known the enticement of Lady Nicotine, what could be more incomprehensible than the filthy practice of consummating a fine meal by drawing into one's lungs the noxious fumes of a burning weed?

Thus, the relationship between evaluation and motivation is intricate. With respect to many of our activities, evaluation depends upon the possibility of our being moved to act independently of our judgement. So the distinction I have been pressing—that between desiring and valuing—does not commit one to an inevitable split between Reason and Appetite. Appetitively motivated activities may well constitute for a person the most worthwhile aspects of his life.[8] But the distinction does commit us to the possibility of such a split. If there are sources of motivation independent of the agent's values, then it is possible that sometimes he is motivated to do things he does not deem worth doing. This possibility is the basis for the principal problem of free action: a person may be obstructed by his own will.

A related possibility that presents considerable problems for the understanding of free agency is this: some desires, when they arise, may 'colour' or influence what appear to be the agent's evaluations, but only temporarily. That is, when and only when he has the desire, is he inclined to think or say that what is desired or wanted is worthwhile or good. This possibility is to be distinguished from another, according to which one thinks it worthwhile to eat when one is hungry or to engage in sexual activity when one is so inclined. For one may think this even on the occasions when the appetites are silent. The possibility I have in mind is rather that what one is disposed to say or judge is temporarily affected by the presence of the desire in such a way that, both before and after the 'onslaught' of the desire, one judges that the desire's object is worth pursuing (in the circumstances) whether or not one has the desire. In this case one is likely, in a cool moment, to think it a matter for regret that one had been so influenced and to think that one should guard against desires that have this property. In other cases it may not be the desire itself that affects one's judgement, but the set of conditions in which those desires arise—e.g. the conditions induced by drugs or alcohol. (It is noteworthy that we say: 'under the influence of alcohol'.) Perhaps judgements made in such circumstances are often in some sense self-deceptive. In any event, this phenomenon raises problems about the identification of a person's values.

---

[8] It is reported that H. G. Wells regarded the most important themes of his life to have been (1) the attainment of a World Society and (2) sex.

Despite our examples, it would be mistaken to conclude that the only desires that exhibit an independence of evaluation are appetitive or passionate desires. In Freudian terms, one may be as dissociated from the demands of the super-ego as from those of the id. One may be disinclined to move away from one's family, the thought of doing so being accompanied by compunction; and yet this disinclination may rest solely upon acculturation rather than upon a current judgement of what one is to do, reflecting perhaps an assessment of one's 'duties' and interests. Or, taking another example, one may have been habituated to think that divorce is to be avoided in all cases, so that the aversion to divorce persists even though one sees no justification for maintaining one's marriage. In both of these cases, the attitude has its basis solely in acculturation and exists independently of the agent's judgement. For this reason, acculturated desires are irrational (better: non-rational) in the same sense as appetitive and passionate desires. In fact, despite the inhibitions acquired in the course of a puritan up-bringing, a person may deem the pursuit of sexual pleasure to be worthwhile, his judgement siding with the id rather than the super-ego. Acculturated attitudes may seem more akin to evaluation than to appetite in that they are often expressed in evaluative language ('divorce is wicked') and result in feelings of guilt when one's actions are not in conformity with them. But, since conflict is possible here, to want something as a result of acculturation is not thereby to value it, in the sense of 'to value' that we want to capture.

It is not easy to give a non-trivial account of the sense of 'to value' in question. In part, to value something is, in the appropriate circumstances, to want it, and to attribute a want for something to someone is to say that he is disposed to try to get it. So it will not be easy to draw this distinction in behavioural terms. Apparently the difference will have to do with the agent's attitude towards the various things he is disposed to try to get. We might say that an agent's values consist in those principles and ends which he—in a cool and non-self-deceptive moment—articulates as definitive of the good, fulfilling, and defensible life. That most people have articulate 'conceptions of the good', coherent life-plans, *systems* of ends, and so on, is of course something of a fiction. Yet we all have more or less long-term aims and normative principles that we are willing to defend. It is such things as these that are to be identified with our values.

The valuation system of an agent is that set of considerations which, when combined with his factual beliefs (and probability estimates), yields judgements of the form: the thing for me to do in these circumstances, all things considered, is *a*. To ascribe free agency to a being presupposes it to be a being that makes judgements of this sort. To be this sort of being, one must assign values to alternative states of affairs, that is, rank them in terms of worth.

The motivational system of an agent is that set of considerations which move him to action. We identify his motivational system by identifying what motivates him. The possibility of unfree action consists in the fact that an agent's valuational system and motivational system may not completely coincide. Those systems harmonize to the extent that what determines the agent's all-things-considered judgements also determines his actions.

Now, to be sure, since to value is also to want, one's valuational and motivational systems must to a large extent overlap. If, in appropriate circumstances, one were never inclined to action by some alleged evaluation, the claim that that was indeed one's evaluation would be disconfirmed. Thus one's valuational system must have some (considerable) grip upon one's motivational system. The problem is that there are motivational factors other than valuational ones. The free agent has the capacity to translate his values into action; his actions flow from his evaluational system.

One's evaluational system may be said to constitute one's standpoint, the point of view from which one judges the world. The important feature of one's evaluational system is that one cannot coherently dissociate oneself from it *in its entirety*. For to dissociate oneself from the ends and principles that constitute one's evaluational system is to disclaim or repudiate them, and any ends and principles so disclaimed (self-deception aside) cease to be constitutive of one's valuational system. One can dissociate oneself from one set of ends and principles only from the standpoint of another such set that one does not disclaim. In short, one cannot dissociate oneself from all normative judgements without forfeiting all standpoints and therewith one's identity as an agent.

Of course, it does not follow from the fact that one must assume some standpoint that one must have only one, nor that one's standpoint is completely determinate. There may be ultimate conflicts, irresolvable tensions, and things about which one simply does not know what to do or say. Some of these possibilities point to problems about the unity of the person. Here the extreme case is pathological. I am inclined to think that when the split is severe enough, to have more than one standpoint is to have none.

This distinction between wanting and valuing requires far fuller explication than it has received so far. Perhaps the foregoing remarks have at least shown *that* the distinction exists and is important, and have hinted at its nature. This distinction is important to the adherent of the familiar view—that talk about free action and free agency can be understood in terms of the idea of being able to get what one wants—because it gives sense to the claim that in unfree actions the agents do not get what they really or most want.

This distinction gives sense to the contrast between free action and intentional action. Admittedly, further argument is required to show that such unfree agents are *unable* to get what they want; but the initial step toward this end has been taken.

At this point, it will be profitable to consider briefly a doctrine that is in many respects like that which I have been developing. The contrast will, I think, clarify the claims that have been advanced in the preceding pages.

III

In an important and provocative article,[9] Harry Frankfurt has offered a description of what he takes to be the essential feature of 'the concept of a person', a feature which, he alleges, is also basic to an understanding of 'freedom of the will'. This feature is the possession of higher-order volitions as well as first-order desires. Frankfurt construes the notion of a person's will as 'the notion of an *effective* desire—one that moves (or will or would move) a person all the way to action' (8). Someone has a second-order volition, then, when he wants 'a certain desire to be his will'. (Frankfurt also considers the case of a second-order desire that is not a second-order volition, where one's desire is simply to have a certain desire and not to act upon it. For example, a man may be curious to know what it is like to be addicted to drugs; he thus desires to desire heroin, but he may not desire his desire for heroin to be effective, to be his will. In fact, Frankfurt's actual example is somewhat more special, for here the man's desire is not simply to have a desire for heroin: he wants to have a desire for heroin which has a certain source, i.e. is addictive. He wants to know what it is like to *crave* heroin.) Someone is a *wanton* if he has no second-order volitions. Finally, 'it is only because a person has volitions of the second order that he is capable both of enjoying and of lacking freedom of the will' (14).

Frankfurt's thesis resembles the Platonic view we have been unfolding in so far as it focuses upon 'the structure of a person's will' (6). I want to make a simple point about Frankfurt's paper: namely that the 'structural' feature to which Frankfurt appeals is not the fundamental feature for either free agency or personhood; it is simply insufficient to the task he wants it to perform.

One job that Frankfurt wishes to do with the distinction between lower and higher orders of desire is to give an account of the sense in which some

---

[9] 'Freedom of the Will and the Concept of a Person', *Journal of Philosophy* (1971), 5–20 [Essay 16, this volume].

wants may be said to be more truly the agent's own than others (though in an obvious sense all are wants of the agent), the sense in which the agent 'identifies' with one desire rather than another and the sense in which an agent may be unfree with respect to his own 'will'. This enterprise is similar to our own. But we can see that the notion of 'higher-order volition' is not really the fundamental notion for these purposes, by raising the question: Can't one be a wanton, so to speak, with respect to one's second-order desires and volitions?

In a case of conflict, Frankfurt would have us believe that what it is to identify with some desire rather than another is to have a volition concerning the former which is of higher order than any concerning the latter. That the first desire is given a special status over the second is due to its having an n-order volition concerning it, whereas the second desire has at most an $(n-1)$-order volition concerning it. But why does one necessarily care about one's higher-order volitions? Since second-order volitions are themselves simply desires, to add them to the context of conflict is just to increase the number of contenders; it is not to give a special place to any of those in contention. The agent may not care which of the second-order desires win out. The same possibility arises at each higher order.

Quite aware of this difficulty, Frankfurt writes:

There is no theoretical limit to the length of the series of desires of higher and higher orders; nothing except common sense and, perhaps, a saving fatigue prevents an individual from obsessively refusing to identify himself with any of his desires until he forms a desire of the next higher order (16).

But he insists that

It is possible . . . to terminate such a series of acts [i.e. the formation of ever higher-order volitions] without cutting it off arbitrarily. When a person identifies himself decisively with one of his first-order desires, this commitment 'resounds' throughout the potentially endless array of higher orders . . . The fact that his second-order volition to be moved by this desire is a decisive one means that there is no room for questions concerning the pertinence of volitions of higher orders . . . The decisiveness of the commitment he has made means that he has decided that no further question about his second-order volition, at any higher order, remains to be asked. [Ibid.]

But either this reply is lame or it reveals that the notion of a higher-order volition is not the fundamental one. We wanted to know what prevents wantonness with regard to one's higher-order volitions. What gives these volitions any special relation to 'oneself'? It is unhelpful to answer that one makes a 'decisive commitment', where this just means that an interminable ascent to higher orders is not going to be permitted. This *is* arbitrary.

What this difficulty shows is that the notion of orders of desires or volitions does not do the work that Frankfurt wants it to do. It does not tell us why or how a particular want can have, among all of a person's 'desires', the special property of being peculiarly his 'own'. There may be something to the notions of acts of identification and of decisive commitment, but these are in any case different notions from that of a second- (or *n*-) order desire. And if these are the crucial notions, it is unclear why these acts of identification cannot be themselves of the first order—that is, identification with or commitment to courses of action (rather than with or to desires)—in which case, no ascent is necessary, and the notion of higher-order volitions becomes superfluous or at least secondary.

In fact, I think that such acts of 'identification and commitment' (if one finds this way of speaking helpful) are generally to courses of action, that is, are first-order. Frankfurt's picture of practical judgement seems to be that of an agent with a given set of (first-order) desires concerning which he then forms second-order volitions. But this picture seems to be distorted. As I see it, agents frequently formulate values concerning alternatives they had not hitherto desired. Initially, they do not (or need not usually) ask themselves which of their desires they want to be effective in action; they ask themselves which course of action is most worth pursuing. The initial practical question is about courses of action and not about themselves.

Indeed, practical judgements are connected with 'second-order volitions'. For the same considerations that constitute one's on-balance reasons for doing some action, *a*, are reasons for wanting the 'desire' to do *a* to be effective in action, and for wanting contrary desires to be ineffective. But in general, evaluations are prior and of the first order. The first-order desires that result from practical judgements generate second-order volitions because they have this special status; they do not have the special status that Frankfurt wants them to have because there is a higher-order desire concerning them.

Therefore, Frankfurt's position resembles the platonic conception in its focus upon the structure of the 'soul'.[10] But the two views draw their divisions differently; whereas Frankfurt divides the soul into higher and lower orders of desire, the distinction for Plato—and for my thesis—is among independent sources of motivation.[11]

---

[10] Frankfurt's idea of a wanton, suitably construed, can be put to further illuminating uses in moral psychology. It proves valuable, I think, in discussing the problematic phenomenon of psychopathy or sociopathy.

[11] Some very recent articles employ distinctions, for similar purposes, very like Frankfurt's and my own. See, for example, Richard C. Jeffrey. 'Preferences among Preferences', *Journal of Philosophy* (1974), 377–91. In 'Freedom and Desire', *Philosophical Review* (1974), 32–54. Wright Neely appeals to higher-order desires, apparently unaware of Frankfurt's development of this concept.

IV

In conclusion, it can now be seen that one worry that blocks the acceptance of the traditional view of freedom—and in turn, of compatibilism—is unfounded. To return to Berlin's question above, it is false that determinism entails that all our actions and choices have the same status as those of 'compulsive choosers' such as 'kleptomaniacs, dipsomaniacs, and the like'. What is distinctive about such compulsive behaviour, I would argue, is that the desires and emotions in question are more or less radically independent of the evaluational systems of these agents. The compulsive character of a kleptomaniac's thievery has nothing at all to do with determinism. Rather, it is because his desires express themselves independently of his evaluational judgements that we tend to think of his actions as unfree.

The truth, of course, is that God (traditionally conceived) is the only free agent without qualification. In the case of God, who is omnipotent and omniscient, there can be no disparity between valuational and motivational systems. The dependence of motivation upon evaluation is total, for there is but a single source of motivation: his presumably benign judgement.[12] In the case of the Brutes, as well, motivation has a single source: appetite and (perhaps) passion. The Brutes (or so we normally think) have no evaluational systems. But human beings are only more or less free agents, often less. They are free agents only in some respects. With regard to the appetites and passions, it is plain that in some situations the motivational systems of human beings exhibit an independence from their values which is inconsistent with free agency; that is to say, people are sometimes moved by their appetites and passions in conflict with their practical judgements.[13]

As Nietzsche said (probably with a rather different point in mind): 'Man's belly is the reason why man does not easily take himself for a god.'[14]

[12] God could not act *akratically*. In this respect, Socrates thought people were distinguishable from such a being only by ignorance and limited power.

[13] This possibility is a definitive feature of appetitive and passionate wants.

[14] *Beyond Good and Evil*, s. 141.

18

THE SIGNIFICANCE OF CHOICE

1. INTRODUCTION

Choice has obvious and immediate moral significance. The fact that a certain action or outcome resulted from an agent's choice can make a crucial difference both to our moral appraisal of that agent and to our assessment of the rights and obligations of the agent and others after the action has been performed. My aim in these lectures is to investigate the nature and basis of this significance. The explanation which I will offer will be based upon a contractualist account of morality—that is, a theory according to which an act is right if it would be required or allowed by principles which no one, suitably motivated, could reasonably reject as a basis for informed, unforced general agreement.[1]

I believe that it is possible within this general theory of morality to explain the significance of various familiar moral notions such as rights, welfare, and responsibility in a way that preserves their apparent independence rather than reducing all of them to one master concept such as utility. The present lectures are an attempt to carry out this project for the notions of responsibility and choice.

Lecture I in *The Tanner Lectures on Human Values* (1988), edited by Sterling M. McMurrin, 151–77. Reprinted courtesy of the University of Utah Press and the Trustees of the Tanner Lectures on Human Values.

This is a revised version of [one of] three lectures presented at Brasenose College, Oxford, on May 16, 23, and 28, 1986. I am grateful to the participants in the seminars following those lectures for their challenging and instructive comments. These lectures are the descendants of a paper, entitled "Freedom of the Will in Political Theory," which I delivered at a meeting of the Washington, D.C., Area Philosophy Club in November 1977. Since that time I have presented many intervening versions to various audiences. I am indebted to members of those audiences and to numerous other friends for comments, criticism, and helpful suggestions.

[1] I have set out my version of contractualism in "Contractualism and Utilitarianism," in Amartya Sen and Bernard Williams, eds., *Utilitarianism and Beyond* (Cambridge: Cambridge University Press, 1982), pp. 103–28. What follows can be seen as an attempt to fulfill, for the case of choice, the promissory remarks made at the end of section III of that paper.

2. THE PROBLEMS OF FREE WILL

Quite apart from this general theoretical project, however, there is another, more familiar reason for inquiring into the basis of the moral significance of choice. This is the desire to understand and respond to the challenge to that significance which has gone under the heading of the problem of free will. This problem has a number of forms. One form identifies free will with a person's freedom to act otherwise than he or she in fact did or will. The problem, on this view, is the threat to this freedom posed by deterministic conceptions of the universe. A second, related problem is whether determinism, if true, would deprive us of the kind of freedom, whatever it may be, which is presupposed by moral praise and blame. This version of the problem is closer to my present concern in that it has an explicitly moral dimension. In order to address it one needs to find out what the relevant kind of freedom is, and this question can be approached by asking what gives free choice and free action their special moral significance. Given an answer to this question, which is the one I am primarily concerned with, we can then ask how the lack of freedom would threaten this significance and what kinds of unfreedom would do so.

The challenge I have in mind, however, is not posed by determinism but by what I call the Causal Thesis. This is the thesis that the events which are human actions, thoughts, and decisions are linked to antecedent events by causal laws as deterministic as those governing other goings-on in the universe. According to this thesis, given antecedent conditions and the laws of nature, the occurrence of an act of a specific kind follows, either with certainty or with a certain degree of probability, the indeterminacy being due to chance factors of the sort involved in other natural processes. I am concerned with this thesis rather than with determinism because it seems to me that the space opened up by the falsity of determinism would be relevant to morality only if it were filled by something other than the cumulative effects of indeterministic physical processes. If the actions we perform result from the fact that we have a certain physical constitution and have been subjected to certain outside influences, then an apparent threat to morality remains, even if the links between these causes and their effects are not deterministic.

The idea that there is such a threat is sometimes supported by thought experiments such as the following: Suppose you were to learn that someone's present state of mind, intentions, and actions were produced in him or her a few minutes ago by the action of outside forces, for example by electrical stimulation of the nervous system. You would not think it appropriate to blame that person for what he or she does under such conditions. But if the Causal Thesis is true then all of our actions are like this. The only differences are in the form of outside intervention and the span of time over which it occurs, but surely these are not essential to the freedom of the agent.

How might this challenge be answered? One strategy would be to argue that there are mistakes in the loose and naive idea of causality to which the challenge appeals or in the assumptions it makes about the relation between mental and physical events. There is obviously much to be said on both of these topics. I propose, however, to follow a different (but equally familiar) line. Leaving the concepts of cause and action more or less unanalyzed. I will argue that the apparent force of the challenge rests on mistaken ideas about the nature of moral blame and responsibility.[2]

It has sometimes been maintained that even if the Causal Thesis holds, this does not represent the kind of unfreedom that excuses agents from moral blame. That kind of unfreedom, it is sometimes said, is specified simply by the excusing conditions which we generally recognize: a person is acting unfreely in the relevant sense only if he or she is acting under post-hypnotic suggestion, or under duress, is insane, or falls under some other generally recognized excusing condition. Since the Causal Thesis does not imply that people are always acting under one or another of these conditions, it does not imply that moral praise and blame are generally inapplicable.

I am inclined to think that there is something right about this reaffirmation of common sense. But in this simple form it has been rightly rejected as

---

[2] In his admirably clear and detailed defense of incompatibilism. Peter van Inwagen observes that if one accepts the premises of his argument for the incompatibility of determinism and free will (in the sense required for moral responsibility) then it is "puzzling" how people could have the kind of freedom required for moral responsibility even under indeterministic universal causation. (See *An Essay on Free Will* [Oxford: Oxford University Press, 1983], pp. 119–50). On the other hand, he takes it to be not merely puzzling but inconceivable that free will should be impossible or that the premises of his arguments for incompatibilism should be false or that the rules of inference which these arguments employ should be invalid. This leads him, after some further argument, to reject determinism. "If incompatibilism is true, then either determinism or the free-will thesis is false. To deny the free-will thesis is to deny the existence of moral responsibility, which would be absurd. Moreover, there seems to be no good reason to accept determinism (which, it should be recalled, is *not* the same as the Principle of Universal Causation). Therefore, we should reject determinism" (p. 223).

My response is somewhat different. Determinism is a very general empirical thesis. Our convictions about moral responsibility seem to me an odd basis for drawing a conclusion one way or the other about such a claim. In addition, whatever one may decide about determinism, it remains puzzling how moral responsibility could be compatible with Universal Causation. I am thus led to wonder whether our initial assumptions about the kind of freedom required by moral responsibility might not be mistaken. Rather than starting with a reinterpretation of the principle of alternative possibilities (along the lines of the conditional analysis), my strategy is to ask first, Why does the fact of choice matter morally? and then, What kind of freedom is relevant to mattering in that way?

question begging. It begs the question because it does not take account of the claim that commonsense morality itself holds that people cannot be blamed for what they do when their behavior is the result of outside causes, a claim which is supported by our reactions to imaginary cases like the thought experiment mentioned above and by more general reflection on what a world of universal causality would be like.

In order to show that moral praise and blame are compatible with the Causal Thesis, it is necessary to rebut this claim. The most promising strategy for doing so is to look for a general account of the moral significance of choice, an account which, on the one hand, explains why the significance of choice is undermined both by commonly recognized excusing conditions and by factors such as those imagined to be at work in the thought experiment described above and, on the other hand, explains why the moral significance of choice will not be undermined everywhere if the Causal Thesis is true. Such an account, if convincing, would provide a basis for arguing that our initial response to the Causal Thesis was mistaken. At the very least, it would shift the burden of argument to the incompatibilist, who would need to explain why the proffered account of the moral significance of choice was inadequate. Before beginning my search for an account of the significance of choice, however, I will take a moment to examine some other forms of the free-will problem.

The problem of free will is most often discussed as a problem about moral responsibility, but essentially the same problem arises in other forms as well. It arises in political philosophy, for example, as a problem about the significance of choice as a legitimating condition. We generally think that the fact that the affected parties chose or assented to an outcome is an important factor in making that outcome legitimate. But we also recognize that there are conditions under which acquiescence does not have this legitimating force. These include conditions like those listed above: hypnosis, brain stimulation, mental incapacity, brainwashing, and so on. To many, at least, it seems plausible to maintain that these conditions deprive choice of its moral significance because they are conditions under which the agent's action is the result of outside causes. But if the Causal Thesis holds, this is true of all actions, and it would follow that choice never has moral significance as a legitimating factor.

. . .[3] Let me mention a further, slightly different case. We think it important that a political system should, as we say, "leave people free to make up their own minds," especially about important political questions and questions of

---

[3] Note omitted.

personal values. We regard certain conditions as incompatible with this important freedom and therefore to be avoided. Brainwashing is one extreme example, but there are also more moderate, and more common, forms of manipulation, such as strict control of sources of information, bombardment with one-sided information, and the creation of an environment in which people are distracted from certain questions by fear or other competing stimuli. What is it that is bad about these conditions? If they count as conditions of unfreedom simply because they are conditions under which people's opinions are causal products of outside factors, then there is no such thing as "freedom of thought" if the Causal Thesis is correct. It would follow that defenders of "freedom of thought" who accept the Causal Thesis could rightly be accused of ideological blindness: what they advocate as "freedom" is really just determination by a different set of outside factors, factors which are less rational and no more benign than those to which they object. There may be good reasons to favor some determining factors over others, but the issue cannot be one of "freedom." Here again, then, the problem is to show that "determination by outside causes" is not a sufficient condition for unfreedom. To do this we need to come up with some other explanation of what is bad about the conditions which supporters of freedom of thought condemn.[4]

These are versions of what I will call the political problem of free will. As I have said, they have much the same structure as the more frequently discussed problem about moral praise and blame. In addition to these problems there is what might be called the personal problem of free will. If I were to learn that one of my past actions was the result of hypnosis or brain stimulation, I would feel alienated from this act: manipulated, trapped, reduced to the status of a puppet. But why, if the Causal Thesis is correct, should we not feel this way about all of our acts? Why should we not feel trapped all the time? This is like the other problems in that what we need in order to answer it is a better explanation of why it is proper to feel trapped and alienated from our own actions in cases like hypnosis, an explanation which goes beyond the mere fact of determination by outside factors. But while this problem is like the others in its form, it differs from them in not being specifically a problem about morality: the significance with which it deals is not *moral* significance. This makes it a particularly difficult problem, much of the difficulty being that of explaining what the desired but threatened form of significance is supposed to be. Since my concern is with moral theory I will not address this problem directly,

---

[4] I have said more about this version of the problem in section IIB of "Freedom of Expression and Categories of Expression," *University of Pittsburgh Law Review*, 40 (1979).

though the discussion of the value of choice in lecture 2 [omitted here] will have some bearing on it.

I will be concerned in these lectures with the first two of these problems and with the relation between them: to what degree can the "better explanation" that each calls for be provided within the compass of a single, reasonably unified theory? My strategy is to put forward two theories which attempt to explain why the conditions which we commonly recognize as undermining the moral significance of choice in various contexts should have this effect. These theories, which I will refer to as the Quality of Will theory and the Value of Choice theory, are similar to the theories put forward in two famous articles, P. F. Strawson's "Freedom and Resentment,"[5] and H. L. A. Hart's "Legal Responsibility and Excuses."[6] My aim is to see whether versions of these two approaches—extended in some respects and modified in others to fit within the contractualist theory I espouse—can be put together into a single coherent account. We can then see how far this combined theory takes us toward providing a satisfactory account of the moral significance of choice across the range of cases I have listed above.

3. THE INFLUENCEABILITY THEORY

Before presenting the Quality of Will theory, it will be helpful to consider briefly an older view which serves as a useful benchmark. This view, which I will call the Influenceability theory, employs a familiar strategy for explaining conditions which excuse a person from moral blame.[7] This strategy is first to identify the purpose or rationale of moral praise and blame and then to show that this rationale fails when the standard excusing conditions are present. According to the Influenceability theory, the purpose of moral praise and blame is to influence people's behavior. There is thus no point in praising or blaming agents who are not (or were not) susceptible to being influenced by moral suasion, and it is this fact which is reflected in the commonly recognized excusing conditions.

[5] In Strawson, ed., *Studies in the Philosophy of Thought and Action* (Oxford: Oxford University Press, 1968), pp. 71–96 [reprinted as Essay 4, this volume].

[6] Chapter 2 of Hart, *Punishment and Responsibility* (Oxford: Oxford University Press, 1968).

[7] See J. J. C. Smart, "Freewill, Praise, and Blame," *Mind*, 70 (1961), 291–306; reprinted in G. Dworkin, ed., *Determinism, Free Will, and Moral Responsibility* (Englewood Cliffs, N.J.: Prentice-Hall, 1970; page references will be to this edition) [reprinted as Essay 3, this volume]. The theory was stated earlier by Moritz Schlick in chapter 7 of *The Problems of Ethics*, trans. D. Rynin (New York: Prentice-Hall, 1939), reprinted as "When Is a Man Responsible?" in B. Berofsky, ed., *Free Will and Determinism* (New York: Harper and Row, 1966; page references will be to this edition).

The difficulties with this theory are, I think, well known.[8] I will not go into them here except to make two brief points. The first is that the theory appears to conflate the question of whether moral judgment is applicable and the question of whether it should be *expressed* (in particular, expressed to the agent). The second point is that difficulties arise for the theory when it is asked whether what matters is influenceability at or shortly before the time of action or influenceability at the (later) time when moral judgment is being expressed. The utilitarian rationale for praise and blame supports the latter interpretation, but it is the former which retains a tie with commonsense notions of responsibility.

The Influenceability theory might explain why a utilitarian system of behavior control would include something like what we now recognize as excusing conditions. What some proponents of the theory have had in mind is that commonsense notions of responsibility should be given up and replaced by such a utilitarian practice. Whatever the merits of this proposal, however, it is clear that the Influenceability theory does not provide a satisfactory account of the notions of moral praiseworthiness and blameworthiness as we now understand them. The usefulness of administering praise or blame depends on too many factors other than the nature of the act in question for there ever to be a good fit between the idea of influenceability and the idea of responsibility which we now employ.[9]

4. QUALITY OF WILL: STRAWSON'S ACCOUNT

The view which Strawson presents in "Freedom and Resentment" is clearly superior to the Influenceability theory. Like that theory, however, it focuses less on the cognitive content of moral judgments than on what people are doing in making them. The centerpiece of Strawson's analysis is the idea of a reactive attitude. It is the nature of these attitudes that they are reactions not simply to what happens to us or to others but rather to the attitudes toward ourselves or others which are revealed in an agent's actions. For example, when you tread on my blistered toes, I may feel excruciating pain and greatly regret that my toes were stepped on. In addition, however, I am likely to resent the malevolence or callousness or indifference to my pain which your action indicates. This resentment is what Strawson calls a

---

[8] Some are set forth by Jonathan Bennett in section 6 of "Accountability," in Zak van Straaten, ed., *Philosophical Subjects* (Oxford: Oxford University Press, 1980).
[9] Broadening the theory to take into account the possibility of influencing people other than the agent will produce a better fit in some cases, but at the price of introducing even more considerations which are intuitively irrelevant to the question of responsibility.

"personal reactive attitude": it is my attitudinal reaction to the attitude toward me which is revealed in your action. Moral indignation, on the other hand, is what he calls a "vicarious attitude": a reaction to the attitude toward others in general (e.g., lack of concern about their pain) which your action shows you to have. All of these are what Strawson calls "participant attitudes." They "belong to involvement or participation with others in inter-personal human relationships."[10] This is in contrast to "objective attitudes," which involve seeing a person "as an object of social policy; as an object for what in a wide range of senses might be called treatment; as something certainly to be taken account, perhaps precautionary account, of; to be managed or handled or cured or trained."[11]

It follows from this characterization that the discovery of new facts about an action or an agent can lead to the modification or withdrawal of a reactive attitude in at least three ways: (a) by showing that the action was not, after all, indicative of the agent's attitude toward ourselves or others; (b) by showing that the attitude indicated in the act was not one which makes a certain reactive attitude appropriate; (c) by leading us to see the agent as someone toward whom objective, rather than participant, attitudes are appropriate.

Commonly recognized excusing conditions work in these ways. The most extreme excusing conditions sever any connection between an action (or movement) and the attitudes of the agent. If your stepping on my toes was a mere bodily movement resulting from an epileptic seizure, then it shows nothing at all about your concern or lack of concern about my pain. It would therefore be inappropriate for me to resent your action or for someone else, taking a more impartial view, to feel moral disapproval of you on that account.

Other excusing conditions have the less extreme effect of modifying the quality of will which an action can be taken to indicate, thus modifying the reactive attitudes which are appropriate. If I learn, for example, that you stepped on my foot by accident, then I can no longer resent your callousness or malevolence, but I may still, if conditions are right, resent your carelessness. If I learn that you (reasonably) believed that the toy spider on my boot was real, and that you were saving my life by killing it before it could bite me, then I can no longer *resent* your action at all, although it remains indicative of a particular quality of will on your part.

Actions produced by posthypnotic suggestion are a less clear case. Much depends on what we take the hypnosis to do. Hypnosis might lead you to

---

[10] Strawson, "Freedom and Resentment," p. 79.
[11] Ibid.

perform the intentional act of stamping your foot on mine but without any malice or even any thought that you are causing me harm. In this case a criticizable attitude is indicated by your act: a kind of complacency toward touching other people's bodies in ways that you have reason to believe are unwanted. But this attitude is not really attributable to *you*. *You* may not lack any inhibition in this regard: it is just that your normal inhibition has been inhibited by the hypnotist. The case is similar if the hypnotist implants in you a passing hatred for me and a fleeting but intense desire to cause me pain. Here again there is a criticizable attitude—more serious this time—but it is not yours. It is "just visiting," so to speak.

Strawson's account of why conditions such as insanity and extreme immaturity excuse people from moral blame is less satisfactory. The central idea is that these conditions lead us to take an "objective attitude" toward a person rather than to see him or her as a participant in those interpersonal human relationships of which the reactive attitudes are a part. Strawson's claim here can be understood on two levels. On the one hand there is the empirical claim that when we see someone as "warped or deranged, neurotic or just a child . . . all our reactive attitudes tend to be profoundly modified."[12] In addition to this, however, there is the suggestion that these factors render reactive attitudes such as resentment and indignation *inappropriate*. But Strawson's theory does not explain the grounds of this form of inappropriateness as clearly as it explained the grounds of the other excusing conditions. In fact, aside from the references to interpersonal relationships, which are left unspecified, nothing is said on this point.

In other cases, however, Strawson's theory succeeds in giving a better explanation of commonly recognized excusing conditions than that offered by the idea that a person is not to be blamed for an action which is the result of outside causes. The mere fact of causal determination seems to have little to do with the most common forms of excuse, such as accident and mistake of fact. It is a distinct advantage of Strawson's analysis that it accounts for the force of more extreme excuses such as hypnosis and brain stimulation in a way that is continuous with a natural explanation of these less extreme cases as well. Moreover, his theory can explain the relevance of "inability to do otherwise" in several senses of that phrase. Sometimes, as in the case of brain stimulation, the factors which underlie this inability sever any connection between an action and the agent's attitudes. In other cases, "inability to do otherwise" in the different sense of lack of *eligible* alternatives can modify the quality of will indicated by an agent's willingness to choose a

---

[12] Ibid. My appreciation of this straightforwardly factual reading of Strawson's argument was aided by Jonathan Bennett's perceptive analysis in "Accountability."

particular course of action. For example, if you stamp on my toes because my archenemy, who is holding your child hostage next door, has ordered you to do so, this does not make you less *responsible* for your act. The act is still fully yours, but the quality of will which it indicates on your part is not blameworthy.

As Strawson observes, these appeals to "inability to do otherwise" do not generalize. The truth of the Causal Thesis would not mean that either of these forms of inability obtained generally or that actions never indicated the presence in the agent of those attitudes or qualities of will which make resentment or moral indignation appropriate.

Like the unsuccessful defense of common sense mentioned above, Strawson's analysis is internal to our moral concepts as we now understand them. Its explanation of the conditions which negate or modify moral responsibility rests on a claim that, given the kind of thing that moral indignation is, it is an appropriate response only to actions which manifest certain attitudes on the part of the agent. This internal character may be thought to be a weakness in Strawson's account, and he himself considers an objection of this sort. The objection might be put as follows: You have shown what is and is not appropriate given the moral notions we now have; but the question is whether, if the Causal Thesis is correct, it would not be irrational to go on using those concepts and holding the attitudes they describe. Strawson's direct response to this objection is to say that the change proposed is "practically inconceivable."

The human commitment to participation in ordinary interpersonal relationships is, I think, too thoroughgoing and deeply rooted for us to take seriously the thought that a general conviction might so change our world that, in it, there were no longer any such things as inter-personal relationships as we normally understand them; and being involved in inter-personal relationships as we normally understand them precisely is being exposed to the range of reactive attitudes and feelings that is in question.[13]

But there is another reply which is suggested by something that Strawson goes on to say and which seems to me much stronger.[14] This reply points out that the principle "If your action was a causal consequence of prior factors outside your control then you cannot properly be praised or blamed for performing it" derives its strength from its claim to be supported by commonsense morality. Consequently, if an analysis such as Strawson's succeeds in giving a convincing account of the requirements of freedom implicit in our ordinary moral views—in particular, giving a systematic explanation of why commonly recognized excusing conditions should excuse—then this is

[13] Strawson, "Freedom and Resentment," p. 82.
[14] Ibid., p. 83.

success enough. Succeeding this far undermines the incompatibilist challenge by striking at its supposed basis in everyday moral thought.[15]

Plausible and appealing though it is, there are several respects in which Strawson's analysis is not fully satisfactory. One of these has already been mentioned in connection with insanity. Strawson suggests that the attitudes which moral judgments express are appropriately held only toward people who are participants in certain interpersonal relationships and that these attitudes are therefore inhibited when we become aware of conditions which render a person unfit for these relationships. But one needs to know more about what these relationships are, about why moral reactive attitudes depend on them, and about how these relationships are undermined or ruled out by factors such as insanity.

A second problem is more general. Strawson explains why certain kinds of unfreedom make moral praise and blame inapplicable by appealing to a fact about interpersonal reactive attitudes in general (and moral ones in particular), namely the fact that they are attitudes toward the attitudes of others, as manifested in their actions. But one may wonder whether anything further can be said about why attitudes of moral approval and disapproval are of this general type. Moreover, it is not clear that moral judgments need always involve the *expression* of any particular reactive attitude. For example, I may believe that an action of a friend, to whom many horrible things have recently happened, is morally blameworthy. But need this belief, or its expression, involve a feeling or expression of moral indignation or disapproval on my part? Might I not agree that what he did was wrong but be incapable of feeling disapproval toward him?

Here Strawson's analysis faces a version of one of the objections to the Influenceability theory: it links the content of a moral judgment too closely to *one* of the things that may be done in expressing that judgment. Of course, Strawson need not claim that moral judgment always involves the expression of a reactive attitude. It would be enough to say that such a judgment always makes some attitude (e.g., disapproval) appropriate. But then one wonders what the content of this underlying judgment is and

---

[15] Compare Thomas Nagel's comments on Strawson's theory in *The View from Nowhere* (Oxford: Oxford University Press, 1986), pp. 124–26 [reprinted as Essay 12, this volume]. The response I am advocating here does not deny the possibility of what Nagel has called "external" criticism of our practices of moral evaluation. It tries only to deny the incompatibilist critique a foothold in our ordinary ideas of moral responsibility. It claims that a commitment to freedom which is incompatible with the Causal Thesis is not embedded in our ordinary moral practices in the way in which a commitment to objectivity which outruns our experience is embedded in the content of our ordinary empirical beliefs. The incompatibilist response, obviously, is to deny this claim. My point is that the ensuing argument, which I am trying to advance one side of, is internal to the system of our ordinary moral beliefs.

whether the requirement of freedom is not to be explained by appeal to this content rather than to the attitudes which it makes appropriate.

In order to answer these questions one needs a more complete account of moral blameworthiness. A number of different moral theories might be called upon for this purpose, but what I will do is to sketch briefly how a Quality of Will theory might be based on a contractualist account of moral judgment.

5. QUALITY OF WILL: A CONTRACTUALIST ANALYSIS

According to contractualism as I understand it, the basic moral motivation is a desire to regulate one's behavior according to standards that others could not reasonably reject insofar as they, too, were looking for a common set of practical principles. Morality, on this view, is what might be called a system of co-deliberation. Moral reasoning is an attempt to work out principles which each of us could be expected to employ as a basis for deliberation and to accept as a basis for criticism. To believe that one is morally at fault is just to believe that one has not regulated one's behavior in the way that such standards would require. This can be so either because one has failed to attend to considerations that such standards would require one to take account of or because one has consciously acted contrary to what such standards would require. If one is concerned, as most people are to at least some extent, to be able to justify one's actions to others on grounds they could not reasonably reject, then the realization that one has failed in these ways will normally produce an attitude of serious self-reproach. But this attitude is distinct from the belief which may give rise to it. Similarly, to believe that another person's behavior is morally faulty is, at base, to believe that there is a divergence of this kind between the way that person regulated his or her behavior and the kind of self-regulation that mutually acceptable standards would require. For reasons like those just mentioned, this belief will normally be the basis for attitudes of disapproval and indignation. This view of morality grounds the fact that moral appraisal is essentially concerned with "the quality of an agent's will" in an account of the nature of moral reasoning and moral motivation. The analysis of moral judgment which it supports is essentially cognitivist. It can explain why moral judgments would normally be accompanied by certain attitudes, but these attitudes are not the basis of its account of moral judgment.

Contractualism also gives specific content to the idea, suggested by Strawson, that moral judgments presuppose a form of interpersonal relationship. On this view, moral judgments apply to people considered as possible participants in a system of co-deliberation. Moral praise and blame can thus be rendered inapplicable by abnormalities which make this kind of participation impossible. (The implications of this idea for excusing conditions such as insanity will be discussed below.)

6. THE SPECIAL FORCE OF MORAL JUDGMENT

Insofar as it goes beyond Strawson's theory in committing itself to a fuller account of the nature of moral blameworthiness, the contractualist view I have described leaves itself open to the objection that this notion of blameworthiness requires a stronger form of freedom, a form which may be incompatible with the Causal Thesis. In order to assess this objection, it will be helpful to compare the contractualist account of blame with what Smart calls "praise and dispraise." According to Smart, we commonly use the word "praise" in two different ways.[16] On the one hand, praise is the opposite of blame. These terms apply only to what a person does or to aspects of a person's character, and they are supposed to carry a special force of moral approval or condemnation. But we also praise things other than persons and their character: the California climate, the flavor of a melon, or the view from a certain hill. In this sense we also praise features of persons which we see as "gifts" beyond their control: their looks, their coordination, or their mathematical ability. Praise in this sense is not the opposite of blame, and Smart coins the term "dispraise" to denote its negative correlate. Praise and dispraise lack the special force of moral approval or condemnation which praise and blame are supposed to have. To praise or dispraise something is simply to grade it.

Smart takes the view that the kind of moral judgment involved in praise and blame as these terms are normally used must be rejected because it presupposes an unacceptable metaphysics of free will. However, we can praise and dispraise actions and character just as we can grade eyes and skill and mountain peaks. The primary function of praise in this "grading" sense, according to Smart, is just "to tell people what people are like."[17] However, since people like being praised and dislike being dispraised, praise and dispraise also have the important secondary function of serving to encourage or discourage classes of actions. Smart suggests that "clear-headed people," insofar as they use the terminology of praise and blame, will use it only in this "grading" sense and will restrict its use to cases in which this important secondary function can be fulfilled.

---

[16] Smart, "Freewill, Praise, and Blame," p. 210.
[17] Ibid., p. 211.

Most people would agree that moral praise and blame of the kind involved when we "hold a person responsible" have a force which goes beyond the merely informational function of "telling people what people are like." The problem for a compatibilist is to show that judgments with this "additional force" can be appropriate even if the Causal Thesis is true. The prior problem for moral theory is to say what this "additional force" is. What is it that an account of moral judgment must capture in order to be successfully "compatibilist"?

As I have said, Smart's analysis is not compatibilist. His aim is to replace ordinary moral judgment, not to analyze it. Strawson, on the other hand, is offering a compatibilist analysis of (at least some kinds of) moral judgment, and his analysis clearly satisfies one-half of the compatibilist test. The expression of interpersonal reactive attitudes is compatible with the Causal Thesis for much the same reason that Smart's notions of praise and dispraise are. These attitudes are reactions to "what people are like," as this is shown in their actions. As long as the people in question really are like this— as long, that is, as their actions really do manifest the attitudes in question— these reactive attitudes are appropriate.

Strawson's theory is more appealing than Smart's because it offers a plausible account of moral judgment as we currently understand it, an account of how moral judgment goes beyond merely "saying what people are like" and of how it differs from mere attempts to influence behavior. But his theory is like Smart's in locating the "special force" of moral judgment in what the moral judge is *doing*. The contractualist account I am offering, on the other hand, locates the origin of this distinctive force in what is claimed about the person judged. It is quite compatible with this analysis that moral judgments should often be intended to influence behavior and that they should often be made as expressions of reactive attitudes; but such reforming or expressive intent is not essential. What is essential, on this account, is that a judgment of moral blame asserts that the way in which an agent decided what to do was not in accord with standards which that agent either accepts or should accept insofar as he or she is concerned to justify his or her actions to others on grounds that they could not reasonably reject. This is description, but given that most people care about the justifiability of their actions to others, it is not *mere* description.

This account of the special force of moral judgment may still seem inadequate. Given what I have said it may seem that, on the contractualist view, this special force lies simply in the fact that moral judgments attribute to an agent properties which most people are seriously concerned to have or to avoid. In this respect moral judgments are like judgments of beauty or intelligence. But these forms of appraisal, and the pride and shame that can go with accepting them, involve no attribution of responsibility and hence raise no question of freedom. To the extent that moral appraisal is different in this respect, and does raise a special question of freedom, it would seem that this difference is yet to be accounted for.

One way in which freedom is relevant to moral appraisal on the Quality of Will theory (the main way mentioned so far) is this: insofar as we are talking about praising or blaming a person on the basis of a particular action, the freedom or unfreedom of that action is relevant to the question whether the intentions and attitudes seemingly implicit in it are actually present in the agent. This evidential relevance of freedom is not peculiar to moral appraisal, however. Similar questions can arise in regard to assessments of intelligence or skill on the basis of particular pieces of behavior. (We may ask, for example, whether the occasion was a fair test of her skill, or whether there were interfering conditions.) The objection just raised does not dispute the ability of the Quality of Will theory to explain *this* way in which moral judgments may depend on questions of freedom, but it suggests that this is not enough. It assumes that "blameworthy" intentions and attitudes are correctly attributed to an agent and then asks how, on the analysis I have offered, this attribution goes beyond welcome or unwelcome description. Behind the objection lies the idea that going "beyond description" in the relevant sense would involve holding the agent *responsible* in a way that people are not (normally) responsible for being beautiful or intelligent and that this notion of responsibility brings with it a further condition of freedom which my discussion of the Quality of Will theory has so far ignored.

I do not believe that in order to criticize a person for behaving in a vicious and callous manner we must maintain that he or she is responsible for becoming vicious and callous. Whether a person is so responsible is, in my view, a separate question. Leaving this question aside, however, there is a sense in which we are responsible for—or, I would prefer to say, *accountable for*—our intentions and decisions but not for our looks or intelligence. This is just because, insofar as these intentions and decisions are *ours*, it is appropriate to ask us to justify or explain them—appropriate, that is, for someone to ask, Why do you think you can treat me this way? in a way that it would not be appropriate to ask, in an accusing tone, Why are you so tall? This is not to say that these mental states are the kinds of thing which have reasons *rather than causes* but only that they are states for which requests for reasons are in principle relevant.

Moral criticism and moral argument, on the contractualist view, consist in the exchange of such requests and justifications. Adverse moral judgment therefore differs from mere unwelcome description because it calls for particular kinds of response, such as justification, explanation, or admission of fault. In what way does it "call for" these responses? Here let me make three points. First, the person making an adverse moral judgment is often literally asking for or demanding an explanation, justification, or apology. Second, moral criticism concerns features of the agent for which questions about reasons, raised by the agent him- or herself, are appropriate. Insofar as I think of a past intention, decision, or action as *mine*, I think of it as something which was sensitive to my assessment, at the time, of relevant reasons. This makes it appropriate for me to ask myself, Why did I think or do that? and Do I still take those reasons to be sufficient? Third, the contractualist account of moral motivation ties these two points together. A person who is concerned to be able to justify him- or herself to others will be moved to respond to the kind of demand I have mentioned, will want to be able to respond positively (i.e., with a justification) and will want to carry out the kind of first-person reflection just described in a way that makes such a response possible. For such a person, moral blame differs from mere unwelcome description not only because of its seriousness but also because it engages in this way with an agent's own process of critical reflection, thus raising the questions, Why did I do that? Do I still endorse those reasons? Can I defend the judgment that they were adequate grounds for acting?

Whether one accepts this as an adequate account of the "special force" of moral judgments will depend, of course, on what one thinks that moral judgment in the "ordinary" sense actually entails. Some have held that from the fact that a person is morally blameworthy it follows that it would be a good thing if he or she were to suffer some harm (or, at least, that this would be less bad than if some innocent person were to suffer the same harm).[18] I do not myself regard moral blame as having this implication. So if a compatibilist account of moral judgment must have this consequence, I am content to be offering a revisionist theory. (The problem of how the fact of choice may make harmful consequences more justifiable will, however, come up again in lecture 2 [omitted here].)

7. BLAMEWORTHINESS AND FREEDOM

It remains to say something about how this contractualist version of the Quality of Will theory handles the difficult question of moral appraisal of the insane. Discussion of this matter will also enable me to draw together

---

[18] This idea was suggested to me by Derek Parfit in the seminar following the presentation of this lecture in Oxford.

some of the points that have just been made and to say more about the kind
of freedom which is presupposed by moral blameworthiness according to
the theory I have been proposing.

As I said earlier, to believe that one's behavior is morally faulty is to
believe either that one has failed to attend to considerations which any
standards that others could not reasonably reject would require one to
attend to or that one has knowingly acted contrary to what such standards
would require. Let me focus for a moment on the first disjunct. Something
like this is a necessary part of an account of moral blameworthiness, since
failure to give any thought at all to what is morally required can certainly be
grounds for moral criticism. But the purely negative statement I have given
above is too broad. The class of people who simply fail to attend to the
relevant considerations includes many who do not seem to be candidates for
moral blame: people acting in their sleep, victims of hypnosis, young children, people suffering from mental illness, and so on. We need to find, within
the notion of moral blame itself, some basis for a nonarbitrary qualification
of the purely negative criterion.

According to contractualism, thought about right and wrong is a search
for principles "for the regulation of behavior" which others, similarly motivated, have reason to accept. What kind of "regulation" is intended here? Not
regulation "from without" through a system of social sanctions but regulation "from within" through critical reflection on one's own conduct under
the pressure provided by the desire to be able to justify one actions to others
on grounds they could not reasonably reject. This idea of regulation has two
components, one specifically moral, the other not. The specifically moral
component is the ability to reason about what could be justified to others.
The nonmoral component is the more general capacity through which the
results of such reasoning make a difference to what one does. Let me call this
the capacity for critically reflective, rational self-governance—"critically
reflective" because it involves the ability to reflect and pass judgment upon
one's actions and the thought processes leading up to them; "rational" in the
broad sense of involving sensitivity to reasons and the ability to weigh them;
"self-governance" because it is a process which makes a difference to how
one acts.

The critical reflection of a person who has this capacity will have a kind of
coherence over time. Conclusions reached at one time will be seen as relevant
to critical reflection at later times unless specifically overruled. In addition,
the results of this reflection will normally make a difference both in how the
person acts given a certain perception of a situation and in the features of
situations which he or she is on the alert for and tends to notice.

This general capacity for critically reflective, rational self-governance is not specifically moral, and someone could have it who was entirely unconcerned with morality. Morality does not tell one to have this capacity, and failing to have it in general or on a particular occasion is not a moral fault. Rather, morality is addressed to people who are assumed to have this general capacity, and it tells them how the capacity should be exercised. The most general moral demand is that we exercise our capacity for self-governance in ways that others could reasonably be expected to authorize. More specific moral requirements follow from this.

Since moral blameworthiness concerns the exercise of the general capacity of self-governance, our views about the limits of moral blame are sensitive to changes in our views about the limits of this capacity. We normally believe, for example, that very young children lack this capacity and that it does not govern our actions while we are asleep. Nor, according to some assumptions about hypnosis, does it regulate posthypnotic suggestion, and it is generally believed to be blocked by some forms of mental illness. These assumptions could be wrong, but given that we hold them it is natural that we do not take people in these categories to be morally blameworthy for their actions. (Whether we think it is useful to blame them is of course another question.) It is important to our reactions in such cases, however, that what is impaired or suspended is a *general* capacity for critically reflective, rational self-governance. If what is "lost" is more specifically moral—if, for example, a person lacks any concern for the welfare of others—then the result begins to look more like a species of moral fault.

As a "higher order" capacity, the capacity for critically reflective, rational self-governance has an obvious similarity to the capacities for higher-order desires and judgments which figure in the analyses of personhood and freedom offered by Harry Frankfurt and others.[19] I have been led to this capacity, however, not through an analysis of general notions of freedom and personhood but rather through reflection on the nature of moral argument and moral judgment. Basic to morality as I understand it is an idea of agreement between individuals *qua* critics and regulators of their own actions and deliberative processes. Critically reflective, rational self-governance is a capacity which is required in order for that idea not to be an idle one. It follows that moral criticism is restricted to individuals who have this capacity and to actions which fall within its scope.[20]

---

[19] See Harry Frankfurt, "Freedom of the Will and the Concept of a Person." *Journal of Philosophy*, 68 (1971), 5–20 [reprinted as Essay 16, this volume]; Wright Neely, "Freedom and Desire." *Philosophical Review*, 83 (1974), 32–54; and Gary Watson, "Free Agency," *Journal of Philosophy*, 72 (1975), 205–20 [reprinted as Essay 17, this volume].

[20] The idea that moral criticism is applicable only to actions which are within the scope of a capacity of self-governance which normally makes a difference in what a person does marks a point of tangency between the Influenceability theory and the analysis I am offering. I am not

In Frankfurt's terms, these restrictions correspond roughly to a restriction to persons (as opposed to "wantons") and a restriction to actions which are performed freely. In my view, however, this last characterization is not entirely apt. Aside from external impediments to bodily motion, what is required for moral appraisal on the view I am presenting is the "freedom," whatever it may be, which is required by critically reflective, rational self-governance. But this is less appropriately thought of as a kind of freedom than as a kind of intrapersonal responsiveness. What is required is that what we do be importantly dependent on our process of critical reflection, that that process itself be sensitive to reasons, and that later stages of the process be importantly dependent on conclusions reached at earlier stages. But there is no reason, as far as I can see, to require that this process itself not be a causal product of antecedent events and conditions.[21] Calling the relevant condition a form of freedom suggests this requirement, but this suggestion is undermined by our investigation into the moral significance of choice.

8. CONCLUSION

The contractualist version of the Quality of Will theory which I have described seems to me to provide a satisfactory explanation of the significance of choice for the moral appraisal of agents. This theory offers a convincing and unified account of familiar excusing conditions, such as mistake of fact and duress, and explains our reactions to questions about moral appraisal of very young children, the insane, and victims of hypnosis. It can explain the special critical force which moral judgments seem to have, and it does this without presupposing a form of freedom incompatible with the

suggesting, however, that particular acts of moral criticism are aimed at influencing people or that moral criticism is always inappropriate when there is no hope of its making any difference to what people do. Morality as I am describing it is in a general sense "action guiding"—moral argument concerns principles for the general regulation of behavior. But moral "ought" judgments need not be intended as action guiding, and insofar as they do guide action they need not do so by being prescriptive in form. Rather, they guide action by calling attention to facts about the justifiability of actions—facts which morally concerned agents care about. In these respects my view differs from R. M. Hare's prescriptivism, though we would say some of the same things about free will. See his "Prediction and Moral Appraisal," in P. French, T. Uehling, and H. Wettstein, eds., *Midwell Studies in Philosophy*, vol. iii (Minneapolis: University of Minnesota Press, 1978), pp. 17–27.

[21] For more extended discussion of this issue, see Daniel Dennett's *Elbow Room* (Cambridge, Mass.: MIT Press, 1984), especially chs. 3–5. I make no claim to be advancing beyond what other compatibilists have said about the nature of deliberation and action. My concern is with the question of moral responsibility. Here I differ with Dennett, who goes much further than I would toward accepting the Influenceability theory. See ch. 7 of *Elbow Room* and Gary Watson's criticisms of it in his review in *Journal of Philosophy*, 83 (1986), 517–22.

Causal Thesis. But the theory applies only to what I called earlier the moral version of the free-will problem. A parallel account may, as I will suggest later, have some relevance to the case of criminal punishment, but it does not offer a promising approach to the other problems I have mentioned. The significance of a person's choices and other subjective responses for questions of economic justice and freedom of thought may have something to do with the fact that these responses reflect what might loosely be called "the quality of the person's will," but this is not because what we are doing in these cases is judging this "quality" or expressing attitudes toward it (since this is not what we are doing). So, in search of an explanation that might cover these other cases, I will look in a different direction.

19

SANITY AND THE METAPHYSICS OF RESPONSIBILITY

SUSAN WOLF

Philosophers who study the problems of free will and responsibility have an easier time than most in meeting challenges about the relevance of their work to ordinary, practical concerns. Indeed, philosophers who study these problems are rarely faced with such challenges at all, since questions concerning the conditions of responsibility come up so obviously and so frequently in everyday life. Under scrutiny, however, one might question whether the connections between philosophical and nonphilosophical concerns in this area are real.

In everyday contexts, when lawyers, judges, parents, and others are concerned with issues of responsibility, they know, or think they know, what in general the conditions of responsibility are. Their questions are questions of application: Does this or that particular person meet this or that particular condition? Is this person mature enough, or informed enough, or sane enough to be responsible? Was he or she acting under posthypnotic suggestion or under the influence of a mind-impairing drug? It is assumed, in these contexts, that normal, fully developed adult human beings are responsible beings. The questions have to do with whether a given individual falls within the normal range.

By contrast, philosophers tend to be uncertain about the general conditions of responsibility, and they care less about dividing the responsible from the nonresponsible agents than about determining whether, and if so why, any of us are ever responsible for anything at all.

In the classroom, we might argue that the philosophical concerns grow out of the nonphilosophical ones, that they take off where the nonphilosophical questions stop. In this way, we might convince our students that even if they are not plagued by the philosophical worries, they ought to be. If they worry about whether a person is mature enough, informed enough, and sane enough to be responsible, then they should worry about whether that person is metaphysically free enough, too.

The argument I make here, however, goes in the opposite direction. My aim is not to convince people who are interested in the apparently nonphilosophical conditions of responsibility that they should go on to worry about the philosophical conditions as well, but rather to urge those who already worry about the philosophical problems not to leave the more mundane, prephilosophical problems behind. In particular, I suggest that the mundane recognition that *sanity* is a condition of responsibility has more to do with the murky and apparently metaphysical problems which surround the issue of responsibility than at first meets the eye. Once the significance of the condition of sanity is fully appreciated, at least some of the apparently insuperable metaphysical aspects of the problem of responsibility will dissolve.

My strategy is to examine a recent trend in philosophical discussions of responsibility, a trend that tries, but I think ultimately fails, to give an acceptable analysis of the conditions of responsibility. It fails due to what at first appear to be deep and irresolvable metaphysical problems. It is here that I suggest that the condition of sanity comes to the rescue. What at first appears to be an impossible requirement for responsibility—the requirement that the responsible agent have created her- or himself—turns out to be the vastly more mundane and noncontroversial requirement that the responsible agent must, in a fairly standard sense, be sane.

FRANKFURT, WATSON, AND TAYLOR

The trend I have in mind is exemplified by the writings of Harry Frankfurt, Gary Watson, and Charles Taylor. I will briefly discuss each of their separate proposals, and then offer a composite view that, while lacking the subtlety of any of the separate accounts, will highlight some important insights and some important blind spots they share.

In his seminal article "Freedom of the Will and the Concept of a Person,"[1] Harry Frankfurt notes a distinction between freedom of action and freedom of the will. A person has freedom of action, he points out, if she (or he) has the freedom to do whatever she wills to do—the freedom to walk or sit, to vote liberal or conservative, to publish a book or open a store, in accordance with her strongest desires. Even a person who has freedom of

---

[1] Harry Frankfurt, "Freedom of the Will and the Concept of a Person," *Journal of Philosophy*, LXVIII (1971), 5–20 [reprinted as Essay 16, this volume].

action may fail to be responsible for her actions, however, if the wants or desires she has the freedom to convert into action are themselves not subject to her control. Thus, the person who acts under posthypnotic suggestion, the victim of brainwashing, and the kleptomaniac might all possess freedom of action. In the standard contexts in which these examples are raised, it is assumed that none of the individuals is locked up or bound. Rather, these individuals are understood to act on what, at one level at least, must be called *their own desires*. Their exemption from responsibility stems from the fact that their own desires (or at least the ones governing their actions) are not up to them. These cases may be described in Frankfurt's terms as cases of people who possess freedom of action, but who fail to be responsible agents because they lack freedom of the will.

Philosophical problems about the conditions of responsibility naturally focus on an analysis of this latter kind of freedom: What *is* freedom of the will, and under what conditions can we reasonably be thought to possess it? Frankfurt's proposal is to understand freedom of the will by analogy to freedom of action. As freedom of action is the freedom to do whatever one wills to do, freedom of the will is the freedom to will whatever one wants to will. To make this point clearer, Frankfurt introduces a distinction between first-order and second-order desires. First-order desires are desires to do or to have various things; second-order desires are desires about what desires to have or what desires to make effective in action. In order for an agent to have both freedom of action and freedom of the will, that agent must be capable of governing his or her actions by first-order desires *and* capable of governing his or her first-order desires by second-order desires.

Gary Watson's view of free agency[2]—free and responsible agency, that is—is similar to Frankfurt's in holding that an agent is responsible for an action only if the desires expressed by that action are of a particular kind. While Frankfurt identifies the right kind of desires as desires that are supported by second-order desires, however, Watson draws a distinction between "mere" desires, so to speak, and desires that are *values*. According to Watson, the difference between free action and unfree action cannot be analyzed by reference to the logical form of the desires from which these various actions arise, but rather must relate to a difference in the quality of their source. Whereas some of my desires are just appetites or conditioned responses I find myself "stuck with," others are expressions of judgments on my part that the objects I desire are good. Insofar as my actions can be governed by the latter type of desire—governed, that is, by my values or

---

[2] Gary Watson, "Free Agency," *Journal of Philosophy*, LXXII (1975), 205–20 [reprinted as Essay 17, this volume].

valuational system—they are actions that I perform freely and for which I am responsible.

Frankfurt's and Watson's accounts may be understood as alternate developments of the intuition that in order to be responsible for one's actions, one must be responsible for the self that performs these actions. Charles Taylor, in an article entitled "Responsibility for Self,"[3] is concerned with the same intuition. Although Taylor does not describe his view in terms of different levels or types of desire, his view is related, for he claims that our freedom and responsibility depends on our ability to reflect on, criticize, and revise our selves. Like Frankfurt and Watson, Taylor seems to believe that if the characters from which our actions flowed were simply and permanently *given* to us, implanted by heredity, environment, or God, then we would be mere vehicles through which the causal forces of the world traveled, no more responsible than dumb animals or young children or machines. But like the others, he points out that, for most of us, our characters and desires are not so brutely implanted—or, at any rate, if they are, they are subject to revision by our own reflecting, valuing, or second-order desiring selves. We human beings—and as far as we know, only we human beings—have the ability to step back from ourselves and decide whether we are the selves we want to be. Because of this, these philosophers think, we are responsible for our selves and for the actions that we produce.

Although there are subtle and interesting differences among the accounts of Frankfurt, Watson, and Taylor, my concern is with features of their views that are common to them all. All share the idea that responsible agency involves something more than intentional agency. All agree that if we are responsible agents, it is not just because our actions are within the control of our wills, but because, in addition, our wills are not just psychological states *in* us, but expressions of characters that come *from* us, or that at any rate are acknowledged and affirmed *by* us. For Frankfurt, this means that our wills must be ruled by our second-order desires; for Watson, that our wills must be governable by our system of values; for Taylor, that our wills must issue from selves that are subject to self-assessment and redefinition in terms of a vocabulary of worth. In one way or another, all these philosophers seem to be saying that the key to responsibility lies in the fact that responsible agents are those for whom it is not just the case that their actions are within the control of their wills, but also the case that their wills are within the control of their *selves* in some deeper sense. Because, at one level, the differences among Frankfurt, Watson, and Taylor may be

[3] Charles Taylor, "Responsibility for Self," in A. E. Rorty, ed. *The Identities of Persons* (Berkeley: University of California Press, 1976), pp. 281–99.

understood as differences in the analysis or interpretation of what it is for an action to be under the control of this deeper self, we may speak of their separate positions as variations of one basic view about responsibility: the *deep-self view*.

THE DEEP-SELF VIEW

Much more must be said about the notion of a deep self before a fully satisfactory account of this view can be given. Providing a careful, detailed analysis of that notion poses an interesting, important, and difficult task in its own right. The degree of understanding achieved by abstraction from the views of Frankfurt, Watson, and Taylor, however, should be sufficient to allow us to recognize some important virtues as well as some important drawbacks of the deep-self view.

One virtue is that this view explains a good portion of our pretheoretical intuitions about responsibility. It explains why kleptomaniacs, victims of brainwashing, and people acting under posthypnotic suggestion may not be responsible for their actions, although most of us typically are. In the cases of people in these special categories, the connection between the agents' deep selves and their wills is dramatically severed—their wills are governed not by their deep selves, but by forces external to and independent from them. A different intuition is that we adult human beings can be responsible for our actions in a way that dumb animals, infants, and machines cannot. Here the explanation is not in terms of a split between these beings' deep selves and their wills; rather, the point is that these beings *lack* deep selves altogether. Kleptomaniacs and victims of hypnosis exemplify individuals whose selves are *alienated* from their actions; lower animals and machines, on the other hand, do not have the sorts of selves from which actions *can* be alienated, and so they do not have the sort of selves from which, in the happier cases, actions can responsibly flow.

At a more theoretical level, the deep-self view has another virtue: It responds to at least one way in which the fear of determinism presents itself.

A naive reaction to the idea that everything we do is completely determined by a causal chain that extends backward beyond the times of our births involves thinking that in that case we would have no control over our behavior whatsoever. If everything is determined, it is thought, then what happens happens, whether we want it to or not. A common, and proper, response to this concern points out that determinism does not deny the causal efficacy an agent's desires might have on his or her behavior. On the contrary, determinism in its more plausible forms tends to affirm this connection, merely adding that as one's behavior is determined by one's desires, so one's desires are determined by something else.[4]

Those who were initially worried that determinism implied fatalism, however, are apt to find their fears merely transformed rather than erased. If our desires are governed by something else, they might say, they are not *really* ours after all—or, at any rate, they are ours in only a superficial sense.

The deep-self view offers an answer to this transformed fear of determinism, for it allows us to distinguish cases in which desires are determined by forces foreign to oneself from desires which are determined *by* one's self—by one's "real," or second-order desiring, or valuing, or deep self, that is. Admittedly, there are cases, like that of the kleptomaniac or the victim of hypnosis, in which the agent acts on desires that "belong to" him or her in only a superficial sense. But the proponent of the deep-self view will point out that even if determinism is true, ordinary adult human action can be distinguished from this. Determinism implies that the desires which govern our actions are in turn governed by something else, but that something else will, in the fortunate cases, be our own deeper selves.

This account of responsibility thus offers a response to our fear of determinism; but it is a response with which many will remain unsatisfied. Even if my actions are governed by my desires and my desires are governed by my own deeper self, there remains the question: Who, or what, is responsible for this deeper self? The response above seems only to have pushed the problem further back.

Admittedly, some versions of the deep-self view, including Frankfurt's and Taylor's, seem to anticipate this question by providing a place for the ideal that an agent's deep self may be governed by a still deeper self. Thus, for Frankfurt, second-order desires may themselves be governed by third-order desires, third-order desires by fourth-order desires, and so on. Also, Taylor points out that, as we can reflect on and evaluate our prereflective selves, so we can reflect on and evaluate the selves who are doing the first reflecting and evaluating, and so on. However, this capacity to recursively create endless levels of depth ultimately misses the criticism's point.

First of all, even if there is no *logical* limit to the number of levels of reflection or depth a person may have, there is certainly a psychological limit—it is virtually impossible imaginatively to conceive a fourth- much less an eighth-order, desire. More important, no matter how many levels of self

---

[4] See, e.g., David Hume, *A Treatise of Human Nature* (Oxford: Oxford University Press, 1967), pp. 399–406, and R. E. Hobart, "Free Will as Involving Determination and Inconceivable Without It." *Mind*, 43 (1934).

we posit, there will still, in any individual case, be a last level—a deepest self about whom the question "What governs it?" will arise, as problematic as ever. If determinism is true, it implies that even if my actions are governed by my desires, and my desires are governed by my deepest self, my deepest self will still be governed by something that must, logically, be external to myself altogether. Though I can step back from the values my parents and teachers have given me and ask whether these are the values I really want, the "I" that steps back will itself be a product of the parents and teachers I am questioning.

The problem seems even worse when one sees that one fares no better if determinism is false. For if my deepest self is not determined by something external to myself, it will still not be determined by *me*. Whether I am a product of carefully controlled forces or a result of random mutations, whether there is a complete explanation of my origin or no explanation at all, *I* am not, in any case, responsible for my existence; I am not in control of my deepest self.

Thus, though the claim that an agent is responsible for only those actions that are within the control of his or her deep self correctly identifies a necessary condition for responsibility—a condition that separates the hypnotized and the brainwashed, the immature and the lower animals from ourselves, for example—it fails to provide a sufficient condition of responsibility that puts all fears of determinism to rest. For one of the fears invoked by the thought of determinism seems to be connected to its implication that we are but intermediate links in a causal chain, rather than ultimate, self-initiating sources of movement and change. From the point of view of one who has this fear, the deep-self view seems merely to add loops to the chain, complicating the picture but not really improving it. From the point of view of one who has this fear, responsibility seems to require being a prime mover unmoved, whose deepest self is itself neither random *nor* externally determined, but is rather determined *by* itself—who is, in other words, self-created.

At this point, however, proponents of the deep-self view may wonder whether this fear is legitimate. For although people evidently can be brought to the point where they feel that responsible agency requires them to be ultimate sources of power, to the point where it seems that nothing short of self-creation will do, a return to the internal standpoint of the agent whose responsibility is in question makes it hard to see what good this metaphysical status is supposed to provide or what evil its absence is supposed to impose.

From the external standpoint, which discussions of determinism and indeterminism encourage us to take up, it may appear that a special metaphysical status is required to distinguish us significantly from other members of the natural world. But proponents of the deep-self view will suggest this is an illusion that a return to the internal standpoint should dispel. The possession of a deep self that is effective in governing one's actions is a sufficient distinction, they will say. For while other members of the natural world are not in control of the selves that they are, we, possessors of effective deep selves, are in control. We can reflect on what sorts of beings we are, and on what sorts of marks we make on the world. We can change what we don't like about ourselves, and keep what we do. Admittedly, we do not create ourselves from nothing. But as long as we can revise ourselves, they will suggest, it is hard to find reason to complain. Harry Frankfurt writes that a person who is free to do what he wants to do and also free to want what he wants to want has "all the freedom it is possible to desire or to conceive."[5] This suggests a rhetorical question: If you are free to control your actions by your desires, and free to control your desires by your deeper desires, and free to control those desires by still deeper desires, what further kind of freedom can you want?

THE CONDITION OF SANITY

Unfortunately, there is a further kind of freedom we can want, which it is reasonable to think necessary for responsible agency. The deep-self view fails to be convincing when it is offered as a complete account of the conditions of responsibility. To see why, it will be helpful to consider another example of an agent whose responsibility is in question.

JoJo is the favorite son of Jo the First, an evil and sadistic dictator of a small, undeveloped country. Because of his father's special feelings for the boy, JoJo is given a special education and is allowed to accompany his father and observe his daily routine. In light of this treatment, it is not surprising that little JoJo takes his father as a role model and develops values very much like Dad's. As an adult, he does many of the same sorts of things his father did, including sending people to prison or to death or to torture chambers on the basis of whim. He is not *coerced* to do these things, he acts according to his own desires. Moreover, these are desires he wholly *wants* to have. When he steps back and asks, "Do I really want to be this sort of person?" his answer is resoundingly "Yes," for this way of life expresses a crazy sort of power that forms part of his deepest ideal.

In light of JoJo's heritage and upbringing—both of which he was powerless to control—it is dubious at best that he should be regarded as responsible for

---

[5] Frankfurt, p. 16.

what he does. It is unclear whether anyone with a childhood such as his could have developed into anything but the twisted and perverse sort of person that he has become. However, note that JoJo is someone whose actions are controlled by his desires and whose desires are the desires he wants to have: That is, his actions are governed by desires that are governed by and expressive of his deepest self.

The Frankfurt–Watson–Taylor strategy that allowed us to differentiate our normal selves from the victims of hypnosis and brainwashing will not allow us to differentiate ourselves from the son of Jo the First. In the case of these earlier victims, we were able to say that although the actions of these individuals were, at one level, in control of the individuals themselves, these individuals themselves, qua agents, were not the selves they more deeply wanted to be. In this respect, these people were unlike our happily more integrated selves. However, we cannot say of JoJo that his self, qua agent, is not the self he wants it to be. It *is* the self he wants it to be. From the inside, he feels as integrated, free, and responsible as we do.

Our judgment that JoJo is not a responsible agent is one that we can make only from the outside—from reflecting on the fact, it seems, that his deepest self is not up to him. Looked at from the outside, however, our situation seems no different from his—for in the last analysis, it is not up to any of us to have the deepest selves we do. Once more, the problem seems metaphysical—and not just metaphysical, but insuperable. For, as I mentioned before, the problem is independent of the truth of determinism. Whether we are determined or undetermined, we cannot have created our deepest selves. Literal self-creation is not just empirically, but logically impossible.

If JoJo is not responsible because his deepest self is not up to him, then we are not responsible either. Indeed, in that case responsibility would be impossible for anyone to achieve. But I believe the appearance that literal self-creation is required for freedom and responsibility is itself mistaken.

The deep-self view was right in pointing out that freedom and responsibility requires us to have certain distinctive types of control over our behavior and our selves. Specifically, our actions need to be under the control of our selves, and our (superficial) selves need to be under the control of our deep selves. Having seen that these types of control are not enough to guarantee us the status of responsible agents, we are tempted to go on to suppose that we must have yet another kind of control to assure us that even our deepest selves are somehow up to us. But not all the things necessary for freedom and responsibility must be types of power and control. We may need simply to *be* a certain way, even though it is not within our power to determine whether we are that way or not.

Indeed, it becomes obvious that at least one condition of responsibility is of this form as soon as we remember what, in everyday contexts, we have known all along—namely, that in order to be responsible, an agent must be *sane*. It is not ordinarily in our power to determine whether we are or are not sane. Most of us, it would seem, are lucky, but some of us are not. Moreover, being sane does not necessarily mean that one has any type of power or control an insane person lacks. Some insane people, like JoJo and some actual political leaders who resemble him, may have complete control of their actions, and even complete control of their acting selves. The desire to be sane is thus not a desire for another form of control; it is rather a desire that one's self be connected to the world in a certain way—we could even say it is a desire that one's self be *controlled by* the world in certain ways and not in others.

This becomes clear if we attend to the criteria for sanity that have historically been dominant in legal questions about responsibility. According to the M'Naughten Rule, a person is sane if (1) he knows what he is doing and (2) he knows that what he is doing is, as the case may be, right or wrong. Insofar as one's desire to be sane involves a desire to know what one is doing—or more generally, a desire to live in the real world—it is a desire to be controlled (to have, in this case, one's *beliefs* controlled) by perceptions and sound reasoning that produce an accurate conception of the world, rather than by blind or distorted forms of response. The same goes for the second constituent of sanity—only, in this case, one's hope is that one's *values* be controlled by processes that afford an accurate conception of the world.[6] Putting these two conditions together, we may understand sanity, then, as the minimally sufficient ability cognitively and normatively to recognize and appreciate the world for what it is.

There are problems with this definition of sanity, at least some of which will become obvious in what follows, that make it ultimately unacceptable either as a gloss on or an improvement of the meaning of the term in many of the contexts in which it is used. The definition offered does seem to bring out the interest sanity has for us in connection with issues of responsibility, however, and some pedagogical as well as stylistic purposes will be served if we use sanity hereafter in this admittedly specialized sense.

---

[6] Strictly speaking, perception and sound reasoning may not be enough to ensure the ability to achieve an accurate conception of what one is doing and especially to achieve a reasonable normative assessment of one's situation. Sensitivity and exposure to certain realms of experience may also be necessary for these goals. For the purpose of this essay, I understand "sanity" to include whatever it takes to enable one to develop an adequate conception of one's world. In other contexts, however, this would be an implausibly broad construction of the term.

THE SANE DEEP-SELF VIEW

So far I have argued that the conditions of responsible agency offered by the deep-self view are necessary but not sufficient. Moreover, the gap left open by the deep-self view seems to be one that can be filled only by a metaphysical, and, as it happens, metaphysically impossible addition. I now wish to argue, however, that the condition of sanity, as characterized above, is sufficient to fill the gap. In other words, the deep-self view, supplemented by the condition of sanity, provides a satisfying conception of responsibility. The conception of responsibility I am proposing, then, agrees with the deep-self view in requiring that a responsible agent be able to govern her (or his) actions by her desires and to govern her desires by her deep self. In addition, my conception insists that the agent's deep self be sane, and claims that this is *all* that is needed for responsible agency. By contrast to the plain deep-self view, let us call this new proposal the *sane deep-self view*.

It is worth noting, to begin with, that this new proposal deals with the case of JoJo and related cases of deprived childhood victims in ways that better match our pretheoretical intuitions. Unlike the plain deep-self view, the sane deep-self view offers a way of explaining why JoJo is not responsible for his actions without throwing our own responsibility into doubt. For, although like us, JoJo's actions flow from desires that flow from his deep self, unlike us, JoJo's deep self is itself insane. Sanity, remember, involves the ability to know the difference between right and wrong, and a person who, even on reflection, cannot see that having someone tortured because he failed to salute you is wrong plainly lacks the requisite ability.

Less obviously, but quite analogously, this new proposal explains why we give less than full responsibility to persons who, though acting badly, act in ways that are strongly encouraged by their societies—the slaveowners of the 1850s, the Nazis of the 1930s, and many male chauvinists of our fathers' generation, for example. These are people, we imagine, who falsely believe that the ways in which they are acting are morally acceptable, and so, we may assume, their behavior is expressive of or at least in accordance with these agents' deep selves. But their false beliefs in the moral permissibility of their actions and the false values from which these beliefs derived may have been inevitable, given the social circumstances in which they developed. If we think that the agents could not help but be mistaken about their values, we do not blame them for the actions those values inspired.[7]

---

[7] Admittedly, it is open to question whether these individuals were in fact unable to help having mistaken values, and indeed, whether recognizing the errors of their society would even have required exceptional independence or strength of mind. This is presumably an empirical question, the answer to which is extraordinarily hard to determine. My point here is simply that *if* we believe

It would unduly distort ordinary linguistic practice to call the slaveowner, the Nazi, or the male chauvinist even partially or locally insane. Nonetheless, the reason for withholding blame from them is at bottom the same as the reason for withholding it from JoJo. Like JoJo, they are, at the deepest level, unable cognitively and normatively to recognize and appreciate the world for what it is. In our sense of the term, their deepest selves are not fully *sane*.

The sane deep-self view thus offers an account of why victims of deprived childhoods as well as victims of misguided societies may not be responsible for their actions, without implying that we are not responsible for ours. The actions of these others are governed by mistaken conceptions of value that the agents in question cannot help but have. Since, as far as we know, our values are not, like theirs, unavoidably mistaken, the fact that these others are not responsible for their actions need not force us to conclude that we are not responsible for ours.

But it may not yet be clear why sanity, in this special sense, should make such a difference—why, in particular, the question of whether someone's values are unavoidably *mistaken* should have any bearing on their status as responsible agents. The fact that the sane deep-self view implies judgments that match our intuitions about the difference in status between characters like JoJo and ourselves provides little support for it if it cannot also defend these intuitions. So we must consider an objection that comes from the point of view we considered earlier which rejects the intuition that a relevant difference can be found.

Earlier, it seemed that the reason JoJo was not responsible for his actions was that although his actions were governed by his deep self, his deep self was not up to him. But this had nothing to do with his deep self's being mistaken or not mistaken, evil or good, insane or sane. If JoJo's values are unavoidably mistaken, our values, even if not mistaken, appear to be just as unavoidable. When it comes to freedom and responsibility, isn't it the unavoidability, rather than the mistakenness, that matters?

Before answering this question, it is useful to point out a way in which it is ambiguous: The concepts of avoidability and mistakenness are not unequivocally distinct. One may, to be sure, construe the notion of avoidability in a purely metaphysical way. Whether an event or state of affairs is unavoidable under this construal depends, as it were, on the tightness of the causal connections that bear on the event's or state of affairs' coming about. In this sense, our deep selves do seem as unavoidable for us as JoJo's and the

they are unable to recognize that their values are mistaken, we do not hold them responsible for the actions that flow from these values, and *if* we believe their ability to recognize their normative errors is impaired, we hold them less than fully responsible for the relevant actions.

others' are for them. For presumably we are just as influenced by our parents, our cultures, and our schooling as they are influenced by theirs. In another sense, however, our characters are not similarly unavoidable.

In particular, in the cases of JoJo and the others, there are certain features of their characters that they cannot avoid *even though these features are seriously mistaken, misguided, or bad.* This is so because, in our special sense of the term, these characters are less than fully sane. Since these characters lack the ability to know right from wrong, they are unable to revise their characters on the basis of right and wrong, and so their deep selves lack the resources and the reasons that might have served as a basis for self-correction. Since the deep selves *we* unavoidably have, however, are sane deep selves—deep selves, that is, that unavoidably *contain* the ability to know right from wrong—we unavoidably do have the resources and reasons on which to base self-correction. What this means is that though in one sense we are no more in control of our deepest selves than JoJo et al., it does not follow in our case, as it does in theirs, that we would be the way we are, even if it is a bad or wrong way to be. However, if this does not follow, it seems to me, our absence of control at the deepest level should not upset us.

Consider what the absence of control at the deepest level amounts to for us: Whereas JoJo is unable to control the fact that, at the deepest level, he is not fully sane, we are not responsible for the fact that, at the deepest level, we are. It is not up to us to *have* minimally sufficient abilities cognitively and normatively to recognize and appreciate the world for what it is. Also, presumably, it is not up to us to have lots of other properties, at least to begin with—a fondness for purple, perhaps, or an antipathy for beets. As the proponents of the plain deep-self view have been at pains to point out, however, we do, if we are lucky, have the ability to revise our selves in terms of the values that are held by or constitutive of our deep selves. If we are lucky enough both to have this ability and to have our deep selves be sane, it follows that although there is much in our characters that we did not choose to have, there is nothing irrational or objectionable in our characters that we are compelled to keep.

Being sane, we are able to understand and evaluate our characters in a reasonable way, to notice what there is reason to hold on to, what there is reason to eliminate, and what, from a rational and reasonable standpoint, we may retain or get rid of as we please. Being able as well to govern our superficial selves by our deep selves, then, we are able to change the things we find there is reason to change. This being so, it seems that although we may not be *metaphysically* responsible for ourselves—for, after all, we did not create ourselves from nothing—we are *morally* responsible for ourselves, for we are able to understand and appreciate right and wrong, and to change our characters and our actions accordingly.

SELF-CREATION, SELF-REVISION, AND SELF-CORRECTION

At the beginning of this chapter, I claimed that recalling that sanity was a condition of responsibility would dissolve at least some of the appearance that responsibility was metaphysically impossible. To see how this is so, and to get a fuller sense of the sane deep-self view, it may be helpful to put that view into perspective by comparing it to the other views we have discussed along the way.

As Frankfurt, Watson, and Taylor showed us, in order to be free and responsible we need not only to be able to control our actions in accordance with our desires, we need to be able to control our desires in accordance with our deepest selves. We need, in other words, to be able to *revise* ourselves—to get rid of some desires and traits, and perhaps replace them with others on the basis of our deeper desires or values or reflections. However, consideration of the fact that the selves who are doing the revising might themselves be either brute products of external forces or arbitrary outputs of random generation made us wonder whether the capacity for self-revision was enough to assure us of responsibility—and the example of JoJo added force to the suspicion that it was not. Still, if the ability to revise ourselves is not enough, the ability to create ourselves does not seem necessary either. Indeed, when you think of it, it is unclear why anyone should want self-creation. Why should anyone be disappointed at having to accept the idea that one has to get one's start somewhere? It is an idea that most of us have lived with quite contentedly all along. What we do have reason to want, then, is something more than the ability to revise ourselves, but less than the ability to create ourselves. Implicit in the sane deep-self view is the idea that what is needed is the ability to *correct* (or improve) ourselves.

Recognizing that in order to be responsible for our actions, we have to be responsible for our selves, the sane deep-self view analyzes what is necessary in order to be responsible for our selves as (1) the ability to evaluate ourselves sensibly and accurately, and (2) the ability to transform ourselves insofar as our evaluation tells us to do so. We may understand the exercise of these abilities as a process where by we *take* responsibility for the selves that we are but did not ultimately create. The condition of sanity is intrinsically connected to the first ability; the condition that we be able to control our superficial selves by our deep selves is intrinsically connected to the second.

The difference between the plain deep-self view and the sane deep-self view, then, is the difference between the requirement of the capacity for self-revision and the requirement of the capacity for self-correction. Anyone with the first capacity can *try* to take responsibility for himself or herself. However, only someone with a sane deep self—a deep self that can see and appreciate the world for what it is—can self-evaluate sensibly and accurately. Therefore, although insane selves can try to take responsibility for themselves, only sane selves will properly be accorded responsibility.

TWO OBJECTIONS CONSIDERED

At least two problems with the sane deep-self view are so glaring as to have certainly struck many readers. In closing, I shall briefly address them. First, some will be wondering how, in light of my specialized use of the term "sanity," I can be so sure that "we" are any saner than the nonresponsible individuals I have discussed. What justifies my confidence that, unlike the slaveowners, Nazis, and male chauvinists, not to mention JoJo himself, we are able to understand and appreciate the world for what it is? The answer to this is that nothing justifies this except widespread intersubjective agreement and the considerable success we have in getting around in the world and satisfying our needs. These are not sufficient grounds for the smug assumption that we are in a position to see the truth about *all* aspects of ethical and social life. Indeed, it seems more reasonable to expect that time will reveal blind spots in our cognitive and normative outlook, just as it has revealed errors in the outlooks of those who have lived before. But our judgments of responsibility can only be made from here, on the basis of the understandings and values that we can develop by exercising the abilities we do possess as well and as fully as possible.

If some have been worried that my view implicitly expresses an overconfidence in the assumption that we are sane and therefore right about the world, others will be worried that my view too closely connects sanity with being right about the world, and fear that my view implies that anyone who acts wrongly or has false beliefs about the world is therefore insane and so not responsible for his or her actions. This seems to me to be a more serious worry, which I am sure I cannot answer to everyone's satisfaction.

First, it must be admitted that the sane deep-self view embraces a conception of sanity that is explicitly normative. But this seems to me a strength of that view, rather than a defect. Sanity *is* a normative concept, in its ordinary as well as in its specialized sense, and severely deviant behavior, such as that of a serial murderer or a sadistic dictator, does constitute evidence of a psychological defect in the agent. The suggestion that the most horrendous, stomach-turning crimes could be committed only by an insane person—an inverse of Catch-22, as it were—must be regarded as a serious possibility, despite the practical problems that would accompany general acceptance of that conclusion.

But, it will be objected, there is no justification, in the sane deep-self view, for regarding only horrendous and stomach-turning crimes as evidence of insanity in its specialized sense. If sanity is the ability cognitively and normatively to understand and appreciate the world for what it is, then *any* wrong action or false belief will count as evidence of the absence of that ability. This point may also be granted, but we must be careful about what conclusion to draw. To be sure, when someone acts in a way that is not in accordance with acceptable standards of rationality and reasonableness, it is always appropriate to look for an explanation of why he or she acted that way. The hypothesis that the person was unable to understand and appreciate that an action fell outside acceptable bounds will always be a possible explanation. Bad performance on a math test always suggests the possibility that the testee is stupid. Typically, however, other explanations will be possible, too—for example, that the agent was too lazy to consider whether his or her action was acceptable, or too greedy to care, or, in the case of the math testee, that he or she was too occupied with other interests to attend class or study. Other facts about the agent's history will help us decide among these hypotheses.

This brings out the need to emphasize that sanity, in the specialized sense, is defined as the *ability* cognitively and normatively to understand and appreciate the world for what it is. According to our commonsense understandings, having this ability is one thing and exercising it is another—at least some wrong-acting, responsible agents presumably fall within the gap. The notion of "ability" is notoriously problematic, however, and there is a long history of controversy about whether the truth of determinism would show our ordinary ways of thinking to be simply confused on this matter. At this point, then, metaphysical concerns may voice themselves again—but at least they will have been pushed into a narrower, and perhaps a more manageable, corner.

The sane deep-self view does not, then, solve all the philosophical problems connected to the topics of free will and responsibility. If anything, it highlights some of the practical and empirical problems, rather than solves them. It may, however, resolve some of the philosophical, and particularly, some of the metaphysical problems, and reveal how intimate are the connections between the remaining philosophical problems and the practical ones.

20

FREEDOM IN BELIEF AND DESIRE

PHILIP PETTIT AND MICHAEL SMITH

People ordinarily suppose that there are certain things they ought to believe and certain things they ought not to believe. In supposing this to be so, they make corresponding assumptions about their belief-forming capacities. They assume that they are generally responsive to what they think they ought to believe in the things they actually come to believe. In much the same sense, people ordinarily suppose that there are certain things they ought to desire and do and they make corresponding assumptions about their capacities to form desires and act on them. We chart these assumptions and argue that they entail that people are responsible and free on two fronts: they are free and responsible believers, and free and responsible desirers.

In the first section, we characterize some assumptions that people make about one another and about themselves within what we call *the conversational stance*. Drawing on this characterization, we go on in the second section to describe people's specific assumptions about their capacities as believers. In the third section, we extend the characterization to encompass the assumptions people make about their capacities as desirers. In the fourth section, we show that these assumptions about the formation of belief and desire commit people to a belief in their responsibility. And then in the fifth and final section, we connect this belief in responsibility with a belief in freedom. We argue that to be responsible in desire is to hold your desires freely—if you like, to enjoy free will—and that to be responsible in belief is to hold your beliefs freely: to enjoy free thought.

The ideals of free will and free thought are not usually connected and we are conscious of offering a relatively novel view of their relationship. As we

From the *Journal of Philosophy*, 93/9 (1996), 429–49. Reprinted by permission of the publisher and the author.

We would like to thank John O'Leary-Hawthorne, Galen Strawson, and Susan Wolf for their very helpful comments. We are also grateful for comments received when the paper was presented to the Australasian Association of Philosophy, University of New England (1995), and at the Human Action and Causality Conference, University of Utrecht (1996), and, as well, when it was read to staff seminars at the Australian National University, the University of Hong Kong, and the University of Caen.

see things, philosophers have taken a unified perspective on freedom to be unavailable because of an unfortunate tendency to overstate the differences between belief and desire. The paper is part of a more general project of undermining this unfortunate tendency.[1]

I. THE CONVERSATIONAL STANCE

One of the most striking things about human beings is conversation, in particular conversation conducted to intellectual effect. People do not set out just to form their own intellectual beliefs and then inform others of them. They listen to one another in the course of belief formation and they invest one another's responses with potential importance. They are prepared often to change their own minds in the light of what they hear from others and, if they are not, then they usually feel obliged to make clear why they are not and why indeed the others should alter their views instead.

It is true, of course, that most human exchange is not primarily intellectual in character. Conversation is the means whereby we recognize others and seek recognition from them. It is the forum in which we tell our jokes, confess our antipathies and form our friendships, coax and persuade and flatter in the furthering of our ends, and, in general, ring changes on the basic themes that engage the human sensibility. But for all that conversation achieves in these respects, it is also in some part a forum in which we put our beliefs on the line and expose them to the reality test that others represent for us. It often assumes an intellectual character.

Conversation of an intellectual kind is such a common feature of everyday life that it is easily taken for granted, but such conversation involves assumptions that are actually rather remarkable.[2] First, people assume that they each form beliefs or judgments and that these beliefs bear on common questions. This appears in the fact that people balk at any perceived discrepancy between their respective attitudes: they take the discrepancy to signal that someone is in the wrong. Second, people assume that they are each authorities worth listening to, even if the likelihood of error varies from individual to individual. No one commands or expects to command universal deference, and no one gets dismissed out of hand or expects to get dismissed out of hand. And third, people assume that when they differ in their judgments, a review of the evidence commonly available can usually

---

[1] See our "Backgrounding Desire," *Philosophical Review*, XCIX (1990), 569–92, and "Practical Unreason," *Mind*, CII (1993), 53–79.

[2] Pettit, *The Common Mind: An Essay on Psychology, Society and Politics* (New York: Oxford, 1993; 2nd ed., with new postscript, 1996), ch. 4.

reveal who is in the wrong and thereby establish agreement; they assume that good evidence, if there is good evidence available, will serve to put the mistaken ones right.

This recourse to evidence will not always be successful in resolving differences. But even then it is striking that people do not happily acquiesce in the existence of the discrepancy. They make the auxiliary assumption that there is probably a certain sort of explanation available. They judge that one or the other does not have access to all the evidence—that the evidence is not equally available on all sides—and try to put that right. Or they judge that the available evidence, or even all the evidence possible, leaves the difference between them unresolved—it is not good enough to constrain belief uniquely—and that, within certain limits, no one is blocked from going his own way. Or they judge that those who dissent are misled by something like inattention or illogic or just laziness of mind. By taking one or another of these views, people are saved from having to conclude that those who dissent are out of their minds and not worthy of attention: that they are not even presumptive authorities. They may be driven to the out-of-their-minds conclusion as a last resort but the default position is more optimistic.

A final feature of conversation is that not only do people make all these assumptions—the three basic assumptions together with this auxiliary assumption—they apparently each accept that the assumptions are a matter of common belief. Each person believes them, each person believes that everyone else believes them as well—or at least no one disbelieves that everyone else believes them[3]—and so on. That everyone believes them shows up, as indicated, in their responding appropriately: they balk at every discrepancy, look for a resolution, and try to explain any failure to achieve it. That everyone believes that everyone believes the assumptions shows up in the fact that no one is surprised at anyone's responding in that way. That everyone believes that everyone believes that everyone believes them shows up in the fact that no one is surprised that no one is surprised at anyone's responding in that way. And so on.

Do many conversations have the intellectual character that engages these assumptions? It is true that people often only go through the motions of pretending that there is a common subject matter under intellectual discussion with others, or that others are really worth listening to on that subject matter, or that they have anything to say. But we take it that the very fact of such pretense is itself testimony to the effect that everyone has a notion of what properly intellectual conversation is and that they all assume that it at

[3] David Lewis, "Languages and Language," reprinted in his *Philosophical Papers, Volume 1* (New York: Oxford, 1983), p. 166.

least occasionally occurs. People do genuinely, if only intermittently, reach out toward others and seek a meeting of minds with them: they authorize their interlocutors and in turn assume authorization by them.

Conversation in the sense characterized need not involve different people in exchange at or over the same time. As someone makes up his mind about what to believe on some matter, conscious that he will return to the topic again, or as someone reflects on what he came to believe earlier, assessing the worth of the reasons that moved him, he enters into a sort of conversation with himself. He takes it, whether at the earlier or later moment, that there is a common content at issue; that neither self can spurn the voice of the other; that any discrepancy ought to be subject to resolution; that if it is not, then that is probably due to limited evidence or a local failure on one or the other side; and that these are matters of common belief between his different, interlocuting selves.

This characterization of intrapersonal conversation is borne out, not by appeal to introspection, but by reflection on the assumptions implicit in the ways people conduct their thought. An earlier self will always balk at the prospect of a later discrepancy, as of course the later self will balk at the experience of such discrepancy with the past: the prospect of later discrepancy may even give an earlier self reason now to rethink commitments.[4] We see in evidence here the assumption on each side that there is a common content addressed by the two selves: or addressed, if you prefer, by the same person at different times. Again, in face of perceived discrepancy, neither the earlier nor the later self defers to the other, or dismisses the other out of hand; and so there is also an assumption of shared authority at work. More-over, to go to the assumptions relating to resolution, the earlier self will try in anticipation, or the later self in recollection, to come to a common mind in the light of common evidence or, failing that, will look for some contingent explanation of the expected or actual lack of consensus. And, finally, that these various assumptions are endorsed by earlier and later selves is a matter of common belief between the two: they chime with their expectations, and their expectations about expectations, in the required manner.

II. BELIEF

It only makes sense to adopt the conversational stance in relation to someone—yourself or another person—if three conditions are satisfied:

[4] Bas C. van Fraassen, "Belief and the Will," JOURNAL OF PHILOSOPHY, LXXXI, 5 (May 1984), 235–56; and Richard Holton, "Deciding to Trust, Coming to Believe," *Australasian Journal of Philosophy*, LXXII (1994), 63–76.

first, there are norms relevant to the issue of what she ought to believe; second, she is capable of recognizing this to be so; and third, she is capable of responding appropriately to the norms: that is, capable of believing in the way she should.

Consider the first condition. There are belief-relevant norms that apply, by everyone's lights, to any conversational interlocutor. When you ascribe beliefs to someone you identify certain propositions as the contents of those beliefs. You say that what she believes is that eucalypts are evergreen or that Princeton is not in England or that ripe tomatoes are red or whatever. So far as certain propositions are the contents of the subject's beliefs in this way, it is right for her to maintain those beliefs in certain circumstances, or in certain apparent circumstances, wrong for her to do so in others. This follows, at least under plausible assumptions, from the fact that beliefs are representations of the subject's environment. Furthermore, it is right for the subject to form certain new beliefs, wrong for her to form certain alternatives, depending on what follows from what: it is right for her to believe that this eucalypt is evergreen, that this English town is not Princeton, that this green tomato is unripe, and so on.

The general lesson is that when you ascribe beliefs you assume, in effect, that certain belief-relevant norms apply to the performance of the believer. There are norms that govern what the subject ought to believe in the presence of certain facts. And there are norms, therefore, that govern what the subject ought to believe in the light of the corresponding evidence—the apparent facts—so far as that evidence is determinate. Are the norms that you postulate in this way objectively valid? Yes, in at least one sense. Such norms are not like the conventional norms of behavior that might be recognized in a given club or circle: they are not norms, such that subjects can be imagined deciding whether to embrace them or not, depending on their contingent attitudes or alignments. To be a thinker who believes in certain determinate contents is to be subject to norms like: believe that p if and only if p; believe that p if and only if all the evidence points to p; and believe that p when p is entailed by some of the things you believe, and is not inconsistent with anything else you believe! The relevance of such norms—such evidential norms, as we will call them—is *inescapable*.

Consistently with acknowledging this you can, of course, admit the possibility that your own view of the relevant norms is inadequate or distorted. For all anyone can guarantee, there may be reasons for casting evidential norms quite differently from the way they are habitually cast. There may be reasons, for example, for revising the received view on what follows from what, or what supports what: standard views on deductive and inductive logic may be mistaken. To think that there are objectively valid norms of evidence is not necessarily to pretend to be infallible on the matter of what those norms are. It is only to hold that believers fall willy nilly under norms of evidence, and that the norms in question apply across the different groups to which the subjects belong. They do not segregate on lines of culture or class or gender.

Consider now the second condition. Does the conversational stance suppose that a conversational interlocutor recognizes evidential norms? Someone will recognize such norms if she has beliefs with contents of the form: it is true that p or it is false that p; the evidence supports the hypothesis that p or is against the hypothesis that p; q, and the fact that q implies or entails that p; and so on. To believe that a certain proposition—a certain potential belief content—is true or is supported by the evidence or is entailed by something that is itself accepted is to believe, in effect, that it is right to believe the proposition, wrong to disbelieve it: it is to believe that there are norms that require the attitude, at least when other things are equal.

We think that in order to attract and sustain authorization, the conversational interlocutor must manifest beliefs involving notions like truth and support and entailment and that in this sense she must recognize certain belief-relevant norms. When you authorize someone in conversation, you hold her to the expectation that she will balk at discrepancies between the two of you, and do so in a way that invites the ascription of beliefs like the following: that you each have different belief attitudes toward the same content, that the evidence available may rule out one of those beliefs as unsupported or false, and that attention to the evidence may reveal which, if either, of the beliefs should be given up. If an interlocutor failed to live up to that expectation, if she failed to manifest any notion of there being a common content of belief or a common fund of evidence, for example, then you would have no reason to take her attitudes seriously; you would have no reason to invest her responses with any authority. But this is to say, then, that in authorizing someone in conversation, you treat her as recognizing certain familiar norms for beliefs. You take her to see that for any content believed there may be evidence for or against the proposition, and that the state of this evidence may make it right or wrong to entertain the belief.

The third condition is that people not only be disposed to recognize the demands of evidential norms in their own case but that they also be disposed to respond to those registerings: that they be disposed to maintain beliefs that comply with the norms and to reject beliefs that fail to do so. What would happen if, on being challenged about a certain belief—say, in virtue of a discrepancy between the two of you—an interlocutor was disposed to examine the belief for its compliance with evidential norms but was not disposed to maintain or reject the belief, depending on what the examination revealed? Suppose the person was unrevisably committed to her beliefs, for example, or that examination of her beliefs occasioned an arbitrary pattern of maintaining or rejecting the belief in question. What would happen then?

In such a case you would, once again, have no reason to invest such a person with the authority of a conversational interlocutor. You might use them, in the way you might use a clock, as a prima facie check on your beliefs. But you could not assign to her the sort of role that you must expect a conversational interlocutor to fulfill. You could not treat her as a subject such that it may well be possible to achieve the resolution of any discrepancy that appears between you. You would not treat her as a subject such that the failure to achieve such resolution is a serious challenge for each of you to face. There will be no possibility of resolution, if she is not disposed to respond to what she registers in her own case as the demands of evidential norms.

This is not to say that the subjects we invest with conversational authority must be cognitive saints or god-like creatures. As already noticed, there are all sorts of obstacles, by the light of our conversational assumptions, that may stop our partners from responding on some particular occasion in the way they know and we know they should. Some of these obstacles are seen as disabling, others as not disabling. We may think that though someone failed to respond on a given occasion—say, through inattentiveness—further conversational pressure would have brought her around. Such nondisabling obstacles are readily countenanced. But we may also think that when other sorts of obstacles are in place, conversational pressure can do no good; on the topic affected—say, by bias—or over the period affected—say, by passion—the person is disabled as a conversational partner. Such obstacles are difficult to countenance since they force us to regard the interlocutor as unworthy of being taken seriously on the topic, or at the time, in question. But still they can be countenanced, provided they are sufficiently insulated from the person's general performance.

To sum up, then, authorizing a subject as a conversational interlocutor makes sense only if there are certain norms governing what that subject ought to believe, the subject is disposed to recognize those norms, and she is disposed to respond in the way required. Whether it be yourself or someone else, authorization involves postulating that the subject has a variety of sophisticated belief-forming capacities.

III. DESIRE

We turn now to the assumptions that people make about their capacities, not in forming beliefs, but rather in forming and acting on desires. Our argument is that these capacities are assumed to be on a par with belief-forming capacities.

Desire-forming capacities will be on a par with belief-forming capacities so far as they fulfill three conditions: first, there are norms governing what agents should desire and do at any moment; second, agents are capable of recognizing these demands; and third, agents prove generally responsive in their desires and actions to the impact of the norms they recognize. Insofar as people converse, not just about more or less theoretical questions, but also about practical matters—about what it is right or wrong, good or bad, rational or irrational, sensible or stupid, to do in a given situation—we think that they are more or less bound to treat one another—and, of course, themselves—as satisfying the three conditions mentioned.

The first condition is that there are norms governing what the agent should desire and do. Why does conversing with someone about practical matters—why does conversationally authorizing him in this role—presuppose that he satisfy this condition? Imagine a difference with someone about whether it would be rational or irrational for someone—say, the interlocutor—to act in a certain way. Such a difference often has the very same characteristics as a disagreement about any ordinary matter of fact. The pair of you balk at the conversational discrepancy and seek out ways in which you might resolve your evaluative difference. You assume that both of you cannot be right, and you assume further that a careful weighing of your reasons for your different judgments will reveal which of you is right, which of you is in error.

When you take yourselves to be concerned in this way with facts that support or undermine the claim that an act is rational or irrational, you treat it as a matter of fact—a matter of agreed fact—that there are norms available to govern the things that the agent should desire and do. While the norms countenanced may leave certain choices open—while they may be permissive of various differences—you are agreed that this is not one of those cases. And by your lights, the business of seeing what the norms require in such a case—the business of deciding whether it is rational or irrational for the agent to act in a certain way—is a serious enterprise. It is not one of just sorting out your respective feelings, for example, nor one of just manufacturing a mutual accommodation, nor anything of the kind. As you practice it, practical evaluation amounts to a world-directed enterprise of sifting out fact from fiction; a matter of trying to determine what, in light of the facts, the agent is required to desire and do.

Of course, it is one thing to argue that practical evaluations make claims that can be justified by appropriate reasons, quite another to give an account of the metaphysical underpinnings of this idea. Should we be antirealists, or quasirealists, or realists with regard to the contents of our practical evaluations?[5] In the present context, we can afford to be ecumenical. Different theorists are free to give the idea of a practical evaluation their preferred treatment. All that our argument requires is that the accounts they give be consistent with the truism that practical evaluations are indeed conversationally interrogable. We return to the issue of metaphysical underpinnings later, but for the moment we may let it pass.

So much for the claim that people presuppose that there really are norms governing desire and action. The other two claims we need to defend are that you have to presuppose with any interlocutor in a conversation about what he ought to do—yourself included, of course—that he is disposed to recognize the demands of those norms and that he is disposed to respond appropriately. These claims do not have to hold true for absolutely every desire. Just as otherwise perceptive and responsive believers may be subject to certain disabling obstacles, so otherwise perceptive and responsive desirers may be subject to similar constraints: they may be the victims of certain restricted fetishes and obsessions, for example, and they may be susceptible to certain disabling moods or passions. And even where they are not so disabled, they may be subject to obstacles that give way only with efforts at self-control or under conversational challenge.

Once we recognize these escape clauses, we can have little hesitation in agreeing that when you authorize someone in conversation about matters of practical evaluation, and in particular on matters that bear on what he ought to do himself, you must treat him as being disposed both to register those demands and to respond appropriately. You will expect him to change his evaluations in light of the evidence, and his desires in light of his evaluations.

Were you to think that your interlocutor lacked the dispositions to register and respond to the demands of the norms governing evaluations that you both countenance, and lacked them even in the provisoed measure allowed, you would either have to put his evaluative understanding or commitment in serious question or you would have to regard him as something close to a

---

[5] For quasirealist and antirealist accounts, see Simon Blackburn, *Spreading the Word* (New York: Oxford, 1984); and Allan Gibbard, *Wise Choices, Apt Feelings* (Cambridge: Harvard, 1990). For realist accounts, see Smith, *The Moral Problem* (Cambridge: Blackwell, 1995); Frank Jackson and Pettit, "Moral Functionalism and Moral Motivation," *Philosophical Quarterly*, XLV (1995), 20–40.

zombie or psychopath. How could the interlocutor agree that doing such and such is irrational, so you will ask, but not see that the prescription applies to him? Or, if he does admit that it applies to him, how could he fail to adjust his desires and actions accordingly? In particular, how could he fail to do these things, when the failure is not to be explained by reference to familiar obstacles? The only answer available would seem to be that he is not seriously or sincerely involved in the business of practical evaluation, or that if he is, then he is not reliably attuned to the practical values in question. In either case, you lose solid grounds for authorizing him as a conversational interlocutor. You must cease to see any point in conducting a conversation that is supposed to bear on how he should behave.[6]

The upshot is that to take someone as a serious conversational partner on questions of value, and in particular on questions of what he ought to do, is to take him to recognize norms governing his desires and actions and to be disposed to register and respond to those norms in his own case. But we cannot stress sufficiently that this is not necessarily to regard him as a paragon of insight and virtue. You can authorize him fully—authorize him fully in domains where there are no disabling obstacles—and yet see him as seriously mistaken on a wide variety of matters: seriously mistaken in some of his evaluations. Here, we recall the similar point made in the last section. And equally you can authorize him fully and recognize that he may often be slow to see the implications of his evaluations for his own behavior, or that when he does see the implications, he may be slow to bring his own desires and actions into line. You may see your interlocutor, for example, as someone who can only manage to bring his behavior into line by resort to direct or indirect methods of self-control: methods of coping with weakness of will and the like.[7] The important point is simply that you cannot fully authorize a conversational interlocutor on matters of value, and see him as someone with whom to discuss what he ought to do, while expecting to find him only

---

[6] The argument of this paragraph requires us to assume that there is an internal connection between evaluative judgment and the will. Externalists will not allow this assumption. Unfortunately, this is not the place to provide a full-scale defense of internalism (but see Smith, ch. 3, and "The Argument for Internalism: Reply to Miller," forthcoming in *Analysis*). Suffice it to say that, since the account of freedom in the sphere of desire and action which we go on to characterize assumes internalism, externalists will be unable to accept the account. They are therefore bound to see a huge gulf between freedom in the sphere of belief, and freedom in the sphere of desire and action, where we see a continuity. Whether this provides yet another argument against externalism presumably depends on the plausibility of the externalist's account of freedom in the two spheres.

[7] See our "Practical Unreason," *Mind*, CII (1993), 53–79; Jeanette Kennett, "Mixed Motives," *Australasian Journal of Philosophy*, LXXI (1993), 256–67; Kennett and Smith, "Philosophy and Commonsense: The Case of Weakness of Will," in Michaelis Michael and O'Leary-Hawthorne, eds, *Philosophy in Mind* (Dordrecht: Kluwer, 1994), pp. 141–57; and our "Brandt on Self-control," in Brad Hooker, ed., *Rationality, Rules and Utility* (Boulder: Westview, 1994), pp. 33–50.

randomly sensitive to the demands of the values. You must be able to see him as having a reliable disposition, however limited and unspontaneous, to track the values in his evaluations, and to link his evaluations to his self-prescriptions and so to his choices and actions.

An example of Gary Watson's[8] illustrates the point. Watson describes a man who suffers an ignominious defeat in a game of squash. As a result, he finds himself wanting very much to smash his opponent in the face with his racquet. Let us stipulate, with Watson, that by the man's lights, there is nothing whatsoever to be said in favor of acting on this desire. Even the satisfaction he would feel if he were to smash his opponent in the face counts for nothing with him, given that the satisfaction would have been obtained by inflicting undeserved harm. He wants to hurt his opponent, but can provide no justification for doing so. To the extent that you authorize such a person in conversation, and see some point in discussing what he ought to do with him, you must take him to be capable of recognizing the demands his own values make upon him: to be capable, that is, of seeing that smashing his opponent in the face with his racquet would be a completely unjustifiable thing to do. And you have to assume further that, having recognized that fact, he is capable of responding appropriately in his desires and actions. He may find it impossible to resist smashing his opponent in the face if he stays on the court, but you must suppose him to be capable of removing himself from the scene and settling himself down, or something of that sort. Were you to reject either of these assumptions then you would weaken the grounds for taking him seriously as a conversational interlocutor on relevant matters of value. Certainly, you would remove any point from conversing with him about what he in particular ought to do. In the old phrase, you might as well be talking to the wall.[9]

---

[8] "Free Agency," JOURNAL OF PHILOSOPHY, LXXII, 8 (April 24, 1975), 205–20 [reprinted as Essay 17, this volume].

[9] The fact that there are norms governing what people should desire and do, norms that they have the capacity to recognize and respond to, is thus implicit in what we have elsewhere called the *deliberative* perspective on human agency: see our "Backgrounding Desire"; "Practical Unreason"; Smith, "Valuing: Desiring or Believing?" in David Charles and Kathleen Lennon, eds., *Reduction, Explanation and Realism* (New York: Oxford, 1992), pp. 323–60; *The Moral Problem*. Human beings do not just house desires to do this or that, desires that come and go without invitation or welcome. They can and do often deliberate about which action to choose and, in the course of their deliberations, they invariably make evaluations of this or that object of desire. They ask whether the course of action desired is right or wrong, good or bad, rational or irrational, sensible or stupid, or whatever, and, insofar as they function properly as rational deliberators, their answers to these questions have an impact upon what they desire and do. They do not just *observe* that acting in a certain way would be rational or sensible or whatever, they at least sometimes do what they do *because* they judge it to be the rational or sensible thing to do. Thus, to suppose that the squash player in Watson's example did not have the capacity to recognize and respond to his own values would be to imagine someone who is incapable of effective deliberation.

To sum up, then, authorizing someone as an interlocutor on certain questions of practical evaluation makes sense only under three conditions: first, there are relevant norms governing desires and actions; second, the interlocutor has the capacity to recognize the demands of these norms; and third, the interlocutor has the capacity to respond appropriately to the demands he recognizes. In other words, the person's desire-forming capacities satisfy conditions that parallel the conditions that you take his belief-forming capacities to satisfy.

IV. RESPONSIBILITY

We have argued in the last two sections that human beings treat themselves as possessed of belief-forming and desire-forming capacities that satisfy three conditions. There are norms governing what they should believe and desire; they are capable of recognizing the demands of those norms in their own cases; and by and large they are capable of responding appropriately, if only via stratagems of self-control, to those demands.

The message in each case can be restated in the language of responsibility. People who engage in conversation suppose that it is appropriate to address a certain 'ought' to their interlocutor, on three grounds. There is a relevant norm in play, as the first condition has it; the interlocutor can see what the norm requires, as the second condition makes clear; and the interlocutor can do what the norm prescribes, as the third condition spells out. The message is that as you see someone in the role of a suitable conversational interlocutor, you cannot help but see her as the addressee of certain 'oughts' and, by the same token, as the realizer of certain 'cans'. You must ascribe the 'can' of perception involved in the second condition, and the 'can' of performance associated with the third: you must see the interlocutor as capable both of recognizing and of responding to the norms.

To see someone in this way is to see her as a responsible subject in the relevant domain. The interlocutor whose beliefs are engaged is depicted as someone who can be made to answer to the norms of evidence governing what is the case. And the interlocutor whose desires and actions are in question is depicted as someone who can be made to answer to the sorts of reasons that can be offered for and against evaluative claims. The one person can be held responsible, as we say, for what she believes; the other person can be held responsible for what she desires and does.

This picture of responsible believing and responsible desiring is very different, it should be noted, from the standard picture associated with talk of what Daniel Dennett[10] calls *the intentional stance*. Under the standard image, believers and desirers may be extremely rational, being well-attuned to demands of evidence, demands of consistency, and the like. They may realize almost perfectly, for example, the Bayesian model of theoretical and practical coherence. But under that image, people can remain passive or mechanical subjects who harmonize and update their beliefs and desires in a more or less autonomic way. Such adjustments as are involved may happen within them without any recognition of why they should happen and without any efforts on their behalf to help them happen.

The picture of responsible believing and desiring that we associate with the conversational stance suggests a very different style of attitude formation.[11] The subject may or may not be particularly rational, may or may not be particularly in tune with the demands of evidence, consistency, and the like. But the subject is certainly not a mere passive or mechanical system. She does not just revise her beliefs and desires autonomically, or at any rate, not when they operate beyond the reach of the occasional disabling obstacles that get in her way. She revises them under the spur of recognizing what the relevant norms require of her. She revises them, in particular, when that spur is applied in the interactive business of conversation, whether the conversation be with one another or with herself.

We have argued elsewhere that it may be useful to give up on the ideal of autonomy or self-rule in favor of the ideal of "orthonomy" or right rule.[12] Responsible believers and desirers are orthonomous subjects, in the sense that they recognize certain yardsticks of right belief and right desire and can respond to the demands of the right in their own case. They may vary among themselves in how far they actually conform their beliefs and desires to those yardsticks; they may be more or less thoroughly ruled by the right. But outside the domain of disabling obstacles, they are all equally orthonomous in at least this sense: they are all able to answer the call that the right makes upon them.

Orthonomy will be taken to be of lesser or greater significance, whether in belief or desire, to the extent that the nomos or rule to which people are said to be responsible is cast as being more or less objective in its standing. The point is worth remarking because, while the norms that govern evidence for ordinary matters of fact are generally taken to enjoy a robust objectivity, there are different theories about the metaphysical underpinning of values, and these theories have a differential impact on the objectivity of the norms governing desire and action. Depending on which of these theories is

---

[10] *The Intentional Stance* (Cambridge: MIT, 1987).
[11] See also Pettit, chs. 2 and 3.
[12] Our "Backgrounding Desire" and "Practical Unreason."

adopted, orthonomy in desire will be taken to be of lesser or greater significance.

The force of this observation appears when we consider the importance attaching to the notion of autonomy which Harry Frankfurt[13] defends: the notion that agents are autonomous to the extent that they act only on first-order desires by which they have a second-order desire to be moved; they are not the victims, as it were, of wanton first-order desires, first-order desires that fail to attract second-order support. One objection to this view is that second-order desires need not be anything special, being inherited perhaps from childhood conditioning.[14] The idea is that Frankfurt's condition stipulates only that one sort of desire should have a controlling influence over others, and that while this condition may be realized by some agents and not by others—while second- or higher-order desires may be more effective in some than in others—this does not mark any significant difference between them. It may serve only to distinguish those with relatively powerful hang-ups from those with hang-ups that they manage often to defeat. It may serve to distinguish one pattern of internal conflict resolution—one internal state of harmony—from a different but no less eligible pattern.

To be orthonomous, as distinct from autonomous, an agent's evaluations and desires have to be sensitive to his recognition of normative requirements: reasons that may be offered in support of evaluative claims. To the extent that there are normative requirements to be satisfied, the achievement of orthonomy will therefore represent something distinct from any sort of internal harmonization; it will represent a way of coming into line with something outside the realm of desire: with the reasons in favor of the relevant evaluative claims. But some accounts of the metaphysical underpinnings of the norms governing our desires and actions may fare better than others in substantiating our image of ourselves as orthonomous subjects. Go for an antirationalist, reductive, psychological account of what values are—go, say, for a crude subjectivist or emotivist account—and the significance of orthonomy will be diminished. Coming into line with what the norms require may be only barely distinguishable from internal harmonization. Go for a more rationalist or realist account and the significance of orthonomy will be magnified. Coming into line with the norms will require either a sensitivity to rationally binding reasons or attunement with the world.

Our own preference is for a more rationalist or realist account of practical

---

[13] "Freedom of the Will and the Concept of a Person," JOURNAL OF PHILOSOPHY, LXVIII, 1 (January 14, 1971), 5–20 [reprinted as Essay 16, this volume].
[14] See Watson.

evaluations, though we differ in the details of the accounts we prefer.[15] Our own disposition is therefore to take practical orthonomy as enjoying great importance: the sort of importance, indeed, that we see in theoretical orthonomy. But others may take a different view on this matter, consistently with sharing our belief in practical orthonomy, and we do not want to contest the issue here. For them, the sort of responsibility people have for their desires and actions will lack the significance of the responsibility they have for their beliefs. For us, the two are on a par.

V. FREE WILL AND FREE THOUGHT

We want to show why the account of responsible believing and desiring defended in the previous section is, precisely, an account of how responsible believers and desirers can enjoy freedom in the matter of what they believe and of what they desire and do. Responsibility or orthonomy in belief means that people enjoy free thought. Responsibility or orthonomy in desire means that people enjoy free will.

Freedom in the sense associated with free will is traditionally defined in terms of the ability of the agent, for anything they do, always to have done otherwise.[16] A believer or desirer would be free in this sense to the extent that no matter what he believes or desires, he is such that he could always have believed and he could always have desired otherwise. Freedom in such an unqualified sense—if, indeed, it deserves to be called "freedom" at all— would not be particularly attractive from our point of view. If an agent believes or desires rightly according to the evidence and the values, then there will be nothing attractive in itself about being such that he could have believed or desired otherwise. Believing or desiring otherwise will simply be a matter of his getting it wrong, and so doing much worse than he actually did. The ability to have believed or desired otherwise will be something inherently attractive from our point of view only so far as it is the person's ability for anything that is not rightly believed or desired always to have believed or desired otherwise. We argue that responsible believers and desirers are free in the sense of having this ability.[17]

Before looking at the argument, we have one short comment on the conception of freedom just mentioned. While freedom is a person's ability, in the event of getting things wrong, to get them right, the question of whether

[15] Smith, *The Moral Problem*; Pettit and Jackson, "Moral Functionalism and Moral Motivation."

[16] O'Leary-Hawthorne and Pettit, "Strategies for Free-will Compatibilists," forthcoming in *Analysis*.

[17] We therefore find much to agree with in Wolf, *Freedom within Reason* (New York: Oxford, 1990).

someone believes or desires freely arises in the case where he gets things right as well as in the case where he gets things wrong. Suppose a person believes or desires rightly: the norms require, or, due to underdetermination, allow that belief or desire. He may do so out of brute luck, in the sense that he would have had that belief or desire no matter how the world was or seemed to be. In that case, he does not hold the belief or desire freely even though he believes or desires rightly. Alternatively, he may believe or desire rightly, not out of pure luck, but in such a way that, were the belief or desire wrong, still he has the ability in such an event to get it right. In such a case he does hold his belief or desire—the belief or desire that is actually right but might have been wrong—freely. To hold a belief or desire freely is to hold it in the presence of an ability, should the belief or desire be wrong, to get it right. The question of whether someone believes or desires freely thus arises both for the case where he gets things right and for the case where he gets things wrong.[18]

Now let us turn to the argument that responsible believers and desirers possess the ability associated with freedom. Suppose that you conversationally authorize someone in a given domain, taking him to be a responsible believer in regard to those topics. The fact of conversationally authorizing the person gives you certain expectations; indeed, these expectations are part of what it is to authorize him. You expect that, whether or not he in fact believed in accordance with the evidence in the domain in question, were he to be challenged about the demands of the evidence then he certainly would do so. Perhaps he would not do so immediately, because of some surmountable obstacle, but he would do so under sustained conversational pressure. The expectation means that, if you find that your interlocutor does not believe in accordance with the evidence, as you see things, then you must believe that were you to challenge him with that evidence, he would come to adjust his beliefs appropriately. In entertaining this expectation, so we claim, you display the assumption that the interlocutor has the ability for anything wrongly believed—or at least for anything wrongly believed by available lights—to believe otherwise.

---

[18] Wolf claims that freedom is asymmetrical: "being psychologically determined to perform good actions is compatible with deserving praise for them, but being psychologically determined to perform bad actions is not compatible with deserving blame" (*op. cit.*, p. 79). Our position in the text is that people only deserve praise for getting things right if their getting them right is governed by an ability which in the nature of things will not be displayed in the actual world, where they get things right, but only in the possible world in which they get things wrong. Presumably someone attracted to the asymmetry view of these matters (a view in the spirit of Wolf's remark) will say that what is important is not that that ability is present in the actual world but that it would come to be present in such a possible world. We think that this position gives praise where something else is due: something like congratulations on the good fortune that these people enjoy. But someone who sticks with the asymmetry view can still go along, of course, with the rest of our argument.

When will an interlocutor have the ability, for anything wrongly believed, to believe otherwise? Following a well-established tradition, we postulate that two conditions are going to be necessary and sufficient: first, the interlocutor would believe otherwise in the event of it being impressed on him that he believes wrongly, and second, the possibility that this is impressed on him is suitably accessible: it is not a possibility that could only be realized, for example, via a total transformation of his nature.[19] You are bound to think that your interlocutor meets both of these conditions. So far as you continue to authorize the person in conversation, you have to think that he would come around to the right belief in the event of your pressing him with the demands of the evidence. And so far as you regard yourself as an agent who can realize at will the options you discern, in particular the option of challenging your interlocutor with the evidence, you have to think that the possibility of pressing the demands of the evidence on him is suitably accessible. Thus, you have to think that for anything that the interlocutor wrongly believes, or at least wrongly believes by available lights, he is capable of believing otherwise.

This means, in our sense, that you have to believe of the interlocutor that in the domain in question, and at least so far as available lights go, he is a free believer or a free thinker. His beliefs do not just come and go in a natural procession of events. His beliefs are subject to an ability on his part that is characteristic of being free. The beliefs come and go in a manner that is consistent with the person's being able to get anything right that he happens to get wrong: or at least that he gets wrong by lights that are available to him in conversation.

Indeed, not only do you have to believe of any interlocutor that you authorize, including yourself, that the person has the sort of ability described: the ability to adjust to evidence that you are in a position to produce. Since you recognize the interlocutor as himself capable of challenging you with the demands of evidence, you must also believe that he has a *self-starting* version of the ability in question. You must suppose that he has the ability to adjust, not just to evidence that you are in a position to produce, but also to evidence that he will often be in a position to produce himself. The interlocutor does not necessarily depend on you, or on any other, for enjoying the freedom of thought that he is presumed to have insofar as you adopt the conversational stance. He may have it by grace of the conversational community he establishes with himself.

---

[19] See, for example, Roderick Chisholm, "Human Freedom and the Self" [reprinted as Essay 1, this volume].

We have argued that to acknowledge someone as a responsible or orthonomous believer, as we do in conversationally authorizing a person, is to see him as possessed of free thought. An analogous argument will show that to acknowledge someone as a responsible or orthonomous desirer, as we do in conversing with him about what he ought to do, is to see him as possessed of free will. You cannot hold out any values as matters to which your interlocutor is answerable without thinking of him in the image of a subject who can get any desires right that by available lights he actually gets wrong. You have to envisage that in the suitably accessible event of your drawing his attention to the demands of the values, he will come to adjust what he desires and does. And you have to envisage, indeed, that he will often be in a position himself to play the role here allotted to you: he will often be in a position to require and promote such an adjustment in himself.

The fact that you cannot think of an interlocutor, or indeed of yourself, as a responsible believer or desirer without postulating freedom of thought and will does not in itself establish the fact of such abilities. Perhaps you cannot fail to think in this way, and yet this way of thinking is mistaken. We acknowledge that this possibility is logically open. We acknowledge that people may be in massive error when they take one another to be responsible believers and responsible desirers and so to be possessed of free will and free thought. But if people were to embrace that possibility they would have to adopt a wild and self-defeating stance on one another and on themselves. They would have to discount everything they must assume in order to practice conversation, and relate more broadly in an interpersonal fashion.[20] Indeed, since thinking itself is a kind of intrapersonal conversation, as we saw earlier, they would have to discount everything they must assume in order to practice conversation with themselves: everything they must assume in order to think.

We are therefore happy to embrace the conclusion that people rightly treat one another, and they rightly treat themselves, both as responsible and free believers and as responsible and free desirers. The conclusion is inscribed in habits of thought that we can scarcely imagine anyone being prepared to give up. The conclusion, moreover, looks capable of being reconciled with what the sciences have taught us about the natural world. We see no reason, in principle, why we might not each be purely physical, even deterministic, systems and yet it be true that we are individually capable of responding to the call of the right. Freedom of will and thought, as we have characterized

<hr>

[20] Peter Strawson, "Freedom and Resentment" [reprinted as Essay 4, this volume].

and supported it, looks capable of being realized in quite nonspooky subjects.[21]

We would like to discuss one more issue, in conclusion. Free thought is a matter of just as much interest from our perspective as free will. It is a matter for congratulation not just that we are free in the formation of desire and the performance of action, where indeed we are free, but also that we are free in the formation of belief. But the prevailing orthodoxy is that the sort of freedom we enjoy, when we enjoy freedom of thought, has nothing whatsoever to do with the sort of freedom we enjoy when we enjoy freedom of the will. How can it be that the tradition has left us with such divergent understandings of free thought and free will? The answer we propose is this. On at least many occasions where a person fails to exercise the ability associated with free will, that failure will be manifest to them, but nothing of the same kind holds for failures to exercise the ability associated with free thought.

Imagine that your beliefs run counter to what evidence and fact require. In such a case, your beliefs will not allow those requirements to remain visible because the offending beliefs themselves give you your sense of what is and your sense of what appears to be. You are therefore denied an experience whose content is that you are believing such-and-such in defiance of the requirements of fact and evidence. This is why, as G. E. Moore[22] observed, you cannot simultaneously think that while you believe that p, yet it is not the case that p.

Now, the same is true on the evaluative side, of course, to the following extent. Imagine that you are firmly committed to a particular evaluative claim even though the reasons available to you favor an alternative. As in the belief case, you are once again denied an experience whose content is that you have a particular evaluative commitment in defiance of the reasons available to you. But nonetheless the evaluative case is different in a further crucial respect. You may be denied any experience of evaluating contrary to reasons, but you are by no means denied the experience of desiring contrary to evaluation. On the contrary, it is an all too common experience that your evaluative commitments lead you on one path but that you go nonetheless on

---

[21] What are we to say about the nature of free choice? What we have said so far is that a subject's beliefs and desires are free to the extent that they are the product of an ability, in the event of his being wrong, to get them right. The natural position for us to take is therefore that a subject's choices are free to the extent that they are the product—product, no doubt, "in the right way"—of beliefs and desires that are themselves free. Note that the claim that beliefs and desires are free in our sense is not equivalent to the claim that they are freely chosen, on pain of an infinite regress familiar in discussions of free will.

[22] In P.A. Schilpp, ed., *The Philosophy of G.E. Moore* (Evanston: Northwestern, 1942; 3rd ed., Open Court, 1968), p. 543.

another: the spirit is willing but the flesh is weak. Agents are aware in such an experience of what the right requires them to desire and do, at least in the light of their evaluative commitments, despite the fact that their actual desires and actions do not conform to that requirement.

Failures to exercise free will—say, through weakness or compulsion or whimsy—are matters of everyday experience, but failures to exercise free thought—say, through being careless or conditioned or subject to group pressure—are not: they are essentially elusive. We believe that this asymmetry may explain why people are keenly aware of free will, being conscious of how their will may fail, but are more or less oblivious of free thought. Not being conscious of the ways in which thought may fail, they do not recognize the ideal of thinking freely as one that parallels the ideal of free will. They do not see that as caution and self-control are necessary for achieving freedom of their will, for example, so vigilance and self-criticism are needed for attaining freedom of thought. They do not see that in this respect, as in others, freedom is one and undivided.

21

FREEDOM OF WILL AND FREEDOM OF ACTION[1]

ROGERS ALBRITTON

Descartes held that the will is perfectly free, "so free in its nature that it cannot be constrained."[2] "Let everyone just go down deep into himself," he is reported to have said to Frans Burman, "and find out whether or not he has a perfect and absolute will, and whether he can conceive of anything which surpasses him in freedom of the will. I am sure that everyone will find that it is as I say."[3] Not everyone has so found, and one might think: "No wonder! We aren't gods. How could our wills not have their limits, like our digestions? Don't we quite often—or occasionally, at a minimum—have no freedom of will, in some matter or other? And mustn't it be like that? Whatever the will is, or was, mustn't it, under whatever name or names, be good for something? And in our case, mustn't it be something in the *world* that the will is good for? But if so, its freedom can't be perfect and unconditional. What in the world, that might reasonably be called a freedom, could be so absolute? If the will in the world were some faculty, say, of never mind what, wouldn't it be possible somehow to restrict its exercise? How could that be impossible? No doubt we're free as birds. We know it, God knows how, or as good as know it. Or better than know it, as perhaps we better than know that twice two is four. But how free *are* birds? Let no bird preen itself on its freedom. There are cages. There are tamers of birds. There's a *lesson* in birds, namely that a certain modesty about our famous freedom is very much in order, in the order of nature to which we so palpably belong." One

Rogers Albritton, 'Freedom of Will and Freedom of Action', from *The Proceedings and Addresses of the American Philosophical Association*, 59/2 (1985), 239–51. Reprinted by permission of the APA, University of Delaware.

Presidential Address delivered before the Fifty-ninth Annual Pacific Division Meeting of the American Philosophical Association in San Francisco, California, March 22, 1985.

[1] What follows is for the most part the text read on the occasion, with minor defensive alterations. One passage, about alcoholism, has been rewritten and is now perhaps intelligible, for better or worse.

[2] *Passions of the Soul*, I, Article XLI. I got this reference from Paul Hoffman.

[3] *Conversation with Burman*, tr. by John Cottingham (Clarendon Press, Oxford, 1976), sec. 31, p. 21.

might think something like that. Nevertheless, I am inclined to agree with Descartes. And of course I have some company. Foreigners, mostly, but there it is.

Not much company, however, as far as I know. Most philosophers seem to think it quite easy to rob the will of some freedom. Thus Elizabeth Anscombe, in an essay called "Soft Determinism," appears to suppose that a man who can't walk because he is chained up has lost some freedom of will. He "has no 'freedom of will' to walk," she says, or, again; no "freedom of the will in respect of walking."[4] "Everyone will allow," she says, "that 'A can walk, *i.e.* has freedom of the will in respect of walking' would be gainsaid by A's being chained up."[5] And again, "External constraint is generally agreed to be incompatible with freedom",[6] by which she seems to mean: incompatible with perfect freedom of *will*, because incompatible with freedom of will to do, or freedom of the will in respect of doing, whatever the constraint prevents.

The horrid tribe of "soft determinists" are supposed by Anscombe to allow, of course, what "everyone will allow," namely that a physical impossibility of, say, walking does restrict one's freedom of will *if* it comes of some external constraint. What they won't admit is that *every* such physical impossibility, from whatever cause, external or internal, is equally fatal to some fraction of one's freedom of will. Anscombe, on the other hand, has "never thought that freedom was compatible with physical impossibility"[7]—that is, with physical impossibility of any derivation, whether from chains or from brains, so to speak. I hope I am not misunderstanding her. At any rate I am not misquoting her. She believes, as she says, that a "'can' of freedom" which holds in face of physical impossibility is pure nonsense.[8]

Well, it's awfully difficult about brains. I won't really get into our brains, this evening. But I do want to dispute, first, what Anscombe thinks "everyone will allow." I don't allow it. I don't see (do you?) that my freedom of will would be reduced at all if you chained me up. You would of course deprive me of considerable freedom of movement if you did that; you would thereby diminish my already unimpressive capacity to *do* what I will. But I don't see that my *will* would be any the less free. What about my "freedom of will to walk," you will ask (or perhaps you won't, but there

[4] G. E. M. Anscombe, *Collected Philosophical Papers*, vol. ii. *Metaphysics and the Philosophy of Mind* (University of Minnesota Press, 1981), pp. 166, 167.

[5] Ibid., p. 167.

[6] Ibid., p. 170.

[7] Ibid., p. 172.

[8] Ibid., p. 172.

the phrase is, in Anscombe's essay); what about my "freedom of the will in respect of walking"? I reply that I don't understand either of those phrases. They seem to me to mix up incoherently two different things: free will, an obscure idea which is the one I am after, on this expedition, and physical ability to walk, a relatively clear idea which has nothing to do with free will.

If instead of being perfectly free in the matter of whether, all things considered, to walk over there or not, I were absolutely restrained somehow from deciding that option in favor of walking, nothing would follow as to my physical ability or inability to walk. And if, having decided to walk over there, I found that I could not, after all these years of being carried about by my devoted pupils, nothing would follow as to my freedom or unfreedom of will. Not according to *my* idea of free will, anyway. I wonder if Anscombe is operating with another one, or what? How can it seem so clear to her that every physical impossibility of doing this or that reduces one's little portion of free will, as if only an impossible creature for whom nothing was physically impossible, not even eating Chicago, could satisfy a clear necessary condition of perfect freedom of will? What about God, for example? He can't eat Chicago any more than I can, after all.

But here someone might reply (in effect) that in God's case that limitation ought to be counted as "grammatical" or "conceptual" or "logical," not physical, and therefore as nothing against His perfect freedom of will. And this reply would make for a possibility of reconciling my idea of free will with what Anscombe says, up to a point. Why am I not inclined to think that my will is any less free than it might be, in that I can't if I like eat Chicago? In one view of me, what gets in the way of that meal isn't, of course, "logic"; it's my *size*, for example. I'm simply not big enough. But perhaps, in thinking as I do "that's no skin off my free will," I am tacitly treating my size as given and treating the impossibility of eating Chicago as geometrical, in my case, rather than physical. If so, and if one were to allow a certain legitimacy to that way of looking at the matter, one might allow that I don't have to think myself deficient in free will because I am too small to wolf down whole cities and too big to live in a shoe. One might similarly make room for my disinclination to count my will as any the less free for my being in no position right now to throw myself into the Seine. That is, one might agree that various trivial consequences of location—of what H. H. Price once called the misfortune that we are not ubiquitous—can be written out of the question how free the will is as in a (very) broad sense logical embarrassments, not physical impossibilities of the kind that straightforwardly restrict our freedom of will, like the physical impossibility of walking if you are properly chained up.

But this line of reconciliation could go only so far, because I still don't see that my freedom of will would be affected even by chains. Especially obviously not if I didn't know about the chains: Suppose I am chained up so that I can't walk, but don't yet know it. I deliberate about what to do next and decide on a little tour of my cell. Then I discover that I can't walk. They've chained me up, the swine! But wasn't the part of my "will to walk" in these events antecedent to that discovery? Do I have reason to think not only, "They've chained me up!" but, "Good God, they've been tampering with my will!"? No, I don't. Of course, one wants not just freedom, in a will, but efficacy too, so to speak. One might well find the possibility of embracing one's fate, however authentically, unconsoling, and wish instead for some effective power of resisting it. But all such power is a different thing from free will.

I am inclined to defend this intuition as follows: What we propose to do is up to us, if our wills are free. But what the world will make of what we do is of course up to the world. (I think I am echoing Brian O'Shaughnessy here.) It's nothing against my freedom of will if I earnestly move my feet in the right sort of way but it isn't in the world to make *walking* out of my so moving them because, as it happens, I am upside down with my legs in the air. It's nothing against my freedom of will if I "can't walk" because the floor will collapse, or because it has been arranged for me to explode if I shift my weight. These difficulties in the way of my actually getting any walking accomplished are on the side of the world, not the will; and they don't in themselves interfere with the will's part in walking (that is, in these cases, its part in deciding and trying to walk). They don't affect its freedom, therefore. Where there's a will, there just isn't always a way. After the christening, the ship majestically slides to the bottom of the harbor, and so we haven't managed after all to launch her, though that was our intention and our wills were in perfect working order. We freely did what we could do, and hoped that it would turn out to have been a launching, so to speak; but the world declined to cooperate . . . Sometimes . . . the car won't start. That's life. But it's much too remote from the springs of action to pass for a shackle on the will.

It's no accident, I imagine, that in Anscombe's example the man is chained up. If you chain somebody up, you seem to be getting closer to where the will is than if you build a high wall around him at a radius of ten miles from where he sits reading Spinoza. You seem to be working in toward the connection in him between will and world, which might strike you as a good point at which to try disabling his will itself. An even better idea might be a judicious injection of curare, if it works as I've been told it does. There he will be, fully conscious but physically so relaxed that he cannot move a muscle. One might hope, even, to have incapacitated him from *trying* anything physical, and thereby definitely constrained his will, because one might hope that it was right to suggest that one logically can't try to perform a "basic" physical action, and that trying to perform any other, nonbasic, physical action must consist in actually performing one or more that are basic.

But that suggestion was wrong, it seems to me. I don't see why the prisoner incapacitated by curate shouldn't be trying and failing to move, if he isn't too far gone to try anything. And I therefore don't see that we've managed to subvert his freedom of will. (I'm out of jail and we're working on somebody else, here.) We have radically disabled this man from exerting his will to any physical effect. Indeed, we have gone as far as possible, without killing him, in the direction of as it were dislodging his will from his body, which we don't want to do. We don't want him *disconnected*, as from an odd piece of furniture: that (if it were possible) would alter his situation "logically," again, which isn't what we're after. We want to get at his will. But this business with the curare hasn't taken us far enough. We have in this (for all we can tell, still defiant) prisoner a limiting case of physical disability, which does involve a sort of disability of the will too. (Why not say so? His will is physically powerless, one might say.) But do we have what (I'm supposing) we wanted: a man not only powerless and flat on his back, but robbed of some *freedom* of will? I don't see that we do. Perhaps he loves us by now, and can't wait to show it. Or on the other hand, perhaps he has other plans.

I don't mean to be thrilling about man's unconquerable will. Or at any rate, not very thrilling. We can just be knocked out, after all, without bothering about our freedom. And even cold sober I sometimes find that I have done quite complicated things "automatically," so to speak, an automatism that is most vivid when it goes awry: What on earth am I doing in the bathroom? Oh, I meant to fetch a certain book from the (adjacent) bedroom, of course. But I have nevertheless gone straight to the bathroom, not in unfreedom of will but in ridiculous absence of mind. No doubt this sort of thing happens to me more often than it did to Marco Polo, and even I don't find that I have in this curious way gone to San Francisco. But there is a portent in everyday automatism, all the same. Why shouldn't it be brought under control and greatly extended in range, by horrible new techniques? This method of getting people to do what you want would just bypass the will, as far as I can see. Or one can leave the will alone and get excellent results even now, by manipulating belief instead. Convince me that your enemy is the Antichrist and I will no doubt behave satisfactorily, in full freedom of will. How else should one behave toward Antichrist?

So I'm not proposing a round of self-congratulation. But all the same, isn't there a distinction between something obscure that might reasonably be called "freedom of will" and every kind of freedom to *work* one's will, to *do* as one will, to *have* one's will or way, so to speak? The living dead might unfortunately have lots of freedom of action. Or freedom of movement, anyway. And a human being of intact free will might have almost *no* freedom of action, indeed no freedom of physical action at all. So it seems to me.

And what goes for physical impossibility goes for physical necessity too, in whatever sense there is any such thing. If I'm forcibly carried to your rotten garden party, or deposited in the middle of it by a defective parachute, I'm there against my will, no doubt; I'm not there of my own free will. But then, I'm not there "of my will" at all, am I? It's *your* will that has been done by these brutes; or it's nobody's will, in the case of the parachute. It's none of *my* doing that I have shown up or appeared at, or come to, your party (if those phrases can be Griced, as perhaps they can). I haven't *put in an appearance* at your party. They can't say I *attended* it. And so they can't say I attended it of an unfree will, so to speak, or in unfreedom of will, or any such thing. My will was free as ever, as I landed in your garden. Why else was I so angry?

An annoying ambiguity of the noun "will" must be dealt with, however summarily. Consider: "She went to work with a will" (what will? well, a will to please, or to succeed, or the like); or "He has a fierce will to live"; or the cartoon in the *New Yorker* of a televised message card reading "Please stand by. We have temporarily lost the will to continue." In these contexts "will" is a noun like "wish," though for some reason it has no such common plural as in "They ignored my wishes." (One doesn't have *wills*. I can't think why not.) But a will, in this sense, is a will that ... or a will to ... A will in this sense may, like a wish, be strong or not so strong. Or one may have *no* particular will in some matter. ("What is your will, majesty?" Answer: "For God's sake leave me alone. Just do anything. This crown is killing me.") Is a will in this sense "free", or "not free"? One might *say* so: "What is your will, sire?" Answer: "Do as this man with the grenade says. But remember: that's not my *free* will." This dark utterance suggests the guess that his "free will", and therefore his *real* will, is something else. Perhaps his eyesight has improved and he can see that it's only a pineapple. What a puzzle! How can he have no "free will" in the matter of this demented peasant? Perhaps he hasn't made up his mind whether to hurt the fellow's feelings or not, and is temporizing. Or of course he may think it *is* a grenade. But then what does he mean, it isn't his "free will" that we do what the fellow says? Perhaps he means that it wouldn't have been his will in pleasanter circumstances, and we're to remember *that*. But in the meantime, if it *is* his will, we'd better do it. He gets so furious when he's crossed. And so forth.

But this talk of a will in some case that's not one's free will is very opaque.

I don't know what to make of it, really. The word "will" in the usual sense of the expressions "free will" and "freedom of the will" is different: it's like "intellect," "mind," "heart," "imagination," not like "wish." "We know the will is free" doesn't invite the question "The will to what?" Of course the idea of freedom of the will is a hard idea to get hold of. But at least one has it, and needn't make it up. One isn't supposed to believe in the will any more, perhaps, not even as one believes in the mind or the imagination. But on the other hand, we say "She has a strong will," "They broke his will," "He has no will of his own," "He didn't do it of his own free will," "He has brain power but no will power," and so on. So we do still believe in the will, however vaguely. And why not? Vows of ontological commitment are another and more dubious matter, but free will is what we've got if the will is free, as of course it is. I don't exactly know what any of that means, but I don't know how to doubt that we've got free will, either. The will is free, whatever that means. Indeed, the ulterior motive of this paper was to discover something about what these expressions do mean by discovering why, hopelessly American as I am, I am so strongly inclined to agree with Descartes' prima facie absurd estimate of *how* free the will is. It seems to me not a grandiosity but a simple truth. Maybe so simple that there's nothing in it, in a sense. But if so, that might be instructive.

Suppose I am right so far. Chains, or the curare of my imagination, can't get at the will directly and can't in themselves affect its freedom. I would say the same, of course, about other sorts of "external" limitation on what one can do. (External to the will, I mean.) Lack of opportunity, for example, or lack of means. I would shoot him, but where is he? There he is, but now where's the gun? Incompetence: here's the gun, and here's the safety catch, but I can't remember how to release it. And so forth. All that kind of thing, not all of it "physical," is nothing to do with free will. Or at any rate, it can't affect my free will directly. Suppose you were to agree. But now, can't that kind of thing constrict the operations of the will indirectly, nevertheless, by way of one's *knowledge* or *conviction* that, for whatever reason, one can't do this or that? Never mind the chained man's physical incapacity. What about his recognition of it? Knowing or believing that he can't walk, how can he so much as try? And trying things is a function of the will, surely: one in which it can be partially paralyzed after all, it seems. Indeed, it needn't even be a *fact* that (say) I can't walk. Convince me that I can't, by suitably arranged illusions and lies, and there goes some former freedoms of my will: my freedom to decide to walk, for example, or to choose to walk, or even to try to walk, and therefore my freedom to decide or choose to try to walk. I can, of course, still *wish* I could walk. But if wishing is an operation of the will— as perhaps it is, in contrast with perfectly passive desire—it isn't much of one. So: convince me that I can't walk, and sooner or later I do lose some freedom of will. Or do I?

I think not, again. In the familiar, obscure sense of "free will" that I am trying to get into clearer view here, it seems to me no deficiency of free will that one can't just up and go against knowledge and belief (insofar as one can't) because that "can't" is, again, not psychological, or metaphysical either, but "grammatical" or "conceptual" or "logical." (I'll just go on saying "logical," if I may, as if I didn't know any better.) It isn't that the will is hobbled by the prospect of an impossible project. It's that "I know I can't do it, but I've decided to do it anyway," for example, is either a figurative way of speaking or a kind of nonsense. Perhaps it is even a contradiction.

Well, perhaps it is, and if so it might be conceded that what gets in the way of *deciding* to walk when you know you can't, or think you know you can't, is in the language, not in the will. But there's no such contradiction in *trying* to do the impossible, knowing one will fail, as far as I can see. So why can't I (as surely I can't) try to jump over this hotel, say? I can't even try to do fifty consecutive pushups, I think. Not really. Why not? Isn't it that my will is in these matters disabled, in a way that has to be seen as robbing it of some freedom? I hope not, but I confess that I have sunk into a little swamp about trying to do the impossible, and don't know how to get out of it gracefully. It isn't an enthralling swamp, so I'll just flounder on here. Consider the following speech: "Of course you won't be able to do it, we know that, but *try*. You promised to try. You will certainly be unable to do it, at first, but if you don't try and try again, you will never be able to do it, whereas if you keep on trying you may eventually succeed." That seems all right. So one can knowingly try to do the impossible—the not yet possible—under certain conditions. Can one, even, try and try again, although one knows perfectly well that the attempt will never succeed, without even hope against hope that it might? I'm not sure that one can't desperately do that. Indeed, I think one might even do it cynically, to please the authorities. They will be very displeased, say, if I don't at least try to lift a certain sacred boulder, which is obviously much too heavy for me to lift. So I try. That is, I grasp the thing and strain hard, thinking, "When will these savages learn?" Am I only *pretending* to try? I don't see that one has to say so. Not in every case.

But then how is it that I can't (if, as I think, I can't) try to jump over this building?[9] If I went sufficiently mad, I could. If I went mad, I could try to fly around it by flapping my arms. Suppose I am pressed to admit that after all trying to fly is a perfectly conceivable little act of the will, which needs no

---

[9] Read "try to jump over this building" opaquely. That I might mistake a building in the distance for a miniature building at my feet, and try to jump over it, is irrelevant, I hope, even if true. (This counterexample, or one like it, was put to me by Palle Yourgrau, as I recall.)

other description. Birds do it. Maybe even bees. So let's do it. But of course
we can't. Why not? Because the logic of trying excludes trying to do what
you know you can't do? Unfortunately, it doesn't. So what's my problem
about trying to fly, or trying to jump over hotels? Isn't it a blot on my
freedom of will? Shouldn't I just admit that?

I don't admit it. And I think I know, more or less, how to handle cases like
trying to jump over this building, as follows: I could go outside, get down
into a crouch, and jump up into the air, thinking (perhaps), "Well, it isn't a
necessary truth that I won't somehow be carried on up and over the building." But that wouldn't be *trying to jump over the building*, as I might try to
jump over this lectern. What would? Nothing I can think of, in these present
circumstances, including of course the circumstance of my present cognitive
"state." It isn't that it's an iron law of the will that someone in that state
can't possibly try, no matter how he strains, to leap tall buildings. It's that
nothing I can think of to do this evening would be rightly *described* as trying
to jump over this building, in a straightforward sense, unless for example my
beliefs were to alter or go very dim. It's the same in principle as if I were
invited to try to wiggle my teeth. Given what I vaguely think about human
teeth, as contrasted with ears, I am not inclined to count anything I might
conceivably do now as "trying to wiggle my teeth" . . .

One can, often, try to do what one sees no point in trying. (Or maybe one
can't be bothered.) But the sort of case I've just been discussing seems
different. It seems over the edge: a logical edge, as I am stupidly putting it. In
my present cognitive state, that is, I'm not inclined to count anything I might
succeed in doing as "wiggling my teeth," "jumping over this building," "flying around it by flapping my arms," and that's why I'm not inclined to count
anything I might do as trying to do any of those things; and that's why my
prima facie incapacity to try to do any of them isn't an incapacity, and
doesn't show any lack of freedom in my will.

Will that do? Perhaps it might for such exotica as these. But I know exactly
what I would count as doing fifty consecutive pushups, or reciting the first
four pages of *The Wings of the Dove*. I can even make what would in someone else's case be a beginning on just those projects. One pushup, perhaps.
I'll spare you that. The first four words of *The Wings of the Dove*. I'll spare
you them, too. So why can't I so much as try for fifty pushups; for four
pages? I want to say: it's not that I can't, it's that those descriptions of me, as
I am—"He's trying for fifty" and so forth—would be inept *whatever* I did.
And so for the chained man: either he *can* try to walk, or if he can't, it's not
that he *can't*, any longer. It's that in his present cognitive position and state
of mind that description of him would be inept whatever he did. Trying to
walk *isn't* a perfectly imaginable little act of the will, separate and distinct

from all belief and contingently blocked in him by belief. Folk psychology is my favorite kind, and I hope it never withers away, but one must not think of such folk-psychological items as trying in *that* way.

Well, again, suppose you were to agree, though God knows why you should, that there is enough for my purposes in this admittedly messy idea of logical limits on the will that ought not to prejudice our estimate of its freedom even though they are not logical limits of the comforting type that rule out (not only in my case but in practically any case, even on Twin Earth) trying to stand at attention while lying down. You might then agree that chains and so forth can't bind the will either directly or indirectly. Not by way of laying on it powerful spells of knowledge and belief, at least.

Of course, chains and the like can in a certain sense undermine apparent choices. But it isn't the *freedom* of those choices that chains can abolish, it's the *choices*, in an objective sense. Determined to remain seated during the national anthem, say, I may think I have done so and then discover that I was firmly stuck to the seat of my chair anyway and am now marooned in the balcony. So I did not, after all, "remain seated by choice," unpatriotic as my intentions were. Of course not, because in the relevant sense I did not, though I thought I did, remain seated. Stuck to my chair as I was, I had no choice of remaining seated or standing, and *didn't do either* of those things. In *this* use of "choice," mere physical circumstance can, of course, deprive us of choices, whether we know it or not. But, again, that's nothing to do with the will's freedom. Stuck in the balcony, am I? Well, then, alternatives between which I might have chosen have gone glimmering. *Both* of them have. They are out of logical range, so to speak again. The thought, as the auditorium empties, "Well, I'll just stay here in the balcony, then, *that's* what I'll do" isn't even an expression of *amor fati*. It's just fatuous.

Where am I, now? Some cases have perhaps turned out not to be cases in which there is any lack or loss of free will. But I must of course consider the obvious objection that I have been looking much too far from home for unfreedom of the will. What if it were urged on me that the will's freedom (if it has any) is diminished all the time in everyday life? Every decisive, compelling reason to make one choice rather than another reduces one's freedom of will, someone might object. Luther said, and he meant it. "Ich kann nicht anders." We say all the time, and not always in bad faith, "I'd love to, but I really can't", "I'm afraid we must go", "I couldn't possibly, she's my sister", "I can't help it, I gave him my word," and the like. Some of us do, anyway. Shall I say we never mean it in good faith? Of course we do, often. Shall I say we mean it, all right, often enough, but it's never true? No, again. It's often true. Well, then mustn't I say that when we do mean it, and it is true, we are reporting a constraint, deep inside, on the will itself, which really does deprive it of some little freedom, or even of some big freedom? Why do so many of us in a way envy criminals, especially if we haven't intimately known any? Isn't it their freedom? And not only, not even principally, their freedom of action, such as it is. (Stone walls do, after all, a prison make.) Isn't it their freedom of *will* that's in a way enviable, or at any rate envied? They may not get far on the wild side; but they walk there, when they can, by choice. Aren't we incapable of that choice? So much stands in the way of it: nervousness, habit, addiction to our comforts, including our spiritual comforts, and to our accustomed pleasures, including such cheap moral thrills as pointing out to the waitress that she has undercharged us. And reason bars the way, too, of course: the awful majesty of duty, or just duty, majestic or not; obligations; other engagements; ordinary prudence; common sense; the usual constraints of cognitive sanity. But in default of reason, wouldn't desire and aversion and so forth do, to keep the will hogtied? We may like to think that if we threw off the restraints of reason we could do appalling things. But could we? Aren't most of us probably too squeamish, if nothing else? And anyway, *can* one throw off the restraints of reason?

Well, the first thing to be said in the matter of what we rationally speaking "cannot" and "must" do is that these modal laments and excuses and so on are standardly not introspective autobiography. "We have to go" isn't a report to the effect that we are about to be frog-marched out of the house by invisible forces. "We really must" isn't falsified if in the end we don't, any more than "You must believe me" is falsified by your not believing me.[10] These "can't"s and "must"s belong to the system of what's getting *considered*, not to the considering of it. "I must go" is false if, for example, the pressing engagement I have in mind was actually for yesterday, not today. What's wanted for the discovery that after all I can stay a little longer is (for example) a look at the calendar, not a more searching look within, much less the observation that I *do* stay a little longer.

To be sure, a man who keeps saying "I really must go" and nevertheless stays on until he is physically incapable of going may be suspected of insincerity; but what he kept saying wasn't therefore *false*, as may be seen by recasting it in the second person and putting it in the mouth of his host: "You really must go!" There is a kind of contradiction in acting against decisive reason to act otherwise; and if you do it often enough you're impossible. But impossible people, given for example to sarcasms like, "Oh can't I? Just watch me," aren't impossible to find. We, of course, aren't like that, except in some of our worst (and, conceivably, some of our best) moments. But *unfreely* not like that? As if it weren't up to us to act, or not act, as there

---

[10] I think it was John Koethe who suggested this analogy.

is compelling reason to do? As if so acting were otiose, and we might instead just wait for the compelling reason to work? I am inclined to say (but I know I have barely begun to argue) that even the most irresistible case for doing a thing isn't irresistible like *that*. How could it be? It's a mere *case*. Can't one always not do what one must? I am on duty; I can't go on fooling around in the linen closet like this; I must make my rounds. I absolutely must. And yet of course from another point of view I needn't at all. I could just stay here, couldn't I, and my station and its duties be damned. And if in a sense I couldn't, because I would become hysterical, and hysteria isn't what you had in mind when you whispered "Stay!", that's irrelevant, isn't it? What I would need in order to do what you *want* isn't more freedom of will, it's stronger *nerves*.

The point is: I have to make my rounds, that's true, and it follows, trivially, that I can't stay. But I don't have to make my rounds in any sense that binds my will. Even Luther's reasons were only *reasons*. Even the reasons that favor obliging a man with a gun are only reasons. Naturally, one gives them a lot of weight, insofar as one acts for reasons at all in such a case. One does. Or one doesn't. "It's entirely up to you," the man with the gun says, smiling ironically. He's right. It *is* up to you, even if his smile is right too. Everyone will gravely agree, later—or perhaps they won't, depending on the case—that you had no choice but to do as he said. There was no alternative. What else could you do? But these remarks are not even psychological, much less absolute. They are like "You had no alternative; there was nothing else to be done" in reviewing a game of chess, which doesn't imply that *you* couldn't have made some quite other, idiotic move instead—or stormed out of the room, for that matter. They are not, in that sense, remarks about you. You occur vacuously in them, so to speak, and they have no bearing on your freedom of will in making the move you made.

Well, I shouldn't quite say that. They have *this* sort of bearing: You have been ordered by God himself to shoot me, and do. Later on, you insist that you had no free will in the matter, no choice. It isn't as if you shot me of your own volition. You hated doing it. Indeed, you shot me again to put me out of my misery. In all this, you were only doing what you had to do. All right. *In religious obedience* (if we believe you) you had no freedom of choice in the matter of whether to shoot me or not. But why did you have no choice between religious obedience and *disobedience*? The same answer won't do, and eventually, as these questions proliferate, we will arrive at a formulation of what you did under which you won't be able to say, in this way of saying it, that you had no free will in the matter of whether to do the thing or not. You will run out of constraining reasons.

Or is there some system of reasons in which you can hole up from which there is no exit except into nonsense? Well, maybe. But even if there is, and yes, one quite sees that every alternative to shooting me *was* ruled out in that system, from which you could not intelligibly have prescinded even in the particular case, still—what of it? You had to do it. You absolutely had to do it. That was the objective position, or anyway you thought so, in your craziness. But having to do a thing does not settle magically the question whether to *do* it or not. Reasons, of whatever species, logically can't close that question. It's a question of a different genre, and is not relative to any system of reasons. It isn't for *reasons*, in the end, that we act for reasons. "I'm sorry, I have no choice," "You leave me no alternative," and so forth, are *objective*. They are misused or used in bad faith (there is bad faith in English as well as in French) if they are put on offer as reporting the sad results of scrupulous introspection. "I *must* shoot you. I can't help it." Well, yes. That's the intrasystematic position. I see what you mean. Now *give* me that gun!

That's all I'm going to say about reasons, because I must say at least something about desire and aversion, and all that lot. That is, I am determined to. But it won't be nearly enough. First, insofar as the role of these items in conduct is that of giving us *reason* to behave well or badly, this species of reason is in itself as powerless as any other. It has to be *treated* with the respect that it may or may not deserve. It's no good your just running it up the flagpole to see if you salute. But of course there is another role of desire and the rest in action. Acting in view of one's desire is one thing, like acting in view of someone else's desire. Acting *from* desire is quite another and commoner thing. Indeed, pure cases of acting in consideration of a (felt) desire but not at all from it must be rare at best. (Your new policy is to satisfy your desires. You notice that, by George, you feel a faint desire for chalk, and rush out into the night, hoping the desire won't vanish before you can satisfy it.) Well, is the will perfectly free in action *from* desire, *out of* fear, *on* impulse, and so on? It certainly can seem not. And a parallel question arises for action from such motives as malice and greed. And for compulsive or obsessional conduct, and so on. But I don't see unfreedom of will even in this most promising part of the forest. Of course if it's really like chains, or like being violently thrown into bed, then it is, and there's no unfreedom of will in it. You haven't in the relevant sense *done* anything. You froze. Or it was a seizure. Why shouldn't there be seizures of whatever you like: curtseying, bowing, waltzing? There are seizures of obscenity, one reads. They must be embarrassing, unless one is obscene anyway.

But addiction, alcoholism, child molesting and so forth—to begin with a very complicated kind of case—aren't patterns of bizarre physical seizure. There is automatism in them, in the sense of finding a cigarette in your hand. And again, that's not unfreedom of will, according to me. But there is a lot else in them. The individual drink, say, is typically not quite automatic, or even not automatic at all. It may be coldly deliberate, in fact, and not preceded by any notable craving. (There is nihilistic drinking that makes one think of *possession* rather than unfreedom of will.) It's simply not true, locally, that the alcoholic can't help himself. I mean: he could perfectly well, and sometimes does, empty the bottle into the sink, or the like. But usually he doesn't. He drinks it, in (as far as I can see) full freedom of will. And goes on like that, year after year. How very odd that the obvious reasons to stop behaving in this way don't weigh with him as decisively as one might expect! Well, yes, it is odd, but there it is: they don't, and he doesn't stop, though other drinkers have just stopped, no doubt. After all, people have on purpose stopped eating and died.

Is there reason to believe about any ordinary alcoholic that he literally *couldn't* stop, even at the cost of devoting his life to not drinking and letting everything else go? I wonder. But in any case, he probably isn't *going* to stop, except by taking extraordinary steps which would be inconvenient and humiliating. (Or worse, he may feel. Who could ask Odysseus to spend a lifetime lashed to the mast?) And since in the usual case he knows this as well as we do, or better, he is in no position to *decide* to stop drinking as one might decide to stop shaving. He is past that point. One can't simply decide to stop doing what one knows one probably *won't* in that way stop doing. But that's "logic" again, not unfreedom. And it doesn't get in the way of a good deal of *pretending* to decide to stop drinking, of course. Indeed, even *really* deciding to stop isn't altogether ruled out by terrible experience of oneself. *This* time, the alcoholic thinks, he'll really stop. Then he doesn't, again.

Is it possible that he *can't*? Of course he could by extraordinary means, but setting such means aside, as he is likely to do, is he perhaps actually incapable of stopping? Perhaps. Perhaps he just hasn't the strength of will to hold out, as one might be unable to withstand torture. (That sort of thing isn't in one's repertoire. One just will, after a time, decide to tell them what they want to know while one still has one's faculties.) All right. But *strength* of will is one thing and *freedom* of will is another. Isn't it? Or do you think not? I think it is.

Besides, the alcoholic may *love* drinking. Moreover, a few drinks ("just one more time") and he alters. He's a changed man. This changed man thinks whatever he thinks, pours the stuff down, gets belligerent with the bartender, imagines that no one can tell, and so forth. That's what he's like. The alcoholic *in propria persona* doesn't quite know about this alteration, of course. How could he? Well, video-tapes might help. But one despairs. What's the *matter* with him? In a word: alcoholism, and I see no unfreedom of will anywhere in it. Unfreedom of will would be a marvelous excuse for the complex misbehavior of such disorders. But there are other causes for pity in them. There's no need to drag *that* one in.

Or to drag it into simpler cases either: flying off the handle, say, and its relatives. Again, if it's like literally exploding, it is, and the will doesn't come into it. But perhaps it isn't quite like that. Rather: you didn't control yourself. Perhaps you actually *couldn't* have controlled yourself much longer, anxiously knew that, anxiously didn't know what form the coming disintegration would take, and (in the nick of time) preempted it. One does that.

But controlling yourself is a *project*, possible or impossible, like controlling a dog. If you try hard and can't do it, better luck next time. You gave it your best shot. Or you didn't, in perfect freedom of will. And, what about your shouting and stomping and smashing the china while we say sayonara to your better self, as if to an incompetent spirit control? We're all dismally used to Mr. Hyde, here, yelling "I am the famous Dr. Jekyll, by God, and you will keep a civil tongue in your head if I have to sew it in myself!" Has he no free will? Why not? He's having a marvelous time. Look at him! Thinks he's a regular force of nature, he does!

You see how this is going to go. "Daddy is not himself." And that's right, he isn't. He'll be back, lachrymose as always. But he's out of the picture at the moment, again. Or is *this* he, after all, raging in monstrous freedom? Either way, how absurd to say to him later, "You had no free will, there. You suffered another of your sad lapses of free will, that's all. Don't take on so." I bet I can handle any case you like, though I know I have only begun to deal with even these few. I hope I haven't cheated. I doubt that I am going to see unfreedom of will anywhere in our lives. Suppose that indeed I am not, not because, miraculously, it isn't there, but because the idea of it is incomprehensible, a picture without application! But I've asked you to do a lot of supposing. You may well be sick of supposing. What about *determinism*, you may wonder. Fortunately, Elizabeth Anscombe has taught me, by her essay "Causality and Determination," that I needn't go in for Laplacean fantasies, and I gather than John Earman is intent on conveying the same reassurance. That's fine. But one wouldn't care to think one's freedom of will secured by the physical possibility in pure theory that one will stay in bed for the rest of one's life, with Russian explanations ready in case anyone asks, much less by the theoretical possibility that instead of doing one's duty one will suddenly deliquesce into a nasty liquid all over the rug. Are we or aren't we as approximately deterministic as alarm clocks, say? That *seems* an awful question.

Unlike Anscombe, Wittgenstein thought it didn't matter, I find. At any rate there is a set of rather bad notes on a lecture about freedom of the will given by Wittgenstein in perhaps 1945 or 1946, from which it appears that he saw no contradiction (or other incoherence) in the idea that a free decision might nevertheless be "determined" by natural laws. He seems to have been quite clear in his mind about that. I, on the other hand, am not. I am foggy about it, possibly because I am bogged down in superstitions about natural law and the causal nexus. Still, I do sometimes think I see that logical inconsistency isn't the real trouble between determinism and free will: that they aren't in strict truth inconsistent. It then seems to me that their conflict comes rather of our being lured by the hypothesis of determinism into an alarming view of ourselves as a species of *objects*, which as such can't be thought to *do* anything (in a sense in which we had supposed that we did things), however busy and smiling they are. Automata are just *automata*, after all, whether physical through and through or on the contrary psycho-physical. And, on second thought, whether deterministic or indeterministic. If one had hoped for a friend, or at least a pet, even a rather unpredictable object is cold comfort.

I think one might be able to hang onto one's friends, and enemies, in spite of these objects. One might begin by questioning the success of any attempt to introduce them into the conversation, by ostension or by description. It really is not clear that if I pat myself all over, saying, "You know: this *thing* here," you do know what thing I mean, or that I can explain what thing I mean, either. So Douglas Long argued explicitly years ago, and others have held too.[11] Anscombe seems to be among them, actually, and perhaps Wittgenstein was as well.[12] They have not been widely believed. Nevertheless, they may be absolutely right.[13] That would help. A new inquiry into the very idea of physical necessity would help.[14] And even what I have said tonight *might* help. But I can't go on about any of that, I really can't. It's out of my hands, I absolutely must stop. So, I will. Thank you.

[11] See Long's articles "The Philosophical Concept of a Human Body," *Philosophical Review*, LXXIII (July, 1964) and "The Bodies of Persons," *Journal of Philosophy* LXXXI, 10 (May 30, 1974), and now also Jay Rosenberg, *Thinking Clearly about Death* (Prentice-Hall, 1983). Strawson's *Individuals* is not a case in point, as far as I can tell, since the "material bodies we possess" of that book seem to be just the bodies in question.

[12] See Anscombe's "The First Person," *loc. cit.*, p. 33, 3rd full paragraph, and on Wittgenstein, John Cook's "Human Beings," in *Studies in the Philosophy of Wittgenstein* ed. by P. Winch (New York Humanities Press, 1969), an interpretation that Cook would now repudiate, if I am not mistaken.

[13] Though not necessarily for the reasons they give, where they give any.

[14] And another into my relation to the necessities, if any, of my nervous system's operations and their bodily consequences. Am I *under* all these necessities? Do they all *face* me with impossibilities, in the sense of Anscombe's rejection of any 'can' of freedom that holds "in face of physical impossibility"?

22

ADDICTION AS DEFECT OF THE WILL: SOME PHILOSOPHICAL REFLECTIONS

R. JAY WALLACE

It is both common and natural to think of addiction as a kind of defect of the will. Addicts, we tend to suppose, are subject to impulses or cravings that are peculiarly unresponsive to their evaluative reflection about what there is reason for them to do. As a result of this unresponsiveness, we further suppose, addicts are typically impaired in their ability to act in accordance with their own deliberative conclusions. My question in this paper is whether we can make adequate sense of this conception of addiction as a volitional defect. In particular, I want to focus on some philosophical assumptions, from the theory of action, that bear directly on the very idea that addiction might impair the agent's volitional capacities. Understanding this idea, I shall argue, requires that we start out with an adequate conception of the human will. Only if we appreciate the kinds of volitional capacities characteristic of normal agents can we conceptualize properly the impairment of those capacities represented by addiction, and assess the implications of such impairment for questions of responsibility.

It might be thought that there is no particular problem understanding how the impulses of an addict could constitute forms of volitional defect. Such impulses are often depicted in the philosophical literature as literally irresistible, and irresistible impulses impair our volitional capacities by artificially restricting the class of actions that it is open to us to perform. Alternatively, addictive conditions are sometimes pictured as bypassing the will altogether, causing us to do things that do not even satisfy the minimal conditions of voluntariness. But neither of these suggestions can be taken very seriously. Addicts typically behave in ways that are at least minimally voluntary, doing things that they themselves intend to do, with basic knowledge of the consequences and so on. Nor is there any sound reason to suppose that the impulses underlying such intentional behavior are, in the

R. J. Wallace, 'Addiction as Defect of the Will: Some Philosophical Reflections' from *Law and Philosophy*, 18/6 (1999), 621–54. Copyright © 1999 Kluwer Academic Publishers. Reprinted with kind permission of Kluwer Academic Publishers.

vast majority of cases of addiction, literally irresistible. If there were, it would be an utter mystery how people ever succeed in overcoming their addictive conditions by exercising strength of will, and yet this seems to happen all the time.

The question that will concern me in this paper is whether addiction can appropriately be thought of as a volitional defect, once we have departed from the simplifying assumptions that addictive behavior is non-voluntary and that the impulses generated by addiction are irresistible. What is it about such impulses that makes it fitting to speak of them as impairments of our volitional capacities, if they neither bypass the will altogether, nor constitute forces that it is impossible for us to resist? Some theorists have voiced a healthy skepticism about the very idea that addiction could be a volitional defect, if it does not function in one of the two ways just mentioned.[1] I hope to show that there may still be some sense to this idea, even after we have rejected the false pictures about how the impulses of the addict operate. To see why this is the case, however, we shall need to consider the more basic issues of how desires in general provide motivations to action, and of the relation of such motivations to our choices and intentions.

An influential approach to these issues in motivational psychology is what I shall call the hydraulic conception of desire. On this conception, desires are thought of as vectors of causal force to which we as agents are subject, and which determine the actions we end up performing. The leitmotiv of this approach is the idea that agents always do what they most want to do, where the concepts of desire and strength of desire are construed in substantial terms, with genuine explanatory work to do. I shall argue that this approach should not be accepted as it stands. It goes wrong in basically depriving agents of the capacity for self-determination, turning all cases of action on wayward desires into cases in which the agent was subject to forces that were irresistible under the actual (psychological) circumstances. This yields a false understanding of our powers of deliberative agency, collapsing the important distinction between those states of desire to which we are merely subject, on the one hand, and motivational states that are under our immediate control on the other.

I contend that these difficulties can be avoided by adopting in their place a volitionalist motivational psychology. The leading idea of this approach is that motivations divide into two fundamentally different kinds. Some motivations are states with respect to which we are passive, conditions that we more or less find ourselves in. These given desires, as they might be called,

---

[1] See, for example, Stephen J. Morse, "Causation, Compulsion, and Involuntariness," *Bulletin of the American Academy of Psychiatry and the Law*, 22 (1994), pp. 159–180.

are to be contrasted with other motivations that are directly up to us, such as choices and decisions. By acknowledging this fundamental distinction, we can avoid the problems that confront the hydraulic model of desire, arriving at a more satisfactory account of the volitional capacities of normal agents. This in turn will pave the way for an improved understanding of how addiction could constitute a form of volitional impairment. That, at any rate, is what I hope to establish in my discussion.

The paper divides into five sections. The first offers some general reflections about the concept of addiction. In the second, I consider different ways of modelling the volitional capacities of ordinary agents, defending the volitionalist approach over the hydraulic model. In part three I address questions about the nature of desires and about their contribution to reflective agency, once such agency is conceived in terms of the volitionalist model. The fourth section brings these abstract considerations to bear on the specific problem of understanding addiction as a form of volitional defect, while the conclusion briefly explores some implications of the favored volitionalist model for questions of moral and legal responsibility.

1. THE CONCEPT OF ADDICTION

What is addiction? What distinguishes the impulses that are due to addiction from other kinds of desire to which we are subject? These are vexed questions, and I am far from competent to give a complete answer to them.[2] But I should like to begin my discussion with a few general remarks about the concept of addiction.

In the popular understanding addiction is typically pictured as a long-term, dispositional condition, characterized by a susceptibility to distinctive kinds of impulse to action, which we might refer to as A-impulses or A-desires. Such desires seem to be distinctive in at least the following respects.[3] First, A-impulses are unusually resiliant; they persist or assail us periodically during periods when they are left unsatisfied, in a way that seems detached from our own deliberative verdicts about the value to be gained by satisfying them. Second, they are experienced as unusually intense, leading us to speak

---

[2] For a helpful overview of current approaches, see Jerome H. Jaffe, "Current Concepts of Addiction," in Charles P. O'Brien and Jerome H. Jaffe, eds., *Addictive States* (New York: Raven Press, 1992), pp. 1–22.

[3] My conclusions here are broadly in agreement with the characterization of addiction as an acquired appetite offered by Gary Watson, in "Disordered Appetites", in *Addiction: Entries and Exits*, edited by Jon Elster (New York: Russell Sage Publications, 1999), pp. 3–28.

of addicts' *cravings* for the substances to which they are addicted.[4] Third, A-desires are linked in various ways with our conceptions of pleasure and pain. Satisfying A-impulses can be a source of often visceral satisfaction, while the failure to satisfy them is in turn painful and unpleasant (producing withdrawal symptoms and the like). Finally, the susceptibility to A-impulses typically has a physiological basis; it can be connected, for instance, with transformations induced by repeated consumption of a particular substance in the reward system of the person's brain.[5]

These characteristics clearly cannot be understood as specifying strict criteria for addiction. This seems true even if we leave aside the cases in which social scientists and others speak of addictive personality traits in an extended or metaphorical sense, as in talk about addiction to shopping or internet surfing as characteristically modern phenomena. Thus I myself seem to be subject to a mild addiction to caffeine, yet prolonged periods without coffee do not induce in me anything aptly characterized as a genuine craving for the substance, only feelings of drowsiness, mild discomfort, light headache, and the like. So urgency cannot be construed as a strictly necessary condition for the status of an impulse or desire as addictive. Still, in the philosophically most interesting cases, A-impulses tend to be experienced as especially intense—this is one of the features, after all, that makes it attractive to think of addiction as impairing our volitional capacities in some way. We might perhaps best respond to this point by thinking of the four characteristics I have identified as defining an ideal type of the A-impulse, while allowing that there are individual examples of A-desires that do not display all the mentioned features.

A further interesting question is raised by the fourth condition, that A-impulses are typically based in physiological transformations induced by (prolonged) ingestion of a chemical substance of some kind, such as ethynol, nicotine, cocaine, amphetamine, or opium. That this is the case is of course an immensely important fact when it comes to understanding the etiology of addiction. It also seems to be reflected in common understanding of what addiction is. Thus the line between literal and extended or metaphorical cases of addiction (such as the aforementioned cases of addiction to shopping and surfing the web), in ordinary thinking about these matters, would seem to correspond roughly to whether or not the A-impulses an

---

[4] I use the word craving here in a non-technical sense, to designate desires of particular intensity; I do not mean the technical use sometimes found in discussions of addiction, according to which cravings are literally irresistible impulses that overwhelm all ordinary capacities for deliberate self-control. For criticism of the technical use, see Herbert Fingarette, *Heavy Drinking: The Myth of Alchoholism as a Disease* (Berkeley: University of California Press, 1988), pp. 41–43.

[5] Compare George Ainslee, "A Research-Based Theory of Addictive Motivation," *Law and Philosophy*, 19 (January 2000), pp. 77–115.

agent experiences are grounded in a physiological condition or not. In cases that do not involve ingestion of a chemical substance, we are (perhaps mistakenly) inclined to suppose that the nonstandard behavior patterns will not be correlated systematically with identifiable kinds of neurophysiological transformation, and we therefore tend to regard those behavior patterns as at best analogous to genuine cases of addiction.

Nevertheless, for my immediate philosophical purposes it does not seem to matter all that much whether or not A-impulses actually have a physiological basis. Perhaps there are other, nonphysiological conditions that dispose a person to experience impulses otherwise just like the impulses of the literal addict, impulses, that is, that are resiliant, urgent, and connected with the person's conception of pleasure and pain. If so, those conditions will raise precisely the same issues concerning potential volitional impairment that are raised by strict cases of addiction. In making this claim, I am assuming that it is not possible for a physiological condition to interfere with our volitional capacities if it is not constitutively linked to impulses that exhibit the characteristics of urgency, resilience, and connection with pleasure and pain. Perhaps volitional impairment by a strictly neurophysiological condition would be possible, if we thought of such impairment as a completely non-voluntary phenomenon or symptom. But I have already expressed doubts about whether this is the right way to conceive addictive behavior, which typically seems to exhibit the kinds of focus and goal-directedness characteristic of much garden-variety intentional action.

Granted, there is probably a lot of simple automatism—the unthinking, habitual performance of ritualized executive tasks—in the daily activities of somebody subject to addiction: think in this connection of the routine lighting-up of a cigarette by the ordinary smoker.[6] But automatism of this variety would be hard to make sense of as a direct effect of neurophysiological conditions that were completely unconnected from the kinds of desires, emotions, and sensations that are phenomenologically accessible to us. Such automatic routines as the addict exhibits presumably develop through habituation, as adjustments to one's state of dependency, ways of staving off the unpleasant effects of continued substance deprivation. It is difficult to imagine how such routines might become established if the neurophysiological condition of dependency was not directly linked with the kinds of conscious psychological phenomena I have spoken of. In any case, automatism itself, though perhaps a kind of bypassing of the will, does not seem to me to represent necessarily an impairment of the agent's volitional

---

[6] Compare Rogers Albritton's discussion of alcoholism, in "Freedom of Will and Freedom of Action," *Proceedings of the American Philosophical Association*, 59 (1985–1986), pp. 239–251 [Essay 21, this volume].

capacities. Thus it is far from obvious that persons who perform certain executive tasks automatically are in any way *unable* to control their behavior through reflection; from the fact that one did not engage in a particular activity deliberately, it clearly does not follow that one lacked the power to exercise deliberate control over what one was doing at the time. For these various reasons, it seems to me that the physiological side of addiction can safely be ignored, for purposes of my discussion of volitional impairment. What is at issue is whether and how addiction might constitute a defect of the will, and in this context the aspects of the phenomenon that are of interest are the ones capable of registering phenomenologically within the agent's point of view.

The questions I have been discussing to this point concern the adequacy of the characteristics identified above as necessary conditions of addiction. It has emerged that we may regard the three features of resiliance, urgency, and connection with pleasure and pain to be necessarily exhibited by those A-impulses that represent potential defects of the will, even if they are not strictly necessary conditions for addiction in all its forms. Further questions can be raised, however, about whether the features I have mentioned, when jointly present, are sufficient conditions of addiction. Consider, for instance, the large class of bodily human appetites, including the elemental impulses associated with food, drink, elimination, sexual gratification, and basic physical comfort. These impulses seem to exhibit all of the characteristics I have proposed. To proceed in reverse order: the bodily appetites have a (neuro)physiological grounding; they are plainly connected with our most primitive experiences of pleasure and pain; they display the kind of urgency typical of cravings, especially when gratification is delayed for a prolonged period of time; and they seem resiliantly independent of our own deliberative reflection. In all these respects natural appetites appear to resemble the paradigm cases of A-impulses I have been focussing on, and yet we do not ordinarily think of ourselves as being (say) addicted to food or water or sex.

Underlying this verdict is presumably the assumption that it is a good (or acceptable) thing to indulge one's bodily appetites, at least when this is done in moderation, with due regard to moral norms, prevailing social conventions, and the like. This brings out a normative element in ordinary thinking about addiction. We label an impulse addictive only if its satisfaction is something that we tend to disapprove of—as being, for instance, difficult to reconcile with a worthwhile, dignified human life—and this does not seem to be the view we take of the bodily appetites. This point about common classification, however, is not of much philosophical depth. For one thing, the negative normative judgments associated with classifications of desires as addictive amount to very rough generalizations at best. Even if satisfaction of bodily appetites is generally good or acceptable, this is far from being the case in every individual situation in which such appetites are felt, as cursory reflection on virtually everyone's experience with hunger and sexual longing will confirm. Furthermore, there are equally cases in which consumption of chemical substances ordinarily classified as addictive must be counted, under the circumstances, highly desirable. Consider an elderly patient suffering from debilitating pain that can only be relieved significantly by an addictive drug, such as morphine, where the risks of treatment with the drug are otherwise no worse than those of the alternative and less effective medications that are available.[7] It would be a kind of narrow dogmatism to insist that prescription of the addictive drug to the patient under these circumstances could not possibly be a good thing to do, simply because consumption of the drug will dispose the patient to the kind of resilient, urgent impulses I have been talking about.

This suggests that the normative presumptions reflected in our classification of impulses as cases of addiction are not by themselves terribly significant. In particular, they do not seem significant when it comes to the question of whether A-impulses can constitute impairments of our volitional capacities. What is significant for this latter question is a different normative dimension of both A-impulses and bodily appetites, namely the condition I have referred to under the heading of resilience. Desires are resilient, in this sense, when they are unresponsive to the agent's own deliberative reflection. Whether a given desire exhibits this kind of responsiveness is not, it should be stressed, simply a matter of its being in actual alignment with the agent's reflective verdict about what they ought to do. At least since Harry Frankfurt's influential discussion of the willing addict,[8] philosophers have been accustomed to the idea that the status of a desire as an A-impulse need not preclude its being one that the agent also endorses, from the standpoint of evaluative reflection. What distinguishes A-impulses of this variety as products of addiction is, above all, a counterfactual property that they possess: A-impulses that are actually endorsed by their agent are desires that would continue to assail the agent—and would retain much of their urgency—even if the agent did not view their objects as good or worthwhile. It is the fact that A-impulses are unresponsive to deliberative reflection in this way that makes them resilient, and resilience in turn is perhaps the philosophically most interesting and salient feature of A-impulses.

In respect of resilience, however, A-impulses and bodily appetites are largely on all fours. The normative dimension discussed above would lead us

---

[7] For a sensible discussion of some actual cases of this kind, see Graham Oddie, "Addiction and the Value of Freedom," *Bioethics*, 7 (1993), pp. 373–401.

[8] In "Freedom of the Will and the Concept of a Person" [reprinted as Essay 16, this volume].

to expect, perhaps, that bodily appetites would more often be in actual alignment with the agent's deliberative reflection than is the case with A-impulses. But desires of both kinds seem to be resilient in the sense just specified. This is the case, even if we accept the Aristotelian view that our bodily appetites are susceptible to a degree of habituation, which brings it about that our conception of the pleasant is directly responsive to our views about the good. (Persons who are virtuous by Aristotle's lights would ordinarily not take pleasure in a meal or a sexual act if they did not think that such activities were right to engage in, under the circumstances, and to this extent even their bodily appetites will exhibit a degree of counterfactual responsiveness to reasoned reflection.) There are, after all, fairly clear limits beyond which bodily appetites are no longer subject to domestication—sexual longing that has gone unsatisfied for a prolonged period, for want of a fitting occasion or partner, generally does not just go away by itself. This becomes even more apparent when we expand our view to consider persons who are not virtuous in Aristotle's sense.

Resilience thus does not seem characteristic of A-impulses alone but is also exhibited to a certain extent by the natural bodily appetites. Moreover, it is the feature of A-impulses that is of greatest importance for the idea that such impulses can be defects of the will. A defect of the will, I suppose, should be understood as a condition that impairs our ability to act well, without necessarily depriving us of the capacity to think clearly and rationally about what we are to do. That is, agents subject to such a defect may succeed in deliberating correctly about what they ought to do, but will nevertheless be impeded in their capacity to translate their deliberated verdicts into action. It is the resilience of A-impulses that makes them candidates for being volitional defects of this kind, and it is presumably the case that their urgency and connection with pleasure and pain further contribute to their playing this role. In all these respects, however, A-impulses often resemble our natural bodily appetites. I conclude that an adequate explanation of addiction as a volitional impairment will have a degree of generality, applying potentially not merely to cases of addiction in the strict sense but also to other desires that exhibit the combined features of resilience, urgency, and connection to pleasure and pain.

2. MODELS OF THE WILL

The remarks of the preceding section suggest that we must focus on the transition from deliberation to action if we are to make sense of the idea that A-desires represent potential defects of the will. Offhand, it would seem that the urgency of wayward A-impulses must somehow impair our capacity to act in accordance with our own deliberated conclusions, if such impulses are to be counted as volitional defects. To understand whether and how such impairment might be possible, we need to look at the phenomenon of deliberative agency more generally. What goes on when agents succeed in translating their deliberated conclusions into action, and what are the potential contributions of desire both to facilitating and to thwarting this process?

It will assist the discussion of these questions to begin by considering an influential way of thinking about the role of desire in deliberative agency. This model, which I shall dub the hydraulic conception, pictures desires as vectors of force to which persons are subject, where the force of such desires in turn determines causally the actions the persons perform. This approach may be thought of as offering a particular and contentious interpretation of the more or less truistic dictum that persons always do what they most want to do. That dictum is truistic so long as the notion of desire is construed liberally enough to include any of the so-called "pro-attitudes" ordinarily thought to play a role in the etiology of action, including such states as intention, decision, and choice. The latter states can themselves often be identified, more or less, with the actions we perform; what exactly I am doing in executing a certain course of boldily movements is thus typically a matter of the intention in action with which those movements are made. In such cases, the idea that the desires on which one acts are the desires that are strongest says merely that they are the intentions with which one acts. There is nothing in this idea to rule out the possibility that the agent who does x could have chosen to do y instead, even holding fixed the other intentional states to which the agent was subject at the time. To say that we always do what we most want, where "want" can be interpreted in this sense of intention in action, is thus to say nothing more interesting than that human action is an intentional or goal-directed phenomenon.[9]

The hydraulic conception extracts from the dictum a more interesting and controversial thesis by assuming a different and more restrictive notion of desire. According to this more restrictive notion, desires are conceptually and empirically distinct from our intentions in action, in the sense that one can want to do something without necessarily intending or choosing to do it. They are given to us, states that we find ourselves in rather than themselves being primitive examples of agency, things that we ourselves do or determine. The hydraulic conception maintains, furthermore, that desires that are given in this way have a substantive explanatory role to play in the etiology

---

[9] Compare G. F. Schueler's discussion of the "pro-attitude" conception of desire, in his *Desire* (Cambridge, Mass.: MIT Press, 1995), chap. 1.

of intentional action. They determine which action we perform by causing the bodily movements that we make in acting, the assumption being that the strength of a given desire is a matter of its causal force in comparison to the other given desires to which we are subject.

The hydraulic conception thus goes beyond the truistic thesis that all actions are intentional, by postulating a causal explanation of such actions in terms of states of given desire with which the actions themselves are not to be identified. Distinctive of the conception is the answer it gives to the question of whether the agent who does x could have chosen to do y instead, holding fixed all the agent's desires, beliefs, and intentional states other than those that are partially constitutive of the action of x-ing itself. The hydraulic model conceives of strength of desire in such a way that this is not possible. The claim that we always do what we most want to do is taken to entail that the agent who does x could not have chosen to do y instead, given the full configuration of intentional states to which that agent was subject immediately prior to action. The desire that leads agent S to do x is postulated to be stronger causally than the other motivations to which S was subject, and from this it follows that no other action was strictly possible for S so long as the attitudes to which S was subject at the time are held fixed.

The hydraulic model is in fact rarely endorsed explicitly in this bald form. More typically, philosophers accept the truistic dictum I articulated above, and then proceed to interpret it in terms that only make sense if the hydraulic conception is implicitly taken for granted.[10] A good test for whether the dictum has been developed in this way is a philosopher's account of *akrasia*, in which agents fail to comply with their deliberated verdicts in the face of temptation. A characteristic assumption in discussions of this phenomenon is that the wayward desire that leads the agent to act *akratically* must have been the desire that was causally strongest, at the time of action—it was, after all, the desire that actually won out. But if this is the case, the question naturally arises as to why cases of ordinary weakness do not simply collapse into cases of psychological compulsion or addiction. The comparative causal strength of the *akratic* desire renders it impossible to resist, under the postulated psychological circumstances, and this apparently traces weakness to the kind of volitional incapacity represented by compulsion and addiction.

The response to this problem favored by those to whom I attribute the hydraulic model is couched in counterfactual terms. Take a case of ordinary

---

[10] Compare the formulation and interpretation of the "motivational perspective" on action offered by Philip Pettit and Michael Smith, in "Backgrounding Desire," *Philosophical Review*, 99 (1990), pp. 565–592 and "Practical Unreason," *Mind*, 102 (1993), pp. 53–79; see also Alfred R. Mele, *Autonomous Agents* (New York: Oxford University Press, 1995), chap. 2.

akrasia, in which I conclude that finishing work on the paper for the conference is the action I ought to perform, but I end up going shopping at the mall instead. About this case, we may suppose that the comparative strength of my desires to work on the paper and to go shopping would have been sufficiently altered to bring it about that the former prevails, if a certain thought had only occurred to me at the time (such as the thought that Mike Corrado will be very angry if the paper is not finished soon).[11] Or we may point to a third desire, say to exercise control, which is sufficiently strong that it could have motivated a distinct course of action—for example, issuing a self-command—even in the face of the powerful temptation to shop; this distinct action, it is suggested, would in turn eventually have altered the overall balance of desire, causing me to work on the paper after all.[12] In cases of psychological compulsion or addiction, by contrast, we may suppose that the counterfactual postulation of similar thoughts and desires would not have altered the balance of motivation sufficiently to bring it about that I do what I believe best.

Accounts of *akrasia* that are developed in these terms are, I maintain, implicitly committed to the hydraulic model. Desires are conceived as vectors of force, independent of the actions performed, that motivate actions by their exertion of causal influence. There is a kind of psychological determinism at work in this approach, which reveals itself in the suggestion that the only scenarios in which *akratic* agents would have succeeded in complying with their deliberated verdicts are scenarios in which they are subject to a different configuration of desires and beliefs. Given the causal force of the various desires to which they are actually subject, together with their actual beliefs, it turns out that *akratic* agents simply lack the capacity to do what they judge best.

This kind of psychological determinism is in my view the underlying philosophical commitment of the hydraulic model; but it is also its undoing. The problem, in broad terms, is that the model leaves no real room for genuine deliberative agency. Action is traced to the operation of forces within us, with respect to which we as agents are ultimatly passive, and in a picture of this kind real agency seems to drop out of view.[13] Reasoned action requires the capacity to determine what one shall do in ways independent

---

[11] Compare Philip Pettit and Michael Smith, "Freedom in Belief and Desire," *Journal of Philosophy*, 93 (1996), pp. 429–449 [reprinted as Essay 20, this volume]. See also Jeanette Kennett and Michael Smith, "Frog and Toad Lose Control," *Analysis*, 56 (1996), pp. 63–73.

[12] See Alfred R. Mele, *Irrationality: An Essay on Akrasia, Self-Deception, and Self-Control* (New York: Oxford University Press, 1987); see also his *Autonomous Agents*, chap. 3.

[13] On this point, see J. David Velleman, "What Happens When Someone Acts?" *Mind*, 101 (1992), pp. 461–481. (Velleman's presentation of this problem is exemplary, though I do not agree with the reductionist solution he proposes.)

from the desires that one merely finds oneself with, and an explanatory framework that fails to leave room for this kind of self-determination cannot be adequate to the phenomenon it is meant to explain. In this respect, the hydraulic model falls short.[14]

The hydraulic model does offer a strategy for distinguishing between ordinary weakness and cases of addiction and compulsion, in the counter-factual terms sketched above. A-impulses are treated as distinctive, insofar as their causal strength is sufficiently great that they would still have pre-vailed, even if (contrary to fact) the agent had been equipped with the sorts of beliefs and desires ordinarily implicated in self-control. At the same time, A-impulses can be distinguished from strictly irresistible desires insofar as there are counterfactual conditions, involving the application of *extraordin-ary* techniques (12-step programs and the like), under which they would be defeated. But this merely enables us to classify A-desires appropriately, as distinct both from the wayward desires ordinarily involved in *akrasia* and desires (if indeed there are such) that are literally irresistible. Lost in this classificatory scheme is the important idea that *akratic*, addicted, and com-pelled agents retain a capacity to initiate a regime of self-control that cannot itself plausibly be reconstructed in terms of responses under various contrary-to-fact conditions. We think of such agents as possessing the power to struggle against their wayward impulses, not merely in counterfactual circumstances in which the desires and beliefs to which they happen to be subject are different, but in the psychological circumstances in which they actually find themselves. Holding those circumstances fixed, the hydraulic model places *akratic*, addicted, and compelled agents in what is essentially the same boat: the causal forces of the desires to which they are actually subject leave them with no real alternative to the wayward actions that they all end up performing.

These considerations make the hydraulic conception ultimately unaccept-able, as an interpretation of the motivating role of desires within deliberative agency. The alternative I would favor is the one referred to earlier as the volitionalist model; its distinctive features can best be introduced by

---

[14] These remarks may seem to have a libertarian cast that fits poorly with my other published views about responsibility and agency (in *Responsibility and the Moral Sentiments* [Cambridge, Mass.: Harvard University Press, 1994]). So to set the record straight: I take the emphasis on the capacity to rise above one's given desires to be an appealing feature of libertarian and agent-causation theories, something that they get right. Unlike the proponents of such theories, however, I do not believe that this important capacity must be incompatible with determinism in every form (though it is irreconcileable with the kind of psychological determinism I have attributed to the hydraulic conception). For more on these matters, see my "Moral Responsibility and the Practical Point of View," in Ton van den Beld, ed., *Moral Responsibility and Ontology* (Dordrecht: Kluwer Academic Publishers, forthcoming).

contrasting them with those of the hydraulic conception. The latter approach pictures deliberative agency as consisting, essentially, in two distinct moments. There is, first, the agent's practical or evaluative judgment about what there is most reason to do, or what it would be best to do on the whole; and there is, second, the agent's motivational state, which is a function of the causal strength of the desires to which the agent is subject.[15] If the agent is lucky, these two states will be in alignment with each other, so that the agent is most strongly motivated to perform the action that the agent believes, at the time, to be best.[16] But whether this kind of alignment is achieved is not really something that is up to the agent to determine.[17]

True, the hydraulic model makes available a notion of self-control, which we ordinarily think of as a matter of bringing it about that one does what one believes best in the face of temptation. This is interpreted according to what might be called the "cold shower" paradigm: we achieve control by devising strategies to influence causally the motivational strength of the desires to which we are subject, such as exposing ourselves to a cold shower, or thinking of the queen, when an access of inappropriate sexual appetite overcomes us. Now I do not doubt that strategies of this kind can sometimes be effective ways of bringing our wayward desires into line, thereby helping us to translate our deliberated verdicts into action. But to suppose that self-control must always conform to the cold shower paradigm turns us into passive bystanders at the scene of our own actions. We don't really determine which actions we perform directly, rather we attempt to manipulate the psychological influences to which we are subject, in the hope that *they* will eventually bring it about that we do what we judge to be best. Agency, to the extent it survives at all, seems restricted to the initiation of such strategies of indirect self-manipulation. But consistent development of the hydraulic approach banishes it from the scene even there. Either the exercise of control gets traced to the occurrence of a psychological event—such as the agent's thinking a certain thought—that is not an intentional action at all. Or room is left for the deliberate initiation of a strategy of control, but this in turn is

---

[15] Some versions of the hydraulic model tend to collapse this distinction, treating practical judgments in noncognitivist terms, as themselves expressions of our given desires. This variant gives us a nonaccidental connection between practical judgment and motivation, but at the considerable cost of depriving practical judgment of its potential autonomy from given desire.

[16] Compare the ideal of orthonomy advocated by Pettit and Smith in "Practical Unreason," p. 77: "The important thing is not to assume control . . . [but] to be someone in whom desires are neither too strong nor too weak."

[17] There are more sophisticated versions of the hydraulic approach that better capture our sense of ourselves as agents, though they remain inadequate in other respects; Velleman's favored reductionist account of agency in "What Happens When Someone Acts?" might be an example. For discussion, see the remarks about "meta-internalism" in my paper "Three Conceptions of Rational Agency," *Ethical Theory and Moral Practice*, 2 (1999), pp. 217–242.

conceived as the result of further causal forces operative within the agent's psychological economy at the time when the exercise of control began.[18]

To avoid these problems, we need in my view to expand our conception of the basic elements involved in reflective agency, acknowledging a third moment irreducible to either deliberative judgment or merely given desire. This is the moment of what I shall call volition. By "volition" here I mean a kind of motivating state that, by contrast with the given desires that figure in the hydraulic conception, are directly under the control of the agent. Familiar examples of volitional states in this sense are intentions, choices, and decisions. It is distinctive of states of these kinds that we do not think of them as belonging to the class of mere events in our psychological lives, along with sensations, moods, passing thoughts, and such ordinary states of desire as being very attracted to the chocolate cake in front of one at the café. Rather intentions, decisions, and choices are things we do, primitive examples of the phenomenon of agency itself. It is one thing to find that one wants some chocolate cake very much, or that its odor reminds one of one's childhood in Detroit, quite another to resolve to eat a piece. The difference, I would suggest, marks a line of fundamental importance, the line between the passive and the active in our psychological lives.[19] Agency is not merely a matter of subjection to motivational states, understood as vectors of force. It is manifested in our exercising the capacity to choose for ourselves what we are to do. An adequate conceptualization of reflective agency must do justice to this point, postulating a distinctively volitional moment in addition to the moments of deliberative judgment and merely given desire.

The volitionalist model just sketched is not meant as a detailed contribution to the philosophy of action. It is offered instead as a schematic framework for thinking about the kind of agency distinctive of those creatures capable of practical reason. From the first-personal standpoint of practical deliberation we take it that we are both subject to and capable of complying with rational requirements, and the volitionalist approach enables us to make sense of this deliberative self-image. Persons who are equipped with the power of self-determining choice retain the basic capacity to comply

---

[18] For these two options, see the following debate: Alfred R. Mele, "Understanding Self-Control: Kennett and Smith on Frog and Toad," *Analysis*, 57 (1997), pp. 119–123, and Jeanette Kennett and Michael Smith, "Synchronic Self-control is Always Non-actional," *Analysis*, 57 (1997), pp. 123–131.

[19] I should stress here that many motivational states seem to straddle this distinction in ways that make them difficult to classify. Most salient among these are states of being attracted to a course of action precisely because one judges that it would be good to perform. The involvement of evaluative judgment in these states makes it misleading to describe them as states with respect to which we are merely passive (as Angela Smith has helped me to see). And yet, being attracted to a course of action is not under our direct control in the way our intentions, choices, and decisions seem to be.

with their judgments about their reasons, even when their merely given desires are feeble or rebellious. Their actions are not merely the causal products of psychological states that they happen to find themselves in at the time, rather they have the power to determine for themselves what they are going to do. By exercising this power, such persons can bring about a kind of rational action that is not merely due to the fortuitous coincidence of rational judgment and given desire, but that is a manifestation of the very capacities that make them, distinctively, *agents*.[20]

3. DESIRES AND REFLECTIVE AGENCY

The volitionalist model accounts for rational agency in terms of motivating states with respect to which we are distinctively active. Action is an expression of choice or decision, not the result of psychological forces operating on us. This raises an important question, however. If ordinary, given desires are not needed to account for the capacity of persons to comply with their deliberated verdicts about action, what role is left for them to play in the etiology of reflective agency? Don't they become fifth wheels, spinning pointlessly in relation to the processes responsible for human action? I do not think that this is the case, and seeing why it is not will be important if we are to make sense of the idea that A-impulses can be forms of volitional incapacity.

Let us start with the context of practical deliberation that leads to the formation of a judgment about what one has reason to do. One way in which given desires could contribute to the processes of reflective agency is by providing data to be taken account of in such practical deliberation. There are influential theories according to which the normative reasons for action that provide the subject matter for this kind of deliberation are exclusively a function of our desires. These theories hold that one can have a reason to do, say, x only if one has some antecedent desire that could lead one to be motivated to do x.[21] For the record, such theories do not seem to me very plausible. Indeed, the volitionalist model sketched in the preceding section undermines the most serious consideration advanced in favor of them, namely the alleged need to postulate a connection between normative reasons and antecedent desires in order to explain the motivational effects of reflection about our reasons. But I don't want to get into that right now. The more important point for the present is that even those who reject the thesis

[20] For further development of these points, see my "Three Conceptions of Rational Agency."

[21] See, most influentially, Bernard Williams, "Internal and External Reasons," as reprinted in Williams, *Moral Luck* (Cambridge: Cambridge University Press, 1981), pp. 101–113.

that all reasons for action are grounded in desires should concede that our given states of desire are often relevant to normative reflection about our reasons. This is one important contribution they have to make to the processes of reflective agency.

Granted, it is easy to be misled about the precise nature of their contribution in this context.[22] One natural way of picturing this contribution is to suppose that agent S's reason for doing x will consist, in many cases, simply in the fact that x-ing would satisfy one of S's given desires. But this picture, however natural, seems to me distorted. In the normal cases in which our reasons are conditional on our given desires, it is not simply the fact that those desires would be satisfied by a given course of action x that gives us reason to choose to do x. At least it is not, so long as we avoid equivocating on the notion of satisying a desire. In the most general sense, satisfaction is a purely formal concept. To say that a desire is satisfied, in this formal sense, is merely to say that the state of affairs that is desired has come to pass; with many desires, this can be the case independently of the subjective facts about the original bearer of the desire, including that person's knowledge of whether or not the desire has been satisfied.[23]

In another sense, however, satisfaction is precisely a subjective condition, a sensation or complex of sensations that is initiated by, or itself consists in, the satisfaction in the purely formal sense of some desire that a person has. Thus if all goes well and the case is otherwise normal, S's desire to eat a crab cake will actually give way to satisfaction in this second sense—to an experience of culinary pleasure—when the desire is formally satisfied. Clearly, satisfaction or pleasure of this kind can be a normative reason for acting, one moreover that is conditioned by our desires, since what one takes pleasure in at a given time is at least in part a function of one's desires at that time: what one feels attracted to, is in the mood for, is crazy about, and so on.[24] This is not the only way in which given desires can contribute to determining what we have normative reason to do, but it is a basic and important way, one moreover that is especially relevant to the operation of A-impulses. I shall return to this point below.

The contribution of desire to reflective agency just discussed may be considered a positive contribution, part of the successful translation of practical reason into autonomous, reasoned behavior. But desire can exert an

[22] I am indebted here to Warren Quinn, "Putting Rationality in its Place," as reprinted in Quinn, *Morality and Action* (Cambridge: Cambridge University Press, 1993), pp. 228–255.

[23] Thus my preference that a long-lost friend should be thriving may be satisfied, in this sense of formal fulfillment, even if I never find out what has become of him.

[24] Our reasons in these cases have what T. M. Scanlon calls "subjective conditions"; see his *What We Owe to Each Other* (Cambridge, Mass.: Harvard University Press, 1998), chap. 1.

influence on the processes in which such agency consists that is negative rather than positive, inhibiting the orderly progression from deliberative reflection through to corresponding action. What makes this possible is, in the first instance, the unruliness of desire, the fact that many desires are not responsive to our practical reasoning about how we ought to act. To take a banal example: I may believe that I ought not to go for a second piece of cake, but find that I continue to desire to eat some more all the same. Here we may suppose that fact that I want another piece of cake has already been taken into account in arriving at the verdict that I ought not to have one; reflecting on this fact in light of the other considerations that speak against having a second piece, I correctly conclude that the desire by itself is not sufficient to override or outweigh those considerations. And yet the desire persists all the same. When this sort of thing happens, our desires can present obstacles to the processes in which deliberative agency consists. Indeed this is precisely what must happen in the case of A-desires, the resilience of which expresses itself in their unresponsiveness to deliberative reflection. The question is how exactly such resilient desires can interfere with deliberative agency, and whether the form of interference they provide is well thought of as a defect of the will. Before we can answer this question, we need to look more closely at the nature of desires. I shall concentrate primarily on examples that share the characteristic features of A-impulses: resilience, urgency, and connection with pleasure and pain.

The first thing to note is that there are various ways of thinking about the the link between such desires and pleasure and pain. One might, for instance, treat the desire itself as an intrinsically dysphoric condition; in these terms, the pleasure or satisfaction associated with the fulfillment of the desire would be (or at least be related to) the cessation of this dysphoric sensation, while the pain attendant on non-fulfillment would simply represent the continued and increasingly intense experience of desire itself. Now I am not convinced that this is the best way to think about all impulses related to pleasure and pain. While there are no doubt some desires and appetites that are themselves dysphoric—extreme hunger is perhaps the best example—in many other cases it seems that we can have desires for the pleasant that are not accurately thought of on the model of intrinsically painful sensations. Furthermore, the dysphoria picture threatens to generate a vicious regress. It suggests that the motivating power of desire is connected with its experiential painfulness; but this suggestion can only be made sense of on the assumption that we have a basic desire to avoid painful sensations, and the obvious question arises as to how the motivating power of *that* background desire is to be accounted for. Sooner or later, it seems, we shall have to postulate a primitive disposition to avoid pain and go for pleasure that is not construed on the model of a dysphoric state. In that event, however, we may as well admit that there are first-order desires relating to prospective pleasure and pain that are not themselves literally painful.

An alternative and to my mind more satisfactory approach to such desires is to think of them on the model of perceptions rather than sensations.[25] Desires to obtain some prospective pleasure or to avoid a prospective pain may be conceived as quasi-perceptual modes of presentation of these anticipated sensations. They are like perceptions in exhibiting conceptual structure, without necessarily being or resting on full-blown judgments. Thus, in cases that are distinctly irrational one can desire an experience under the aspect of the pleasant, while judging on reflection that the experience in question would probably not be all that pleasant after all, on the whole; an example might be a case of commodity fetishism, where one finds oneself wanting to possess, say, a new toaster oven or lawn mower that one doesn't really need, while knowing from experience that fulfillment of such free-standing consumerist desires is generally a source of disappointment and mild depression rather than satisfaction. In such a case, the desire consists in part in one's thinking about the potential course of action or experience in terms of some evaluative category, its persistently presenting itself to one as, say, pleasant.

Furthermore, like other forms of perception (optical illusions, for example), the presentation of a potential course of action under an evaluative category of this kind is not necessarily something that is fully under one's voluntary control. This is what makes possible the kind of divergence of desire and considered judgment just mentioned, where one continues to desire something as pleasant, while not really believing that it would be all that pleasant on the whole. This in turn is connected with a third and still more distinctive feature of the class of desires we are considering, *viz.*, the way one's attention is focussed on the possibility for action that strikes one as pleasant.[26] It is part of the mode of presentation characteristic of appetitive desire that the prospective action or experience one thinks of under an

---

[25] For some suggestive remarks in a similar vein, see Dennis W. Stampe, "The Authority of Desire," *The Philosophical Review*, 96 (1987), pp. 341–381. (I would reject, however, the conclusions Stampe draws from the perceptual analogy concerning the role of desire in practical reasoning.) I should also stress in this context that the points I shall make about desires for pleasure are not meant to apply to all states that are referred to as desires in philosophical parlance (which include, among other things, the distinctive kind of "pro-attitudes" I have referred to as volitions). The phenomenological account I shall develop is an account of that sub-class of desires, of which A-desires are an example, that can present an agent with temptations in contexts of deliberation and decision.

[26] Compare Scanlon's remarks about desire in the "directed attention" sense, in *What We Owe to Each Other*, chap. I, and Watson's discussion of the ways in which desires can be *compelling*, in "Disordered Appetites," sec. 3.

evaluative category should tend to dominate one's conscious experience. Gleaming images of the toaster oven from the advertisements keep appearing before one's mind's eye, and one's thoughts turn repeatedly to questions related to the acquisition of such an item. The focussing of one's attention in a certain direction is one of the most salient characteristics of A-desires, and it helps to explain their resilience in the face of conflicting judgment, especially when temporal distinctions are taken into account. Someone in the grip of an intense impulse to smoke some crack cocaine, for instance, will find their thoughts focussed very relentlessly on the immediate pleasure associated with that course of action, even if they judge that there is more pleasure and less agony to be gained in the long term from desisting.

Desires for pleasure, then, may be thought of as quasi-perceptual modes of presentation of a course of action under the aspect of the pleasant, which are not under one's voluntary control, and which manifest themselves consciously in the direction of one's attention onto the desired activity or experience. To say that a desire of this kind is strong or urgent, something approaching a craving, is accordingly to say that it is a state in which one's thoughts and attention are directed onto the desired activity or experience with particular force or intensity. We have, in other words, a *phenomenological* conception of strength of desire. Desires are not urgent in virtue of their causal force; that approach, as we have seen, renders exercises of strength of will in the face of strong temptation something close to a conceptual impossibility. What makes some desires particularly urgent is rather the way things seem experientially to the person who is in their grip. Urgent desires can seem to take over the course of one's thoughts, presenting one with highly vivid candidates for action, colored in an evaluative light, that one is unable simply to ignore. In many cases urgency may be manifested further in the experience of dysphoric sensations and other emotions, including anxiety, fear, and excitement. As I argued above, dysphoric and emotional elements of this sort do not seem to be present in all cases of desire for the pleasant, but when such desires become particularly intense they are doubtless often accompanied by discomfort and other dysphoric sensations and feelings.

Once the urgency of A-impulses is understood in these phenomenological terms, however, we can begin to gain a realistic appreciation of the ways in which those impulses can impede reflective agency. It is to this issue that I now turn.

4. A-IMPULSES AND THE IMPAIRMENT OF REFLECTIVE AGENCY

In considering the obstacles posed by A-desires to reflective agency I want to put to the side the following possibilities: that individual acts of drug consumption might be justifiable, in moral and prudential terms, and that addiction itself might operate as a kind of excuse. Obviously many A-impulses, construed as quasi-perceptual representations of a prospective course of action or experience as pleasant, are veridical. The reason why it strikes one vividly that ingesting some more of a certain drug would be very pleasant is that it would in fact be so, whereas the failure to take the drug is likely to be quite unpleasant, involving eventually the various painful symptoms customarily referred to under the heading of withdrawal. When this is the case, the comparative pleasure to be gained by consumption could be such as to render that option justified, especially if such conditions as the following are also satisfied: the drug is readily available, in plentiful supply, at reasonable cost; its use would not interfere with one's other important life pursuits; the side-effects of consumption for one's health are otherwise negligible; its use would not require one to breach one's responsibilities to friends, family, and others; and so on.

Even when these conditions of ordinary justification are not satisfied, however, addiction might function to excuse the addicted agent from blame for the act of consumption.[27] This possibility is raised by cases in which the painful withdrawl effects of abstention are unusually great. In such cases, it could become permissible for the agent to embark on a course of action that would ordinarily be prohibited (morally and otherwise), in order to avoid the painful effects of abstaining from consuming the drug to which they are addicted. This scenario, in which it is assumed that addiction functions much like ordinary coercion or duress to excuse the agent from blame for a deed that would otherwise be impermissible, clearly cannot be extended to cover very many of the offenses of interest to the law. Rudeness and incivility, and such minor offenses as littering and jaywalking, might conceivably be excusable in this way, if they were sincerely believed by the agent to be necessary to avoid the anticipated and severe distress of withdrawal; but the strategy would not apply to more serious violations of legal and moral norms. The reason for this is that a duress defense is generally recognized under the law only when the agent is plausibly threatened with death or grievous bodily harm, and the discomfort of withdrawal from a substance to

---

[27] For a general account of the conditions that excuse persons from blame, see my *Responsibility and the Moral Sentiments*, chap. 5.

which one is addicted can hardly be compared with such effects.[28] In any case, I shall simply bracket such issues, assuming that we are dealing with situations in which the anticipated painful effects of abstention would not constitute an excuse analogous to coercion or duress, and in which the balance of risks and benefits is not such as to justify consumption in ordinary moral and prudential terms.

Consider, then, a person addicted to a drug such as heroin, who is considering whether to obtain some more of the drug for another fix. The issue, just to be clear, is not the effect of actual consumption of the drug on the person's capacities for deliberative agency, but rather the effects on those capacities of the urgent A-desires to which the addiction disposes the person. We may suppose, to begin with, that such desires might interfere with the person's capacity to deliberate rationally about the normative considerations that speak for and against the act of shooting up. To be sure, even the most intense A-desire would presumably not deprive one altogether of the ability to appreciate the most fundamental moral, legal, and factual parameters of one's situation. Supposing that the case really is one in which consumption is not justifiable in terms the agent would accept, these parameters might include such facts as the following: that possession of heroin is legally sanctioned; that its purchase therefore involves certain prudential dangers; that use of the drug poses significant risks to one's longer-term health; that such use interferes in still more significant ways with activities and relationships one values, and so on. What may be impaired by an intense A-impulse, however, is one's capacity to weigh these normative factors accurately and judiciously, in reflection leading to a verdict about what one has most reason to do on the whole.

On the phenomenological account I have offered, A-desires involve the intense focussing of one's attention onto the anticipated pleasures of (say) drug consumption, perhaps accompanied by other painful sensations and emotions. But someone subject to such a quasi-perceptual state will presumably find it difficult to think clearly about the overall balance of reasons bearing on the decision to consume or abstain from consuming the drug. Let us suppose that the anticipated pleasure and release from discomfort is of little normative significance in comparison to the clear prudential and moral disadvantages of continued heroin consumption, and that the agent in question would agree that this is the case when reflecting calmly about the issue in circumstances that do not involve the presence of intense A-desires. Adding

---

[28] Compare Morse, "Causation, Compulsion, and Involuntariness," and Herbert Fingarette, "Addiction and Criminal Responsibility," *Yale Law Journal*, 84 (1975), pp. 413–444, at pp. 437–438. See also Gary Watson's paper, "Excusing Addiction", *Law and Philosophy*, 18/6 (1999), pp. 589–619.

such a desire to the mix, it seems, would make it much harder for the agent to reach this conclusion and to keep it firmly in view. The focussing of one's attention onto the pleasures of consumption that is brought about by A-desires is apt to encourage one to overestimate the value and importance of those pleasures, in reflecting about what one is to do, and this distorting effect can be considered an impairment of the agent's capacities for practical rationality.[29]

In saying this, I do not suppose that such an impairment should be thought of on the model of total incapacitation. The urgent A-desire is not itself a belief or judgment to the effect that the desired state or action is good on the whole, but merely a presentation of that state or action that is colored in evaluative terms; in this respect, it is unlike the delusional false beliefs to which some forms of mental illness may dispose those whom they affect. Furthermore, I see no reason to conclude that such quasi-perceptual presentations of an alternative for action should render an agent altogether unable to think clearly about the normative considerations that actually bear on the decision to perform the action. Reaching the conclusion that short-term pleasure does not justify the decision to consume a given drug, in light of the other factors that need to be taken into account, is not altogether beyond the psychological powers of persons who are subject to intense A-impulses. It is merely difficult to do, something that requires effort, concentration, strength of will, and so on; moreover that this is the case is perfectly intelligible once we are operating with the phenomenological conception of strength of desire. My claim is that this effect of A-impulses on the processes of deliberation deserves to be thought of as at least a partial impairment of our capacities for reflective agency.

It does not yet amount to a defect of the will, however. The forms of interference with reflective agency just discussed represent impairments of our capacities for rational thought about the normative issues bearing on action. A defect of the will, by contrast, would be a form of interference with the processes of reflective agency that goes beyond, and is independent from, deficiencies in respect to rationality alone. To home in on the question of whether addiction can constitute such a defect of the will, we need to imagine a case in which an agent correctly arrives at the conclusion that abstention would be the best course of action on the whole, while nevertheless remaining subject to urgent A-impulses to shoot up. That such a scenario is possible follows from the point that A-impulses are resilient, since, as we have seen, resilience precisely consists in the unresponsiveness of desires

---

[29] The effects of strong A-desires on the rationality of the agent subject to them are emphasized in Stephen Morse's "Hooked on Hype," *Law and Philosophy*, 19 (January 2000), pp. 3–49.

to evaluative reflection.[30] So our imagined agent is one who judges that abstention would be best, but retains an especially intense desire to consume some more of the drug. Should we think of this condition as a potential defect of the will?

We should not, if such a defect is understood as a complete incapacitation of our volitional powers. The power to choose in accordance with one's deliberative judgments would be completely obliterated by A-desires only on the assumption that those desires are literally irresistible, and I have already rejected that assumption (along with the related causal interpretation of strength of desire). But I see no reason to think that a defect of the will must amount to a form of total incapacitation of the will. We saw above that it can be appropriate to speak of impairment of our powers of practical reasoning even in cases in which such impairment is partial rather then complete. Similarly, I believe we should be prepared to grant that there are impairments of our volitional powers that do not amount to cases of complete incapacity to act in ways we ourselves deem best. Moreover, the phenomenological conception of strength of desire I have been developing makes it fairly clear why urgent A-impulses should amount to volitional defects of this kind. To be in the grip of such an impulse is to be made vividly aware of a concrete alternative for action, presented in terms that appear highly attractive. Even if one succeeds, in the face of such a desire, in reasoning correctly to the conclusion that it should not be acted on, its continued presence and urgency will make it comparatively difficult to choose to comply with the deliberated verdict one has arrived at. The A-impulse that persists in a situation of this kind is the extreme case of the phenomenon of temptation, a psychological condition that facilitates the choice of an action the agent believes ill-advised, by directing the agent's thoughts onto the alleged attractions to be gained through that action. An intense and systemic temptation of this variety, I submit, is appropriately thought of as a kind of volitional defect.

Consider as an analogy a different kind of temptation, in which A-desires are not at issue. Suppose that after consultation with my doctor I have reached the conclusion that it would be best on the whole to reduce substantially my cholesterol level. Suppose further that, without being in any way addicted to the things, I am very fond of certain high-fat foods (Belgian chocolates and premium Vermont ice cream, let us say) that I need to avoid if I am to attain my goal of reducing my cholesterol level. It seems obvious

---

[30] That is, from reflection about what one has most reason to do. It is compatible with resiliance in this sense that A-desires are connected to thoughts about the prospective pleasure to be gained through action, in the ways outlined in sec. 3 above.

that it will be far easier for me to comply with my deliberated judgment about what to do if there are not large supplies of chocolate and ice cream lying about in my cupboards and refrigerator. The physical presence of such items presents me vividly with concrete possibilities for action that are undeniably attractive in a certain respect, even if they are not the alternatives I favor on the whole. My reflective judgment about what to do represents one option for the will, but the vivid awareness of a very pleasant alternative, prompted by my literal perception of chocolate and ice cream in my environment, represents a different possibility, one whose rewards would be immediate and visceral.

This is an understandable effect of the perception of the forbidden food-stuffs on what might be called the phenomenological field of agency—one's immediate awareness of a set of options as concrete and appealing alternatives for action. It seems clear that an alteration of this kind in the field of agency would make it more difficult for me to act well by my own lights—and not merely by interfering with my capacity to think clearly about the pros and cons of a rich diet. Even if I remain convinced that it would be best on the whole to stay away from ice cream and chocolates, the vivid presentation of these items as dietary alternatives may impair my capacity to choose in accordance with this verdict, by making the act of choice itself much harder than it otherwise would be. If this is correct, however, then it should be equally clear that urgent A-impulses can also represent impairments of our powers of choice. On the phenomenological conception of them I have sketched, such impulses are to be understood as involuntary, quasi-perceptual presentations of experiences and actions as unusually pleasant. But the effects of such conceptualized presentations of concrete options on the field of agency are in the relevant respects just like the effects of my literal perception of chocolates and ice cream in the case described above.[31] By making one vividly aware of alternatives for action that promise an immediate and visceral pleasure, A-impulses bring it about that compliance with one's settled better judgment would require effort, concentration, strength of will. In these ways, A-impulses represent potential impairments not only of our capacities for rational deliberation but also of our volitional power to comply with the verdicts of such deliberation.

[31] In fact, the two scenarios I have described here are really two instances of the same basic kind of case. In the first scenario, we must suppose that the literal presence of the forbidden foodstuffs incites in us a desire to consume them, since chocolate and ice cream would not make us "vividly aware" of pleasant possibilities for action if they did not give rise to such a desire. The difference between the scenarios is simply that in the first, an intense desire is caused by the literal perception of the substance that is to be consumed, while this is not so in the second case. On the general role of situational cues in giving rise to A-desires, see George Loewenstein, "Willpower: A Decision-theorist's Perspective," *Law and Philosophy*, 19 (January 2000), pp. 51–76.

Against this, it might be urged that my account of volitional defects due to addiction does not succeed in distinguishing them adequately from impairments of an agent's rationality. The account builds on the effects of A-desires on the phenomenological field of agency; but, the reply would go, any agent who is subject to these effects is also necessarily subject to an impairment of rationality. Such an agent may succeed in judging (correctly, as I have been supposing) that it would be best on the whole not to satisfy their intense A-desire. But the continued presence of the desire will necessarily distract their attention from the practical judgment they have arrived at. Much in the way of Aristotle's *akrates*, they will find themselves unable to focus with full concentration on the normative conclusions that they accept. Doesn't this mean that the threat posed by addiction to deliberative agency is at bottom a threat to our rationality, and not a defect of the will?

In answer to this question, I would offer the following observations. First, facts about the direction of one's attention occupy a curiously liminal position in respect to the divide between the rational and the non-rational in our psychological lives. In themselves, attention, interest, vivid presence to consciousness and the like would seem to be features of our emotional and desiderative biographies.[32] According to the phenomenological account of A-desires I have endorsed, for instance, to be subject to such a desire is (*inter alia*) to have one's attention directed onto certain possibilities for action, conceived of as pleasant in some way. This is, in part, a cognitive phenomenon, involving a susceptibility to thoughts of distinctive kinds, but it is not on that account unequivocally a defect of rationality. The focussing of attention that is constitutive of desire becomes a clear defect of rationality only to the extent that it impinges on our ability to form true beliefs and to draw correct inferences from them; but in the sorts of cases I have been considering we were to suppose that A-desires do not cause impairments of these kinds.

To be sure, the failure to choose in accordance with one's correct practical judgment about what one ought to do may be counted a failure of rational inference in the broadest sense. This will be the case on the plausible assumption that it is a requirement of rationality that we choose in accordance with our conclusive practical judgments about what we have reason to do.[33]

---

[32] They are treated this way, for instance, by Michael Stocker, in *Valuing Emotions* (Cambridge: Cambridge University Press, 1996), chap. 1.

[33] This is one version of the thesis referred to as internalism in discussions of normative reasons for action; see, for example, Christine M. Korsgaard, "Skepticism about Practical Reason," as reprinted in her *Creating the Kingdom of Ends* (Cambridge: Cambridge University Press, 1996), pp. 311–334.

Note again, however, that a failure in this respect does not license the conclusion that the agent was altogether incapable of choosing correctly. It is attractive, but misleading, to picture our motivational psychology in terms of standing dispositions to action that are triggered causally if (and only if) the agent's attention is focussed sufficiently on the possibilities for action that are to be chosen. This picture is really just a variant of what I earlier referred to as the hydraulic conception. On the volitionalist alternative I have recommended as superior to the hydraulic model, the capacity for self-determination is not something that can be reconstructed in terms of a deterministic theory of the operations of the mind. This means, in particular, that the basic capacity to choose in accordance with our evaluative beliefs can survive even in the presence of psychological conditions that tend to direct our attention away from the objects of those beliefs. Intense A-desires may make the exercise of reflective self-control difficult, but they do not render it impossible.

In the end, the admission that there are norms of rationality governing volition as well as belief deprives the distinction between defects of rationality and defects of the will of its theoretical interest. The relevant distinction to draw in this area is within the class of defects of rationality, between impairments of our capacity for practical judgment and impairments of our capacity to choose in accordance with our practical judgments. The kinds of volitional impairments I have tried to characterize in this section represent ways in which A-desires can lead us astray even when we succeed in judging correctly what we should do. If choice in accordance with one's practical judgments is itself a requirement of reason, however, then such volitional impairments will also be defects of rationality, in an extended sense.

For this reason (among others), I am uncertain whether the position I have defended in this paper provides support for the jurisprudential thesis that the law should acknowledge the category of volitional defect in addition to that of defect of rationality. I strongly suspect that a legal code that only allows for the latter form of impairment of deliberative agency can reach the same verdicts about particular cases of addiction as a code that acknowledges both rational and volitional forms of impairment. For purposes of philosophical self-understanding, however, it is important to be clear that a phenomenon such as addiction can present different kinds of obstacles in the way of our acting well. Doing so helps us to appreciate not only the variety of things that can go wrong when we try to translate our values into action, but also the complexity of our capacities for deliberative agency even when they are functioning well.

5. CONCLUSION

The main themes of my discussion can be summarized very succinctly. I have defended a volitionalist conception of the will as against the hydraulic conception of the contribution of desire to action. In terms of the volitionalist theory, I have tried to explain how addiction might impair our capacity to choose in accordance with our deliberated verdicts about what we ought to do. What are the implications of this position for questions about the moral responsibility of addicts for their actions?

I would like to make three brief, concluding observations by way of answering this question. The first is that dichotomizing approaches to the responsibility of the addict are not very helpful, and should be avoided. Discussions of this issue sometimes convey the impression that there are basically only two options: either the behavior of the addict is viewed as fully voluntary, or it is treated as the completely involuntary symptom of a disease. But moral accountability is not in general an all or nothing matter.[34] The capacities for deliberative agency that render us accountable are not only complex, they are also liable to various degrees of development or defect. The specific kinds of defect that I have traced to addiction are best understood as impairing our powers of reflective self-control, without depriving us of those powers altogether. Agents who are subject to urgent A-impulses are not thereby rendered unable to deliberate well about action, or to choose in accordance with their deliberated verdicts; it is rather that the correct exercise of their powers of deliberative agency is considerably more difficult in the presence of persistent A-impulses than it would otherwise be. Addiction, in other words, should be thought of as producing a condition of potentially diminished accountability. It moves an agent into that grey area in which the powers that make us accountable, though still present, are present only in a reduced degree. This may be frustrating to our desire for clear-cut, yes/no answers to questions about the accountability of addicts for their behavior, but it seems to reflect well the inherent difficulty both of the phenomenon and of the normative problems it raises.

Even if we make due allowances for this kind of intractability, however, it seems to me that the range of behaviors from which addiction might plausibly be thought to exempt an agent from accountability is rather restricted; this is the second of my concluding observations. Consider, in particular, the kinds of "other-regarding" criminal behavior often associated with addiction to controlled substances, such as theft, assault and battery, homicide, and so on. A person subject to urgent A-desires might find that their

---

[34] Compare my *Responsibility and the Moral Sentiments*, chaps. 6–8.

satisfaction would be facilitated by a criminal action of one of these kinds, and so we may suppose that refraining from such an action might be somewhat more difficult for the addict than for a person not subject to similar impulses. It would be incredible, however, to claim that the difficulty involved here is sufficiently great to constitute an exemption from accountability for such criminal behavior.[35] That is, we reasonably expect and demand that people refrain from theft, assault, homicide, and the like, even when doing so means that they must forgo the intense satisfactions to which their attention is directed by the A-impulses to which they are subject. In this respect, the situation of the addict seems little different from that of other agents who have strong personal motives, apart from literal self-defense, for engaging in such criminal activity (such as financial exigency or an intense desire for revenge).

The forms of behavior to which the status of diminished accountability would seem primarily relevant are the self-regarding activities directly associated with satisfaction of A-desires themselves: purchase and consumption of a controlled substance, for instance. Understanding addiction as a partial impairment of one's capacities for reflective self-control, we may be led to view it as diminishing the agent's moral accountability with respect to such questionable self-regarding activities. (I bracket here, of course, the difficult issues of whether consumption of addictive substances ought to be morally and legally sanctioned, and of the responsibility of the addict for becoming addicted in the first place.[36]) My final observation is that this result is likely to be most significant when it comes to our personal interactions with those who suffer from addiction. The acknowledgment that addiction impairs one's capacities for reflective agency can encourage understanding for the addict's plight, helping us to move away from cartoonish, "just-say-no" approaches to the problem, and to appreciate the contribution that sophisticated techniques of self-control and social support can make in overcoming urgent A-impulses. At the same time, the volitionalist conception that I have defended should discourage the equally cartoonish image of the addict as a mere victim, someone helpless in the presence of a force that is beyond the human capacity to resist. Addicts are not rendered completely powerless by the A-impulses to which they are subject. By acknowledging this fact in our interactions with those who are addicted—treating them as moral persons, equipped in a basic degree with with the powers of reflective

---

[35] Compare Morse, "Causation, Compulsion, and Involuntariness."

[36] Questions about the justifiability of legislation proscribing addictive drugs, and their connection with the issue of whether addiction can function as a defense under the criminal law, are explored by Douglas Husak in "Addiction and Criminal Liability", *Law and Philosophy*, 18/6 (1999), pp. 655–684.

self-control—we may encourage in them a more empowering self-conception, thereby enhancing the chances that they shall succeed in overcoming the obstacles placed by their condition in the way of acting well.[37]

---

[37] I received much helpful feedback on earlier versions of this paper from the other participants in the Carolina Workshop in Law and Philosophy in September 1998, as well as from audiences at the Universities of Oxford and Reading in March 1999. I owe a special debt to Karin Boxer, Kirsten Petzold, and Angela Smith for detailed and probing comments: and to my "Hilfskräfte" Ninja Kaiser and Jacob Klingner for excellent research support.

NOTES ON THE CONTRIBUTORS

RODERICK M. CHISHOLM was Professor of Philosophy and Andrew W. Mellon Professor of Humanities at Brown University.

PETER VAN INWAGEN is John Cardinal O'Hara Professor of Philosophy at the University of Notre Dame.

J. J. C. SMART was Professor Emeritus at the Australian National University.

SIR PETER STRAWSON is Professor Emeritus at the University of Oxford.

DAVID WIGGINS is Wykeham Professor of Logic Emeritus in the University of Oxford and Emeritus fellow of New College, Oxford.

DAVID LEWIS was Class of 1943 University Professor of Philosophy at Princeton University.

HILARY BOK is a member of the Philosophy Department and Luce Professor in Bioethics and Moral and Political Theory at Johns Hopkins University.

HARRY G. FRANKFURT is Professor of Philosophy Emeritus at Princeton University.

DAVID WIDERKER is a member of the Philosophy Department at Bar-Ilan University, Israel.

JOHN MARTIN FISCHER is Professor of Philosophy at the University of California, Riverside.

GALEN STRAWSON is Fellow of Jesus College, University of Oxford.

THOMAS NAGEL is Professor of Philosophy and Law at New York University.

TIMOTHY O'CONNOR is a member of the Philosophy Department at Indiana University.

RANDOLPH CLARKE is a member of the Philosophy Department at the University of Georgia.

ROBERT KANE is University Teaching Professor of Philosophy at the University of Texas, Austin.

GARY WATSON is Professor of Philosophy at the University of California, Riverside.

T. M. SCANLON is Alford Professor of Natural Religion, Moral Philosophy, and Civil Polity at Harvard University.

SUSAN WOLF is Edna J. Koury Professor of Philosophy at the University of North Carolina.

PHILIP PETTIT is Professor of Social and Political Theory in the Research School of Social Sciences, Australian National University.

MICHAEL SMITH is Professor of Philosophy in the Research School of Social Sciences, Australian National University.

ROGERS ALBRITTON was Professor of Philosophy at the University of California, Los Angeles.

R. JAY WALLACE is Professor of Philosophy at the University of California, Berkeley.

SELECTED BIBLIOGRAPHY

ANTHOLOGIES

Buss, S., and Overton, L. (eds.). *The Contours of Agency: Essays on Themes from Harry Frankfurt*. Cambridge, Mass.: MIT Press, 2002.

Ekstrom, L. W. (ed.). *Agency and Responsibility*. Boulder, Colo.: Westview Press, 2001.

Fischer, J. M. (ed.). *God, Freedom, and Foreknowledge*. Stanford, Calif.: Stanford University Press, 1989.

—— and Ravizza, M. (eds.). *Perspectives on Moral Responsibility*. Ithaca, NY: Cornell University Press, 1993.

Kane, R. (ed.). *Free Will*. Oxford: Blackwell Publishers, 2002.

O'Connor, T. (ed.). *Agents, Causes, and Events*. New York: Oxford University Press, 1995.

Pereboom, D. (ed.). *Free Will*. Indianapolis: Hackett Publishing Company, 1997.

Widerker, D., and McKenna, M. (eds.). *Freedom, Responsibility and Agency*. Aldershot, UK: Ashgate Press, 2000.

BOOKS

Berofsky, B. *Freedom from Necessity*. London: Routledge & Kegan Paul, 1997.

Dennett, D. C. *Elbow Room*. Cambridge, Mass.: MIT Press, 1984.

Ekstrom, L. W. *Free Will: A Philosophical Study*. Boulder, Colo.: Westview Press, 2000.

Fischer, J. M. *The Metaphysics of Free Will*. Cambridge, Mass.: Blackwell Press, 1994.

—— and Ravizza, M. *Responsibility and Control*. Cambridge: Cambridge University Press, 1998.

Frankfurt, H. *The Importance of What We Care About*. New York: Cambridge University Press, 1988.

—— *Necessity, Volition, and Love*. New York: Cambridge University Press, 1999.

Ginet, C. *On Action*. Cambridge: Cambridge University Press, 1990.

Haji, I. *Moral Appraisability*. New York: Oxford University Press, 1998.

Hampshire, S. *Freedom of the Individual*. New York: Harper and Row, 1965.

Honderich, T. *A Theory of Determinism*. 2 vols. Oxford: Clarendon Press, 1988.

Kane, R. *The Significance of Free Will*. New York: Oxford University Press, 1996.

Klein, M. *Determinism, Blameworthiness and Deprivation*. Oxford: Oxford University Press, 1990.

Magill, K. *Experience and Freedom: Self-Determination without Illusions*. London: Macmillan, 1997.

Mele, A. *Autonomous Agents: From Self-Control to Autonomy*. New York: Oxford University Press, 1995.

O'Connor, T. *Persons and Causes: The Metaphysics of Free Will*. New York: Oxford University Press, 2000.

Pereboom, D. *Living without Free Will*. Cambridge: Cambridge University Press, 2001.

Pettit, Philip. *A Theory of Freedom*. Oxford: Oxford University Press, 2001.

Scanlon, T. M. *What We Owe to Each Other*. Cambridge, Mass.: Harvard University Press, 1998.

Smilansky, S. *Free Will and Illusion*. Oxford: Clarendon Press, 2000.

Strawson, G. *Freedom and Belief*. Oxford: Oxford University Press, 1986.

Wallace, R. J. *Responsibility and the Moral Sentiments*. Cambridge, Mass.: Harvard University Press, 1994.

Wolf, S. *Freedom Within Reason*. New York: Oxford University Press, 1990.

ARTICLES

Aune, B. 'Hypotheticals and "Can": Another Look'. *Analysis*, 27 (1967), 191–5.

Ayer, A. J. 'Freedom and Necessity', in A. J. Ayer, *Philosophical Essays*. London: Macmillan, 1954.

Bennett, J. 'Accountability', in Zak van Straaten (ed.), *Philosophical Subjects: Essays in Honor of P. F. Strawson*. Oxford: Oxford University Press, 1979.

Benson, P. 'Freedom and Value'. *Journal of Philosophy*, 84 (1987), 465–86.

Buss, Sarah. 'Autonomy Reconsidered', in P. French, T. Uehling, Jr., and H. Wettstein (eds.), *Midwest Studies in Philosophy XIX: Philosophical Naturalism* (1994).

Chisholm, R. 'He Could Have Done Otherwise'. *Journal of Philosophy*, 64 (1967), 409–17.

Clarke, R. 'Agent Causation and Event Causation in the Production of Free Action'. *Philosophical Topics*, 24 (1996), 19–48.

Davidson, D. 'Freedom to Act', in D. Davidson, *Essays on Actions and Events*. Oxford: Clarendon Press, 1979.

Dennett, D. C. 'Mechanism and Responsibility'. Reprinted in D. C. Dennett, *Brainstorms*. Montgomery, Vt.: Bradford Books, 1978.

——. 'On Giving Libertarians What They Say They Want'. Reprinted in D. C. Dennett, *Brainstorms*. Montgomery, Vt.: Bradford Books, 1978.

Fischer, J. M. 'Responsibility and Control'. *Journal of Philosophy* 89 (1982), 24–40.

——. 'Recent Work on Moral Responsibility'. *Ethics*, 110 (1999), 93–139.

Frankfurt, H. 'Concerning the Freedom and Limits of the Will', in H. Frankfurt, *Necessity, Volition, and Love*. New York: Cambridge University Press, 1999.

Gallois, A. 'Van Inwagen on Free Will and Determinism'. *Philosophical Studies*, 32 (1977), 185–99.

Ginet, Carl. 'A Defense of Incompatibilism'. *Philosophical Studies*, 44 (1983), 391–400.

Hoffman, P. 'Freedom and Strength of Will: Descartes and Albritton'. *Philosophical Studies*, 77 (1995), 241–60.

Horgan, T. 'Compatibilism and the Consequence Argument'. *Philosophical Studies*, 47 (1985), 339–56.

Korsgaard, C. M. 'Creating the Kingdom of Ends: Reciprocity and Responsibility in Personal Relations', in C. M. Korsgaard, *Creating the Kingdom of Ends*. New York: Cambridge University Press, 1996.

Lehrer, K. 'Cans Without Ifs'. *Analysis*, 29 (1968), 29–32.

Malcolm, N. 'The Conceivability of Mechanism'. *Philosophical Review*, 77/1 (Jan. 1968), 45–72.

O'Connor, T. 'Indeterminism and Free Agency: Three Recent Views'. *Philosophy and Phenomenological Research*, 53 (1993), 499–526.

Rowe, W. 'Two Concepts of Freedom'. *Proceedings of the American Philosophical Association*, 62 (1987), Presidential Address, 43–64.

Slote, M. 'Selective Necessity and the Free Will Problem'. *Journal of Philosophy*, 79 (1982), 5–24.

Smith, M. 'A Theory of Freedom and Responsibility', in G. Cullity and B. Gaut (eds.), *Ethics and Practical Reason*. Oxford: Oxford University Press, 1997.

Stump, E. 'Sanctification, Hardness of the Heart, and Frankfurt's Concept of Free Will'. *Journal of Philosophy*, 85 (1988), 395–412.

——. 'Libertarian Freedom and the Principle of Alternative Possibilities', in M. Beatly (ed.), *Christian Theism and the Problems of Philosophy*. Notre Dame, In.: Notre Dame University Press, 1996.

Taylor, C. 'Responsibility for Self', in A. Rorty (ed.), *The Identities of Persons*. Berkeley: University of California Press, 1976.

Van Inwagen, P. 'The Incompatibility of Free Will and Determinism'. *Philosophical Studies*, 27 (1975), 185–99.

Velleman, J. D. 'What Happens When Someone Acts?' in J. D. Velleman, ed., *The Possibility of Practical Reason*. New York: Oxford University Press, 2000.

——. 'Epistemic Freedom', in J. D. Velleman, ed., *The Possibility of Practical Reason*. New York: Oxford University Press, 2000.

Vivhelin, Kadri. 'Stop Me Before I Kill Again'. *Philosophical Studies*, 75 (1994), 115–48.

——. 'Libertarian Compatibilism', in James E. Tomberlin (ed.), *Philosophical Perspectives*, 14 (Oxford and Boston: Blackwell Publishers, 2000), 139–66.

Watson, G. 'Free Action and Free Will'. *Mind*, 96 (1987), 145–72.

Widerker, D. 'Frankfurt's Attack on the Principle of Alternative Possibilities: A Further Look'. *Noûs*, 34 (2000), 181–201.

——. 'Farewell to the Direct Argument'. *Journal of Philosophy*, 94/6 (2002), 316–24.

Williams, B. 'How Free Does the Will Need to Be?' Reprinted in B. Williams, *Making Sense of Humanity*. Cambridge: Cambridge University Press, 1995.

Wolf, S. 'Asymmetrical Freedom'. *Journal of Philosophy*, 77 (1980), 151–66.

——. 'The Importance of Free Will'. *Mind*, 90 (1981), 386–405.

Yaffe, G. 'Free Will and Agency at its Best', in James E. Tomberlin (ed.), *Philosophical Perspectives*, 14 (Oxford and Boston: Blackwell Publishers, 2000), 203–30.

Zagzebski, L. 'Does Libertarian Freedom Require Alternative Possibilities?' in James E. Tomberlin (ed.), *Philosophical Perspectives*, 14 (Oxford and Boston: Blackwell Publishers, 2000), 231–48.

INDEX OF NAMES

Abbott, T. K. 36n
Ainslee, G. 427n
Albritton, R. 9n, 11, 20–1, 24, 408n, 428n
Alston, W. P. 178n
Anscombe, G. E. M. 234, 288n, 409, 410, 422–3
Anselm, St 36, 37n
Aquinas, St T. 28
Aristotle 26n, 30–1, 32n, 62n, 109n, 215, 431
Armstrong, D. M. 259, 293n
Audi, R. 290n
Austin, J. L. 66, 99n, 308
Ayer, A. J. 2n, 38, 322n

Babloyantz, A. 307n
Balchin, N. 59–60, 62, 71
Baskin, W. 151n
Bayes, T. 339
Beckermann, A. 263n
Bennett, J. 98n, 230n, 358n, 360n
Benson, P. 18n
Berlin, I. 351
Bernstein, M. 299n, 303, 304n
Berofsky, B. 177n, 187n, 209n, 299n, 304n, 308n, 310, 312n, 357n
Bigelow, J. 293n, 294n
Bishop, J. 267n, 288n, 289n
Blackburn, S. 396n
Blumenfeld, D. 164n, 177n, 192n
Bok, H. 5–6, 9, 11, 13, 18n, 24, 130n
Boswell, J. 1n
Bradley, F. H. 283
Brand, M. 204n, 277n, 285n
Branson, J. 321n
Broad, C. D. 268–9, 285n
Brody, B. 268n
Burman, F. 408

Buss, S. 190n, 203n, 204n, 211

Cahn, S. M. 303n
Calley, W. 242–3, 255–6
Campbell, C. A. 26n, 59–60, 62–8, 225n, 283
Carr, E. H. 217, 218n
Cato 27–8
Charles, D. 398n
Chellas, B. F. 123n
Chisholm, R. M. 10–11, 13, 26n, 94n, 134n, 234, 262n, 270, 272–3, 285–7, 292, 297, 334, 404n
Clark, R. 24n
Clarke, R. 11–12, 13–14, 276n, 299n, 304n, 308n, 312n
Compton, A. H. 302n
Cook, J. 423n
Costa, M. 185n
Coste, P. 35
Cottingham, J. 408n

Dante 153
Davidson, D. 38–9, 101n, 104n, 177n, 178, 261, 265–8, 277
Davis, L. 279
Della Rocca, M. 198
Dennett, D. 13n, 25, 138, 147, 164n, 177n, 299–300, 370n, 400
Descartes, R. 20, 114, 248, 292n
Destexhe, A. 307n
Donagan, A. 283n
Double, R. 275n, 299n, 303, 304n, 212n
Dretske, F. 267n, 271n
Dworkin, G. 357n

Earman, J. 422
Eccles, J. 302n
Eddington, A. S. 113–14

Edwards, J. 28
Edwards, P. 58n
Eells, E. 288n
Ekstrom, L. 193n, 194, 198, 202n, 209, 299n, 308n
Eliot, G. 226n
Elster, J. 426n
Erdmann, N. 35n

Farrer, A. 234
Feinberg, J. 190–1
Feynman, R. 43–4
Fingarette, H. 427n, 444n
Fischer, J. 5n, 7–8, 18n, 25, 135–6, 137n, 177n, 181n, 195n, 196n, 197n, 198n, 199n, 203n, 204n, 205n, 211n, 299n, 305n
Fisk, M. 104n
Flanagan, O. 313n
Flohr, H. 263n
Foot, P. 308
Foster, L. 101n
Frankfurt, H. 6–8, 17–18, 20–1, 106n, 162n, 163n, 177–84, 187–211, 229, 304n, 348–51, 369–70, 373–7, 379–80, 385, 401
Freeman, W. 307n
French, P. 370n

Gallois, A. 50n
Gardner, M. 54n
Genet, J. 115
Gibbard, A. 396n
Gide, A. 227
Ginet, C. 178n, 182n, 187n, 193n, 268n, 269, 272n, 279, 280n, 282, 285n, 289n, 308n
Goetz, S. 273n, 277
Goldman, A. 178n, 281n
Graham, G. 299n
Greene, T. M. 162n
Greenwood, J. 283n

Habermas, J. 19n
Haji, I. 299n, 303, 304n, 312n

Hampshire, S. 234n
Hare, R. M. 370n
Harre, R. 260, 283
Hart, H. L. A. 99n, 357
Hazen, A. 126n
Heathcote, A. 293n
Heinaman, R. 177n
Hempel, C. G. 101n
Henry, D. P. 37n
Heraclitus 94n
Herman, B. 162n
Hill, C. 299n
Hirsch, S. M. 243n
Hobart, R. E. 377n
Hobbes, T. 34, 38, 105n, 338
Hodgson, D. 299n
Hogg, G. 307n
Holton, R. 391n
Homstrom-Hintikka, G. 305n
Honderich, T. 38n, 94n, 95n, 264n, 273n
Honore, A. M. 99n
Hook, S. 26n, 58n, 101n, 285n
Hooker, B. 397n
Horgan, T. 204n
Hornsby, J. 116n
Howard-Snyder, D. 195n
Huberman, P. 307n
Hudson, H. H. 162n
Hume, D. 3, 38, 60, 112–20, 258, 261, 268, 283, 339–40m 377n
Hunt, D. 195
Husak, D. 451n
Huxley, A. 201n

Jackson, F. 396n, 402n
Jacobivits, L. 97n
Jaffe, J. H. 426n
James, W. 206–7, 300
Jeffrey, R. C. 350n
Johnson, S. 1, 2
Jordan, J. 195n

Kane, R. 10, 12–14, 193n, 199–208, 215n, 223–4, 275n, 276, 285n, 293n, 304n

Kant, I. 4, 24, 34–6, 120, 162n, 163n, 217, 218n, 255n, 300
Katzoff, C. 185n
Kennett, J. 397n, 434n, 437n
Kenny, A. 39n
Kim, J. 1n, 263n
Klein, M. 202n
Korsgaard, C. 163n, 448n

La Rouchefoucauld, F. 75
Lamb, J. W. 177n, 180n
Laplace, P. S. 45n, 60n, 62–4, 67, 101n, 133–4, 422–3
Lee, W.-C. 211
Lehrer, K. 125n, 204n, 285n, 334n
Leibniz, G. W. 35–6, 274, 303n
Lennon, K. 398n
LePore, E. 296n
Levison, A. 264n
Lewis, D. 5, 108, 209, 288n, 294n, 390n
Locke, J. 34, 38, 195n
Loewenstein, G. 447n
Loewer, B. 9n, 299n
Lombard, L. 185n
Long, D. 423
Lucas, J. R. 95n, 235n, 236n
Luther, M. 235n, 419

Mabbott, J. D. 90
MacKay, D. M. 145n, 217n
Madden, F. 260, 283
Magill, K. 299n
Malcolm, N. 13n
Martin, R. 54n
McCann, H. 185n, 299n, 305n
McCarthy, T. 19n
McLaughlin, B. 263n, 296n
McMurrin, S. M. 295n, 352n
Melden, A. I. 31, 34–5
Mele, A. 185n, 195, 206, 215n, 299n, 303–4, 310–11, 315, 433n, 434n, 437n
Michael, M. 397n
Mill, J. S. 164n

Miller, C. B. 397n
Montague, R. 45n
Moore, G. E. 28, 38, 406
Morse, S. J. 425n, 444n, 445n, 451n

Nagel, T. 1, 9n, 11, 13, 22–4, 45n, 229n, 251n, 283, 302n, 362n
Narveson, J. 46n, 54n
Nathan, N. 299n, 312n
Naylor, M. 177n
Neely, W. 350n, 369n
Nietzsche, F. 220, 227, 351
Nitschke, R. 208
Novalis 226
Nowell-Smith, P. H. 73n, 74n

O'Brien, C. P. 426n
O'Connor, T. 11, 13, 278n, 299n, 304n, 208n, 312n
Oddie, G. 430n
O'Leary-Hawthorne, J. 397n, 402n
O'Shaughnessy, B. 230, 411
Overton, L. 190n, 211
Owens, D. 19n

Parfit, D. 252n, 253n, 367n
Pargetter, R. 293n, 294n
Passmore, J. 101n
Patten, J. 217–18
Pears, D. F. 101n, 104n
Peirce, C. S. 94n
Penner, T. 340n, 341n
Pereboom, D. 201, 299n
Perry, D. 147n
Perry, R. B. 341n
Petit, P. 19, 22, 389n, 396n, 400n, 402n, 433n, 434n, 436n
Plantinga, A. 47n, 178n, 180
Plato 120, 339–41, 343n, 348, 350
Popper, K. R. 61, 145n
Price, H. H. 410
Prigogine, I. 299n

Quine, W. V. 23n, 103n
Quinn, W. 439n

Raab, F. V. 65
Ravizza, M. 18, 177n, 203n, 205n, 211n
Rawls, J. 23n
Reid, T. 10, 26n, 27–8, 33, 35, 178n, 262n, 263, 268n, 270–1, 283
Rensing, L. 307n
Rescher, N. 209n
Robb, D. 195
Robson, J. M. 164n
Rosenberg, J. 423n
Rowe, W. 299n
Russell, B. A. W 101n, 113–14
Ryle, G. 61, 145n

Sade, D. A. F. de 59–60, 62, 71
Sanford, D. H. 296n
Satre, J.-P. 114–16, 151, 217, 218n
Scanlon, T. M. 9, 16–18, 295n, 439n, 441n
Schacht, R. 227n
Schlick, M. 38, 357n
Schlipp, P. A. 406n
Schueler, G. F. 432n
Searle, J. 185n, 262–3, 283
Sen, A. 352n
Senor, T. 299n
Shoemaker, S. 260–1
Sidgwick, H. 255n
Skarda, C. 307n
Skinner, B. F. 202
Smart, J. J. C. 9–10, 14–16, 24, 58n, 338,. 357n, 364–5
Smilansky, S. 227n, 299n
Smith, M. 19, 23, 396n, 398n, 433n, 434n, 436n, 437n
Socrates 351n
Sosa, E. 1n
Spinoza, B. 234n, 411
Stalnaker, R. 209
Stampe, D. W. 441n
Steinberg, D. 97n
Stevenson, C. L. 38
Stocker, M. 448n
Strawson, G. 11, 14, 18–19, 165n, 212n,

274–6, 293n, 299n, 302n, 303, 310, 312n
Strawson, P. F. 15–16, 98n, 117–19, 230, 243–5, 322n, 357–64, 405n, 423n
Stroud, B. 245n
Stump, E. 177n, 195–6
Suarez, F. 32n
Swanson, J. W. 101n

Taylor, R. 26n, 94n, 104–5, 230n, 270–1, 283, 285–7, 292, 373, 375–7, 380, 385
Thalberg, I. 277n, 285n
Tomberlin, J. E. 23n, 305n
Tooley, M. 259n, 288n, 293n, 294
Tuomela, R. 305n

Uehling, T. 370n

van den Beld, T. 435n
van Fraassen, B. C. 391n
van Inwagen, P. 2, 5n, 126–8, 134n, 135, 152–5, 156n, 178n, 185n, 186, 275n, 292, 299n, 205n, 354n
van Straaten, Z. 98n, 358n
Velleman, J. D. 9n, 158n, 434n, 436n
Vesey, G. 94
Vihvelin, K. 148n

Wallace, R. J. 18n, 20–2, 424n
Waller, B. 299n, 303–4, 310
Walton, D. 204n, 277n, 285n
Warnock, G. J. 104n
Watson, G. 1n, 95n, 115n, 134n, 161n, 162n, 252n, 262n, 285n, 293n, 295n, 299n, 312n, 369n, 370n, 373–6, 380, 385, 398, 401n, 426n, 444n
Wefald, S. 235n
Wells, H. G. 345n
Wettstein, H. 370n
Widerker, D. 8, 185n, 193n
Wiggins, D. 3–4, 9, 10, 12–14, 16n, 22, 234, 234, 235n
Williams, B. A. O. 101n, 352n, 438n

Wittgenstein, L. 299, 422–3
Wolf, S. 18, 143n, 234n, 372n, 402n, 403n
Woo, E. 24n
Wyma, K. D. 193n

Yaffe, G. 23n
Yovel, Y. 163n

Zimmerman, M. 177n, 187n, 207n, 211